STUDIES IN MEDIEVAL AND RENAISSANCE HISTORY

Volume IX
(Old Series, Volume XIX)

STUDIES IN
Medieval and Renaissance History

Volume IX
(Old Series, Volume XIX)

EDITORS:

J. A. S. EVANS

R. W. UNGER

AMS PRESS
New York

AMS PRESS, INC.
56 EAST 13th STREET
NEW YORK, NY 10003

Copyright © 1987 by AMS Press, Inc.
All rights reserved.

ISSN 0081-8224
ISBN 0-404-62850-8 (Set)
ISBN 0-404-62859-1 (Vol. IX)

Library of Congress Catalog Card Number 63-22098

Manufactured in the United States of America

CONTENTS

INTRODUCTION

Studies in Medieval and Renaissance History is a series designed for original major articles in all fields of medieval and renaissance history. Volumes will appear approximately once a year.

Studies in Medieval and Renaissance History was formerly published by the University of Nebraska Press, and the impetus for the creation of the series came from the belief that there was a need for a publication that would accommodate the study that was too long to be included regularly in scholarly journals, but too short to appear as a book. The editors will consider articles in all areas of history from approximately the third to the sixteenth centuries—economic, social and demographic, political, intellectual and cultural, and studies that do not fit neatly into a single traditional category of historical investigation.

While the series is devoted primarily to the publication of major studies, it contains occasional bibliographic essays, and briefer articles dealing with unpublished archival and manuscript resources. The *Studies* also makes available in translation original articles by scholars who do not write in English or French.

Studies in Medieval and Renaissance History is published by AMS Press for the Committee for Medieval Studies at the University of British Comunbia, and the editors welcome submissions from all scholars doing research in medieval and renaissance fields, including those whose interests are not strictly historical.

J.A.S.E.

MEDIEVAL SETTLEMENT IN BASILICATA

Carola M. Small
University of Alberta

MEDIEVAL SETTLEMENT
IN BASILICATA

The justiciarate of Basilicata was constituted by the Emperor Frederick II some time before 1230.[1] Broadly speaking, it covered the area of the former Roman province of Lucania, which had been revived by the Byzantines in the 10th century; but it was significantly smaller than the Roman province and reached further north than the Byzantine one. Modern Basilicata includes roughly the same area but with certain important differences, notably that Matera, now the capital of one of the two provinces of Basilicata, was in Apulia in the Middle Ages. Stretching from the east slopes of the Apennines to the sea near Metaponto, Basilicata contained a varied terrain ranging from the mountainous slopes round Potenza to the wide flat plains of the lower Basento, Agri, and Sinni valleys. It was more or less at the centre of the mainland kingdom of south Italy and consequently vulnerable to the numerous political disturbances which beset the kingdom throughout the Middle Ages. It contained few towns of major importance but among them was Melfi, the first headquarters of the Norman rulers of south Italy and an important administrative center until Angevin times. Thereafter, Melfi's importance waned somewhat but it remained the chief stronghold for the defence and policing of Angevin Basilicata.

The medieval settlement of the south of Italy has not hitherto attracted much in the way of detailed study[2] and many of such studies as do exist have tended to concentrate more on Apulia and Calabria than on Basilicata. One reason for this comparative neglect is perhaps the destruction of the Neapolitan Archives in 1943, which removed much of the evidence for the history of medieval south Italy. It has, however, been possible to recover some of the lost documentation from copies and from secondary sources. Among the documents still available is a number of administrative documents relating to the communities of medieval Basilicata. They are very disparate, so that a direct comparison of their evidence is in most cases inadmissable; but cumulatively they can be used for a cautious reconstruction of the settlement of Basilicata in the medieval period. All of them have been studied in some depth; but no attempt has hitherto been made to bring them together to show the general trends in the period which they cover.

The earliest of the documents on which our evidence for the settlement of this area is based, is the famous catalogue of the barons, compiled about 1156 on the orders of William I (though some of its data are later). This antedates the formation of the justiciarate of Basilicata; and the entries for the area later included in the justiciarate are somewhat scattered. They constitute, however, the earliest evidence for the settlement of the area.[3]

The next document to be analysed is a list of castles in Basilicata compiled towards the end of the reign of Frederick II, probably in 1242.[4] This indicates which communities were responsible for the upkeep of the various imperial castles. Its main value is in indicating the number and location of communities in the mid-13th century, though some inferences as to their size, importance, and links with other communities at the local level can be made from their grouping.

For the Angevin period the evidence is more abundant & since, even though the famous Angevin registers, which contained copies of a large number of the documents issued by the Angevin chancery, have been lost, a substantial part of them is recoverable. This includes various orders to the Justiciar of Basilicata concerning castle garrisons; tax lists of 1276 and 1320 specifying the amount of tax due to the crown from the various communities of the area; the tax total for various years for individual provinces and for the Regno as a whole; and a number of references to individual villages, most of which deal with the relationship of the villages to their lords. Two not very complete tithe lists also survive from the Angevin period in the Vatican archives.[5] Of these documents, the most valuable are the two tax assessments for the general subvention.[6] These give, for the first time, some indication of the relative size of communities in Basilicata. They are not good evidence for this, for they record only the amount of tax for which each community was assessed; and this, given that we do not know how that amount was arrived at, is rather vague evidence. It is unlikely that the correlation between the sum of money paid in taxes and the size of the community was exact. Nevertheless, it is absurd to suggest that there is no correlation at all and the tax lists must be accepted as better evidence for the size and prosperity of places in Basilicata than anything which preceded them.

Unfortunately the tax lists, like most of the other surviving Angevin documents, come from the early part of the Angevin period. The standard of royal record keeping declined drastically under Giovanna I and her successors; and has, in any case, attracted fewer copyists. There is therefore a serious gap in the records between about 1343 and the late fifteenth century. Thereafter, more tax lists become available, this time containing not the actual assessments but, more usefully, the numbers of hearths in each community which provided the basis for assessments. These lists will be discussed briefly for the light they shed on Basilicata at the end of the Middle Ages and on the changes which had taken place there between the 14th and 16th centuries.

The Norman Period

The catalogue of the barons mentions some ninety–five places which would later be included in the justiciarate of Basilicata as it is described in later documents[7] (Table I). All but twelve of these appear again later. There are some lacunae. Potenza was not included in the catalogue except incidentally,[8] although it was a bishopric and a place of some importance; and both Melfi and Acerenza (the one a bishopric, the other an archbishopric) are mentioned only because certain, but not all, episcopal fiefs interested the compilers of the catalogue.[9] These large towns were presumably in the royal domain and, as such, the service due from them could not be listed, so that only fortuitously were they included. It is likely, then, that other domanial fiefs were unlisted and escaped even incidental mention. Nevertheless, the number of domanial fiefs cannot have been large—the crown is unlikely to have retained many small fiefs in its own hand—and the error resulting from the omission of domanial fiefs is probably very slight.

A second, more serious problem is that the catalogue does not cover the area of Basilicata south of the Sinni, for which the relevant pages do not survive. This does not, of course, in any way invalidate its evidence for the area north of the Sinni, but it does mean that comparison with later documents, which deal with the whole of Basilicata, must be undertaken with care.

Finally, the possibility must be borne in mind that some communities were subsumed into neighbouring fiefs. We know, for example, that Avigliano existed and had a *domina* in 1129.[10] It is not listed in the catalogue. This could be because it had become part of the royal domain but more probably it is because Avigliano is in an area of land held, in the middle of the century, by the counts of Conversano. This area comprised the fiefs of Ruoti and Lagopesole in one of which, probably Ruoti, Avigliano must have been included. The catalogue then is imperfect evidence for Norman settlements in Basilicata. Still, at least the inclusion of a place is evidence that it did exist, and the evidence of the catalogue makes it clear that these fiefs were fairly widespread over Basilicata.

As to when these settlements arose, there is in most cases very little evidence. Some places can be shown to have existed by the ninth century. These included most of the episcopal towns (and even such of these towns as did not acquire bishops until the tenth or eleventh century can probably be assumed to have been functioning earlier—new bishoprics could not spring to life from nothing all in a year). They also included a number of monasteries which, like the Greek Kyr Zosimo (Cerchosimo) or the Latin Santa Maria di Banzi, attracted surrounding settlements early on.

These early settlements in Basilicata seem to have been most concentrated in the south, perhaps as a result of Greek eremitic settlement (paradoxical though that may seem) in the Val Sinni. Perhaps on the other hand, the seeming concentration is simply a result of the haphazard survival of the records. It would at all events, be rash, given the nature of the evidence, to suggest that all Greek and Lombard settlements in pre-Norman Basilicata are known.[11] It is, however, worth commenting that in one relatively restricted area for which a thorough archeological survey has been undertaken, there is no archeological evidence for early Lombard settlements other than those for which documentary evidence also exists. In the Avigliano-Ruoti area, where the survey was carried out, no sites were found certainly dateable to the period between the sixth and the ninth centuries. It is true that dating such sites would not be easy, for the domestic pottery of the period cannot yet be accurately dated on stylistic grounds; but it seems that if Lombards sites existed at all, other than those recorded in written documents, they were sparse and relatively humble—farms rather than villages.[12]

It was then between the end of the ninth century and the middle of the twelfth that most settlements described in the catalogue of the barons for Basilicata probably emerged. This is more or less in line with what happened elsewhere. This was the great period in Italy of *incastellamento,* a process widespread enough in the rest of Italy for it to be inconceivable that it should not have happened in Basilicata. *Incastellamento* could take various forms, from the establishment of fortified centers among existing villages which altered the structure of local power but not the settlement pattern,[13] to the regrouping of the population in nucleated settlements round a castle.[14] It was evidently the latter process which took place in Basilicata as indeed it did everywhere in south Italy for which records survive. Probably then, many of the places listed in the catalogue of the barons already existed by the time of the Norman Conquest. Some, however were added later. The castles at San Fele and San Mauro, for example are Norman constructions and probably denote Norman foundations.

The establishment of new settlements in Basilicata was at least partly caused by a rise in the population of the area. This rise, like the process of *incastellamento,* can be paralleled throughout Italy and indeed, throughout Europe. Some of the new places may have been formed simply because the inhabitants had migrated from scattered farms in the countryside and resettled but, given the apparent paucity of scattered settlement earlier, this can hardly be the only factor in the emergence of new settlements. Some of the population growth was, of course, the result of immigration. In fact, however, the number of Norman immigrants was relatively small,[15]

Although the appearance of the new settlements almost certainly marks a rise in population between Lombard and Norman times, the new places were, judging by such few indications of size as can be extracted from the catalogue, very small. Each entry in the catalogue notes the amount of service due in return for each fief, along with the *augmentum* or additional service required for specific crises. The service with the *augmentum* was normally twice the normal service but not invariably so: sometimes it seems to have been imposed almost at random. At all events, the normal service is a better guide to the size and value of a fief than service with the *augmentum.* In normal conditions, only four places in Basilicata owed the service of more than six knights. Seventeen owed four to six knights and the majority owed three or less. (Twenty owed three, twenty-two owed two or two ½, and twenty-three, one or a little more.) Other places were mentioned without service but these were included with other fiefs. Now the data of the catalogue for the Regno of South Italy as a whole show that holdings elsewhere could be much larger. The largest mentioned for anywhere in the Regno were for more than twenty knights, and twenty-six places owed more than ten knights. Comparatively speaking, then, no holding in Basilicata was large by the standards of south Italy generally.

It is impossible to estimate with any precision how a knight's fief was calculated. Probably it depended on the whim of the monarch and the historical circumstances of the creation of the fief as much as on the size or population of the fief. Nevertheless, a few indications of size appear in the catalogue. In some places, there were no knights' fiefs, but instead, a large number of lords holding villeins, whose service was computed on the number of villeins they had. In many cases, these villeins were said to constitute a knight's fief. The number required for this varied considerably. It was never less than eighteen, but sometimes as many as forty villeins consituted a single knight's fief.[16] It would be unwise to assume that all knight's fiefs everywhere in south Italy had on them between eighteen and forty villeins: obviously a fief which, for example, consisted of acres of sheep pasture would be less populous than one of similar value consisting of small mixed farms; but, given that an economy of small mixed farms was prevalent in Basilicata,[17] there is some justification for accepting that, within the region of which that was true, a fief of one knight contained on average somewhere between eighteen and forty villeins with their families. The majority of villages in the area, then, would have contained a population of between eighteen and 120 households while some twenty places would have had more, none, however, except perhaps the large towns, having more than 440 or so households. This takes no account of the non-villein population. In the smaller villages the non-villein was probably negligeable: the lord's household and little else; but there were also some towns which would have contained many more non-villeins. The size of these cannot even be guessed from the catalogue. Prominent among them were Melfi and Potenza, which, judging by contemporary chronicle evidence, were places of some importance. Then there were a further nine bishoprics (at Rapolla, Venosa, Lavello, Muro, Tricarico, Anglona, Marsico, Satriano and Acerenza—the last an archbishopric) and an ex-bishopric at Montepeloso. Without even a hint as to the size of these, it is impossible to form an estimate of the total population of Basilicata in the Norman period; but the pattern of settlement, with numerous small villages intermixed with a few large towns, is clear enough.

The Hohenstauffen Period: New Settlement

During the years which followed the Norman conquest, the number of settlements in Basilicata further increased. By the time of Frederick II, there were 176 places in Basilicata liable for contributions to the upkeep of royal castles and *domus* or hunting lodges (including the settlements round the castles and *domus* themselves—map 2 and table IV), as opposed to ninety-five in the catalogue of the barons. The increase is partly explained by the inclusion of some thirty-nine places south of the Sinni in the area not covered by the catalogue. A few other places like Avigliano are known to have existed earlier and the Greek names of one or two others like Andriace and San Basilio suggest that they too had survived or revived from an earlier period.[18] Still, a minimum of some 30 new places had appeared; and this number should in fact be slightly higher, since fourteen of the places listed in the catalogue do not appear in the castle list (*v* Table II). Thus the total number of new settlements seems to be around forty-three. Moreover, at least two places listed in the catalogue and left out of the castle list, Picerno and Colobraro, reappear in 1276 and so were presumably not totally defunct in the 1240s. Thus, even allowing for some omissions in the catalogue, the number of settlements in Basilicata would seem to have increased fairly dramatically over the century between the compilation of the catalogue and the compilation of the castle list.

There are two possible explanations for this growth of new settlement. One is that the inhabitants of Basilicata, many of whom must have inhabited villages at some distance from the lands they cultivated, had moved to smaller, more convenient locations;[19] or alternatively, the population was rising, forcing the inhabitants to clear fresh land and to establish new settlements near it. Colonization caused by a rising population would be likely to occur on "marginal" land or in previously uncleared areas of forest: the foundation of new settlements for convenience of access would not. Can we then, establish any general pattern for the new settlement in Basilicata?

Firstly, the pattern of settlement, including that of new settlement, appears to bear very little relation to the nature of the soil. This is not, perhaps, very surprising. The geology of Basilicata is extremely complex, comprising a variety of terrains dating from the mesozoic to recent formations and including both sedimentary deposits of various types—limestones, sandstones, clays, agglomerates etc.—and volcanic deposits. There is a broad division between the sandy pleiocene deposits to the west of the province flanking the lower reaches of the great river valleys and the earlier agglomerates, schists and limestones of the more mountainous eastern sector. Very little of the region is stable, being subject to frequent earthquakes and landslides—indeed it is more menaced by the latter than anywhere else in Italy with, at present, some 70 percent of its communes damaged or threatened with damage by landslides.[20] The problems of this basic instability have recently been compounded by the destruction of forest cover, overgrazing and consequent erosion on a scale which has turned parts of the lower Bradano, Basento and Agri valleys into virtual desert. This problem, however, was probably less serious in the Middle Ages than it is now, though there is no doubt that landslides always posed a certain threat.

A comparison of the distribution of settlements with the geological map of Basilicata shows that settlements existed on virtually every type of soil to be found in Basilicata and that new settlements, as much as old, were distributed rather evenly among the different types of terrain in the region. The only terrains that consistently lacked settlement were, then as now, the lowest levels of the river valleys which are subject to annual flooding on a scale that makes cultivation impossible, particularly as the rivers dry up completely or almost completely in summer. These valleys apart, neither geology nor topography can be shown greatly to have affected the pattern of settlement in Basilicata. With regard to the latter, it is perhaps true that the coastal plain was less popular for settlement than the hills and mountains further inland: it was more subject to malaria and settlements there could not be very easily defended. But even there, settlements existed.

Most of Basilicata, except in the extreme west and in the river valleys, was probably covered with forest in the early Middle Ages but naturally a good deal of this had been cleared for cultivation to support the settlements that had emerged by the time of the Normans. In most cases the additional settlements established between 1156 and 1242 were also established at the expense of the forest. This can be most easily demonstrated for those which appeared near the royal forests. Although we do not know the exact boundaries of all of these, we do have a description of the boundaries of the forest of Lagopesole.[21] We know also that there was forest round Cisterna and Gaudiano, though not its exact limits, and it is reasonable to assume that all the royal hunting lodges were surrounded by some forest. Settlement was not impossible within a royal forest—there was, for example, a community at Lagopesole; and in the eleventh century there seems to have been not only a settlement at Vitalba, within the forest of Lagopesole, but a settlement large enough to support a bishop.[22] On the other hand, by the fourteenth century, nearly all settlement inside the forest of Lagopesole had ceased except at Lagopesole itself, and even there it was not thriving. New settlement did appear, however, on the edge of the forest, effectively reducing its size. Caldane, Casal Aspro, Casal Sant'Andrea and Rionero all appeared on the edge of the forest of Lagopesole. It would seem, then, that the forest was being somewhat eroded under the pressure of new settlement.

Further south, Stigliano almost certainly encroached on the forest of Petrolla. Non–royal reserve forests are less easy to trace but we know that by the thirteenth century there was one at Santa Sophia which is likely to have existed earlier and at the expense of which Castelluccio di Santa Sophia must have emerged. And it is reasonable to suppose that San Nicola de Silva was established in a wood if not a forest.[23] By and large then, where there is any evidence for the nature of the land before new settlement took place, the land seems to have been forested. We are dealing here with new assarts. Certainly the alternative, that new settlement took place in land already cleared, merely for convenience of access, is not one that seems particularly convincing. We have here then, a pattern of assarting for new settlement common throughout late twelfth and thirteenth century Europe.

Some of the settlements not mentioned in the catalogue of the barons but attested earlier probably also come into the category of new assarts. Their reappearance in the castle list probably implies that they had either been resettled or had expanded. They include Monte Serico and Petra Castalda, inhabited in Roman times but subsequently abandoned, Pierno, which had a Norman church founded in the eleventh century by Gilbert of Balvano but which probably attracted

enough people to constitute a village only somewhat later, San Basilio
and Andriace on the western coastal plain and Metaponto in the same
region, the last once a thriving Greek city but, since the silting up of its
harbour, situated in some of the least productive land of Basilicata.
The revivals are almost better evidence of the need to bring "marginal" land into production than the new foundations, for many were on
land that had before proved unsatisfactory and would do so again—
few survived the Middle Ages.

New assarts are normally taken to mean increased population. Unfortunately for Basilicata the increase between 1156 and 1246
can only be inferred. It can, however, be demonstrated to have
occurred by 1276 and, as we shall see later, it was by then considerable. Given that the number of settlements was, as we shall see later,
appreciably higher in 1246 than it was in 1276, we may surmise that
the rise in population between 1156 and 1246 was even greater—that
in fact the demographic trend had begun to move downwards after
Frederick II's death in 1250. But even if this is not the case, it seems
that the rise in population between the mid-twelfth and the mid-
thirteenth century must have been considerable.

These new settlements, like those of Norman times, seem in
many cases to have been nucleated settlements near a fortified dwell-
ing or, more rarely, an ecclesiastical establishment. Caldane, Vigianel-
lo and Calvello, for example had their castles; and the list could
perhaps be extended. Tramutola had its abbey (founded as an
offshoot of the great monastery of La Cava in 1154).[24] Some of the
new settlements were, however, break-away offshoots of earlier settlements with no "feudal" presence. Castelluccio di Santa Sophia is some
distance from the castle of Santa Sophia and was probably created by
a grouping together of outlying tenants of Santa Sophia. *Incastellamento*, in the sense of nucleation for defense without there
being necessarily a castle within the nucleus, continued in Europe well
into the twelfth and even thirteenth century.[25] It was not, I think,
common in thirteenth-century Basilicata, but there are examples.

As for the places in the catalogue of the barons which do not
appear in Frederick's list, seven were very small, owing the service of
one knight or less. They cannot all be located now but it seems that
most were isolated rural strongholds. The rest, however, were somewhat larger and it is difficult to know why they failed to survive.
Revisco, a little north of Potenza, owing service of three knights and
probably reasonably large, perhaps declined when its lords, the family

of Santa Sophia, established their headquarters in Potenza itself rather than in Revisco. The most interesting victim was the former bishopric of Vitalba. This was still extant in 1278 when it was described as a *casale* and valued at twenty-eight *uncie* per annum.[26] At the same period (1279) its *difesa* (forest or hunting preserve) was in the hands of the crown and described as *guasta*.[27] Since it was already omitted from Frederick's list of castles, the "waste" must have occurred some time previously, but we do not know what had happened. Vitalba, Revisco, and Tur (of which last there is no other record) are, however, the only significant places to vanish between the mid–twelfth and mid–thirteenth centuries and their disappearance is more than offset by the new foundations. This pattern is not uncommon—it is paralleled for instance in Lazio[28]. Toubert has suggested that here the commonest causes of abandonment were either that the places had been founded with too great a regard to defense and too little to their economy—an explanation which does not seem very plausible for either Vitalba or Revisco, neither of which was particularly badly situated; that a place suffered from the proximity of a more prosperous place next to it, as Revisco may well have sufferred from Potenza; or that the lord had sufferred some kind of set back—a plausible explanation in the case of Vitalba and Tur, though one for which there is no proof, but one that seems less likely in the case of the lords of Revisco, the Santa Sophia family, who were among the supporters of the Hohenstauffen and enjoyed their favor. Whatever the reason for their disappearance, the number of places to vanish between 1156 and 1250 is relatively unimportant.

Overall, the castle list shows a rise in settlement. It also gives some idea of the administrative grouping of settlements under the Hohenstauffen. Each royal castle had assigned to it a group of villages responsible for its upkeep. In these assignments, ease of communication between the castle and the contributing village seems to have been a minor consideration. The official who drew up the list did try to group contributing villages to one side of the castle, normally the south, but he was prepared to go very far afield to find his villages. It is over fifty kilometres as the crow flies and about 115 by road from Seleuci to Rocca Imperiale and people from Salandra had to go ninety-three kilometres to Acerenza. This is too far for the castle to have counted for much in local administration, and indeed the practice of demanding contributions from villages all on one side of the castle, rather than surrounding it, should warn us against seeing the castle as a center of local political or administrative activities. The castles were intended as a defensive network for the region and the assignment of responsibilities for them to the villages was dictated probably largely by considerations of how best to match necessary contributions with the ability of the villagers to pay—and to some extent also, by considerations of ease of collection.

The Angevin Period

The castle list contains the largest listing of settlements in Basilicata for the whole of the Middle Ages. The next full listing of places in the area is a tax schedule for 1276 (v Table III). This includes 145 places, twenty-four less than the castle list. Since, however, it includes five places which were not mentioned in the castle list, the total number of places dropped since the compilation of the castle list is twenty-nine. Some of these were near the border and were transferred to other administrative districts under the Angevins. They include Agromonte south of the Sinni; Ayeta, Turtura and Castrocucco near Maratea; Metaponto, which was moved to the Terra d'Otranto[29] and possibly some other places in the south on the border (though it is equally possible that these, which no longer exist, vanished at this time). In the north Montemilone and San Nicola de Ofido may have been transferred; though the latter, being a hunting lodge, may not have had communities of taxable size near it anyway. Still, even allowing for as many as twelve transfers out of Basilicata—and this is generous—we are left with sixteen places fewer in 1276 than in 1246 (v Table V).

A large proportion of these vanished places were new appearances in the castle list. In fact, only two of the sixteen places are listed in the catalogue of the barons. The rest seem to be failed colonies of the twelfth century. We do not know why they failed— their lands seem to be no better and no worse than those of other settlements but it seems that more recently established villages were more vulnerable to the troubles of the late thirteenth century than longer established ones.

Whether they were also exceptionally small is, unfortunately, impossible to determine with any accuracy. The only indications of size which we have before 1276 must be drawn from the data of the catalogue of the barons and the castle list. The former is admittedly some help for the two places mentioned in it and shows that one of them, Petrolla, was indeed very small, the fief of one knight. The other, Marmore, owing the service of three knights and part of a fourth calculated on some additional villeins, was not markedly small. It was divided among several lords, which may not have helped its prosperity; but there seems no very obvious reason why it should have vanished when other places equally troubled by a plurality of lords did not. The evidence of the catalogue of the barons is not, then, very enlightening.

The other evidence, from the castle list itself is, though less quantifiable, perhaps more valuable. The places which vanished were generally grouped with a large number of other villages in taking responsibility for their allotted castle (v Table IV). At first sight it might seem that a large number of contributors merely reflects the importance of the castle. This, however, was not the case, for we know that Melfi, which had very few contributors was one of the largest and strategically most important castles of Basilicata. We can more reliably assume that the royal castles which remained in the hands of the crown in Angevin times were, on the whole the most important. Charles of Anjou drastically reduced the number of royal castles from twenty to five. Those which remained were Acerenza, Melfi, Metaponto (later transferred to the Terra di Otranto), San Fele, and Muro. The list shows a heavy concentration in the north west of the region— probably a distortion occasioned by the intensity of the opposition to the Angevins in that area. For the Hohenstauffen period we must substitute Rocca Imperiale for Metaponto. The contributors to these five or so major castles, however, ranged in number from twenty-seven (for Rocca Imperiale) to three (for Melfi). It seems then, that the number of places that contributed to a given castle bore little relation to its importance. On the other hand, it is likely that the more places were asked to contribute to a castle, the poorer those places were. There are a few anomalies—Potenza, among the fourteen contributors to Acerenza, was an episcopal city and can hardly have been desperately poor, and Montepeloso was also fairly large and important. But this would imply that the other contributors to Acerenza were even poorer than might at first be assumed. Poverty need not of course be equated with smallness but in the majority of cases the two are likely to have gone together.

If numbers of places in a group of contributors to the up-keep of castles are any guide, then several of the places that vanished between 1250 and 1276 were definitely small. Four were among the

twenty-seven contributors to Rocca Imperialis. The high number of
contributors suggests that none was very large, and we shall see that
this is substantiated by later evidence. Similarly three of the deserted
villages were among thirteen contributors to Anzi and one from
among fourteen contributors to Acerenza. On the whole, then the
indications are that those places which were deserted were small—but
how small we cannot say. Even assuming, however, that they were
very small indeed, a decline which entails the disappearance of at least
fifteen communities is by no means negligable.

Various reasons for the decline can be suggested. The main
one was probably a tendency on the part of the peasants to abandon
their fields in the wake of the political upheavals attendant on the
Angevin takeover. We know that lands at Petrolla and Policoro, both
among the missing communities in 1276, were deserted;[30] and we
know that other communities which survived suffered the same problem. Among these were Muro, Lagopesole and Pisticci, Montalbano
and Roccanova, all of which reported abandoned fields in the 1270s
and '80s, and also a small *casale*, San Marco, which is not otherwise
known but which is said to have had only very few fields cultivated in
1280.[31] There are references to places that are *dishabitati* which presumably means much the same thing.[32] These included Pulsandrana,
Calabra, Trisagia, and the Terra Tancredi di Guarino, the last said to
have been destroyed in 1272.[33] though it still paid a minimal tax of six
tari in 1276. Acerenza was also said to be "quasi exhabitata" in 1270,[34]
a manifest exaggeration, since the same document, while reducing its
taxes, still assessed it for the substantial sum of fifty-four *uncie*, but
still an indication that all was not well. Finally, Satriano claimed—
though in this case we do not know the government response—that it
was "habitatoribus derelictus" in 1270.[35] These various references,
haphazard though they are, are sufficient to show that there was
extensive migration from many settlements in the province, and that
the decline was not limited to communities which were actually deserted. In one case, Acerenza, we even have some evidence for the
scale and rapidity of the decline. Acerenza was apparently taxed over
100 *uncie* in 1269. It had its assessment reduced to fifty-four *uncie* in
1270 and to twenty-three *uncie* 13 *tari* by 1276. This may not mean
that it had lost precisely 77 percent of its population in seven years but
it does imply a very sharp drop. Roccanova and Lagopesole too, both
of which were listed in 1276 but not taxed, must have suffered a very
rapid decline. This may have been compounded by poor harvests for
which there is evidence in 1270.[36]

Evidently the government hoped that this trend was reversible and that the inhabitants could be persuaded to return to their abandoned fields. We cannot therefore attribute the desertions to large scale mortality as a result of war or other disasters. On the contrary, it seems that they were largely occasioned by relatively minor political upheavals, particularly in the north where resistance to Charles of Anjou in the late 1260s had been markedly strong, and where the inhabitants simply fled from his vengeance. Some of them doubtless took to the forest. Others fled to neighboring communities where, in due course, several were found and despatched home.[37] This migration almost certainly explains the disappearance of Pierno, never a large settlement, which was involved in a savagely repressed rebellion in 1272,[38] and perhaps also that of Marmore which had probably belonged to one of the main leaders of the resistance, the lord of Santa Sophia. Such communities may not have been physically destroyed, but were probably abandoned by their frightened inhabitants.

Migrants must obviously move somewhere and it has been suggested that desertions elsewhere were occasioned by people moving to the towns. It would be difficult to substantiate this for Basilicata. There were few large towns there, the only really large one being Melfi. This was clearly already large by 1250, judging by its importance in Norman times; it may well have grown more thereafter—certainly as we shall see, it was very large indeed (by some computations enormous) by 1276,[39] and this may reflect immigration from surrounding villages. The same could perhaps be true of Potenza, Rapolla, Venosa, Montescaglioso, and Montepeloso. On the other hand Acerenza, the archbishopric, was declining—perhaps it was too inaccessible to thrive. By and large, however, if the decline of rural settlements in thirteenth-century Basilicata was caused by migration to the towns, the migrants were going a very long way. This is of course possible; some of the coastal towns in Apulia became huge in the late thirteenth century.[40] But there is no evidence of such movement. There is, on the other hand, evidence of local migration. The rebels against Charles of Anjou were rarely found more than 50 kilometres away from their former homes,[41] and most were in small villages where they were clearly living illegally and precariously. It seems likely then that the chief effect of migration in Basilicata in the late thirteenth century was a rise in the number of outlaws and brigands in a mountainous countryside that was always troubled by such people.

Of course a few cities really were destroyed. Rapolla was razed to the ground by Manfred in 1253,[42] Sant Arcangelo was burned down *casualiter* in 1274,[43] Accetura was reduced from 100 households to 12 as the result of a fire in 1273,[44] and a little later Tramutola claimed to have been destroyed as the result of an incident (not specified) in 1304, followed by an invasion in 1306.[45] Powers of recuperation in medieval Basilicata were good, however. Rapolla must have recovered fairly completely by 1276 when it was taxed over 102 *uncie*—the fifth highest assessment for the province. Tramutola was assessed for five *uncie* twenty-seven *tari* in 1307—up from six *tari* in 1276, which accords ill with its tale of disasters. Sant' Arcangelo did have its assessment reduced in 1276 when it payed only eleven *uncie* but it was up again to some forty-six *uncie* in 1320. Accetura paid nothing in 1276. It was, however, listed, so the government presumably expected its troubles to be temporary. In this it was correct for Accetura was assessed over two *uncie* by 1307. Roccanova, also assessed nothing but listed in 1276, did even better: it was paying five *uncie* twenty-three *tari* in 1307. Of the communities listed but not assessed in 1276, only Lagopesole and Rodiano failed to recover. They were dropped entirely by 1307, the former at least having successfully protested against attempts to re-assess it shortly before that.[46]

One other factor may have accounted for the decline of certain villages between 1246 and 1276. In 1272, Potenza claimed to be in serious straits as the result of an earthquake that had inflicted widespread destruction. Obviously, the effects of such an earthquake cannot have been confined to Potenza alone, and the communities nearest to it must also have sufferred. This could explain or partly explain the disappearance of at least Vaglio and Gloriosa.[47]

The decline in numbers of settlements continued after 1276, but was very slight. A further twelve settlements were dropped from the next listing in 1307 but seven others, not taxed in 1276, were taxed by 1307. Two of these seven were Roccanova and Accetura and another three had been recorded at some time earlier. The only really new appearances in 1307 were Casal San Martino and Grassano, both as yet very small, though Grassano was destined to survive and grow. On the other hand, of the places dropped from the tax schedule, again four were left out only temporarily (Rotunda Maris, San Mauro, Grottole, and Trifogium). Only four then disappeared permanently. Still, their disappearance undoubtedly marks a further decline.

Three of the places to disappear need occasion no surprise. Lagopesole and Rodiano were, as we have seen, already in difficulties and, although it was still paying taxes in 1276, the same is true of Calabra. But what happened to explain the temporary eclipse of the other four in 1307–20 is obscure. Two of them, San Mauro and Viggiano, were paying taxes substantial enough to imply that they were very considerable communities in 1276, and the others, Grottole and Trefoglie, though they paid rather less, paid by no means minimal sums. In the case of Grottole one possible explanation is that many or all of its inhabitants migrated to the newly founded town of Grassano, not far along the ridge above the River Basento. In the long term Grassano did not replace Grottole, for both were functioning in 1532. Nevertheless, Grassano must have been populated from somewhere, and the coincidence of its foundation and the disappearance of Grottole may suggest that the inhabitants of the latter, initially at any rate, simply moved to the former. There are parallels for such migration and also for a return of the population later.[48] Again the reasons for it are conjectural. An earthquake or landslide might be one possible explanation, though some record of at least the former might be expected. Political troubles might also account for migration. The war between the Aragonese and the Angevins was waged fitfully from 1282 to 1312 and, though it troubled the island of Sicily far more than it did the mainland, must have caused considerable disturbance to the latter. Nevertheless, on the whole this period seems to have been politically less active for southern Italy than most. The likeliest explanation for the eclipse of the three communities is, then, that they were the victims of local disasters—fires, landslides or earthquakes—as Accetura and others were earlier, but lacked the capacity for quick revival.

A close analysis of the villages that disappeared between 1276 and 1307 indicates that the fall in the number of taxable communities was not very serious. On the other hand, it should be noted that it was also accompanied by a fall in the total tax assessment for Basilicata. This implies that the area was continuing to decline in prosperity, since it is inconceivable that the government deliberately lowered its tax demands while the war with Aragon was still going on. The assessors must therefore have considered that the area as a whole had less ability to pay taxes in 1307 than it had had in 1276.[49] The decline was not, however, uniform. Some communities paid more in 1307 than they had paid previously, and moreover, to some extent, these can be grouped into areas: the area northwest of Potenza, for example, was apparently prospering more in 1307 than it had done earlier. Still, of 148 communities, ninety-three paid less in 1307 than they had in 1276 (including nine which were listed in 1307 but paid nothing). Of these, twenty were paying more than 25 percent less. In absolute terms, some of the reductions were remarkable. The assessment on Petra Pertosa was reduced by fifty *uncie* and five more places had their assessments reduced by eighteen *uncie* or more. The transfer of three relatively large towns to other provinces exaggerates the difference[50] but probably not seriously. Satriano at least we know to have been paying substantially less in the early fourteenth century than it was earlier.[51]

The 1320 tax assessment shows a further reduction in total from that of 1307 of thirty *uncie*. This is not a serious reduction and this time the problem can be pinpointed. It arose from a further decline in three big communes, Spinazzola, Rocca Imperialis and Tito. The tax list of 1320 notes the decline, and notes also the need to tax other places extra in order to make up for it, but unfortunately gives no clue as to what had happened. It is unlikely that migration could, on its own, account for it. No one natural disaster is likely to have affected all three places, which are widely separated, without discernably troubling anywhere in between. We are forced to accept then that they were victims of local disruptions. It is interesting to note however, that, despite the taxation of five new settlements and an increase in taxation on another fifteen, the crown could not make good its losses.

The pattern of taxation is also significant here. It was not the big towns which had their taxes raised in order to make good the deficiencies of Spinazzola, Rocca Imperialis and Tito but the relatively small villages and some newly taxed *casali*. This pattern, particularly the appearance of the new *casali*, suggests that at this period, there was a tendency, already perhaps becoming apparent in 1307 when the *casale* San Matteo was newly taxed, towards the establishment of new settlement in the open countryside—a reversal, at last, of the *incastellamento* which, though administratively and militarily desirable, must have been remarkably inconvenient for agriculture. This in turn may reflect some relaxation after the peace of Caltabellota in 1304 of the perennial violence and disorder to which southern Italy had so long been subject.

Despite this tendency, the overall impression to be gained from the 1320 tax adjustments does not suggest that the region was prospering. Not only did the crown fail to recoup its losses on three major communes: it could not, even in the communities on which it raised the taxes in an attempt to do so, necessarily restore assessments to their 1276 level. Seven of the communities taxed extra in 1320 had already been assessed more in 1307. They must have been prospering, at least in relation to other communes. Ten, however, had been assessed less in 1307 than in 1276 and the higher assessments in 1320 did not restore them to their former level of taxation. Only one place, Marsico Vetere, paid less in 1307 than in 1276 but more in 1320 and even then, the rise was marginal.

On the whole, then, the prosperity of Basilicata had declined although the decline was by no means drastic. In this the province was no different from the rest of the Regno. The share of Basilicata in the total assessment of 1276 was 11.7 percent. In 1320, it was 11 percent Basilicata had then declined more than some other areas but not appreciably more.

The decline was not, however uniform. The twenty-one places (including the new *casali*) assessed for extra tax in 1320 were widely scattered. Clearly their propinquity to Spinazzola or Rocca was not a factor in choosing them. On the whole, however, they again show a slight concentration to the north west of Potenza. The reasons for this can only be guessed but we know that the area was punished for its resistance to Charles of Anjou. By the fourteenth century, it may perhaps have been recovering from a certain amount of deliberate repression by the earliest of the Angevins. If this is indeed the explanation we should be cautious in attributing any real improvement in prosperity to the area—it was more a matter of catching up.

The tax assessments for 1307 and 1320 contain the only detailed break-downs of tax allocations in Basilicata extant for the Angevin period after the death of Charles I. Their information can be supplemented from tithe lists of 1310 and 1325[52] (*v* Table VI), but in fact these latter add little to our knowledge. They list, naturally, only places with churches and are, moreover, very incomplete. They do contain one or two places not listed in the tax documents— Marmore is a case in point—showing that the ommission of a village from a tax document may not have implied the total abandonment of a site. But such instances are few and, I think, unimportant. Even in the twentieth century, throughout Europe churches can be found in regular or intermittent use standing in open countryside from which all other settlement has vanished. The tithe lists can tell us where people worshipped: at least 105 out of 150 villages had their own churches (v Table VII). They can also tell us which places had a large number of clergy who were expected to pay the tithe. Thus, for example, Avigliano, paying a disproportionately high tithe, must already have been something of a religious centre in the Middle Ages. But for Basilicata at any rate, and indeed for any part of the Regno for which detailed tax lists survive, the tithe lists are of minor use.[53]

We do have other totals for both Basilicata and for the Regno as a whole, which show that until shortly before the middle of the fourteenth century, tax assessments remained more or less stable, with only minor adjustments. We can probably infer, therefore, that the prosperity of the area during this period did not greatly decline. Perhaps the burden imposed by the hearth tax became somewhat heavier, as it did elsewhere in Europe, but not remarkably so. The main fall in prosperity came at the time of the war of the Sicilian Vespers, between 1285 and 1304.

This picture must be qualified a little. Basilicata was not immune from the epidemics which beset Europe in the early fourteenth century. Melfi asked for tax relief apparently because of an epidemic in 1313.[54] In 1330 its tax quota was reduced to fifty *uncie* though only temporarily. In 1336 it was allegedly abandoned because of another epidemic.[55] In 1333, Genzano and Banzi also complained of epidemics.[56] If these places were suffering in this way, it is reasonable to suppose that other places were also periodically in trouble. Nevertheless, that trouble did not affect the overall tax assessments.

The Later Angevin and Aragonese Period

After 1348 the story presumably changes, with the onset of the Black Death; though this can be no more than a presumption since records for the second half of the fourteenth century are almost totally lacking. The next one we have for Basilicata is for 1415, reported by Racciopi.[57] This shows that the number of places recorded in Basilicata dropped to 101.[58] By 1445 it had declined still further to ninety-seven (v Table VIII). Since we know that two of the places in these lists were new, this implies that at least fifty-one places in all disappeared. Since we have only the overall figures for the fifteenth century, it is impossible to say precisely which of the ninety-seven places listed in 1445 actually were. We can, however, get a rough indication of which they were from later lists. We possess the names and hearth estimates of ninety-three communities in 1532. This list is not quite complete but it is reasonable to assume that in most cases the places on it would have been the same as for 1445. A comparison of the 1532 and 1320 lists will therefore tell us not only what places disappeared between those dates but will also indicate, though we must allow some margin for error here, what had already changed by 1445 (v Table IX).

Predictably enough there were few new settlements. The 1532 list names three, Atella, Spinosa, and Ferrandina. The first two can be shown to have been founded in the fourteenth century[59] while Ferrandina dates from late in the fifteenth. In addition some six settlements were transferred into Basilicata from elsewhere in a reorganization of regional boundaries under the Aragonese.[60] By contrast sixty-three places in all were dropped from the 1320 list (v Table X). Some four or five of these may perhaps have been transferred elsewhere.[61] About five were ommitted in error.[62] Five revived by the end of the sixteenth century[63] and, in addition, some six or more have revived since.[64] But about forty-three settlements which stopped paying taxes between 1320 and 1532 have vanished leaving either no trace or, more usually, a few ruins behind; and one other, Faracum, although listed in 1532, was already paying no taxes by that date and vanished later. These figures, though high, are considerably lower than the raw data of the tax lists would imply and should caution us against too facile an acceptance of their statistics.[65]

In addition to the lost communes, some smaller hamlets, which were always included for purposes of taxation with a neighbouring commune, seem to have disappeared in this period. The nature of our documentation makes these hard to trace but we know of one near Anzi, six near Montescaglioso, one of which (Cornu) had a church listed in the tithe lists, and seventeen near Muro in addition to Platano and Marmore.[66]

The proportion of fourteenth-century villages in Basilicata deserted by the fifteenth century was very high—some 28 percent of the communes. How does this compare with elsewhere? The phenomenon of deserted villages was a common one throughout Italy and, for that matter, Europe in the fourteenth and fifteenth centuries. In the District of Rome, some 25 percent of villages vanished though the disappearances were by no means evenly distributed throughout the District: for instance only 4 percent came from Sabina and 55 percent from Tuscia.[67] About 25 percent of the villages round

Volterra and San Gimignano vanished.[68] In the Capitanata nearly 50 percent vanished.[69] Outside Italy numbers were lower but still fairly high—some 26% in Germany,[70] around 25 percent in Provence[71] and 20 percent or less in northern France. They were many fewer in Artois and the Netherlands,[72] and few still in England.[73] The questions then arise: why did Basilicata lose a number of settlements in the fourteenth and fifteenth centuries, why were its losses apparently greater than in most other areas and is there any pattern discernable which might explain why some places vanished and others did not?

To the first question, which concerns a problem which Basilicata shared with the whole of Europe, many answers have been suggested. One is to link the desertion of villages to a fall in the population and to claim that, as the population fell, many settlements, particularly those on "marginal" land were abandoned. The fall in the European population itself is undoubted, though its size and chronology are still to some extent disputed. It is generally held, however, that the population of Europe, having reached its maximum somewhere around the middle of the 13th century or shortly thereafter, began to level off and then slowly decline, the decline becoming apparent at different times in different places but being general throughout Europe by the second decade of the fourteenth century. This decline was greatly accelerated during the middle years of the fourteenth century by the Black Death and its subsequent visitations, until at least the end of the fourteenth century. There are few reliable statistics concerning the impact of the first visitation of the Black Death in 1347–49, but plenty of contemporary accounts of the horror which it occasioned. These, taken in conjunction with a series of statistics from various parts of Europe showing huge drops in the populations of various towns between the 1330s and 1360s are evidence that the mortality caused by the plague must have been very great. Precisely how great is harder to determine. Reasonably precise figures from Givry in Burgundy suggest a mortality of 33 percent and most other evidence seems to point to the same conclusion. There were however wide variations particularly in rural areas.[74] Still, we can suggest with some confidence that at least 25 percent of the population of Europe and at most perhaps as much as 45 percent died.[75] Subsequent outbreaks of the plague reduced the population still further, and certainly retarded any replacement of it. Nevertheless at different times during the fifteenth century the population did begin to recover. It had probably returned to pre-plague levels throughout Europe by the late sixteenth century.

Certainly the trends in European population sketched above fit in well with the chronology of deserted villages in Basilicata. The number of villages reaches its peak in the earlier part of the thirteenth century and begins to decline slowly from about 1250 onwards. It drops rapidly during the fourteenth century when the plague is at its height and then continues to drop rather more slowly until the middle of the fifteenth century. Thereafter the number is stabilised and in the sixteenth century begins at first gradually and then very rapidly to rise again. It is tempting then to blame the desertion of villages on population decrease and on the plague in particular. But does what we know of population in Basilicata conform to the general European pattern? And if so, can we necessarily link the phenomenon of deserted villages with demographic trends?

For Basilicata itself there is no direct evidence for demographic trends in the 14th century, or even for the Black Death. The Black Death is recorded for Naples in late 1347 and for the Regno as a whole in May 1348.[76] Giovanna I deplored its ravages throughout her realm,[77] and it is reasonable to suppose that Basilicata suffered from it like everywhere else, and that its population fell accordingly.[78] We can therefore, I think, assume a population decline of some magnitude but we have no statistics to indicate how great it was. Equally it is reasonable to assume a further decline in subsequent outbreaks of the plague. These again are not recorded for Basilicata but they are recorded for Naples in 1371, 1398, 1463, 1476, 1493, and 1522, according to del Panta;[79] and in 1382, 1394, 1402, 1422, 1448, 1458, 1463, 1479 according to A. Filangieri.[80] It is unlikely that Basilicata escaped all—or probably any—of these. There were also other outbreaks of disease, notably one, probably related to malnutrition caused by famine, in 1340–42.[81] Famine itself was also a serious problem in the fourteenth century. It is not recorded for the early part of the century when northern Europe suffered badly,[82] but there were bad harvests in the early 1340s and a serious famine in 1374–75.[83] Again it is impossible to assert categorically that Basilicata was affected but the liklihood is that it was; and that both disease and famine caused a fall in the population. The best data we have in this regard are from a series of records for the town of Altamura in Apulia. Altamura is about 40 kms from the medieval boundary of Basilicata and was always situated in a relatively sparsely settled area of the Regno. It is not therefore ideal for comparison but it is near enough to Basilicata for its history to be of some relevance. The records from Altamura for the fourteenth and fifteenth centuries were published before the destruction of the Naples Archive[84] and these show a steady and fairly drastic reduction in taxation between 1276 and 1437, followed by a sudden and even more drastic rise between 1437 and 1465. The reductions are expressly linked to a fall in population. Whether the rise reflects a subsequent upswing in the population is more doubtful. It may equally be a result of more savage taxation by the Aragonese on which we have at present very little data.[85] But at any rate, the fall in population in Altamura up to 1437 is attested and it is likely to have been paralleled in areas in its immediate vicinity.

Further information on the population of Basilicata can be extrapolated from various indications in the tax lists for the fourteenth and fifteenth centuries. These are partial and potentially misleading, but they are better than nothing. They are slightly more reliable for the later fifteenth century because, after the Aragonese takeover in the fifteenth century, an administrative reform led to the compilation of household lists on which tax assessments could be based, rather than lists of the assessments themselves. We know, therefore, from 1445 onwards, the total number of taxable households in the realm in various years. This figure is not completely accurate: some households were not taxed and were not therefore included in the taxation lists. These included new immigrants, who were often given tax remission to encourage them to settle; but there are other discrepancies also between the hearth lists prepared for taxation and other data still extant on numbers of hearths. Thus, whereas the tax lists would imply that by 1532 Melfi had been overtaken by Tursi in numbers, other evidence suggests that in fact Melfi had many more hearths than the tax lists imply and was still the largest town in Basilicata (v Table XI). Nevertheless, though they are not wholly accurate, the tax lists do at least give the numbers of taxable hearths which should provide a reasonable basis of comparison with earlier data also taken from tax documentation.

In 1448–65, then, the total number of taxable households in southern Italy was between 23,000 and 24,000. It dropped slightly to 21,500 in 1485, and rose again to over 25,000 by the end of the century. This figure remained more or less stable until 1518, and then began to shoot up rapidly. Basilicata, however, seems not to have been quite in line with these developments. Beloch published a figure for Basilicata of 13,708 hearths in ninety-three places in 1455. Admittedly the hearth list for that year was incomplete and the figure must be higher. Nevertheless it omits at most seven places, so it cannot be far off. The population of Basilicata, therefore, must have grown rapidly in the late fifteenth century, for by 1505 there were some 22,000 hearths in ninety-seven places in Basilicata. By contrast it grew more slowly than anywhere else except the Capitanata in the early sixteenth century, so that by the middle of the century the differences had evened out (v Table VIII). By and large, however, it may be said that demographic recovery in Basilicata began relatively early, but as elsewhere in the south, did not reach its full extent until the mid-sixteenth century.

How then does the population of Basilicata in about 1500 compare with the population of the fourteenth century? To answer this question, we need to arrive at some means of estimating the fourteenth century population based on the amount of tax it was paying since this last is the only datum we have. Such an estimate is not easy to achieve, though it has frequently been attempted. The first problem is that neither Frederick II, who introduced the hearth tax,[86] nor Charles of Anjou, who systematised it, levied the same tax on each household. Frederick expressly stated that the wealthier were to help the poor, and indeed, to require them to do so was standard medieval practice. It was even possible for local authorities to alter the basis of taxation altogether—we know that on one occasion a sales tax was substituted for the normal hearth tax.[87] The most we can hope for then, is to establish the *average* sum paid by each household throughout the kingdom. This also can be difficult for sometimes the king clearly demanded more than at others (e.g., in 1275, when the amount of tax assessed was half as much again as that of the following year. This however, does seem to have been exceptional and to have been based quite literally on a double levy.) On the whole, however, it seems likely that there was a normal basis of assessment under Charles of Anjou yielding around 4000–5000 *uncie* from Basilicata and a constant one from about 1294 onwards yielding between 3,600 and 3,800. The minor fluctuations in this probably do represent changes in the population or prosperity of individual places rather than changes in the the basis of assessment.

In order to arrive at any reasonable correlation between the taxes paid and the hearths paying them, we need to rely on the very few documents which show both the number of hearths taxed and the amount of tax paid. The first historian seriously to tackle this problem, P. Egidi,[88] found four such instances, none of them unfortunately in Basilicata[89]. These showed that to divide the tax of a given place by the number of households in it produced highly improbable quotients involving fractions of a *granus:* secondly that the tax per household fluctuated wildly from 128 ⅔ *grani* to twenty-nine. Nevertheless, while accepting the existence of the problems, Egidi postulated a mean, based on his four places, of 32–35 *grani* per household. This certainly is not much—the wages of a donkey driver with one donkey at Melfi in the 1280s were eight *grani* a day[90]—and, as we shall see it implies a very large population. Nevertheless, it has the merit among modern hypotheses of being based exclusively on the evidence, making minimal use of unsubstantiated modifications to the conclusions.

The problem of quotients involving fractions of a *granus* led Pardi[91] to suggest that the tax should perhaps be computed on a per capita basis: that is, he assumed that the unit of assessment was the individual rather than the household. He postulated, on evidence drawn from the tax assessments of Calabria, the area in which he was chiefly interested, a tax of twelve *grani* a head, pointing out that this could be divided into the tax totals for Calabria to produce whole quotients. His arguments may be correct for Calabria—as we have seen, regional variations were possible—but the attempt to apply it to the whole Regno is less happy. Twelve *grani* does in fact produce a whole quotient when divided into the tax total for Basilicata in 1275–76, but there are serious objections to the hypothesis. Firstly, although the total tax demanded in Basilicata in 1275–76 is exactly divisible by 12, that asked in 1276–77, for which we know the total sum demanded from Basilicata (though not the detailed breakdown), is not. This might be explained on the grounds that no new census was made in the interim and temporary adjustments were made on the basis of households rather than of individuals, but such a procedure seems odd. Secondly, many of the tax assessments of other regions are not exactly divisible by twelve, though of course we could suggest different divisors for different regions. Finally—perhaps the most serious objection—when the crown entertained pleas for reduction of taxes on behalf of a locality, it was interested in the number of households, not the number of individuals therein. These arguments, taken together, seem to me conclusive and Pardi's solutions must therefore, I think, be rejected.

Beloch, in his magisterial work on the Italian population,[92] was not perturbed by fractions of a *granus* in quotients—the relationship between households and taxes could after all be expressed only by averages—but he was unhappy with the size of population implied by Egidi's conclusions. For the whole Regno this would be about 3,400,000, about the same as in the late sixteenth century, when there was alleged to be pressure of population on the pasture land and cultivation of marginal land far up the mountains. The objection seems valid, though it may be pointed out that there was probably less land given over to pasture in the thirteenth century than in the sixteenth and there would certainly have been strong vested interests opposing its re-conversion to arable in the later period. Still, Beloch was able to cast some doubt on Egidi's figures. He pointed out that Egidi's data came mostly from the Cilento region which was badly hit by war in the late thirteenth century, and that quotas per hearth were markedly higher in the early fourteenth century than in the thirteenth. He argued that post war data were probably more reliable than war time data and applied the former also to the tax lists of 1276. He thus postulated a mean tax of sixty-six *grani* (one ninth of an *uncia*) per hearth. Beloch's estimate of the population is thus considerably lower than that of Egidi—about 2,000,000 in all.

Most recently, Angerio Filangieri has returned to the problem.[93] In his opinion, Beloch's figures for the cities are still too high, making Bari, with some 25,000 inhabitants, as large as all but the greatest of the north Italian cities and giving Barletta an even more startling a population of some 31,000. He therefore postulates a graded tax whereby the inhabitants of large cities paid ninety *grani* per household, those of medium-sized towns sixty, and those of the villages thirty. For the Regno, this brings the total population to about 3,000,000, less than in the sixteenth century but still substantially more than Beloch's total. For Basilicata, which contained few towns or cities, the effect is in fact to push the population up to nearly the total suggested by Egidi, though Melfi, Venosa, and one or two other cities emerge as considerably smaller. The chief objection to Filangieri's hypothesis is that it seems to have virtually no evidence to support it. Its chief justification is its plausibility. Given, however, that no theory is based on very satisfactory evidence, it deserves some consideration.[94]

In each theory outlined above, the total is, of course, merely the number of households in the area. This gives rise to a further problem of what multiplier to use to convert households into population numbers. This again has been a subject of much debate, but

Beloch, extrapolating from rather late evidence, suggests between 5 and 5.5 people per household and his arguments have been fairly generally accepted.[95]

There seems little point in adding to the current theories on the relationship between taxes and population, but some further light may be thrown on the subject by approaching it from another angle. The attacks on Egidi were made on two grounds. The first was that 3,500,000 people were more than southern Italy could have supported in the Middle Ages. The number is greater than that of about 3,000,000 known to have been reached at the end of the sixteenth century when there are also known to have been distinct population pressures in Italy. Secondly, as we have seen, the towns seem implausibly large. It is difficult to believe that Melfi in the thirteenth century could have been nearly as large as London, with a population of 27,000. Egidi's estimates seem on the whole less plausible than those of his successors. There remain the estimates of Beloch and Filangieri. For Basilicata, that of Beloch gives us some 38,500 hearths in 1276 or 211,150 people and 33,363 hearths (183,500 people) in 1320. Filangieri gives 204,859 people for 1320. He gives no figures for 1276 but on a rough calculation his 1320 figure can be increased by about 12 percent to some 229,443 people. This gives a density of, for Beloch, some twenty–two persons per sq.km. assuming an area of about 9,384 square kilometers for Basilicata[96] in 1320 and for Filangieri twenty-nine persons per sq. km. By comparison with other areas, these figures are not exceptionally high. They are also, however, not very enlightening since they include both urban and rural populations and any estimate of their implications would have to take into account the quality of the land in Basilicata. To determine how great were the population pressures, it is probably more useful to look at a restricted area and determine what size of population it could have supported.

To do this completely satisfactorily would presumably involve estimating the proportion of produce requisitioned by the landlords, the proportion sold, the proportion available for those who worked the soil and the numbers of individuals dependent for their nourishment on these last; not to mention the quality of the soil and the techniques used.[97] This is obviously impossible in the present state of the records but the possibilities for subsistence in a small rural community do offer scope for investigation. One such community in the northwest of Basilicata, round the commune of Ruoti, has been studied.[98] Here, in an area of roughly 125 sq.kms., the late thirteenth century population was, using Filangieri's calculations, about 3,226 people, and using Beloch's, about 1,466. These figures are based on the returns of four villages in the area, which latter forms a natural geographic unit surrounded on all sides by high ridges except for a narrow outlet to the west for the Fiumara di Ruoti.[99] (It is worth noting that one of these villages, Caldane, paid a tax of only five *tari* which, on Beloch's calculations would give it a population of at most two families which seems improbably small.[100]) With regard to density, this would be twenty-two persons per sq.km according to Filangieri and 11.5 according to Beloch. We can, however, be a little more precise. Not all land in the area is cultivable. Some is too precipitous and some, in the river valleys, is subject to heavy annual flooding and virtually sterile. In all about eighty-five square kilometres is cultivable. In fact then, in the improbable event that every household in the valley had the same amount of land, the size of farmland available was either 16.9 or 31.8 hectares depending on the calculation. This is not to suggest that every peasant in the valley would have enjoyed that amount of land—obviously distributions were unequal—or that any peasant would have enjoyed all the produce of it, much of which would have been absorbed by his landlords. Nevertheless, even by Filangieri's calculations there is little evidence of overcrowding here. The size of farm necessary to supply a peasant with a reasonable subsistence on cereal without many supplements would have been, in the thirteenth and fourteenth centuries, in this area about six hectares, allowing for moderately productive soil and rather poor farming techniques. Families could, and in many cases did survive on much less.[101]

On Filangieri's figures, there was not much surplus in the Ruoti valley, given unequal holdings and the need to find money to pay tenant dues and taxes. Nevertheless, given that most places in Europe were experiencing some population pressure by the late thirteenth century, his figures seem more plausible than those of Beloch, which in fact imply very little pressure at all. On the other hand, if Filangieri is correct, there were more people in Basilicata in 1320 than at any time later before the late seventeenth century. This is by no means improbable: in parts of northern France, the medieval population was not again equalled until the nineteenth century. Indeed even the high figures of Egidi seem from this viewpoint not impossible though his towns still seem on the large side. In what follows, Filangieri's figures will therefore be accepted as the most probable. Those of Egidi are ignored as being very close to those of Filangieri except in the instances (i.e., the towns) in which they are least probable and in which they are also least substantiated. Beloch's figures are given in the notes. Of course the area of Ruoti was not necessarily typical of the whole of Basilicata. A further series of studies is needed, though in many areas it might be difficult to establish the boundaries necessary to make them. Still a preliminary comparison with other villages in Basilicata which fall into obvious groups does not suggest that their population densities would be very significantly higher.

There were then, in Basilicata, in 1320 about 50,000 hearths.[102] What sort of demographic development do these figures suggest for the period before 1276? If the calculations used previously for the Norman period have any validity at all, they show a very large rise in the rural population. The "average" village of some twelve households has risen to around 300.[103] Only some forty places have fewer than 150 households. And the largest villages (not counting the bishoprics which were classified as urban centres under the Normans) have upwards of 600 households. In addition, the number of settlements has itself risen. When this population increase reached its zenith we cannot say. The number of settlements was greatest in or before 1246, but if settlements were abandoned while their population fled elsewhere, the reduction in population need not have kept pace with that in settlements. Probably, however, the reign of Manfred and the early years of Charles I did see the reversal of the earlier demographic trend. Certainly the population was falling, albeit slowly, after 1276.

The fall became more marked in the last centuries of the Middle Ages. Some 50,000 hearths in 1320 present a violent contrast with the figure of perhaps 15,000 which is the most we can postulate for 1445, or even 22,295 in 1510; 41,964 in 1561 is still appreciably lower. There is every reason, therefore, to accept that the decline in the number of settlements in the late Middle Ages was matched by a decline in population. Was it also caused by that decline?

It is true that disease could sometimes cause the disappearance of villages—in other countries the Black Death carried off the whole population of some places, or at any rate so much of it as to force the rest to move.[104] Others may have gone in the wake of successive outbreaks of the plague or of other diseases.[105] Herlihy, discussing the decline of Pisa suggests that malaria was a major factor in this[106] and certainly the evidence for south Italy suggests that malaria, having been a relatively minor problem in the earlier thirteenth century, became more serious from the middle of the century. Siponto was abandoned for Manfredonia in the late thirteenth century supposedly because of malaria. Charles of Anjou stayed near Foggia, later highly malarial, but subsequent kings avoided the area.[107] Unfortunately our detailed records of the middle years of the fourteenth century are too scanty to show the impact of disease but it was probably considerable. Nevertheless, though it may account for some disappearances, it is unlikely to explain the abandonment of all the lost villages of Basilicata.

The most obvious alternative, that the number of settlements declined because people migrated to larger centers, will not work. Such a phenomenon has been documented for other areas, eg. England where the population of York actually rose by 50 percent between 1348 and 1377.[108] For Basilicata we lack such precise evidence but a comparison of numbers of households in the larger cities is instructive here. In 1320 Melfi had 1,914 hearths.[109] In 1532 it had 781 taxable hearths: and though there is some evidence that this is an underestimate—it had perhaps nearer 1,000 hearths in all—this is still a big drop. Venosa in 1320 had 986 hearths;[110] In 1532 it had 695. Montepeloso in 1320 had 760 hearths;[111] in 1532 it had 314. The dates are too far apart to make a good basis of comparison but it is difficult to see here, even given a general drop in population, or a higher mortality in the cities than in the countryside—in itself by no means proved to have been always the case[112]—any evidence of substantial migration to the towns.

Of course there must have been some local migration. Unless we suppose that the entire population of abandoned villages died off, the survivors must have gone somewhere. But where they went was to neighboring villages. Thus Avigliano rose from 73 households to 133.[113] Presumably it accomodated some population from the vanished neighboring villages of Caldane, Santa Sophia, and Ruoti. Episcopia rose from 87 households to 143,[114] doubtless reflecting the disappearance of Faratum, Pulsandrana, and Calvera in the south. One of the few new foundations of the fifteenth century, Ferrandina, was populated largely from the abandoned neighboring town of Oggianum after an earthquake; and the fourteenth century foundation of Atella probably similarly collected together the former inhabitants of villages thenceforth deserted in or near the Valle di

Vitalba—Monte Marcone, Monticchio, Rionero, and perhaps even Ruoti.[115] Grassano, Gorgoglione, Marsico Vetere, and Tursi also increased in size.[116] But none of these places except perhaps Tursi and Ferrandina can be called towns—the effect of migration was merely to enlarge a few villages to compensate for a larger number which were deserted.[117]

If this is the case, it still does not explain the migration. It has been argued that elsewhere, on the fertile land and productive areas of western Europe there was a contraction in settlement size, but abandonments were rare. In central Europe small settlements on marginal land were abandoned,[118] and in England too, villages which were abandoned tended to be among the smaller settlements of a given area.[119] What we know of Basilicata does not fit either category very well. Obviously settlements were abandoned, so we are not looking merely at a contraction in their size. On the other hand, although small places were certainly likely to disappear—the small *casali*, newly taxed in 1320, were no longer separately listed in the household lists and had presumably either been abandoned or included with neighbouring communities (without, however, appreciably enlarging them)—nevertheless some small places did survive (e.g., Grassano and Episcopia); and those abandoned were not necessarily, or even usually on notably poor land. Furthermore, some of the deserted places were quite large, like Monte Serico, Santa Sophia, Irsi, and, most remarkable of all, Oggiano.

Some of these deserted places we know to have been victims of natural disasters. There was a great earthquake in 1456 which must have affected much of the region.[120] Oggiano, its most notable victim, was in fact abandoned and its population in due course moved to the newly founded settlement of Ferrandina. Casal Aspro was also abandoned as a result of this earthquake.[121] Nevertheless, we should be cautious in attributing the desertion of villages exclusively to natural disasters. This was after all a European phenomenon and not all places in Europe suffered from earthquakes. Moreover, a thriving community will survive even the worst earthquake. Besides, on the evidence of the numbers of settlements in the 1445 tax lists, most of these settlements had already gone by 1446. They could of course have been destroyed in earlier earthquakes but on these, if they existed, we have no information.

An alternative explanation is that the deserted villages were destroyed in war.[122] Certainly, in the case of Satrianum, it is said that it was abandoned after the troops of Giovanna II had razed it to the ground; but the story is suspect and the event is supposed to have taken place in 1420, five years after a tax assessment was made from which Satrianum is known to have been omitted so the explanation does not carry much conviction.[123] And apart from Satrianum, the documents do not report the deliberate and successful destruction of villages, though there were complaints that companies of soldiers were destroying the harvests in the 1330s.[124] As with earthquakes, however, enemy activities in the Middle Ages rarely led to the permanent destruction of a thriving community. Rapolla for example was "razed to the ground" by Manfred in the mid 13th century but it was one of the most highly taxed places in Basilicata by 1276. Moreover, unlike Northern Europe, where the impact of war was very much greater in the fourteenth century than it had been in the twelfth and thirteenth, Basilicata had suffered from almost constant unrest throughout the Middle ages. It is difficult to believe that war had a greater effect on Basilicata in the fourteenth and fifteenth centuries than it had done earlier—indeed for the reign of Robert the Wise at least, war must have been rather less of a problem than was usually the case.

Finally, there is the explanation that the main reason for deserted villages was a change in the pattern of agricultural exploitation. In the thirteenth century most places in Basilicata practised small scale polyculture, each village producing some cereal, mostly wheat and barley, and usually some vines. Most also had some cattle and pigs. The evidence for all this is not extensive, consisting largely of a few descriptions of the sources of landlord's income from various fiefs made at the time of the Angevin conquest,[125] but taken in conjunction with sporadic references in the Angevin Registers, it is sufficient. An obvious change which could have been made in the fifteenth century would be from arable to sheep farming. This would have been a sensible response to the declining population. It would also have countered to some extent, at least for the landlords, the ill effects of declining grain exports from south Italy,[126] though it is unlikely that the peasant economy of Basilicata was affected by these to the same extent as areas further east in the Regno.[127] We know that such a change took place on a large scale in Apulia.[128] Whether it also took place in Basilicata is less certain—except for the extreme northeast around Monte Serico, the documents of the *Dogana della mena pecore* do not cover Basilicata—but there is every liklihood that Monte Serico itself fell victim to sheep rearing at this point, and other places in what subsequently became important sheep country may well have done the same. There had been some sheep rearing in the south round Lagonegro in the earlier Middle Ages, whence the sheep were taken to the coast round Metaponto for the winter. There was also transhumance in the thirteenth century between the uplands of Basilicata south of Potenza and the Tavoliere of Apulia through the forest of Lagopesole.[129] But there seems to have been some additional land given over to sheep rearing in the north for, by the sixteenth century, there were alleged to be important sheep pastures round Melfi, Lavello, Genosa, Banzi, Palazzo San Gervasio, Montemilone, Spinazzola, and Montepeloso,[130] and this perhaps accounts for the disappearance of some places in the area.

Other places in good hunting country were probably abandoned also. Among the places to disappear were Lagopesole, Gaudiano, Caldane, Monte Marcone, and Armentum, all in or close to royal forest; and Santa Sophia, in an area known for its seigneurial forest.[131] Finally, some areas were indeed perhaps abandoned as marginal land not worth cultivating. But these, as we have seen, can only rarely be proved to be more marginal than those of their surviving neighbors. A more plausible explanation is that some settlements were abandoned because they were inconvenient. There is nothing wrong with the soil of Irsi and Monte Serico, on hills rising sharply from the surrounding plain, but they are tiring to reach and must have relied on cisterns for water, for there is no source close at hand. Again, it cannot be said that all abandoned villages were short of water—much of Basilicata is well supplied with natural springs and Caldane, for example, has an abundance of excellent water. Equally, many hill top towns fully as inconvenient as Irsi and Monteserico survived. Nevertheless, in these cases at least and possibly one or two others, difficulty of access and poor water supply may well have been factors in their abandonment.

The conversion of land to sheep rearing or hunting forest, where it was done, was obviously the result of an initiative by landlords since it had to be done on a larger scale than any peasant could have managed. Cherubini has emphasised the importance of proprietors in determining not only land use but the pattern of settlement in any area, specifically linking changes in Tuscan settlement to the increase, in the late Middle Ages, of urban proprietors.[132] In Basilicata, most communes were, and remained until long after the Middle Ages under the control of a feudal nobility—feudal in the literal sense that they held their land in fief of the crown. Nevertheless there are some changes to be observed in the nature of the landed aristocracy of Basilicata towards the end of the Middle Ages, which may have affected settlement. In the catalogue of the barons, most lords are resident on their fiefs. They may hold of other lords; but with a few exceptions, such as the fiefs of the counts of Marsico and Tricarico, most fiefs have a lord who lives at least part of the time locally. Even the crown, the greatest (though rarely the worst) of all absentee landlords, held little land except for Potenza and Melfi in Basilicata. Under Frederick II, though there were more absentee landlords, the crown was still little represented. The castles and *domus* were held directly by Frederick, but few other places.[133] By the time of the Angevins, this is no longer true. Charles of Anjou made many grants to his French followers and in doing so, tended to lump together a large number of fairly scattered fiefs.[134] The inevitable result was that as absenteeism among landlords became more widespread, landlords became less concerned with their fiefs than formerly. This tendency became even more marked in the Aragonese period when many fiefs were concentrated in the hands of very few great lords—the San Severini, the Caracciolo, the Guevara, and later the Doria.[135] Bad landlords may have been a significant factor in the reduction or prosperity in southern Italy which led to the abandonment of some rural settlements and the shrinkage of others.

There is then no one explanation for the abandonment of villages in late medieval Basilicata. It can be said, however, that while Basilicata reacted to the problems of depopulation in the later Middle Ages much as other countries in Europe did, its problems of disease and war, common to most places, were compounded by natural disasters—hence perhaps its exceptionally though not uniquely high number of abandoned sites. The reduction in the number of sites was more or less permanent. The number of sites in Basilicata did rise again in the modern period. In particular, an attempt to encourage new settlement led to the immigration in the late fifteenth and sixteenth centuries of numbers of Slavs from the Balkans who founded a few new villages, repopulated Ruoti and San Chirico and established colonies in one or two other places.[136] But numbers of settlements never again attained anything like those of the 13th century.

Conclusion

How then does the history of settlement in Medieval Basilicata fit in with general European trends? In broad outline, it fits well into the European picture, in so far it is possible to generalize for all of

Europe. Like many other regions, it began with a small population in the Lombard period, which increased steadily to the second half of the thirteenth century, declined slightly and then, between the mid fourteenth and later fifteenth century plummeted, rose slowly, and had almost or completely regained its thirteenth century level by the mid sixteenth century. The number of settlements more or less fluctuated with the population until the last rise which was not matched by a similar rise in the number of inhabited settlements. The earlier population expansion, however, led to a significant number of new settlements. There were more places in Basilicata in 1246 (176) than there are communes now—though admittedly there are now some *frazioni* of communes which are in fact separate villages of some size.

Nevertheless, although in broad outline Basilicata fits well into the European picture, it also presents some anomalies. Firstly, whatever may be said about the population—and the evidence on that is ambiguous—the first decline in numbers of settlements took place between 1250 and 1276. This is not in itself surprising, for the troubled period of the Angevin conquest clearly had an adverse effect on the countryside. Still, the previous equally troubled periods of the Norman and Hohenstauffen conquests did not see a fall in either the population or the number of places inhabited in Basilicata; but rather the reverse. More significantly, the decline, when it came, antedates that of most other places in Europe.[137] It is true that there was a very minor decline in these years elsewhere[138] and even in Italy,[139] but these lost villages were few in number and usually offset by new foundations. Admittedly there were new foundations in Basilicata too, but certainly not in sufficient numbers to offset the losses.

Secondly, although there is certainly some evidence of an epidemic in Melfi in 1312, on the whole the appalling troubles of the second decade of the fourteenth century in Northern Europe did not reach Basilicata. Italy further north was certainly affected[140] though perhaps less gravely than places like Flanders,[141] but in Basilicata our evidence, scanty as it is, seems definitely to indicate that the population declined only slightly. It did perhaps show a tendency, albeit short-lived, to move to hamlets in the countryside more convenient for agriculture than the previous fortified settlements.

From 1330 onwards the population in most places began to decline rather more rapidly. There was another epidemic in Basilicata but the little evidence we have suggests that the population continued stable for at least another decade. Thereafter there are no reliable data until the fifteenth century. It is unlikely that Basilicata escaped the famine of 1340 which hit the south exceptionally hard and we can probably assume a fall in the population from that time onwards. On the impact of the plague itself we know only that Giovanna I lamented that she could not, in 1349, raise a tenth of the taxes which she had formerly enjoyed because of its ravages. But it was probably the subsequent as much as the initial outbreaks of plague which led, at least in part, to the depopulation and shrinkage in the number of settlements which took place in the late fourteenth and early fifteenth centuries. Other factors contributing to these would include famine, diseases other than the plague, war, earthquakes and other natural disasters and perhaps changes in land use, though these last were perhaps more likely to have been a result than a cause of a fall in the number of settlements.

That the region of Basilicata suffered a drastic demographic decline in the fourteenth and fifteenth centuries because it was over-populated to the point of saturation is extremely unlikely, given that in the Ruoti area there was apparently sufficient land to go round even in the 1270s. The so-called "Malthusian" debate over the de-population of the fourteenth century has been continuing for many years now with ever more qualifications being added to each side of the argument. What we know of Basilicata does not support the theories of the "Malthusians." Certainly the area had reached a pop-ulation density not again to be attained until the sixteenth century but it had by no means reached saturation point—or if it had, it was because landlords were taking too large a share of the available resources, not because the resources were lacking. Yet the population did decline greatly, and more settlements were abandoned than in most parts of Europe. This is not to argue that there was no problem of overpopulation anywhere in thirteenth century Europe: it seems very probable that there was. But overpopulation will not explain the disasters and the fall in population over the whole continent and certainly does not seem to be a valid explanation for settlement patterns in late Medieval south Italy.

The evidence for the history of settlement in Basilicata is fragmentary and imprecise compared with that for many places in Europe. Nevertheless, one conclusion is clear: no single cause will explain the changes in settlement and more particularly the abandon-ment of villages in the fourteenth and fifteenth centuries. It need arouse no surprise that many places disappeared, weakened as they were by a fall in population caused by disease, vulnerable to acts of war and to seismic disturbances, perhaps in a few cases overpopulated and relying on unsuitable land, and in some cases victims of irresponsible landlords. The general causes of decline were many, but the immediate reason for the disappearance of villages in Basilicata varied from place to place.

NOTES

[1] Art. 18 of an agreement between Frederick II and Gregory IX ordering officials in the justiciarates of Basilicata and Bari not to bring clergy before secular justices except in matters concerning fiefs. *Monumenta Germaniae Historiae* (hereafter MGH), *Epistolae selectae saeculi XIII* I (1883), p. 598.

[2] There are of course some studies: C. Klapisch and J. Day, 'Villages désertés en Italie', in *Villages désertés et histoire économique*, École pratique des Hautes Études, & VIe section, Centre de Recherches Historiques: Les Hommes et la Terre, XI, Paris, 1965, p. 437; A. Filangieri, *Territorio e popolazione nell'Italia Meridionale. Evoluzione storica*, Università di Napoli. Centro di specializzazione e ricerche economico-agrarie per il mezzogiorno. Collana di studi e ricerche 13, (Milan, 1980); C. Klapisch-Zuber, "Villagi abbandonati ed emigrazione interne," *Storia d'Italia*, ed. Giulio Einaudi, V, 1, (Turin, 1973); Maurice Aymard, Henri Bresc, "Problemi di storia dell'insediamento nella Sicilia medievale e moderna, 1100–1800," *Quaderni Storici*, 8 (1973), 945–976. Nevertheless, southern Italy hardly gets adequate coverage in many general histories. *v.* e.g. Wilhelm Abel (trans.O. Ordish), *Agricultural fluctuations in Europe from the 13th to the 20th centuries* (London, 1980), pt. I, which mentions southern Italy not at all or Norman Pounds, *An Economic History of Medieval Europe*, (London, 1974), which says very little about it.

[3] *Catalogus Baronum* in *Fonti per la Storia d'Italia* 101, ed. E. Jamison, 1972.

[4] Eduard Winkelmann, *Acta Imperii Inedita Saeculi XII et XIV* I, no. 1005, pp. 768–80. *v* also, for a very full discussion, E. Sthamer, *Die Bauten der Hohenstauffen in Unteritalien. I. Die Verwaltung der Kastelle im Königreich Sizilien unter Kaiser Friedrich II und Karl I von Anjou.* Konigl. Preussisches Historisches Institut in Rom, (Leipzig, 1914).

[5] Published by Domenico Vendola, "Rationes Decimarum nei secoli XIII e XIV: Apulia-Lucania-Calabria," *Studi e Testi* LXXXIV (Vatican City, 1939).

[6] The first, for 1276, is published by G. Racioppi, "Geografia e demografia della provincia di Basilicata," *Archivio Storico per le provincie Napoletane* (hereafter ASPN), XV, 1890, pp. 565–82 (document printed pp. 565–73). The second for 1307–1320 is printed by Camillo Minieri-Riccio, *Notizie Storiche tratte da 62 Registri Angioini del Archivio di Stato di Napoli*, (Naples, 1877), pp. 177 ff.

[7] In the mid-12th century, the area of the later Justiciarate of Basilicata fell into four major and several minor subdivisions. For the purposes of this paper, I have taken into account all fiefs listed in the Catalogue which would at any time later, before 1600, have been included in the justiciarate. *v* table 1. For a fuller discussion of the structure of administration in the Catalogue, *v* E. Jamison, "The Norman administration of Apulia and Calabria," *Papers of the British School at Rome* (hereafter PBSR)

(1913), 211–481. Further discussion of the Catalogue may be found in B. Capasso, "Sul Catalogo dei feudi e dei feudatari delle Provincie Napoletane," *Atti della Reale Accademia di Archeologia, Lettere e Belle Arti*, 4 (1896), 293–371; Claude Cahen, *Le régime féodale de l'Italie Normande*, (Paris, 1940); E. Jamison, "Additional work on the *Catalogus Baronum*," *Bull. Istit. Italiano per il Medioevo e Archivio Muratoriano* (1971), pp. 1–63; and, on Basilicata, Tommaso Pedio, *Per la storia del mezzogiorno d'Italia: note e appunti*, pp. 92 ff.

8 It was mentioned once—Jamison, *Cat.Bar.* no. 932. "et de feudo Pontiscurvi et Sugii quod judicie Curie recuperavit aput Potentiam quod est, sicut ipse dixit, feudum unius militis."

9 Jamison, *Cat.Bar.* nos. 402, 146.

10 Giustino Fortunato, *Avigliano nei secoli XII e XIII*, Avigliano, 1905, doc. I, citing Archivio della Badia de la Cava, perg.grec.28.

11 The difficulty is not lessened by the tendency of south Italian communes to claim Lombard origins on little or no evidence. e.g. the gateway at Avigliano and the castle at Ruoti are both allegedly Lombard: *v* Vincenzo Claps, *Avigliano: Brevi cenni sulle origini e gli sviluppi*, 3rd ed. (1966), pp. 12, 17 and Gerardo Salinardi, *L'Antica Terra di Ruoti*, Ruoti (1973), p. 8. Neither gives any evidence and the remaining buildings certainly show no trace of Lombard origins. The following places existed in Lombard times but the list is not necessarily complete. (The source is André Guillou, "L'Italia Byzantina dalla caduta di Ravenna all'arrivo dei Normanni," in Giuseppe Galasso ed., *Storia d'Italia III, Il Mezzogiorno dai Byzantinti a Federico II*. Turin, 1983.)

Marsico Vetere	Laurenzana
Corleto Perticara	Pietrapertosa
Acerenza	Tricarico
Tolve	Viggiano
Roccanova	Senise
Noepoli/Noha	Cerchosimo
Oriola	San Chirico Raparo
Castelsaraceno	Teana
Carbone	Calvera
Episcopia	Lauria
Lagonegro	Rivello
Castellucio Inferiore	Mormanno
Castelluccio Superiore	Rotonda
Laino	Pisticci
Stigliano	Colobraro
Montalbano	Tursi
Nova Siri (Bollita)	

12 The survey round San Giovanni di Ruoti, in the forthcoming publication on San Giovanni di Ruoti, ed. A. M. Small and R. J. Buck.

13 Chris Wickham, 'Settlement problems in early medieval Italy: Lucca territory', *Archeologia medievale* 5 (1978), 495–503.

14 Chris Wickham, *Early medieval Italy: central power and local society, 400–1000* (London, 1981), pp. 163–5; Pierre Toubert, *Structures du Latium Mediévale* (Rome, 1973), cp. 4, pp. 303–68; Vera von Falkenhausen, "I Longobardi Meridionale," in G. Galasso, ed., *Storia d'Italia*, III, pp. 298–302.

15 D. C. Douglas, *The Norman Achievement* (London, 1969) p. 77, doubts that there

were even as many as three thousand mounted Normans at the battle of Civitate. L. R. Ménager, "Pesanteur et étiologie de la colonisation normande en Italie" in *Hommes et institutions de l'Italie normande* Variorum (London, 1981), also indicates how relatively few the incoming Normans were.

[16] In this analysis, the contribution of those assessed for the service of one knight under the *augmentum* only has been ignored, since, for this, even lords of only one villein were expected to give service. The service of two knights under the *augmentum* has, however, been taken to imply the obligation of one knight's service in normal circumstances, even if this is not expressly stated. This may occasionally be misleading but it is probably generally valid. Eighteen communities were counted: numbers of villeins are as follows:

15 plus a mill; 26; 40; 46; 24 plus a mill; 45; 23; 29; 33; 22; 35; 30 plus a mill; 26; 19; 18. plus some more (number unspecified) plus a mill; 28; 22; 28 plus a mill.

[17] *v* below p. 35.

[18] Filangieri, pp. 226–7.

[19] On this *v* G. Duby, *Rural Economy and Country Life in the Medieval West*, (trans. C. Postan) (London, 1968), pp. 81–4.

[20] Luigi Ranieri, *Basilicata*, Le Regione d'Italia ed. R. Almagià XV (Turin, 1961), p. 43.

[21] Gennaro-Maria Monti, 'Cinque postilli di storia Calabro-Lucana', ACL I (1931), pp. 93–4.

[22] *v* Giustino Fortunato, *Badie, Feudi e Baroni della Valle di Vitalba*, ed. Tommaso Pedio, 3 vols., Manduria, 1968, II, p. 15.

[23] On the distinction between woods and forests *v* Pierre Toubert, "Paysages ruraux et techniques de production," in *Potere, Società e popolo nell'età dei due Guglielmi*. Centro di Studi Normanno-svevi; Università di Bari, Atti 4 (1979).

[24] L Mattei-Ceresoli, "Tramutola," ACL XIII (1943), p. 106.

[25] *v* e.g. Toubert, (at note 14), pp. 308–63.

[26] Reg.Ang. XIX, reg.81, no. 247.

[27] Reg.Ang. XIX, reg.82, no. 223.

[28] Toubert, (at note 14), pp. 303–50.

[29] Sthamer, (at note 4), I, p. 16

[30] Policoro might be supposed to have been transferred to Calabria for it was right on the border. This may indeed have been done at some point in the Middle Ages but it was still in Basilicata in 1270 and should therefore probably have been taxed with that province in 1276 if it was taxable. *I registri della Cancelleria Angioina ricostruitti da R.Filangieri. Testi e documenti di storia Napoletana*, Accademia Pontaniana (Naples, 1950), (hereafter Reg.Ang.) XVIII, reg.80, no. 673. For Petrolla *v* ibid. III, reg.12, no. 249.

[31] For Pisticci and Montalbano *v* Reg.Ang., loc.cit. For Muro, *v* Reg.Ang. VII, reg.28, no. 199; IX, reg.41, no. 253. For Roccanova, *v* Reg.Ang. XI, reg.63, no. 385. For Lagopesole, ibid., *v* no. 376. For San Marco, *v* Reg.Ang. XXII, reg.92, no. 198.

[32] "*Dishabitatus*"/ "*desabitato*" clearly does not mean totally deserted for many of the places so described continued to be assessed for taxes. It means rather that such places had suffered a serious fall in population.

[33] Camillo Minieri-Riccio, *Studi Storici su Fascicoli Angioini della regia zecca di Napoli*, (Naples, 1863), p. 63.

[34] Reg.Ang. VII, reg.24, no. 152.

[35] Reg.Ang. VII, reg.24, no. 210.

[36] A. Filangieri, (at note 2) p. 178

[37] Giustino Fortunato, (at note 10), doc.3.

[38] Lorenzo Lanzetti, "Il Vespro della valle di Vitalba," *La Basilicata nel Mondo* ann 1, no. 1, pp. 123–6. This has no references and may be unreliable but it is presumably not total fabrication. See also Paolo di Grazia, "L'Insurrezzione della Basilicata contra Carlo d'Angio," ACL VIII (1938), pp. 225–64; Giuliano Vitale, "Potenza nell cozzo tra Svevi ed Angioini per il possesso del regno di Napoli," ASPN, n.s. 38 (1958), 137–151; Tommaso Pedio, *Potenza dai Normanni agli Aragonesi* (Bari, 1964).

[39] By one reckoning, it could have had as many as 27 000 inhabitants while the smallest number suggested would be about 10,000. Venosa would have had anything from 5,000 to 12,000. (*v* below p. 29.)

[40] According to one estimate, Barletta would have had 31,500, Trani 26,000, Bitonto 25,000 and Bari 22,500: *v* Beloch, p. 200. On the lowest possible estimate, they would have been about one third this size—still substantial for the period in question. (*v* below, p. 29.)

[41] 5 citizens of Potenza were found in Avigliano. 5 other rebels were found in Ruoti, 3 in Santa Sophia, one in Casal Sant'Andrea and others in Tramutola, Vignola and Pietrafesa. *v* G. Fortunato, (at note 10), doc.III.

[42] Niccolo Jamsilla, *Storia* ed. G. del Re, *Cronisti e Scrttori sincroni della Dominazione Normanna nel Regno de Pugli e Sicilia*, 2 vols (Naples, 1845), 8, II, p. 151.

[43] Reg.Ang. XI, reg.63, no. 386.

[44] Reg.Ang., IX, reg.41, no. 259. "Cum in casale Accepturi igne combusto de focularibus c vix remanserunt xii . . ."

[45] Mattei-Ceresoli, "Tramutola," p. 201.

[46] "Cartulario del Vulture," in Fortunato, (at note 22) III, p. 241.

[47] Reg.Ang. XI, reg.54, no. 151.

[48] N. Coulet, "Villages disparus en Provence," *Annales:*ESC., 28 (1973), 1463–1483.

[49] It should be noted that the *uncie auri* in which the taxes were assessed were units of weight. The assessments would not therefore have been affected by fluctuations in the value of the currency (which, in any case was well known to be stable: *v* e. g. Yves Renouard, *Les Villes d'Italie de la fin du Xe siècle au début du XIV siècle*, (Paris, 1969) 2, p. 59)

[50] Marsico Nuovo was transferred to the Principate at some time between 1307 and 1320 and transferred back at some time after 1415. Nocera was transferred to Calabria between 1276 and 1320; it too was transferred back after 1320. The third was Satriano, similarly transferred back later.

[51] Satriano paid 15 *uncie* 14 *tari* 2 *grani* as opposed to 37 *uncie* 22 *tari* 4 *grani* in 1276.

[52] Domenico Vendola, *Rationes decimarum Italiae nei secoli XIII e XIV: Apulia, Calabria, Lucania, Studi e Testi, LXXXIV* (Città del Vaticano, 1939).

[53] Note that the map in Vendola's edition, though useful, contains many places which are not in the tithe lists with no indication of which are and which are not.

[54] R. Caggese, *Roberto d' Angio e i suoi tempi* (Florence, 1922–30), I, p. 635 quoting the Reg. Ang.

[55] Ibid., p. 236

[56] Filangieri, (at note 2), p. 186.

[57] art.cit. p. 82

[58] According to Racioppi (*v* note 6), the list omitted, *inter alia*, Avigliano, Rionero, Rotondella, San Chirico di Tolve, Trevigno, Cerchosimo, and Campomaggiore.

Avigliano was again assessed by 1445, Rotondella by 1532, San Chirico by 1561 and Cerchosimo by 1595. Campomaggiore was regarded as "new" by Giustiniani in 1798 and had in fact revived in a different location. Rionero was taxed with Atella in the 17th century but regained its separate identity in the 18th. Trevigno was not listed by Giustiniani, though it is now a commune.

[59] S.de Pilato, "Atella e gli Atellani," ACL XV (1945), pp. 79–92.

[60] Marsico Nuovo, v above; Nocera, v above; Metaponto, transferred to the Terra di Otranto in about 1270 (Sthamer, at note 4, I, p. 16) and transferred back at some time after 1320; Montemilone, transferred to the Terra di Bari between 1246 and 1276 and transferred back after 1320; Genosa, transferred to the Terra di Bari between 1246 and 1276 and transferred back after 1320; Brienza, always formerly in the Principate but near enough the border for Frederick II to have made some places in Basilicata responsible for its upkeep.

[61] Maratea was certainly transferred to Calabria though it has since been restored to Basilicata. Other possible transfers include Avena, Miglionico, Scansana.

[62] Potenza, Teana and Picerno (though the last was also left out of the tax list of 1320, so its eclipse may have been genuine. It was paying taxes by 1561—P. Summonte, *Storia della città e Regno di Napoli*, 2nd ed. (Naples, 1675), pp. 140–140bis.

[63] San Chirico Nuovo, Cerchosimo, (v above) Ruoti (recorded by Giustiniani, VIII, p. 80 as *desabitato* in 1508—actually in 1608 but this is certainly a misprint—but assessed again by 1561 after an influx of slavic settlers repopulated it), Papasidero (assessed again by 1648) and Brindisi di Montagna (assessed by 1669).

[64] Vaglio, Trevigno, Missanello, Rionero, Campomaggiore, Banzi. The last of these probably never wholly vanished. It had an *università* or commune which was involved in litigation in 1522 (Giustiniani, p. 168) but appeared in no 16th or 17th century tax list. Various other places like Monticchio and Lagopesole now have modern hamlets but are still only *frazioni* of other communes.

[65] C. Klapisch-Zuber, (at note 2) pp. 311–64, citing overall numbers from tax lists for Calabria almost certainly exaggerates the number of lost villages there. It is fair to add that this is not an error of which she is normally guilty.

[66] Giustiniani, I, p. 211, II, pp. 138–41, 183.

[67] C. Klapisch and J. Day, (at note 2) . . .', p. 437.

[68] Enrico Fiumi, "La popolazione del territorio volterano-sangimignanese ed il problema demografico del età communale," *Volterra e San Gimignano nel medioevo*, Sienna, 1983.

[69] C. Klapisch-Zuber, (at note 2) pp. 311–64. v also Klapisch and Day, (at note 2), p. 447.

[70] W. Abel, *Agricultural fluctuations* (London, 1980), p. 81.

[71] J.-M. Pesez and E. Le Roy Ladurie, "Le cas français: vue d'ensemble," in *Villages désertés et histoire èconomique*, pp. 159–61

[72] Abel, (at note 70), p. 83 ff.

[73] Maurice Beresford, *The Lost Villages of England* (London, 1954), pp. 158–60.

[74] J. N. Biraben, *Les hommes et la Peste en France et dans les pays Européens et méditerranéens*. Ecole des Hautes Etudes en Sciences Sociales. Centre de recherches historiques: Civilisations et sociétés, XXXV (1975), I, p. 148 ff. esp. pp. 170–1. from P. Gras, "Le registre paroissal de Givry (1334–57) et la peste noire en Bourgogne," *Bibliothèque de l'École des Chartes*, C (1939), 295–308. v also E. Carpentier, "Famines

et épidémies dans l'histoire du XIVe siècle," *Annales.E.S.C.* 17 (1962), 1062–1093; and Robert Gottfried, *The Black Death: Natural and Human Disaster in Medieval Europe* (London, 1984), esp.pp. 54–76.

[75] *v* Y. Renouard, 'Conséquences et intérêt démographiques de la Peste noire de 1348', *Études d'histoire médiévale*, Bibliothèque générale de l'École des Hautes Études, VIe section (Paris, 1968), p. 161 "Ainsi la proportion des décés dû à la peste par rapport à l'ensemble de la population semble avoir oscillé entre les deux tiers et la huitième, selon les régions." J. C. Russell, *British Medieval Population* (Albuquerque, 1948), p. 367 suggested as little as 20% though his views are not generally popular. *v* the summing up of P. Ziegler, *The Black Death* (London, 1969), p. 231. "To maintain that one European in three died during the period of the Black Death can never be proved but equally cannot be widely far from the truth."

[76] Biraben, (at note 74), p. 74

[77] A. Filangieri, (at note 2), p. 189 and, for the diffusion of the plague in Italy, Lorenzo del Panta, *Le Epidemie nella Storia demografica Italiana (secoli XIV–XIX)* (Turin, 1980), pp. 112, 113.

[78] There is some confirmation for this assumption in the fact that Melfi, the only place for which any 14th century tax figure has been recorded was assessed 140 *uncie* under Giovanna I compared with 287 in 1320. *v* G. Monti, "Da Carlo I a Roberto di Angio. Ricerche e documenti. part IX. Sul reddito dell secrezie e sul bilancio erariale del Regno di Sicilia," A.S.N. ns.19 (1933), p. 70.

[79] del Panta, *Le epidemie*, p. 117

[80] A. Filangieri, (at note 2), p. 186 ff.

[81] Carpentier, p. 1081.

[82] Abel (at note 70), pp. 38–40; H. S. Lucas, "The European famine of 1315, 1316 and 1317," *Speculum*, 5 (1930) Carpentier, p. 1075

[83] Carpentier, (as note 74), p. 1077

[84] A. Granuzzi, *Le carte di Altamura. Codice diplomatica Barese XII* (Bari, 1935), pp. 36; 331; 372; 407; 447.

	uncie	tari	grani
1276	154	7	4
1289	60	2	5
1374	60 reduced to 45		
1406	45 reduced to 30		
1437	30 reduced to 22.5		
1465	92	10	2

[85] But see on this Alan Ryder, *The Kingdom of Naples under Alfonso the Magnanimous: the making of a modern state* (Oxford, 1976), p. 211. He believes that the new Aragonese taxation did not, at least under Alfonso, bring in substantially more in taxes than did the old.

[86] Winkelmann.936, pp. 711–2.

[87] P. Egidi, "Ricerche sulla popolazione dell'Italia meridionale nei secoli XIII e XIV," *Miscellanea di Studi storici in onore di Giovanni Sforza* (Lucca, 1920), p. 27; pp. 727–50; This was done at Rapolla in 1303.

[88] Historians prior to Egidi based their calculations on a misunderstanding of one document which they thought implied a tax of one *uncia* to every four households. Egidi showed that this was a special and deliberately punitive levy. Conclusions

based on any other interpretation of it (eg. by Galanti, Capasso etc.) can be discounted.

[89] Egidi, (at note 87) pp. 740–50.

[90] Sthamer, (at note 4), II, p. 184, no. 1107

[91] G. Pardi, 'I registri Angioini e la popolazione calabrese del 1276', ASPN ns.ann VII, pp. 27–60.

[92] Karl Julius Beloch, Bevolkerungsgeschichte Italiens, 3 vols. (Berlin, 1937–61), III, pt. 3, pp. 169 ff.

[93] A Filangieri, (at note 2), pp. 131–3.

[94] For the whole Regno, Beloch would have a population of around 2,000,000, Filangieri one of about 3,000,000 and Egidi one of about 3,400,000.

[95] Roger Mols, Introduction à la démographie historique des villes d'Europe du XIVe au XVIIIe siècle. 3 vols. (Louvain, 1954–6), II, esp. pp. 110–15, 128 And see, on later Neapolitan households G. Delille, "Numérations des feux et état des ames dans le royaume de Naples," in Populatie si Societate ed. Stefanu Pascu, Cluj "Dacia" III (1980), pp. 171–3, discussing the very full census lists by household formerly in the Archivio di Stato of Naples

[96] Beloch, p. 281

[97] D. Grigg, Population growth and Agrarian Change: an historical perspective. Cambridge Geographical Studies 13 (Cambridge), 1980, cp.7, pp. 66–7.

[98] What follows is condensed from a fuller discussion in my chapter in the forthcoming publication on San Giovanni di Ruoti, ed. A. M. Small and R. J. Buck.

[99] For one of the four villages in the area (at note 11), a 15th-century description of the boundaries survives, (printed by Salinardi, Ruoti, p 20). The others can only be estimated but the margin of error cannot in fact be very great.

[100] It is not impossible: one or two 16th century villages were listed as having only two or three hearths and assuming that Caldane families paid lower taxes than the average, we might push the number of families up a little. Still it cannot have been much of a village.

[101] Grigg, (at note 97) pp. 68–9. In some places peasant families had as little as 3 hectares or even less.

[102] Filangieri, on the basis of 30 grani per hearth tax in communities assessed less than 50 uncie, 60 per hearth in communities assessed 50–100 uncie and 90 grani per hearth on communities assessed more than 100 uncie and 5 persons per hearth calculated 285 742 persons for the modern region of Potenza—that is about 57,000 hearths. (Territorio p. 282.) Medieval Basilicata was however rather smaller and my calculations on the basis of the 1320 tax list suggest that the number of persons was only about 204, 859 (see above) or 50,000 hearths.

[103] This figure is obtained by taking the average number of households counting all settlements which paid less than 100 uncie in taxes. Communities which paid more than 100 uncie were, by definition, towns, and since we have seen that there is no way of arriving at even a rough estimate of the number of people in towns in the Norman period, they had to be left out of the calculations for the Angevin period. Even then the comparison is no more than approximately valid, since our data are fuller (though perhaps not necessarily more reliable) for the later period. It is, however, adequate to show the general trend and to give some idea of the magnitude of the rise in population. Beloch's figures would of course suggest that this rise was considerably less great: but even his calculations would show a rise from about 120 to 200 households per settlement on average.

[104] Instances of the disappearances of villages which were unequivocally caused by the Black Death of 1348–9 are very few but see eg. Ambion, Tilgarsley, Tusmore and Standelf in England: Alan R. H. Baker, "Changes in the later Middle Ages," cp. 5 of *A new Historical Geography of England before 1600*, ed. H. C. Darby (Cambridge, 1976), p. 190 and Beresford (at note 73), pp. 159–160. But even in England, villages depopulated as a result of the Black Death of 1348 were few.

[105] Baker, p. 193; Beresford, pp. 162–3.

[106] D. Herlihy, *Pisa in the early renaissance: a study of Urban growth* (New Haven, 1958), pp. 48–53.

[107] See A. Filangieri, (at note 2), pp. 208–9.

[108] Baker (at note 104), p. 190.

[109] Beloch (at note 92), calculates 2610.

[110] Beloch calculates 1345.

[111] Beloch calculates 1040.

[112] It is difficult to obtain, anywhere in Europe, adequate statistics to calculate the mid 14th century mortality over a large area of countryside and the variations seem to be immense. Since a given village could lose as much a 100% of its population, it seems misleading to imply that the towns were necessarily worse hit than the countryside: it depended on which bit of countryside. *v* on this Biraben (at note 74), I, pp. 192–228.

[113] Beloch calculates 33.

[114] Beloch calculates 37.

[115] Rionero survived as a subdivision of Atella and Ruoti revived but neither was taxed in the late 15th and early 16th centuries

[116] On Beloch's showing another 30 places show a rise in the number of households.

[117] This phenomenon was not confined to southern Italy. There are, for example good parallels in Provence. M. Hebert, 'La peste noire et les mouvements de population dans le midi de la France aux XIVe et XVe siècles', *Europa: Revue d'Etudes Interdisciplinaires* I, no. 2 (1978), pp. 173–86.

[118] N. Pounds, *An economic history of Medieval Europe*, London, 1974, p. 186 summarises this view, first argued in detail by W. Abel, *Geschichte der deutschen Landwirtschaft* (Stuttgart, 1962).

[119] Beresford, pp. 160–1.

[120] A Filangieri, *Territorio*, p. 83. There were 1200 dead in Acerenza, and further north 9 cities were destroyed in Abruzzo, 19 in Molise and 2 in Benevento. Many others were seriously damaged. Atella was also badly damaged (see Pilato, 'Atella . . .' p. 79.)

[121] Giustiniani, p. 192.

[122] Pounds, (at note 118) p. 187. "But of all the secondary reasons for the loss of villages, the formost was war."

[123] David Whitehouse, 'Excavations at Satriano', PBSR 38 (1971), p. 191.

[124] Caggese, (at note 54) p. 499.

[125] N. Cianci Sanseverino, *I campi pubblici di alcuni castelli del Medioevo in Basilicata*, (Naples, 1891), pp. 113ff. (Documents from the *Fascicoli Angioini*)

[126] On these *v* H. A. Miskimmin, *The Economy of Early Renaissance Europe, 1300–1460*, (Englewood Cliffs, N.J., 1969), p. 66.

[127] Basilicata still exported some grain in the 15th century. *v* Giuseppe Coniglio, *Il Regno di Napoli al Tempo di Carlo V. Amministrazione e Vita Economico-sociale* (Naples, 1951), p. 123.

[128] *L'Archivio del Tavoliere di Puglia, Archivio di Stato di Foggia. Pubblicazzioni degli Archivi di Stato LXXII*, ed. Pasquale di Cicco and Dora Musto (Rome, 1970), Introduction. On the astonishingly large numbers of sheep in 15th century Apulia *v* A. Ryder (at note 85), p. 361.

[129] Fortunato, (at note 22), III, p. 241. Order to Castellans of Lagopesole to permit freely the pasturing and watering of royal flocks from Apulia followed by mastiff dogs.

[130] Andrea Gaudiani. *Notizie per il buon governo della regia dogana della mena delle pecore di Puglia*, ed. by Pasquale di Cicco, *Societá Dauna di Cultura. Testi e documenti per la Storia della Capitanata* 5 (Foggia, 1981), p. 199. (reprint of a text of 1700, part of the purpose of which was to prove that the inhabitants of Basilicata were liable for the *dogana*.

[131] Cianci-Sanseverino (at note 125), doc.XII, p. 142. This shows that under Charles of Anjou, hunting rights were worth 18 *uncie* 15 *tari* of a total of 28 *uncie* to the lord of Santa Sophia.

[132] Giovanni Cherubini, "Qualche considerazione sulle campagne dell'Italia centro-settentrionale tra l'XI e il XV secolo" in *Signori, Contadini, Borghesi; ricerche sulla società italiana del Basso medioevo*, La Nuova Italia; Biblioteca Storica 17 (Florence, 1974).

[133] In this connection it is worth noting that the castle list makes a deliberate distinction between villages which owe *(debet)* service and those which can *(potest)* be asked for it. It is not clear what gave rise to the distinction but one plausible explanation is that lands held of the *curia* owed service whereas from other lands it *could* be demanded in case of necessity. If this is the case, no villages in Basilicata were held directly by the *curia*, for the word *potest* is used in connection with all villages in Basilicata.

[134] eg. Pierre de Saumur held Oppido, Albano, Trevigno and Casalaspro in Basilicata and other fiefs in the Capitanata. Geoffroi de Terzarello held Marsico, Ripacandida, Ruoti, Santa Sophia and Bella and four places in the Capitanata. Raymond de Poncelles had Pescopagano, Vignola, Balvano, Brienza and two other places outside Basilicata. The list could be prolonged.

[135] see Alessandro d'Alessandro, 'Aspetti della storia dei feudi in Basilicata', A.S.C.L. XXVII (1958), pp. 187–205 and N. Cortese, "Feudi e feudatari Napoletane della prima metà del cinquecento," ASN 54 (1929), pp. 5–150.

[136] Cirillo Koralevsky, "Le vicende ecclesiastiche dei paesi Italo-Albanesi della Basilicata e della Calabria," ASCL I (1931), p. 43. *v* also A. Filangieri, p. 238

[137] Compare, for example San Gimignano, the region of which saw the disappearance of many villages from the beginning of the 14th century onwards (Fiumi, at note 68), Tuscany where the number of villages was at its height at the end of the 13th century (Cherubini, p. 148.) and Lazio (Toubert, *Structures*, p. 366—after the middle of the 12th century "on n'enregistre plus . . . ni fondations nouvelles ni, au moins jusqu'au XIVe siècle abandons notables.")

[138] Pesez and Le Roy Ladurie (at note 71), pp. 140–51, concentrating mainly on Artois; Beresford, pp. 156–158.

[139] Klapisch and Day (at note 2), on lost villages in Lazio, Sicily and Sardinia

[140] Gottfried (at note 74), p. 28, citing Villani

[141] Abel, (at note 70), pp. 38–40

Table I. Places in Catalogue of Barons.

k = knights, v = villeins, * denotes places now abandoned. ** denotes places not in castle list but appearing later. Places appearing only in Catalogue shown in square brackets.

name	service	mod. name
Aliano Superiore	(see Aliano Inf.)	Aliano
Sanctus Felice	inquiretur	San Fele
Castrum Novum	000 (probl)	Castronovo
Moliterno	000 (?)	Moliterno
Potencia	000 (domain)	Potenza
Minganellum	000 (see Aliano Inf.)	Missanello
Raczanum	000 (see Camarda)	Pisticci
Trifogium (Grisegium)	000 (see Campomaggiore)	Trefoglie
Rocca Nova	000 (see Colobraro)	Roccanova
Sanctus Arcangelus	000 (see Colobraro)	Sant'Arcangelo
Petraperciata	000 (see Mons Albanus and Campomaggiore)	Pietrapertosa
Mons Caveoso	000 (county)	Montescaglioso
Turris Curiliani	01 k	Corigliano*
Trivinea	01 k	Trevigno
[Pulliano]	01 k	Pugliano*
Petrulla	01 k	Petrolla
Minganellum	01 k	Missanello
Rocca de Acino	01 k	Rocca di Acino
[Castelluccio (nr.S.Angelo le Fratte)]	01 k	Castelluccio
Tursi	01 k	Tursi
Castrum Medianum	01 k	Castelmezzano
Vineola	01 k	Pignola
Garagusium	01 k	Garagusi
Sanctus Felice	01 k	San Fele
Camarda	01 k	Bernalda
Petra de Acino	01 k	Pietra di Acino
[Castellionum]	01 k	unknown*
Labella	01 k 127 v	Bella
Gallipoli	01 k(+?)	Gallipoli*
[Gagnanum]	01 k(?)	unknown*
[Petrasicca]	01 k(?)	unknown*
Boreano	01 k(?)	Bareano*
[Tora]	01 k(?)	La Tora*
[Ingurgum]	01 k(?)	Castro Cicurio*
Accetura	01.5 k	Accetura
Armatera	02 k	Armatera*
Marsico Vetere	02 k	Marsico Vetere
Montepeloso	02 k	Irsina
Rocca Nova	02 k	Roccanova

Table I *(continued)*

k = knights, v = villeins, * denotes places now abandoned. ** denotes places not in castle list but appearing later. Places appearing only in Catalogue shown in square brackets.

name	service	mod. name
Abriola	02 k	Abriola
Oliveto	02 k	Oliveto Lucano
[Roccetta]	02 k	unknown*
Corneto	02 k	Corleto Perticara
Laurenciana	02 k	Laurenzana
Raponum	02 k	Rapone
Columbarium**	02 k	Colubraro
Perticara	02 k	Perticara*
Gurgulionum	02 k	Gorgoglione
Lacus Pensilis	02 k	Lagopesole
Pomaricum	02 k	Pomarico
[Acchium]	02 k	Torre Accio*
Acernum	02 k	Agromonte
Petragalla	02 k	Petragalla
Oppido	02 k (?04)	Oppido Lucano
Tiganum	02 k (Roccheta nr.Teggiano)	Teana
Ageroncia	02 k +?	Acerenza
Picerno**	02 1/2 k	Picerno
Aliano Superiore	03 k	Aliano
Castrum de Grandis	03 k	Castelgrande
Salandra	03 k	Salandra
Mons Morconis	03 k	Monte Marcone*
Guardia	03 k	Guardia Perticara
Rotum	03 k	Ruoti
Rapolla	03 k	Rapolla
Banzi	03 k	Banzi
Albanum	03 k	Albano
[Vitalba]	03 k	Vitalba*
Anzi	03 k	Anzi
[Tur]	03 k	Turri (nr.Guardia)
Gloriosa	03 k	Gloriosa*
[Riviscum]	03 k	Revisco*
Platano	03 k	Platano*
Tito	03 k	Tito
Altus Joannes	03 k	Altogianni*
Ripa Candida	03 k + 8 villeins + 9 individuals	Ripacandida
Marmore	03 k 20 v	Marmore*
Campus Maior	03 k (with Trifogium)	Campomaggiore
Aliano Inferiore	04 k	Alianello
Tulba	04 k	Tolve

name	service	mod. name
Venosa	04 k	Venosa
Gaudianum	04 k	Gaudiano
Criptole	04 k	Grottole
Cracum	04 k	Craco
Armentum	04 k	Armento
Bellus Mons	04 k	Belmonte*
Muro	04 k 153 v (+)	Muro Lucano
Mons Albanus	05 k	Montalbano
Irsi	05 k(?)	Monte Irsi*
Melfia	06 k+?	Melfi
Anglona	06 k	Anglona
Cisterna	06 k	Cisterna
Spinaciole	06 k (see Fiorenza)	Spinazzola
Santa Sophia	06 k (with Baragiano etc)	Castelluccio di Santa Sophia*
Barayano	06 k (with Sta Sophia etc)	Baragiano
Sanctus Arcangelus	07 k	Sant'Arcangelo
Milionicum	09 k	Miglionico
Tricarico	09 k+	Tricarico
San Giuliano	1 k(?)	Grumento Vetere (or San G.nr.Miglionico)
Florencia	11 k	Forenza
Marsico Novo	11 k	Marsico Nuovo

Table II Fiefs in Catalogue of Barons
not mentioned in Castles list.

name	Service
Acchium	02 k
Castellionum	01 k
Castelluccio (nr.S.Angelo le Fratte)	01 k
Columbarium	02 k
Gagnanum	01 k(?)
Ingurgum	01 k(?)
Petrasicca	01 k(?)
Picerno	02 1/2 k
Pulliano	01 k
Riviscum	03 k
Roccetta	02 k
Tora	01 k(?)
Tur	03 k
Vitalba	03 k

Note. A query in the "Service" column means that the place in
question is listed with another fief and the service has therefore
had to be estimated.

Table III.   Angevin Tax Assessments for Basilicata.

Sums given are in Uncie, Tari and Grani.

Place	tax. 1276	tax. 1307	tax. 1320	Modern name
Banzi	0	006 11 04	006 11 04	Banzi
Rocca Nova	0	005 23 16	005 23 16	Roccanova
Grisosutrum	0	018 10 16	018 10 16	unknown*
Casal Rubio	0	003 13 10	003 03 10	Rubeo
Sanctus Theodorus	0	0	000 25 00 (R.I.)	San Teodoro
Grassanum	0	001 00 00	003 00 00 (Spin.)	Grassano
Casale Sancti Martini	0	000 22 14	002 22 14 (Spin.)	Casal San Martino
Casal Lupicoso	0	0	002 25 00 (Spin. 0 25. R.I. 2.)	unknown*
Casal Sancte Marie de Cornu	0	001 16 15	001 16 15	unknown*
Casal Sancti Mattei	0	001 00 00	002 20 00 (Spin.)	unknown*
Altus Joannes	0	004 00 00 (unnoted)	005 00 00 (Spin.)	Altogianni*
Sanctus Salvator	0	0	000 25 00 (Spin.)	San Salvatore*
Accetura	000 00 00	002 28 00	002 28 00	Accetura
Lacus Pensilis	000 00 00	0	0	Lagopesole
Turris Curiliani	000 00 00	010 28 16	010 28 16	Corigliano*
Rodiano	000 00 00	0	0	Rodia*
Rocca de Acino	000 05 00	000 00 00	000 00 00	Rocca di Acino
Caldaria	000 05 00	000 15 00	000 15 00	Caldane / San Cataldo
Terra Tancredi de Guarino	000 06 00	000 05 11	000 05 11	unknown*
Tramutola	000 06 08	005 27 05	005 27 05	Tramutola
Pulsandrana	001 08 08	005 00 16	005 00 16	Pulsandra*
Casale Sanctus Nicola de Silva	001 16 04	001 11 07	001 11 07	San Nicola de Silva
Petra de Acino	001 18 12	001 17 09	001 17 09	Pietra di Acino
Trisagia	002 11 08	003 20 12	003 20 12	Trisagia*
Casal Aspum	002 12 12	006 21 05	006 21 05	Casalaspro*

Place	tax. 1276	tax. 1307	tax. 1320	Modern name
Prisinachum	003 00 12	005 01 01	005 01 01	Presiniaco*
Bactiboranim	003 02 08	003 15 18	003 15 18	Battifarano
Episcopia	003 04 04	004 11 00	004 11 00	Episcopia
Castrum Bellocte	003 17 04	004 00 07	004 00 07	Castelbellotto
Platano	003 22 15	007 03 00	007 03 00	Platano*
Campus Maior	003 22 16	005 00 00	005 00 00	Campomaggiore
Boreano	003 27 00	005 01 06	005 16 06 (Spin.)	Bareano*
Calabra	004 03 00	0	0	Calabra*
Sanctus Basilius	004 03 00	003 20 01	003 20 01	San Basilio
Avillanum	004 07 04	003 21 04	003 21 04	Avigliano
Barayano	004 25 04	005 25 06	005 25 06	Baragiano
Marsico Vetere	004 25 16	004 10 10	005 20 10(R.I.=1u, Spin=10t)	Marsico Vetere
Minganellum	005 00 12	004 14 17	004 14 17	Missanello
Raponum	005 04 16	007 00 00	007 00 00	Rapone
Trivinea	005 09 00	002 08 02	002 08 02	Trivigno
Petragalla	005 21 05	009 19 16	010 04 16 (Spin.)	Petragalla
Mons Morconis	005 23 08	006 21 18	006 21 18	Monte Marcone*
Scansana	006 03 03	003 23 10	005 13 10 (Spin.)	Scansana
Bellus Mons	006 09 12	007 29 14	007 29 14	Belmonte*
Andriacum	006 20 08	004 13 09	004 13 09	Andrachio
Acernum	006 20 08	004 13 09	004 13 09	Agromonte
Rotum	006 26 08	006 04 15	006 19 15 (Spin.)	Ruoti
Gurgulionum	007 13 04	006 19 13	006 19 13	Gorgoglione
Armatera	007 26 08	007 29 16	007 29 16	Armatera*
Tofaria	008 00 12	004 25 05	004 25 05	Tofaria
Baglio	008 26 08	011 24 08	011 24 08	Vaglio
Appium	008 27 00	001 16 14	003 16 14 (R.I.)	Appio*
Petra Castalda	009 01 16	008 03 03	008 03 03	Pietracastalda*
Vineola	009 18 00	008 10 13	008 10 13	Pignola
Oliveto	009 22 08	006 11 08	006 11 08	
Cervaricio	009 22 16	014 05 17	014 05 17	Cervarezza

Table III   (continued)

Sums given are in Uncie, Tari and Grani.

Place	tax. 1276	tax. 1307	tax. 1320	Modern name
Sanctus Iulianus	010 00 00	012 01 16	012 01 16	Grumento Vetere (or San G.nr.Miglionico)
Aliano Inferiore	010 03 00	008 01 02	008 01 02	Alianello
Casal Sant'-Andrea	010 07 16	015 12 00	015 12 00	Casal Sant'Andrea*
Rotunda Maris	010 08 08	0	0	Rotondella
Laurisellum	010 08 08	005 09 04	005 09 04	Lauriosello*
Cancellara	010 15 00	010 27 06	011 27 06 (Spin.)	Cancellara
Gallucium	010 16 16	011 00 00	011 15 0 (R.I.)	Gallichio
Gallipoli	010 24 12	007 10 07	007 25 07 (Spin.)	Gallipoli*
Sanctus Arcangelus	011 15 12	026 02 11	046 02 11	Sant'Arcangelo
Monticuli	011 24 00	015 03 15	015 18 15 (R.I)	Monticchio
Triclina	011 28 04	007 20 10	007 20 10	Trecchina
Casal Pisticci	012 01 14	008 13 06	009 13 06 (Spin.)	Sta.Maria di Pisticci
Castrum Novum	012 02 08	012 02 08	012 02 08	Castronovo
Petra fixa	012 12 00	011 02 11	012 02 11 (Spin.)	Satriano di Lucania
Garagusium	012 18 00	004 16 04	004 16 04	Garagusi
Rionero	012 22 16	011 12 10	011 12 10	Rionero
Avinella	013 12 12 (Rocca Imp)	003 00 16	003 15 16	Avenella
Genzano	013 16 16	023 24 01	023 24 01	Genzano
Gloriosa	013 26 00	013 26 00	012 12 09	Gloriosa*
Labella	015 026 08	017 09 09	018 09 09 (Spin.)	Bella
Anglona	015 12 00	015 09 18	015 09 18	Anglona
Castrum Medianum	016 00 08	009 21 10	009 21 10	Castelmezzano
Latronicum	016 07 04	014 15 16	014 15 16	Latronico
San Mauro	016 09 12	0	0	San Mauro Forte
Tiganum	016 19 16	014 27 12	014 27 12	Teana

Place	tax. 1276	tax. 1307	tax. 1320	Modern name
Faratum	016 19 16	014 27 02	014 27 02	Fardello
Cersosimo	017 04 04	023 17 14	023 17 14	Kyr Zozimo
Santa Sophia	018 01 04	016 04 05	017 04 05 (Spin.)	Castelluccio di Santa Sophia*
Moliterno	018 04 16	016 07 10	016 07 10	Moliterno
Castrum de Grandis	018 18 00	011 29 02	011 29 02	Castelgrande
Camarda	019 04 04	017 03 00	017 03 00	Bernalda
Abriola	019 18 12	017 16 10	017 16 10	Abriola
Nocara	020 03 00	0 (moved)	0(moved)	Nocera
Noha	020 09 12	018 05 06	018 05 06	Noepoli
Ripa Candida	020 15 00	023 00 03	023 00 03	Ripacandida
Criptole	020 18 00	0	0	Grottole
Lavena	020 18 00	018 12 17	018 12 17	Avena
Cracum	020 22 04	028 26 11	028 26 11	Craco
Clarus Mons	021 06 12	018 29 10	018 29 10	Chiaramonte
Papasiderum	021 16 08		011 07 17	Papasidero
Laurenciana	022 10 16	020 00 00	020 00 00	Laurenzana
Sarconium	022 22 06	020 10 05	020 10 05	Sarconi
Monte Sellicole	022 27 00	020 14 12	020 14 12	Monte Serico*
Ageroncia	023 13 06	027 29 11	027 29 11	Acerenza
Sanctus Clericus Vallis Signi	023 24 00	024 07 00	024 07 00	San Chirico Raparo
Anzi	024 14 08	021 27 00	021 27 00	Anzi
Picerno	024 15 00	021 27 07	021 27 07	Picerno
Favale	025 00 16	001 16 10	001 16 10	Val Sinni
Guardia	025 03 00	020 03 11	020 03 11	Guardia Perticara
Corneto	025 09 12	022 19 10	022 19 10	Corleto Perticara
Armentum	025 24 16	023 02 16	023 02 16	Armento
Lavello	026 27 12	024 02 08	025 02 08 (R.I.)	Lavello
Albanum	027 00 04	020 09 17	020 09 17	Albano
Raczanum	027 09 00	045 28 15	045 28 15	Pisticci
Rotunda Vallis Layni	028 04 16	017 12 07	017 12 07	Rotonda
Irsi	028 18 12	025 18 00	025 18 00	Monte Irsi*
Salandra	030 00 00	011 16 14	011 16 14	Salandra
Lacus nerus	030 00 00	026 25 03	026 25 03	Lagonegro
Columbarium	031 21 12	028 11 03	028 11 03	Colubraro
Tricarico	031 21 12	028 11 03	028 11 03	Tricarico

Table III   *(continued)*

Sums given are in Uncie, Tari and Grani.

Place	tax. 1276	tax. 1307	tax. 1320	Modern name
Castelluccio	032 00 00	028 27 09	028 27 09	Castelluccio Superiore
Tulba	033 03 12	027 08 17	027 08 17	Tolve
Brundusium de montana	034 01 16	030 14 00	030 14 00	Brindisi di Montagna
Trifogium (Grisegium)	035 01 01	0	0	Trefoglie
Biganellum	036 03 03	032 08 13	032 08 13	Viggianello
Castrosarraceno	036 28 16	025 14 17	025 14 17	Castel Saraceno
Sinisium	037 18 12	027 12 17	027 12 17	Senise
Satrianum	037 22 04	015 29 06	015 14 02 (Spin.)	Satriano
San Martino	040 18 12	036 10 00	036 10 00	San Martino
Spinaciole	040 27 00	044 20 00	024 11 00	Spinazzola
Calvellum	041 05 08	036 25 02	036 25 02	Calvello
Sanctus Clericus de Tulbia	042 05 08	031 14 03	031 14 03	San Chirico Nuovo
Oppido	046 00 00	033 17 08	033 17 08	Oppido Lucano
Sanctus Felice	046 06 00	036 19 18	036 19 18	San Fele
Marathia	047 13 04	047 26 09	047 26 09	Maratea
Bianum	051 00 08	0	0	Viggiano
Muro	053 18 00	054 28 06	054 28 06	Muro Lucano
Mons Albanus	055 02 08	043 24 15	043 24 15	Montalbano
Stigliano	055 14 08	055 02 04	055 02 04	Stigliano
Marsico Novo	057 03 12	0	0 (moved)	Marsico Nuovo
Perticara	060 00 00	030 08 00	030 08 00	Perticara*
Tursi	060 03 00	069 09 10	069 09 10	Tursi
Lauria	060 08 08	038 20 17	038 20 17	Lauria
Petrapagana	062 17 08	065 09 03	065 09 03	Pescopagano
Aliano Superiore	065 03 00	058 07 07	058 07 07	Aliano
Montemurro	065 22 16	058 24 14	058 24 14	Montemurro
Pomaricum	066 03 00	054 03 18	054 03 18	Pomarico
Rivello	067 01 04	054 15 13	054 15 13	Rivello
Milionicum	069 10 16	062 01 04	062 16 04 (Spin.)	Miglionico
Petraperciata	070 04 04	020 00 00	020 00 00	Pietrapertosa

Place	tax. 1276	tax. 1307	tax. 1320	Modern name
Florencia	070 12 00	072 09 04	072 09 04	Forenza
Tito	080 07 04	062 13 03	040 00 00	Tito
Mons Caveoso	093 03 12	075 15 12	075 15 12	Montescag- lioso
Gaudianum	098 03 12	087 23 00	087 23 00	Gaudiano
Rocca Im- perialis	098 25 24	065 02 04	049 02 04	Rocca Im- perialis
Saponaria	100 17 08	0 (moved)	0 (moved)	Grumento
Oggianum	100 29 08	090 09 15	090 09 15	Oggiano*
Rapolla	102 03 14	091 10 06	091 10 06	Rapolla
Montepeloso	114 13 04	110 04 03	110 04 03	Irsina
Potencia	121 05 08	133 22 07	133 22 07	Potenza
Venosa	137 03 00	147 29 10	147 29 10	Venosa
Melfia	287 19 06	287 03 06	287 03 06	Melfi

Notes:
1. Places not appearing in a given tax list shown with one 0. Places appearing but assessed nothing shown thus: 000 00 00.
2. Spin. in Tax. 1320 column indicates that the extra assessment in taxes for that year was to make up for reduced contributions from Spinazzola. R. I indicates a similar arrangement for Rocca Imperialis.
3. An asterisk in the Modern Name column indicates that the place no longer exists.

Table IV.   Castles and Villages in Frederick II's list.

Castle	Village
Acerenza	Genzano
	Albanum
	Casal Aspum
	Potencia
	Oppido
	Salandra
	Tulba
	Calciano
	Cancellara
	Criptole
	Montepeloso
	Baglio
	Tricarico
	Sanctus Clericus de Tulbia
Agromonte	Florencia
Anzi	Guardia
	Laurenciana
	Cirigliano
	Montemurro
	San Martino
	Bianum
	Turris Curiliani
	Sanctus Iulianus de Petra
	Sanctus Iulianus
	Oriens
	Perticara
	Minganellum
	Corneto
	Gallucium
Bareano	Cervaricio
	Banzi
Brienza	Marmore
	Petra fixa
	Marsico Novo
Brindisi	Trivinea
	Campus Maior
	Oliveto
	Laurisellum
	Garagusium
	Gallipoli
	Petraperciata
	Castrum Medianum
	Radia
	Castrum Bellocte
	Trifogium (Grisegium)

Castle	Village
	Accetura
Calvello	Sarconium
	Moliterno
	Saponaria
Calvello	Marsico Vetere
	Tramutola
castle (sole)	Abriola
Cisterna	Rapolla
domus (sole)	Mons Albanus
	Gaudianum
	Monte Sellicole
Gorgoglione	Aliano Inferiore
	Rocca Nova
Lagonegro	Triclina
	Rivello
Lagopesole	Barayano
	Castelluccio (di Sta. Sophia)
	Gloriosa
	Santa Sophia
	Vineola
Lavello	Monte Milone
Maratea	Biganellum
	Lauria
	Lavena
	Castrocucco
	Castelluccio
	Rotunda Vallis Layni
	Papasiderum
	Nemoli
	Turtura
	Ayeta
Melfi	Casal Sant'Andrea
	Venosa
	Monticuli
Metaponto	Raczanum
	Camarda
	Sanctus Basilius
	Cracum
	Casal Pisticci
	Avinella
Monte Marcone	Caldaria
	Rotum
	Avillanum
	Petragalla
Montescaglioso	San Mauro
	Pomaricum
	Altus Joannes

Table IV *(continued)*

Castle	Village
	Milionicum
Montescaglioso	Oggianum
Muro	Platano
	Satrianum
	Petra Castalda
	Marmore
	Tito
	Saxo
	Marsico Novo
Pescopagano	Tofaria
	Castrum de Grandis
Petra di Acino	Armentum
	Aliano Superiore
	Rocca de Acino
Petrulla	Andriacum
	Casale Sanctus Nicola de Silva
	Stigliano
Policastro	Tuclani
	Brigetti
Policoro	Trisagia
	Sanctus Arcangelus
	Scansana
	Culicleari
	Rotunda Maris
	Bullice
Rocca Imperialis	Sanctus Clericus Vallis Signi
	Pulsandrana
	Clarus Mons
	Rodiano
	Castrum Novum
	Castrosarraceno
	Favale
	Casal Rubio
	Anglona
	Calabra
	Episcopia
	Armentana
	Prisinachum
	Calvera
	Noha
	Sanctus Aniane
	Tiganum
	Solucium
	Sinisium

Castle	Village
	Casal Canne
	Latronicum
	Nocara
	Tursi
	Acer Mons
	Faratum
Rocca Imperialis	Bactiboranim
San Fele	Sanctus Thoma de Robo
	Labella
	Raponum
	Pierno
San Nicola de Ofido	Rionero
	Ripa Candida
	Armatera
Spinazzola	Irsi
	Bellus Mons

Table V.   Places listed under Frederick II
but not in 1276.

Place	Castle
Calciano	Acerenza
Sanctus Iulianus de Petra	Anzi
Cirigliano	
Oriens	
Banzi	Bareano
Marmore	Brienza
Radia	Brindisi
Petrulla	castle
Policoro	
Burgencia	
Metaponto	
Cisterna	domus
Sanctus Nicolaus de Ofido	
Rocca Nova	Gorgoglione
Castelluccio (di Sta.Sophia)	Lagopesole
Monte Milone	Lavello
Ayeta	Maratea
Nemoli	
Castrocucco	
Turtura	
Altus Joannes	Montescaglioso
Marmore	Muro
Saxo	
Tuclani	Policastro
Brigetti	
Culicleari	Policoro
Bullice	
Casal Rubio	Rocca Imperialis
Armentana	
Sanctus Aniane	
Casal Canne	
Calvera	
Solucium	
Acer Mons	
Sanctus Thoma de Robo	San Fele
Pierno	

Table VI.   Places in Basilicata paying tithes in early 14th century.

Sums given in Uncie, Tari and Grani
(in order of size of tithe assessed in 1310.)

Place	tithe. 1310	tithe. 1324	tax. 1276
Lacus nerus	0	00 06 00	030 00 00
Rotum	0	00 08 00	006 26 08
Montemurro	0	00 24 00	065 22 16
Oliveto	0	00 06 00	009 22 08
Trifogium (Grisegium)	0	00 02 00	035 01 01
Tricarico	0	11 12 00	031 21 12
Trivinea	0	00 02 12	005 09 00
Sanctus Basilius	0	00 02 00	004 03 00
Gallucium	0	00 07 10	010 16 16
Baglio	0	00 18 00	008 26 08
Armatera	0	00 01 00	007 26 08
Salandra	0	00 06 00	030 00 00
Armentum	0	00 12 00	025 24 16
Mons Albanus	0	00 18 00	055 02 08
Cracum	0	00 21 00	020 22 04
Rapolla	0	12 19 00	102 03 14
Sanctus Iulianus	0	00 01 00 (?)	010 00 00
Biganellum	0	00 04 10	036 03 03
Rionero	0	00 01 00	012 22 16
Caldaria	0	00 00 00	000 05 00
Gallipoli	0	00 07 00	010 24 12
Garagusium	0	00 05 00	012 18 00
Papasiderum	0	00 19 10	021 16 08
Albanum	0	00 12 00	027 00 04
Guardia	0	00 23 00	025 03 00
San Mauro	0	00 15 00	016 09 12
Mons Morconis	0	mentioned	005 23 08
Rotunda Vallis Layni	0	00 04 10	028 04 16
Accetura	0	00 07 00	000 00 00
Boreano	0	00 07 10	003 27 00
Marathia	0	00 26 04	047 13 04
Ripa Candida	0	01 08 00	020 15 00
Gurgulionum	0	00 05 00	007 13 04
Aliano Inferiore	0	00 05 00	010 03 00
Turris Curiliani	0	00 02 10	000 00 00
Minganellum	0	00 07 00	005 00 12
Stigliano	0	00 12 00	055 14 08
Perticara	0	00 08 00	060 00 00
Raczanum	0	12 19 00	027 09 00
Aliano Superiore	0	00 28 10	065 03 00
Corneto	0	00 02 10	025 09 12

Table VI *(continued)*

Sums given in Uncie, Tari and Grani
(in order of size of tithe assessed in 1310.)

Place	tithe. 1310	tithe. 1324	tax. 1276
Lavena	00 00 10	00 00 10	020 18 00
Faratum	00 01 00	0	016 19 16
Calvellum	00 01 00	01 11 00	041 05 08
Rocca Nova	00 01 10	0	0
Platano	00 01 10	0	003 22 15
Cersosimo	00 02 00	0	017 04 04
Castelluccio	00 02 00	0	032 00 00
Banzi	00 02 00	00 02 00	0
Moliterno	00 03 00	0	018 04 16
Petra Castalda	00 03 00	0	009 01 16
Marmore	00 04 00	0	0
Appium	00 04 00	00 04 12	008 27 00
Gloriosa	00 04 00	00 04 00	013 26 00
Castrum Bellocte	00 04 00	00 05 00	003 17 04
Altus Joannes	00 05 06	0	0
Irsi	00 05 10	00 10 00	028 18 12
Castrum Novum	00 06 00	0	012 02 08
Columbarium	00 06 00	0	031 21 12
Marsico Vetere	00 06 00	0	004 25 16
Laurisellum	00 06 00	0	010 08 08
Tulba	00 07 00	00 09 00	033 03 12
Campus Maior	00 07 10	00 13 10	003 22 16
Barayano	00 07 10	0	004 25 04
Camarda	00 07 10	00 13 10	019 04 04
Cervaricio	00 08 00	00	009 22 16
Santa Sophia	00 08 00	0	018 01 04
Sanctus Arcangelus	00 08 00	0	011 15 12
Sanctus Felice	00 08 00	0	046 06 00
Raponum	00 09 00	0	005 04 16
Brundusium de montana	00 09 00	00 11 08	034 01 16
Castrum de Grandis	00 09 00	0	018 18 00
Sinisium	00 09 00	0	037 18 12
Labella	00 10 00	0	015 026 08
Casal Aspum	00 10 00	00 09 00	002 12 12
Petrapagana	00 10 03	0	062 17 08
Petra fixa	00 12 00	0	012 12 00
Noha	00 12 00	0	020 09 12
Casal Sant'Andrea	00 12 00	00 12 00	010 07 16
Nocara	00 12 00	0	020 03 00
Castrum Medianum	00 13 00	00 16 00	016 00 08
Vineola	00 14 10	00 16 00	009 18 00
Petragalla	00 15 00	00 15 00	005 21 05

Place	tithe. 1310	tithe. 1324	tax. 1276
Anzi	00 15 00	00 10 00	024 14 08
Cancellara	00 15 00	00 10 00	010 15 00
Rocca Imperialis	00 15 00	0	098 25 24
Avillanum	00 15 00	00 15 00	004 07 04
Laurenciana	00 15 00	00 19 00	022 10 16
Monte Sellicole	00 15 00	00 15 00	022 27 00
Abriola	00 15 00	00 15 00	019 18 12
Criptole	00 15 10	00 19 00	020 18 00
Tito	00 16 00	00 24 00	080 07 04
Genzano	00 18 15	0	013 16 16
Pomaricum	00 20 00	00 18 00	066 03 00
Tursi	00 23 00	0	060 03 00
Spinaciole	00 24 00	0	040 27 00
Picerno	00 24 00	00 20 00	024 15 00
Sanctus Clericus de Tulbia	00 24 00	00 05 00	042 05 08
Florencia	00 25 00	0	070 12 00
Milionicum	00 25 10	00 25 10	069 10 16
Oppido	01 00 00	01 00 00	046 00 00
Petraperciata	01 00 00	01 02 00	070 04 04
Prisinachum	01 00 00	01 12 00	003 00 12
Saponaria	01 00 00	0	100 17 08
Gaudianum	01 04 18	03 17 03	098 03 12
Mons Caveoso	01 10 00	01 10 00	093 03 12
Oggianum	01 10 00	01 10 00	100 29 08
Lavello	01 16 00	0	026 27 12
Montepeloso	01 26 00	02 00 00	114 13 04
Satrianum	03 24 00	0	037 22 04
Anglona	05 01 10	0	015 12 00
Marsico Novo	05 02 10	0	057 03 12
Muro	07 08 00	0	053 18 00
Potencia	15 18 00	07 34 10	121 05 08
Ageroncia	17 10 00	22 13 10	023 13 06
Melfia	40 17 01	33 14 01	287 19 06
Venosa	52 07 06	11 06 14	137 03 00

Table VII. Early fourteenth century tithe payments.

name	First	Second	mod. name
Lacus nerus	0	00 06 00	Lagonegro
Rotum	0	00 08 00	Ruoti
Montemurro	0	00 24 00	Montemurro
Oliveto	0	00 06 00	Oliveto Lucano
Trifogium (Grisegium)	0	00 02 00	Trefoglie
Tricarico	0	11 12 00	Tricarico
Trivinea	0	00 02 12	Trevigno
San Basilio	0	00 02 00	San Basilio
Gallucium	0	00 07 10	Gallichio
Baglio	0	00 18 00	Vaglio
Armentum	0	00 01 00	Armatera*
Salandra	0	00 06 00	Salandra
Armentum	0	00 12 00	Armento
Mons Albanus	0	00 18 00	Montalbano
Cracum	0	00 21 00	Craco
Rapolla	0	12 19 00	Rapolla
San Giuliano	0	00 01 00	Grumento Vetere (or San G.nr.Miglionico)
Biganellum	0	00 04 10	Viggianello
Rionero	0	00 01 00	Rionero
Caldaria	0	00 00 00	Caldane/San Cataldo
Gallipoli	0	00 07 00	Gallipoli*
Garagusium	0	00 05 00	Garagusi
Albanum	0	00 12 00	Albano
Guardia	0	00 23 00	Guardia Perticara
San Mauro	0	00 15 00	San Mauro Forte
Ripa Candida	0	01 08 00	Ripacandida
Rotunda Vallis Layni	0	00 04 10	Rotonda
Accetura	0	00 07 00	Accetura
Papasiderum	0	00 19 10	Papasidero
Marathia	0	00 26 04	Maratea
Boreano	0	00 07 10	Bareano*
Gurgulionum	0	00 05 00	Gorgoglione
Aliano Inferiore	0	00 05 00	Alianello
Turris Curiliani	0	00 02 10	Corigliano*
Minganellum	0	00 07 00	Missanello
Stigliano	0	00 12 00	Stigliano
Perticara	0	00 08 00	Perticara*
Raczanum	0	12 19 00	Pisticci
Aliano Superiore	0	00 28 10	Aliano

Corneto	0	00 02 10	Corleto Perticara
Lavena	00 00 10	00 00 10	Avena
Faratum	00 01 00	0	Fardello
Calvellum	00 01 00	01 11 00	Calvello
Rocca Nova	00 01 10	0	Roccanova
Platano	00 01 10	0	Platano*
Cersosimo	00 01 00	0	Kyr Zozimo
Castelluccio	00 02 00	0	Castelluccio Superiore
Banzi	00 02 00	00 02 00	Banzi
Moliterno	00 03 00	0	Moliterno
Petra Castalda	00 03 00	0	Pietracastalda*
Marmore	00 04 00	0	Marmore*
Appium	00 04 00	00 04 12	Appio*
Gloriosa	00 04 00	00 04 00	Gloriosa*
Castrum Bellocte	00 04 00	00 05 00	unkonwn*
Altus Joannes	00 05 06	0	Altogianni*
Irsi	00 05 10	00 10 00	Monte Irsi*
Castrum Novum	00 06 00	0	Castronovo
Columbarium	00 06 00	0	Colubraro
Marsico Vetere	00 06 00	0	Marsico Vetere
Laurisellum	00 06 00	0	Lauriosello*
Tulba	00 07 00	00 09 00	Tolve
Campus Maior	00 07 00	00 13 10	Campomaggiore
Barayano	00 07 10	0	Baragiano
Camarda	00 07 10	00 13 10	Bernalda
Cervaricio	00 08 00	00	Cervarezza
Santa Sophia	00 08 00	0	Castelluccio di Santa Sophia*
Sanctus Arcangelus	00 08 00	0	Sant'Arcangelo
Sanctus Felice	00 08 00	0	San Fele
Raponum	00 09 00	0	Rapone
Brundusium de montana	00 09 00	00 11 08	Brindisi di Montagna
Castrum de Grandis	00 09 00	0	Castelgrande
Sinisium	00 09 00	0	Senise
Labella	00 10 00	0	Bella
Casal Aspum	00 10 00	00 09 00	Casalaspro*
Petrapagana	00 10 03		Pescopagano
Petra fixa	00 12 00	0	Satriano di Lucania
Noha	00 12 00	0	Noepoli
Casal Sant'Andrea	00 12 00	00 12 00	Casal Sant'Andrea*
Nocara	00 12 00	0	Nocera
Castrum Medianum	00 13 0	00 16 00	Castelmezzano

Table VII. (*Continued*)

name	First	Second	mod. name
Vineola	00 14 10	00 16 00	Pignola
Petragalla	00 15 00	00 15 00	Petragalla
Anzi	00 15 00	00 10 00	Anzi
Cancellara	00 15 00	00 10 00	Cancellara
Rocca Imperialis	00 15 00	0	Rocca Imperialis
Avilanum	00 15 00	00 15 00	Avigliano
Laurenciana	00 15 00	00 19 00	Laurenzana
Monte Sellicole	00 15 00	00 15 00	Monte Serico*
Abriola	00 15 00	00 15 00	Abriola
Criptole	00 15 10	00 19 00	Grottole
Tito	00 16 00	00 24 00	Tito
Genzano	00 18 15	0	Genzano
Pomaricum	00 20 00	00 18 00	Pomarico
Tursi	00 23 00	0	Tursi
Spinaciole	00 24 00	0	Spinazzola
Picerno	00 24 00	00 20 00	Picerno
Sanctus Clericus	00 24 00	00 05 00	San Chirico
de Tulbia			Nuovo
Florencia	00 25 00	0	Forenza
Milionicum	00 25 10	00 25 10	Miglionico
Oppido	01 00 00	01 00 00	Oppido Lucano
Petraperciata	01 00 00	01 02 00	Pietrapertosa
Prisinachum	01 00 00	01 12 00	Presiniaco*
Saponaria	01 00 00	0	Grumento
Gaudianum	01 04 18	03 17 03	Gaudiano
Mons Caveoso	01 10 00	01 10 00	Montescaglioso
Oggianum	01 10 00	01 10 00	Oggiano*
Lavello	01 16 00	0	Lavello
Montepeloso	01 26 00	02 00 00	Irsina
Satrianum	03 24 00	0	Satriano
Anglona	05 01 10	0	Anglona
Marsico Novo	05 02 10	0	Marsico Nuovo
Muro	07 08 00	0	Muro Lucano
Potencia	15 18 00	07 34 10	Potenza
Ageroncia	17 10 00	22 13 10	Acerenza
Melfia	40 17 01	33 14 01	Melfi
Venosa	52 07 06	11 06 14	Venosa

*Denotes a place which no longer exists

Table VIII. Table of tax and hearth totals for Basilicata and the *Regno* of South Italy (excluding Sicily).

Date	Tax in Basilicata in uncie	Source for tax or hearths in Basilicata	Hearths in Basilicata	No. of sites in Basilicata	Source for site nos.	Total tax for Regno	Source for taxes and hearths in Regno	Total hearths in Regno	Proportion rep. by Basilicata
1238	7000	Winkelmann p. 631–2				82000	Winkelmann p. 631–2		8.5%
1242	8800[1]	Winkelmann p. 666–7				48800	Winkelmann p. 666–7		
1248	9000	Winkelmann p. 712				107000	Winkelmann p. 712		8.4%
1270	5848	Reg. Ang. 7 reg. 24, 188				58414[2]	Reg. Ang. 7 reg. 24, 188		10.1%
1271	6133[3]	Reg. Ang. 7 reg. 27, 13.				57237	Reg. Ang. 7 reg. 27, 13		10.7%
1272	8000[4]	Reg. Ang. 8 reg. 37, 70.				87268	Reg. Ang. 8 reg. 37, 70		9.1%
1275	7144	Beloch, 191				75366	Beloch, 191		9.4%
1276	4283	Racioppi & Beloch, 191		148	Racioppi	45230[5]	Beloch, 191		9.4%
1277	4924	Reg. Ang. 18 reg. 80, 27		150	Reg. Ang. 18 reg. 80, 10 reg. 80, 125	52045	Reg. Ang. 18 reg. 80, 27		9.4%
				140[6]					
1278	5069	Beloch, 191				53442	Beloch, 191		9.5%
1294	3836	Beloch, 192				32867[7]	Beloch, 192		11.7%
1307	3700[8]	Minieri-Riccio		145	Minieri-Riccio				

Table VIII (*continued*)

Date	Tax in Basilicata in uncie	Source for tax or hearths in Basilicata	Hearths in Basilicata	No. of sites in Basilicata	Source for site nos.	Total tax for Regno	Source for taxes and hearths in Regno	Total hearths in Regno	Proportion rep. by Basilicata
1313	3755	Caggese, 612							
1317	3755	Caggese, 612							
1320	3670	Minieri-Riccio		150	Minieri-Riccio	33187	Beloch, 192		11%
1325	3670	Caggese, 612							
1327	3670	Caggese, 612							
1332	3670	Galanti, 21							
1339	3670	Monti, 70				23662[9]			
1342	3670	Beloch, 192				33261	Beloch, 192		11%
1415				101	Racioppi				
1445				97	Racioppi				
1455		Beloch, 260	13708[10]	93	Beloch, 260				
1465							Beloch, 212	232896	
1485							Beloch, 212	215107	
1501							Giustiniani cxxxviii-x	254380	
1505		Beloch, 260	22295	97	Beloch, 260		Beloch, 212	251823	8.8%
1507		Coniglio, 149	22302				Coniglio, 152	267324	8.3%
1510		Coniglio, 150	20141				Coniglio, 151	263510	7.6%
1511		Coniglio, 150	22295				Beloch, 212	264916	
		Coniglio, 156	22245						
1514		Coniglio, 150	22295				Coniglio, 152	261377	
1518		Coniglio, 156	22245				Coniglio, 152	268345	
1532		Giustiniani	26542[11]	89[12]	Counted fr. Giusti-		Beloch, 212	247866	
							Beloch, 212	316000	
							Coniglio, 152	315990	

Date							
1542	Coniglio, 156	24971					
1545	Beloch, 260	32318	103	Beloch, 260	Beloch, 212	422080	7.6%
1533					Coniglio, 151	425837	
1559					Coniglio, 151	470589	
1561	Cagnazzi, 274	41964	98	Cagnazzi, 274	Cagnazzi, 274	498431	8.4%
	Giustiniani	38753			Giustiniani	455504	8.5%
					Beloch, 212	481745	
1565					Coniglio, 151	485522	
1573					Coniglio, 151	487378	
1595	Beloch, 260	45881	108	Beloch, 260	Beloch, 260	540090	8.5%

Notes.

In the above, figures are taken from Beloch where possible. The figures given by Cagnazzi, Galanti and Giustiniani, where they differ from those of Beloch have not been noted unless data from these sources have been used to supply other information about a given year. Coniglio's figures are taken from a series in the Archivo General di Simancas, Estado leg. 1003, 4, 27, 30, 46, 64 not used by Beloch. Where his figures differ from those of Beloch, both have been given.

[1] Includes total also for Capitanata. Proportion represented by Basilicata could not therefore be shown.

[2] Excludes Calabria and the Val di Crati.

[3] Calculated from a schedule for the distribution of new money, for which the basis was the assessments for the general subvention.

[4] Aid for the knighting of the king's eldest son.

[5] Total listed by Beloch under 1274–5.

[6] These figures are from orders of 1277/8 for the appointment of judges in Basilicata. The first is presumably the correct one.

[7] This and the totals for 1320 and 1342 exclude Calabria and the Val di Crati.

[8] Calculated from data in the 1320 assessment.

[9] Total reached by adding sums assessed at various different dates on individual provinces. Dates range from 1330–1340. Most are for 1339.

[10] Both the sum for Basilicata and the number of places therein are incomplete.

[11] Incomplete.

[12] Incomplete. Underestimates the number of places by at least four and more probably eight and reduces the total number of hearths accordingly.

Table IX.   Sixteenth Century Household Lists.

(in order of size in 1532).

Place	1532	1545	1561	1595	Modern Name
Monte Milone	0003	0003	0055	0133	Montemilone
Rotunda Maris	0015	0020	0023	0087	Rotondella
Oppido	0024	0235	0301	0309	Oppido Lucano
Garagusium	0026	0033	0034	0050	Garagusi
Gallucium	0027	0032	0040	0098	Gallichio
Raponum	0034	0040	0050	0077	Rapone
Aliano Inferiore	0040	0049	0062	0042	Alianello
Metaponto	0041	0041	0026	0057	Metaponto
Rocca Nova	0055	0069	0090	0169	Roccanova
Corneto	0057	0109	0157	0225	Corleto Perticara
Saxo	0059	0065	0104	0151	Sasso di Castalda
Barayano	0064	0069	0092	0109	Baragiano
Bactiboranim	0064	0069	0092	0109	Battifarano
Grassanum	0069	0114	0124	0178	Grassano
Accetura	0070	0118	0182	0301	Accetura
Castrum de Grandis	0078	0088	0113	0162	Castelgrande
Guardia	0079	0105	0122	0183	Guardia Perticara
Petra fixa	0081	0118	0150	0194	Satriano di Lucania
Camarda	0099	0135	0284	0673	Bernalda
Ripa Candida	0100	0133	0163	0115	Ripacandida
Labella	0115	0205	0199	0275	Bella
Rapolla	0123	0140	0179	0193	Rapolla
Triclina	0126	0226	0207	0286	Trecchina
Castrum Medianum	0131	0164	0091	0126	Castelmezzano
Avillanum	0133	0176	0216	0439	Avigliano
Ruvo	0133	0156	0223	0269	Ruvo
Vineola	0136	0167	0238	0318	Pignola
Sanctus Felice	0136	0160	0128	0401	San Fele
Biganellum	0141	0211	0264	0260	Viggianello
Anzi	0141	0197	0337	0517	Anzi
Episcopia	0143	0178	0205	0247	Episcopia
Moliterno	0144	0184	0251	0345	Moliterno
Cancellara	0149	0169	0216	0387	Cancellara
Petrapagana	0153	0119	0165	0354	Pescopagano
Petragalla	0154	0116	0146	0173	Petragalla
Castelluccio	0164	0210	0344	0356	Castelluccio Superiore
Sanctus Clericus Vallis Signi	0164	0215	0268	0249	San Chirico Raparo

Place	1532	1545	1561	1595	Modern Name
Burgencia	0168	0199	0243	0391	Brienza
Gurgulionum	0173	0224	0203	0145	Gorgoglione
Aliano Superiore	0175	0299	0324	0271	Aliano
Laurenciana	0183	0236	0462	0520	Laurenzana
Genzano	0186	0247	0319	0365	Genzano
Calvellum	0194	0248	0426	0498	Calvello
Rotunda Vallis	0202	0291	0332	0245	Rotonda
Layni					
Favale	0204	0260	0148	0069	Val Sinni
Salandra	0206	0236	0266	0348	Salandra
Tulba	0208	0235	0327	0385	Tolve
San Mauro	0220	0267	0340	0409	San Mauro Fort
Anglona	0223	0280	0221	0400	Anglona
Clarus Mons	0235	0204	0216	0206	Chiaramonte
Tramutola	0240	0302	0402	0603	Tramutola
Abriola	0249	0292	0376	0228	Abriola
Latronicum	0254	0357	0319	0385	Latronico
Lavello	0257	0358	0574	0702	Lavello
Marsico Novo	0260	0300	0456	0574	Marsico Nuovo
Castrosarraceno	0260	0387	0437	0486	Castel Saraceni
Calciano	0266	0284	0236	0144	Canciano
Armentum	0274	0450	0448	0316	Armento
Albanum	0279	0395	0388	0480	Albano
Marsico Vetere	0286	0326	0356	0574	Marsico Vetere
Mons Albanus	0294	0569	0604	0479	Montalbano
Tito	0294	0507	0508	0567	Tito
Stigliano	0294	0420	0514	0692	Stigliano
Saponaria	0311	0273	0312	0317	Grumento
Montepeloso	0314	0426	0586	0914	Irsina
Florencia	0325	0412	0600	0717	Forenza
Bianum	0326	0410	0482	0578	Viggiano
Cracum	0342	0507	0518	0465	Craco
Lacus nerus	0344	0414	0516	0706	Lagonegro
Columbarium	0345	0245	0470	0583	Colubraro
Ageroncia	0350	0368	0418	0269	Acerenza
Noha	0361	0431	0216	0079	Noepoli
Ferrandina	0379	0499	0686	1031	Ferrandina
Rivello	0381	0448	0546	0651	Rivello
Pomaricum	0386	0515	0551	0670	Pomarico
Lauria	0391	0551	0720	1097	Lauria
Sinisium	0402	0524	0522	0274	Senise
Montemurro	0410	0560	0539	0317	Montemurro
Rocca Imperialis	0425	0577	0688	0342	Rocca Imperialis
Muro	0430	0552	0721	0486	Muro Lucano
Criptole	0433	0525	0557	0648	Grottole
Petraperciata	0521	0521	0543	0332	Pietrapertosa
Atella	0532	0593	0622	0582	Atella
Mons Caveoso	0545	0760	0846	0856	Montescaglioso

Table IX   *(continued)*

(in order of size in 1532).

Place	1532	1545	1561	1595	Modern Name
Tricarico	0607	0867	1773	1059	Tricarico
Venosa	0695	0841	1095	1095	Venosa
Melfia	0781	1042	1772	2180	Melfi
Tursi	0866	1339	1799	1400	Tursi
San Martino	0	0	0343	0246	San Martino
Minganellum	0	0	0138	0210	Missanello
Sarconium	0	0	0198	0118	Sarconi
Rotum	0	0058	0091	0097	Ruoti
Oliveto	0	0070	0059	0034	Oliveto Lucano
Papasiderum	0	0	0251	0243	Papasidero
Castrocucco	0	0	0012	0012	Castrocucco*
Milionicum	0	0	0293	0656	Miglionico
Marathia	0	0	0467	0560	Maratea
Turris Curiliani	0	0	0177	0178	Corigliano*
Cersosimo	0	0	0	0017	Kyr Zozimo
Sanctus Clericus de Tulbia	0	0	0053	0029	San Chirico Nuovo
Palazzo San Gervasio	0	0	0001	0082	Palazzo San Gervasio
Spinaciole	0	0	0390	0516	Spinazzola
Castelluccio Inferiore	0	0	0	0023	Castelluccio Inferiore
Baglio	0	0	0254	0328	Vaglio
Sanctus Arcangelus	0	0	0186	0350	Sant'Arcangelo
Castrum Novum	0	0	0	0046	Castronovo
Picerno	0 (misl aid)	0	0468	0548	Picerno
Raczanum	000	0	0783	0938	Pisticci

Table X. Places taxed in 1320 no longer listed in 1532.

Tax of 1320 in Uncie, Tari and Grani.

Place	tax. 1320
Rocca de Acino	000 00 00
Terra Tancredi de Guarino	000 05 11
Caldaria	000 15 00
Sanctus Theodorus	000 25 00 (R.I.)
Sanctus Salvator	000 25 00 (Spin.)
Casale Sanctus Nicola de Silva	001 11 07
Casal Sancte Marie de Cornu	001 16 15
Petra de Acino	001 17 09
Trivinea	002 08 02
Casal Sancti Mattei	002 20 00 (Spin.)
Casale Sancti Martini	002 22 14 (Spin.)
Casal Lupicoso	002 25 00 (Spin.0.2 5,R.I.2)
Casal Rubio	003 03 10
Avinella	003 15 16
Appium	003 16 14 (R.I.)
Sanctus Basilius	003 20 01
Trisagia	003 20 12
Castrum Bellocte	004 00 07
Acernum	004 13 09
Andriacum	004 13 09
Minganellum*	004 14 17
Tofaria	004 25 05
Campus Maior*	005 00 00
Altus Joannes	005 00 00 (Spin.)
Pulsandrana	005 00 16
Prisinachum	005 01 01
Laurisellum	005 09 04
Scansana	005 13 10 (Spin.)
Boreano	005 16 06 (Spin.)
Banzi*	006 11 04
Oliveto*	006 11 08
Rotum*	006 19 15 (Spin.)

Table X. *(continued)*

Tax of 1320 in Uncie, Tari and Grani.

Place	tax. 1320
Casal Aspum	006 21 05
Mons Morconis	006 21 18
Platano	007 03 00
Gallipoli	007 25 07
	(Spin.)
Bellus Mons	007 29 14
Armatera	007 29 16
Petra Castalda	008 03 03
Casal Pisticci	009 13 06
	(Spin.)
Turris Curiliani	010 28 16
Papasiderum*	011 07 17
Rionero	011 12 10
Baglio*	011 24 08
Sanctus Iulianus	012 01 16
Castrum Novum	012 02 08
Gloriosa	012 12 09
Cervaricio	014 05 17
Faratum	014 27 02
Tiganum*	014 27 12
Casal Sant'Andrea	015 12 00
Satrianum	015 14 02
	(Spin.)
Monticuli	015 18 15
	(R.I.)
Santa Sophia	017 04 05
	(Spin.)
Grisosutrum	018 10 16
Lavena	018 12 17
Sarconium	020 10 05
Monte Sellicole	020 14 12
Cersosimo	023 17 14
Spinaciole*	024 11 00
Irsi	025 18 00
Perticara	030 08 00
Brundusium de montana*	030 14 00
Sanctus Clericus de Tulbia*	031 14 03
San Martino*	036 10 00
Sanctus Arcangelus	046 02 11
Marathia*	047 26 09
Milionicum*	062 16 04
	(Spin.)
Gaudianum	087 23 00
Oggianum	090 09 15
Potencia*	133 22 07

Note: Places marked with an asterisk recovered later and are now communes.

Table XI. Table showing numbers of
hearths in various places in Basilicata.

Figures for 1507 and 1531 from Aragonese surveys,[1]
figures for 1532 from Giustiniani.

	1507	1531	1532
Atella		600	536
Forenza		400	325
Grottole	360		433
Maratea	360		
Melfi		1000	781
Montescaglioso	150		545
Pomarico	255		386
Rapolla		100 (with	123
		Barile	
Ripacandida		110	100
San Gervasio	60		
San Mauro	Inhabited		
Scanzana	Inhabited		
San Fele		30	136
Tursi	800		866

[1]See note 63.

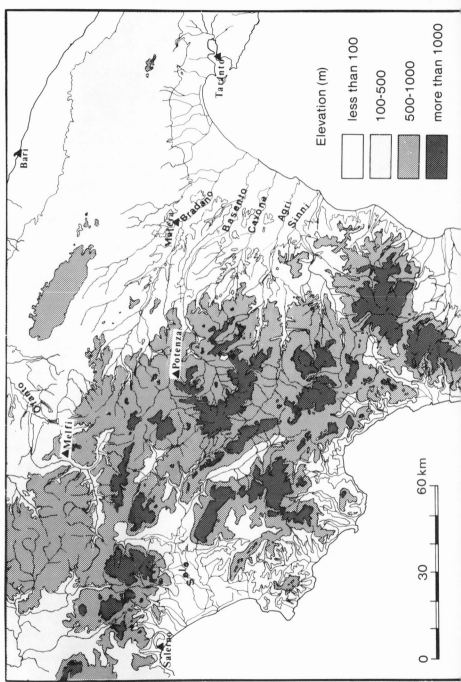

MAP 1. Relief and rivers of Basilicata.

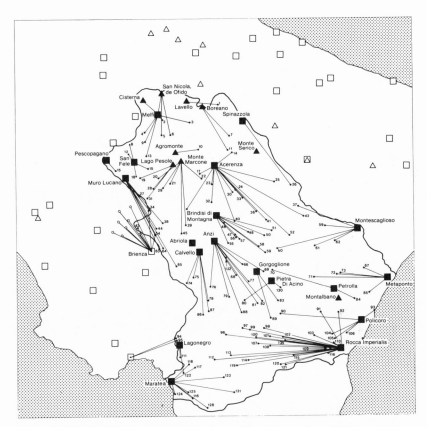

Map 2. Castles of Frederick II and villages serving them

Map References

1	Monte Milone	2	Rapolla
3	Venosa	4	Monticchio
5	Ripacandida	6	Rionero
7	Cervarezza	8	San Tomaso di Ruvo
9	Casal Sant'Andrea	10	Forenza
11	Banzi	12	Rapone
13	Armatiera	14	Genzano
15	Castelgrande	16	Pierno
17	Casalaspro	18	Bella
19	Castelluccio di Santa Sophia	20	Caldane
21	Avigliano	22	Pietragalla
23	Cancellara	24	Oppido
25	Montepeloso	26	Irsi
27	Platano	28	Santa Sophia
29	Ruoti	30	Tolve
31	Baragiano	32	Vaglio
33	San Chirico Nuovo	34	Marmore
35	Potenza	36	Tricarico
37	Altogianni	38	Tito
39	Pignola	40	Albano
41	Calciano	42	Grottole
43	Salvia	44	Satriano
45	Gloriosa	46	Trevigno
47	Trifoglie	48	Gallipoli
49	Campomaggiore	50	Oliveto
51	Garaguso	52	Salandra
53	Miglionico	54	Pietrafesa
55	Castelbelloto	56	Castelmezzana
57	Pietrapertosa	58	Accetura
59	Raja/Radia	60	San Mauro Forte
61	Oggiano	62	Pomarico
63	Sasso	64	Pietracastalda
65	Marsico Nuovo	66	Perticara
67	Camarda	68	Corleto
69	Cirigliano	70	Stigliano
71	Craco	72	Pisticci
73	Casal Pisticci	74	Tramutola
75	Marsico Vetere	76	Viggiano
77	Guardia	78	Saponaria
79	Montemurrone	80	Armento
81	Gallichio	82	Missanello
83	Alianello	84	Andriace
85	San Basilio	86	Moliterno
87	Sarconi	88	San Martino
89	Roccanova	90	Sant'Arcangelo
91	Tursi	92	Anglona

Map References *(continued)*

93	Scansana	94	Brigetti
95	Tuclani	96	Castelsarraceno
97	San Chirico Vallis Layni	98	Castronovo
99	Pulsandrana	100	Calvera
101	Battifarano	102	Senise
103	Favale	104	Rontondella
105	Bollito	106	Trisagia
107	Teana	108	Chiaramonte
109	Nocara	110	Presiniaco
111	Rivello	112	Seleuci
113	Latronico	114	Episcopia
115	Noha	116	Canna
117	Lauria	118	Nemoli
119	Agromonte	120	Rubio
121	Faraco	122	Trecchina
123	Castelluccio	124	Catrocucco
125	Tortora	126	Ayeta
127	Rotunda Vallis Layni	128	Papasidero
129	Culicleari	130	Aliano
131	Viggianello	132	Laurenzana
133	Avena	134	Tofaria

THE CAPETIAN KINGS AND ST. MARTIN OF TOURS

Quentin Griffiths
Inverness, California
*Emeritus, California State
University, Chico*

THE CAPETIAN KINGS AND ST. MARTIN OF TOURS

Any student of the Middle Ages is familiar with the kings' heavy reliance on the high clergy for counsel and even administrative services. He is apt to be less familiar with the French and English kings' ability to maintain some influence over the choice of their clergy in the face of the Gregorian reforms of the eleventh and twelfth centuries. He may even be unaware that the kings enjoyed a free hand in confering benefices on certain officers in their collegiate churches (or "royal free chapels" in England) well before the championing of the "national church" in the fourteenth century. If he has read in Joinville that St. Louis consulted with his clerical advisors at length to insure that these benefices be given to worthy persons, he may be surprised that some of these church officers were royal administrative functionaries.[1] The professional historian, on the other hand, assuming that the king's rights in these churches had always existed, might be surprised that by the mid-thirteenth century, only three churches were providing this financial support for the royal bureaucracy: St. Martin of Tours (in formerly English territory to the west of Paris); St. Aignan of Orléans (on the southern border of the old domain); and St. Frambaud of Senlis, fifty-one kilometers to the north. It is the purpose of this paper to explain the preeminent role which St. Martin had assumed from the early thirteenth century in this productive partnership between church and state, and, conversely, to account for the late introduction of the practice in France, in contrast to its more widespread use in England.

The Development of the Partnership between the King and His Collegiate Churches

The basis of the partnership was the "spiritual liberties" of collegiate churches. The study of the origins of these liberties has benefited from English and French comparative scholarship, especially from Jeffrey H. Denton's book in 1970 which draws heavily on the Guillaume Mollat's work in 1951.[2] But neither considers at any length their implications for royal government, nor the particular status or significance of St. Martin of Tours. By "spiritual liberties," Mollat refers to the king's right to "confer, give and dispose, as absolute master and without ecclesiastical interference, the benefices subject to his collation." Freedom from diocesan control was one of the countercurrents against Gregorian reform, like the king's rights to present candidates to offices in cathedral churches, or the more general right of patronage. But this right of collation *pleno jure,* which Mollat has defined, was derived from actual or factitious foundations by the king, from inheritances, or from donations to churches. By the mid-thirteenth century it was far more comprehensive and undisputed than his regalian rights in the cathedrals,[3] and more significant as a supplement to the royal budget than ordinary rights of patronage, as the evidence from St. Aignan and St. Frambaud as well as St. Martin will demonstrate.

By the mid-twelfth century it was a right being exercised, though in varying degrees, in both England and France. The liberties of the English royal free chapels probably go back to the Anglo-Saxon minsters. There is no evidence, however, of their furnishing maintenance for royal personnel until the twelfth century, except for the king's priest or chaplain. Likewise, on the continent clerks in the writing-office were closely identified with the Carolingian palace chapels.[4] The link with the king's regular entourage almost disappears here too until the days of Louis VI, who presented his favorite, the chancellor Étienne, as candidate for the deanship of St. Aignan. The treasurer of St. Martin of Tours, who administered St. Martin as part of the king's domain, seems to have been a king's man even during the alienation of the territory to the Angevins. But the right of collation is not clearly articulated until 1236 by the English king, and 1267 by the French king.[5] And there is no firm evidence that the French king tapped an office in a collegiate church for advice and service on the "king's business" (as distinct from a sinecure for a royal son or favorite official) until 1192, when Dean Anselme of St. Martin began to serve Philip Augustus.[6] There is other evidence of the enjoyment of such liberties besides that for St. Martin and St. Aignan: for the duke of Burgundy's chapel at Dijon in 1207, and for the French king's chapel at Chateauneuf-sur-Loire in 1213.[7] And there are many examples even before 1200 of the king's exercise of his rights of spiritual regalia to compensate or reward a royal chancellor for his services by promoting him to bishop. But only at St. Martin does a royal functionary (other than a chancellor) appear as early as 1213, when Eudes Clément became preoccupied, as he was for a major part of his years as dean, "with the administration of royal affairs,"[8] notably on the Norman Exchequer, and only at St. Martin do we find such functionaries before the middle of the century.

Before examining the unique combination of circumstances which explains the preeminent role of St. Martin, we need to understand how the king's privileges were actually exercised at certain collegiate churches and where we find the first use of their officers as royal agents. The first Capetians exercised limited control in the few collegiate churches where actual royal patronage survived. For example, as late as Louis the Fat's reign, the king could do no better than reserve his right to *invest* the dean of St. Frambaud of Senlis, who was elected by the canons.[9]

Yet St. Frambaud is cited as a model "royal church."[10] Perhaps the kings had nominated the treasurer, until the office was appropriated by the Bouteillers de Senlis (off and on Great Officers of the crown), but there is no evidence of crown control until the royal clerks appear there in the second half of the thirteenth century.[11] Indeed, however extensive these prerogatives were claimed to be in later centuries,[12] the early Capetians either did not or could not exercise them, often because the church was outside their territorial domain. For example, at the church of St. Quentin in Vermandois the right of collation to the office of warden was still in the hands of the count until the time of Philip Augustus.[13]

Hugh Capet's and Robert's ecclesiastical interests lay in another direction, the encouragement of monastic reform, and the collegiate churches were not the objects of munificence as they were under the Carolingians; but the extension of occasional favors enhanced the king's influence in the area. Among the *collégiales*, St. Aignan of Orléans seems to have been favored by Robert, as Henry I and Philip I favored those involved in canonical reform.[14] However, such favoritism may have been due to the fact that one of the canons was the king's beneficiary Edelin, present when the king confirmed privileges to the abbey of Micy, and he was surely the dean in 1029 who is ordered by the king to translate some relics to that abbey.[15] Robert's reputation at St. Aignan probably rests on his generosity in restoring and enlarging the church after a fire, and on the donation of another church; the rest of his acts were simply confirmations of earlier concessions.[16] Hugh Capet, who first combined the roles of lay abbot and king at both churches, also had been generous to St. Martin when he enlarged the area covered by the immunities granted by his grandfather. Although even his son Robert the Pious in that same capacity could and did grant away church properties to lay barons,[17] one of Robert's foundations, in 1007, was made at the request of his representative at St. Martin, the likewise "pious" treasurer Hervé.[18]

More important for the purpose of our study than favors or occasional new foundations by the first four Capetian kings, is the disproportionate representation of these two churches among the small but growing number of minor ecclesiastics who witnessed and subscribed royal diplomas. To be sure, at this early stage, they were wanted, not for advice or service, but to make known locally the royal presence.

The subscribers in 1007 include, besides four former, current, and future treasurers of St. Martin (dignitaries whom Professor Lemarignier ranks roughly with archdeacons), the dean Ulgerius.[19] He and the cantor Gautier are among the only three or four "minor ecclesiastics" who appear on diplomas in this reign.[20] In Henry I's reign St. Aignan and St. Martin are represented by a sub-dean and a dean, respectively, and the number of all "minor ecclesiastics" has risen to about seven, though, again, none of them subscribed more than once.[21] During Philip I's reign four officers of St. Martin and St. Aignan are among the fourteen minor ecclesiastics and archdeacons to witness royal acts.[22] In contrast to St. Martin and St. Aignan, the collegiate church of St. Quentin is represented only once by Jean, probably the warden, when the king confirms a liberty from the bishop's authority at the request of the count of Flanders.[23]

Thus the three Capetians following Hugh Capet increasingly used the dignitaries of these *collégiales* as members of their local entourages to witness their acts, however token or routine. As king's men, they helped make evident the royal presence, even on the periphery of the royal domain, where their own churces were located.[24] At the same time, the offices of treasurer and dean provided the kings with opportunities to reward the families loyal to the crown: those of Amboise, Montigny, and Preuilly at St. Martin or Garlande at St. Aignan. But even these *fideles* cannot yet be considered royal counselors in a regular sense, let alone the nascent civil servants who enjoyed the same benefices in the thirteenth century. The first Capetians were probably more interested in assuring canonical reform in their churches, in a growing competition of prestige with the pope, than in strengthening their political and economic resources; but these latter motives always seem dominant at St. Martin, where even modest reforms awaited the thirteenth century.[25]

Extending his protection and favors to "royal houses" became a deliberate policy under Louis VI and Louis VII, and it was the latter's "trump card" in reinforcing royal authority, according to Pacaut. Sometimes the king reminded the chapter that he acted as lay abbot as well as king, as in 1114.[26] The policy was continued by Philip Augustus, who confirmed earlier privileges.[27] And these kings went a step further: their nominees at St. Martin and St. Aignan became the eyes and ears of the king, while the churches helped support a royal chancellor and members of the royal family.

There is indeed some evidence from such extensions of favors that the kings were purposely reinforcing their prerogatives in "royal houses," especially now that their control of cathedral churches was being challenged by the Gregorian reform. Pacaut identifies fifty-odd churches in this category which Louis VII "controlled regularly." Almost half of them are Augustinian or reformed chapters, and they include the collegiate churches we have been considering. We know far less about the king's relations with the deans than with the bishops, and Pacaut admits it is "hard to tell over which ones he was able actually to revive the prerogatives which he held by the fact of their establishment by his ancestors, and which might have been forgotten in his time." Though he does not acknowledge Mollat's definition of the right of collation *pleno jure,* Pacaut's definition of a true "royal house" is remarkably similar, and he suggests the examples of St. Martin and St. Aignan, where, as lay abbot, the king was "surely patron, entitled to intervene in elections."[28] Yet the king had not extended his prerogatives to this point at St. Frambaud, as we have noted. Louis the Fat made no more than a token appearance in 1135 for the revelation of the relics. Still, he and his son considered it a "royal abbey" like Ste. Geneviève of Paris, and concluded a pariage of a village with the canons. It was probably the same Ebroin, the Queen Mother's chaplain, elsewhere referred to as dean of St. Frambaud, to whom the king granted a dispensation from residence, when he was invested as chaplain of St. Denis of Senlis.[29] But there is not even a suggestion that he designated the treasurer till perhaps 1202, when Philip Augustus sent the treasurer "W." on a mission to Pope Innocent to obtain more time to dissolve his marriage with Ingeborg.[30] At St. Quentin, too, patronage did not necessarily imply the right of nomination.[31]

By contrast there is early evidence of the king's special advantages at St. Martin and St. Aignan. They are suggested by the application of *fidelis* as early as 988 to Dean Archambaud of St. Martin, in 1164 to Barthélemy de Vendôme, and then in 1196 to Anselme. At St. Aignan it is obvious at least from Louis VI on, that the king is naming the deans, like Peter of Pisa, "made dean by the k." in 1161 or 1162.[32] This prerogative was often the key to controlling other benefices and prebends like the cantor's.[33] There was the increasing use of the office of treasurer at St. Martin to support surplus members or relatives of the royal family, no longer just to assure the loyalty of a local noble family. Louis VI's son Philippe (the second by that name) may have been dean of both St. Aignan and St. Martin; the evidence is scanty. He already enjoyed a host of other dignities, heaped upon him by his brother the king, mindful perhaps of their father's troublesome step-brother Philippe de Mantes who had remained a layman.[34] But there is no doubt about the treasurership of Tours where Louis VII placed his other brother Henri. Their father had started him out on his ecclesiastical career as abbot of St. Mellon of Pontoise at the age of five. After a frustrated marriage he had entered the Cistercian order. He was placed over most of the royally-founded abbeys where Philippe was not already abbot. Though he quarrelled later with Louis VII, he ended up as archbishop of Reims.[35] The practice of so employing the treasurership continued with Renaud III and Rotrou.[36]

After Philippe and until the mid-thirteenth century, the deanship at St. Aignan was no more than a supplemental reward for a favorite clerk—sometimes a chancellor, sometimes a chaplain. Louis the Fat's chancellor, the infamous Etienne de Garlande, enjoyed the deanship of St. Aignan from 1114 presumably until his death about 1149, but the appointment came after he had been made archdeacon of Paris, dean of St. Samson and dean of the cathedral church of Ste. Croix of Orléans, and it was only one of the many favors heaped upon a man of substantial family, whose brothers and ancestors were also Great Officers, and who himself took over the office of seneschal in addition to the chancery. Forced out of the court by the reform party of Queen Adelaide in 1127, he exercised a remarkable influence on the king, and resumed the title of chancellor from 1132 to 1137, though he shortly lost the exercise of the great seal to his notary or vice-chancellor Algrin, the king's chaplain—perhaps to mollify the reformers.[37] Cadurc, Louis VII's chancellor from 1140 to 1147 and briefly in 1150, may seem to be a parallel case: another royal favorite, deprived of his ecclesiastical honors and endangering his master's soul for contesting an election to the bishopric of Bourges, then made archdeacon by his late rival, and, despite Cadurc's opposition to Suger during the crusade, stubbornly pampered by the king thereafter with appointments as his representative, gifts of land, the abbacy of St. Sulpice of Bourges, and finally in 1183, the deanship of St. Aignan.[38] Surely he was just as greedy and ambitious. Unlike Etienne he might be the harbinger of the "new man" in the chancery, whose origins we are tracing: a career royal servant from (presumably) the modest nobility, like the deans of these two churches in the thirteenth century. But there is an important difference: the deanship came *after* he had retired, and it came from Philip Augustus, perhaps as a gesture to his father's memory, and not as a source of maintenance for royal service. To support his chaplain in royal service, Louis VII, again exercising his rights as abbot, while confirming the requirement for the cantor to remain in the cloister, requested a lifetime exemption for the incumbent Geoffroy.[39] He remained at court at least till 1185.[40] From 1201 to 1207, Philip Augustus used the office of dean to support his chaplain Guillaume who obtained privileges for his church.[41] Renaud of St. Gilles, dean around 1212 to 1217, defended the king and the "king's church" when Innocent III intervened in an issue between St. Aignan and Bishop Manassée of Orléans, even though, we are told, he was dean "at the chapter's request."[42] Thereafter the officers of St. Aignan had no apparent royal functions until we reach the series of royal clerks beginning about 1245 with Dean Etienne de St-Samson. We know only of a Thomas de la Chapelle, probably from the family which produced royal bailiffs and a pantryman, and of a Dean Henri, two cantors and a subdean.[43]

The roles played in government by the officers of St. Martin from the later years of Louis VII were far more active, until by 1212 they were functioning in key administrative positions. It is tempting to identify, with an otherwise obscure Dean Barthélemy, Louis VII's chancellor during the brief interval of the Second Crusade.[44] If the identification does not rest simply on a coincidence of names, the credit was probably Abbot Suger's for first using the deanship at St.

Martin to maintain a functionary of presumably modest means, albeit in this instance a chancellor. In any case, a subsequent Barthélemy played an important role representing the king with the bourgeois of Chateauneuf and as an observer of the English king's movements, and we shall consider later the diplomatic and administrative roles of deans like Anselme and Eudes Clément under Philip Augustus and his successors.

Even before the reconquest of Touraine, it is clear that St. Martin had become a more regular and substantial source of royal agents than St. Aignan or the other collegiate churches.

St-Martin's Unique Situation under the Early Capetians

The initial aim of this paper was to determine the reasons for St. Martin's pre-eminent role. The answer lies in the unique combination of circumstances which had linked the Capetians with that church. Matthew Paris recognized this special link when he reported the protests of the king and clergy in 1245 over papal interference in the collation of benefices "even in . . . the special churches of the lord king, as in the church of St. Martin of Tours and several others . . ."[45] The chapter of St. Martin had acquired significant wealth and temporal privileges under earlier dynasties; the kings tenaciously maintained their links with the church throughout the feudal period.

The wealth and the temporal rights of the church grew rapidly from the time of the foundation of the fifth-century basilica, which contained the remains of the first bishop of Tours—virtually a patron saint of France like St. Denis. It became the object of pilgrimages and therefore of revenues which produced the town of Chateauneuf around it—a bustling community distinct from the archiepiscopal city of Tours one kilometer to the west. (Today the two are separated only by the north-south highway which bridges the Loire.)[46] St. Martin had been loaded with gifts and privileges by the Carolingian kings, as well as by the Holy See. Already a mix of monks and secular clerks when Alcuin was abbot in the time of Charlemagne,[47] by the ninth century the abbey had become a church under a college of canons, and was governed by a dean appointed directly by the lay abbot. From the reign of Charles the Bald in 866 the lay abbot of St. Martin was one of the Robertian counts of Neustria (also called dukes of Francia), the ancestors of the Capetian kings.[48] In 888 the abbacy became hereditary in their family, 100 years before Hugh Capet permanently joined the office of abbot to the crown.

Hugh's oath to defend and protect the church's possessions, rights and immunities, a tradition inherited from the Carolingians, reflects St. Martin's importance, and the oath was one which he and his descendants kept.[49] It implied a continuing control over the choice of the church's governing dignitaries. The unusual relationship that existed at the accession of Hugh Capet between the king, the chapter, the surrounding feudal lordships, and the local bourgeosie requires some explanation.

What was it that allowed the Capetians to enjoy this island of royal domain in a feudal sea? For St. Martin was more like one of the German *Reichskirche* than many of the French bishoprics, where the king received little more than titular recognition. In the tenth century, the church and Chateauneuf were surrounded by the barony of Blois, and then, early in the eleventh century, by that of the more formidable count of Anjou. How could the king rely on the dignitaries at St. Martin even to witness a royal act, let alone install his own candidates in these offices when they were vacant? The answer seems to lie in the feudal rivalry between these two great baronies at the beginning of the eleventh century, a rivalry that played into the kings' hands, even before the challenge of an aggressive bourgeoisie in Chateauneuf invited royal intervention in the twelfth century. Even after the conquest of Tours and its county, the rivalry among the successors of Geoffroy Martel allowed an otherwise feeble monarchy to keep its appointees at St. Martin beholden to it. The diplomatic rivalry is reflected in the game of "musical chairs" over which baronial house or which faction was to be represented in the offices of dean and treasurer. Although Geoffroy Plantagenet was to restore order in Anjou by the second quarter of the twelfth century (before conquering Normandy for his son, the future Henry II of England), King Louis the Fat took advantage of the disarray in the county at the beginning of his reign, and in 1139 reasserted that the "abbey and its lands" were an integral part of the royal domain.[50]

But let us go back and trace briefly the origins of this rivalry which prevented the two great baronial houses, or any of their vassals, from achieving a monopoly over the major offices at St. Martin. The Angevin involvement seems to have been more than a material interest in their holdings in Chateauneuf, around the year 1000 still a modest commercial suburb of Tours. The interest went back to the days of Count Foulques the Good in the tenth century, who had probably been made a canon of St. Martin by Hugh Capet's ancestor, Hugh the Great. According to the chroniclers, Foulques liked to sing with the other canons, and occupied a stall next to the dean's: a tradition revived (or continued?) when Arthur of Brittany was count under Philip Augustus' protection at the end of the twelfth century, until King John did him in.[51] The tradition was certainly nourished in the eleventh century by the pious deeds of the treasurer Hervé of Buzançais, a house loyal to the count of Anjou. Hugh Capet, both as duke of Francia and as king, continued the alliance with Foulques Nerra in order to resist the expansionism of Eudes of Blois. Thereafter cooperation with Blois or Anjou was determined by the needs of royal diplomacy, if one may so characterize the familiar Capetian style of reacting to the situation at hand.

The shifting pattern of family affiliations of the deans and treasurers at St. Martin with one or the other baronial faction, when it is set against the background of diplomatic alliances, suggests that there was far from a monopoly of power at St. Martin, but rather a sharing of interest between the king on the one hand, and Blois or Anjou on the other.

The first treasurer under Hugh Capet was Renaud, almost certainly the same person as Foulques' viscount of Angers, known as the Thuringian, whom the count wanted to pry loose from a tempting arrangement with the Blois faction, as Professor Bachrach has demonstrated. The new dean at about this time (and our dates are anything but precise) was named Archambaud. Because that name is so common in the house of Buzançais, it suggests he was likewise an Angevin partisan. Yet he was simultaneously a *fidelis* of the king, who doubtless nominated him, and who granted him and the chapter a renewed favor of protection and immunities.[52]

The appointment of the next treasurer was obviously governed by the "diplomatic revolution" precipitated by King Robert's passion for Berthe, widow of Count Eudes, and which inaugurated a period of Capetian-Blois unity (996–1003). Gautier was almost certainly from that family of Blois loyalists which produced the count's overseers with headquarters at Tours, and he may even have been the father of the better-known Ganelon, three treasurers down the line. Eudes, the new dean that year, could well have been from a family of viscounts of Tours, still the Blois capital of Touraine.

On the other hand, if this reaction to momentary needs

suggests a challenge to the king's authority at St. Martin, note that Dean Eudes outlasted the next revolution, when King Robert decided to marry Foulques's cousin Constance (1003). Moreover, the tide had already turned against Blois at St. Martin in 1001, when the pious Hervé was installed as treasurer. A king's man as much as an Angevin partisan, he survived the briefly renewed royal liaison with Berthe, while the next dean Ulger appears to have been a beneficiary of it! A king's representative was not, it seems, turned out of office because of a shift in diplomatic alliances.

The next treasurer was Hervé's nephew, the notorious Sulpice, warlike castellan of Amboise (where today you can spend an elegant holiday in his castle overlooking the Loire). His appointment reflects, we are told, the king's "hardening attitude" toward Blois, though he was the king's direct vassal. But at the end of his career, in a last joint effort to confront the Angevin power, the new King Henry and Count Eudes II attempted unsuccessfully to besiege him. His successor Ganelon was the last Blois partisan at St. Martin. Overseer for the count at Tours, he held the treasurer's office for twenty years. Notably he was not evicted from his church office, as he and his fellow tenants were from their lay holdings when Geoffroy Martel defeated Blois in 1044. These evictions were probably approved by the king, according to Guillot, but the king would not have looked kindly at the expropriation of his treasurer's possessions. It is completely consistent, too, with earlier examples that the dean Jaubert likewise outlasted the fall of his Blois lord.

Let us consider a few other examples of how the king was able to maintain an effective "liege lordship" at St. Martin, once peace was made with Anjou, and he could no longer count on a Blois alliance. If the king had effectively "alienated" the office of treasurer, as once suggested by Professor Boussard, would the office have lain vacant for almost five years after Ganelon's death?[53] Even when one recognizes that all the treasurers and deans whose families we can identify were Angevin loyalists till the appointment of the son of Louis the Fat in the mid-twelfth century, there is evidence that the king kept his hand on the affairs of St. Martin and Chateauneuf. Geoffroy of Preuilly, whose *seigneurs* were vassals of both king and count, exercised his judicial rights as treasurer over the local royal domain from the castle of Chateauneuf. Both he and his successor Renaud revolted against the legitimate count, who was supported by the king, but the latter helped establish a truce with Foulques Rechin, the leader of the revolt, and indeed Renaud's appointment seems to reflect a royal entente with the new count. Renaud did become a counselor of Foulques, and acknowledged the latter's rights in Chateauneuf. We do not know when these specific rights were obtained, but the fact that they are acknowledged by the king's representative—perhaps held of him—indicates that the town is basically royal territory, and the acknowledgment anticipates the *enquête* of 1190, discussed below. The suggestion that Geoffroy took some of his "official rights" into his family heritage is not documented, and although there was at least one more treasurer from Preuilly in the twelfth century, there were no direct successions within this or any other family, as far as we can tell. Even when Geoffroy Plantagenet reestablished strong rule in Anjou, we find a cantor of St. Martin serving as judge in the count's court, and the cantor was appointed by the dean, a royal designee.[54]

We have referred already to the continuing appearance of the treasurers and increasingly the deans in active roles in the king's entourage from the reign of Louis VII, Angevin-involved though they were. And they enjoyed his support: Barthélemy of Vendôme, Louis's agent in keeping an eye on the Angevin Henry II of England, was rewarded with the archbishopric of Tours. After 1190, all had origins outside the Touraine. The offices were never really feudalized, even though the incumbents recognized the king as their overlord for their church dignities, as well as the count for their families' lay holdings, and though they received homage for possessions held of them as officers of the church.

These dignitaries had remained the king's representatives in his royal domain, and their considerable prerogatives, which we will consider in further detail below, were to be spelled out in the *enquête* in 1190 leading to the Treaty of Corbigny between Richard Lionheart and Philip Augustus.[55] Louis VI had made sure that, as the administrator of most of the chapter's temporalities, the treasurer would not be a tool of his Plantagenet foe, and probably assured the appointment of his son Henri by Louis VII. Until St. Louis chose Simon de Brion, the office after the accession of Philip Augustus was held by sons or relatives of the royal family, like Renaud de Mouzon and Philip's bastard son Pierre Charlot. He had first to be a canon with a prebend, but it was only the latter's defect in birth and not his ecclesiastical shortcomings to which the chapter objected. Of course the king assumed during vacancies in the treasurership all its revenues and privileges.[56] In the twelfth century to protect his representatives at Chateauneuf, the king had another major opportunity for involvement in church affairs.

It was explicitly to protect their domain that Louis VI and his successors made occasional concessions to the bourgeoisie but consistently supported the chapter and treasurer in their periodic confrontations. These began in 1122, when arson destroyed the chapter's buildings. Soon the bourgeoisie were at odds with the royal authority[57] because they had failed to assure themselves of Louis VI's protection. (Louis, we are reminded by Touraine's historian, "did not refuse to confirm rights to those who paid.")[58]

Chateauneuf and its inhabitants had been both a gold mine and a sore spot, especially from the days of the Viking attacks. In 903, while still duke of France, Robert I as lay abbot had fortified the town—hence the name: Chateauneuf. This was the "real town," while Tours itself remained the sleepy ecclesiastical and feudal capital with its cathedral and castle.[59] Immunities had been granted earlier in the ninth century both to the church (jurisdiction over Chateauneuf and its environs) and to the bourgeoisie under this jurisdiction (such as freedom from the "tallage of royal ministers").[60] These immunities now had to be confirmed periodically to maintain the fortifications, if not also the royal revenues.

Whatever revenues the king may have lost during the Angevin ascendancy, Chateauneuf remained a "dependency of the church and of the king simultaneously."[61] But the inhabitants never gave up the struggle to wrest from the chapter such tangible benefits as exploiting the pilgrims. Around 1141 they demanded through their leaders (the usual small group of those who were "already fat") a share of the chapter's monopoly on the operation of taverns and the sale of wine, an important part of the tourist trade. Louis VII agreed, but reprimanded them for occupying forts and "royal rights of way" and otherwise infringing on his rights and those of his brother the treasurer. He confirmed their ancient privileges, but subject to heavy fines. Freedom from royal tallages was confirmed in 1143, but with the concomitant obligation to submit to the treasurer's court of justice.[62] And in 1180 the famous John of Salisbury, bishop of Chartres, heard a dispute at the pope's request: he denied further claims for privileges, condemned the secret sworn association of bourgeois, and excommunicated the leaders.[63] The chapter fought with the usual ecclesiastical weapons, like excommunication, and was usually sup-

ported by the pope as well as the king; but on one complex issue
extending from 1145 to 1164 between a canon and a bourgeois, the
pope and his episcopal arbitrator were supporting the bourgeois (who
was also receiving protection by the English king's officers) while the
French king was supporting—as always—the canon and his church.[64]
The inhabitants were granted extensive financial and police powers at
the outset of Philip Augustus's reign, but were still subject to the
treasurer's judicial authority. The pope again condemned the commune in 1184, and the new liberties were effectively squelched in
1212, when the king imposed an accord on the parties, which gave the
treasurer power to authorize the future exercise of the town's
liberties.[65] There was more violence in 1231, when the bourgeois
attacked the house of St. Louis' bastard uncle, the treasurer Pierre
Charlot. This incident was followed by the usual arbitration and fines,
and the renewed grant of rights in exchange for oaths to respect the
privileges and property of the church.[66]

Most of the surviving evidence of continuing control by the
king comes from the history of these disputes with Chateauneuf. But
after seizing Tours and Chateauneuf from the forces of the aging
English king Henry II, Philip Augustus and Richard Lionheart (as
count of Anjou and Tours) in the Treaty of Corbigny (July, 1190)
agreed on a condominium of Chateauneuf and Tours. The *enquête*
reflects the pre–existence of such an arrangement rather than the
restoration of domainal rights to the French king. It clarifies (especially for us) what had probably been simply customary practice:
the functioning of a French royal enclave inside English-Angevin
territory, as Boussard describes the territory and revenues of the
church.[67] Had any major new concessions by the new Angevin king or
count been attributable to Philip's military presence, they would certainly have been revoked when he traded Chateauneuf and Tours for
other concessions in the more comprehensive settlement of Gisors.
Although John Lackland ceded Tours to Philip Augustus during
Richard's absence on crusade with a guarantee to St. Martin of her
ancient rights,[68] the inhabitants of Chateauneuf remained loyal to
their immediate English lord, Richard, and were rewarded with 1000
marks on his return in 1194. The canons of St. Martin were driven
out and their goods confiscated for their open attachment to the
French king; and they were restored only after intervention of the
papal legate the following year.[69] With Richard's death, the young
Arthur of Brittany, having done homage to Philip Augustus, seemed

at last to be entering into his inheritance, and as count of Anjou was received as an honorary canon at St. Martin (1199).[70] During a truce with John, Philip Augustus visited St. Martin's tomb, and on that occasion received old Queen Eleanor's homage for Guienne and Poitou. However, it was only in November of 1202, after Tours and Chateauneuf had changed hands several times, and been burned and pillaged, that Philip Augustus, on a diversion from his conquest of Normandy, brought Touraine under permanent French occupation, and only after the armistice of 1206 was Philip Augustus formally "received" as lay abbot of St. Martin.[71]

What the Treaty of Corbigny had confirmed was a sharing of privileges and obligations that left the preponderance of control in the hands of the king and chapter, whose rights were still "confounded indistinguishably." The condominium included the domains of the abbey in Chateauneuf, the city of Tours, and "much of the surrounding territory as much as twenty kilometers away." There the treasurer received the homages of lay lords and collated church offices as well as the revenues therefrom.[72] Justice in the cloister was held of the king, and exercised by the treasurer (in high justice cases), or by other dignitaries or by the chapter itself. In Chateauneuf, the treasurer (representing the king again) and *viguiers* (or *voyers*) representing the count of Anjou rendered justice and shared the jurisdiction and proceeds. The count carried out corporal punishments from the treasurer's court and shared fines. The count of Anjou's prebend was temporarily returned to the church by Philip Augustus; then Louis VIII reactivated the title for his son Charles, the new count. Twice a year the count joined the king's sergeant for an assize, and shared certain other specific but seemingly minor rights. The count's rights, in sum, as Professor Boussard observes, seem rather recent and limited.[73]

The agreement of 1190 fails to inform us whether the chapter had retained its ancient right to strike the "money of Tours," renewed in the charter of Hugh Capet.[74] There is no evidence that Henry I or Philip I confirmed any right of coinage to St. Martin, as they did to the churches of St. Valerian (Tournus) and St. Philibert.[75] When the striking of the traditional *tournois* (with the legend of St. Martin and the *chatel*) resumed after Philip Augustus's conquest, the profits may or may not have been shared; Mme. Dumas is uncertain. In view of our ignorance of how any profits may have been shared under the Angevins, it would be a mistake to overemphasize financial gain as a major aim of Philip Augustus. But when he subsequently suppressed the chapter's *tournois* in favor of his own, it drove the Angevin *denier* out of circulation, and helped to achieve the universal recognition of a royal coinage.[76] As late as 1316, the chapter tried unsuccessfully to have its right to strike money recognized by virtue of ancient royal concessions.[77] One may suppose, therefore, that even if his Angevin vassal was his chief rival with respect to the money of Tours, rather than the chapter of St. Martin itself, Philip Augustus had good reason to associate the right of coinage with control of the church as he completed the dispossession of the English king in the region.

The Dignitaries of St. Martin and Their Contributions in the Thirteenth Century

The king's domainal rights had remained virtually intact during Angevin control, and directly under the chapter and the treasurer. Control of the treasurership was a foot-in-the-door for the king in reasserting his rights of collation to other offices. Yet, with the sole exception of Simon de Brion, the treasurers of the thirteenth century were clearly not professionally trained clerks in the king's employ, but the beneficiaries of political patronage and diplomatic alliances.[78] Even Simon held the treasurership long after he gave up the keepership of the king's seal, suggesting that it was a reward for past service rather than the equivalent of a salary. The very extent of the treasurer's temporal wealth doubtless made the office unsuitable for the support of a royal functionary in the thirteenth century.

Ironically, then, this role fell to the deanship, normally associated as it was with the cure of souls, as in England, and therefore usually reserved for a priest. The requirement proved to be no great stumbling block, since the dean had a year to meet it, and it may have been circumvented for Louis VI's son Philippe, and probably for others.[79] Philip Augustus and St. Louis may have been more cautious than their English counterparts in transforming the office into a source of support for royal clerks. Objections to royal nominees by the chapter seem confined to defect in birth, as in Pierre Charlot's case, or to absence of ordination.

The most complete contemporary statement of the king's control of the deanship—and the earliest—comes from the *Rituale,* drawn up just before his death in 1227 by a canon named Péan

Gastineau. It is a "book of customs," fortunately reproduced in the seventeenth century though probably with some additions, as part of a defense of the church's privileges. The *Rituale* states that when the king gives the deanship he presents the person by letters patent to the chapter.[80] Like the treasurer, that person, according to his oath, must be already a canon of the choir provided with a prebend. The oath was probably included in the extensive reforms of Nicolas de Roye around 1221. But none of these seemed to tie the king's hand.[81] Upon receiving his office, the dean did homage to the king, and not until Philip III's reign was the obligation remitted of providing hospitality when the king visited Tours.[82] For comparison, the king of England in 1189 and 1199 was conferring the deanship on royal clerks at St. Martin-le-Grand "with the gift of prebends and churches." By 1250 Henry III had gone far beyond canonical exemptions and was claiming complete authority in all "royal free chapels" independently of bishop, archbishop or pope.[83]

Just as Innocent III was told that to the dean of St. Martin-le-Grand belonged the donation of prebends, so the dean of St. Martin of Tours enjoyed substantial "spiritual liberties" besides his lucrative benefices.[84] He nominated candidates for cantor, schoolman, cellarer, subdean and granger. The cantor Gilles *Raderii* was chosen in 1235 by dean Aubry Cornut (then keeper of the seal and a doctor of "both laws") in accord with the *Rituale,* which did not require ordination, but against the chapter's wishes; Gilles later became keeper of the seal and archbishop of Tyre.[85] The dean also nominated the provosts and priors of the fourteen dependent collegiate churches and priories, many with similar "liberties"—all of whom had to do him homage, even before doing so to the chapter of St. Martin.[86] In some of these churches, like Léré, he appointed the cantor. There were prebends held of the dean in fief and homage, such as the one sold in 1243 to Dean Jean de la Cour, another keeper of the seal.[87] In 1253 a subcantorship was established after a compromise between the dean and the chapter over its collation.[88]

At Tours the dean was entitled to special honors at his installation and during the performance of daily offices and at religious festivals. He was the first dignitary of the church, subordinate only to the king as "lay abbot."[89] His oath included the obligation to make his principal residence in this *villa*. Since he was not required to officiate more than fifteen days a year,[90] this apparently did not prevent the deans in the thirteenth century from spending most of their time with the court in Paris and elsewhere. Moreover, the indulgence granted in March, 1255 by Alexander IV to Guy de Neaulphe provided that "each time he resides in the territory of the church he will be considered resident," subject only to the chapter's approval. The territories of St. Martin were widely distributed in the royal domain! On the same date the pope granted him a "proper travelling staff": one or two canons when he was travelling on the church's business. This concession was made "because of the status of your person and the honor of your church." St. Louis must have been aware of these exceptions for "illustrious or lettered" persons despite the testimony of his chroniclers.[91]

While the dean's rights of justice were not as extensive as the treasurer's, they did include the cloister and seem to have run the gamut from manifest heresy, blasphemy and sacrilege, to rape, adultery, and incest.[92] In 1292 the jurist Philippe de Beaumanoir, as bailiff of Touraine, was still assuring the immunity of the cloister.[93]

Not surprisingly, the dean and the church were recipients of a number of royal favors besides the privileges acknowledged in 1190[94]: there were others extended by Philip Augustus every year from 1212 through 1218; a chaplaincy by St. Louis in 1255, subject to his presentation of the candidates; and gifts by Philip III and IV.[95] *Parlement,* also not surprisingly, generally supported the church's rights. In 1232 royal arbitrators allowed Chateauneuf to elect six "good men" to inquire into the violence against the treasurer, but made no concessions to the town.[96] The king was limiting direct control to a castellan in the chateau,[97] and judgments of the *Parlement* in 1260 and 1263 again favored the chapter over the bourgeoisie and other dependent men there. Other judgments in 1263 and 1269 similarly protected St. Martin's rights elsewhere.[98]

St. Martin was worth more to the king than simply the deanship: for example, the tallage that was imposed on Chateauneuf for "the king's gift."[99] But the financial advantages of maintaining his clerks through the deanship cannot be overstated. The first extant household ordinance of 1261 provided for paying five sous a day plus three in lieu of livery to the treasurer of St. Martin, then Simon de Brion, as keeper of the seal (who had usually been the dean). The dean of St. Aignan, Etienne de Montfort, king's clerk, received four sous a day plus four in lieu of livery. These pittances, the highest paid to any clerks—a total of eight sous each—make a striking comparison with the salaries paid even the minor lay officers of the household.[100]

In England, too, the clerks received little or no government salary, and salaries were forbidden in the English ordinance of 1279, if the clerk had a benefice from the king.[101] We should not forget, of course, the inducements to the French clerks of future ecclesiastical preferment. Five of the deans of St. Martin in the thirteenth century became bishops; and four treasurers became bishops and one a pope.[102]

Could this happy coincidence of need and availability have occurred without the willingness of the collegiate churches? Denton thinks not; it was in the self-interest of deans and canons to preserve their links with the crown. It is significant that most of the royal clerks in England came from St. Martin-le-Grand and Wolverhampton, where, by 1249, the king had his general spiritual rights, as well as his rights of donation, recognized by the English clergy. Though the "initiative [for obtaining spiritual liberties] was usually indistinguishable from the king himself," it was the beneficiaries in the king's employ who fought for the privileges of the royal chapels. The situation could have been little different in France, where such initiatives might have come from the beneficiaries in the chancery or the *Parlement*—probably one of St. Louis's reasons for prohibiting multiple benefices. Indeed, the administrator if not the "spiritual superior" of the free colleges, may have been the keeper of the seal himself, like Aubry Cornut in the absence of a chancellor, who later served this function as in England.[103] Whether anyone advised Louis and his successors regularly on nominations is no more certain: Mollat thinks it was the confessor who at the time was Robert de Sorbonne; Louis's biographers say the chancellor of Notre Dame furnished him a list. In any case candidates for administrative tasks surely included clerks who were *vertueux* in Joinville's judgment—if in a different sense than the Brothers Minor and Preacher who were so favored in the early *enquêtes* and who have received so much attention from historians.[104]

The major difference between the freedoms enjoyed by the French collegiate churches as against the English was, according to Denton and Mollat, the retention by the English chapels of the responsibility for the cure of souls and the success of the king in obtaining exemptions from episcopal visitation. No doubt, by contrast with France, control by bishop or king in England was "much less obnoxious" in the eyes of reform-minded clergy than control by ordinary laymen, to whom many of the collegiate churches had been alientated in France. But by the last half of Louis's reign, was he not

obtaining many of the same sorts of exemptions and issuing dispensations from residence on his own? The distinction is therefore
blurred. Denton admits, moreover, that even in an exempt deanery,
without the cure of souls, the dean must have supervised or had the
right to supervise the performance of spiritual duties at subordinate
churches, as he did at St. Martin-le-Grand. Besides having to be a
priest, the dean of St. Martin of Tours certainly had responsibility for
its parishes, like the really "free" secular colleges of England.[105]

St. Martin of Tours would have seemed more like a "corpo-
ration of government officials than a real religious house," as Tout
describes St. Martin-le-Grand,[106] had it not been for the "little clerks"
from the subordinate collegiate church of Léré, whose canons performed the offices at the mother church. The dean's fifteen required
days of officiating included five religious festivals, and the canons of
St. Martin were held only to a six or seven months' residency, even
after the reforms of 1221.[107] At least the situation was apparently not
as bad thereafter as at Wolverhampton, where the former dean Peter
of Blois observed that the canons were "completely undisciplined, as
though they were Welshmen or Scots."[108]

Finally, the effective availability of collegiate benefices to the
king rested on a new relationship between kings and popes. As in
England, the king's control over the royal colleges was subject to little
more than titular papal jurisdiction. True, the popes of the thirteenth
century recognized no blanket exemptions of the colleges from episcopal jurisdiction. Their willingness to accede to limited privileges,
such as freedom from excommunication, may show simply their
willingness to recognize those established by custom. The timing of
Aubry Cornut's nomination—when the see of Tours was vacant—
seems deliberate. Clement IV was still holding to the principle that
the clergy themselves were not free from diocesan supervision, even if
the college *was* free. Yet Urban IV had issued a whole series of
privileges to the French kings. Certainly aware of the actuality of
royal control, Clement IV—himself a former king's clerk, Guy
Foucaud—not only confirmed them, he explicitly supported the view
that "to serve the king was to serve the church." Clement, who inaugurated the practice of "reservations," as well as Urban, who had
collated to a benefice at St. Martin, were not far behind the king in
carving out rights of appointment at the expense of local chapters.[109]
In any case, the French kings, if slower than their English counterparts in asserting their rights of collation, may actually have encoun-

tered less ecclesiastical interference. Having had less ground to lose during the twelfth-century Gregorian reforms, they now regained it with less challenge. And at St. Martin they reacquired their rights intact.

The second question we proposed at the outset can be more briefly dealt with here: why didn't the French kings make earlier use of this method of economizing on the household budget through the "ecclesiastical sector?"—and especially at St. Aignan, a more convenient place than St. Martin to install a royal clerk before the reacquisition of Touraine? For Etienne de Garlande the deanship had been only partial support, particularly since he was already chancellor, a Great Officer of the crown. Although Louis VII might have continued to use a more modest functionary like Algrin to handle the seal after Louis VI's death, instead, following the tradition, he promoted him to chancellor.[110] Algrin and his successors continued to handle it until another fractious and overweening chancellor, Hugues de Puiset, caused Philip Augustus to leave the office vacant, which it remained in the thirteenth century (except for its tenure by Brother Guérin under Louis VIII). These benefices in themselves were probably not enough for a chancellor, who, almost always a member of an important family, was looking forward to a bishopric. (Two disappointed chancellors, Algrin and Cadurc, left royal office under a cloud.) Yet the benefices were seemingly more than was needed at the time to support an ordinary chancery clerk—that is, until he was saddled with keeping the seal, or attending the Exchequer (or later the *Parlement*) as he was at the end of Philip Augustus's reign; tasks which became more demanding in time and in skill. Parallel with the changing demands on the clerks of the chancery was its disassociation from the chapel;[111] rarely do we find a royal chaplain with a deanship after Guillaume at St. Aignan. The answer, then, to this second question is that the need for professionally-trained administrators was relatively recent, or at least the kings' awareness of it was.

The need did not escape Philip Augustus's attention; he drew, perhaps, as in other innovations, on English experience. In England the royal free chapels began to serve as centers for royal patronage at this same time, and especially the deanates, as at St. Martin-le-Grand and at Wolverhampton. This development, which Denton admits merits its own detailed examination, unfortunately has not received much attention except for Professor Cuttino's work on the clerks of Edward III.[112] In France from the later years of Philip

Augustus these and other royal functionaries are increasingly apparent in a variety of advisory, diplomatic, and bookkeeping roles, but most particularly in the chancery and in the nascent *Parlement*, where clerks outnumbered laymen in the judicial sessions in the last half of St. Louis's reign. Administration was more sophisticated: it was Philip Augustus who (according to the story too useful to dismiss completely as fabrication) took the royal filing department "off the road" after Richard Lionheart captured his baggage train, and began to register his acts.[113] In the *Parlement* a knowledge of canon, and even Roman law was a distinct asset.

The king's interests in St. Martin and other collegiate churches were therefore transformed rapidly at the beginning of the thirteenth century. The deanship, briefly like the treasurership a lucrative emolument for sons and relatives under Louis the Fat, came to be filled by royal functionaries. We have noted that Barthélemy de Vendôme (about 1162–71) was used by Louis VII to keep track of Henry II's military movements in 1167 (as was Geoffroy the treasurer) and perhaps in diplomatic negotiations.[114] Deans Philip II and Thibaut, like the treasurers, leave no evidence of royal service, though they enjoyed the backing of the pope and Philip Augustus in a contest with the commune in 1184. However, Anselme (1192–97) played definite diplomatic roles in 1194 and 1196 with the English, the archbishop of Rouen, and the pope.[115] As noted earlier, too, Eudes Clément (1211–16) must have spent as much time on royal business as on the church's.[116]

Royal service by the next dean, Nicolas de Roye, cannot be documented till he became bishop, but, beginning with the deanship of Aubry Cornut in 1229, the new needs of the king explain an unbroken succession of royal clerks at St. Martin. Since Aubry went on a mission for the king as early as 1226, it is likely he was a "king's clerk" before his presentation as dean in 1229 and the appointment as keeper of the seal in 1231. In any event, from 1231, if not from 1210, the deans of St. Martin were, from even our fragmentary evidence in Exhibit A, fully occupied with the king's business. To our knowledge the king had not in the past asserted his right of appointment for a major functionary like the keeper of the seal, unless one considers Étienne de Garlande. But no one could object if Aubry was promoted to keeper of the seal in 1231, and had to stretch the liberality of the dean's residency requirements recently adopted.

Like St. Martin-le-Grand in England, St. Martin of Tours set the pattern for exploiting two other collegiate churches in the mid-thirteenth century for the benefit of the civil service. As we have observed, at St. Framband of Senlis, it was the treasurership that began to support royal functionaries; at St. Aignan, the deanship; and at St. Quentin, the office of warden, along with a few canonries. Louis's brother Alphonse exercised the same right over the treasurer of St. Hilaire of Poitiers, who became an important royal administrator, though Philippe's title had been "chaplain" to the count.[117]

Twice St. Louis came back to St. Martin as a source of maintenance for his keepers of the seal, once to the cantorship and once to the treasurership and all of them obtained bishoprics. Every dean was a royal clerk. Philip III and IV followed the pattern. Ultimately, it was the deanship of St. Martin which Louis X conferred in 1315 on the first royal chancellor created since the time of Louis VIII.[118]

Both the wealth and the king's continuing control of St. Martin of Tours therefore were major contributors to the transformation of the French state into an administrative monarchy. It and increasingly the other collegiate churches supplemented the modest fiscal resources of a feudal household until a system of public taxation began to take shape.

The tapping of these resources, though a positive development in the growth of a more centralized monarchy, was a weak spot in the Gregorian reform movement. The practice contributed in the fifteenth and sixteenth centuries to abuses like the transmitting of ecclesiastical benefices in favorem, and probably to the use, sale and transmission of royal offices for laymen as well. Louis IX was more scrupulous than most medieval rulers. But he was still the pragmatic Capetian, willing to reconcile reasons of state with canon law, and to exploit, however unconsciously, royal sacrosanctity. By the time Boniface VIII "loudly revoked" privileges granted the French kings, it was too late.

NOTES

*This article is the outgrowth of papers read to the Medieval Association of the Pacific in February, 1974, and to the Rocky Mountain Medieval and Renaissance Conference in April, 1982. I am grateful to Pierre Gasnault of the Bibliothèque Mazarine for his comments. Abbreviations used for other works: Newman: Wm. M. Newman, ed., Les Actes de Robert le Pieux (Paris, 1937). Lay.: Layettes du Trésor des Chartes, ed. Teulet et al. (Paris, var. dates). Lem.: Jean-François Lemarignier, Le Gouvernement royal aux premiers *temps Capétiens* (Paris, 1965), with *tableaux des souscripteurs.* Luchaire, *Louis VI:* Achille Luchaire, *Louis VI: annales de sa vie et de son règne* (Paris, 1890). Monsnyer: Raoul Monsnyer; *Celeberrimae Sancti Martini Turonensis ecclesiae historia.* Luchaire, *Actes:* A. Luchaire, *Etudes sur les actes de Louis VII* (Paris, 1885). *Actes de P-A: Recueil des Actes de Philippe Auguste,* ed. H.-Fr. Delaborde el al. (Paris, 1916 ff.). HF: *Recueil des historiens des Gaules et de la France,* ed. Bouquet et al. (Paris, var. dates). Nobilleau, *Necr.: Necrologium beatissimi Martini Turonensis, 804-1495* (Tours, 1875), an incomplete and not very useful embellishment of Baluze's MS copies. Bibl. Nat.: Bibliothèque Nationale. Bibl. Mun.: Bibliothèque Municipale. Other abbreviations: d. = died; s.-seigneur; K. = king; dept. = département; ar. = arrondissement; n.s. = new style dating.

1 Joinville, *Histoire de St. Louis,* ed. Natalis de Wailly (Paris, 1874), p. 364, para. 662, and p. 380, para. 692.

2 *English Royal Free Chapels, 1100–1300: a constitutional study* (Manchester, England, 1970); cf. Guillaume Mollat, "Le Roi de France et la collation plénière des bénéfices ecclésiastiques," *Mémoires présentés par divers savants à l'Academie des Inscriptions* 14 (1er série):2 (Paris, 1951), pp. 107–286. Perhaps because the king's rights of St. Martin were too obvious, or because there is no *pouillé* like those for the other two churches, Mollat only refers incidentally to the appointment by the king of the dean of St. Martin, when citing a case before *Parlement* in 1412 (pp. 111–112), and omits the church in his incomplete list (p. 154 ff.): *v* n. 105.

3 Mollat, op. cit., p. 110. Cf. Noël Didier, *La Garde des églises au XIIIè siècle* (Grenoble, 1927), p. 82.

4 Denton, op. cit. p. 7. L. M. Larson, *The King's Household in England before the Norman Conquest* (New York, 1902), pp. 139, 141.

5 Louis IX excepted from concessions at Orléans to Prince Philippe the collation to and homage of the deanship of St. Aignan of Orléans (June, 1267) (*Lay:* 4, p. 227, no. 5289). The earliest example cited by Mollat (pp. 127–128, 149) from the three collegiate churches supporting deans or treasurers in royal service concerns the treasurer of St. Frambaud of Senlis, whose benefice by 1397 was conferred by the king (*Pouillés de Reims: Recueil des historiens de France* 6:1, p. 463.) St. Aignan is in the sixteenth century *Pouillés de Sens* 4:335. Cf. Denton, op. cit., pp. 19–21; and my article "St. Louis and the New Clerks of Parlement," *Studies in Medieval Culture* 4:2 (1974), 271–273, regarding the appearance of royal clerks at French churches besides St. Martin.

6 His diplomatic role is emphasized by the church's seventeenth century protagonist. *v* Monsnyer, 1, p. 227. *v* Exhibit A and note on documentation.

7 Denton, (at note 2). pp. 20–22.

8 Monsnyer 1:p. 231. *v* Exhibit A.

9 At the same time (1109) he gave up taking an ounce of gold on prebends conferred by the dean. *v* Achille Luchaire, *Louis VI: annales de sa vie et de son règne* (Paris, 1890), no. 83. The king's rights with respect to the dean were the same in the thirteenth century (*Gallia Christiana* 10, col. 1472).

10 The liberties of St. Frambaud, founded about 996, like Ste-Geneviève's of Paris, were extended in 1129 to a more recent foundation, St. Vincent of Senlis (Luchaire, no. 446).

11 *Gallia Christiana* 10, col. 1472 and *Instr.* no. 55 and no. 168. *v* n. 5.

12 Cf. Mollat, (at note 2), esp. pp. 159, 163, 164.

[13] The count's suzerain, Robert the Pious, was assured of no more than a token fine if the terms of a gift to the church were violated: Charles Pfister, *Études sur le règne de Robert le Pieux* (Paris, 1885), p. 155.

[14] Jean-François Lemarignier, "Aspects politiques des fondations de collégiales dans le royaume de France au XIè siècle," *La Vita commune del clero nei secoli XI e XII* (Milan, 1962), pp. 27, 30 and 37. *v* Pierre Gasnault, "Les actes privés de l'abbaye de St-Martin", *BEC* 112 (1954), p. 40 and n. 2.

[15] HF 10:605 (1022). HF 10:370, where he appears as *decano domino Tedelino*: forged.

[16] Lem. p. 93. *Gallia Christiana* 8, col. 1518; Newman, no. 53 (between 1008 and 1021) and 103 (1031); HF 10:110–111. Henry I donated new altars in 1038 when Robert was dean (*Gallia Christiana* 8, col. 1522).

[17] HF 10:550–552: undated but authentic (Ferdinand Lot, *Études sur le règne de Hugues Capet*, p. 231, n. 2). Cf. Pfister, (at note 13), pp. 105 and 108.

[18] 1007: Newman, no. 30, pp. 37–38. Lem., p. 47 and n. 28.

[19] Lem. ibid, pp. 57, 93 and n. 69 and the tableaux of subscribers for Robert's reign. Unaccountably he omits the dean, and another future treasurer Sulpice, listed with other members of the chapter. He correctly associates Galterus and Wanillo (listed without title in HF 10:590–1 following Count Eudes of Blois) with the former and future treasurers Gautier and Ganelon. *v* Exhibits A and B.

[20] They subscribe a donation by King Robert to the abbey of Marmoutier in 1029. In his *tableau* of subscribers for this reign, Lemarignier excludes treasurers and archdeacons from "minor ecclesiastics." The sources cited by Newman (no. 77), who omits subscribers, were not available to me.

[21] The Geoffroy of St. Aignan, according to Lemarignier, subscribes an act at Paris in 1048, and the Geoffroy of St. Martin, one at Orléans in 1052 (*Gouvernement royal*, p. 101 and *tableau* of subscribers for Henri Ier). For 1048, the subscribers are omitted in F. Soehnée, *Cat. des actes d' Henri Ier*, (Paris, 1907), no. 79, pp. 83–84; and in the sources he cites: *Gallia Christiana, Instr.* col. 300; HF 11:583; and *Spicilegium* 3:398. For 1052, *v* Exhibit A.

[22] Lemarignier's categories change from reign to reign, and, in addition, there is a discrepancy in totals between his table of subscribers and his *tableau numérique*. Listed in 1067 among a large assembly of witnesses to the king's rededication of the church of St. Martin-des-Champs of Paris is Renaud, treasurer of St. Martin of Tours. His name appears nine years later, next to the king's chamberlain's, in a confirmation of donations to a monastery near Poitiers by the king's brother the duke of Aquitaine and some of the great vassals. In 1079 Sancion, dean of St. Aignan and Godefroy, the cantor, subscribe an act of donation to a church in Orléans, alongside representatives of Ste. Croix, and in 1095 a Sancion subscribes a royal confirmation of the donation of the abbey of Mozac to Cluny by the count of Auvergne. Since Hélias was dean from 1093, the Sancion, "dean of Orléans" in 1095, must have been dean of Ste. Croix, the cathedral church, and perhaps a different person (contrary to Lemarignier's table). In 1093 the new dean and the canons of St. Aignan secure reconfirmation of grants to their church. For St. Martin, *v* Exhibits B and C. For St. Aignan, M. Prou, *Recueil des actes de Philippe Ier*, nos. 97 (1079), 135 (1095), and 332 (1093).

[23] Prou, no. 115 (1085).

[24] Lem., p. 101.

[25] There is no evidence of the king's influence in the reforms of Nicolas de Roye in

1221 (Exhibit A), though it is tempting to associate his appointment with an effort to improve the royal image after the dispute over Pierre Charlot, or simply to continue intervening (cf. n. 56).

26 Marcel Pacaut, *Louis VII et son royaume* (Paris, 1964), pp. 106 and 115. In 1114 Louis VI granted St. Aignan judicial and tax privileges, and in the following year protection from the demands of the lords of Le Puiset. (Luchaire, *Louis VI*, nos. 176, 177 and 200.) At St. Martin, at the request of Dean Eudes and Treasurer Gautier, he confirmed donations by Queen Bertrade of the church and town of St. Pierre-Puellier (1118 and 1119; *v* Exhibit A and B). Louis VII confirmed the donation and privileges, and gave up his right of hospitality when he visited Tours: *v* Luchaire, *Actes*, no. 137 (1143–44). When Philippe II was dean, the church received a share of the king's revenues near Léré (Luchaire, *Actes*, no. 752).

27 For St. Martin, *v* Exhibits A and B. For St. Aignan: H.-Fr. Delaborde el al., *Recueil des actes de Philippe Auguste* (Paris, 1916 ff.), 2:432–437, nos. 852 and 853, and p. 526, no. 934 (1204/5 and 1206). Note, too, the protection of St. Aignan's personnel conceded to the king by the bishops in 1212 (*Lay.* 1:382, no. 1020).

28 Pacaut, *Louis VII*, pp. 103–106.

29 Luchaire, *Louis VI*, no. 556 (Act of 1135). Luchaire, *Actes*, nos. 90, 217, 365 and 792. Eric Bournazel identifies the chaplain at Senlis as Ebroin de Chatenay, *Le Gouvernement Capétien au XIIè siècle*, (Paris, 1975), pp. 24 & 81.

30 *HF* 19:414b-c.

31 Mollat, (at note 2) p. 164. Philip Augustus begins to extend favors (Luchaire, *Actes*, 4, no. 1683) and is referred to as *inclitus patronus ecclesie nostre* when he requires the citizens of St. Quentin to protect the church (*Lay*, 1:393a, no. 1051 (1213). Louis VI had simply added a token confirmation of a grant approved by the Count of Vermandois (Luchaire, *Louis VI*, no. 528).

32 No doubt this was to please Pope Alexander, whose envoy he was. The date is 1161 (*Gallia Christiana*, 8, col. 1522) or 1162 (*Martirologium ecclesiae regalis Sancti Aniani Aurelianensis* (1739): Bibl. Mun. Orléans MS 329, fol. 134v–135 (hereafter referred to as Mart 329). St. Aignan was one of three churches where there was not even the formality of an election by the chapter: *v* Mollat, (at note 2) p. 149.

33 HF 10:550; HF 16: 141–142, no. 178; Raoul de Diceto, HF 17:652.

34 For St. Aignan our evidence is curiously limited to *Gallia Christiana* 8, col. 1522, which refers to a concession by him of some plowland, and a reference to his burial in the church of Paris in *Gallia Christiana* 8, col. 61. He is listed as dean in 1142 in the Mart 329, fol. 134v, and this would mean that Etienne was dispossessed before his death. *v* Exhibit A for his other offices. In 1147 he is referred to simply as "brother of the king" (Luchaire, *Actes*, no. 200). For St-Martin, *v* Exhibit A.

35 Luchaire, *Louis VI*, p. cliv and Luchaire, *Actes*, nos. 265 and 468.

36 *v* Exhibit B.

37 Lucien Perrichet, *La Grande Chancellerie de France*, (Paris, 1912), pp. 55 and 498–501; Charles Cuissard, *Chanoines et dignitaires d'Orléans* (Orléans, 1900), pp. 147–148; Luchaire, *Louis VI*, pp. xliii–lii and 303–305. In 1115, Adelaide's first year as queen, Étienne was deprived of a prebend in favor of the fabric of the church, in order that it be independent of anyone with royal authority! (Luchaire, *Actes*, no. 199.

38 *Gallia Christiana* 8, col. 1522–1523; Perrichet, (at note 37) p. 503; Luchaire, *Actes*,

nos. 541 and 552. Philip Augustus confirmed a donation by him in 1192/3: *v Actes de P-A*, 1: p. 517). Mart. 329 records him as dean only from 1185.

39 Luchaire, *Actes*, no. 574 (1169–70); reconfirmation in 1204–05 (*Actes de P-A*, 2:432–433, no. 852). One of the clerks who are "just names" to us in the k.'s suite (Bournazel, *Gouv. royale*, pp. 24 & 81).

40 *Lay* 1, p. 144b, no. 336, records him as witness to an act.

41 *Actes de P-A*, 2, p. 432, no. 852; pp. 526–527, no. 934.

42 HF 19:548, n. (a). *Gallia Christiana* 8, col. 1523.

43 RHF: *Obituaires de Sens*, vol. 3: Cathédrale d'Orléans, p. 74A; St. Avit, p. 196D, Bibl. Mun. Orléans, MS 329: *Martirologium ecclesiae regalis Sancti Aniani Aurelianensis*, fols. 136v and 135v; GC 8, col. 1523.

44 *v* Exhibit A for Luchaire's documentation of the chancellor but only E. R. Vaucelle suggests (without any citations) that a Barthélemy was dean in 1150: *v La Collégiale de St Martin de Tours des origines à l'avènement des Valois* (Paris, 1908), p. 440.

45 ". . . nam in quaelibet ecclesia, etiam in illis ecclesiis quae sunt speciales ecclesiae domini regis, utpote in ecclesia Sancti Martini Turonensis et quibusdam aliis, contulistis multas praebendas . . ." (*Chronica Majora: Additamenta*, ed. Luard [1872–83], pp. 103–104.)

46 Bernard Chevalier, "La Cité de Tours et Chateauneuf du Xè au XIIIè siecle," *Cahiers d'histoire* 17:3 (1972), p. 238.

47 *Gallia Christiana* 14:154.

48 Jacques Boussard, "L'Enclave royale de St. Martin de Tours," *Bulletin de la Société Nationale des Antiquaires de France* (1958), p. 158 and "Le Trésorier de St-Martin de Tours," *Revue d'Histoire de L'Église de France* 47 (1961), pp. 71–72.

49 HF 10:550–552, apparently based ultimately on the copy by Dom Housseau (Bibl. Nat., MS Collection de Touraine, t. 7, no. 2811).

50 Boussard, "Le Trésorier," pp. 73–76, and "L'Enclave", pp. 158–9.

51 According to Olivier Guillot (*Le Comte d'Anjou et son entourage au XIème siècle* [Paris, 1972], 1:23 & 171) the earlier alliance between Anjou and the dukes of Francia was reinforced by the ability of Foulque's father Geoffroy Grisegonelle to capitalize on the benefices he held of the church by regranting them to his *fideles*. Cf. Richard W. Southern, *The Making of the Middle Ages* (New Haven & London, 1953), p. 83. The bulk of the citations in this discussion of family affiliations will be found in the notes for Exhibit A & B for the individual involved. On the events concerning Arthur *v* n. 70.

52 Explicitly designated as *fidelis* or vassal were, besides Archambaud, Dean Barthélemy II and Treasurers Sulpice, Ganelon and Geoffroy I.

53 "Le Trésorier", pp. 72–3; and the k. had the right to confer the treasurership well *before* the "beginning of the 13th c." (p. 85).

54 J. Boussard, *Le Comté d'Anjou sous Henri Plantagenet* . . . (Paris, 1938), p. 158, n. 1, citing Josèphe Chartrou, *L'Anjou de 1109–1151* (Paris, 1928), pp. 386–87, no. 55(53). In 1119 Queen Bertrade's chaplain Guillaume was a canon of St. Martin (Chartrou, *L'Anjou*, no. 47 of the *catalogue*).

55 *Layettes* vol. 1, no. 371 (especially pp. 160–61) and the *Actes de P-A*, 1, p. 437, no. 361.

56 Vaucelle, (at note 44) pp. 200–01. Philip acknowledged he was not to keep the treasurership vacant in his hands more than a year, and that he intended to receive

Pierre as "his man" only when he had a prebend (*Actes de P-A*, nos. 1450 and 1493 [1216 and 1217]).

[57] Arthur Giry, *Les Établissements de Rouen* I (Paris, 1883), p. 187.

[58] J. T. Chalmel, *Histoire de Touraine* 2 (Paris/Tours, 1828), p. 9.

[59] Chevalier, "Tours," pp. 239–41.

[60] Giry, op. cit., I:185.

[61] Boussard, "L'Enclave," pp. 163–64.

[62] Chevalier, "Tours," p. 244. Giry, 1:188 and 190, citing in vol. 2: pièce justificative no. 19. Luchaire, *Actes*, no. 75.

[63] Giry, op. cit., I:194–95. HF 16:624, no. 104.

[64] Giry, op. cit., I:192–93. HF 15:820 and 822, nos. 140, 144 and 145; HF 16:95–101, nos. 290–95 and 306–13.

[65] Chevalier, "Tours," p. 247. *Gallia Christiana* 14, *Instrumenta*, col. 86, no. 67. Giry, op. cit., II:p.j. no. 20. *Actes de P-A*, 3:325, no. 1241.

[66] Giry, op. cit. I:203–04; 2:p.j. nos. 21 and 22.

[67] *v* note 56. See the ff. paragraph for relevant provisions.

[68] St. Martin's rights and customs throughout Angevin territory (*Lay*. 1:175b, no. 412).

[69] Chalmel, (at note 58) 2:46–51, 56–57.

[70] Vaucelle, (at note 44), p. 177. Chalmel op. cit., 2:65.

[71] Vaucelle, op. cit., p. 122. Chalmel, op. cit., 2:67, 78–89.

[72] Boussard, (at note 48), p. 172 and n. 50 above.

[73] Vaucelle, op. cit., pp. 173–74, 180–81. Boussard, op. cit., pp. 173–74. Philip Augustus conceded the prebend for upkeep of the luminary (*Actes*, 4, no. 1513, year 1218).

[74] A. de Barthélemy, "Note sur l'origine de la monnaie tournoise," *Mémoires de l'Académie des Inscriptions et Belles Lettres* 35:2 (1896), pp. 285–87. He found nothing in the archives of St. Martin suggesting the chapter's involvement, and must have been aware of Pfister's citation of Hugh's charter from HF 10:56lb (*Robert le Pieux*, p. 125).

[75] Jean Lafaurie, *Les Monnaies des rois de France* (Paris, 1951), p. 6. nos. 42–44; p. 11, no. 92.

[76] Lafaurie (p. 22, no. 193) suggests Philip Augustus' first *denier* was issued by the *collégiale* in the king's name. More recent is Françoise Dumas, "La monnaie au temps de Philippe Auguste", in *La France de Philippe Auguste* (Paris, 1982), pp. 546–47 & pl., nos. 9 & 10.

[77] De Barthélemy, "Note . . . sur la monnaie tournoise," p. 281.

[78] *v* Exhibit B from about 1200. Foreign diplomacy explains the choice of Philippe de Castille and Philippe de Majorque.

[79] Vaucelle, op. cit., p. 201, nos. 2 and 4, which include the dean's oath (Bibliothèque Municipale-Tours MS 193, fols. 196v–197r).

[80] Monsnyer 2, p. 496. The *Rituale* by the canon Péan Gastineau (died about 1227) was published defectively by Paul Nobilleau, *Rituale seu Liber Consuetudinum Beatissimi Martini Turonensis*, (Tours, 1873). M. Pierre Gasnault, who has been working on a new edition, advises that the only reliable existing one is the rare book by the abbé A. Fleuret. Péan's work is considered fairly reliable, but includes nothing about himself or his colleagues. The same drawback is in his *Chronicon Turonense* (ed. E. Martène and U. Durand, *Amplissima Collectio*, vol. 5).

[81] *v* note 79. The "tradition" of Touraine origin is probably a post-thirteenth century addition to the document. Other rights of the king are summarized in Vaucelle, pp. 201–03. The charter of Dean Nicolas and the chapter was copied by Housseau, Bibl. Nat., MS Coll. de Touraine, t. 6, no. 2663.

[82] Archives d'Indre et Loire, MS G. 414, no. 7 (confirmation of 1294 of a concession to Pierre Chalon).

[83] Denton, (at note 2), pp. 34–35 and 95.

[84] Denton, op. cit., p. 43. Paul Nobilleau's estimate of their value at £15,000 a year is unsupported: *La Collégiale de St-Martin de Tours* (Tours, 1869), p. 64.

[85] Vaucelle, op. cit., p. 207. The Egidius listed by him as cantor in 1255, who became archbishop of Tyre, may be a second individual.

[86] Vaucelle, op. cit., pp. 203–04 and 266–67, based in part on Archives d'Indre et Loire, MS G. 415, p. 909 (drawn up in 1753). *v* Monsnyer 1:79–80, 87, 89, 90. St. Martin was also patron of five churches in the archipresbytery of Tours (RHF: *Pouillés de Tours* 3:11, dated about 1275).

[87] Archives d'Indre et Loire, MS G. 414, liasse 5, no. 3.

[88] Vaucelle, op. cit., p. 266. Monsnyer, 1, p. 79–80.

[89] Monsnyer, 2, p. 524.

[90] "Ligiam mansionem in hac villa" (note 79 above). Cf. Vaucelle, op. cit. p. 193.

[91] *Registres d'Alexandre IV* 15:102 and 109, nos. 342 and 359. Cf. HF 20:12 and 408.

[92] Monsnyer, 2, pp. 496–501, published defectively in Nobilleau, (at note 80), p. 4. Cf. *Lay.* 1:159.

[93] Archives d'Indre et Loire, MS G. 381, no. 4 (a later copy).

[94] *Lay.* 1, no. 371. There was also an exchange of rights between the king and chapter in 1189–90 (*Actes de P-A.* 1, p. 320, no. 269).

[95] There was a further definition of the king's, dean's, treasurer's and canons' rights in Chateauneuf in 1211–12; and guarantees of protection of St. Martin's men and goods in 1212 (*Actes de P-A*, 3, p. 325, no. 1214 and 3:359–62, no. 1241). Other favors from 1213 through 1218: *Actes*, 4:9, no. 1407; 4:41, no. 1432 and 1513. Philip yielded his bailiff's jurisdiction over certain "men" in 1214 (Bibl. Nat., MS Coll. Housseau, t. 6, no. 2377). For 1255: Vaucelle, op. cit., p. 215. *v* Exhibit A under Guy de Neauphle, Pierre Chalon and Gilles Lambert.

[96] Chalmel (at note 58), 2:117–19) thought this led to a confirmation of communal liberties by the king in 1258, but he must have been looking at the *vidimus*, dated 1258, of Louis VII's letter (Giry, 1:188 and 2:p.j. 19). The arbitrators were the archbishop of Sens, Gautier Cornut (Aubry's uncle), and the king's chamberlain, Jean de Beaumont (Giry, (at note 60) II:p.j. no. 21).

[97] Giry, op. cit, I:205. *Lay.*, 2, p. 494, no. 3032.

[98] *Actes du Parlement de Paris*, ed. E. Boutaric, 1:38, no. 432 and 44, no. 496 (in 1260); 74, no. 818A (in 1263, when the king himself conceded rights of high justice in Chateauneuf to the treasurer and church); nos. 744, 1330, 1335 and 1390 (in 1263 and 1269) on their rights elsewhere.

[99] *Actes du Parlement* 1:365, no. 412.

[100] Q. Griffiths, "St. Louis and the New Clerks," p. 270. *v* Perrichet, *La Grande Chancellerie*, p. 155 and Appendix V, p. 548; Louis C. Douët d'Arcq, *Comptes de l'hôtel des rois de France* . . . (Paris, 1865), p. 5, citing Archives Nationales, MS JJ 57, fol. 5r, 16v and 23r.

[101] Cuttino, "King's Clerks," p. 409.

[102] Exhibit A and B.
[103] Mollat, (at note 2), p. 171. Denton, (at note 2) pp. 24–25 and 145. Regarding multiple benefices, see Mollat, pp. 204–05 and Griffiths, op. cit., p. 273. Lawyers like Aubry and Simon were exceptions.
[104] Mollat, (at note 2). pp. 176–77; HF 20:12 and 409. Joinville's esteem for Louis' principles does not rule out advisers other than "men of religion," *Histoire de St. Louis,* ed. Natalis de Wailly (Paris, 1874), p. 364, para. 662 and p. 380, para. 692. Griffiths, pp. 269–70 and n. 4. Cf. William Chester Jordan, *Louis IX and the Challenge of the Crusade* (Princeton, New Jersey, 1979), p. xii, 51–63, 153 and passim.
[105] Denton, (at note 2) pp. 6–7, 25, 29, 39. Mollat, (at note 2) pp. 111–12; he seems equivocal on how critical was retention of the cure of souls in the *collégiales* (p. 149); on residence, see pp. 145–46. In his recent work on *Robert Winchelsey and the Crown, 1294–1313* (Cambridge, 1980), pp. 269, 272 and 293, Denton distinguishes between the king's right of *presentation* to the "custodian of spiritualities" (the episcopal ordinary, here the archbishop, who reserved the right of institution in churches with the cure of souls) from his broader right of *collation.* The latter was never generally recognized by the English episcopacy, while by the thirteenth century the king was effectively "appointing" seven of the ten deans even in royal chapels *with* the cure of souls (p. 285). Pacaut makes no distinction (n. 28 above). Presentation is probably the proper term for St. Martin's dean, since it is used in two of our three contemporary sources (the *Rituale,* n. 80 above, where the king presents the person receiving the deanship *to the chapter,* and the act of 1315, n. 118 below, where the king presents *to the deanship*). The exception is Matthew Paris's use of collation, which may reflect English royal practice (*Chronica majora,* pp. 103–104). But there is no evidence at St. Martin of any need to present the nominee to any spiritual authority beyond the Chapter, such as the archbishop of Tours, even though Eudes Clément had to struggle for "all [other?] parochial rights and jurisdiction" (Monsnyer, 1, p. 231), and Jean de la Cour's appointment during a vacancy in the see of Tours may have been deliberate.
[106] T. F. Tout, *Chapters in the Administrative History of Medieval England* 2:15, quoted by Denton, (at note 2), p. 40.
[107] Vaucelle, (at note 44), pp. 184 and 193. n. 79 above.
[108] Denton, op. cit., p. 148.
[109] Griffiths, (at note 100), pp. 273–74. Even St-Martin was a victim (Matthew Paris, loc. cit.).
[110] Perrichet, (at note 37), pp. 501–02.
[111] Perrichet, op. cit., p. 55.
[112] Denton, op. cit., p. 133.
[113] Charles Petit-Dutaillis, *Actes de Philippe Auguste,* vol. 2, intro. pp. vi–ix.
[114] Monsnyer, 1, p. 223; HF 16:141–42, nos. 178 and 179.
[115] *v* Exhibit A.
[116] Monsnyer, 1, p. 231. Thibaut was partial to the king, if not active in royal affairs. *v* Exhibit A.
[117] Cf. note 5 above. CF. Denton, op. cit. pp. 41–42.
[118] Archives d'Indre et Loire, MS G. 415, p. 46 (eighteenth century). It had been applied loosely to some earlier keepers of the seal.

Exhibit A DEANS OF ST. MARTIN OF TOURS
UNDER THE CAPETIAN KINGS*

	*Royal Activity/Affiliation***	*Ecclesiastical Offices*
Archambaud (de Buzançais ?)[1]	Secures protection/ immunities from Hugh Capet. *Fidelis* of Anjou? & of the k.	Dean 987/8
Eudes I (Odo)[2]	From family of viscounts of Tours, *fideles* of Blois?	Dean 996–1001
Ulger de *Bresis* (Brayes ?)[3]	Subscribes diplomas of Robert II. Probably Blois partisan.	Dean 1006/7–1023
Bove *(Bovo/ Bono)*[4]	Subscribes a royal charter	Dean 1024–29 (–35?)
Jaubert (Gosbert)[5]	Related to house of Blois, Ste-Maure or Maillé?	Dean 1029–47
Geoffroy I[6]	Subscribes diploma of Henry I (1052). *Fidelis* of Anjou.	Dean 1047–d. ca. 1062 (self-styled from 1044)
Raoul[7]		Dean 1063–70
Geoffroy II de (Langeais)[8]	Brother of castellan of Langeais, loyal to Angevins.	Dean/cantor 1068/70–1087.
Pierre I de Doué *(de Doado)*[9]	From important family in court of Anjou.	Dean 1087–1101
Eudes II[10]	A "considerable landowner" from house of Langeais.	Dean 1109/11–1143/4
Barthélemy I (Payen ?)[11]	Royal chancellor 1147–49	Dean in 1150?

Exhibit A *(Continued)*

	*Royal Activity/Affiliation***	*Ecclesiastical Offices*
Philippe de France[12]	Younger son of Louis VI	Dean 1154/5? Archdeacon of Paris. Abbot of St. Spire of Corbeil. Treas. of St. Corneille of Compiègne. Abbot of Mantes.
Barthélemy II de Vendôme[13]	*Fidelis,* agent & counselor of Louis VII.	Dean 1163–71? Archbsp. of Tours 1174?–d.1206
Vacancy		1172?–1175 (March)
Philippe II[14]	No direct activity known, but receives royal support. Related to house of Langeais.	Dean 1176–91
Anselme[15]	K.'s envoy ca. 1190, 1194. K.'s clerk 1196.	Dean 1192–1196 Probably the Bsp. of Meaux ca.1197– d.ca.1207
Thibaut de Perche[16]	No direct activity known, but supported k. on excommunication	Dean 1197–1210 Archdeacon of Reims
Eudes III Clément[17]	K.'s clerk in all but name Master of Norman Exchequer ca. 1213–1216/7	Archdeacon of Paris 1175/80-1209. Vicar of St. Spire, Corbeil. Dean of St.Martin 1211–1216/7.
Nicolas de Roye[18]	Nephew of Chamberlain Barthélemy from Picardy K.'s counselor in the *curia* 1232–37	Dean 1217–1228. Chancellor, Bsp. of Noyon 1228–d. 1240

Aubry Cornut[19]	K.'s envoy (1226); clerk by 1229; keeper of the seal 1231–36; on the Exchequer	Dr. of civil & canon law, U. of Paris Canon of Paris, Sens & Chartres Dean of St.Martin 1229–36 Bsp. of Chartres 1236–d. 1243
Jean de la Cour d'Aubergenville[20]	K.'s clerk from 1231; on the Exchequer; keeper of the seal 1236–44	Master; canon of Paris ca. 1234 Dean of St. Martin 1236–44 Bsp. of Evreux 1244– d. 1256
Guy de Neauphle[21]	K.'s clerk 1253–70 Envoy Counselor of Philip III	Master Dean 1244–69 Pope's chaplain (1255)
Pierre Chalon[22]	Counselor & administrative *enquêteur* (1277); keeper of the seal 1282–1290	Master. Archd. of Autun. Dean 1269–90 Bsp. of Senlis 1291–d. 1294
Gilles Lambert[23]	Counselor 1286—till after 1307	Master Dean 1290–d. ca 1315 (n.s.)
Etienne de Mornay[24]	Chancellor Louis X Jan. 1315 (n.s.)–Jy. 1316; counselor to Charles IV & Philip VI 1322–1332	Master in civil law Canon of Auxerre Dean of St.Martin 1316 (n.s.)–d. 1332

Notes for Exhibit A

* Documentation is largely confined to supporting activities and associations with the royal entourage and dates of ecclesiastical office. Principal reliance for dates has been placed on the following three sources, unless otherwise indicated, and in this order: Emile Mabille, ed., *La Pancarte Noire de St-Martin de Tours* (Paris, 1866), reconstructed from the MS copies by Housseau and Baluze in the Bibl. Nat., and especially pp. 32–37 of the Intro. containing a list of officers (presumably based after 1131 on the *Pancarte Blanche*, which survives only in the same MS collections); E. R. Vaucelle, *La Collégiale de St-Martin de Tours* . . . (Paris, 1908), App. pp. 440–43, which does not cite sources; *Gallia Christiana* 14: cols. 171–81, with *Instrumenta* referred to by no. Where documented, it often depends on the 17th c. history of the church by Raoul Monsnyer, *Celeberrimae Sancti Martini Turonensis ecclesiae historia,* published only to p. 206 in 1670, then ostensibly continued, but probably also altered by Michel Vincent, a canon of St. Martin, in 1702–03; volumes 1 and 2 constitute Bibl. Mun. Tours, MSS 1294–1295. André Salmon's MS collection at Tours was destroyed in World War II.

** All deans served in the judicial sessions of the *Parlements* from Nicolas de Roye on. See Lists II & III of my article, "St. Louis and the New Clerks of Parlement," *Studies in Medieval Culture* 4:2 (1974).

Family and partisan affiliations for the early Capetian period are drawn mainly from the work of Jacques Boussard, "L'Origine des familles seigneuriales dans la région de la Loire moyenne," *Cahiers de Civilisation médiévale* 5:3 (1962); his *Le Comté d'Anjou sous Henri Plantagenet et ses fils* (Paris, 1938); and Olivier Guillot, *Le Comte d'Anjou et son entourage au XIè siècle,* 2 vols. (Paris, 1972). The speculations based on first names recurring in a family were inspired by Bernard Bachrach, "Robert of Blois, abbot of St-Florent de Saumur . . .," *Revue Bénédictine* 88 (1978), pp. 123–46. Uncertain dates are shown thus: 1175/80.

1. *Lem.,* p. 188, n.l; Ferdinand Lot, *Etudes sur le règne de Hugues Capet* (Paris, 1903), p. 231, n. 2; HF 10:550 (undated: 988?). Judging from the name, he was probably from the family of Buzançais, *fideles* of Anjou (Guillot, 1:24, n. 15). An Archambaud appears as nephew of Hervé and brother of Sulpice from the house of Buzançais, both later treasurers (Louis Halphen, *Le Comté d'Anjou* [Paris, 1906], pp. 18–19, n. 4).

2. Members of the house of Blois styled themselves irregularly in the early tenth century as viscounts of Tours (Boussard, "Origines", p. 309). The initial date coincides with that for the treasurer Gautier and a brief period of Blois-Capetian solidarity. The cartulary of Marmoutier records under 1001 a meeting between officers of that abbey and of St. Martin, including Dean Eudes and the prévot Sulpice (the future treasurer?), in the house of the canon Ulger (*Odulgerius,* the next dean?) to resolve a dispute between St. Martin's canons and a knight (Bibl. Nat., MS Coll. Housseau, t. 2, no. 330).

3. If the Latin refers to Braye(s), dept. Indre et Loire, ar. Tours, he is from the family of a twelfth century bishop of Angers with the same name. He may have begun as a Blois partisan: he is associated with Blois *fideles* Gautier and Ganelon in his subscription of a diploma for the convent of Beaumont in 1007 (HF 10:590e; Newman, no. 30; cf. Exhibit B). On the diplomatic shifts, *v* Bachrach, "Robert of Blois . . .", p. 134. But he seems to be on the other side by 1023, when he joins with then-Treasurer Sulpice d'Amboise, the Angevin castellan, in requesting a confirmation of the above act (HF 10:607–09; Newman, no. 92). And in 1023 or 1024 he joins Sulpice in subscribing a

renunciation by Foulque Nerra of "all the bad customs" imposed on possessions of St. Martin (Halphen, *Anjou,* pp. 254–55, no. 35). He was probably related to, if he was not the uncle of Sulpice, as suggested in his son's renunciation of some claims against the abbey of Marmoutier, a confirmation of an act made in the son's youth with his brother Sulpice (Bibl. Nat., MS Coll. Housseau, t. 2, no. 701, Feb. 1067).

4. *Collection de documents inédits sur l'histoire de France* 1:116, charter dated ca. 1024. Origin unknown.

5. Under a variety of spellings the name occurs in all three houses. Gauzbert de Bourgueil (dept. Indre et Loire, ar. Chinon) was made abbot of Marmoutier two years after the appointment of Dean Eudes I at St. Martin (Guillot, 1:174). The castle of Ste. Maure (same ar.) was besieged by Geoffroy Martel, who may have pressed the king to replace Jaubert even before 1047; see n. 6).

6. Subscription: HF 11:590; F. Soehnée, *Cat. des actes de Henri I,* no. 91. He styled himself dean prematurely with Angevin encouragement when he joined in an act of 1044 with other nobles of Angevin centers (Guillot 2: no. C85). He probably served till his death ca. 1062, when his son ceded to La Trinité of Vendôme part of his *honor,* a church in Les Alluyes (dept. Eure et Loir, ar. Chateaudun—Guillot 2: no. C240). This and his name suggest a relationship to the viscounts of Chateaudun (Boussard, "Origine", p. 313). He witnessed a donation by Geoffroy Martel in 1055, confirmed by the k. (A. Trémault, *Cartul. de Marmoutier pour le Vendomois* [Paris, 1893], no. 117).

7. Origin unknown.

8. He was from the family of Langeais, Angevin castellans, and vassals of Mayenne. In 1070 and 1078, with his brothers including (then-castellan?) Hamelin, he granted charters to the abbeys of Corméry and Bourgueil (Halphen, *Anjou,* p. 194, n. 5; he dates the deanship from 1068). In 1080 he accompanied his brother Hugues (whom Halphen identifies as *seigneur* of Langeais) in a concession to Corméry (Guillot 2: no. C355 & n.; and 1:172, n. 182, & pp. 254 & 294; he faults Halphen for connecting our Geoffroy with Geoffroy de Tours, future bp. of Angers, dean of Tours, cantor of St. Martin—p. 252). In an undated entry but during Raoul's archbishopric, he and the canons received guarantees from Hugues de Ste. Maure to desist from taxing their men of St. Espain (Bibl. Nat., MS Coll. Housseau, t. 3, no. 804). Halphen attributes his elevation to bishop to Count Foulque le Réchin, whom St. Martin supported against the archbishop (*Anjou,* p. 198, n. 3); but Guillot reports no such promotion, and the Archives de St. Martin recorded under 1086 that Dean Geoffroy restored to the mayor of Ligueil a privilege held of him in fief (Bibl. Nat., MS Coll. Housseau, t. 3, no. 885).

9. Doué-la-Fontaine is in the dept. of Maine et Loire, ar. Saumur (Boussard, *Anjou,* p. 34, n. 3). On Easter of 1091 he and the canons have their land in Lombardy restored by the marquis Hugo on a personal visit to Tours (Bibl. Nat., MS Coll. Housseau, t. 3, no. 927).

10. An unidentified martyrology describes him as a "considerable landowner (GC 14: cols. 175–76). Since his nephews included Bsp. Hamelin of Le Mans, and Hamelin I founded the house of Langeais (Halphen, *Anjou,* p. 159, n. 1), he doubtless belonged to that castellan family like Geoffroy II. In 1114 he confirms to the monastery of Noyers possession of the church of Pouzay (Indre et Loire, ar. Chinon), inaugurating a series of joint acts with the treasurer Gautier, who apparently made the gift a year before, if one allows for a difference in spelling (Exhibit B; Bibl. Nat., MS Coll. Housseau, t. 4, no. 1354). He enjoyed the support of both the count of Anjou and the king. Before 1116 he and his nephew Jacquelin join as witnesses of a gift of land to the abbey of

Fontevrault by Count Foulque the Younger (Foulque de Jérusalem) *v* Josèphe Chartrou, *L'Anjou de 1109–1151* (Paris, 1928), pp. 326–27, no.6. With Gautier he secures the
king's confirmation of St. Martin's possession of the priory of St. Côme and St. Damien
(1118); papal confirmation of St. Martin's possessions at the king's request; and the gift
of St. Pierre-Puellier (both in 1119:Luchaire, *Louis VI*, nos. 238, 266 and 278; Mabille,
Panc. Noire, no. 122). Some time between 1129 & 1136 he & Gautier receive assurance
from Count Geoffroy Plantagenet that he will defend the chapter's interests against
Sulpice d'Amboise and Guillaume Bucelle, who was appropriating the canons' revenues
from their *Burgus regum francorum* (Chateauneuf?—Chartrou, p. 389, no. 58[56]). At
the end of his long deanship he and the new treasurer Henri obtain exemption from
the royal *gîte* (Luchaire, *Actes*, no. 117).
11. Luchaire has traced his movements with the king to Châlons-s-Marne and Reims in
1147, then to the Orient, and back to France in advance of the k. "in the interest of the
kingdom" (to relieve Suger of Chancellor Cadurc?) between July of 1148 and April of
1149 (Martène and Durand, *Veterum scriptorum . . . Amplissima collectio* [Paris, 1704],
1:803; Luchaire, *Actes*, nos. 221 & 238; Arch. Dépt. Loiret, *Cartul. de Fleuri*, no. 13).
Except for the last source, probably destroyed in WWII, he is identified only as
chancellor. He appears only on Vaucelle's list of deans (p. 440), but without any source.
There were several Payens *(Pagani)* among the canons of St. Martin (as well as the
bourgeois leaders of Chateauneuf!). Boussard's note that he was an influential friend of
the *prévot* of La Trinité of Vendôme suggests an Angevin link (*Anjou*, p. 135, n. 4).
12. A younger son by the same name as the first heir-apparent. Mabille's inclusion of
Philippe for 1155 and 1160 must rest on the *Pancarte Blanche* via copies by Baluze or
Housseau, which I have not identified (See note on documentation above). None of
Luchaire's *Actes*, including nos. 432 and 438, referring to his death, so identify him.
The GC 14: col. 176, simply follows Monsnyer 1:222, who quotes the story of an
anonymous of Marmoutier that Philippe turned down the bishopric of Paris in favor of
Peter Lombard. On his other dignities, *v* Luchaire, *Actes*, nos. 148, 257 & 276; GC 7:
col. 61. He was abbot of St. Mellon of Pontoise in 1138 *after* his brother Henri (Andrew
Lewis, *Royal Succession in Capetian France* [Cambridge, Mass., 1981], p. 250). Dead by
1161, not 1163, as in GC 14: col. 175.
13. Though it would make him almost an octogenarian when he died, we are told he
was the son of Count Geoffroy Grisonelle of Vendôme in whose presence he founded
a chapel *(cella)* at Chauvigny-en-Perche (Loir et Cher, ar. Vendôme); his mother was
Mathilde of Chateaudun (GC 14: col. 92). In 1163 he and the chapter raise the church
of Gres to the status of a priory dependent on St. Martin (Bibl. Nat., MS Coll.
Housseau, t. 5, no. 1851). In the same year they make a lifetime grant of the town of
Charentilly (ar. Tours) to Jaubert, son of Hugues of Ste. Maure, whom Boussard was
the first to identify as treasurer (*Le Comté*, pp. 50 & 141, citing Bibl. Nat., MS Coll.
Housseau, t. 5, no. 1855, fol. 146v). He requests Louis VII's support against the
bourgeois of Chateauneuf in 1164, adding "In vobis enim post Deum unicum meum
refugium est" (HF 16: 95–96, nos. 290 & 292); against the treasurer and members of
the chapter who are threatening his authority in the *prévoté* of Chablis, which he held in
fief of the king and by right as dean (HF 16:99, nos. 308 & 309); and in the same year
joins with the chapter to protest to the king the threats against their rights in Chablis
(HF 16:100, nos. 311–313). In 1167 he and Treasurer Guillaume are asked by the king
for information on Henry II's movements in Poitou (HF 16:141–42, nos. 178 & 179).

Even as archbishop and while papal legate in France, he continues to be a royal counselor; Louis himself writes the pope to explain why Barthélemy's illness prevented his attending the Lateran Council of 1179. He is well enough to attend Philip-Augustus's coronation in that year, and in 1182 the king tells the pope he needs Barthélemy's industry, presence, counsel & help (GC 14: cols. 92–95). Nobilleau includes him in his *Necr.*, p. 35.

14. Nephew of Eudes II and brother of Bsp. Hamelin of Le Mans. He receives the king's support and a share of revenues near Léré in 1178/9 (Luchaire, *Actes*, no. 752). John of Salisbury informs him of the excommunication of the bourgeois conspirators in 1180 (HF 16:624, no. 104). In 1184 he and the treasurer are informed by the papal delegates of the sentence against the conspirators (GC 14: cols. 86–87, no. 67). Nobilleau, *Necr.*, p. 28.

15. As dean in 1193 he recognizes that a house in the prévoté of Ligueil belongs to the canons (Bibl. Nat., MS Coll. Housseau, t. 31, I: charte originale no. 2). We are told he drew up the instrument proclaiming the truce between Philip-Augustus and Richard Lionheart at Vaudreuil in 1194 (GC 14: cols. 177–78). Roger of Hoveden reports he represented the king, along with the archbishop of Reims, the counts of Nevers and Bar, and "many others" (HF 17:569). In 1196 he reports to Innocent III on difficulties with the citizens of Tournai in a dispute with their church, and on their efforts to "circumvent the royal authority"; the pope writes to him as king's clerk to urge perseverance. (HF 19:300, nos. 30 & 31). In the same year the king sends him with the chamberlain Ours to deliver a message of goodwill to the archbishop of Rouen, a former partisan of the English king (L. Delisle, *Catalogue des actes de Philippe Auguste*, p. 115, no. 478; HF 17:652). Gilles of Paris, a contemporary canon of St. Marcel of Paris, refers to him as a *nobilis Parisinus* (patrician or Parisian?) and *aulicus* (courtier) of the king, according to Fr. Duchesne, *Historia Francorum Scriptores coaetanei* . . . 5:324 (Paris, 1649), as cited in GC 8: col. 1618. His first act as bishop (on the assumption it was the same man) was in July, 1197. In 1202 (n.s.) he facilitated the issuance of the papal bull legitimizing the king's children by Agnès. When in 1204 a council was convened at Meaux by the papal legate to make the peace with England, the French bishops, rather than leaving it to him, appealed to Rome; Anselme was among those who visited the pope. Gilles's verses praise his expertise in canon and civil law (*Gallia Christiana* 8, cols. 1618–1620). Date of installation and death: *v* P. B. Gams, *Series Episcoporum* (Graz, 1957), p. 575.

16. Son of Count Geoffroy of Perche. The statutes drawn up by Bishop Hamelin of LeMans on Innocent III's orders, for the internal discipline of St-Martin, were put in place by 1204 (Arch. Dépt., Eure et Loir, MS G. 3592—Chap. de St-Martin); Monsnyer is vague on Anselme's or Thibaut's role, if any (*Celeberrimae* . . . 1:227–30). According to the *Gallia Christiana* (14:177) without indication of source, "He angrily looked the other way when the papal court took up a sentence of interdict against the king." Though Dom Housseau admits his inability to determine the cause of the quarrel between the dean and the chapter, he was obliged by the canons to seek papal grace for St. Martin's failure to observe Innocent's interdict against the king, and to travel to Rome at his own expense (Bibl. Nat., MS Coll. Housseau, t. 6, nos. 2180–bis and -ter). In the same year 1203, however, he took an opposing position to the king's, as archdeacon of Reims (HF 19:425). In 1205 and 1209 he was occupied with internal affairs of the chapter (E. Mabille, ed. *Catalogue analytique des diplomes, chartes et actes* . . . *Dom Housseau* [Tours,

1863], nos. 2203, where the T. does not stand for Thomas, and 2485). He was the last appointee from Angevin territory, (Perche was just east of Tours), but in any case he was related to Philip-Augustus like the Treasurer Rotrou and his predecessor.

17. The Clément family, which included a dean and another archdeacon of Notre-Dame of Paris also called Eudes, and two marshals of France, was generous with gifts to the subordinate church of Léré in particular, dept. Loiret (*Cartulaire de Notre-Dame de Paris* [Paris, 1850] 4:63, no. 124). Eudes succeeded this archdeacon about 1209 (4:187, no. 322). He demonstrated his piety by founding a chaplaincy at St. Perpet, subject to the presentation of the sub-dean (his appointee), and fought for the rights of St. Martin against the pretensions of the Archbishop of Tours (Monsnyer, 1:231–32; Vaucelle, p. 215). He was assured the protection by the king's bailiffs and *prévots* from 1211 (*Actes de Philippe Auguste*, 3:335–36) and the redefinition of his and the church's rights in Chateauneuf in 1211–1212 (note 95 of the text above); acquired through an exchange of rights the mayoralty of Ligueil for himself and his successors as dean in 1213; and reached an accord by 1216 on jurisdiction there with the lord of Loches (Arch. Dept. Indre and Loire, G. 399; *Actes de Philippe Auguste*, 3:418, no. 1293, and 4:18, no. 1415; *Lay.* 1:426–27, no. 1159). Yet he was "occupied for the major part of his five (*sic*) years as dean with the administration of royal affairs" (Monsnyer, 1:231), especially on the Norman Exchequer, over which he presided on at least one occasion (L. Delisle, *Recueil de jugements de l'Echiquier* [Paris, 1865], nos. 109, 114, 134, 162).

18. For his family, see Fernando Pico, "Membership in the Cathedral chapter of Laon", *Catholic Historical Review*, 61:1 (1975), p. 18. In 1221 (n.s.) Nicolas and the chapter issued new statutes and regulations for the *collégiale*, which included the requirement of priesthood for the seven regular dignitaries like the dean (Bibl.Mun. Tours, MS 193, fol. 192v). Monsnyer tells us the regulations were approved by the pope 17 years later (i.e. 1237 old-style—1:236–37). Nicolas seems to have been more active in the church than in the royal court before his elevation to bishop, though he received St. Louis solemnly at St. Martin in February, 1227. *v Gde. Chronique de Tours* ed. A. Salmon (Paris, 1864), p. 159. *v* note ** for column two of this exhibit. He is called king's clerk uncharacteristically after his promotion to bp.

19. Aubry was nephew of Eudes Clément and nephew or brother of Gautier, archbishop of Sens. The family was from Villeneuve-la-Cornue (today Salins, dept. Seine-et-Marne, ar. Provins). They enjoyed various rights in Rozoy, where he was prévot for Notre-Dame of Paris in 1218. *v* Paul Quesvers, *Notes sur les Cornus . . .* (Montereau, 1893, pp. 11–13). Among his activities for the churches of St. Martin and Chartres, we mention only: his dispute in 1235 with the chapter of St. Martin over his giving the cantorship to Gilles *Raderii* (another king's clerk—*v* Exhibit C), in which the arbiters decided the latter should take the orders of priest within a year (Vaucelle, op. cit., p. 207)—as already provided in Nicolas' regulations!—and his efforts in 1234 to settle disputes of the treasurer Pierre Charlot, Philip-Augustus's bastard son, with outside parties (Bibl. Nat., MS Coll. Housseau, t. 7, no. 2770) and from 1230 on with the inhabitants of Chateauneuf (*v* Exhibit B). "Master Aubry's" first royal assignment was in 1226 as envoy of Queen-regent Blanche, with the pantryman Hugues d'Athies, to obtain oaths guaranteeing arrangements with the county of Flanders (*Lay.* 2:102, no. 1830). The first references to him as king's clerk and dean of Tours coincide in 1231 in the *pallia militum et clericorum* for the royal household; and he appears in the accounting of 1234, at which time he was given papal dispensation from residence at St. Martin in order to serve the king (L. Perrichet, *Grande Chancellerie*, pp. 509–10; he thinks Aubry

may have assumed responsibility for the seal from 1231). In 1233 the king turned over to St-Martin a "false knight" from Chablis, whose fine he proposed to share with the church (*Lay.* 2:254, no. 2250). From 1234 on he served frequently on the Exhequer, on which clerks now predominated (L. Delisle, *Recueil de l'Echiquier*, nos. 497, 511, 564, 539, and 590). In 1235 he and his brother Gautier, together with two other royal officials, affixed their seals to letters setting forth the dowry of Mathilde de Dammartin, widow of Count Philippe Hurepel of Boulogne (*Lay.* 2:288, no. 2368). Following his elevation to the bishopric of Chartres, he and St. Louis agreed on arbitration of the king's collation of two prebends and an archdeaconry while the see was vacant (*Lay.* 2:371, no. 2694—year 1238). He died in 1243 in Nevers, after a frustrated attempt to rally behind the pope in Rome (*Dict. de biogr. franc.* v. 4:col.292,9:697; his family connections and generosity to various churches are celebrated in the obituaries of Nevers, Chartres and Paris, along with his preeminence in the king's councils and his expertise in canon and civil law, which he taught at Paris. ("Necrologium B. M. Carnutensis," in *Cartulaire de Notre-Dame de Chartres*, ed. Lépinois and Merlet [Chartres, 1863] 3:197; "Obituarium," in *Cartulaire de Notre-Dame de Paris* 4:50, no. 111).

20. Jean, whose family seems to have had close ties with the Poussins of Aubergenville (dept. Yvelines, ar. Mantes), may also have been of bourgeois origin (L. Delisle, *Cartulaire Normand* [Caen, 1852], no. 469; Houth, *Recueil de chartes de St-Niçaise de Meulan*, p. 122, no. 120 and passim). He had been king's clerk well before assuming the deanship, which coincided with taking over the seal (according to the *pallia* and accounting of 1231 and 1234 cited by Perrichet, *Grande Chancellerie*, pp. 165 and 510–511). Besides witnessing payments like Aubry, according to the *pallia* of 1239 the "dean of [St. Martin of] Tours" was accountable for the products of the seal until he was "discharged" by the receipts of the *caisse*. (L. L. Borrelli de Serres, *Recherches sur divers services publiques* . . . [Paris, 1895] 1:381, ns. 5 and 6, citing HF 22:588, 593, 606 and 610). In 1231 he had his own clerk to send on a mission to the count of Flanders (*Lay.* 5:119, no. 360). In 1234 he was to be paid £100 (Money of Paris) for obtaining exemption from military service by the bishop of Amiens (*Lay.* 2:264, no. 2285). From that year, when he witnessed the sale of Blois and Chartres to the king at royal assembly (HF 23:676, no. 322), he was a regular member of the *curia* and its judicial sessions (Lists I and II of my article, "St. Louis and the New Clerks"), and from 1236 "filled the functions of chancellor of the kingdom" (L. Delisle, HF 24:*313). Not surprisingly he obtained the usual dispensations from residence requirements (Perrichet, p. 510), and little evidence has survived of activities in the internal affairs of St. Martin (*Gallia Christiana* 14, col. 180; the dean purchased the fruits of a prebend held of him in 1243 (Arch. Dept. Indre and Loire, MS G414, no. 3). He presided at his first recorded session of the Exchequer in 1235, and was a member on three other occasions as bishop. (L. Delisle, *Jugements*, nos. 572, 789, 791, and 792). He was nominated to the bishopric of Evreux, ostensibly by papal direction (Lebeurier, "Mémorial des éveques d'Evreux," *Annuaire de l'Eure* [1865], pp. 72–73), but doubtless on St. Louis's insistence, as were many of his successors when they gave up the seal. He continued to be an active counselor to Queen Blanche as regent during the king's crusade and after, witnessing the report of an arbitration ordered by the king, subscribing a charter, and witnessing the return of the regalia to the archbishop of Tours (*Cartulaire de Notre-Dame de Paris* 2:395–98, no. 17, and Delisle, HF 24:*312, no. 134, both in the year 1248; *Lay.* 3:150, no. 3977, year 1252). In 1248, in recognition of his services, the king had given a manor to his nephew Guillaume d'Aubergenville on the occasion of the latter's marriage

(*Cartulaire Normand*, no. 469, cited above). A concession in 1275 by King Philip III to Bishop Philippe de Cahors (another royal counselor) tells us that the cathedral's exemption from regalian rights was acquired by Jean (Arch. Dept. Eure, MS G6: Evéché d'Evreux, charte no. 175). The Obituary of Evreux commemorates his death in 1256, when Louis ordered a sum paid to his executors (HF 23:461; Arch. Dept. Eure, MS G6, charte no. 228); Nobilleau's *Nec.*, p. 22, cites Monsnyer, 1:242. His ring and cross were found in 1884 in his tomb in the cathedral and are in the Musée d'Evreux (Canon Motte, "St. Louis et le diocèse d'Evreux," *La Vie diocésaine d'Evreux*, no. 1 [January, 1961], pp. 3–4).

21. Guy was the brother of the castellan of Neauphle (dept. Vvelines, ar. Rambouil-let—L. Merlet, *Cartulaire des Vaux de Cernay* 1:452–53, nos. 492–93; J. Depoin, *Chartes . . . d'Abbécourt*, p. 44, nos. 36–37). His earliest known royal association was as dean in August, 1249, when he was named among the executors of the king's brother Alphonse of Poitiers (*Lay.* 3:76, no. 3796) whose entourage had produced more than one royal clerk. (A debt owed him was among those owed to Alphonse in 1269 [*Lay.* 4:402, no. 5601]). In 1247 he had been referred to simply as "clerk" in a transaction with the canons of Abbécourt (J. Depoin, *Chartes d'Abbécourt*, p. 71, no. 99). According to Monsnyer (1 pp. 242–243), in 1251 he obtained papal exemption for the church's personnel from interdict and excommunication by any ordinary court, and in 1255 the establishment of a foundation by the king in honor of St. Martin. In the same year he obtained new privileges from Alexander IV covering his own residency and that of the canons in his company (*Registres d'Alexandre IV*, ed. B. de la Roncière, p. 109, no. 359 and p. 102, no. 342). Guy was active not only in the internal affairs of St. Martin, which we pass over, but with the treasurer Simon in a transaction with the Hospitallers and over rights of high justice and the jurisdiction of the church's schoolman in Chateauneuf (*Lay.* 4:13, no. 4694; Boutaric, *Actes du Parlement*, no. 818A, year 1263; MS Coll. Housseau, t. 7, no. 3220, year 1268). He was an active arbitrator between private parties during his last ten years (*Cartulaire de Chartres* 2 pp. 181–183, no. 342; MS Coll. Housseau, t. 7, no. 3221), a regular member of the *Parlements*, and an envoy to England for the ratification of the Treaty of Paris of 1259 (*Lay.* 3 p. 443, nos. 4461–4462; Rymer, *Foedera* I p. 1, pp. 380, 391). He could not have resigned his deanery to go to the Holy Land until 1270, which was probably the year of his gift of a meadow to St. Martin (the gift is dated March, 1269 [o.s.]; Easter was the 24th—Bibl. Nat., MS Coll. Housseau, t. 7, nos. 3223 and 3225). Though not with the king on his second crusade, he was chosen as his substitute executor (*Lay.* 4 pp. 468 and 470, nos. 5730 and 5734). In 1271 he was designated a counselor by Philip III (Arch. Nat., MS J401, no. 2).

22. Pierre II was born of "noble stock" (*Gallia Christiana* 14:180–81) from Chalon in Burgundy (Monsnyer 1:246). He was in a Toulouse *Parlement* in 1280. *v Textes relatifs à l'histoire du Parlement*, ed. Charles V. Langlois [Paris, 1888], p. 108, no. 77; 1283 (*Gallia Christiana* 14:181); in the Paris *Parlement* in 1284 when it condemned Charles of Anjou on the issue of Poitiers and Auvergne (*Actes du Parlement* 1: App. by Delisle, pp. 388–89, no. 537); and in 1285, as "dians de Tours" (Langlois, p. 124, no. 91). He styled himself "vice chancellor" in 1282 (Perrichet, *Grande Chancellerie*, pp. 153 and 519). He was named in that year to execute the will of the Count of Alençon (*Gallia Christiana* 14:180–81). In 1277 he and a knight were sent to the sénéchaussée of Agenais to wind up the *enquête* (J. Glenisson, *Les Enquêteurs-Réformateurs*, unpub. thesis, Ecole des Chartes, pp. 2 and 9). Philip III had renounced his right of hospitality from the dean in

exchange for an annual payment of £15: Philip IV's confirmation in 1294 (Arch. Dept. Indre and Loire, MS G414, no. 7, a copy of the lost original). I am obliged to M. Pierre Gasnault for a copy of a concession in 1286 (n.s.) by Philip the Fair to his *dilecto clerico et fideli nostro* of some structures adjoining the dean's *hôtel* in Paris, which were no longer needed for the defense of the city (Léopold Delisle, "Instructions addressées par le Comité des travaux historiques et scientifiques aux correspondants du Ministère de l'Instruction publique et des Beaux Arts," *Litterature latine et histoire du Moyen Age* [Paris, 1890], pp. 80–81, from Salmon's Ms. collection now destroyed.) Because the king refers to him as keeper of the seal, it helps to close the gap in dates before Pierre's elevation to the bishopric of Senlis. He was still dean in 1290 (*Gallia Christiana* 14, col. 181, citing Baluze) but appeared in *Parlement* in that year as *electus Silvanectensis* (H. Klimrath, *Travaux sur l'histoire du droit français* [Paris, 1843], p. 113). He sat as bishop from April, 1291, till his death after June, 1294 (Arch. Dept. Indre et Loire, G414, no. 7; Cf. P. B. Gams, *Series Episcoporum* [Graz, 1957], p. 628. On his political role, v F. J. Pegues, *The Lawyers of the Last Capetians* (Princeton, 1962), pp. 189–90.

23. He is a counselor on organization of the king's *hôtel* in 1286—listed by name, without title of dean (Langlois, *Textes*, p. 129, no. 97). He may have been preoccupied with church affairs until 1307 (another dispute with Chateauneuf, restoring discipline at Léré [Monsnyer 1 p. 80], and jurisdiction at St. Epain [Bibl. Nat., MS Coll. Housseau, t. 8, nos. 3439 and 3444]). In that year he contributed to the *ordonnance* on the *Parlement* (Langlois, *Textes,* p. 178), but was not in the large *Parlement* of 1298, though we are told he sat in that body till his death about 1315 (*Gallia Christiana* 14, col. 181). He possessed the priory of St-Rémy of Beaulieu near Chevreuse, dept. Yvelines: v J. LeBeuf, *Histoire de la ville de Paris* (Paris, 1883–93), 3, pp. 377–378. In 1309 he and the chapter received a gift from Philip the Fair of £40 annual rent (Bibl. Nat., MS Housseau, t. 8, no. 3454).

24. Etienne had been chancellor of Charles of Valois. From Berri, he was a nephew of Pierre, keeper of the seal and bishop under Philip the Fair. He was presented to the "deanship vacant by the death of Me. Gilles," but the date should be 1316 (n.s.) (Arch. Dept. Indre and Loire, MS G415, no. 2; Perrichet, *Chancellerie,* p. 532; Francis Guessard, "Etienne de Mornay: chancelier de France sous Louis Hutin," BEC 5 [1843], pp. 373–76 and 379). Louis X's letter of notification to the Chapter of 21 February, 1315, apparently did not result in a formal presentation till 11 February, 1316 (n.s.). Nogaret had effectively recreated the chancellorship according to Jean Favier (*Philippe le Bel* [Paris, 1978], p. 73). Etienne's tenure was as short as his master's reign, but his service to the crown resumed under Philip's third son (Guessard, pp. 381–82).

Exhibit B   TREASURERS OF ST. MARTIN OF TOURS UNDER
THE CAPETIAN KINGS*

	*Royal Activity/Affiliation***	*Ecclesiastical Offices*
Renaud ("the Thuringian")[1]	Viscount of Angers under Foulque Nerra	*Archiclavis* 987
Gautier I[2]	Probably of family from Chouzé-s-Loire, Blois *fideles*	Treas. 996–
Hervé (de Buzançais)[3]	Requests royal diploma. *Fidelis* of Anjou	*Archiclavis* 1001–d. 1022
Sulpice d'Amboise[4]	Angevin castellan of Amboise, vassal of King Robert II	Treas. 1022/3–d. 1027
Ganelon de Montigny[5]	Royal vassal & Blois *fidelis*	Treas. of St. Maurice of Tours ca. 1023–7? Treas. of St. Martin 1028/31–d. 1048/50
Vacancy?		ca. 1050–55
Geoffroy I de Preuilly[6]	Of Touraine family whose s. is royal vassal; Angevin partisans.	Treas. 1056/9–66
Renaud de Montreuil-Bellay[7]	Related to Angevin Langeais. Subscribes diplomas of Philip I.	Treas. 1067–83 Archbsp. of Reims 1083–d. 1096
Hardouin[8]	From Touraine family	Treas. 1086
Gautier II[9]	Another Preuilly	Treas. 1087–1136 (!)
Henri de France[10]	Son of Louis VI	Abbot of St. Mellon of Pontoise & 6 others Treas. 1139/41–49 Bsp. of Beauvais 1149– Archbsp. of Reims 1162–d. 1175
Giraud/ Guillaume/ Jaubert[11]	Jaubert was the son of the seigneur of Ste. Maure	"G." between 1149–69 Jaubert in 1163
Geoffroy II[12]	Receives k.'s support; a Preuilly or Buzançais?	Treas. 1169/75–1178/9

Renaud III de Mouzon[13]	Cousin of Philip-Augustus	Treas. 1178/80–1182 Bsp. of Chartres 1182–1217
Rotrou de Perche	Another royal first cousin from family of counts	Treas. 1183/5–1190 Archdeacon of Reims Bsp. of Châlons-s-Marne 1190–d. 1201
Pierre (le Chambellan de Nemours)[14]	Son of Gautier, royal chamberlain?	Treas. 1190–1203/8 Bsp. of Paris? 1208–19
G.[15]		Treas. 1203
Robert II de Mehun[16]	From family holding fiefs of the Courtenays	Treas. 1209–1215. Bsp. of Le Puy 1215–d. 1219
Vacancy		Mar. 1216–Nov. 1217
Pierre Charlot[17]	Bastard son of Philip-Augustus	Treas. 1217–ca. 1241 Bsp. of Noyon 1240–d. 1249
Archambaud (de Buzançais?)		Treas. 1241 & 1242
Philippe I de Castille[18]	A diplomatic appoint-ment	Canon of Toledo. Treas. 1243–1256
Simon de Brion[19]	Keeper of the seal 1259–61 Member of *Parlement* Adviser to Charles of Anjou	Canon of St. Quentin ca. 1238 Archdeacon of Rouen (Caux) 1248–59 Treas. of St. M. 1256–81 Cardinal-legate 1261–Pope Martin IV 1281–d. 85
Simon de Nesle[20]	Son of Raoul de Cler-mont, s. of Nesle	Prévot of Courçay Treas. 1281/9–1296 Bsp. of Noyon 1297–Bsp. of Beauvais 1301–12
Philippe II de Majorque[21]	Cousin of Philip the Fair	Treas. 1297–1341 Warden of St. Quentin 1303–d. 1341?

Notes for Exhibit B

*v note on documentation.

**v note for Exhibit A on family and partisan affiliations. Our starting-place has been Jacques Boussard, "Le Trésorier de St-Martin de Tours", *Revue d'histoire de l'église de France* 47:144 (1961), pp. 68–87.

1. Employing, like Boussard, the analysis of first names recurring in certain families, Professor Bachrach concludes he must have been the Angevin viscount ("Robert of Blois", pp. 126 & 128–9). He and Dean Archambaud secure a grant in 988 (HF 10:550). In his last year as treasurer and Eudes of Blois' first year as count (995) he obtains the latter's confirmation of a gift to St. Martin of vineyards purchased from a citizen of Tours. (Léonce Lex, *Eudes, comte de Blois* . . . (Troyes, 1892), p. 120, no. 73).

2. Affiliation: Guillot, 1:25; Boussard, "Le Trésorier", pp. 77–78. Mabille, in his detailed *Notice* on a later treasurer, Ganelon de Montigny and his family, makes no attempt to associate our Gautier with that family. But his association with Ganelon in subscribing Robert II's diploma of 1007, and the frequency with which the name did occur in that family, suggest a close relationship; perhaps he *was* Ganelon's father, uncle of Hugue, s. of Montigny before Ganelon. The family, ironically, was of Angevin origin: Chouzé-s.-Loire, dept. Indre & Loire, ar. Chinon, con. Bourgueil, to the abbey of which they were generous (Emile Mabille, *Cartul. de Marmoutier pour le Dunois* [Chateaudun, 1874], p. xx & n.l, citing Bibl. Nat., MS Coll. Housseau, no. 549, and p. xxii). Gautier joins in subscribing Robert II's diploma of 1007 for the convent of Beaumont, when he is no longer treasurer but the k. has renewed his liaison with Count Eudes's widow Berthe (Bachrach, "Robert of Blois", p. 134). Gautier and Ganelon are simply listed with members of the chapter of St. Martin (Lem., p. 47, n. 28 & *Tableau des souscripteurs;* Newman, no. 30; HF 10:590e).

3. Affiliation: Guillot, 1:26; Boussard, "Le Trésorier", p. 78. For his request to the k.: HF 10:272 and the refs. in n. 2 above. The date of d. is from the *Chronique de Tours* (HF 10:283). In 1001 he had rebuilt the church of St. Martin after a fire (*Chronicon Turonense,* attributed to Péan Gastineau, in *Veterum Scriptorum . . . Collectio,* ed. Martène & Durand, vol. 5, col. 995). He was renowned for a pious life (HF 10, pp. 29–30 & *passim*), and this may have helped him survive the royal about-face which renewed the pro-Blois alliance (Bachrach, op. cit., p. 144), though it also supports Guillot's argument that even the early Capetians maintained their rights and were able to protect their officers & St. Martin's interests (pp. 88–89). It is Hervé, an Angevin *fidelis*, who apparently secures Eudes of Blois's approval for including Luzé in the foundation of Beaumont (Lex, *Eudes,* p. 105, no. 23), and who seems to have initiated the k.'s grant of 1007 witnessed by important partisans of Blois; and at an unknown date he adds to a donation by St. Martin to Marmoutier in the suburbs of the city of Tours, still an outpost of Blois. (Lex, p. 102, no. 14).

4. He was Hervé's nephew, and reflects the k.'s "hardening attitude" toward Blois (Guillot, 1:32; & n. 160; Boussard, "Le Trésorier", p. 79). But the following dean, Jaubert, was probably a Blois partisan, and in 1027 the warlike "clerk-castellan" is besieged (unsuccessfully) by Eudes II of Blois and the young k. Henry I (Guillot, pp. 34–5)—the last year in which he styles himself treasurer (Mabille, *Cartul. de Marmoutier,* p. xxvi) and presumably the year of his death. He and the contemporary dean Ulger subscribed Foulque of Anjou's renunciation of "bad customs" imposed on St. Martin (Exhibit A). In 1023 he requests reconfirmation of the act of 1007 for Beaumont (Newman, no. 92; HF 10:607–609).

5. His father was Gautier de Tours (of Angevin origin), so-called because he served Eudes I, Thibaut & Eudes II, counts of Tours, as their *provisor* (something "between a viscount and a *prévot*"), collecting revenues through the *viguiers)*—a function in which Ganelon succeeded him around 1024 (Mabille, *Cartul. de Marmoutier*, pp. xix–xxi; & n. 2 above). He had subscribed the royal diploma of 1007 along with the former treasurer (his father?) Gautier (*Lem.*, p. 57, n. 69), and he and his brothers were present in 1015 when Eudes II required their father Gautier to give up the rights with which he was unduly oppressing the abbey of Marmoutier (Lex, *Eudes de Blois,* pp. 142–43, no. 12; Mabille, *Cartul.*, p. xxv, and pp. xxiv–xxxi for the entire *notice* on Ganelon). His first (& only ?) act as treasurer of the *cathedral* church of Tours was in 1023, and Mabille believes he succeeded Sulpice at St. Martin on the latter's d. in 1027 (pp. xxv & xxvi). Probably soon after 1028 he inherited Montigny (Eure & Loir, ar.Chateaudun) and other land in the Dunois & Blésois (Loir & Cher), on which he could fall back after 1044 when he lost his lands in Touraine (dept. Indre & Loire, ar. Chinon; n. 2 above; Mabille, pp. xxii & xxvii).

The one royal diploma he subscribed as treasurer was Henry I's (undated, GC 14, Instr. no. 48). Between 1034 & 1037 he subscribed an act of Marmoutier announcing a gift by Eudes of Blois of land once belonging to St. Martin—a royal concession to Blois? (Lex, *Eudes de Blois*, p. 162, no. 26; cf. Mabille, p. xxvi, n. 5, from Bibl. Nat., MS Coll. Housseau, t. 2, no. 430). "Overzealous like his father" in his lay capacity, he also was forced by the count to renounce exactions imposed on Marmoutier by him and his *prévot* (Lex, *Eudes de Blois*, p. 164, no. 28, from MS Coll. Housseau, t. 12^2, no. 6750— a suppl. vol. of copies; Mabille, p. xxvii, cites Dom Martène, *Hist. de Marmoutier*, t. III, no. 221).

His treasurership of St. Martin survived the Angevin victory over Blois at Nouy in 1044, though he & other tenants of Blois were evicted from their now-Angevin lands (Boussard, "L'Eviction des tenants d'Eudes de Blois . . .", *Moyen Age* 69 [1963], pp. 142 & 145). He was on sufficiently good terms with Geoffroy Martel between 1042 & 1044 to obtain his consent (as overlord?) to a donation of St-Hilaire-s-Yerre (in the same ar. as Montigny) to Marmoutier, an act confirmed by King Henry as his *dominus* (Mabille, *Cartul.*, pp. 22–4, no. 22, cited by Halphen, *Anjou*, p. 265, no. 70). His last known act was in 1045: the restoration of the abbey of St. Avit in the diocese of Chartres, where he had benefices (Mabille, *Cartul.*, p. xxviii, n. 4—a re-ed. of GC 8, Instr. no. 15); he was apparently dead by 1051 (Mabille, p. 31, no. 32), survived by his wife, who made a donation of some vineyards between 1032 & 1037 (Lex, *Eudes de Blois*, p. 110, no. 17; Mabille, pp. 90–91, no. 97), and two nephews named Ganelon (!), one of whom inherited Montigny. Cf. Guillot, 1:63 and n. 280.

6. His family was friendly to the Buzançais (Guillot 1:90, n. 404; Boussard, "L'Origine", p. 320). His witnessing of a diploma of Henry I in 1052, alongside Dean Geoffroy, symbolized the new alliance between the k. and Count Geoffroy Martel (Guillot 1:91; Exhibit A above). He held his court of justice as treasurer in the castle of Chateauneuf (Guillot 2: app., p. 468; from Bibl. Nat., MS Coll. Housseau, t. 2, no. 686). He had a vicar (like the count), identified in an undated act in which he gave up some serfs to the chapter (Housseau, t. 2, no. 303). But Guillot does not support his suggestion that some of the treasurer's jurisdiction slipped into his *lignage*. Housseau's date of 1080 (t. 3, no. 931), for a consent by him & Foulque le Réchin to a donation, must be in error; or else he gave up his treasurership to fellow-rebel Renaud long before his death.

7. He first appears as s. of Montreuil in 1067, in the first of two diplomas of Philip I (Lem., p. 101 & *tableau;* M. Prou, *Recueil des Actes de Philippe Ier,* nos. 30 & 84 [for year 1076]; Guillot 1:113–14). Though Renaud and his predecessor Geoffroy had rebelled against Count Geoffroy le Barbu, who was supported by the k., the latter had established a temporary truce, and Guillot does not regard his appointment as treasurer as a "cave-in" by the k. to the rebel leader Foulque le Réchin. He did become one of Count Foulque's counsellors (Guillot 2: C313 & n.; C344), and joined him in approving a gift by one of his vassals (Halphen, *Anjou,* p. 315, no. 244). And he subscribed an act setting forth Foulque's rights at Chateauneuf (Guillot 2: app., pp. 467–68). At an unknown date he renounced his efforts to impose "unjust burdens" on the abbey of St. Aubin of Angers (Bibl. Nat., MS Coll. Housseau, t. 3, no. 895). Halphen places at the end of 1083 his elevation to archbishop (*Anjou,* p. 314; no. 243 & n.). Nobilleau, *Necr.,* p. 15.

8. His name suggests he belonged to the Rochecorbon group of families, originally located in the ar. of Tours (Boussard, "L'Origine", p. 318). Guillot's index indicates a relationship to the s. of Maillé (dept. Indre et Loire, ar. Chinon); an Hardouin, son of Agnès *de Malliaco,* was a witness in the *Cartul. de Marmoutier* (ed. Mabille, p. 122, no. 132)—or to the s. of Trèves (Maine & Loire, ar. Saumur), in either case an old Touraine family. Appointed by the k. during a period of Angevin weakness, probably after a vacancy of some length.

9. If there was more than one "G" or Gautier during this long period, at least one was surely a Preuilly Guillot 2: app., p. 468); in 1113 he makes a gift of the church of *Pausai* (La Roche-Pozay?, S.E. of Preuilly, Indre & Loire, ar. Loches) to the monastery of Noyers (Bibl.Nat., MS Coll. Housseau, t. 4, no. 1330). *v* Exhibit A for Eudes's confirmation & other acts.

10. For his ecclesiastical career, *v* n. 35 of the text and GC 9: col. 88. He benefited from the fine levied against the bourgeois of Chateauneuf in 1141 (Luchaire, *Actes,* no. 75).

11. For this period Vaucelle lists a Guillaume, and Mabille a Giraud, whom he confuses with a dean (*Panc. Noire,* p. 34, n. 2). It was indeed a Giraud who destroyed the house of the count of Anjou's *viguier* (or *voyer—Lay.* 1:161). Only Boussard includes a "Josbert de Ste-Maure", and solely on the basis of a grant by the chapter in 1163 (Exhibit A, n. 13). The confusion stems from the ambiguous "G's" in the MSS. In 1173 the (unnamed) treasurer is warned about excessive rents charged by townspeople in anticipation of a papal council (Luchaire, *Actes,* no. 471)—evidence of his jurisdiction in Chateauneuf. See Exhibit A regarding his and Barthélemy's dispute with the chapter.

12. *v* Exhibit A under Philippe II for the act of 1178/9.

13. He was a son of the count of Barre and Mouzon and of Agnès of Champagne & Brie, and a cousin of Philip Augustus (Boussard, "Le Trèsorier", p. 80). The GC (8: cols. 1152–6) Gallicizes *Moncionis* as Monçon, (prob. Monceaux, dept. Brie, arr.Seine & Marne; Mouzon is in dept. Ardennes, arr. Sédan); but it is clear that the k. is no longer drawing his treasurers from Angevin territory. Mabille lists him as treasurer as late as 1185, a confusion with his successor with the same initial? He was a *prévot* of Chartres like his brother Hugues when he is elected bishop in 1182. He accompanies Philip-Augustus on the Third Crusade, and takes the cross against the Albigensians in 1209 *(ibid.).*

14. If he was the son of Pierre de Courtenay, he would be a grandson of Louis VI (Boussard, "Le Trésorier", pp. 80–81). But if, as is more likely, our Pierre was the son of Gautier I, s. of La Chapelle-en-Brie and Villebéon, the k's chamberlain, and Aveline

de Nemours, he became bishop of Paris in 1208, one of three brothers to become prelates (GC 7: cols. 86–87). Unlike Dean Eudes he played no special royal function as treasurer, though he is mentioned in this capacity in 1190 (*Lay.* 1:158, no. 371).

The Josbert referred to by Boussard in 1199 (*Le Comté,* p. 182) was cantor of St. Maurice of Tours, the cathedral church (his P.J. no. 9).

15. Bibl. Nat., MS Coll. Housseau, t. 4, no. 2180. None of our published lists speculates on this person.

16. Boussard, p. 81. *v* Exhibit A under Eudes III for the act of 1211/1212 defining rights in Chateauneuf. He was involved in a dispue with this dean and the chapter in August, 1213 (Bibl. Nat., MS Coll. Baluze, vol. 76, fol. 186). As bishop: C. Eubel, *Hierarchia Catholica Medii Aevi* (Regensburg, 1913), 1:91.

17. *v* note 55 of the text. Although Pope Honorius felt "unable" at this time (1217) to legitimize Pierre, the chapter seems to have backed down and provided the prebend on which his reception as treasurer was contingent. The *Pancarte Noire* lists an Archambaud for 1241–42, as does Boussard with a question mark (p. 82); but Monsnyer says nothing of Pierre's resigning *before* his elevation to the bishopric (p. 242). He was elected bishop in 1240 (Gams, p. 590).

18. Son of Frederick III of Castille and a student in Paris in 1245 (Boussard, op. cit., p. 83). There is uncertainty regarding a vacancy, especially from 1253 (see note 20 ff.). A dispute over Philippe's qualifications, similar to those over Pierre Charlot's and Philippe de Majorque's (note 21 below), may account for an alleged vacancy in July of 1245 (Bibl. Nat., MS Coll. Housseau, t. 7, no. 2945) and the appearance of another "G., treasurer" in April, 1247 in a settlement with the bourgeois of Chateauneuf; this "G," is accounted for by none of our authorities. (Bibl. Nat., MS Coll. Housseau, t. 7, no. 2969.)

19. Despite claims of Touraine or other origins, he was probably from a knightly family in the Brie française (Seine-et-Marne); his father was *grand-juge-maire* for a holding of St. Martin's: *v* Richard Kay, "Martin IV and the Fugitive Bishop of Bayeux," *Speculum* 40:3 (1965), 461–62. He studied law in Parma: *v* Edward M. Meijers, *Etudes d'histoire du droit* 3 (Leiden, 1959), 17, n. 61, citing Salimbene, *Chronicon,* MGH SS 32:508. Since Simon was already archdeacon of Rouen, the date 1256, supported by Vaucelle and others for Simon's appointment (Kay, op. cit., p. 464, n. 18) would make him another royal clerk of St. Louis guilty of multiple benefices; is that why he is still listed in the *Parlement* of September, 1258, simply as archdeacon? (*Actes du Parlement* 1:23, no. 285A). He was still treasurer of St. Martin in 1280, according to the *Pancarte blanche* (Bibl. Nat., MS Coll. Housseau, t. 7, no. 3309), though long-since cardinal legate. (Anything is possible if one is a lawyer under the patronage of a saint!). Borelli de Serres pointed out (*Recherches,* p. 263) that the higher-pay (five sous) received in 1261, according to the ordinance on the household, by the treasurer of St. Martin and the dean of St. Aignan (then Etienne de Montfort) indicated they had special financial functions (Arch. Nat., MS JJ57, fol. 23r, published by Perrichet, *Grande Chancellerie,* App. V, p. 548). A more important reason might be that the one was keeper of the seal, and the other, a master of the Exchequer, both regular members of the *Parlements* (List II of my article, "St. Louis and the Clerks"). *v* Exhibit A under Guy for their exchange with the Hospitallers. He was cardinal-priest of St. Cecilia and papal legate when in 1266 he served as counselor to Charles of Anjou and organizer of his campaign into Italy (HF 20: 559e). By 1268 he was instructed by the pope to take over the collection of funds for St. Louis' crusade (E. Berger, "Les Derniers années . . .," Intro. to *Lay.* 4, p.

liii; 4, p. 254, no. 5355). He announced a special royal exemption from the tithe for certain clerks of Alphonse of Poitiers (*Layettes* 5:286, no. 828), which suggests a close relationship with that prince's entourage, perhaps through association with Guy de Neaulphe. As pope in 1282 he conceded to the Dean of St. Martin permanent occupancy of his house (Vaucelle, 203). In 1283 he communicated to his future chaplain, then dean of Chartres, Guillaume Durand (the canon laywer?), an indulgence granted the French king and prelates against excommunication (*Cartulaire de Chartres* 2:226, no. 373).

20. Boussard suggests that Simon de Nesle was not treasurer before March, 1289, which would mean there was another long vacancy (Bibl. Mun. Amiens, MS 1077, fol. 73v, no. 123). Simon de Clermont, lord of Nesle, had been one of St. Louis' closest associates.

21. He became treasurer at age 16 or 17; the office had reverted to an earlier function! Probably he was already warden of St. Quentin in 1296, when he was at a *Parlement* (Klimrath, *Histoire du droit*, p. 113). He may have been "received" by the chapter as late as 1314 (Boussard, p. 83), but there is evidence he was treasurer in 1297 and 1299 (Bibl. Nat., MS Coll. Baluze, t. 76, fol. 194r and v and 196); in 1303, when he was still warden of St. Quentin (Arch. Nat., MS LL985B, fols. 14 and 27v–32, cited by Boussard); in 1306 and thereafter, except for 1307? (Vaucelle, p. 201, n. 3; Bibl. Nat., MS Coll. Baluze, t. 76, fol. 197). King Philip had already been pressing the chapter for his reception when he delivered his mandate of 23 March, 1298 (n.s.) (Bibl. Nat., MS Coll. Housseau, t. 7, fol. 354v, no. 3408).

EXHIBIT C

Other Officers of St-Martin in Royal Service or Entourage*

	Royal Service	Ecclesiastical Office
Gautier[1]	Subscribed diploma of Robert II	Cantor 1007–1029
Gilles Raderii[2] (or Guy)	Keeper of Seal 1249– 1252	Cantor 1235–1249/55? Bsp. of Damietta 1249–1252 Archbsp. of Tyre 1252/54–d. by 1266
Eudes de Lorris[3]	King's clerk: variety of roles by 1248: di- plomatic, financial, and judicial.	Sub-dean 1251–1253? Chevecier of Angers 1252 Chevecier Orléans 1259 Treas. of Bayeux, 1252–1259 Bishop 1263–d. 1274
Gilles de Bonneval[4]	Clerk of Alphonse of Poitiers (King's brother), ca. 1248	Canon from 1211 Sub-dean 1257–1262 Granger 1265–1271 Dean of St–Maurice of Tours?

1. Lem., tableau des souscripteurs, citing Newman, no. 77, whose sources I could not verify. The act was a donation to Marmoutier.

2. v note 81 in the text. He became archbishop in 1254 according to Jean Richard (Bibliothèque de l'Ecole des Chartes 120 [1962], 51). In 1245 he was also prévot of St. Martin in Anjou (Bibl. Nat., MS Coll. Housseau, t. 7, fol. 75, no. 2853). See Perrichet, p. 512. From 1263–65 he helps collect the tithe for the king's crusade, but complains of the competition from Charles of Anjou's campaign (Lay. 4:52 and 81, nos. 4804 and 4893; 5:258, no. 767; 4:161, no. 5119).

3. For more information on his royal service and ecclesiastical advancement, v my article, "St. Louis and the Clerks," p. 274, Lists I–III and App. He was not dean of St. Aignan, and may have resigned as sub-dean before becoming chevecier.

4. He was enquêteur, executor, procureur, and vice–regent for Alphonse in 1270–71. He may also have been cantor. (Enquêtes administratives d'Alphonse de Poitiers, ed. Four-nier and Guebin, pp. xxxvi–xxxvii and ns. 18–22.) A later vidimus records a gift in 1277 by Gilles de Bonneval, as dean of St. Maurice of Tours, the cathedral church (Arch. Dept. Eure and Loire, MS G.1438, liasse: côte K, no. 5).

THE REBELS OF VÉZELAY (1152–55)

Rosalind Kent Berlow
Associate, Rogers & Wells

THE REBELS OF VÉZELAY
(1152–1155)

Now, "commune" is a new and evil name for an arrangement for them all to pay the customary head tax, which they owe their lords as a servile due, in a lump sum once a year, and if anyone commits a crime, he shall pay a fine set by law, and all other financial exactions which are customarily imposed on serfs are completely abolished.[1]

So wrote the Abbot Guibert de Nogent to introduce his account of the communal revolt at Laon in 1112.[2] The communal movement had swept over Northern France in the late eleventh century. Communes were established in Huy in 1066, in Le Mans in 1070, in Cambrai in 1076, and in Beauvais in 1099. Two years after the revolt at Laon, the communes appeared at Amiens and at Valenciennes and, in 1127, at Saint Omer.[3] The passage from Guibert is frequently cited to exemplify the hatred and contempt felt by the established order for this novel institution. As a definition of the commune, however, it is seldom taken seriously.

Pirenne considered arbitrary financial exactions to be one of several aspects of the traditional order which were incompatible with the needs of the new merchant class and which therefore led directly to urban revolts. He denied that any meaningful distinction could be drawn between the communes and other towns. The term "commune" was merely reserved for "those episcopal cities of the north of France where municipal institutions were the result of insurrection."[4] Petit-Dutaillis agreed that the privileges and/or institutions of communes were not significantly different from those found in other towns, except that the citizens of communes had the right to enter into a sworn pact with each other: "C'est une association jurée, pas autre chose."[5] Vermeesch concluded that the commune was not characterized by the participation of any one social or economic class, but, in the course of the twelfth century, it came to be restricted in territory to the town and its environs, and in function to defense.[6]

The difficulty in finding a satisfactory definition of the commune results in large part from the fact that there is so little information available for the earliest period when it was frequently under attack. Guibert's attitude is typical of the hostility of the early narrative accounts. As for the rebels themselves, no evidence is to be expected from their pens. They were, after all, engaged in a highly subversive activity. More reliable evidence comes from the handful of early communal charters,[7] which Pirenne declared responded to the program of the rebels.[8] Those who benefitted the most from the establishment of the commune, he asserted, were the men responsible for the revolt. But is this a valid assumption? Can one assume that those who benefit from a rebellion caused it? Were the communal charters a program for revolution or, as Vermeesch has suggested, a compromise?[9] If we knew who were the rebels, we might find the answer to these questions.[10]

The case of the revolt of Vézelay (1152–55) in central France may suggest some answers.[11] The monastery of Vézelay had been established in the mid-ninth century.[12] After almost two hundred years of obscurity, it suddenly leaped to prominance in the eleventh century as the center of a major pilgrimage route.[13] The lay community grew rapidly outside the walls of the monastery.[14] By the first half of the twelfth century, the settlement at Vézelay had all of the primary attributes of a town. Its inhabitants were personally free and enjoyed a diversified economy.[15] The influx of pilgrims spawned a host of establishments to service their needs. Innkeepers and moneychangers prospered.[16] Taverns flourished, distributing the produce of the vineyards which surrounded the town.[17] Merchants from Vézelay travelled to the fairs of northern France.[18] By the end of the century, the town received a charter defining its liberties,[19] and was surrounded by a protective wall.[20]

Despite the importance of the pilgrimage which the monastery sponsored, there was constant friction between the lay and religious communities. The Abbots of Vézelay claimed secular as well as religious authority and demanded tithes on all produce, rents on lands, hay for the horses of the abbot, hospitality for his guests.[21] Disputes over such obligations led, in 1106, to the assassination of Abbot Artald,[22] and, in the 1120s, to the exile of Abbot Renald.[23] Abbot Alberic forestalled an uprising in 1137 by submitting the issues in dispute between the "burghers" and himself to arbitration.[24] Seven representatives of the burghers were directed to swear on behalf of themselves and the others that they had neither participated in nor had knowledge of the participation of others in a conspiracy against the Abbot.[25] Peace was restored—for the moment.

The prosperity of the town during the decade of the forties[26] postponed the confrontation for a while, but, in 1151, it broke out with explosive force.[27] The local populace complained that year of "new and unjust customs,"[28] which, unfortunately, were not specified. One can imagine the types of complaints from the issues raised by the burghers in 1137. The largest number of complaints at that date concerned agriculture. The burghers complained, for example, that the Abbot had increased the rent on the vineyards, that his officials demanded payment in coin rather than in kind and computed the obligation at a rate higher than the amount for which the wine was sold in the town, that the *decanus* sent his servants into their vineyards to gather grapes without their permission, that the marshall demanded hay for the Abbot's horses, whether or not he was in town, that pastures which were held in common had been withdrawn from their use.[29]

The year, 1151, was also a year of famine.[30] Then there occurred an incident which would probably have gone unrecorded at any other time. A monk patrolling the forests of the monastery came upon a man in the act of felling a tree. The monk attempted to seize the axe as evidence. The man resisted and, in the ensuing struggle, unhorsed the monk and made good his escape. The monastic community was infuriated by this outrage to one of their number. That evening, a band of servants of the monastery attacked the culprit in his home and blinded him.[31] The Abbot of Vézelay, Ponce of Montboissier (1138–61), made no effort to punish those responsible for the assault, belittling the whole episode. When Count William III of Nevers (1147–61), whose lands surrounded the estates of the monastery, sought to intervene, his authority was rejected.[32] The Count therefore withdrew his protection from the territory of Vézelay which was soon overrun by petty local lords who preyed on peasants and merchants alike.[33]

The following year, in 1152, the men of Vézelay, with the encouragement of Count William, established the commune. Leaders and judges were chosen and given the title of *consul*.[34] A local militia was organized. Arms and shields were later found in the homes of rebels after the suppression of the commune.[35] Meetings were held day and night, but their substance has not been preserved. The Abbot fled to the safety of Cluny.[36] The *History of Vézelay* then accuses the rebels of committing sacrileges in the church, invading the monastery and occupying its tower, assaulting the monks and destroying monastic property and facilities. The rebels were excommunicated and reacted furiously when the sentence was pronounced in the parish church. When the monks refused to permit them to use the oven and the mill, the rebels sought the advice of Count William who instructed them, "Go and light the oven with your wood and bake. If anyone prevents you, burn him alive, and if the miller objects, crush him alive with the millstone."[37]

The commune lasted three years. During this period, there was a celebration attended by hundreds of rebels in the neighboring village of Asquins.[38] Abbot Ponce appealed repeatedly to the royal court for help, but Louis VII (1137–80) delayed taking action. At one point, the authority of the Abbot was temporarily restored and Robert the Baker was ordered to submit to a trial by combat. He begged to be excused, but to no avail. An angry crowd gathered at the site for the duel and attacked the monks.[39] Finally, in 1155, Ponce appeared at the royal court and did homage to the King.[40] Thereupon, Louis commanded his vassal, the Count of Nevers, to suppress the rebellion he had been instrumental in launching.[41] On November 3, 1155, a group of more than forty men was required to swear renewed fidelity to the Abbot in the presence of King Louis at Auxerre. The King imposed a penalty of 40,000 *solidi* on these "traitors made loyal," and the Abbot appointed some of them to collect the fine.[42]

These facts are known from the contemporary account of the uprising written by Hugh of Poitiers, a monk of Vézelay and eye-witness to many of the events he narrated.[43] Hugh's *History of Vézelay* is preserved in only one twelfth–century manuscript. Portions of this manuscript, including the section containing the account of the time of the communal regime, were deliberately mutilated under circumstances which remain obscure, probably within about half a century of its final entry.[44] The sequence of events in the mutilated portions can only be perceived in its broadest outlines, precluding definitive statements as to events and institutional developments during the period of the commune at Vézelay.[45]

The loss of the information reported on the mutilated pages is somewhat alleviated by the incorporation of a curious document into the manuscript which was inserted at the end of the section which tells of the suppression of the commune. This document lists a number of criminal acts and names the men charged with these acts.[46] Although the list may not be complete, it probably contains the names of the most active rebels, since the greatest care would have been taken to record the most serious incidents. The information gleaned from this list can be related to the data contained in other sections of the *History* to provide a profile of the rebels of Vézelay in the mid–twelfth century.

The names which appear in the *History* and on the list, in themselves, provide considerable information. The use of a second name to distinguish men with the same first name was just becoming a common practice at this time, but the second name was not yet permanent.[47] Thus, one finds the use of variant forms in the documents of Vézelay conveying the same meaning, such as *Rotbertus furnarius* or *de furno*, or the use of different names for the same man, such as *Aimo de Sancto Christophoro qui dicitur insanus* who appears as *Aimo de Sancto Christophoro* or as *Aimo insanus*. The meaning of the second name is often ambiguous.[48] While one cannot put too much emphasis on the evidence of a single name, the names of over two hundred members of the lay community in the area of Vézelay around the time of the communal revolt are preserved.[49] More than half of these can be identified from the sources as rebels.[50] The names provide information as to occupations, family relationships, and origins.

The discussion which follows is based primarily on the following six sections from the twelfth-century manuscript of the *History of Vézelay:*

A list of men who were called upon to testify in 1146 at the hearings between the Abbot of Vézelay and the Count of Nevers with regard to jurisdiction over the routes leading into the town. These witnesses were frequent travelers, and probably included representatives of the town's merchant class. Sixteen men were so named.[51]

A list of names which appears on a mutilated portion of the manuscript of the chronicle.[52] Those names known from other references are all rebels, so it is assumed that others also are rebels. Thirty-two names can be recovered in whole or in part.[53]

Another list of names which appears on the mutilated pages seems to identify men who were loyal to the Abbot when the monastery was under siege. Thirty-nine names can be recovered in whole or in part.[54]

The names of men who were punished after the suppression

of the commune in 1155. Twelve men were punished by the confiscation of all their property. Six men received a milder penalty of the loss
of wine.[55]

A list of rebels which appears to be an archival document
copied into the manuscript between sections of the narrative account.
Thirteen different criminal activities are listed. Ninety-five different
names appear, some of them being charged with several offenses.[56]

In 1166, the elders (seniores et potentiores) of the town took
refuge in the monastery when the men of the Count of Nevers
invaded the town. Twenty-five names are recorded.[57]

The list of the rebels is the most valuable since it is the most
extensive and provides the most explicit evidence as to the identity of
the rebels. For convenience of reference to the chart of Activities of
the Leaders appended to this article, I shall identify the various
sections of this list by letters. The first three sections of the list relate
to the destruction of vineyards. The very first section of the list (A)
declares, "These caused the uprooting of the vineyards of the dean
and others," and lists nine names.[58] The following sections charge,
(B) "These are the uprooters" (forty–nine names), and (C) "From
Vézelay, there were these at the vineyards of Arnulf of Ferrières"
(seven names).[59] Such distinctions permit one to identify those who
were considered the instigators on this occasion and reveal that both
townspeople and non-residents of the town were involved.

The next group of charges on the list of the rebels relates to
the celebration held at the home of Robert Quarrel in Asquins, a
village at the foot of the hill of Vézelay. Six men were accused of
confiscating the grain of the Marshall (D),[60] while ten men were
alleged to have received flour from them (E), the amount received
being noted next to each name.[61] The first six men were also charged
with taking eleven pigs which they slaughtered at the home of Robert
Quarrel and divided among the leaders of the revolt (F). These six
and twenty-two others seized hens, chickens, geese, and pigeons (G).
This section ends with the statement, "The rabble ate the others."[62]

The list of the rebels continues, recording the names of the
men who destroyed the grange of Pâtis (H), the mill of the Dean (I),
the mill of the granary (J), and those who absconded with the supplies
of the grange of Saint-Père (K). It concluded on an ominous note:
"These swore death to the Abbot" (L), and "Death to William the
Constable" (M).[63] The pages of the Chronicle describe the destruction
of property,[64] but the oaths were evidently ineffectual. Abbot Ponce

survived the commune by six years.[65] There is no further information
as to the fate of the Constable. The list of the rebels makes no specific
accusations of violence against persons except for these threats. The
Chronicle does refer to assaults resulting in death and injury, but
never mentions either a victim or an assailant by name.[66] Such a lack
of specificity raises doubts as to the credibility of the accusations.

Thirteen men appear on the list of the rebels in the capacity
of leaders. The Chronicle names twelve men who can be presumed to
be leaders since they received the more severe punishment for their
role in the revolt. The two lists agree in the cases of five men: Hugh of
Saint-Père, Peter of Saint-Père, Peter Galimard, Renald Daudet, and
Robert the Baker.[67] Since the lists were compiled for different reasons, the discrepancies should not be considered contradictory. To
the extent that they agree, they highlight the prominence of these five
men. While the list of the rebels was concerned with assigning
culpability for specific acts, the narrative was concerned with the
confiscation of property and may simply have omitted mentioning the
landless and/or the non-residents of the town. The punishments seem
more indicative of the responsibility ascribed to the participants than
to the violence of their acts or intentions. One would expect those who
swore death to the Abbot to be punished severely, but, in most cases,
their fate has gone unrecorded.

One of the five men named above, Hugh of Saint-Père, was
always mentioned in the Chronicle with particular venom. A suprascript on one of the mutilated leaves of the manuscript describes him
as one of the "principes factionis."[68] He was introduced as "*Hugo de
Sancto Petro advena,* ignoble by birth and manners, to whom nature
offered little, but skill in mechanical arts brought wealth."[69] This
introduction has proven to be fertile soil for the imaginations of
nineteenth-century historians. Augustin Thierry described Hugh as
an immigrant from Saint-Pierre in the Midi, who introduced southern French concepts of municipal government, such as the use of the
title *consul,* into his new home.[70] To Aimé Chérest, author of the basic
three-volume monograph on Vézelay, Hugh was a "rich industrialist"
to whom the Count of Nevers turned in a time of financial embarrass-
ment.[71]

The name, *de Sancto Petro,* was the excuse for connecting
Hugh with southern France. Since the name has obvious connections
with local communities, including upper Saint-Père on the hill of
Vézelay and lower Saint-Père at its base, a reference to a southern

French community seems unlikely.[72] Nor does the use of the title *consul* indicate contact with the south, since it was known in the region. The Counts of Nevers used that title.[73] Officials of popular brotherhoods also were known as *consuls*.[74] As for the suggestion that Hugh lent money to the Count, the Chronicle provides no evidence to indicate that he was a money-lender. All we know is that his property was in real estate and his economic interests were those related to the local agrarian society.[75] The connotations of the term "rich industrialist" are certainly inappropriate for such a man who would probably be more aptly described as a prosperous peasant.

At the time of the revolt, Hugh was a resident of the town of Vézelay in the parish of Upper Saint-Père.[76] He was a mature man with a son and perhaps grandsons *(nepotes)* old enough to participate in the rebellion.[77] Hugh may have been born outside the territory of Vézelay,[78] but, on the eve of the revolt, he was probably a long-time resident, if one can judge from his contacts and properties. In 1151, when the conflict first erupted, Hugh was mentioned as an intermediary between the Count of Nevers and the rural populace living on the lands of the monastery.[79] Hugh owned mills and ponds,[80] properties consistent with his "mechanical skills" as well as his rural connections. After the establishment of the commune, when the monks of Vézelay refused to let the excommunicated rebels use their mill and press,[81] Hugh constructed a wine-press in the basement of his home.[82] After the suppression of the commune, his property was destroyed and confiscated.[83] Hugh disappears from the record.

Of the twenty leaders who are known, only four, Hugh of Saint-Père, Peter of Saint-Père, Odo of the Marsh, and Robert Little-Boot, are identifiable from the sources as inhabitants of the town.[84] John the Pastry-Cook, Michelet, and Robert Champereux were not, and members of the immediate families of three other leaders also lived outside the town. A majority of the twenty men who swore death to the Abbot were probably non-residents.[85] Family attachments are often mentioned among the rebels. There were four leaders whose sons and grandsons or nephews are mentioned as participating in the revolt. Two other leaders, Geoffroy Quentin *(Quintini)* and Peter Galimard *(Galimardi)* are identified by surnames in the genitive case, a contraction of "son of X," which at this date, when the use of a second name was still in flux, may indicate that the names of their fathers were also known in the area. At a time when a large proportion of the residents were recent immigrants,[86] these leaders seem to be drawn from a more stable element of the population.

Several leaders had names which referred to neighboring localities. The name, *de Sancto Petro*, was borne by two leaders, Hugh and Peter, who were probably residents of the parish of Upper Saint-Père within the town, as well as by another rebel, Claude, who was probably from the village of Saint-Père at the foot of the hill of Vézelay.[87] The names of the leaders Odo of the Marsh and Robert of the Cross probably refer to landmarks in the immediate vicinity which would have been known to other members of the community.[88] Other rebels bore names referring to nearby villages, such as Nanchèvre, Esclarlis, Bourgelier, Asquins, and Saint-Christophe.[89] The importance of the role played by inhabitants of nearby villages can be seen in the prominence of charges related to the feast at Asquins. Were this a function of some merchant or craft gild, the activity would probably have been held within the town limits and the participants would have been restricted to members of the appropriate group of townspeople. In this case, however, the feast was held outside the town and included both townsmen and non-residents, including, among others, John the Shepherd. The circumstances and participants were more appropriate to functions of popular groups, such as confraternities, which were widespread at this date.[90]

Attempts have been made to link the rebels of Vézelay with commercially advanced centers of France and Italy,[91] without much success. The case for Hugh of Saint-Père has already been examined and found wanting. Another case is that of Arnulf *de Ferrariis*, who has been cited by scholars as establishing a connection with Ferrara, Italy.[92] It is much more likely that Arnulf came from a place called "Ferrières," of which there are literally hundreds in France, including the *Bois des Ferrières* near Vézelay. Moreover, Arnulf was not a rebel but was so strongly identified with the monastic cause that his vineyards were uprooted in the course of the rebellion.

Simon of Souvigny was the only man whose name refers to a center of any economic importance who was active during the period of the commune. By the time of the communal revolt Simon was probably the wealthiest man in the town.[93] Although Simon was active in Vézelay during the period of the commune,[94] it is not likely that he was allied with the rebels. He enjoyed generous privileges from the monastery at the time of his arrival in the town and the fact that he continued to enjoy local prominence after the restoration of the Abbot precludes a major role on his part in the rebellion.[95] Nevertheless, the chronicler of Vézelay referred to him as "the impious Simon," and to his home as "both the cause and beginnings of all evils,"[96] because it was fortified without authorization. As a money-dealer, Simon would have had great need for protection during the period of unrest attendant with the establishment of the commune.

When the monastic administration took action against Simon, its timing seems to have been coincidental but unrelated to the revolt. On November 21, 1155, shortly after the suppression of the commune, Pope Adrian (1154–59) wrote Abbot Ponce, denouncing the privileges Ponce had granted to Simon as contrary to ecclesiastical custom which prohibited the gift, sale, or alienation of property of the church. The Pope instructed Ponce to revoke these privileges.[97] The monks of Vézelay complied with alacrity, destroying Simon's counter, as well as the entry to his home.[98] This was the only action reported against him and was clearly in response to the papal missive. Had Simon also been guilty of rebellion, it seems probable that this too would have been mentioned as added justification for the rescission of Simon's privileges.

There is little more to suggest that the rebels had distant ties. The name of Stephan Jerusalem is probably a nickname, perhaps referring to a resident who had visited the Holy Land.[99] The names *Alamannus, Normannus, Turonensis,* indicate distant origins but are too vague to be used to demonstrate commercial ties. Gilbert of Toul, a man who must have been considered as a prominent member of the lay community, may be cited as an exception. Gilbert of Toul was one of three men who were mentioned by name out of a group of forty burghers of Vézelay who renewed their oath of loyalty to the Abbot after the suppression of the commune in the presence of the King.[100] This is the only reference to Gilbert who was evidently not active in the revolt.

In 1137, five of the seven oathtakers in the Agreement between the Abbot and the "burghers" of Vézelay, bore occupational names, including Aimo, son of Aimo the Money-Changer, David the Money-Changer, Gilbert the Pastry-Chef, Durand the Innkeeper, and Fulbert the Mercer.[101] Very few of the communal rebels, however, bore occupational names and only one of the leaders, Robert the Baker, is so named. Robert was a central figure in one of the more dramatic episodes during the period of the commune when the Abbot commanded him to take part in a judicial duel. Ponce later referred to the incident as involving a *servus.*[102] Robert's name, referring to a facility maintained in normal times by the lord and often staffed by servile labor, adds credence to this allegation, but since Robert's home was later destroyed and his goods confiscated,[103] servile status was evidently no barrier to owning property.

Of those who swore "Death to the Abbot," only John the Shepherd bears an occupational name. Among the rebels who played less prominent roles, one finds Dodo, the Re-Seller of Hay, an inhabitant of the town, Walter Treading-Hay, a non-resident who was active with his brothers on several occasions and John the Pastry-Cook, who was accused of stealing grain. Other rebels bore names suggesting some connection with the monastic regime, such as Renald, the nephew (or grandson) of Robert the Chaplain, and the Prefect Stephan,[104] who was accused of appropriating a column and two beams from the mill of Pâtis, which the rebels had destroyed. The activities of Jonah, son of the Paganus Seguin, may indicate involvement on the part of a member of the petty rural nobility.[105]

Where were the long-distance merchants? Where were the artisans? Where were the money-dealers? With the possible exception of Simon of Souvigny, these groups are conspicuously absent from the pages of the *History* at the time of the commune. One would expect the author to be particularly concerned with recording the activities of prominent merchants whenever appropriate. Of the seven burghers who represented the townspeople in 1137, the name of only one, Durand the Innkeeper, reappears among the participants in the revolt. Durand suffered the milder punishment after the suppression of the commune, but there is no record of the charges against him.

Perhaps the other oath-takers of 1137 had died in the interim, but other merchants resided in the town on the eve of the outbreak of the revolt. Where was Aimeric the Wax-Dealer or Blancard the Tailor,[106] or any of the other artisans or businessmen who undoubtedly lived and worked in the town? In 1146, when hearings were held concerning jurisdiction over the routes leading to and from the town,[107] witnesses who were called on to testify probably included merchants who would have been familiar with these conditions. One of the witnesses, Renald Dautran, might be the rebel leader listed as Renald Daudet.[108] Goodfriend of Châtel Censoir also testified; was Hugh, son of Goodfriend, who was included with the rebels, his son? Arnulf of Ferrières also testified in 1146, but, as noted above, he was the enemy of the rebels.

One group of local tradesmen was evidently involved in the

revolt. Six men were named as having received the relatively mild punishment of having their wine poured out.[109] They were probably wine-merchants, owners of vineyards, and/or innkeepers. The names of two of them, Durand the Innkeeper and Hugh Frying-Bread (*Fricans-Panum*),[110] suggest occupations servicing visitors to the town. Most of the men whose punishment was mentioned in the narrative account were accused on the list of the rebels of acts which would justify the punishment. Hugh Frying-Bread was an exception, but, while he was not included on the list, he was mentioned elsewhere with a group of rebels. In addition, during the period of the commune, he had constructed a wine-press in the basement of his house which was destroyed after the restoration of the Abbot. Despite their participation in the revolt, both Hugh and Durand continued to reside in Vézelay and enjoy local prominence. Durand appeared again in 1165 as a spokesman for the burghers, and Hugh was mentioned in 1166 as one of a group of men identified as the "elders and most powerful people of Vézelay".

The lack of evidence of participation on the part of the merchant class has already been mentioned. Another important group of townsmen, identifiable on the basis of their political role rather than their economic activity, also seems to have played no part. These are the town elders (*maiores natu*). In 1152, shortly after the formation of the commune, the elders made a futile attempt to resolve the conflict. The chronicler of Vézelay described them as men who "seemed to be the heads of the people,"[111] suggesting that they had no official standing. The fact that they were received by the Abbot militates against interpreting the phrase to mean that they were the leaders of the commune. Moreover, a decade later, long after the suppression of "the detestable commune," the elders were still prominent in Vézelay. At that time, there was a dispute with Count William IV of Nevers (1161–68) about the salt tax. The new Abbot, William of Mello (1161–71), claiming ignorance of the customs, promised to call the elders of the town and other wise men and to follow their advice.[112]

The elders of 1165 were evidently recognized as authorities on local custom. The elders of 1152 had also come to discuss questions of local custom, requesting the remission of "certain new and tyrannical customs."[113] That account of the abortive meeting of 1152 is the earliest appearance of the term "the elders" in the sources from Vézelay, but such a group was undoubtedly in existence long before that date. We may find their trace in the agreement of 1137 which had been concerned with local customs. It does not seem far-fetched to suspect that those men who were called upon to speak and to swear on behalf of their fellow townspeople were none other than the elders. These men were representative of the local business community. The agreement of 1137 also contained provisions which imply the existence of a popular tribunal having jurisdiction particularly over the market-place, another area in which the elders were probably involved. The decisions rendered with regard to punishment for false weights and the right of the Abbot to appeal to extend his ban on wine sales,[114] both imply the existence of some tribunal. Similarly, the demand on the part of the burghers that the Abbot rectify his injuries to the men of Saint-Père and other villages through them,[115] implies some functioning body.

In the 1160s, the most prominent burghers could also count on the protection of the monastery in a time of danger. In 1166, when the men of Nevers attacked the town, twenty-five men, the "senior and most powerful of the people of Vézelay,"[116] found refuge behind the walls of the Abbey. The names of only six of these men appear in the sources from the time of the commune, three of them as rebels. The first, Hugh Frying-Bread, needs no introduction at this stage. The other two, John Girard and Girard *Dalmacii*, appeared in the company of known rebels but there is no other record of their participation. On the other hand, Albert Cardinal was named among those who remained loyal to the Abbot, enduring the siege of the monastery with the monks. Two men, Renald of Saint-Christophe and John Rufus, appear in the chronicle, but their roles cannot be determined. Nineteen men out of twenty-five, however, were not mentioned at all at the time of the communal revolt.

Around the year 1200, the inhabitants of Vézelay finally received a charter, and the "liberties of Vézelay" set a model for grants to several other communities.[117] The charter indicates that the status of the townspeople had declined since the time of the agreement of 1137. The charter abolished *mortmain,* a custom which was not mentioned at all in 1137 when rights of inheritance by descendants were recognized without qualification.[118] In the charter, the fee for the use of the wine-press of the monastery was one pint and eight deniers, as opposed to one pint and one denier in 1137. As for the regulation of commerce, the charter stipulated that the marketplace would continue to be regulated as it had been in the time of

Abbots Alberic and Ponce, over half a century earlier. Nevertheless, the charter of around 1200 did provide the burghers with a written statement of their privileges which clearly distinguished them from the populace of the surrounding countryside. By the time of its issuance, a wall encircled the town, further emphasizing the separation of rural and urban society.

* * * *

The communal revolt, which swept through Vézelay in the mid-twelfth century, involved a broad spectrum of regional society, including townspeople, villagers, peasants, local tradesmen, members of the class of local officials and perhaps even representatives of the petty nobility. Although its manifestations centered around the town, its leadership was drawn from both urban and non-urban localities and included men with close familial, geographic, and economic ties with the rural society. The communal revolt of Vézelay was not limited to the urban community.

Merchants involved in long-distance trade and money-lenders, those representatives of the newly developing commercial class, were conspicuous by their absence. One of their number, Arnulf of Ferrières, was so strongly identified with the monastic regime that his property also suffered from the attacks of the rebels. Those tradesmen who participated in the revolt had occupations involved in the distribution of agricultural products and/or agricultural services. While it is always possible that the picture has been grossly distorted by a practice of identifying the merchants who were active by other names, in the absence of evidence to the contrary, the burden of proof must rest with those who would affirm their participation.

The aftermath of the revolt may provide clues as to how it came to be that, in the course of the twelfth century, the commune was transformed into an urban institution. The role of the elders may provide the key. One of the immediate causes of the communal revolt had been the refusal of Abbot Ponce to respect local custom which the elders represented. After having experienced the fury of the commune, however, Ponce was willing to recognize the position of certain townsmen, probably those who were most prosperous, for the purpose of collecting the fine which had been imposed by the King. His successor, Abbot William, went even further and willingly sought counsel from the elders on a question of local custom. The leading townsmen of his time included only a few who were even marginally involved in the communal revolt. Most had played no part at all in that episode.

There is a connection between the communal revolt and the acquisition of power on the part of the urban leadership, but it is not a direct one. One can assume that a broad-based revolt (or even the threat of one) would lead to some concessions on the part of those in power, but only the minimum necessary to defuse the situation. The urban community included, on the one hand, merchants and money-dealers who already enjoyed the lord's protection and privileges and upon whose loyalty he could generally count, and, on the other, local tradesmen who were potentially the most active element in the revolt and were in direct contact with the rural populace which provided the most volatile element in the rebellion. If the lord could satisfy the urban component and unite these two factions, the commune could be deprived of much of its leadership and focus.

As just one town of thousands in the process of evolution at this time, the example of Vézelay is, of course, too infinitessimal a part of the total picture to prove or disprove a particular theory. It is, moreover, atypical in many respects. Vézelay was not on the mainstream of commercial development and its economy was closely tied to the established order. In addition, the revolt was a failure. It is possible that the peculiar features noted in connection with the communal revolt at Vézelay were the factors which contributed to its ultimate defeat.

The mainstream of commercial development, however, is more apparent in hindsight than it was in the twelfth century. At the time of the revolt, Vézelay was at the height of its importance and the fact that it had no commercial future would hardly have been obvious to contemporaries. As for the fact that the revolt was a failure, defeated movements share the same objectives as successful ones. The unusual nature of the evidence from Vézelay, which reports who actually took part in the revolt, as opposed to the communal charters which record who benefitted from it, is of extraordinary significance for the history of the movement whose success was not immediate or automatic.

It may be that, in the twelfth century, the new commercial class, rather than being the revolutionary bearers of progress on the political scene, were, instead, a conservative force, swept into power in the wake of popular uprisings which they then contributed to control. If we accept this scenario, it would appear that the sharp division between rural and urban society, which characterized the later medieval world was the indirect result of, not the cause of, the communal movement.

NOTES

Earlier versions of this paper were presented at the Columbia University Seminar in the History of Legal and Political Thought, New York City, on February 20, 1975, and at the Tenth Conference on Medieval Studies sponsored by the Medieval Institute, Western Michigan University, Kalamazoo, Michigan, May 5, 1975.

[1] *Guibert de Nogent: Histoire de sa vie,* ed. Georges Bourgin, Collection de textes pour servir à l'étude et à l'enseignement de l'histoire, No. 40 (Paris, 1907), pp. 156–57; English translation by C. C. Swinton Bland, revised by John F. Benton, *Self and Society in Medieval France* (New York, 1970), p. 167. Henceforth the Latin text will be cited as Bourgin; the English translation will be cited as Benton.

[2] Bourgin, p. 183; Benton, p. 188. For the charter granted to Laon in 1128, *v Ordonnances des rois de France* (Paris, 1723–1849), 11:185–87 (hereafter *Ordonnances*).

[3] The literature on the medieval communes of France is enormous. Most of the major communes are included in Philippe Dollinger and Philippe Wolff, *Bibliographie d'histoire des villes de France* (Paris, 1967). *v* also the bibliography in Charles Petit-Dutaillis, *Les communes françaises* (Paris, 1947; repr., 1970, with supplementary bibliography).

[4] Henri Pirenne, *Les villes du moyen âge* (Brussels, 1927); English translation by Frank D. Halsey, *Medieval Cities* (repr. New York, 1956). Reference will be made to the readily available English translation: *v* p. 129. The commune, however, was not limited to episcopal cities; *v* the example of St. Omer, in A. Giry, *Histoire de la ville de St. Omer et de ses institutions jusqu'au XIVe siècle* (Paris, 1877). Vézelay was also originally a monastic foundation: *v* discussion below. Nor was the commune always established by violence: *v* the examples of Laon and Amiens which were originally granted upon payment of a sum of money: *v* Bourgin, pp. 156, 197; Benton, pp. 167, 200. As a corrective to Pirenne's tendency to ignore regional differences, *v* Edith Ennen, "Les differents types de formations des villes européenes," *Le Moyen Age* 62 (1956), 397–411. Pirenne's theory, however, continues to be cited uncritically. For a recent article which continues to adhere to the Pirennist assumptions, *v* Paul H. Freedman, "An Unsuccessful Attempt at Urban Organization in Twelfth-Century Catalonia," *Speculum* 54 (1979), 479–89.

[5] Petit-Dutaillis, (at n. 3), p. 35.

[6] Albert Vermeesch, *Essai sur les origines et la signification de la commune dans le Nord de la France,* Études presentées à la Commission internationale pour l'histoire des assemblées d'états, 30 (Heule, 1966), pp. 175–83.

[7] For those which pre-date the revolt at Vézelay, *v* Beauvais (1144) in L. H. Labande, *Histoire de Beauvais et de ses institutions communales jusqu'au commencement du XVe siècle,* (Paris, 1892), p. j. 8; Laon (1128) in *Ordonnances*, 11:185–87; Mantes (1150) in *Ordonnances*, 11:197; Saint-Omer (1127) in A. Giry, (at n. 4), p. j. 3; Saint-Riquier (1126) in *Ordonnances,* 11:184; Valenciennes (1114) in MGH SS 21:605–10. The contents of others can be known from later confirmations.

[8] H. Pirenne, *Medieval Cities,* (Garden City, N.Y., 1956) p. 136; for a more detailed analysis of the charters along these lines, *v* E. W. Dow, "Some French Communes in the Light of their Charters," *AHR,* 8 (1903), 641–56.

[9] Vermeesch, (at n. 6), p. 178.

[10] For examples of studies of the origins of the urban populace, *v* A. B. Hibbert, "The Origins of the Medieval Town Patriciate," *Past and Present,* 3 (1953), 15–27 and Jean Lestocquoy, "L'Origine des habitants d'Arras aux XIIe et XIIIe siècles d'après les noms de famille," *Annales de la fédération archéologique et historique de Belgique,* 35e congrès (Cambrai, 1954), fasc. 3, pp. 157–62.

[11] For a bibliography of the monographic literature on the history of Vézelay, *v* Rosalind Kent Berlow, "Social and Economic Aspects of the Early History of Vézelay, 9th–12th Centuries" (City University of New York dissertation; University Microfilms No. 72982, 1971), pp. 405–09. Excerpts from this dissertation have been revised for publication in "Spiritual Immunity at Vézelay, 9th–12th Centuries," *Catholic Historical Review* 62 (1976), 573–88; "The Case of André du Marais," *American Journal of Legal History* 24 (1980), 133–44; and "The Case of the Disappearing Abbot," *Studia Monastica* 23 (1981), 325–38.

[12] Three of the four documents which relate to the foundation of the monastery are included in *Monumenta Vizeliacensia,* ed. R. B. C. Huygens (Corpus Christianorum, Continuatio Mediaevalis 42; Turnholt, 1976), pp. 244–258 (henceforth *Monumenta*). The fourth is preserved in a manuscript in the Laurentiana, Plut. XIV, Cod. XXI, published in *Catalogus codicum latinorum Bibliothecae Laurentianae,* ed. A. M. Bandini (Florence, 1774), 1:134–35, and in a manuscript from Saint-Germain published in *Cartulaire général de l'Yonne,* ed. Max Quantin (2 vols., Auxerre, 1854–1860), 2:4–5. On the early status of the monastery, *v* Berlow, *Catholic Historical Review* 62 (1976), 573–88.

[13] For the earliest references to the cult of Mary Magdalene at Vézelay, *v* *Gesta Episcoporum Cameracensium* (ca. 1043–44), MGH SS 7:464, and for the privilege of Pope Leo IX (27 April 1050), *v* *Monumenta,* pp. 291–93.

[14] In 1137, the requirement that the burghers provide hospitality was reduced to half of that required prior to 1106 because of the growth of the population; *v* *Cartulaire* 1:316. In 1155, the Count of Nevers observed that the majority of the inhabitants of the town were newcomers: *Monumenta,* p. 497.

[15] Hugh of Poitiers was inconsistent in the terms he used to describe the locality, referring to it at times as a *vicus* (*Monumenta,* p. 419), a *villa* (p. 421), or an *oppidum* (p. 497). The inhabitants were referred to as *oppidani* or *vicani* (sic) (p. 500) or *burgenses* (p. 504). On the development of the town, *v* Berlow, "Social and Economic Aspects, (n. 11)" pp. 248–341. On the early use of the term *burgus,* *v* Traute Endemann, *Markturkund und Markt in Frankreich und Burgund vom 9. bis 11. Jahrhundert* (Konstanz, 1964), pp. 158–61.

[16] Durand the Innkeeper, for example, appeared as a representative of the townspeople in 1137: *v* *Cartulaire,* 1:321. Simon of Souvigny may have arrived in town shortly after 1138, when Abbot Ponce of Montboissier took office. Ponce actively supported local bankers and granted Simon the privilege of setting up a counter on very generous terms: *v* *Monumenta,* pp. 392–93. Chérest, *Étude,* 1:118, n. 2, suggested the identification of Ponce with an early twelfth-century prior of Souvigny, but this seems doubtful. His career prior to his coming to Vézelay does not seem to have been particularly distinguished. The Little Chronicle of Vézelay, *Monumenta,* p. 226, records only "MCXXXVIII. Poncius abbas Vizeliaci ordinatur.

Hic frater Petri Cluniacensis abbatis de Clusino monasterio assumptus est." During Ponce's exile from Vézelay at the time of the commune, his brother reluctantly granted him the monastery of Souvigny; v the letter of Anastasius IV to Peter, A.-C. Chaix de Lavarène, *Monumenta Pontificia Arnarniae* (Clermont-Ferrand, 1886), pp. 230–31, instructing him to rescind the grant. Pope Adrian's reference to Simon's installation at Vézelay might refer to the brief period around 1153 in which Ponce temporarily was restored after a time in exile at Souvigny. This might explain the apparent delay on the part of the Pope in denouncing the concession to Simon. Ponce also solicited the pope's help on behalf of money-lenders of Vézelay in collecting debts from the Abbot of Chôre; v *Monumenta*, p. 359.

[17] Gui de Bazoches, who joined the crusading armies at Vézelay in 1190, left a description of the town surrounded by verdant vineyards, delightful both in the charm of its site and in the abundance of the liquid "which gladdens the heart"; v Epistola 34 in *Liber Epistularum Guidonis de Basochis*, ed. Herbert Adolfsson, Acta Universitatis Stockholmiensis: *Studia Latina Stockholmiensia*, 18 (1969), 145. In 1137, the largest number of grievances related to the growth, processing and sale of wines: v *Cartulaire* 1:315–23.

[18] In 1152, the pope forbade the bishops of Langres, Troyes, Paris, and Sens to admit the excommunicated burghers of Vézelay to their fairs, and similar instructions were sent to the lay authorities of Burgundy, Bourbon, Chalon, Jovigny, Donzy, Rougemont, Luzy, Monreal, Sens, Vergy, Mont Saint Jean and Château-Landon: v *Monumenta*, pp. 366–69.

[19] The charter of Vézelay has not survived, but its text was incorporated into other charters: v *Cartulaire* 2:507–509.

[20] Victor Petit, *Description des villes et campagnes du département de l'Yonne. II: Arrondissement d'Avallon* (Auxerre, 1870), pp. 251–52, asserted that the construction of the enclosing wall began in the first years of the twelfth century. I have been unable to find any confirmation of that date in the evidence. The facts that, during the period of the commune, the burghers found it necessary to fortify their own homes, *Monumenta*, pp. 504–05, and that, in the 1160s, the men of Nevers had no difficulty in riding into town and harrassing the inhabitants (*ibid.* p. 586), indicate that it was not yet in existence. It must have been built by 1196, when the town of Vézelay was able to withstand a siege, while neighboring villages were burned; v Robert of Auxerre, "Chronicle of Saint Marian of Auxerre," RHF 18:261. The "Little Chronicle of Vézelay," *Monumenta*, p. 229, referred to the campaign but did not mention the siege.

[21] The Agreement of 1137 contains the most complete list of grievances; v *Cartulaire*, 1:314–23.

[22] *Monumenta*, pp. 302, 311, and 433. v also the *Annales Ordinis Sancti Benedicti*, ed. J. Mabillon (Paris, 1703–39), 5:497.

[23] The "Little Chronicle of Vézelay," *Monumenta*, p. 225, mentioned the ordination of Abbot Baldwin in 1124, an event also referred to in the Chronicle, p. 403. Abbot Renald continued to use the title, Abbot of Vézelay, even after the assumption of Baldwin; v RHF 14:232 and *Annales Benedicti* 6:204. The circumstances are discussed in greater detail in Berlow, "The Case of the Disappearing Abbot," pp. 325–38.

[24] v n. 21.

[25] In addition to the five who were identified by profession, there were Durand *Glaiel*

(Gladiolus) and Peter Letard, probably a member of a family which provided officials to both the Abbot of Vézelay and the Count of Nevers; on Hugh Letard, Prévôt of Châtel-Censoir around 1106, and Simon, son of Odo, the Prefect of Vézelay and maternal uncle of Hugh Letard, v *Monumenta*, pp. 535, 538, 571, 586 and 603.

[26] The most spectacular event was the preaching of the second crusade at Vézelay: v *Sacrorum Conciliorum Amplissima Collectio*, ed. J. D. Mansi (Florence-Venice, 1759–98), 21, cols. 691–94.

[27] Huygens, following Aimé Chérest, dated the outbreak of the rebellion in 1150; v *Monumenta* p. 72 and n. 2. A two-year interval between the first outbreak and the establishment of the commune seems excessive and cannot be explained by intervening events.

[28] *Monumenta*, p. 427. On Abbot Ponce of Montboissier, v Giles Constable, *Letters of Peter the Venerable* (Cambridge, Mass., 1967), 2:233–45 and Rose Graham, *An Abbot of Vézelay*, (London: 1918). I cannot agree with their laudatory appraisals of Ponce's character. For the views of Peter the Venerable on his brother, Ponce, v Constable, *Letters*, 1:23, in which he warns Ponce not to spurn "caritas," and *Monumenta*, p. 442, where he chastises his brother who had taken refuge with him during the period of the commune.

[29] *Cartulaire*, 1:314–23.

[30] *Monumenta*, p. 227.

[31] *Monumenta*, p. 425. Huygens, ibid., p. 71, n. 1, recounts another version of the episode preserved in the local lore, involving the murder of a monk who had seduced the wife of an innkeeper.

[32] *Monumenta*, p. 426: "Arridens abbas quasi ludo, utrum iusiusticiae ab eo dignaretur accipere requisivit. Quo negante."

[33] The Count denied responsibility for their actions, ibid., p. 436, but if he had not actually provoked the petty lords, he could certainly have restrained them.

[34] *Monumenta*, p. 435.

[35] *Monumenta*, p. 502. It was probably the army of the commune which attacked the monastery. Unfortunately, the account occurs in the section of the manuscript which was mutilated; v ibid., p. 487.

[36] *Monumenta*, p. 438.

[37] *Monumenta*, p. 439.

[38] *Monumenta*, p. 439.

[39] *Monumenta*, pp. 476–78.

[40] A mutilated page, *Monumenta*, p. 495, preserved the fragment, "Abbas: Ego, ait, in manu tua sum."

[41] On May 21, 1155, the Pope threatened the Count with excommunication: v *Monumenta*, pp. 382–83, apparently without effect.

[42] *Monumenta*, pp. 503–504.

[43] The text is preserved in the Municipal Library of Auxerre, ms. No. 227, fols. 22–176. It is published in *Monumenta*.

[44] *Monumenta*, pp. 443–96 and 591–602.

[45] Achille Luchaire, *Histoire des institutions monarchiques de la France* (2nd ed. Paris, 1891), 2:182, n. 6, denied the existence of a commune at Vézelay. The word "commune," however, is specifically used in the sources: e. g., the Letter of Pope Hadrian IV to King Louis VII of May 21, 1155, *Monumenta*, pp. 388–89, which

directed "et burgenses abiurare communiam quam fecerent . . .," and the Chronicle, ibid., pp. 435, 441, and 446. *v* also Suger, *Gesta Ludovici Regis*, ed. Molinier, in *Vie de Louis le Gros suivie de l'histoire du roi Louis VII* (Collection des textes pour servir à l'enseignement de l'histoire; Paris, 1887), p. 174. The existence of the commune was discussed in the exchange of articles between Léon de Bastard, "Recherches sur l'insurrection communale de Vézelay au XIIe siècle," and F. Bourquelot, "Observations sur l'établissement de la commune de Vézelay," in the pages of the *Bibliothèque de l'Ecole des Chartes*, sér. 3, 2 (1851) 339–65 and 3 (1852) 447–63, respectively.

[46] *v* above, p. 142.

[47] *v* A. Giry, *Manuel de Diplomatique* (Paris: 1894), pp. 351–76; and, for words of caution on the use of this evidence, *v* Richard W. Emery, "The Use of the Surname in the Study of Medieval Economic History," *Medievalia et Humanistica*, 7 (1952), 43–50.

[48] *v Rotbertus Furnarius*, *Monumenta*, p. 507, and *de Furno*, p. 473, or the use of different names or nicknames for the same person, such as *Aimo de Sancto Christophoro qui dicitur insanus*, p. 502. The manuscript contains corrections in a contemporary hand, which underscore the ambiguity; *Guibertus Leucensis* was corrected to read *Lotariensis*, *Monumenta*, p. 504, while *Joslenus de turribus* was corrected to *Turonensis*, p. 473.

[49] It is not possible to give a precise count of the persons named in the manuscript due to the condition of the manuscript and to the possibility that persons may be known by more than one name.

[50] Robert Latouche, "La commune du Mans (1070)," *Mélanges d'histoire du moyen âge dédiées à la mémoire de Louis Halphen* (Paris, 1951), pp. 377–82, studied the names preserved on the documents from Le Mans, but was unable to identify the rebels. Finding little evidence of a commercial class in Le Mans, Latouche concluded that the failure of the commune was due to their absence. He did not consider the alternative, that a commune was not dependent on the existence of a commercial class.

[51] Latouche (at n. 50), p. 422.

[52] Aimé Chérest, *Etude historique sur Vézelay* (3 vols., Auxerre, 1863), reprinted in part in *Monumenta*, pp. 1–194, attempted to reconstruct the events on the mutilated pages, but his account is often suspect. *v*, e.g., Chérest, (*Étude*, 1:227), who concluded that an attempt was made on Ponce's life while *en route* to Lyons. The fragmentary remains of the pages in the manuscript, *v Monumenta*, pp. 483–86, permit one to conclude no more than that the Abbot fled in fear. Again, Chérest (*Étude*, 1:232–33), recounted an incident involving the murder of a messenger by the rebel Aimo of Saint-Christophe. Since an account of a banquet occurs between the interception of the messenger and the description of a throat being slit, *v Monumenta*, p. 491, it seems more than likely that the throat belonged to one of the animals being butchered for the feast.

[53] *Monumenta*, p. 473.

[54] *Monumenta*, p. 487.

[55] *Monumenta*, p. 502.

[56] *Monumenta*, pp. 507–11.

[57] *Monumenta*, p. 587.

[58] *Monumenta*, p. 507: "Isti sunt qui fecerunt extirpare vineas decani et alias."

[59] *Monumenta,* pp. 507–508: "Isti sunt extirpatores . . . De Vizeliaco fuerunt isti ad vineam Arnulfi de Ferrariis."

[60] *Monumenta,* p. 508: "Isti sunt qui ceperunt annonam de Mares." Hugyens, ibid., p. 659, suggested that the last word should be "Maerz," the name of a town in the territory of Nevers. The agreement of 1137 mentioned the marshall as the official responsible for assigning the duty of hospitality to the townspeople and as receiving hay from everyone in the territory who had a meadow; *v Cartulaire,* 1:316–17. A reference to Maerz seems rather far-fetched.

[61] *Monumenta,* pp. 508–509: "De ista farina habuerunt isti." The careful notations next to each name in this section indicates a concern for precision which certainly does not characterize the narrative account. If the measures at Vézelay were comparable to those at Cluny, the amount of flour reported stolen would have been sufficient for about five thousand large loaves of bread; *v Recueil des chartes de l'Abbaye de Cluny,* eds. A. Bernard and A. Bruel (Paris, 1878–1903), 5, no. 4143, in which it is reported, "De uno sextario fiunt CXX panes majores." A banquet is described on the mutilated pages: *v Monumenta,* p. 492.

[62] *Monumenta,* pp. 509–10: "Isti sex ceperunt XI porcos et in domo Rotberti Quarrel fuerunt occisi et inter istos divisi . . . Gallinas, chapones, anseres, columbas cum sex predictis isti ceperunt . . . Alias comederunt garciferi."

[63] *Monumenta,* pp. 510–11: "Isti sunt qui fregerunt grangiam de Pasticio . . . Isti sunt qui fregerunt molendinum decani . . . Isti fregerunt molendinum granetarii . . . Isti abstulerunt annonam de grangia de Sancto Petro . . . Mortem abbatis iuraverunt isti . . . Mortem Guilelmi conestabuli . . ."

[64] *Monumenta,* pp. 439–40.

[65] The oaths may have been intended merely to frighten the individuals, in which case, they certainly succeeded with Abbot Ponce; *v Monumenta,* p. 436.

[66] Several episodes recounted on the mutilated pages may have led to the death of monastic personnel; *v,* esp. *Monumenta,* pp. 479 and 489. King Louis (ibid., p. 504), also declared that those who had killed *pueri ecclesiae* should be pursued and brought to justice. The only time the chronicler mentions assailants by name (*ibid.,* p. 439), the incident did not result in injury.

[67] The other leaders who were named on the list of the rebels are *Robertus Caligalaxa, Petrus Surdellus, Gaufredus Quintini, Odo de Palude, Robertus de Cruce, Michelet, Iohannes Gastellus* and *Nivardus;* the other rebels who received the most severe punishment in the Chronicle were *Aimo de Sancto Christophoro, Aimo de Phalesia, Alardus de Fonte Leonis, Claudus de Sancto Petro, Durannus Gulos, Galterius Normannus,* and *Robertus de Campo-Petroso.*

[68] *Monumenta,* p. 479. Huygens ascribed the suprascript to a thirteenth-century hand. The suprascript also names a Robert, but, since the group of identifiable leaders includes four men named Robert, he cannot be identified.

[69] *Monumenta,* pp. 424–25: "genere et moribus ignobilis, quem natura inopem protulerat, sed manus arte docta mechanica locupletem effecerat."

[70] Augustin Thierry, *Lettres sur l'histoire de France* (1820), pp. 311–13.

[71] Chérest, (at n. 52), 1, p. 78.

[72] The name, *de Sancto Petro,* could refer to either Upper or Lower Saint-Père, but the traces of a name, – – – *tus de Sancto Petro inferioris ville, Monumenta,* p. 478, may indicate that unless otherwise specified, the name was understood to refer to Upper Saint-Père.

[73] The title, *consul*, is found on earlier documents of the Count of Nevers; e. g., *v* Lebeuf, *Mémoire sur le diocèse d'Auxerre* 4, no. 14, and *Gallia Christiana* 12, Instr. no. 6. Documents which include *Guillelmo consule* in the dating formulae may be found in the Bibliothèque Nationale, Champagne 45, fol. 89r and Latin 9885, fol. 25r. Another undated document in a cartulary of Nevers, Bibliothèque Nationale, Baluze 74, fol. 363r, refers to "Raginaldus qui fuit Praepositus qui et ipse dedit vadimonium loco consulis." Hugh of Poitiers also used the word *consulatus* to refer to the office of the Count of Nevers: *v Monumenta*, pp. 419 and 423.

[74] Evidence from a later period indicates that the officials of the confraternities of the Holy Spirit were known as consuls; *v* Duparc, "Confréries," pp. 349–67.

[75] *Ars mechanica* is defined in a marginal note, *Monumenta*, p. 425: "Ars mechanica est genere generalissimo quicquid extra liberales artes rurali officio exercetur, ut fabricium, lanificium, obsonium. Dicitur autem mechanica vel adulterina quia a liberalibus degenerat." Hugh of Saint Victor, (*Didascalicon*, II: ch. 20, ed. Charles Henry Buttimer, Catholic University of America: *Studies in Medieval and Renaissance Latin* 10 (1939), p. 38), included "lanificium, armaturam, navigationem, agriculturam, venationem, medicinam, theatricam." *v* the discussion by Marie-Dominique Chénu, "Arts mécaniques et oeuvres serviles," *Revue des sciences philosophiques et théologiques* 29 (1940), 313–15.

[76] Hugh was one of the townsmen who reacted violently to the pronouncement of the sentence of excommunication in the church of Upper Saint-Père, *v Monumenta*, p. 439, and was presumably a member of that congregation.

[77] Hugh's son, Renald, participated in the oath to kill the Abbot and was also involved in the seizure of grain. Renald, or another son, seized eight hens and took part in the destruction of the mill of the granary. Three of Hugh's grandsons or nephews *(nepotes)* also participated in the destruction of the mill. One of them, or perhaps a fourth, Arbertus, a non-resident of the town, took part in the destruction of the vineyards.

[78] The use of the adjective *advena* would indicate that he was not a native of the area of Vézelay, but not necessarily a foreigner. Elsewhere the chronicler used the term *alienus* for a foreigner: *v* the discussion by de Bastard, "De la commune de Vézelay," p. 538. Rolf Sprandel, "Le fer au moyen âge," *Annales; ESC*, 24 (1969), 307, found the phrase *homines advenae* used in a document of 1155 of the Count of Toulouse to refer to an entrepreneur connected with ironworks. *Advena* was also used at this date to mean a fly-by-night, a good-for-nothing, a man who was here today but gone tomorrow, or, more specifically, a runaway serf: *v* Ducange, *Glossarium Mediae et Infimae Latinitatis:* "Advena."

[79] *Monumenta*, p. 425; "Is ut erat acer ingenio et in omni versutus nequitia comitem modo muneribus illiciebat . . ."

[80] *Monumenta*, p. 502, describes the destruction of his property, including "omnia edificia ipsius, domus et molendina stagnaque aquarum . . ."

[81] Hugh of Poitiers gave a vivid description of the perplexity of the rebels, *Monumenta*, p. 439, but just before this episode he had described their violent acts. It seems inconsistent to depict the rebels as violent determined men one minute and the next as completely at a loss when barred from the use of basic facilities.

[82] *Monumenta*, p. 501.

[83] *Monumenta*, p. 502.

[84] In addition to the list, *v Monumenta*, p. 439.

[85] Of the twenty men who took the oath, "Death to the Abbot," ten were probably

non-residents, three were townsmen, and there is simply no basis for determining the others. None of the eight men who swore death to the Constable appear to have been townsmen.

86   *v* n. 48.

87   *Monumenta*, p. 478, presents the fragmentary line as ". . . tus de Sancto Petro inferioris villae." I am not convinced that the first "t" is warranted by the manuscript. The fragmented name is probably Claudus.

88   The marsh was probably the site of a reclamation project sponsored by monastic authorities. In 1165, the Abbot claimed that André of the Marsh was a serf; *v* Berlow, "The Case of André du Marais," (n. 11), pp. 133–44. On the crosses which marked the approach to Vézelay, *v* René Louis, "Sens successifs et étymologie du nom 'Montjoie'," *Publications annuelles de la Société des fouilles archéologiques et des monuments historiques de l'Yonne: Série toponymique I* (Auxerre, 1939).

89   *v* map, p. 161. The villages of Bourgelier and Esclarlis are mentioned on medieval documents; *v* Max Quantin, *Dictionnaire topographique du département de l'Yonne*, (Paris, 1862), pp. 18 and 49. On Saint-Christophe, *v* A. Pissier, "Notice historique sur Saint-Père-sous-Vézelay," *Bulletin de la Société des sciences historiques et naturelles de l'Yonne* 56 (1902), 172, n. 1.

90   Communal dinners and distributions of food were common features of associations, such as the confraternities of the Holy Spirit, which were not socially exclusive at this early date: *v* Pierre Duparc, "Confréries du Saint Esprit et communautés d'habitants au moyen âge," *Revue historique de droit français et étranger* 4 sér., 36 (1958), 349–67. Gilles Gerard Meersseman, *Ordo fraternitatis: Confraternite e pietà dei laici nel medioevo* 1 (*Italia Sacra* 24, Rome 1977), pp. 204–09, discusses the possible connection between confraternities and communes.

91   E. g., J. Calmette and H. David, *Les grandes heures de Vézelay* (Paris, 1951), p. 143, and criticisms by Richard and Drouot in their review in the *Annales de Bourgogne*, 23 (1951), 65.

92   This error was included in the translation by Guizot, *Collection des Mémoires* (Paris, 1824), 7:95–202 (reprinted in *Chronique de l'Abbaye de Vézelay*, ed. François Vogade (La Charité-sur-Loire, 1969).

93   The chronicler (*ibid.*, p. 505, n. 92) charged that Simon had presumed, on the strength of his "favor and familiarity with princes" to fortify his home and, after the suppression of the revolt, obtained letters from local potentates urging that his home be spared. Simon's relationship with the Count of Nevers was very close in the decade of the 1160s. In 1165, another time of troubles, when Simon and Durand the Innkeeper volunteered to speak to the Abbot on behalf of the burghers, Simon was described as a partisan of the Count's interests: *ibid.*, p. 532. The following year, a rebellious monk reportedly gained access to the Count through Simon: *ibid.*, pp. 553–54. Later that year, the Count and his mother, Ida, were entertained in Simon's home: *ibid.*, pp. 568 and 572. In 1170, a Simon of Vézelay, perhaps the same man known in Vézelay as Simon of Souvigny, appeared as a witness to an act involving the Count of Nevers: *v* J. Lebeuf, *Mémoire sur le diocèse d'Auxerre*, 4, no. 62.

94   *Ibid.*, p. 473.

95   Another rebel named Simon, who suffered the loss of his wine, *ibid.*, p. 502, is identified as the brother of Eustachius, p. 473, and should not be confused with Simon of Souvigny.

96   *Monumenta*, p. 505.

[97] *Monumenta*, pp. 392–93. This letter did not form part of the original manuscript but was written in a similar hand, soon after the original, and crowded into the space left vacant at the end of a section.

[98] *Monumenta*, p. 501.

[99] *Monumenta*, p. 400.

[100] *Monumenta*, p. 504; *Leucensis* (Toul) was crossed out and *Lotariensis* written above.

[101] *Cartulaire*, 1, p. 321.

[102] *Ibid.*, p. 497.

[103] The statement found in Sermon 24 of Julien of Vézelay, *Sermons*, ed. Damien Vorreux (Paris, 1972), 2, pp. 554–56: "Seruus nil habet proprium sed suo domino lucratur, quippe qui ipse suus non est sed est pecus alienum," illustrates Julien's classicizing tendency. Local custom evidently allowed for personal property on the part of a *servus*, for the Abbot would not have ordered property of the monastery destroyed.

[104] Perhaps the same man as the Prefect of Blannay who testified in 1146: *v Monumenta*, p. 422.

[105] In 1119, both *Paganus Buticularius* and *Seguinus de Moncellis* appeared among the henchmen of Nevers who were accused of sacrilege: *Monumenta*, p. 365. A *Seguinus Grosso* witnessed the agreement of 1137, together with other local notables; *Cartulaire*, 1, p. 316. The use of a double surname is unusual. Another possible petty lord is the rebel Robertus de Campo-Petroso, *Monumenta*, p. 502, also known as Rotbertus Champerrus or, probably, simply Champerrus on the list of the rebels. Could he be the Roberto de Campis who also witnessed the agreement of 1137?: *v Cartulaire*, 1, pp. 316, 321.

[106] *Aimericus cerarius* and *Blancard Sartoris* are mentioned in *Monumenta*, p. 402; *Blancard de Sarcitorio* also appears on p. 422.

[107] *Monumenta*, p. 422.

[108] A suprascript, ibid., p. 422, explains, "de Altranno vel de altero anno." The French form, "d'autre année" is easily corrupted to Daudet.

[109] *Monumenta*, p. 502.

[110] The name, *Fricans panum*, is also intriguing because of the prominence of the Frangipane family in Rome; *v* P. Fedele, "Sull'origine dei Frangipane," *Archivio delle Società romana di storia patria* 33 (1910), 493–506, especially p. 505, n. 3, for early forms of the name.

[111] *Monumenta*, p. 435: "Ingressi denique maiores natu quique capita populi esse videbantur . . ."

[112] *Ibid.*, pp. 531–32: "loquar cum maioribus natu ville huius et cum ceteris sapientibus et secundum consilius celitus nobis indultum per proprios comiti nuncios respondebo."

[113] *Ibid.*, p. 435: "postulabant remitti sibi quasdam consuetudines quas novitatis et tirannidis esse dicebant."

[114] *Cartulaire*, 1, p. 317 and p. 323.

[115] *Ibid.*, 1, 320.

[116] *Monumenta*, p. 587.

[117] The contents of the charter of Vézelay is known from the grant to Mont-Saint-Jean in 1222, *Cartulaire* 2:507–509, and other 13th-century Burgundian charters; *v* the discussion in Joseph Garnier, *Chartes de communes et d'affranchissement en Bourgogne* (Dijon, 1918), pp. 67–72.

[118] *Cartulaire*, 1, p. 321.

Map of the Area of Vézelay
Scale - 1:100,000

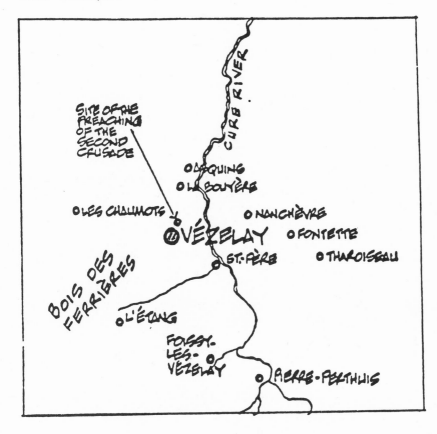

Activites of the
Leaders of the Communal Revolt
at Vézelay, 1152–1155[1]

	Accusations on the List of the Rebels[2]												
	A	B	C	D	E	F	G	H	I	J	K	L	M
Aalardus (de Fonte Leonis)							?						
Aimo de Phalesia													
Aimo de Sancto Christoforo											x		
Claudus de Sancto Petro		f											f
Durannus Golos							x						
Galterius Normannus													
Gaufredus Quintini	x					x	x						
Hugo de Sancto Petro		f		f	x		f			f		b	
Iohannes Gastellus			x	x	x				x	x			
Michelet			x	x	x					x	x	x	x
Nivardus					x	x	x	x					
Odo de Palude	x					x	x						
Petrus Galimardi	x			x	x								
Petrus de Sancto Petro	x				x	x	x					x	
Petrus Surdellus	x				x		x						
Renaldus Daudet	x	f			x	x	b			f			f
Robertus Caligalaxa	x		b		x	x	x					x	
Robertus Champerrus		x		?						x	x		?
Robertus de Cruce	x				x	x	x	x					
Robertus de Furno	x						x						

Accusations in the Narrative:

Communal Oathtakers[3]	Severe Punishment[4]	Other References[5]
	x	
	x	
?	x	491–92
x	x	478
	x	
	x	
?		

?	x	424–25, 428, 439, 453, 478
x		439
x	x	
	x	439, 481
x	x	422
x		
	x	
x	x	476

Key to the Table

x = The leader was mentioned by name.

? = The leader was probably mentioned by name, but either part of the name was lost because of the mutilation of the manuscript, or a variant of the name is given, so that identification is not absolutely certain.

f = A member of the family of the leader was mentioned.

b = Both the leader and a member of his family were named.

1. The Leaders have been identified on the basis of their having been listed as those responsible for uprooting the vineyards (Section A on the List of the Rebels), as having received stolen grain supplies (Section E on the List of the Rebels), or as having received the more severe punishment of having their property confiscated, according to the narrative account. *v* discussion above, p. 143, on identifying the leaders.

2. Hugh of Poitiers, *Chronicle of Vézelay*, published in *Monumenta Vezeliacensia*, ed. R. B. C. Huygens (Corpus Christianorum, Continuatio Mediaevalis XLII, Turnholt: 1976), pp. 507–11. *v* discussion above, p. 142, with regard to the charges listed on the Table from A to M.

3. Ibid., p. 473.

4. Ibid., p. 502.

5. Ibid., *v* pages listed on table.

ROMANESQUE FRENCH RELIQUARIES

Claire Wheeler Solt
Encyclopedia Britannica

ROMANESQUE FRENCH RELIQUARIES

Medieval people collected and valued relics. The famous Shroud of Turin, with its mysterious history, inexplicable composition, enigmatic history and markings evokes wonder, scoffing, curiosity, and skepticism—reactions symptomatic of modern attitudes towards the medieval relic cults. Relic veneration is not much believed in these days, no longer being a dominant feature even of Roman Catholic worship. Relics, where they still exist, are oddities. Even a rural French curé had not thought about exactly what relic might be in a reliquary bust of Saint Theau. It is displayed at Solignac much as it was during the Middle Ages. Today tourists come to Solignac for its art and architecture, not its relics, whereas relics are presumed to have drawn pilgrims to this and other shrines in the Middle Ages. The foreignness of the cult to us and our sense of modern scientific superiority have made us trivialize and minimize an important and distinctively medieval cultural trait.[1]

Medieval people paid serious attention to the service of relics. They built their monuments, particularly the great Romanesque pilgrimage churches, around relics, and displayed costly reliquaries crafted to hold their real treasures, the bodies of their patron saints. Communities used relics for many purposes:[2] relief from natural disasters, protection of monastic property, solemnizing oaths of allegiance,[3] and for healing, as safer and surer means to health than the ministrations of medieval physicians.[4] Relics in rich reliquaries went to councils, to expositions of other relics and on tours to solicit offerings for building funds,[5] and as the symbol and standard of the community away from home. They attracted pilgrims whose offerings at tombs created revenue. They had miraculous powers believed in by all, sought by all, and controlled by the church. Also relics had very real social, economic, religious, medical, and political power. Above all these earthly powers was supernatural power: relics were regarded as miraculous. People believed that relics assured the intercession of particular saints and were themselves tangible pledges of the promised resurrection of the flesh, beliefs most people no longer share.

What we have needed for a long time (Émile Mâle called for it)[6] is an exposition of the central facts of the medieval cult of saints and relics that would help work in several fields. We need definitions of the cult of relics at different times and places, lists of relics churches had, and medieval criteria showing which relics were most valued. Also we seek to know how they were treated (what art was specifically created to house relics) and how beliefs about relics influenced these forms.

After considerable research on the cult of relics, some of these fundamental questions still need to be addressed or readdressed, for our distance in time and temperament disposes us to misinterpret. André Grabar[7] and Peter Brown[8] concentrated on the late antique world, leaving the Romanesque era to others. Some limited studies tend to analyze spiritual manifestations in organizational and socio-economic but not usually theological ways.

Contemporary Bollandists have revealed the synthetic and imitative character of many saints' lives written during the eleventh and twelfth centuries.[9] Patrick Geary uncovered a literary pattern in documents from several monasteries which claimed to have stolen the relics of their patrons. But the *Acta Sanctorum* contains many other kinds of works about saints as well. Art historians have treated majesty reliquaries primarily as Romanesque sculpture stimulating revival of monumental sculpture. Ilene Forsyth argued that the St. Foy majesty and other reliquaries are an iconographically determined group of both reliquary and non-reliquary statues, instead of primarily cult objects: perhaps an anachronistic idea.[10]

Social scientists have applied economic and social theory with interesting results. Topfler used Marxist theory to question the authenticity of monks' beliefs in relics.[11] Heliot and Chastang contributed economics.[12] Most recently, Weinstein and Bell added computers and sophisticated statistical techniques to the arsenal of weapons with which we assault the medieval religious mentality.[13]

Studies of fundamental motivating beliefs behind the cult of saints and relics have been seriously lacking. Ward, on miracles, is a welcome exception in that she treats a peculiarly spiritual phenomenon associated with the cult of saints and relics.[14] Perhaps such sympathetic studies are doomed to oblivion. Audiences, listening to research about relics, often quip that if all of the claimed fragments of the True Cross were put together, one could probably build something very large. This continues in spite of the exhaustive efforts of Anatole Frolow to collect and study reliquaries and relics of the True Cross, including calculating the mass of all known relics.[15] His work is read and cited less than some of the more sensational studies.

Scholars leave open to question whether certain medieval saints ever existed, whether their relics were genuine, and whether the motives of the medieval promoters of relic cults were indeed primarily spiritual. Having neglected to examine carefully the spiritual base of the cult, they reflect contemporary skepticism better than medieval faith. By bringing forth evidence of marginal practices, skeptics have created a picture of fraud, theft, and exploitation: surely corruption, but of what? We lack knowledge of authentic custom undergirded by consistent beliefs, the strong, authentic tradition which fostered wide acceptance of the Christian institution of relic veneration. This implicit question deserves to be made explicit by establishing the basic facts of the cult in its myriad specific saints, shrines, beliefs, and cult practices: the central facts which were true for a great many shrines, and against which one can measure the significance of certain documented practices. Using the concrete elements of the cult as a focus around which to build a synthesis provides a large and tangible data-base from which to work towards establishing this information.

Directing our attention as closely as possible to the medieval focus, we should conduct studies which are authentic in geography, time, and content, and which are broad enough to permit reasonable generalization about shrines and practices. Regional studies which begin with knowledge of the saints, of their cults' dates and characteristics, and of their relics, especially, and which proceed to consider the shrines and how architecture, literature, and art were created to praise these saints will have a wholeness which will make them more useful than the ones we now have. They can establish norms against which certain practices can be measured as characteristic or unusual, healthy or corrupt. Since the cult of relics was an important focal point in life in the Middle Ages, it needs to be specifically documented in all of its aspects putting first things first and the bizarre in its place.

There is reason to believe that the specific character of the medieval relic cults varied significantly with time and place, just as concepts of sanctity changed when the popularity of regional and local saints competed with that of the universal saints Mary and Nicholas in the twelfth century. Poulin's work on the idea of sanctity in Carolingian Aquitaine documented a changing view of preferred standards for what was regarded as holy.[16] Less well-known is the fact that ideas about the best way to care for relics varied and changed even in one locale over time. During the tenth to the thirteenth centuries, tombs of saints were opened, and relics elevated to be placed on or behind the main altar, in shrines or statues which were produced in the finest metals and enamels. In the thirteenth century, still another innovation was brought from Byzantium. Imported rock crystal stimulated the creation of the ostensory reliquary, which allowed the faithful to peer into the reliquary and see the tiny holy particles for themselves.[17]

In the face of such diversity, it is not valid to assume that the late antique Christian relic cult described by Grabar and Brown still prevailed in twelfth–century France. Nor is it wise to assume that the cult was essentially the same in England, Byzantium, and elsewhere in the eleventh and twelfth centuries. This simply was not the case; the cult varied with time and place during the Middle Ages. However, simple variety may not be important, unless it leads to an understanding of important questions such as how and when the cult came to be transformed from a traditional Christian spiritual expression into a macabre and venal institution which was rejected by Luther and ultimately by most Christians as superstitious.

This study asks precisely what relics of what saints were kept at individual shrines and how and where they were kept. It describes the beliefs some medieval people had about their relics and the saints. Finally it treats the creation and elaboration of the reliquary art form within this context. It is based on the study of a large number of shrines in a cultural region throughout a sufficiently long period of time so that the findings have some general though not universal significance. Its geographical scope is southwestern France from Paris to the Pyrenees and from Marseilles to the Atlantic, an area of particular interest because of the great art and architecture presumed to have been fostered partially by the cult of relics and by the pilgrimage to Santiago da Compostela. It deliberately excludes regions which were especially open to other cultural influences, particularly Normandy in the west, and eastern regions susceptible to Ottonian imperial ideas, although there is a growing discussion of the importance of Byzantine influence in Aquitaine in the tenth century, and this region may not have been as insular as is usually supposed. When a map is drawn to plot the shrines which are known to have used reliquaries during this period, it shows that the majority of these shrines were clearly concentrated in southwestern France and presented a geographical pattern typical of cultural diffusion, with some other reliquaries along the roads to the north, east, and west but not in the surrounding regions generally. The time is 950 to 1200 A.D., a time when particular reliquary forms were invented and then spread in popularity. It ends mostly with the Fourth Crusade, which brought many new relics and new ideas about reliquary sculpture to the region.

In the tenth century, in southwestern France, an unusual type of reliquary sculpture emerged at Clermont and Conques. A bishop Stephen seems to have ordered that a statue be made for relics. The idea caught on and other reliquary statues were made. More common than statues were *châsses* or casket reliquaries. The evolution of the majesty has provoked the still-unanswered question of "why?" The less-heralded production of fine metal and then enamel *châsses* combines to make this region one of the most important centers for reliquary manufacture. This study took its lead from the reliquaries of the medieval region of southwestern France. It has sought to place them in their proper context and to consider them primarily as objects which were produced for use by the relic cult of particular saints, more than as objects of art. Here we ask rather, what was the reliquary created to hold? And, since the answer to this question is usually that the reliquary was made to hold the body of a particular saint, we ask who the saint was, when he lived, what type of saint he was, and what his relationship was to the community which had his relics. Then, where was the reliquary kept? How was it used? How does it compare to other similar objects in the region? Finally, what did people of this region believe about relics and reliquaries?

We are concerned with the concrete aspects of the cult of relics, the relics themselves, and the reliquaries made to hold them. Although these are the basic facts of the cult, in the sense that their exposition reveals much about what kind of relic cult it was, no previous study has systematically exposed them. By focusing on the concrete elements we can more nearly approach a medieval view because we are led to all shrines which valued relics enough to write about them or create art to honor them. We are led to imagine this cult of relics within its own primarily religious context, without neglecting entirely, the economic, sociological, literary, artistic, or architectural ones. When we supplement the few remaining examples of reliquaries with textual references to the others which have disappeared, we can begin to measure the magnitude of the phenomena we are studying. The combination of texts and artifacts provides evidence of reliquaries used at a great many shrines during the central Middle Ages. Here we shall study sixty shrines with relics of saints and a total of one hundred and seventy-six reliquaries recorded at these shrines in the period before 1200 in southwestern France.

Table I lists the shrines studied in alphabetical order. Since the list started with shrines with extant medieval reliquaries and then expanded to include those where there is documentary evidence of reliquaries, it is not the usual short list of medieval shrines that share a particular characteristic. Its sheer length indicates the extent of the cult of relics during the period under study. The chart lists the patron saint second because it has been found that, in most cases, reliquaries were made to house the remains of one or more patron saints. Since they were usually obscure local French saints, their identity became part of the study. Most communities usually claimed to possess the complete body of their saint. Evidence of the possession of fragmentary relics or of the division of the relics of one saint among many communities exists but is rare. Usually reliquaries were created to house the remains of the patron saint. It is interesting to note that there is no duplication of saints on this list with each shrine having its own saint or saints. The frequent criticism that shrines had conflicting claims to the relics of the same saints is one that does not seem to have affected this region during this era. Also there is little evidence of monasteries parcelling out relics to dependent houses. Two notable exceptions are the cases of Saint Austremoine, the apostle of the Auvergne, and perhaps Saint Valerie, who was depicted on many enamel reliquaries which may or may not have contained her relics. Finally, saints have been typed according to category: martyr, bishop, hermit, monk, Biblical, because these designations seem best to represent the dominant ideas of sanctity during this era as represented by contemporary sources depicting saints.

Most of the saints were local rather than universal. They lived and died in the immediate vicinity of the shrine which venerated them and were intimately connected with the Christian history of the area. Several, such as Saint Austremoine, the first bishop of the Auvergne, and Cesarius, the first bishop of Arles, were associated with the earliest evangelization of Gaul. Others, like Saint Denis, were prototypical martyrs. Martin of Tours, Martial of Limoges, and Gerauld of Aurillac had been revered as regional heroes for centuries before the Romanesque era, and their names were intimately associated with the locale which kept their tombs. These saints had lived and died in the immediate region, they had been buried in local soil, and they were elevated (or brought forth from their tombs in the ground) only in the course of the tenth and eleventh centuries. Their identity is extremely important, for different cultures adhere to their own concepts of sanctity, and the ideas of sanctity conform to other aspects of the culture.

Eleventh-century Frenchmen sought their models of sanctity in the distant past. It apparently seemed either inconceivable or undesirable to them that anyone living among them could be enough of a saint to merit such an honor, because the record shows that they did not venerate anyone of recent memory as a patron. Their patrons all had lived centuries before. The reasons for this are not entirely apparent or simple, but there was a clear mental set that the age of saints was past, despite the fact that history seems to have corrected their view; statistically, France during the eleventh century seems to have produced an average number of saints.[18] The choice in favor of ancient saints may be usefully related, at least partly, to the reform movement which questioned everyone's holiness, and probably made the whole notion of contemporary sanctity suspect at the same time as it promoted the universal apostolic saint, Peter. Cluny is almost the only listed monastery that claimed its own monks and abbots were indeed saints, and venerated their relics, though Grandmont memorialized its recent founder, Stephen Muret, with a magnificent reliquary which is kept at Ambazac today (v Plate 1). Others all claimed an ancient local patron. This preference for an ancient definition of sanctity also seems to have served as a conservative force resisting change. The ancient patrons who had withstood the test of time and were expected to be loyal to a particular bishopric or monastery, could be counted upon to help their followers resist the pretensions of reformers who offered an universal idea of sanctity and authority vested in far-off Rome instead of the locality.[19] They undoubtedly also helped the monasteries establish or reestablish claims to land and independence in the face of secular and ecclesiastical rivals. Because they belonged to the dim, sometimes almost legendary past, they were not active partisans in rivalries between bishops and abbots, or among monks, canons, and bishops. Their symbolic value could be debated and even altered as the memory of an esteemed man recently dead could not have been. A case in point is the series of eleventh-century Aquitanian councils which deliberated on, and eventually approved the claim by the monastery of Saint Martial of Limoges that their saint should be considered an apostle, thereby outranking Stephen, patron of the cathedral of the same city and most other French patron saints as well. Michel Aubrun considers this debate symptomatic of the struggle between monasticism and other clerical institutions in the region at the time, and Rosenwein has established a context of changing social status of lay patrons in the tenth century. Saint Martial competed both with the bishop and Cluny for its independence, so that the intervention of the papal legate Peter Damien was required to secure its later submission to Cluniac reform, and manipulation of the image of the patron saint played a part in these contests.[20]

        Although Valous spoke of a "contre cour" to the abbey of Cluny,[21] the interesting subject of monastic resistance to the Cluniac reform has not been much investigated, but one medieval monastic source in particular suggested this resistance might be useful in explaining the prevailing idea of sanctity in eleventh- and twelfth-century southern French monasteries. The role of the saint in the conflict between the reform, and a monastery which did not want to be reformed, is strongly suggested in a passage from John of Salerno discussing the possible reform of the Cluniac monastery of Saint-Benoît-sur-Loire at Fleury. In a vision, Saint Benedict objected that the monks were giving him no peace and that he would find a man from Burgundy to reform the monastery. Then he departed, whereupon the monks reacted by going after him in the night on horses to bring him back.[22] Seen from the Cluniac view the saint was on the side of reform, and the behavior of monks who went out into the night after him was laughable. However, from the viewpoint of the monks of Fleury, their actions were understandable because Benedict was their possession and he was a venerable saint fully able to help them defend their ways against the pretensions of Cluny and its patron Peter. Saint-Benoît-sur-Loire never established any more than weak links with Cluny. At the same time it exalted and translated its patron an unusual number of times to richer *châsses* throughout the eleventh and twelfth centuries, creating stronger and stronger claims to independence of ancient origin through the favor of their own universal patron, Benedict. In this case, at least, the history of monasticism and the history of art meet in the study of reliquaries, their uses and purposes.

Medieval Frenchmen wanted saints who had trod the very same soil that they did. They were slow to adopt a foreign patron and most often when they did, they naturalized the saint by a legend that he had in fact lived and died in the region. The most elaborate example of this tendency was the legend that Lazarus and Mary Magdalene had been missionaries to southern France and had been buried at Aix-en-Provence. Later their relics were moved and they became the patrons of Autun and Vézélay.[23] A similar belief was that Saint James was buried at Santiago da Compostela. Thus they took Biblical saints and made their lives and legends conform to those of local saints at surrounding shrines. There is some evidence that they also created lives and legends for nameless corpses which they exhumed from the ground and made into patron saints. Here, too, they made them local when they composed their *vitae*. One example is the story of Saint Savin and Saint Cyprien whose martyrdoms are depicted in famous frescoes on the walls and ceiling of Saint Savin-sur-Gartemps. These frescoes reproduce episodes from the *Passio SS. Savini et Cypriani Martyrum,* a characteristic work dating from the eleventh century which attempted to piece together the life of Saint Savin after presumed relics were found in the ruins of an oratory by a shepherd and were translated to a basilica erected to house them. That the author chose to make Saint Savin an antique French martyr is a clear indication that this was a prevailing idea of sanctity at the time.[24]

Thus, primarily we have the names of purely local saints as the patrons of the churches that used reliquaries. From this list, St. Martin of Tours and Saint Foy were the only French saints recognized by the church outside of the region, although the list includes eight universal saints whose relics had come to France by theft (Benedict), importation (Mamas, Anthony, Blaise), or legend that they had lived in France (Lazarus, Mary Magdalene, and Martha). The others were best known in their own locale. Obscure saints like Bibanus of Figeac, Taurin of Gigny, Libaude of Grandselve, Hydulph of Sens and others complicate the work of research because they are local saints that never have been famous, yet they are as much a part of the record of the cult of saints as the great saints and famous shrines. Benedicta

Ward likewise emphasized the primarily local sphere of influence of even the famous saints, Foy and Benedict.[25] Perhaps we have been misled by overemphasis on pilgrimage roads and interchange to think in terms of crowds of moving pilgrims visiting huge shrines of well-known saints, whereas a more accurate version would include fewer pilgrims and many more local people at all but a few shrines. Also, it was surely the beliefs and practices of local communities that formed the background for those at pilgrimage shrines.

In addition to the emphasis on the local origins of the patrons, the list leads to two more insights into a definition of sanctity in eleventh- and twelfth-century France. First, it contains eighteen martyrs, twenty-one bishops, and only six monks. It is curious that monks seldom chose monastic saints but that bishops were greatly esteemed. The great number of bishops reminds us that the cult of saints and relics was not exclusively a monastic phenomenon but was also practiced in the cities where it had been an important element in episcopal power during the late Roman empire.[26] The emphasis on martyrs is probably best seen as another example of the very conservative character of the cult. The martyrs were the preeminent saints; they were considered holy without question. Hermit saints have been considered typical of the Limousin, but there are only three on this list. Hermits were saints, but they seldom became patrons of churches which used reliquaries.[27]

The patron saints of these churches were not merely patronyms chosen for symbolic reasons, but indicate that the church possessed the relics of the saint and that it was, therefore, a place of particular favor to the saint where his intercession could be obtained. These relics, or corporeal remains of the saints, were kept in reliquaries, works of art designed for the purpose. In the overwhelming majority of the cases, reliquaries were created to house the remains of the patron saint of the church which was dedicated to him, and sometimes the saint had several reliquaries over time. French reliquaries were the distinct creation of this culture and do not resemble reliquaries made elsewhere in the world until the thirteenth century, when other reliquaries influenced the French, and *vice versa*, due to cross-cultural exchanges. A correct understanding of the nature of the cult of relics in France during this period is fundamental to understanding the unusual art that was created.

Scholarship has shown that the ancient Roman prohibition against defiling tombs and dividing up the bodies of saints was first given up in Byzantium and later in Rome, and scholars have assumed that the developments in Rome spread throughout the West.[28] However, this was not always true. The ancient traditions persisted into the central Middle Ages in southwestern France where the cult of saints retained an antique flavor with strong preference for the bodies of local saints in their tombs, and much less interest in relic fragments. Although some, perhaps most, shrines did have relic fragments in their treasuries, they did not usually celebrate them; rather, they elevated the bodies of their patron saints, even though these saints may have seemed obscure to others, and they considered possession of the whole body of the patron saint very important. They continued to be very reluctant to dismember their saint for the purpose of distributing corporeal relics to others, and preferred, rather, secondary relics (created by touching the tomb) or *inventio* (the miraculous discovery of a forgotten saint) whenever more relics were called for.

The importance of possession of all of the relics of the patron saint is elucidated in several ways by different sources. Among these are the legends which asserted that the bodies of certain saints could not be moved. Abbot Stephen was unable to translate the body of Saint Foy at Conques,[29] and Saint Martial had reputedly caused an unceasing deluge on Aquitaine in 830 when he was translated from his tomb against his will.[30] The *Codex Calixtinus* claimed that there were four saints buried along the pilgrimage routes which could not be moved. These included James of Compostela, Martin of Tours, Leonard of Noblat, and Giles of Provence.[31] Although these legends of immovability were probably told to discredit stories of rival communities said to have had relics of important saints,[32] they also indicate the clear undesirability of allegations of the same relics at two locations in the minds of medieval writers, and not necessarily the simple ignorance or gullibility so often presumed. They show, as well, medieval preference for preserving, not dispersing, relics of saints.

It was believed that the saint himself actively protected his body from dismemberment. Accordingly, it was told that Saint Martial had paralyzed a contingent which had sought to take relics from his body[33] and that Saint Denis was so angered when Clovis II removed one of his arms as a relic for his private chapel that he filled the Parisian church with a dark mist. Within an hour the bold monarch lost his mind.[34] Such stories, and others like them, seem designed to frighten would-be relic seekers. The presence of relic-seekers and conflicting claims to relics sometimes may indicate a conflict between personal and community values in the society, for fragmentary relics could be enclosed in phylactery reliquaries and worn around one's neck as Christians had done for centuries. At other times relic seekers are better interpreted as evidence of tension between the conservative institutional pattern expressed in the written legends and the presence of an opposing exploitative tendency toward relics in a minority which has been documented in other studies. Nonetheless, the legends seem to express the dominant, preferred value for keeping the relics of the saint inviolate and integral.

Legendary accounts are buttressed by more historical narratives of *translatio* or relocation of the saints' remains. When relics were stolen, for instance, the whole body of the saint was claimed to have been taken, not just a part of it.[35] Conques asserted that one of its monks had taken the body of Saint Foy from Agen,[36] and the monks of Fleury claimed that they had rescued the body of Saint Benedict from Monte Cassino during the Lombard invasions.[37] In doing so these monasteries had gained patrons, not just relics. The *furta sacra* became a literary *topos*, which casts doubt on the historicity involved, but at the same time provides evidence for the preferred values of the society. Certainly, it would have been easier to steal a relic than a treasured saint; moreover it would have been simpler to gain credence for the possession of a relic than of a famous saint traditionally claimed by another monastery. We can best explain the extravagant claim that the saint was stolen by acknowledging that the society placed great value on having all of the relics of saints together in one place and that relic fragments were not easily distributed nor were they sufficient for the needs of the would-be thiefs.

Reports of *translatio* ceremonies were sometimes made when relics of saints were moved from one reliquary to another. Typically they recorded the careful inventory of relics made by ecclesiastics during the ceremony. An eye-witness account of the translation of Lazarus at Autun emphasized the integrity of the saint's body as attested to by invited dignitaries.[38] Also, in a translation document from Saint-Flour, the monk Abscalon came from Auvergne and, when the bronze reliquary had been opened, he enumerated the parts of the body and proclaimed the contents of the reliquary: "En brachium sancti Florenti! En crus! En costae! Et ita per omnia membra dicendo omnique."[39] Likewise, Hugh of Flavigny was careful to record that one of the saints which was translated at Verdun lacked a foot, not because his body had been defiled by a relic seeker, but because he had lost that foot during his lifetime, as everyone knew.[40] Careful scrutiny of the integrity of the body and proclamation of all of its parts was a characteristic of the *translatio* ceremony and further underlines the value placed on having all of a saint's relics.

The conscious accumulation of relics of a single Eastern saint at Langres provides an extraordinary illustration of the importance of the patron saint's whole body to the individual medieval shrine. Langres obtained the collar bone of the Cappadocian martyr Saint Mamas of Cesaria late in the eighth century and dedicated its church to the saint.[41] However, this relic fragment alone did not satisfy this community. So, during the eleventh and twelfth centuries, it endeavored to acquire additional relics of the same saint. In 1075 Rainard of Langres obtained an arm from Constantinople.[42] After the Fourth Crusade, Walon de Dampierre made a special appeal to the papal legate for the head of Saint Mamas, and he received it.[43] An anonymous account of the translation to Langres concludes by explaining how the four relics then held by the church were regarded as the essential parts of the body through which the saint acted. It is as if Langres thought that it had been able to put the saint back together and could now claim to possess the whole body of its patron. It says:

> The first relic sent was the collarbone which contains the arteries which carry a thought which is in the heart so that the tongue might burst forth into voice; the second was the arm, through which work is perceived; third, a long bone which seems to be from the tibia or femur . . . Fourth and finally, the head came, as if so that he might speak, since thinking, speaking, and acting are communicated through the collarbone and the arm.[44]

Nowhere do we read whether or not this assembly of bones in which the relic of the head was considered of premier importance in activating the power of the saint in this place was regarded as an intact saint by others, but we do know that Saint Mamas was revered as the patron of this community into the nineteenth century and that he came to be thought of as someone from the locality. His Byzantine origins were forgotten so completely that in the eighteenth century, pious Benedictines doubted the authenticity of Greek inscriptions on the reliquary from Constantinople.[45] In a similar way, the community of Angers collected the relics of Saint Sergius.

Guibert of Nogent has been regarded, by some, as the great

medieval skeptic regarding relics. His objections to contemporary practice illustrated the difference between fragmentary and corporeal relics in the medieval mind, but he was, in no way, universally skeptical. Whereas in *De Pignoribus Sanctorum* he criticized many fragmentary relics which he considered specious, in *De Vita Sua* he repeated, and presumably accepted, an incredible story about a king Quillus of England who had brought relics from the Holy Land to Nogent and was considered a saint there. So, although Guibert doubted fragmentary relics of questionable origin at other monasteries, he did not attack the cult of patron saints. Quillus later became the patron saint of the community of Nogent and was depicted on its seal.[46]

Possessing the whole body of the saint was also important in becoming a major pilgrimage center. According to the *Liber Sancti Iacobi*, it was the "bodies of the saints which ought to be visited on the route to Saint James." This pilgrim's guide recommended that the pilgrim visit Saint Foy at Conques where her "very precious body" was kept.[47] The body of the most worthy Saturnin was the reason for visiting Toulouse, *not* its relic collection which, by other accounts, included apostles supposedly deposited there by Charlemagne.[48] The pilgrim should stop at St.-Guillelme-le-Desert to venerate the body of its patron, a revered Saracen fighter. The guide mentions this monastery's relic of the True Cross only in second place and then it seems to stress that its acquisition was an accomplishment of the patron.[49] The head of John the Baptist at Angely was the only relic fragment in all Romanesque France which merited pilgrimage.[50] Everywhere else it was the possession of the *corpus,* or whole body, of the patron saint which recommended a shrine. Raymond Oursel claimed that it was this wholeness of his relics that gave Saint James his prominence; "Saint James enjoyed an incomparable privilege in that his body had never been dismembered, and he remained intact in his tomb."[51] Nonetheless, this privilege was shared by other saints along the pilgrimage routes. Thus Saint James fit the pattern of the other saints along the route where the dominant value was for keeping the whole bodies of patron saints together.

The importance of keeping the saint's body whole is explained by medieval beliefs about saints and the resurrection of the dead, beliefs fully explained by Peter the Venerable in a sermon given in honor of the reception of relics of an unnamed martyr in a rich reliquary.[52] He justified the practice of venerating relics with many allusions to the scriptures. The saint had two existences after death. Whereas his soul was received into heaven where he shone "like a sun in the heavenly Jerusalem" (Matt. xiii. 43), his body persisted on earth, uncorrupted, in affirmation and anticipation of the Savior's promise of the resurrection of the flesh.

> In wonderful largesse he has divided, as if in equal parts, his martyr with divine dignity, so that his spirit might continue to march among the souls of the holy ones and the relics of his holy body he would give for veneration by the faithful still living in the flesh.[53]

In France belief in the dual existences of the saint went back at least as far as Gregory of Tours who spoke of Saint Hilary as being in heaven while "*virtus*" came from his tomb[54]—"*virtus*" being that attribute of sanctity which saints possessed over time but which was subject to redefinition by the culture.

Peter the Venerable considered incorruptibility of the flesh the natural order which most men forsook by sin and which God would restore at judgment. Incorruptibility of the bodies of saints was a sign of their holy and just lives.

> But because, as first He instituted, this was the order, so that if the spirit went forth with justice and the flesh through the spirit of justice remained incorrupt; he established for all mankind justification to proceed in this life, and in the future of the flesh to carry away the incorruptibility or immortality of the flesh. Because he wished to make this the merit of conserving the faith, if that which Christ promised in the future, he would confer in the present.[55]

The condition of the relics themselves was crucial to the belief system and was considered instructive.

> And he (the martyr) teaches us to know from his body, and he shows by his own body what you ought to hope for yours.[56]

Often writers drew an analogy between the saint in heaven and a precious gem as in "verum etiam in terris corpore gemina", referring to Saint Valerian of Tournus.[57] Reliquaries materialized this analogy. Bernard of Angers referred to the reliquary statue containing the head of Saint Foy of Conques as "without doubt a pearl in the heavenly Jerusalem."[58] Peter the Venerable explored the relationship between gems, saints, and reliquaries. He praised the gift of a gold and silver reliquary decorated with pearls as a symbolic representation of the glory of the saint in heaven, saying,

> Today we celebrate on earth one whose merits are forever exalted in heaven. He shines now, according to the promise of the Savior, like a sun in the kingdom of the Father, he whose body this work of art contains.[59]

....

> Thence, this is the cause, that their bodies, which cultivated justice in this life, we do not discard as lifeless; we do not treat contemptfully as "senseless," and we do not despise like the cadavers of brute animals, but we should venerate as temples of the Lord, and we adorn them as the palaces of divinity. We preserve them as pearls befitting crowns of the eternal king, so that the holy spirits having been resurrected, we keep what we can in vessels again associated with devotion.[60]

Thus, the beliefs and practices had unity and logic which, to a very great extent, dictated the reliquary art. Saint's bodies were uncorrupted as a reward from God and were awaiting the day of judgment. Surely, the line of argument continued, man should not disturb this God-given privilege. When he began to do so, he started to erode the very basis for belief in relics.

We cannot assume that the fragmentary relics which the churches had (and they did have them) were believed to have had the same powers or were expected to perform the same functions as the body of the saint in its tomb or reliquary. There seems to have been a hierarchy of relics which was colorfully illustrated by the behavior of frightened brothers when a terrible storm hit Sens. First they sought relief by running to their altar, some carrying crosses and others relics of the saints, while still others sounded church bells and prayed to God. When these measures had no effect on the tempest, they took refuge in the solace of their patron Hydolph in the feretory *châsse* which contained his holy body; and the saint repulsed the storm.[61] To the people of Sens this story was proof that their patron saint was their surest, most powerful recourse among many strong and tested measures, and the historian must note that the reliquaries played an

important part in the acting-out of the rituals of prayer for intercession at Sens.

We can only glimpse the early dim origins of reliquaries in
southwestern France, but certainly their most important predecessor
was the tomb. Ancient tombs survived then (as some do now) and may
have provided prototypes for later sculptors, for the cult had a very
sepulchral character throughout the Middle Ages. In southwestern
France thirty-six, or twenty percent, of the reliquaries we study were,
in fact, tombs. An important characteristic of the tomb was that it was
a fixed place or point of contact between the natural and the supernatural world. In that place, especially, the saint could be counted on
to offer the benefits of his power to men. There was a strong tradition
that these tombs should remain inviolate and it was reinforced by
beliefs and stories that the saint could not be moved. Removal of the
saint from the tomb was, then, a significant break with tradition which
modern scholarship has wrongly associated with elevation and
glorification but which was not sanctioned everywhere because of its
revolutionary implications. For instance, Saints Martin, Martial, Junien, Leonard, Priest, and Germaine all rested in tombs throughout
the Middle Ages, except during brief emergencies, in spite of the
fashion for other kinds of reliquaries. Among these were some of the
most important regional saints. Thus tombs were not necessarily
abandoned for reliquaries as being too old-fashioned. Conversely,
reliquaries gained acceptance partially inasmuch as they imitated
tombs both in their design and in their placement proximate to the
altar.

I have found references to thirty-six tombs for saints during
the period. In general, they were either very old or they were newly
created in the eleventh or twelfth century. The tombs at Le Mas
d'Aire,[62] Aix-en-Provence,[63] and Saint-Guillhelm-le-Desert[64] were
very old Gallo-Roman tombs. All three of these survive. Several
tombs, reputedly made in the seventh century by Saint Eloi at Beauvais, Paris, Tours, Auxerre, and Sens, were fashioned of marble with
gold, silver, and gems.[65] None survives. To be sure, the authenticity
of the record has been questioned, because the combination of working in marble with gold and gems is otherwise unknown.[66] Saint Eloi
became, in legend at least, the patron of goldsmiths and
the father of the gem-encrusted French reliquary. Another seventh-century tomb was that of Saint Austremoine at Volvic.[67] After
this the record of tombs is scanty. Saints Marcellinus and Peter were

placed in a tomb in 826 when their relics were brought from Rome to Soissons.[68] I have found no evidence of new tombs from the tenth century, a fact attributed partly to the decline of the marble industry during the Norman and Saracen invasions of the period.[69]

There was a small renaissance in tomb-making and use in the eleventh and twelfth centuries. In the eleventh century, tombs were made for Saint Mayeul in 1039 and later for Saint Odilon at Souvigny; they were simply tombs cut out of rock.[70] In the Aude one can find an eleventh–century tomb which is a frank imitation of a Gallo-Roman tomb.[71] The tomb of Saint Magnance, created in the twelfth century, adapted the form of the Gallo-Roman sarcophagus, but its bas-relief sculptures recount the legend and miracles of the patron who was believed to have been one of the five Roman women who had accompanied the body of Saint Germaine of Auxerre from Ravenna to Burgundy.[72] At Saint-Guilleme-le-Desert, the patron, Saint William, governor of Aquitaine under Charlemagne and revered Saracen-fighter, was enshrined in a small lapidarium which dates from the sixth or seventh century. Within this is a Gallo-Roman sarcophagus which was worked over in the twelfth century. The elaborate tomb of Lazarus at Autun was made between 1170 and 1189 with marble statues of Mary Magdalene, Aaron, Moses, Martha, and Peter. A new tomb was made for Saint Denis in Paris in the twelfth century.[74]

Saint Junien rested in a large stone tomb (v Plate II) which was under the altar at the church of Saint Junien during the Middle Ages and today stands behind it. On the east side Christ with his hand raised in blessing is shown in an oval surrounded by symbols of the Evangelists. The inscription above reads,

"HIC.JACET.CORP.SCTI.IUNIANI.IN.VASE.IN.QO.
PRIUS.POSITUM.FUIT"

emphasizing continuity in the housing of the remains of the saint, presumably as a guarantee of their authenticity.

The tomb is truly a monumental work. It is approximately four feet high and seven feet long. On one side is the Christ. On another face, Mary is seated in a mandorla with the infant Jesus standing on one of her knees. Most of the rest of the work is taken up by arcades with crowned seated figures sitting on thrones in niches. The entire iconography is a heavenly one which includes Jesus, Mary, and saints, bearing a striking resemblance to Last Judgment tympana on Romanesque churches, and recurring on other tombs and reliquaries as well. On the back is a large wooden door which is closed by iron bars and locked. This reminds us that relics were taken out of reliquaries such as these from time to time and were used for specific purposes. But it also reminds us that relics were carefully guarded against spoilers and that every attempt has been made to keep the pledge of the inscription on the tomb promising that the saint remains in the original container of his burial and is available on this spot for aid and intercession.[74]

A magnificent marble mausoleum which contained the tomb of Lazarus likewise backed up to the altar of the choir at Autun and was decorated with programmed sculpture inside and out. It was made under Stephen II (1170–1189). The sculptor was a monk, Martin, according to the inscription he chiseled into the work. The tomb was a large mausoleum nearly eighteen feet high in the shape of a church or an enormous *châsse*. The sculptured decoration showed Mary Magdalene on the south end and Saint Martha on the north end. At the summit was a lamb surrounded by four evangelists, some of the same motifs that appear on one side of the tomb of Saint Junien. Inside the mausoleum the saint was represented in sculpture, inside his tomb, wrapped in a shroud. Jesus stood at the end of the tomb and bade Lazarus arise. Saint Peter stood at his right and Saint Andrew at his left, facing the statues of Mary and Martha.[75]

The Rolin Museum at Autun conserves the four statues which are all that remain of the tomb. Mary Magdalene raises both hands in a gesture of astonishment and her sister Martha still holds a handkerchief to her nose as if to avoid smelling a noxious odor coming from the open tomb of her brother.

In the case of Autun we can safely surmise that an elaborate tomb was devised to help bolster what must have been even then the dubious claim that Lazarus had come to France and had been the first bishop of Autun. The relics were installed after an elaborate, formal translation ceremony in which regional ecclesiastics certified the relics. Their claim to authenticity was reinforced by the tomb itself. The structure did this in two ways: first by using the traditional tomb structure rather than one of the new types of reliquaries to house its relics, Autun linked its cult with regional tradition. Second, it sculpted its claims into stone for all to see and understand, continuously renewing the idea that Lazarus was at Autun and reinforcing it by using the standard Last Judgment symbols until it became familiar.

Of final interest is the continued use of tombs even beyond
the period under study. Gauthier noted a thirteenth-century tomb for
Saint Stephen at Obasine[76] and there is one from the same date at the
Worcester Art Museum in Worcester, Massachusetts (1949.38). This
sarcophagus (v Plate III a and b) is limestone, carved in relief and of
modest dimensions (18 7/16"×54"×23 11/16"). The iconography re-
peats what were by then familiar motifs. On the front (v Plate III a),
Christ is shown in a mandorla, seated in majesty, holding a book in
one hand with the other hand raised in blessing. Symbols of the four
evangelists and twelve standing apostles flank him beneath crocketed
arches resting on columns. The right end shows the Annunciation,
and on the left end is the Crucifixion. The back side (v Plate III b)
depicts funerary rites in a triple-arched arcade which presumably
refer to the death of the saint whose remains were contained by the
tomb. The museum judges that the decoration indicates that it was
probably used behind an altar.[77]

This and other Romanesque tombs demonstrate that the
traditional stone tomb continued to answer the needs of the cult of
patron saints' relics in some communities throughout the medieval
period. Tombs were customary. They preserved the importance of
place in the relationship between man and saint. They could be
moved to the apse of the church; they could be associated with the
altar either by building the altar over the tomb in the crypt or by
affixing the tomb to the altar. One could keep a patron saint's relics in
a tomb and still design an architectural plan which allowed for smooth
circulation of pilgrims through the church. Similar iconography on
tombs and facades further indicates compatibility between the tomb
and the overall architectural conception and plan of the Romanesque
church. Yet reliquaries were devised and spread during this same
period. We ask what special conditions prompted this innovation,
and, having eliminated some possibilities by the study of the survival
of tombs in this period, we are in a better position to uncover the
unique appeal of these works of art in this context.

* * * *

An important artistic development of tenth- and eleventh-century
France was the creation and elaboration of the reliquary as an art
form. A reliquary is a work of precious materials designed to hold
relics—remains of saints or other holy mementos associated with holy
places or holy people.[78] The appearance of new kinds of reliquaries

coincided with changes in the cult of relics and with architectural innovations as well. All three appear to have been related. By virtue of these changes the cult of saints in southwestern France underwent a fundamental transformation and emerged as a cult with its own unique character partly characterized by a distinctive architecture and an unusual reliquary art.

The most fundamental change in the cult was the partial abandonment of the tomb of the saint and the substitution of one or two reliquaries for the tomb. During this period reliquaries took two distinctive forms: *châsses*, or casket-shaped boxes, and majesties, or reliquary statues. Both originated in this region and both were developed and elaborated on in the Romanesque period. A significant number of churches changed from tombs to reliquaries during the eleventh and twelfth centuries, although this did not happen at all shrines by any means.

According to Ralph Glaber, the turn of the eleventh century was a time for the discovery of a great number of saint's bodies and relics. "The whole world had been clad in new church buildings then . . . the relics of very many saints which had long lain hid, were revealed by diverse proofs and testimonies."[79] This Cluniac historian fixed the date of the inventions, or miraculous discoveries, of hidden saints in 1008 and maintained that the saints were found after the churches had already been built.

Other chronicles attest to the frequent discovery, *(inventio)* of the bodies of saints during this period but show that the phenomenon occurred over a period of seventy-five years and not only in 1008 as Glaber said. They also specifically state that the discovery of the saints preceded church building. In fact, it was the need to accomodate crowds of people who sought to visit tombs of saints which was most often given as the reason for building new churches in this period. The ambulatory and radiating chapel plan of the pilgrimage shrines which were built at this time was probably devised to allow these crowds to circulate easily around relics of the saints.

In the space of seventeen years, saints' bodies were found for Saint-Pierre-le-Vif on three separate occasions. Hydylph and two of his disciples were discovered at Sens in 956. The Virgin Columba and Saint Loup were both found in 998, and in 1015 Abbot Rainard found the bodies of Saint Savinianus and Saint Potentianus which he said he knew had been hidden during the invasions of the ninth century.[80] This names some.

At the same time some communities which had kept their patrons in an underground crypt either moved the saint to the upper church or they enlarged the crypt. The Virgin Columba and Saint Loup were "raised with great honor" from the crypt of Saint-Pierre-le-Vif. Saint Martin was raised from below when the new basilica was consecrated at Tours in 1014.[81] Benedict was moved from the crypt to the upper church at Fleury in 1056.[82] Miraculous discoveries or translations also occurred at Auxerre in 859,[83] St.-Flour in 956–85,[84] St.-Deodat in 1003,[85] Angely in 1014, Fleury in 1027,[86] and Souvigny in 1063. Saints were also translated at Saint Albin of Angers in 1070, 1128, and 1151, Saint Vedast at Beauvais July 15, 1093,[87] Saint Medard of Soissons during the reign of Charles the Bold,[88] and Saint Valerian at Tournus in 979.[89]

When they gave a reason, most of the sources gave congestion as the reason for the abandonment of the crypt and the moving or translation of the saints to the upper church. However, we can be sure that this crucial decision which violated ancient strictures and altered a fundamental aspect of the cult of relics was not made by an architect solely for architectural, creative, or aesthetic reasons. Another possibility which has been suggested is that saints were moved because people had a strong desire to exalt them and to see their relics displayed in a higher place, usually the altar. This too, by itself, is an insufficient explanation, especially in view of contra-indications provided by tradition and law.[90] Together with evidence of humiliation of relics, however, it does provide important symptomatic evidence of fundamental changes in the cult.[91]

The saints of France had lain in their tombs for centuries, and there were very strict prohibitions against disturbing their tombs. According to Ademar de Chabannes, Abbot Gosfridus renovated the basilica of Limoges after fifty people were trampled to death visiting the tomb of Saint Martial in the crypt in 1018.[92] Although this catastrophe could seemingly have provided a compelling reason for abandoning the crypt at Limoges, the body of Saint Martial remained in the crypt throughout the Romanesque period because the monks of Saint Martial believed that their patron did not wish to be moved to the upper church. The saint had amply demonstrated his wish to remain in his tomb, they said, when, in 830, he had caused an unceasing deluge upon Aquitaine until he was replaced in his tomb. Saint Martial was not moved to the upper church so that many people could see his tomb; but people had to peer through a *fenestella* installed for the purpose of looking into the crypt.[93] Nor was he the only saint who stayed in his tomb, respecting ancient beliefs of the inviolability of the tomb, as we have already noted. Elsewhere, once the decision was taken to move a saint, the community was obliged to perform an elaborate ritual with regional ecclesiastical dignitaries present. The formal translation ceremony involved an all-night vigil at the tomb, opening the tomb at dawn, closely examining and verifying the contents, and finally moving the contents to a new tomb or reliquary. The ceremony was apparently necessary to forestall challenges to the authenticity of the relics which had been deprived of their traditional home. In some communities the date of the translation became one of the major feasts. This was true at Sens (VI Nones May), Tournus (January 26), Auxerre, (January 6), Fleury (July 9), and Tours (July 4). At Fleury peasants were warned that they must observe both the traditional feast of Saint Benedict and the feast of the translation, as well, or their crops would not grow. The ceremony, itself, and its annual commemoration show that a community needed very compelling reasons, indeed, to break with tradition and translate a saint from his tomb to a reliquary. Once they had done this, they required frequent reaffirmation of the authenticity of the relics. Both the annual celebration of the translation and also the iconography of the decoration of the reliquaries provided this.

A third possible reason which has been suggested for the development of reliquaries was the need to have the saint portable, for it became customary to carry the relics of saints abroad in elaborate reliquaries. The first recorded instance of this was in the first quarter of the eleventh century when the head of Saint John the Baptist was reported found at the monastery of Saint Jean d'Angely which placed it on display. The story of the discovery spread, and people came from far and wide to see the relic. They travelled with the relics of their own saints. Among these were relics of Saint Martial and Saint Stephen of Limoges. Ademar de Chabannes related that the abbot of Saint Martial and the bishop of Limoges, accompanied by many nobles and innumerable people, carried the relics of their patron from his church in a portable reliquary made of gold and gems. Bernard of Angers noted that it was the custom in the province of the Auvergne to bring the relics of saints to church councils in *châsses* or in golden statues.[94] These practices, required portable reliquaries and surely also inspired the elaborate individualized iconography of some Romanesque reliquaries which identified the saints in a reliquary to people who were from other regions whether they were pilgrims to the saint's church or attendants at an important religious gathering.

In both instances the saint seems to have been used as a legitimate religious patron in a strictly religious context; however, the portable reliquary was a revolutionary change in that it allowed the clerics to move the saint around to use the saint for their purposes and these came to include secular as well as religious causes. The traditional close association between the saint and the special place where he rested was severed, and, with this break, the relationship between men and the supernatural changed. Men sought to evoke miracles through the saints' relics wherever and whenever they sought to carry them. Instead of people having to come to the saint, it was then possible to carry the saint to people or problems. These transmigrations implied that the decision to make miracles was in the hands of the custodians of the relics and was no longer the mysterious purview of the saint. They set the precedent that the saint could be used; questionable practices followed, facilitated by the creation of reliquary art forms.

Processions armed with relics were used in several additional ways during the Romanesque period. The eleventh-century customary of Udalrich described the offices to be followed when necessity required that relics leave the monastery of Cluny. It prescribed a solemn procession to the gates of the monastery where the relics were to be given to the care of laymen. Similar offices were performed at the return. Monks processed to the gates with a cross, two candles, ringing of the church bells, censer, and holy water. Responses were sung, and a special antiphon was used for the reception of the statue of Saint Peter.[95] Although the form prescribed appears very holy, the purposes of these processions were not always sacred, but were instead for what Benedicta Ward has called "miracles of power." To wit, when in 986 the abbot of Fleury and the bishop of Orléans quarreled over possession of a vineyard, the monks came out in procession with the relics of Saint Maurus and Saint Frongentius in a silver shrine, whereupon the episcopal guardian of the vineyard made way for the saints, and the monks harvested their vintage in peace.[96] Bernard of Angers related a similar custom at Conques. Whenever any land belonging to the saint was threatened, a solemn procession of clerics and people was formed. They carried relics of the saint, a golden gem-encrusted processional cross, candles, lamps, texts of the

Evangelists, and holy water. They sounded cymbals and blew an ivory horn to hasten off the usurper.[97] In these instances relics were used for temporal purposes—to protect property—and this use was facilitated by the availability of relics through portable reliquaries.

During the period of the Viking and Saracen invasions some communities moved to safer regions and carried the relics of their saints in portable reliquaries. It has been suggested that this event marked the beginning of portable reliquaries. However, this hypothesis cannot be proved because there is no evidence of continuity.[98] In all cases the relics of saints were returned to tombs when the community returned home after the invasions, and the portable reliquaries were discarded. There is not one example of a portable reliquary from the invasion period which continued to be used in the later period. There was a definite period of discontinuity between the two phenomena.

None of the causes which have previously been advanced are sufficiently compelling reasons, in themselves, for the translation of many saints' bodies from tombs to reliquaries beginning late in the tenth century. Taken together, however, they have in common a sense that man could control the supernatural by the way he treated relics. He sought to conjure miracles by exalting or humiliating relics and by carrying them abroad. To meet these new needs two new forms of reliquary sculpture were devised: the *châsse* and the majesty statue. *Châsses* were by far more numerous than statues, but have received less attention.

A *châsse* reliquary was a casket-shaped rectangular box. Romanesque *châsses* were usually made of oak and covered with a shell of precious metals and gems. Later, in the twelfth century, the shell was made of *champlevé* enamel. The *châsses* could be quite large and heavy, being from three to five feet long. Often it took four men to carry one on a stretcher, or *feretrum*.

The early *châsses* are known mainly from documentary sources where they are indicated by the terms: *arca, capsa, scrinium,* and *theca,* all words which appear to have been synonymous with the modern French word *châsse*. If medieval authors meant anything more specific by any of these terms, we have no indication what the differences might have been. These sources indicate a total of more than twenty-eight reliquaries of this type from the tenth through the twelfth centuries. Of these only fifteen are known to have survived.

One can trace the beginnings of the *châsse* reliquary in literature and in the metalwork traditions of the Franks. The Celts used boxes also called reliquaries to store valuable possessions, especially books. These may have been adapted to hold relics, although the link is very weak. Though *châsses* continued a North European tradition of working in metals and precious gems, their iconographical origins are better sought in the tomb and casket which the *châsse* reliquary supplanted.

In France the earliest *châsses* were attributed to Saint Eloi, a sixth-century goldsmith who later became the patron of French artists. Saint Ouen, his biographer, credited him with a remarkable ability to discover lost bodies of saints and with the creation of beautiful tombs to memorialize them. "The bodies of holy martyrs which hitherto had been hidden from the people for so many centuries were brought forth . . . (He) made sepulchres for many saints from gold, silver, and gems."[99]

For Saint Denis of Paris, Saint Eloi fashioned a metalwork superstructure over a marble tomb. At Tours, he made a tomb of gold and precious stones for Saint Martin. After finding the remains of Saint Quentin, "he moved the body nearer the altar, and then he made a tomb of marvelous workmanship from gold, silver, and gems."[100]

There is some doubt as to whether Saint Eloi actually constructed *châsses* for the bodies of saints or whether he decorated Gallo-Roman tombs. No works survive of either type. *Châsses* from the Merovingian period, such as the seventh-century reliquary of Mumma in the treasury of Conques, are very small and do not at all fit the descriptions of the works attributed to him by Saint Ouen.

There is no way to tell when the works of Saint Eloi might have disappeared or if Romanesque artists had some *châsses* by him to use as patterns for their works. They certainly knew the story of his life by Saint Ouen, and it offers such striking parallels with eleventh-century phenomena that it could have, in itself, served as inspiration for the Romanesque *châsses*, which, like those of the legendary saint, were tombs of precious metals and gems to house the bodies of rediscovered saints and martyrs.

The only *châsse* reliquaries which we know survived from the tenth or eleventh century are two lead *châsses* from Saint Leonard of Noblat. They are undecorated, except for inscriptions which give the contents. One has a flat lid, the other a peaked one. The first is approximately eleven inches wide by twenty four inches long and eight inches high. It bears the inscription "Hic jacet nobilissima bti Leodi". The second (*v* Plate IV) has a pointed roof and feet. It measures approximately eleven inches wide and twenty-eight inches long. The base of the box is six inches high and rises to a height of fourteen inches at the point of the gable. The inscription "Hic requiescit cinerem sti Leonardi confessor dni" runs along both sides.

These two lead reliquaries are curious in three ways. First their precise functions are difficult to estimate, although the inscriptions imply that the first contained the relics of the saint while the other held *cinis* or the debris from the tomb that remained, once recognizable relics had been removed. We wonder how these reliquaries related to the massive stone tomb which remains an active devotional site to this day with the *verrou,* a massive iron chain, draped above it, symbolizing the saint's special favor for prisoners. Most of all the *châsses* are surprising because of their complete simplicity, lack of rich ornament, and lead composition. This suggests that they were probably not meant to be used as reliquaries by themselves. The lead material suggests a coffin liner; these lead boxes were probably placed inside richer *châsses* which have since disappeared. Yet they are the only extant artifacts available to help interpret the documentary evidence of *châsse* reliquaries of the tenth and eleventh centuries.

There are literary references to ten *châsse* reliquaries from the ninth, tenth, and eleventh centuries. The first describes a *"capsa"* for the head of Saint Richarius made in Sens in 864. Unlike the simple reliquaries of Saint Leonard this was made of silver, gold, and gems.[101] Also at Sens in 876, small silver coffretts imitating sarcophagi, which were not of Western workmanship but came from Jerusalem, held the blood of Stephen, Mamas, and Scholastica.[102] At some time prior to the tenth century, Saint Germaine was placed in a cave in a gold *châsse* which was removed and exposed during the tenth century. Also in the tenth century, there was a *"scrinium cornu"* at St.-Flour.[103] A *"capsa"* of Saint Valerian at Tournus contained "majorum reliquiis artuum, ceteris exuviarum corpusve cineribus in sepulcro relictis".[104] Relics of the saints were kept in gold and silver coffers at the Cathedral of Clermont during this period.

The eleventh century supplies what seems to be very scanty information, when one remembers that this was reputedly an important time for the discovery of saints and for translations of their relics to reliquaries. The famous relic of John the Baptist's head was found in 1017, and it was displayed in a "saxea theca instar pyramidis

turrita," an unusual form of reliquary of which no example survives.[105] In 1015 at Sens a very elaborate *châsse* was made for Saint
Savinien. It was made of gold and two large agathas which were
donated by Robert the Pious. The iconography featured inscriptions
and scenes from the life and passion of the saint.[106] St. Martial was
carried to Angely in some sort of reliquary at this time. Otherwise the
record is silent for the eleventh century.

Most of the material evidence for the use of *châsse* reliquaries
dates from the twelfth century, as do the extant examples. Two
wooden coffretts are preserved at Conques and Bellac and date from
the early twelfth century. They are simple boxes with flat lids which
are decorated with enamel medallions and silver nail heads which
form an overall scroll pattern. We can only wonder how much they
are like the *"vasculum"* which was made of gold and silver for the head
of Saint Alban at Angers in 1151[107] or the *"capsa nova"* made for Saint
Flour in 1159.[108]

In 1871 a *châsse* containing most of the body of Saint Foy was
found hidden in one of the walls of the church at Conques. It had lain
there since the Huguenot wars of the seventeenth century.[109] Since its
discovery this important *châsse* has been somewhat neglected by art
historians who have not noticed its singular importance in understanding the history of reliquaries and have concentrated on the
important enamel medallions instead.

The *châsse* of Saint Foy (*v* Plate V) is large (.58 m. long by .39
m. high & wide). It is made of wood covered with black leather and
decorated with small round-headed silver nails which form an overall
scrollwork pattern. The flat lid like that on one of the Saint Leonard
châsses and the geometric decoration suggest that it dates to the ninth
or tenth century. Sometime before the eleventh century it may have
been covered with gold and have been the golden *châsse* described by
Bernard of Angers.[110] A century later the gold layer may have been
removed, perhaps to meet an extraordinary expense, such as funding
participation in a crusade. Abbot Boniface renovated the *châsse* and
added several enamel medallions representing birds. An inscription
on two enamel plaques enables us to establish the date in the twelfth
century at which the *châsse* reached this state. It reads, "Boniface had
this ornamentation made." Of course it is also possible that there was
more than one *châsse* at Conques over this long period.[111]

The *châsse* of Saint Calmine surpasses all known Limoges
enamel *châsses* in beauty and complexity of iconographical scheme. It

too is quite large (82 cm. long by 24 cm. wide by 49 cm. high). Its enamel decoration consists of fourteen panels. Six panels on one side and two panels on the roof are devoted to Saint Calmine and his wife Namidia. Figures on the front of the *châsse* and the figures of Mary and Saint Austremoine on the ends are in relief.

On the back side we see Saint Calmine and his wife Namidia supervising the construction of three monasteries which they are credited with founding. At the left they watch masons climbing a ladder to build the church of the monastery of Saint Chaffre (*v* Plate VIa) in the diocese of Puy. Under another ladder, one sees the altar of the church decorated with holy vessels. At the top and bottom of the panel an inscription reads "S. Calminius construit unam abbatiam in Podiens epatu in onome sti Theofredi martiris." In the center panel (*v* Plate VIb) Calmine and Namidia survey the construction of the monastery of Tulle. The founders stand at the right of the panel. At the left is the church with its two-story bell tower, flanked by two other partly-built towers. The altar is also shown. The inscription at the top and bottom reads, "S. Calminius senatm Roman coarvit scdm abbaiam in Lemovicensi epatu noie Thuellam."

At the right is the church of Mozat (*v* Plate VIc). Under the bell tower of this church a bust of Saint Caprais, the primitive patron of the church, is a singularly important illustration of the custom of placing reliquary statues on altars. Below that, two masons with trowels in hand are mixing mortar in a vat to build a wall. The inscription of this panel reads, "S. Calminius construit tercia abbaiam nomine Mavziacum Narvernensi epatuin." Saint Calmine is depicted as a type of saint which we may call a *builder-saint* and, this is very much at variance with depictions of other patron saints who were early founders and evangelizers in Romanesque art. Calmine is supervising construction of monasteries whereas saints like Nectaire, Benedict, and Martin were shown vanquishing dragons, and cutting down pine trees worshipped by pagans.

The two saints are also represented in two panels on the lid of the *châsse*. These show the saints in their tombs. Two people with haloes kneel at the far edges holding shrouds which will cover the bodies. A bishop is blessing each body. The souls of the saints are shown as small figures ascending to heaven where they are surrounded by angels holding censers. Inscriptions indicate that relics of both of the saints were preserved in the *châsse*. "Hic a Nima ab ange X poltatur ic sepelit S. Calminius confesm Xpi inmu" on the left panel;

"Beata Namidia sepelit ic Hic in monasterio Mausiaco ab angel ducitur" on the center panel; and "Petrus abbas Mauziacus fecit capsam precio" on the right are the inscriptions which identify the contents and give a clue as to the date of the creation of the *châsse*, thought to have been during the abbacy of Peter of Mozac.[112] Little is known of him, but he may have been someone whose values were much like those of abbot Suger of Saint Denis who valued a saint or an abbot by the building program he could accomplish.

Records of the monastery of Saint-Benoît-sur-Loire indicate that the body of Saint Benedict was kept in a series of *châsse* reliquaries from the ninth to the eighteenth centuries. Although the monks of Fleury entombed the body of Saint Benedict after receiving it from Monte Cassino, the threat of Norman invasions prompted Abbot Bernard to remove the holy bones to a *châsse* in 838 so that they could be transported on a stretcher in case of a sudden emergency. This wooden *châsse* was replaced by a bronze one when the church was rebuilt in the early eleventh century. The bronze *châsse* was to be placed in a sculpted pillar in the crypt of a new church, perhaps in a somewhat similar fashion as the stone *châsse* containing the head of John the Baptist was in a pyramid at Angely at the same time. In 1056, however, the monks solemnly translated the *châsse* to a place above the altar in the sanctuary of the church, reflecting an important change in ideas about the best location for relics which affected many congregations.[113] Half a century later, in April 1107, in the presence of an august assembly including bishops, royalty, and everyone whose feet could carry him, the body of Saint Benedict was moved to an elaborate *châsse*. According to an eye-witness account, "The most holy body was translated in full view of all who were there

> . . . and having been raised, a chest precious with gold, silver, and all the rare gems was placed on a *feretrum* made with gold and jewels as is befitting such a great father.[114]

Through several translations the *châsse* of Saint Benedict retained its traditional shape, and the twelfth-century creation continued to hold the relics of the saint until 1793 when a commission of the district of Vien appropriated the silver and bronze of the treasury for civilian coffers.[115]

Most enamel *châsses* which survive from the twelfth century cannot be identified with any particular saint or shrine. They were produced at Limoges for a mass market and have similar iconography. They are generally smaller and less individualized than the *châsses* for saints were. There are examples in churches and museums around the world, including the Cathedral of Albi, Masseret, the Cluny museum, the Louvre and many others. These reliquaries were probably created to hold imported relic fragments and, therefore, are not in the same category as the *châsses* made for the relics of patron saints.

After the tomb, the *châsse* reliquary was the most common kind of reliquary in Romanesque France. Its origins were obscure but certainly ancient. Iconographically it resembled the tomb, its predecessor. Although the whole idea of opening a tomb and removing its contents, for any reason, to any other receptacle must be seen as revolutionary, at least the kind of reliquary was not completely different in that *châsses* were shaped like coffins or tombs. Therefore, they may be regarded as transitional.

Majesty statues, the other new form of reliquary devised in this period, were indeed wholly new. The community which devised the idea of placing relics in a statue not only violated the tradition which held that tombs should not be disturbed but also broke strong Carolingian prohibitions against idolatry which had kept representative sculpture suppressed for two hundred years. When Bernard of Angers first saw these statues, he was shocked and considered them idols. More recently Kenneth Clark made a remarkably similar observation in *Civilization* when he commented on the irony of a rich statue to honor a simple virgin at Conques.[116] The majesties have received a great deal of attention as works of art separate from their function as reliquaries because they are thought to have played an important role in the revival of monumental sculpture in the round.

Altogether, we have found evidence of seventeen reliquary statues used during the central Middle Ages in southwestern France. They include a partially-gilt silver statue of Candidus from the late eleventh century, a head of Saint Maurice with a crown of pearls, rubies, and sapphires,[117] an early twelfth-century statue of Gerauld of Aurillac made of gold and precious gems,[118] and a golden head with a crown at Nevers.[119] Busts of Saint Cesarius of Maurs, Saint Chaffre of Monastier, and Saint Baudimus of Saint Nectaire still exist. Tournus had statues of both Saint Valerian and Saint Porcian in the tenth century,[120] Saint Martial had one, and there were statues of the patrons of the most important pilgrimage shrines, Santiago da Com-

postela and Cluny.[121] There were also majesty statues of Saint
Armand of Rodez and Saint Marius of Vabres. The most famous of
all was and is the golden majesty of Saint Foy at Conques.

The statues or majesties which were reliquaries held the
head of a saint and were paired with a *châsse* or tomb which held the
rest of the relics of the saint. Together they were companion or dual
reliquaries which functioned together as one reliquary for the complete remains of a single saint. The only place where both reliquaries
survive is Conques where both the *châsse* and the majesty are extant.
In Medieval times they did not leave the monastery separately,
according to Bernard of Angers.[122] The system of dual reliquaries for
the relics of one saint is documented at other monasteries as well. At
Tournus, the relics of Saint Valerian were divided between a
mausoleum of gold, silver, and precious stones and an *imago* for the
head of the saint in the tenth century. Likewise, at Nevers, Limoges,
and Monastier there is documentary evidence of the use of two
reliquaries for the relics of the same saint. Indeed the system of using
two companion reliquaries was common for Romanesque churches,
whereas using more than two, as at Saint-Denis where an arm and a
hand reliquary were added, was highly unusual.

Late medieval Cluniac reliquaries conformed to the fashion
for two reliquaries, one for the head and another for the rest of the
relics of the saints. An inventory of 1399 described how the relics of
Saint Hughes were displayed.

And first, in the major reliquary, is the intact body of Saint Hughes,
abbot of Cluny, without his head; which is placed in an image of the
Holy Hughes, newly fashioned. And, in this aforementioned reliquary, there are no other relics.[123]

Therefore, not only must we consider the Romanesque reliquary
statues within the general context of the cult of relics of a particular
saint, but we should also regard them as parts or halves of reliquaries
which required the company of *chasses* to contain the rest of the relics
of the saint. And we must be aware that this was not an isolated
phenomenon at some remote shrine in the Auvergne but was instead
a popular and widespread way of handling relics and statues which
continued to be used during the High Middle Ages, as well.

Modern scholarship has been unable to uncover any certain
reason for the innovation of keeping relics of the heads of saints in

statues. The practice seems to have begun at Clermont in 946 when bishop Stephen ordered a wooden madonna covered with gold from his goldsmith Aleume. Later, as abbot of Conques, the same Stephen enshrined the relics of Saint Foy in a golden statue seated on a throne. This reliquary statue still exists at Conques. So also does the *Book of Miracles* of Bernard of Angers, a cleric who visited Conques from Chartres and saw and commented on the unusual southern French majesties and on their place in spiritual practice.

In the famous statue at Conques (*v* Plate VII), Saint Foy is depicted seated on a throne. Both hands are raised and hold small receptacles which may once have held attributes of the saint. She is clad in splendid robes, bedecked with jewels. The statue was made of carved wood covered with thin sheets of gold hammered to fit the shape of the wood core.[124] The motif of a frontal, seated figure which was used in the Saint Foy majesty was common in medieval manuscripts and has been analyzed as the "throne of wisdom" by Forsythe. It was adapted in art from the representation of kings because, as Jean-Claude Fau noted, the artist who created the Saint Foy majesty did not seek to represent the young girl martyr as she appeared in her earthly life and as she is shown on the tympanum of the west facade at Conques. Rather, he sought to depict the "triumphant virgin, transfigured by her martyrdom, accompanied by her royal attributes, the crown of gold and the throne of honor which symbolizes her glory."[125] A similar motif appears on the tomb of Saint Junien where the triumphant Christ is surrounded by rows of crowned figures, presumably saints, on thrones. However, showing that the motif existed in western medieval art and that it was appropriate imagery for a saint still seems to be an insufficient explanation for the adoption of this wholly new type of reliquary art, the majesty or reliquary statue. So, although contemporary scholarship has been impressive, there remain two unanswered questions: why was the reliquary statue introduced at this time, and what did the Saint Foy majesty originally look like.

An unexplored possible explanation for the sudden appearance of reliquary statues is possible Byzantine influence through Byzantine clerics who are known to have been in Aquitaine at the time. We know from a vision of an unnamed relative of a prefect of Illyricum that there were two statues in the *ciborium* of Saint Demetrius in Thessalonika. These could have provided models for those reliquary statues of the Auvergne which represented saints.

When the attendant had opened the doors, our man, even before he had entered, saw the little silver couch that is set up in the middle—as we may see it also—and at the head of it a splendid throne made of gold and precious stones upon which sat Christ's most glorious martyr Demetrius in the same form as he is depicted on icons, while at the foot of the couch was another splendid throne made entirely of silver on which he saw seated a woman of beautiful and decorous aspect.[126]

It is interesting to compare the vision of the statue of Saint Demetrius sitting on a golden, gem-studded throne and the surviving statue of Saint Foy which displays the same design. Perhaps her origins are Byzantine with some iconographic similarities in manuscripts paving the way for the acceptance of the idea in the West. However, this cannot explain the association of statues and relics, the relic of the head in particular, because the *ciborium* of Saint Demetrius did not necessarily have relics and there is no evidence that the relic of the head was placed in the Byzantine statue.

Depiction of Saint Foy in the Auvergnese statue corresponds closely, but differs in one important respect from the description of Saint Foy as she appeared in a vision to Witbert early in the eleventh century.

He saw a girl, angelic and very serene in appearance, her face shining white, flushed with a tinge of pink, a face which surpassed the beauty of all humans with inestimable vigor. Her clothing was very grand, elegantly woven in gold throughout, and finely woven with various embroidery. Truly, generous sleeves hanging to her feet, their magnitude was lessened by the fact that they fell in the smallest of folds. And her headpiece, intersecting in a circle in four places, gleamed with bright white pearls.[127]

In the statue, and in Witbert's vision, Saint Foy appeared dressed in splendid gold robes and wore a jeweled crown. But in the vision she did not have a gold head, and this leads us to speculate that the statue had a painted white wooden head at this time, as many other early statues had.

We may assume that one purpose of the statue was to exalt the saint on earth as she was exalted in Heaven. She was clothed in gold and precious gems so that she would shine forth "like the sun in the kingdom of the Father," as Jesus had promised that his saints would shine in heaven. Bernard of Angers alluded to this Biblical pledge in his justification of the majesty statue of Saint Foy. It was not, he said, an idol, but a reliquary for the head of the martyr which has been proved so efficacious in interceding in behalf of sinners, that "it is without doubt a pearl in the heavenly Jerusalem."

Both Bernard of Angers and Peter the Venerable needed to justify and defend elaborate reliquaries against charges of idolatry. Although the creation of magnificent reliquary statues and *châsses* can be explained by a desire to elevate and exalt the saints, this must be viewed against the conservative tradition which forbade disturbing the tomb of the saint and banned statues. Furthermore, this tradition offers the best possible explanation for the curious practice of keeping the saint in two reliquaries in his home church, a statue which held the head and a *châsse* which contained the rest of his corporeal remains. The head, as the most important and most individualized relic of the saint, seems to have been used to sanctify what would otherwise have been considered an idolatrous statue.[128] If this analysis is correct, then we have uncovered another example of the tendency to use or exploit the relics of saints, because the saint was violated to satisfy a desire for a statue rather than a beautiful statue being to glorify the saint's memory. On the other hand, both explanations may be correct, if the reason for wanting the statue was to praise and glorify the saint, and this reason is traditional in explaining or justifying religious art.

Bernard of Angers enumerated several majesties which have since disappeared and specified that these statues were created as reliquaries to hold the heads of saints.[129]

It is an old practice and antique custom that in the whole land, Auvergne, or Rourgue, or Toulouse, and in other neighboring regions to construct a statue of gold or silver, or some other pleasing metal, whichever each can, for its saint, in which the head or other major venerable part is enclosed.[130]

He explained that the Majesty statue of Saint Foy was a reliquary for her head and mentioned that there was a "golden *châsse* without which her sacred statue was never carried abroad."[131] The statue which contained her head and the *châsse* which contained the rest of her relics together functioned as a reliquary. In the church at Conques they were kept in front of the altar, and they travelled together. Even though the community had indeed violated the integrity of the corpse by separating the head and putting it in a different reliquary, it tried to keep the spirit, if not the letter of the law, by keeping the two reliquaries together at all times.

The remains of Saint Martial were also kept in two receptacles. Whereas most of the body of the saint was kept in a tomb in the crypt at Limoges, his head was kept in reliquary which most scholars think was a majesty statue. According to Adémar de Chabannes, the statue was made in 985 by Gauzbert, then treasurer of the monastery, "a golden seated statue of the apostle Martial upon the altar, blessing the people with his right hand and holding the book of gospels with his left." This statue was transformed into a reliquary a few years later when Abbot Josfred "made a gold and gem studded reliquary in which the body of Saint Martial is carried, from the golden statue."[132]

Reliquary busts from the late eleventh and twelfth century continued the tradition of enshrining the head of the saint in a statue while the rest of the saint's relics were kept in a *châsse*. These life-sized busts showed the saint from the waist up and used precious metals and jewels. When they were borne aloft on the shoulders of men in procession, it looked as if the saint had descended to earth to walk among his devotees.

Three of these reliquary busts from France survive. Sometimes there is accompanying evidence of a companion *châsse* for the rest of the saint's remains. There is considerable advancement in the skill with which the artists handled the materials and the representation of the human form in the three examples.

Stylistically the most primitive, though not the oldest reliquary bust which still exists, is that of Saint Cesarius (*v* Plate VIII), the first bishop of Arles, whose relics were said to have been brought to the Auvergne after the destruction of the saint's tomb by the Saracens in the eighth century. This statue was made in the workshops of Conques late in the twelfth century. The torso of the statue was made from a tree trunk hollowed and shaped with a gouge. Sheets of *repoussé* silver and copper gilt were fitted on the wooden core. The statue was a reliquary for the head of the saint and bears the inscription, "here is the head of Saint Cesarius, Bishop of Arles." A gold door on the chest of the statue allows the saint's head to be removed and examined.[133]

The statue of Saint Chaffre (*v* Plate IX) contained the relics of an abbot of Monastier who faced a Saracen raid alone and was mortally wounded trying to convert Moslems to Christianty in about 732.[134] Like the bust of Saint Cesarius, the torso is wood covered with sheets of *repoussé* copper, gilt with silver and gold. The hands are wood. However, the head is of cast metal with a hinged opening at the back for placement of relics within the head. The cast head shows greater skill in metalwork and was considered by F. Souchal to be the earliest attempt at portraiture in this medium in France.[135] According to a chronicle, in the late eleventh or twelfth century, the statue wore a golden crown gleaming with precious jewels. There was also a gold and silver *châsse* which contained the other relics of the saint.[136] Both reliquaries contained many other relics including those of Saint Chaffre.

The curé of Solignac showed me a less famous pair of reliquaries for Saint Theau (*v* Plate X), disciple of Saint Eloi and patron of Solignac. The superior of the neighboring monastery explained local ecclestiacal history in August 1982. Both reliquaries date to the twelfth century. A bust of the saint is made of oak and plaster. A small window in the chest with a rib bone of the saint visible under glass appears more recent. The bust supports a head in copper with silver and gilt which could well be twelfth-century workmanship except for a lens on the back of the head which displays a bone. (Open display of bones is not a characteristic of medieval reliquaries.) The statue is 38 cm. high, by 30.5 cm. wide. Its companion reliquary is an oak *châsse* with remnants of enamel and metal decoration and iron hinges. It is 90 cm. long by 54 cm. high by 26 cm. wide, by far the largest extant medieval *châsse*, although, we know from illustrations and other sources that *châsses* were often large and required four men to lift them and carry them in procession. Nailheads and nailholes, as well as fragments of enamel indicate that it was once covered with enamel plaques which were arranged in arcades.

The statue of Saint Baudimus (*v* Plate XI) dates from the twelfth century and shows the most sophisticated handling of the metal of the surviving reliquary busts. Both the hands and the head are of cast copper gilt which are fitted on to wooden stumps at the neck and arm and are held by wooden pegs. The hair, of stylized curls in relief, contrasts with the tooled hair of Saint Chaffre and Saint Theau. The eyes of Baudimus, made of ivory with pupils of horn, lend a more realistic appearance to the saint. Saint Baudimus was traditionally considered a disciple of Saint Nectaire who evangelized the Auvergne in the third century and was represented by a silver statue which disappeared during the Revolution. Perhaps neither of these statues were reliquaries, although the statue of Baudimus is usually assumed to be one, in spite of the absence of any door to a relic compartment inside. Perhaps the relics of the two saints remained undisturbed in their tombs during the Middle Ages until 1488.[137]

Polychrome capitals that depict miracles from the lives of both saints circle the choir of the church. One relates two miracles from the life of Saint Nectaire. First the resurrection of the noble Bradulus is under a model of the church. On the side facing the ambulatory an angel orders the devil, whose mouth is wide with anger and whose hair is standing on end, to transport the saint to the other side of a river. On the side facing the choir the pope comes to revive the abbot Nectaire who had fallen ill at Sutri in Tuscany, but he was already dead. One of the capitals of the side aisle of the nave depicts Baudimus triumphing over a fierce animal which sowed terror and fear in the mountains of the Doré leaving numerous victims in its path. Here the saint is victorious, with his feet crushing the enormous head of the dragon.

These saints certainly had more to conquer than dragons, for the church of Saint Nectaire is half way up a mountain with ancient and competing religious traditions at the foot and at the summit. At the bottom the Romans founded curative spas, at the top people of a forgotten prehistoric faith had erected enormous megaliths, and in the middle Nectaire and Baudimus founded a Christian church with awesome miracle-working saintly patrons. This place which was chosen as holy, indeed miraculous, by three separate, different cultures is still a special spot in the Doré nowadays: a popular tourist and vacation place. The mountainside teams with people during August seeking the cool mountains of the Doré much as they apparently have for thousands of years. The church gets its share of business now from people who come to see its artistic treasures, and the guards vigilantly protect these relics from those who would touch or take photos much as medieval guards prohibited pilgrims from defiling sacred relics. One is led to reflect that there has always been competition at Saint Nectaire, and probably elsewhere, among the appeals of dolmen, church, and spa. Forgotten rivalries and unexplored tensions of competition may help explain why certain shrines had rich reliquaries and others did not. Some places needed stronger attractions than others to meet the competition. Golden statues were then and remain today good drawing cards.

Throughout, this study of the concrete aspects of the cult—of the relics and the reliquaries themselves—has revealed several important characteristics of the cult of saints and relics in southwestern France during the tenth, eleventh, and twelfth centuries. The cult reveals itself as one which originally in the ninth and tenth century seems to have been very conservative and possessed of certain values and characteristics which many have presumed had been discarded earlier because they had been changed elsewhere. Primary among these conservative characteristics was the emphasis on the tomb and the importance of keeping the body of a saint whole and in his place of burial as an aid in intercession for the community, and tombs continued to be important throughout the period, even though many reliquaries were made to supplement their function. The development of reliquaries, however, was an important break with this tradition.

A related phenomenon is that this cult was a cult of saints more than it was a cult of relics. Saints were venerated and appealed to through their relics, but fragmenting the remains of saints and trafficking in relic fragments was not a feature of this culture. Rather, when relics were needed, they were discovered, usually miraculously, and characteristics of the new relic cults were made to conform to the dominant pattern with typical lives, *passios*, and complete, incorrupt bodies. It was a local cult largely sufficient unto itself for its ideas of sanctity and for its supply of relics of holy men who had lived in the same region in ancient times. It did not need to import. Finally, it was conservative in its ideas of sanctity, primarily revering martyrs and founding clerics, the heroes of the earliest days of Christianity in its own region. Traditional patrons, men known only in this region, continued to be preferred in spite of the supposed equalizing influence of the Universal liturgy with its calendar of universal saints which is sometimes supposed to have diminished the popularity of regional saints.

Within this conservative context three unusual forms of reliquary sculpture emerged, the tomb, the *châsse*, and the statue. Each is best understood within the context of a conservative relic cult. New, sculpted, stone tombs created in the twelfth century were most in line with traditional values. Thus, tradition provided the impetus for the revival of the art. Other forces, however, seemed to have prompted new solutions, in particular portable shrines, and shrines that could be placed on altars. *Châsses* and statues, varying in size and form, were created by metalsmiths to meet these demands. Some *châsses* were as big as coffins, while others were much smaller. Some were made of simple materials, and others were of gold, studded with gems. Later they were made of enamel which permitted a rich iconographic program. In a few cases relics of the head of the saint were placed in a statue of the saint while the rest of the saint's relics were kept in a *châsse*. This last idea is the one that had the most influence elsewhere.

The creation and use of portable reliquaries represent a fundamental change in the relationship of the saint and his miraculous power to the community. Whereas traditionally, the saint had rested in a specific place and pilgrims and supplicants went "ad limina sanctorum," and miracles came from God through him at this place, now the saint was moved about like a troubleshooter and taken here and there to perform miracles as the community saw fit. Clearly certain communities decided in the eleventh and twelfth centuries that they could conjure miracles by their own actions. It is well known that they elevated saints in the belief that their actions would influence the saint to act in their interests. Less well known, but well documented, is that they humiliated saints in their reliquaries removing them from exalted positions in the church and punishing their relics because they had not been active enough. Both rituals clearly indicate that they thought they could influence the supernatural by their own actions. This is a fundamental change in the definition of miracles and offers the best explanation for the development of portable reliquaries. By means of these reliquaries clerics took possession of the saint and his miraculous powers and carried him around to lend his miracle-working power and sanction to their activities such as councils, processions, and the like. In a real way they reversed the relationship between the saint and the community. They were cautious about this, to be sure, careful to try to keep some of the traditional appearances, but they clearly violated the ancient traditions of the sanctity of the saint's place of entombment and of the integrity of his body in order to gain power over the miraculous, a power the church was vigorously asserting with the sacramental system.

This picture provides the information necessary for rich contrast with relic cults elsewhere. Preliminary observations include the realization that southwestern France does not seem to have been affected by the practice of dividing and distributing relics which is

documented for Byzantium and later Rome, nor was it affected by the
fashion current in Imperial territories of importing relics, preferring,
instead, its own obscure local heroes. This means that it was not
primarily a cult of relics of witness, those pieces of bone, dust, blood,
and wood which had been brought from the Holy Land and which
always had critics who doubted their authenticity and efficacy. This is
not to say that relics of this sort did not exist in the treasuries of some
Romanesque churches, for they did, and they included two of the
most controversial relics of Christianity. The head of John the Baptist
at Angely caused a real stir when it was first exhibited. Saint-Guillhelm-le-Desert held a prized relic of the True Cross. These are the
two examples of duplicate relics most cited by critics of the cult, but
imported relic fragments of this sort were not generally the focus of
veneration in the way that the patron saints were. In this instance they
constituted the exceptions and not the rule, and it is in this respect
that our investigation has been most instructive.

Our study of the relics themselves reveals a cult that centered
on the careful custody of the physical remains of local religious
heroes, and must conjure a new image in most of our minds, for we
have been accustomed to assuming that references to relics associated
with medieval French churches must have meant that they had grue-
some fingers, miraculous boiling blood, exposed dusty cadavers, or
tiny splinters of wood which are now laminated in clear plastic and
can be seen in various places around the world. These practices make
it easy to scorn a cult of relics and to regard it as a form of exploitation
of the superstitions of the ignorant, and many often draw a parallel
between Mexican women who crawl long distances to the shrine of
Our Lady of Guadaloupe in Mexico and the medieval pilgrims to
Compostela.

But the cult we have described was a good deal more digni-
fied than we generally imagine, and today, a visit to the tomb of Saint
Leonard in his massive stone tomb evokes feelings no more bizarre
than a visit to the tomb of John F. Kennedy in Arlington cemetery
near Washington, D.C. At neither does one actually see any part of
the physical remains of the distinguished leader, and perhaps their
opacity is the single most important feature that all three types of
Romanesque French reliquaries have in common with each other,
with earlier tradition, and with our monuments to decreased leaders.
To be sure, there is a big difference between the medieval and the
American shrines in that, at the one, one might still see a woman

coming to pray and light candles, asking for the saint's help in conceiving a child, and, at the other, people presumably come only to remember and revere a great leader. Nonetheless, the decorum with which the bodily remains are hidden from view and kept protected from those who would like a souvenir is similar, and it is something that allows us to approach this cult with greater sympathy—that is, until we imagine what would happen if enterprising politicians were to dig up Jack Kennedy's bones and put them in statues or boxes so that they could carry them around the country and set them up at conventions and thousand-dollar-a-plate fund-raising dinners. The cult of the American martyr would have been as greatly altered by this as the medieval cult of saints was changed in the Romanesque era. The boxes and the statues of Kennedy would survive in museums as concrete evidence of that change just as Romanesque reliquaries, many now empty, have a story to tell about the cult they were created to serve.

NOTES

[1] Peter Brown, *The Cult of the Saints* (Chicago 1981), pp. 13–18, discusses a two-tiered model of society and religion as developed by Hume and spread by Gibbon. He believes it has inhibited the study of popular religion.

[2] I summarized and documented the diverse uses of relics during the eleventh and twelfth centuries in Claire Wheeler Solt, *The Cult of Saints and Relics in the Romanesque Art of Southwestern France and the Impact of Imported Byzantine Relics and Reliquaries on Early Gothic Reliquary Sculpture*, (Ph.D. dissertation, The Catholic University of America, Washington, D.C. 1977), 99–121. Some material was also presented at conferences: "Relics and Pilgrimages," 1977, University of British Columbia; Midwest Medieval Conference, 1983, University of Kentucky; and University of Missouri Medieval and Renaissance Group, all of which provided useful suggestions.

[3] Patrick Geary traced the custom of swearing oaths on relics to Carolingian custom. *Furta Sacra: Thefts of Relics in the Central Middle Ages, 800–1000* (Diss., Yale University, 1974), 37–38, also *Furta Sacra*, (Princeton, 1978). Frank Stenton, (ed.), *The Bayeux Tapestry*[2] (London, 1965), Charles H. Gibbs-Smith "Notes on the Plates," and Charles H. Gibbs-Smith, *The Bayeux Tapestry*, (London, 1973), offer a plausible explanation of two reliquaries, one containing the relics of a Norman saint and the other of Anglo-Saxon saints. They identify the latter as saints Rasyphus and Ravennus, two British saints who fled to France and were ultimately martyred there but offer no documentation for this identification. In David C. Douglas and G. W. Greenaway, (eds.), *English Historical Documents* (London, 1953), s.v. "The Bayeux Tapestry," pp. 232–78 the authors claim that the relics are fully exposed and may be seen at the bottom of the reliquary on which Harold placed his right hand. Even the best reproductions reveal nothing to me which look like bones exposed by the reliquary. Indeed I would be very surprised to see any such

representation for eleventh–century France when reliquaries were invariably made of solid materials. Ostensories which exposed the relics were introduced in the thirteenth century.

4 Miraculous cures at shrines with relics is the great given subject in the sense that it is readily conceded to have been an important element. It awaits a scholar who is willing to tackle the enormous task of analyzing voluminous miracle literature to ascertain the numbers and types of cures that were claimed, among other things. Benedicta Ward, *Miracles and the Medieval Mind* (Philadelphia, 1982), asserts that miracles of power and protection were more numerous than cures, but an anthropological and psychological study, especially of saints particularly associated with a medical specialty, would be of great interest. Studies of psychological aspects revealed by miracle story collections from other periods and places are: R. Finucane, *Miracles and Pilgrims. Popular Beliefs in Medieval England*, (London, 1977) and M. Rouache, "Miracles, maladies, et psychologie de la foi à l'époque carolingienne en France," *Hagiographie cultures et sociétés*, 319–337.

5 Efforts to compute the value of pilgrim donations include Christopher Robert Cheney, "Church Building the the Middle Ages," *Bulletin of the John Rylands Library*, 34 (1951), 20–36; George Gordon Coulton, *Five Centuries of Religion*, (Cambridge, 1932–50) I; and Otto von Simpson, *The Gothic Cathedral*, (New York, 1964) pp. 172, 179. Reliable estimates by contemporaries include *Gesta S. Trudonis*, XIII, in *Spicilegium*, Luc d'Achery, ed., II, 707; and Abbot Suger, *De Consecratione*, ed. E. Panofsky, in *Abbot Suger on the Abbey Church of Saint Denis*, (Princeton, 1946), pp. 102–03. On the economic impact of feasts *v* P. Huvelin, *Essai historique sur le droit des marches et des foires*, (Paris, 1887), and C. Levillain, "Essai sur les origines du Lendit," *Revue Historique*, 157 (1927), 25–61 on the feast of Saint Denis and the Paris fairs.

6 Émile Mâle, *L'art religieux du XIIe siècle*, (Paris, 1922), p. 36. "A really fine study of relics would be one of the most curious chapters of medieval history, and one which the historian of civilization and the historian of art would find equally instructive." (author's translation)

7 André Grabar, *Martyrium*, 3 vols., (Paris, 1946) is still a fundamental study of the cult of martyrs in the early church, and many of his articles on early Christian and Byzantine reliquaries are collected in André Grabar, *L'Art de la fin de l'Antiquité et du Moyen Âge*, 3 vols. (Paris, 1968).

8 Peter Brown, "The Rise and Function of the Holy Man in Late Antiquity," *JRS*, 61 (1971), 80–101; id., *Religion and Society in the Age of Saint Augustine*, (London, 1972); id., *Society and the Holy*, (Berkeley, Calif., 1982); id., *The Cult of the Saints* (at note 1).

9 Baudouin de Gaiffier, "Les Sources Latines d'un Miracle de Gauthier de Coincy," *Analecta Bollandiana*, 71 (1953), 100–132; "Les Sources de la Passion de S. Eutrope de Saintes dans le 'Liber Sancti Iacobi,'" *Analecta Bollandiana*, 69 (1951), 55–66; "Les Sources de la Passion des Saints Savin et Cyprien," *Analecta Bollandiana*, 73 (1955), 323–41; "Les Sources de la Vie de Saint Cassien, Evêque d'Autun," *Analecta Bollandiana*. 66 (1948), 33–52.

10 Ilene H. Forsyth, *The Throne of Wisdom* (Princeton, 1972), pp. 32–34.

11 Bernard Topfer, "Reliquienkult und Pilgerbewegung zur Zeit der Klosterreform in burgundisch-aquitanischen Gebeit," *Vom Mittelalter zur Neuzeit,* ed. H. Sproemberg and H. Kretzchmar (Berlin, 1956), pp. 420–39.

12 Pierre Heliot and Marie-Laure Chastang, "Quêtes et voyages de reliques au profit

des églises françaises du moyen âge," *Revue d'Histoire Écclesiastique* 59 (1964), 789–822; 60 (1965), 5–32.

[13] Donald Weinstein and Rudolph Bell, *Saints and Society* (Chicago, 1982) builds on the work of Pierre Delooz, "Pour une étude sociologique de la sainteté canonisée dans l'église Catholique," *Archives de Sociologie des Réligions* 13 (1962), 17–43 and his *Sociologie et canonisations*, (Liège, 1969). Their premise that men chose to act like saints because of their reaction to society conflicts with the theological explanation that God chooses certain men to be saints and that sanctity is a result of the indwelling of the Holy Spirit. Patrick Sherry, *Spirit, Saints, and Immortality*, (Albany, 1984) presents a modern model which would certainly have been regarded as heretical in the Middle Ages and is probably too anachronistic to provide a useful explanation of distinguished churchmen. Methodologically this problem could probably be clarified by using a control group of men who chose a religious life but did not become saints instead of a saints-only sample.

[14] Ward, (at note 4), *passim.*

[15] Anatole Frolow, *La Relique de la Vraie Croix*, (Paris, 1961); id., *Les Reliquaires de la Vraie Croix*, (Paris, 1965).

[16] Joseph-Claude Poulin, *L'ideal de sainteté dans l'Aquitaine carolingienne d'après les sources hagiographiques (750–950)*, (Quebec, 1975). Also Andre Vauchez, *La sainteté en occident aux derniers siècles du Moyen Âge: D'après le procès de canonisation et les documents hagiographiques*, (Rome: Bibliothèque des Écoles Françaises d'Athènes et de Rome 1981), p. 241. An important methodological question hinges on whether the ideas of sanctity, or of other ideas for that matter, are better measured by studying the living saints or the saints revered at any certain time. Whereas Delooz, Weinstein, and Bell study the saints in the context of the century in which they lived, we choose to group them in the times in which they were venerated. Although relic cults, by their very nature, concern a relationship with the past, extraordinary exemplars like saints may well offer evidence which is out of tune with contemporary values except when evidence of an active cult shows contemporary acceptance. Measuring concrete evidence of active cults attests to changes in religious sensibilities of a wide segment of the population.

[17] Claire Wheeler Solt, (at note 2), ch. 4, "The Fourth Crusade and Early Gothic Reliquaries," pp. 192–230; and "Byzantine and Gothic Reliquaries," *Byzantinoslavica*, 45 (1984), 212–16.

[18] Weinstein and Bell, (at note 13), pp. 166–93. Studies of saints' birthplaces over time reveal high numbers for France, (forty-six for the eleventh and seventy-four for the twelfth centuries): numbers roughly equivalent to the numbers of saints produced by Italy, seemingly greater than the British Isles during the same period, and less than in the Holy Roman Empire. In all regions, there were more saints during this period than in following centuries. The fact that this period did produce a comparatively high number of saints but that they did not quickly receive great reverence of their communities, as did Thomas Becket in the same period, indicates the conservatism of the cult in this region at this time, as well as problems inherent in choosing a sample from modern compendia of saints which represent the distilled judgment of history on sanctity better than contemporary assessment.

[19] Brown, *The Cult of Saints*, p. 24, enunciated the principle this way. "Excessive celebration of funerary rites, undue expressions of loyalty to the memory or to the

tombs of the dead, could become a lever by which one group might hope to assert themselves, in the name of the departed, among their living fellows."

[20] Michel Aubrun, *L'Ancien Diocèse de Limoges dès Origines au Milieu du XI Siècle,* (Clermont-Ferrand, 1981), pp. 167, 217. John of Lodi, "De Gallica Profectione", MPL, 145, pp. 875–76; *Acta Concilii Lemovicensis II,* MPL 142, pp. 1353–1400.

[21] Valous, *Le Monachism Clunisien*[2] (Paris, 1970) II, p. 179, n. 1.; H. E. J. Cowdrey, *The Cluniacs and the Gregorian Reform* (Oxford, 1970) claimed that Cluny possessed relics of Saint Peter who could therefore "be venerated there as he could be venerated at Rome. It could even be said, by a bishop that to come to Cluny was to come 'ad limina apostolorum.' " (pp. 142–43.) Cowdrey probably exaggerated the appeal of the cult of Saint Peter at Cluny. Whereas it is logical to attribute interest in apostolic saints partly to the vigorous assertion of the primacy of Saint Peter by the reform papacy and Cluny, the type was also rooted in authentic regional tradition: Sulpicius Severus who called Saint Martin "potens et vere apostolicus" in *Vita Martini,* 7.7, trans. B. M. Peewles, *Niceta of Remesiana, Sulpicius Severus, Vincent of Lerins, and Post-Nicene Fathers,* (New York 1949). *v* Peter Brown, "Relics and Social Status in the Age of Gregory of Tours," *Society and the Holy,* (Reading, 1977), pp. 222–50. The customary of Udalrich is the best indication of the Cluniac hierarchy of saints: "Post matutinas regulares (les Laudes) agimus quorumdam commemorationem sanctorum cum antiphonis versibus et collectis, qui nobis est familiare ut appellamus suffragia angelorum, sanctorum, et primo quidem sanctae crucis, sanctorum angelorum, sancti Joannis Baptistae, sanctorum Petri et Pauli, aliorum apostolorum, sanctorum martyrum, sancti Martini, sancti Benedicti, sanctorum simul Patrum Oddonis, Maioli atque Odilonis, et novissime confessorum." MPL, CXLIX, cap. *v,* 650. This list clearly deviates from prevailing regional ideas of sanctity especially in its preference for the dominical relic of the True Cross and the apostles over martyrs as well as its inclusion of contemporary Cluniac saints and "new confessors." The first appearance of the feasts of the translations of these Cluniac saints is in "Calendrier clunisien X-XI s." Valous, I, Appendix III, 396–410 which lists April 29, *translation* S. Maioli; May 11, *translation* S. Maioli; May 13, *translation* S. Hugonis; August 10, *translation* S. Odonis. Feasts of Cluniac saints are given as January 2, Odilonis, and April 29 Hugh. Note that most Cluniac feasts occur in fair weather months, i.e., seasons when pilgrimage was most feasible, whereas the feast dates of the saints of the other shrines cannot be fitted into such a pattern. *v* Dom Hesbert, "Les témoins Manuscrits du Culte de Saint Odilon," *À Cluny, Congrès Scientifique,* (Dijon 1959), pp. 53–120.

[22] John of Salerno, *Vita Sancti Odonis,* III, 8, 81, MPL, p. 133; *Life of St. Odo of Cluny,* trans. & ed. Dom Gerard Sitwell, OSB, (London 1958), p. 79.

[23] In the twelfth century the Lazarus of the parable (Luke 16:19–31) and the Lazarus Christ raised at Bethany (John 11:1–46) were considered the same person. Likewise the sister of Lazarus, Mary of Bethany and Mary Magdalene were one person. A debate on the origins of the legend of Mary Magdalene in Burgundy has turned on the question of whether the legend had early roots in Provençal legends or whether it originated at Vézelay. In the middle of the last century, Étienne M. Faillon published a collection of documents and an argument impassioned by Restoration enthusiam for old traditions to prove the authenticity of the legend of the apostolic mission of Mary Magdalene in the south of France: *Monuments inédits sur l'apostolat de Saint Marie-Madeleine en Provence,* 2 vols. (Paris, 1848). His argu-

ment was based primarily on interpretation of a version of the legend attributed to Rhabanus Maurus, "Rabanus de vita Beatae Marie Magdalenae et sororis ejus," *Monuments* II, pp. 457 ff. The assertion that the legend originated at Vézélay and had no real roots in Provençal tradition was first made by F. Duschesne, "La Legende de Sainte-Marie Madeleine," *Annales du Midi*, 5 (1893) 1–33, and *Fastes Episcopaux*, I, 310. Duschesne pointed out some historical discrepencies. Recent work by Victor Saxer has expanded on the objections of Duschesne and has disproved Provençal origins and associated the legend of Mary Magdalene in France with the reform of the abbey of Vézélay and its subsequent history. He showed the Rhabanus Maurus legend to be a forgery in "La 'Vie de Sainte Marie Madeleine' attribué au Pseudo-Rhaban Maur, oeuvre claravallienne du XIIe s.," *Mélanges S. Bernard*, (Dijon, 1954), pp. 408–21. He then proceeded to investigate the development of the legend of Mary Magdalene at Vézélay in "L'origine des reliques de s. Marie Madeleine à Vezelay dans la tradition historiographique du moyen âge," *Revue des sciences réligieuses*, 29 (1955), 1–18, and in *Le culte de Marie Madeleine en Occident*, (Auxerre and Paris, 1959) which is considered the definitive statement on the subject. Also of interest is his *Le Dossier Vézélien de Marie Madeleine, Invention et Translation des Reliques en 1265–1267, Subsidia Hagiographica*, 57, (Brussels, 1975). R. Louis, *Girart, Comte de Vienne (819–877) et ses fondations monastique* (Auxerre, 1946), hypothesized that a rivalry between monasteries in Provence and Vézélay fostered this legend attributing the transferal of the relics of Mary Magdalene to Girart, and that this legend originated in Provence. The thesis is refuted by Baudouin de Gaiffier, "Hagiographie bourguinone," *Analecta Bollandiana*, 69 (1951), 131–44, who agreed with Saxer that all of the legends of Mary Magdalene in France originated at Vézélay in the eleventh century. However he yields to the evidence of P. de Vregille, "Saint Lazare d'Autun ou la Madeleine de Vézélay? Un problem d'antériorité," *Annales de Bourgogne*, 21 (1949), 34–43 who has discovered traces of a cult of Lazarus at Autun in the tenth century and argues that the tradition and propagandization of relics of the family of Bethany in Burgundy originated at Autun.

[24] de Gaiffier, *Anolecta Bollandiana*, 73 (1955). p. 328; Poulin, (at note 16), p. 33.

[25] Ward, (at note 4), pp. 33–56.

[26] Brown, (at note 1), p. 8.

[27] Jean Maury, Marie Madeleine Gauthier, Jean Porcher, *Limousin Roman* (Zodiaque, n.d.) pp. 17 and 29. In addition to Saints Leonard and Junien included here they cited St. Amand, St. Sylvain d'Ahun, St. Goussard, St. Pardoux, St. Marien en Combraille, and St. Psalmet of Eymoutiers, saints even more obscure than the ones studied here.

[28] For a survey of the development and diversification of the cult of relics in Byzantium beginning with the cult of holy places during the reign of Constantine and growing to include *brandea*, bodies of saints translated to the capital, fragments of saint's bodies, then items of clothing of the Virgin, and finally miraculous portraits v. Claire Wheeler Solt, (at note 2), pp. 128–38. Hippolyte Delehaye, *Les Origines du Culte des Martyres*, (Brussels, 1911); R. Janin, *La Géographie Écclesiastique de L'Empire Byzantin*, t.III: *Les Églises et Les Monastères*, (Paris 1953), and Jean Ebersolt, *Sanctuaires de Byzance*, (Paris 1921). On the cult of holy places, *v* Charles Couason, O, P., *The Church of the Holy Sepulchre in Jerusalem*, trans. J. P. B. and Claude Ross,

(London, 1974), 12; and Gregory Dix, *The Shape of the Liturgy*, (Westminster, 1943), 348. On *brandea v* Jean Lassus, *Sanctuaires Chrétiens de Syrie*, (Paris 1947) and *DACL*, II, 132. For miraculous portraits *v* E. Kitzinger, "The Cult of Images in the Age before Iconoclasm," *Dumbarton Oaks Papers*, 8 (1954) 112–13 and Louis Bréhier, "Icones non faites de main d'homme," *Revue Archéologique* 35 (1932), 68–77. For the cult in Rome and its bibliography, *v* John M. McCulloh, "The Cult of Relics in the Letters and 'Dialogues' of Pope Gregory the Great: A Lexigraphical Study," *Traditio* 32 (1976), 145–184. For documentation of Carolingian importation and even theft of relics of Roman martyrs during the ninth and tenth centuries *v* Geary, *Furta Sacra* (at note 3), who admits that preferences changed in favor of regional saints during the eleventh and twelfth centuries: *v* pp. 93, 124.

29 Dom Hesbert, op. cit. (at note 21), p. 77.
30 Adémar de Chabannes, *Chronique*, ed. J. Chavanon, (Paris 1874); MPL 141, pp. 10–79.
31 *Codex Calixtinus*, ed. Walter Muir Whitehill, (Compostela 1940), p. 364.
32 Jonathan Sumption, *Pilgrimage: An Image of Medieval Religion*, (London, 1975), p. 37.
33 Adémar de Chabannes, (at note 30); *Acta Sanctorum* (AASS hereafter), June 7, 513.
34 Sumner M. Crosby, *The Abbey of Saint Denis*, (New Haven, 1942), p. 44. Also on the cult of Saint Denis, *v* Gabrielle M. Spiegel, "The Cult of Saint Denis and Capetian Kingship," *Journal of Medieval History*, 1975; *Abbot Suger and Saint Denis*, ed. Paula Gerson, (New York: Metropolitan Museum of Art), 1986.
35 Geary, (at note 3), *passim*, treats thefts of relics extensively. Note, however, that thefts were more characteristic of the ninth and tenth centuries than they were in the eleventh and twelfth when "inventio" or discovery of relics was the most frequent way obtaining new relics.
36 There are three main literary records of the cult of Saint Foy at Conques: *The Passion of Saint Faith* (AASS, Oct. 3, 288–89); *Chanson de Ste. Foy* (AASS, Oct. 3, 289–92); and the *Book of Miracles of Saint Foy* (*Liber Miraculorum Sancte Fidis*, ed. A. Bouillet, (Paris, 1877). Benedicta Ward, (at note 4), pp. 36–46, is the important recent survey of the cult of Saint Foy. She classifies all three sources as products rather than causes of the cult because of the late dates of their composition. As such they reflect the values of the cult under study. *v* also AASS, Oct 3, 294–99 for the theft and *Codex Calixtinus*, (at note 31), 1, 365 for the wider reputation of the claim of Conques to have all of the relics of the saint. All of the important works which deal with monastic or art history in this period touch on the cult of Saint Foy. Those which treat it in depth are *The New Catholic Encyclopedia*, *v*, p. 1049 and Jean-Claude Fau, *Conques*, (La Pierre qui Vivre, 1973). Others who treat it in context are Gaillard, *Pélerins*, p. 95; B. de Gaiffier, (at note 9), p. 310 and P. Brown, *Society and the Holy*, (at note 8), p. 330.
37 The cult of Saint Benedict at Fleury is treated by Ward, (at note 4), pp. 42–56, with a good summary of relevant bibliography. On the cult of Saint Benedict at Monte Cassino *v* the *Dialogues* of St. Gregory the Great, *Magni Dialogi*, ed. U. Moricca, *Fonti per la storia d'Italia*, 57 (Rome 1924) and Desiderius, *Dialogi de Miraculis Sancti Benedicti*, ed. G. Schwartz and A. Hofmeister, MGH, 32 (1934). For analysis *v* Pierre Boglione, *Miracle et merveilleux réligieux chez Gregoire le Grand*, Théorie et Thèmes," (Diss., Montréal, 1974), first part published as "Miracle et nature chez

Grégoire le Grand", *Epopées, légendes et Miracles,* (Montréal, 1974); also McCulloh, (at note 28). On the translation of the relics of Saint Benedict to Fleury *v* Peter the Deacon, *Historia Relatio de Corpore S. Benedicti Casini,* AASS, March 3, 288–89; Paul Meyvaert, "Peter the Deacon and the Tomb of St. Benedict," *Benedict, Gregory, Bede and Others* (London, 1977), pp. 3–70; *Il sepolcro du S. Benedetto,* Miscellanea Cassinese, 27 (Montecassino, 1951); and Walter Goffart, "Le Mans, St. Scholastica, and the Literary Tradition of the Translation of St Benedict," *Revue Benedictine,* 77 (1967), 107–41. On the cult of Saint Benedict at Fleury, *v Les Miracles de Saint Benôit,* ed. E. de Certain, (Paris, 1856); Peter Damien, "Sermon for the Vigil of St. Benedict," MPL 144, pp. 545–48; John of Salerno, *Life of Saint Odo;* and Deodat Galli, *Saint Benôit en France,* (Fleury, 1950).

[38] "Relation de l'anonyme", in Faillon, (at note 23), II, pp. 720–21.

[39] "Historia Sancti Florenti Salmurensis", Paul Marchegay and Emile Mabille, eds., *Chroniques des Églises d'Anjou,* (Paris 1869), pp. 309–310.

[40] Hugonis, "Chronicon Virdunense seu Flavinicensis", MGH SS, VIII, 373.

[41] Benedetto Cignetti, "Mama de Cesarea," *Biblioteca Sanctorum,* (Rome, 1961–69), 8, 603–04; AASS, August 3, 423–46.

[42] Bernard Leib, *Rome, Kiev, et Byzance à la fin du XIe siècle,* (Paris, 1924), and Cignetti, op. cit. (at note 41), p. 607.

[43] "Epistola P. sedis apostolicae legati ad canonicus Lingonensis—de reliquiis Sancti Mamantis martyris", MPL, 217, pp. 132–34. This letter was written by the papal legate to authenticate the relic. *v* Janin, (at note 28), III, p. 329 for the church of St. Mamas in Constantinople.

[44] "Canonicus Lingonensis", in *Exuviae Sacrae Constantinopolitanae,* Count Riant, ed., (Geneva, 1877–98), I, 33–34. *v* also A. Coulon, "À propos d'une relique de Saint Mames," *Analecta Bollandiana* 66 (1928), 78–80.

[45] Martène et Durand, *Voyage littéraire de deux religieux benedictins de la Congrégation de Saint Maur,* (Paris, 1717; repr. 1954), pp. 408–21.

[46] Abel Lefranc, "Le Traité des Reliques de Guibert de Nogent," *Etudes d'Histoire du Moyen Age,* (Paris, 1896), pp. 285–306 argued for the exceptional perspicacity of Guibert in *De Pignoribus Sanctorum,* MPL, 156, pp. 607–80. Indeed it is hard to reconcile this criticism with the role relics played in his *De Vita Sua,* (MPL 156, pp. 607–80) unless one understands the importance of patron saints vis à vis fragmentary relics. Guibert scorns the latter, at the minimum considering them less important and sometimes even spurious, while he accepts the dubious patron Quillus without comment. *v Self and Society in Medieval France,* ed. John Benton, (New York, 1979) with interesting introductory notes when Benton argues that Guibert distinguished between corporeal and non-corporeal relics. An earlier English edition was Guibert of Nogent, *Autobiography,* C. Swinton Bland, trans., (Routledge n.d.). *v* also Klaus Guth, *Guibert von Nogent und die hochmittelalterliche Kritik an der Reliquienverehrung* (Ottobeuren 1970).

[47] *Liber sancti Jacobi, Codex Calixtinus,* (at note 31), VIII, p. 365. "De corporibus sanctorum que in ytinere Sancti Iacobi requiescunt, ejus sunt visitanda . . . visitandum deate Fidis virginis et martiris . . . corpus preciossimum in valle que uulgo dicitur Conquas."

[48] *Ibid.,* "Item in eadem via vsitanda est corpus dignissimum beati Saturni episcopi et martiris." At Saint Sernin one can still see the marble sarcophagi in the apsidal chapels which reputedly held the bodies of apostles which Charlemagne deposited

there on his return from Spain. *v* Christopher Robert Cheney, "Church Building in the Middle Ages," *Bulletin of the John Rylands Library*, 34 (1951) 20–36; and Joseph Bédier, *Les Légendes Epiques: recherches sur la formation des chansons de geste*, (4 vols., Paris 1914–21), II, p. 342.

49 *Liber sancti Jacobi*, (at note 47), p. 364. "Sanctissimus Guillemi corpus est visitandum . . . visitandum lignumque dominicum apud Gelloni secum detulit."

50 *Ibid.*, p. 369.

51 Raymond Oursel, *Evocation de la chrétienté romane*, (La Pierre qui Vivre, 1968). Daniel Missione, "Un écrit de saint Gérard de Brogne relatif à une relique de saint Landelin," *Analecta Bollandiana*, 83/1–2 (1965) 105, warned that the term "corpus" could be used for any significant relic and did not necessarily mean possession of the whole body of the saint. However, it most certainly can mean whole body as here where the linguistic evidence is supported by other kinds of proof.

52 "Sermo cuius supra in honore sancti illius cuius reliquiae sunt in presenti," in "Petri Venerabilis sermones tres," ed. Giles Constable, *Revue Benedictine*, 64 (1954), 265–272. Translations mine.

53 *Ibid.*, p. 265.

54 Gregory of Tours, *De Gloria confessorum*, LIII, *MPL*, 71, 867. "Cui quae sit merces in caelo, ad ejus ostenditur tumulum; eumque inhabitare paradisum prodit virtus egrediens de sepulcro." It has been suggested that an interesting avenue of investigation would be to explore relationships between the theory of dual existences of saints and seemingly similar concepts concerning kings in France and the Holy Roman Empire. See Ernst Kantorowicz, *The King's Two Bodies*, and the work of E. A. R. Brown and others on burial and dismemberment of the Capetian kings.

55 "Sermones Tres", (at note 52), p. 266. Apparently incorrupt bodies were not universally accepted as signs of sanctity. In other cultures incorruption could be regarded as a sign of evil.

56 *Ibid.*, 271.

57 Falcon, "Chronicon Trenorchiense", *Monuments des abbayes de Saint Philibert*, ed. René Poupardin, pp. 26; 88.

58 *Liber Miraculnum*, ed. A. Bouillet (at note 36), I, pp. 13, 49.

59 "Sermones Tres", (at note 52), p. 265.

60 *Ibid.*, 266.

61 "Chronicon Sensoniensis", *Spicilegium*, II, p. 611.

62 Frederik Van der Meer, *Cathédrales Méconnues de France* (Brussels 1968), pp. 159–60; fig. 172. Tomb sculpture in Medieval France has not been the subject of serious systematic study, though it merits such attention.

63 Duchesne, (at note 23), p. 32; Faillon, "Ancienne Vie de S. Marie Madeleine," *Monuments*, I, 49; II, 435. (*v*. n. 23).

64 Vera and Hellmut Hell, *The Great Pilgrimage* (New York, 1968), pp. 122; 135; plate 69.

65 Ouen Audeoni, *Vita Sancti Eligii Episcopi*, *Spicilegium*, II, pp. 87–88; 93.

66 Germain Bapst, "Le tombeau de Saint Quentin", *Revue Archéologique*, 14 (1889), p. 271, argued that Saint Eloi probably only decorated Gallo-Roman marble tombs with precious jewels and metals and did not make large metal *châsses* because there are no large *châsses* from so early a date which are extant. Neither are there any marble tombs with Merovingian decoration in gold and gems extant. St. Ouen was

explicit "auro argentoque et gemmis fabricavit sepulcra," but difficult to interpret
in light of material evidence.

[67] Bernard Craplet, *Auvergne Roman*, (Zodiaque, 1958), p. 96.

[68] *Chronicon S. Medari Seussonicus, Spicilegium*, II, p. 487.

[69] On the decline of the marble industry and invasions, Jean Hubert, *L'Art Pre-Romain* (Paris, 1938), p. 98.

[70] Hesbert, op. cit., (at note 21) pp. 61; 77; Topfler, op. cit. (at note 11), p. 427 AASS, May V.II, 690–98.

[71] Joan Evans, *Art in Medieval France*, (Oxford, 1948), p. 24.

[72] *Dictionnaire des Églises de France*, (Paris, 1966–71), IIa, p. 153. In addition to the tomb of Saint Magnance, Joan Evans lists other Romanesque tombs which imitated Gallo-Roman sarcophagi: Saint Hilaire in the Aude, Saint Giles, Saint Libaude at Grandselve, and the tomb of Saint Vincent at Avenas: *v* Joan Evans, *Cluniac Art of the Romanesque Period* (Cambridge, England, 1950).

[73] Erwin Panofsky, *Abbot Suger*, 2, (Princeton, 1979), p. 119.

[74] Saint Junien, *Collegiale Saint Junien*, (Lyon, n.d.). Some information on the cult of the saint is given in Jean Becquet, "Collegiales et sanctuaires de chanoines seculiers en Limousin aux Xe–XIIe siecles," *Bulletin de la Société archéologique et historique du Limousin*, 103 (1976), 93–98.

[75] P. Quarré, "La sculpture du tombeau de Saint Lazare a Autun," *Cahiers de la Civilization mediévale* (1962), pp. 169–74.

[76] Maury, Gauthier, and Porchor, (at note 27), p. 66.

[77] "Recent accessions from the Brummer Collection", *Worcester Art Museum News Bulletin and Calendar*, (Oct., 1949), p. 2; *Worcester Art Museum Handbook*, (n.d.) p. 43.

[78] Good introductory articles on reliquaries can be found in *New Catholic Encyclopedia* 12, pp. 335–36, and DACL, 14, pt. 2, pp. 2294–2359. *v* also A. Ferrua, "Reliquie e reliquiarii," *Civ. Catt.*, 19.3 (1940), 354–61; and E. Meyer, "Reliquie und Reliquiari im Mittelalter," *Festschrift für Carl Georg Heise*, (Berlin 1950) (article unavailable). There is no systematic modern study of Romanesque French reliquaries available. Most useful are the general works of two French art historians: Jean Taralon, *Treasures of the Churches of France*, transl. Mira Intrator, (New York, 1966) which is based on an important 1965 Paris exhibition, and Marie Madeleine Gauthier, *Émaux Limousins* (Paris, 1950). *v* Konrad Hoffman, *The Year 1200* (New York, 1970). Joseph Braun, *Die Reliquiar des christlichen Kultes und ihre Entwicklung* (Freiburg, 1940), pp. 92–100, notes the preference for gold and silver reliquaries from the twelfth to the fourteenth centuries. However, his primary focus is on reliquaries of the Gothic period and later. Still very useful is Ernest Rupin, *L'Oeuvre de Limoges* (Paris, 1890), which drew on two works not available in the United States: Leon Palustre, *Orfèvrérie et émailerie Limousines* (Paris, 1887); and Emile Molinier, *Histoire general des arts appliqués à l'industrie du Ve à la fin du XVIIIe siècle;* IV *Orfèvrérie religieuse et civile*, Part 1 (Paris, 1896–1911). Jean Babelon, *L'Orfèvrérie francaise* (Paris, 1946) and *L'Orfèvrérie* (St. Mande, 1948) also treat the subject briefly. Although often cited, they appear to have been intended for use by tourists in Paris.

[79] Rodolfi Glabri, *Historiarum Libri Quinque*, III; VI, MPL, 142, 665. "Candidato, ut diximus, in novatis ecclesiarum basilicis universo mundo, subsequenti tempore, id est anno octavo infra praedictum millesimum humanati Salvatoris annum, revelata

sunt diversorum argumentorum indiciis, quorsum diu latuerant, plurimorum sanctorum pignora. Nam veluti quoddam resurrectionis decoramen praestolantes Dei nutu fidelium obtutibus patuere, quorum etiam mentibus plurimum intulere solamen."

80 *Chronicon S. Petri Vivi: Spicilegium,* II, 470, 474. These discoveries indicate that early Christian *martyria* outside of Sens were located and their saints were transferred to the monastery of Saint-Pierre-le-Vif. The *martyrium* of Saint Columba was located two kilometers north of Sens. Saint Loup, archbishop of Sens in the early seventh century, visited the *martyria* outside Sens nearly every night and requested burial at the *martyrium* of Saint Columba. He died September 1, 623. In the same era Saint Savinien's body was kept in a Merovingian basilica one kilometer east of Sens. Joseph Perrin, *Le Martyrium de saint Sanctien* (Sens, 1929).

81 Adémar de Chabannes, (at note 30) p. 174.

82 *Miracula S. Benedicti,* auct. Aimoino, mon. Floriacensi, in Victor Mortet, *Textes Relatifs à l'histoire de l'architecture en France* (Paris, 1911), p. 9.

83 R. Louis, (at note 23), p. 43.

84 *Breve Chronicon Sancti Florentii Salmurensis,* Marchegay & Mabille ed., p. 188; *Fragmentum Veteris Historiae Sancti Florentii Salmurensis,* Marchegay & Mabille ed., p. 211; *Historia Sancti Florentii Salmurensis,* pp. 309–10.

85 *Chronicon Senoniensis,* II, xv: *Spicilegium,* II, 616.

86 "Sermo de Relatione corporis Beati Vedasti a Bellovaco ad Proprium Locum", MGH S.S., 15, 402–05.

87 Nithard, *Hist.,* III, 2; *Bulletin de la Société archéologique de Soissons,* 14 (1883), p. 19.

88 *Chronicon Trenorchiense,* ed. R. Pourpardin, 38; 98. Jean Hubert, " 'Cryptae inferiores' et 'cryptae superiores' dans l'architecture religieuse de l'epoque carolingienne," *Mélanges d'histoire du Moyen Age dédiés à la memoire de L. Halphen,* (Paris, 1951) 351–57.

89 Joan Evans (at note 72, p. 25) asserts, "Such shrines and tombs were no longer hidden in a crypt or *confessio,* but were raised high where all men might see them, above, upon, or below the high altar of the church."

90 Only those things necessary for the celebration of the Mass could be placed on the altar, *Liber Pontificalis,* 275–283, I, p. 159 and 314–335, I, 171; Saint Augustine, *De Civitate Dei,* I. 22, c.8; Gregory of Tours, *De Gloria confessoris,* 130. The stringency of the rule was not allowed to lapse until the ninth century. In a homily of Leo IV, relics are allowed on the altar along with the Bible and the pixis. "Super altare, nihil ponatur nisi capsae et reliquiae et quatuor Evangelia, et pixis cum corpore Domini ad viaticum infirmis: caetera in nitido loco recondantur." MPL, 72, 83–84. Although permitted in the tenth century, it was rare for relics to be displayed on an altar. F. J. Mabillon, "Appendix ad opera Sancti Germani Parisiensis: de Liturgica Gallicana," (Paris, 1785) and MPL, 72, 83–84. When the relics of Saint Walburgis were placed on an altar, miracles ceased and the saint appeared to a sick man and warned him that he would not be healed because it was not fitting for his relics to be on the altar. *Ita S. Odo,* Lib. II Collationum, 28, 83. A. Grabar, (op. cit., at note 7) p. 38, explored the importance of associating relics with altars in Western architecture.

91 Patrick J. Geary has written extensively and well on the humiliation of saints and their relics: *sv* "La coercition des saints dans la pratique religieuse médiévale," *La*

Culture Populaire au Moyen Âge, Études presentées au Quatrième colloque de l'Institut d'études médiévales de l'Université de Montréal, (1977), pp. 148–161; and "Humiliation of saints," in Saints and their Cults, ed. Stephen Wilson, (Cambridge, 1982), pp. 123–140; and an earlier version "L'humliation des reliques," Annales, E.S.C., (1979), pp. 27–42.

[92] Ademar de Chabannes, Chronicon, (v. n.30) 173.

[93] The correct identification and function of the fenestellae long eluded scholars. F. Cabrol-Leclercq, "Fenestella", DACL, 5, (1924–30), pp. 1355–58 unconvincingly identified them with small apertures in the faces of sarcophagi. René Louis, Autessiodurum Christianum (Paris, 1952), applied a manuscript illustration for the recontruction of the church of Saint Gall to the problems of the crypt at Saint Germaine, Auxerre and derived a workable explanation of the puzzling fenestellae. At St. Gall he identified the fenestella as the area between two sets of stairs leading from the choir to the altar which is labeled accessus ad confessionem. This clearly could not indicate stairs to a subterranean crypt which are identified in crypta ingressus et egressus. He hypothesized that it was instead an opening which would allow the devout to see the tomb of a patron from the choir and applied this scheme to his reconstruction of the crypt of Saint Germaine at Auxerre.

[94] AASS, June VII, 518; Liber Miraculorum (at note 36), I, pp. 28, 71–72. "Multa sanctorum corpora, que secundum morem illius provinciae feruntur ad concilia ... in capsos vel in imaginibus aureis, sanctorum corpora sunt evecta."

[95] Udalrico, Antiquiores Consuetudines Cluniacensis Monasterii, III; 15, 46, MPL 149, 758–59.

[96] Aimon, Mirac. S. Benedicti, II, p. 19, 123–25. Joan Evans, (at note 72), p. 20 claimed that the monks of Fleury carried the relics of Saint Benedict abroad on this occasion. However, they may have been too precious. The relics of his disciple were used instead.

[97] Liber Miraculorum (at note 36), II; pp. 4, 100; B. Ward, (at note 4), pp. 42, 47.

[98] Le-Brun-Dalbane, "Le trésor de la cathédrale de Troyes," Memoirs de la Société du départment de l'Aube, (1864), pp. 58–59 traced origins to ninth century invasions. Emile Mabille, "Les invasions Normandes de la Loire et les peregrinations du corps de Saint Martin," Bibliothèque de l'école des Chartes, XXX, 50, 6 ème ser., (1869), pp. 147–94 and 425–60 demonstrated that the image of nomadic monks had been exaggerated. Furthermore, most evidence suggests that relics were brought back and placed in a crypt as much as 100 years before the translations to the Romanesque châsses. Saint Martin of Tours's body returned permanently in 919 and was not translated to a châsse in the Romanesque church until 1014.

[99] Audeoni, (at note 65), p. 87.

[100] Ibid., 87, 88, 93.

[101] Hariulf, Chronique de l'abbay de St. Riquier, ed. F. Lot, (Paris 1894), pp. 120–22.

[102] Perrin, (at note 80), pp. 105–07.

[103] Historia S. Florentii Salmurensis, pp. 223, 309–10; Frag. Vet. Hist. Sancti Florentii, p. 211; Breve Chron. S. Florentii, p. 188 (at note 39).

[104] Chronicon Trenchorchiense, (at note 39), Cap. 38–39, 97–99. Evans, Cluniac Art, p. 25.

[105] AASS June VII, 518; Raymond Oursel, Les Pélérins du Moyen Age, (Paris, 1963), p. 63.

[106] Jean Hubert, "Introibo ad altare," *Revue de l'art*, 24 (1974) pp. 15–16.

[107] *Chronicae Sancti Albini Andegavensis*, eds. Paul Marchegay et Emile Mabille, *Chroniques d'Anjou*, (at note 39), p. 36.

[108] *Historia S. Florentii Salmurensis*, (at note 39), pp. 309–10.

[109] Rupin, *L'Oeuvre de Limoges*, p. 60; Fau, *Conques*, pp. 48, 122; Evans, (at note 72), p. 38; Gauthier, *Emaux*, p. 27. On the *châsse* of Bellac, J. Maury & Gauthier, *Limousin*, p. 286.

[110] *Liber Miraculorum* (at note 36), II; 4, 100. "Alia tempestate fuit portata imago sancte Fidis, et capsa aurea quam fertur donavisse Karolus magnus, sine qua etiam numquam ejusdem sacer imaginis loculus bajulantur." The reference to Charlemagne is considered a legendary popular belief of the eleventh century. AASS, Oct. III, 279. Jean Hubert interprets it as a mis-identification of a gift of Charles the Bold. Jean Hubert, "La statue de Sainte Foy," *Bulletin de la Société Nationale des Antiquaires de France*, (1943–44), pp. 390–95.

[111] *Ibid.*, "Schrina Concharum: monstrant opus undique clarum hoc ornamentum Bonesit facii monimentum." Although this inscription can be interpreted to mean that the *châsse* was made in the twelfth century (J. C. Fau, *Conques*, p. 48), it it unlikely that this rustic box was produced at Conques at this time.

[112] On the *châsse* of Saint Calmine (also called the *châsse* of Mozat and the *châsse* of Mozac), v E. Rupin, (at note 78), pp. 102–7; George N. Desdevises du Desert et Louis Bréhier, *L'Auvergne et ses Villes d'Art*, (Paris 1932), pp. 32–39; and K. Hoffman, *1200*, I, #135, p. 131. M. M. Gauthier, *Emaux*, pp. 26, 45, 79. On Saint Calmine, Jean Charles Didier, "Calmino", *Biblioteca Sanctorum*, III, p. 693; J. Baudot, "Calmine," *Vies des Saints*, VIII, pp. 333–34.

[113] B. Galli, *Saint Benoît en France*, pp. 44, 50.

[114] *Chronicon S. Petri Vivi, Spicilegium*, II, p. 478.

[115] Galli, (at note 113), p. 73.

[116] Kenneth Clark, *Civilization*, (New York, 1969), p. 41.

[117] Eva Kovacs, "Le chef de Saint Maurice à la cathédrale de Vienne", *Cahiers de Civilisation Mediévale*, 7.1 (1964), pp. 19–26. Jean Hubert, "Introibo ad altare," p. 17.

[118] De Gaiffier, (at note 36), p. 310; M. Roger Grand, "La Sculpture et l'architecture Romannes à Saint-Géraud d'Aurillac," *Mélanges Martroye*, pp. 239–67; "Breve chronicon Aurelicensis," Mabillon, op. cit., *Vetera Analecta*, II, pp. 237 ff; Lauffray, op. cit., p. 108; *Liber Miraculorum* (at note 36), XIII, p. 47.

[119] Barbier de Montault, "Revue des Inventaires," *Revue d'art Chrétien*, (1890) pp. 240–47 contains a tenth century inventory of the treasure of the cathedral which lists eighteen items.

[120] *Chronicon Trenorchiense*, (at note 39), pp. 98–99; Evans (at note 72), p. 28; B. Topfler, 423–24.

[121] On the statue of St. Peter at Cluny: "Antiquiores Consuetudines Cluniacensis," MPL, 149, 759 & 764; B. Albers, *Consuetudines Monasticae*, (1900–12) II; pp. 1, 184; Forsyth, *Throne of Wisdom*, p. 39.

On the statue of St. James at Compostela, v "Liber Sancti Iacobi," *Codex Calixtinus*, 15–18, 147, 233, 364; Vasquez de Parga J. M. Lacarra, and J. U. Riu, *Las peregrinaciones à Santiago de Compostela*, 3 vols. (Madrid 1949), pp. 40–45,

129–35; Marilyn Stokstad, *Santiago de Compostela*, (Norman, Oklahoma 1978), p. 59.

[122] *Liber Miraculorum* (at note 36), II; pp. 4, 100.

[123] Dom Hesbert, "Manuscrits du culte Odilon," 51–120.

[124] For a report on the recent restoration studies of the statue together with a good overview of other scholarship concerning the Saint Foy statue *v* Jean Taralon, "La majesté d'or de Sainte-Foy du trésor de Conques," *Revue de l'Art*, (1978), pp. 40–47. Another important recent analysis is Forsyth, *Throne of Wisdom*, pp. 49–52.

[125] Fau, *Conques*, 13. Kovacs, "chef de Saint Maurice," considered the reliquary at Vienne the first known example of one representing a crowned saint and that the crown closely resembled the diadem worn by the Saint Foy statue. However, she did not hold it to be a direct antecedent of the majesties because it only depicted the head whereas they represent a full figure and place great emphasis on the hands.

[126] *Miracula S. Demetrii*, 82–84 trans. in Cyril Mango, *The Art of the Byzantine Empire*, (Englewood Cliffs, New Jersey, 1952) pp. 129–30. The silver ciborium was destroyed by the Arabs in 904. For a reconstruction *v* G. A. and M. G. Soteriou *He basilikē toū Hagiou Demetrioū, Thessalonikes*, (Athens, 1952).

[127] *Liber Miraculorum*, (at note 36), I, pp. 17, 53. One part of Witbert's vision, his description of the saint as dressed in gold but having a white face, flushed with pink, makes it difficult to concur with Taralon that we see the original version of the statue which was made to hold a reused Imperial Roman golden head. Also Bernard of Angers emphasized the symbolic value of the colors of the saint's skin in his interpretation of the dream: "bene etiam per candorem, qui nitore sui alios colores vincit, karitas intelligitur, virtutum perfectissima, quem nos ante ruborem, qui martirium insinuat." *Liber Miraculorum* (at note 36), I, pp. 1, 10. To him the white stood for the saint's charity, the pink in her cheeks was for her bloody martyrdom. It seems unlikely that he would have made as much of this if the statue had a golden head at the time. Note also that the saint was represented differently, as a virgin, on the facade. One would expect the two visual representations to agree. Of some interest are Carl Alfred Meir's comments on the relationship of the appearance of Greek gods in dreams and in their cult images. According to Artemidorus, a god which appeared in dreams had to appear true to his attributes and to his cult image in favorable dreams. Gods appearing in false costume could easily lie. "The Dream in Ancient Greece and its Temple Cures," in Gustave E. von Grunebaum and Roger Caillois, eds., *The Dream in Human Societies*, (Berkeley, 1966). An investigation of this belief in the Middle Ages would be of use.

[128] Taralon, "La Majesté," p. 20.

[129] Bernard named three other reliquary statues of patron saints. Two were brought to the synod of Rodez between 1025 and 1031. *Liber Miraculorum* (at note 36), I, pp. 28, 672. "Sancti Marii, confessoris et episcopi aurea majestas, et sancti Amanti, eque confessoris et episcopi, aurea majestas." He also saw a statue of Saint Gerald on the altar at Aurillac. *ibid.*, I, 13, 47. "Sancti Geraldi statuam super altare positam perspexerim, auro purissimo ac lapidus preciosissimis insignem et ita ad humane figure vultum expresse effigitam."

[130] *Ibid.*, I, 13, 46–47.

[131] *Ibid.*, II, 4, 100.

[132] *Commemoratio Abbatum Lemovicensium, Chroniques de Saint Martial de Limoges*, ed., H.

Duples-Agier (Paris, 1874), p. 5. "Isdem Gauzbertus iconam auream Marcialis apostoli fecit sedentem super altare et manu dextra populum benedicentem, sinistra libra tenentem Evangelii." *Ibid.*, p. 6: "Hic de icona aurea loculum fecit aureum cum gemmis, in quo vectum est corpus Marcialis." The accepted reading of these two passages is that a statue became a reliquary. However, they can also be interpreted to mean that a statue was melted down and its materials were used to make a reliquary. Neither of the chroniclers of Limoges mentioned a statue after Josfred. Ademar called the reliquary in which Saint Martial's body was taken to Angely in 1017 "Vectorio ex auro et gemmis." *Chronicon*, III, pp. 56, 180. Bernard of Itier mentioned a reliquary which held the head of Martial twice calling it a "scrinium" and a "capsa". both of which translate châsse instead of statue. *Chronicon*, ed. Duplés-Agier, p. 43, "Josfredus . . . qui fecit ij cruces aureas et scrinium ubi caput apostolici de Icona que erat super sepulchri altare," and 80, "Capse ubi caput Apostolic manet, renovatur." The assumption has been that because there was a statue related to a reliquary, especially one for the head of a saint, that the statue was converted into a reliquary for the head.

On the cult of Saint Martial, AASS, June VII, 518–23; on the monastery C. de Lasteyrie, *L'Abbaye de Sainte-Martial-de-Limoges*, (Paris, 1901); Aubrun, *L'Ancienne Diocèse de Limoges*, L. Duschesne, *Fastes Episcopaux de l'Ancienne Gaule*, 2nd. ed., (Paris, 1907) II, 104–17; On the reliquaries, *v* E. Mâle, *L'art réligieux du XIIe siècle*, pp. 196–97; E. Sakur, *Die Cluniacenser*, (Halle, 1892) 404–05; E. Rupin, *L'Oeuvre de Limoges*, 69.

[133] *Histoire générale des églises de France*, II B, 86; Taralon, *Treasures*, pp. 26, 261. "Hic est caput Sancti Cesari Arlatensis Episcopi." For evidence of the cult of Saint Césaire *v* J. de Lauriere, "Ceinture de Saint Césaire, évêque d'Arles," *Bulletin Monumental* (1877) pp. 240–45; and Evans, (at note 72), pp. 24–25 on the tomb of the saint at Arles.

[134] *Vita S. Theofredi*, AASS, Oct. VIII, 527–32; Baudot, *Vies des Saints*, XI, pp. 616–17.

[135] F. Souchal, "Les bustes reliquaires et la sculpture", *Gazette des Beaux-Arts*, 67 (1966), p. 206.

[136] Ulysse Chevalier, *Cartulaire de l'abbaye de S. Chaffre; chronique de Saint-Pierre du Puy*, 67 (Paris, 1884), pp. 41–42. ca.998 A.D. "De vassibus Ecclesiasticus. Capsulas argenteas, ubi reliquiae sanctorum servantur, IIII vel quinque, cum majori capsa sanctorum Innocentium et arca illa ubi reliquiae sancti Theofredi sanctique Eudonis et quorumdam aliorum repositae sunt, quae circumdata auro et argento fulgere solebat, donec illius qui Jhersolimam properabant datum est pro commutatione possessionum: tali tamen tenore ut ex eisdem possessionibus ibidem restitueretur argentum; in illa quoque imagine sancti martyris multae sanctorum habentur reliquiae, cum quadam dominicae crucis ligni portione, cuius corona capitis ex auro mundo gemmisque pretiosis miri refulget specie venustatis, palmae quoque similtudo totius complet figmentum ipsius operis."

Emile Lesné, *Histoire de la propriété ecclesiastique en France*, III: *L'inventaire de la propriété*, p. 211.

[137] B Craplet, *Auvergne Roman*, p. 107; Marcel Chabozy, *St. Nectaire: L'église et son trésor*, (Clermont-Ferrand, 1978); Taralon, *Treasures*, 263; F. Souchal, "Bustes reliquaires," p. 206; E. Mâle, (at note 6), p. 202.

TABLE I   Shrines of Southwestern France
Which Used Reliquaries X–XII Centuries

LOCATION	PATRON SAINT	TYPE OF SAINT
Agaune	Candidus	martyr
Aix-en-Provence	Maximin	Biblical
Aix-en-Provence	Mary Magdalene	Biblical
Angely	John the Baptist	Biblical
Angers	Albin	bishop
Angers	Serge	martyr
Arles	Cesarius	bishop
Aurillac	Gerauld	confessor
Autun	Lazarus	bishop/martyr
Auxerre	Germaine	bishop
Avenas	Vincent	hermit
Beauvais	Vedast	
Beauvais	Lucien	martyr
Berze la Ville	Blaise	
Blaye	Romain	priest
Chamberet	Dulcide	bishop
Chambon	Valerie	martyr
Cluny	Peter	apostle
Conques	Foy	martyr
Dijon	Benigne	martyr
Figeac	Bibanus	
Fleury	Benedict	monk
Gigny	Taurin	bishop
Grandmont	Stephen Muret	monk
Grandselve	Libaude	
Issoire	Austremoine	bishop
Langres	Mamas	martyr
Le Mas d'Aire	Quiteria	martyr
Limoges	Martial	bishop
Maurs	Cesarius	bishop
Monastier	Chaffre	bishop
Mozac	Calmine	monk
Noblat	Leonard	hermit
Noyen	Eloi	bishop
Pamiers	Anthony	martyr
Perigueux	Front	bishop
Paris	Denis	bishop/martyr
Poitiers	Hilary	bishop
Rocamadour	Mary	Biblical
Rodez	Armand	bishop
Sacillinus (Seclin)	Piat	martyr
Saintes	Eutrope	bishop
Sens	Richard	

Sens	Hydylph	monk
Sens	Columba	martyr
Sens	Leon	bishop
Sens	Stephen	
Sens	Loup	bishop
Soissons	Medard	bishop
Soissons	Crispin	martyr
Solignac	Theau	monk
Souillac	Theophilus	martyr
Souvigny	Mayeul	monk
St.-Deodat	Deodat	bishop
St.-Flour	Flour	teacher
St.-Guilhelm-le-Desert	William	warrior
St.-Junien	Junien	hermit
St.-Nectaire	Baudimus	teacher
St.-Nectaire	Nectaire	teacher
St.-Savin	Savin	martyr
Tarascon	Martha	Biblical
Toulouse	Sernin	bishop/martyr
Tournus	Valerian	martyr
Tours	Brice	bishop
Tours	Martin	martyr
Tulle	Stephen	bishop
Vabres	Marius	bishop
Vezelay	Mary Magdalene	Biblical
Vienne	Maurice	martyr
Volvic	Priest	bishop

TABLE II RELIQUARIES AT MEDIEVAL SHRINES OF SOUTHWEST FRANCE

SHRINE	*RELIQUARY STYLE*
Agaune	statue, Candidus
Aix-en-Provence	tomb, Mary Magdalene
Angely	*châsse,* head John the Baptist
Angers	*châsse,* Albin
Arles	tomb, Cesarius
Aude	tomb, Magnance
Aurillac	statue, *châsse:* Gerauld
Autun	tomb, Lazarus
Auxerre	tomb, *châsse,* hand, cross: Germaine
Avenas	tomb, Vincent
Beauvais	*châsse,* Vedast
Bellac	*châsse*
Belvacus	tomb, Lucien
Brioude	tomb, Julien
Clermont	statue, Virgin; *châsses,* relics saints
Cluny	statue, Peter; *châsse: tabula*
Conques	statue, *châsse:* Foy
Flavigny	arm, vase, *casula*
Fleury	*châsses,* hand: Benedict
Grandmont	*châsse,* Stephen Muret
Langres	disk, arm, phylactery: Mamas
Le Mas d'Aire	tomb, Quiteria
Limoges	tomb, statue, *châsse:* Martial
Limousin	tomb, Stephen
Masseret	*châsse,* Valerie
Maurs	statue, Cesarius
Monastier	statue, *châsse:* Chaffre
Mozac	*châsse,* Calmine
Nevers	head, *châsse*
Noblat	tomb, *châsses* Leonard
Nogent	*châsse*
Paris	tomb, Genevieve
Paris	tomb, *châsses,* arm, head, hand: Denis
Perigeux	tomb, Front
Poitiers	tomb, Hilary
Rodez	statue, Armand
Sacilinus	tomb, Piat
Saone-et-Loire	*châsse,* Hughes Autun
Sens	tomb, *châsse:* Hydulph
Sens	*châsses,* phylacteries: Richard
Sens	*châsse,* Leon
Sens	tomb, Peter
Sens	tomb, Columba
Sens	*châsse,* Savinien

Solignac	statue, *châsse:* Theau
Souvigny	tomb, Mayeul
St.-Deodat	tomb, châsse
St.-Flour	*châsses*
St.-Guilhem-le-Desert	tomb, William
St.-Junien	tomb, Junien
St.-Nectaire	tomb, statue, *châsse:* Nectaire
St.-Nectaire	tomb, statue: Baudimus
Tarascon	tomb, cross: Martha
Toulouse	tomb, *châsse:* Sernin
Tournus	tomb, statue, *châsse:* Valerian
Tournus	tomb, statue: Porcian
Tours	tomb, Brice
Tours	tomb, Martin
Vabres	statue, Marius
Vezelay	tomb, Mary Magdalene
Vienne	tomb, head: Maurice
Volvic	tomb, Priest

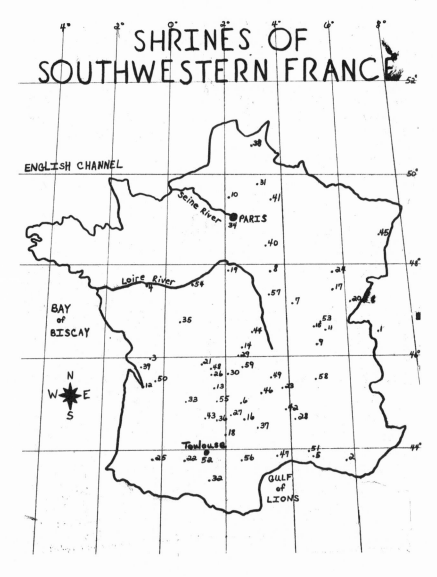

SHRINES OF
SOUTHWESTERN FRANCE

LEGEND FOR MAP SHOWING SHRINES OF SOUTHWESTERN FRANCE WHICH USED RELIQUARIES

X–XII Centuries

1 - Agaune		30 - Noblat
2 - Aix-en-Provence		31 - Noyon
3 - Angeley		32 - Pamiers
4 - Angers		33 - Perigueux
5 - Arles		34 - Paris
6 - Aurillac		35 - Poitiers
7 - Autun		36 - Rocamadour
8 - Auxerre		37 - Rodez
9 - Avenas		38 - Seclin
10 - Beauvais		39 - Saintes
11 - Berze la Ville		40 - Sens
12 - Blaye		41 - Soissons
13 - Chamberet		42 - Solignac
14 - Chambon		43 - Souillac
15 - Cluny		44 - Souvigny
16 - Conques		45 - St. Deodat
17 - Dijon		46 - St. Flour
18 - Figeac		47 - St. Guilhelm-le-Desert
19 - Fleury		48 - St. Junien
20 - Gigny		49 - St. Nectaire
21 - Grandmont		50 - St. Savin
22 - Grandselve		51 - Tarasoon
23 - Issoire		52 - Toulouse
24 - Langres		53 - Tournus
25 - Le Mas d'Aire		54 - Tours
26 - Limoges		55 - Tulle
27 - Maurs		56 - Vabres
28 - Monastier		57 - Vezelay
29 - Mozac		58 - Vienne
		59 - Volvic

Map by: B. Abbot, R. Bax, D. Bure, S. Cowley, L. Damph, J. George, V. Gohlston, D. Jordan, J. Libbert, D. Massman, P. McGuire, B. Prow, M. Schmitz, M. Wieberg

I. Chasse of St. Stephen Muret, Ambasac (photo: Paul Faye)

II. Tomb of S. Julien, 12th century (photo: Guillet Lescuyer)

IIIa. Sarcophagus, Worcester Art Museum, French 13th century, front, Christ in Majesty

IIIb. Sarcophagus, Worcester Art Museum, back, burial of a saint

IV. Lead chasse, St. Leonard de Noblat, 10th century (photo: C. W. Solt)

V. Chasse of Saint Foy, Conques, 10–12th centuries (photo: Auguste Allemand)

VIa. The chasse of Saint Calmine. Building the monastery at St. Chaffre.

VIb. Building the monastery at Tulle (photos: William Keighley)

VIc. Building Mozac
(photos: William Keighley)

VII. Majesty statue,
St. Foy, Conques
(photo: Auguste Allemand)

IX. Bust of St. Chaffre, Monastier,
11th century (after Taralon)

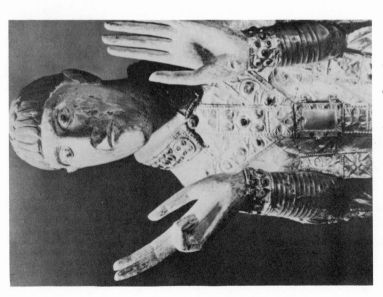

VIII. Bust of St. Cesarius of Arles.,
12th century (after Taralon)

X. Chasse of St. Theau,
Solignac, 12th century
(photo: C. W. Solt)

XI. Statue of St. Baudi-
mus, Nectaire, 12th cen-
tury (after Taralon)

INDEX

CONTENTS OF
PREVIOUS VOLUMES

M. F. VAUGHAN
The Liturgical Perspectives of Piers Plowman.

VOLUME IV (1981)
MARC GLASSER
Marriage in Medieval Hagiography.

ALBERT L. ROSSI
"A L'Ultimo Suo": *Paradiso* XXX and Its Virgilian Context.

RICHARD C. TREXLER
and MARY ELIZABETH LEWIS
Two Captains and Three Kings: New Light on the Medici Chapel.

VOLUME V (1982)
ALAN E. BERNSTEIN
Theology Between Heresy and Folklore: William of Auvergne on Punishment after Death.

ROBERT D. STEVICK
A Formal Analog of *Elene*

ARON JA. GUREVICH.
On Heroes, Things, Gods and Laughter in Germanic Poetry.

PAUL C. BURNS
Beneventan Interest in Vergil.

VOLUME VI (1983)
RICHARD C. HOFFMANN
Outsiders by Birth and Blood: Racist Ideologies and Realities around the Periphery of Medieval European Culture.

KATHRYN L. REYERSON
Land, Houses and Real Estate Investment in Montpellier: A Study of the Notarial property Transactions, 1293–1348.

D. L. FARMER
Crop Yeilds, Prices and Wages in Medieval England.

VOLUME VII (1986)
BERNARD S. BACHRACH
Geoffrey Greymantle, Count of the Angevins, 960–987: A Study in French Politics.

Crosscurrents: Children, Families & Religion

EVELYN KAYE

Crosscurrents:
Children, Families & Religion

Clarkson N. Potter, Inc./Publishers

NEW YORK

To my family

Copyright © 1980 by Evelyn Kaye

Printed in the United States of America
Published simultaneously in Canada by General Publishing Company Limited

Library of Congress Cataloging in Publication Data

Kaye, Evelyn, 1937–
  Crosscurrents.

  Bibliography: p.
  Includes index.
  1. Marriage, Mixed—United States.   2. Family—
United States   Religious life.   3. Religious education
of children.   I. Title
HQ1031.K37   1980   306.8'7   79-26687
ISBN 0-517-5312921   10 9 8 7 6 5 4 3 2 1

Contents

Acknowledgments

In researching, planning, writing, rethinking, and rewriting this book, I have met a wide range of people who have shared ideas, suggestions, information, and advice. I am deeply grateful to every one of them, and in particular to those hundreds of men and women across the country who invited me into their homes to explain how they were educating their children about religion. It is their thoughts, their beliefs, and their experiences that have been faithfully recorded in this book. Because of the personal nature of our discussions, I promised anonymity to those I interviewed. For this reason, all names and some locations have been changed, as well as minor identifying details.

Religious leaders from many faiths have openly and informatively answered my sometimes naïve questions. An informal advisory board read an early version of the manuscript and gave me their comments individually, based on their own particular religious expertise. I would like to thank them for their comments and suggestions:

Reverend Bradford Howe Bryant, Senior Pastor, Church of All Nations (United Methodist), Boston, Massachusetts

Reverend Dajad Davidian, St. James Armenian Apostolic Church, Watertown, Massachusetts

Dr. Leo Fahey, Roman Catholic, psychotherapist, Boston, Massachusetts

Reverend Rollin J. Fairbanks, D.D., Episcopalian; Professor of Pastoral Theology (retd.), Episcopal Divinity School, Cambridge, Massachusetts

Mr. Steve Gilliland, Director, Cambridge Institute of Religion, Church of Jesus Christ of Latter-Day Saints (Mormon), Cambridge, Massachusetts

Ms. G. Heinbockel, Assistant to the Director, Advisory Council on Church and Society, United Presbyterian Church, New York, New York

Reverend Kenneth Joines, Minister of Education, First Baptist Church of Newton, Massachusetts

Rabbi Allen Maller, Temple Akiba, Culver City, California

Dr. Donald Manthei, Lutheran, Director, Interfaith Counselling Center, Newton, Massachusetts

Dr. Edward Peacock, Executive Director, American Institute of Family Relations, Los Angeles, California and United Presbyterian minister, Anaheim, California

Dr. Paul Plummer, Superintendent of Education, Seventh-Day Adventist, Glendale, California

Mr. Clark Power, Center for Moral Education, Graduate School of Education, Harvard University, Cambridge, Massachusetts

Reverend G. William Sheek, Director of Family Ministries, National Council of Churches of Christ, New York, New York

Dr. Marshall Sklare, Professor of American Jewish Studies, Brandeis University, Waltham, Massachusetts

Reverend Robert Zoerheide, Unitarian Universalist, First Parish Church of Lexington, Massachusetts

My thanks also to Jean Kotkin, Joe Chuman, and Charlene Brotman of the American Ethical Union; Aharon G. Aharonian; Gerald B. Bubis; Stella David; Rabbi David Eichhorn; June Judson; Father Richard Little; Professor Egon Maier; and Rabbi Frank Waldorf.

Initial research benefited from the excellent resources of the Newton Public Library, Boston Public Library, Brandeis University's American Jewish Historical Association Library, and Harvard Divinity School Library. Attending meetings of the Newton Catholic-Jewish Committee was very educational during my year's membership, and my thanks to Sister Elizabeth Corbin.

From the beginning, Jane West of Clarkson N. Potter has provided unfailing support. My editors Audrey Soracco and especially Beth Rashbaum suggested constructive changes that improved and strengthened the manuscript. And along the way writer friends provided encouragement and advice, in particular Dian Dincin Buchman and Flora Davis of the American Society of Journalists and Authors. Also to Marion Meade and Wendy Lipkind, my sincere thanks.

Finally my deepest appreciation to my children, Katrina and David, who learned to tread cautiously when they saw me typing frenziedly, and to my husband, Christopher Sarson, who helped me survive the crises and never doubted a book would emerge from the mountains of papers and folders around my desk.

1

Who cares about religion today?

I t was at the surprise birthday party for a friend, given by the young psychiatrist she was living with, that I met a young woman who wanted to know the subject of the book I had just started.

"Families and religion," I said slowly. "It's an attempt to find out what parents are doing to pass on to their children the traditional religious values, observances, ceremonies, philosophical ideas, and moral concepts. In particular, it's a look at how these things are worked out in interfaith marriages, where the parents come from different religious backgrounds, because so many people today are involved in two-faith families."

She looked surprised. "Religion?" she said, picking up a cheese-covered cracker. "Surely no one bothers about religion anymore? How can anyone be interested in that? Does anyone care today?"

Her reaction was one I was to hear many times as I wrote this book, mostly from young people living independently or couples without children, and it was one that reflected what my own views had been before I became a parent and was forced to consider what kind of religious training, if any, I wanted to give my children in our dual-faith family.

1

"Often it doesn't seem to matter when you're single," I said, as she nibbled at her cracker, "or even when you're living with someone or married. The crunch comes when you have a child. That's when you have to make some kind of decision about what religious information you want your child to absorb, and how you will deal with the questions, and what reactions you will have to the information children pick up from television and radio, from their friends and your family. Even parents who say they intend to do nothing find that they have to cope with pressures from the outside world in some way."

She looked thoughtful. "I'm still not sure it matters though," she said. "Take my parents, for example. They were Jewish, and we did things at home once in a while—you know, we celebrated the High Holy Days and went to a couple of services and had a seder at Passover. But now that I am living on my own, I don't do anything. And then there are my two older sisters. They're both married, and they both married guys who aren't Jewish, so I suppose that shows that religion didn't mean much to them." She took a sip of her white wine. "But, you know, now that I think of it, when my sister had her baby this year, there was quite a fuss because she had him circumcised in the hospital, and her husband was mad. He wanted to baptize him, not circumcise him, and she wouldn't let the baby be baptized. Yes, there was quite a fight one day when she was over at my parents and I was visiting to see the baby. Her husband called on the phone, and they screamed at each other, and she got very hysterical and cried. I couldn't believe she would make such a fuss, because she never seemed to care about anything religious before. I mean, it seemed so pointless to me. Ummm . . . you know, I've never really thought about it before, but I'm not sure I could marry someone who wasn't Jewish; I don't know why, but I just don't think I could do it somehow." She took another sip of her wine and added, "It does matter, doesn't it, this religious thing?"

In the liberal, ethical, independent culture of today, religion is often dismissed. But the influence of traditional religious ideas quietly, often invisibly, permeates almost every area of our lives. The majority of Americans were brought up in one or another of the traditional religions, and the values that they learned in their church or temple, as well as the customs, rituals, and ceremonies, still influence their attitudes and thinking. Americans are among the most religiously aware citizens in the Western world, with more than half of the total population belonging to a church, and total church membership estimated at around 131 million.

In a typical week about 40 percent of adults in America attend a church or synagogue, compared to 26 percent in Greece, 20 percent in England, and 18 percent in Uruguay.

The Roman Catholic church has over 48 million members in the United States, about 23 percent of the total population, while the Protestant churches have nearly 70 million members, about 34 percent of the population, including 27 million Baptists, 13 million Methodists, 9 million Lutherans, and 2.5 million Latter-Day Saints (Mormons). There are also some 4.5 million followers of Eastern Orthodox churches and about 5 million Jews.

About one-third of all Americans consider themselves to be "unchurched" and are not affiliated with any religious group, but a 1971 Gallup Poll showed that only 2 percent of all Americans did not believe in God. Some groups with few members, like the Society of Friends (Quakers) with 116,261 adherents, or the American Ethical Union (5,000), have had an impact on American life far in excess of their numbers. And while there's been a great deal of attention paid to new sects and cults, statistically they are almost insignificant compared to the millions of followers of traditional denominations.

Long-held religious traditions are seldom actively cherished as part of the American dream. Our conscious emphasis is on assimilation, on the new, the unexplored. History and morality seem to us to begin in 1776, and the eras before that stretch brief and uncluttered, both in our school texts and in our consciousness. But our laws, our customs, our behavior are irrevocably linked with the past, and our history and our legends reach back far earlier than the arrival of Christopher Columbus, into the days of Romans and Greeks, Egyptians and Israelites. And in ways that often take us by surprise, we find ourselves clinging to our pasts and our traditions, to religious and ethnic customs that we thought we had left behind.

The clear separation of church and state in America protects our public-school children from the parochialism that often distorts the teaching in religiously directed schools. But it has also deprived them of a valuable education about the role of religion in world history. Almost completely ignored is a huge body of cultural and historical knowledge that touches on many facets of our lives and is linked to the art, literature, and music of our heritage. Furthermore, until very recently, concepts of moral values and discussions about ethical behavior were not brought into the classroom.

Today a child is likely to learn about religion only in the home, or from involvement in a religious institution, should the parents decide to join.

The reason children believe that Jesus was born of a virgin, unlike any other baby, is because their parents say so. If children are taught that baptism is essential for entrance to heaven, they will accept that unquestioningly. Children taught that alcohol is sinful and wicked will look askance at others who drink or may, in adulthood, rebel and drink to excess. And if at Easter children are instructed that "the Jews killed Jesus," they will accept that simplistic interpretation, and it may be unrealistic to expect them to show tolerance to the Jews they meet.

Indeed, as we grow up we may find it impossible to shake the ideas and attitudes passed on to us by our parents, no matter how intellectual or sophisticated we have become as adults. "Give me a child for the first seven years of his life and he is mine ever after" is one chilling religious dictum. Those emotional links to our earliest childhood stay with us throughout our lives, and to deny them completely is futile.

There is no way parents can avoid discussing questions about religion with their children. Messages from outside, from friends, from TV and radio reach even the youngest; every parent is forced to make some sort of response. Think of the questions raised by the deluge of Christmas TV specials and the incessant holiday-gift commercials. Your child may be absorbing only the most commercialized and simplistic messages about a Christian festival, but he will be curious about what he sees, and your reaction and explanations are important in interpreting these messages for him.

There's been little research into how children absorb ideas about religion or where they find the information. Dr. David Elkind, a research psychologist and member of the Society for the Scientific Study of Religion, examined over 700 young children between five and twelve to see when they understand the concept of religious identity and know what it means to say, "I am a Catholic" or "He is a Jew."

Children between five and seven years have only a vague concept of religious denomination, he found. They understand it as a kind of name, and cannot comprehend how people can have a religious denomination as distinct from a political or personal name. Several children in his small study said that people could not be an American and a Catholic at the same time. At seven, eight, and nine children begin to recognize the philosophies and practices that mark different beliefs. An eight-year-old when asked what a Catholic is replied: "He goes to mass every Sunday and he goes to Catholic school." But it is not until children are ten and over that they begin to realize what the differences mean intellectually. An eleven-year-old when asked what a Jew is said: "A person who believes in one God and doesn't believe in the New Testament." And a twelve-year-old when asked to define a Catholic replied: "A person who believes in the truths of the Roman Catholic church."

But at some point every child will wonder about the symbols or comments about religion that are around us every day. Questions such as "What is Christmas?" or "Who was Jesus?" will suddenly arise and every parent will be faced with an inquiring young face waiting anxiously for an answer. A father described how, as he sat reading the newspaper one evening, his five-year-old daughter came up and asked, "Daddy, is there a God?" "I didn't know what to tell her," he said. "My wife was bringing up the children as Catholics, and I supported her and never interfered. I don't believe in any religion and consider myself an atheist and have for a long time. But I didn't want to confuse my daughter with different ideas that were contrary to what my wife was saying or whatever they were being told in Sunday school. So I thought for a few seconds and then looked at her and said, Yes. She skipped off very happily because I had given her an answer. That's all she wanted. But I spent the rest of the evening thinking about it and what I should have said and what I wanted her to know about my beliefs."

Even parents who are quite sure of their religious ideas and feel they will have no problems sharing their beliefs with their children are facing new difficulties. Fundamental changes have shaken some of the basic tenets of traditional observances.

Within the Roman Catholic church, for example, any recognition of the realities of divorce was unacceptable. Yet today the number of church-granted marriage annulments is increasing annually, which is one way of permitting the official breakup of a marriage without calling it a divorce. The church has also lifted the ban on divorced and remarried Catholics attending mass. New groups have sprung up to provide emotional and spiritual support for the growing number of Catholics who find themselves divorced or separated.

These changes have come very rapidly since the historic Vatican Council meetings and announcements of the 1960s, and for many families, it's hard to adjust. A woman with grown-up children can see how conservative her attitudes are compared with her children's. "I was married very young," this middle-aged Catholic woman explained, "much too young I realize now, but I thought that was what I should do because I believed everything I had been told. My husband left me after the two children were born, and I brought them up myself. But I felt I could never divorce him because I had been taught not to believe in divorce. Finally, last year I filed for divorce, and when the papers came through in the mail, I picked them up and felt so strange holding them. It was like rejecting everything I had been taught as a child. But I can see those teachings are often foolish, and in fact when my daughter's marriage didn't work out, I urged her to get a divorce and to get a church annulment too, because there's no point in sitting around waiting. I couldn't let her throw away her life as I threw away mine."

In the Episcopal church, divorce was not acknowledged until 1973 when the church's convention ruled to recognize civil divorce and ease the strictures on remarriage. The church also agreed to admit women to the priesthood, and that decision has caused so much controversy that some communities within the Episcopal church have seceded to form their own church in defiance.

Women in traditional religions are slowly making themselves heard and are gaining new access to decision making and to training for leadership positions. These revolutionary changes shake the fundamental concepts of many religious groups and often cause bitter friction and conflict among church members.

One of the results of these new attitudes toward women in religion, together with the growing emphasis on autonomy for women in all areas of their lives, is the growing number of interfaith marriages. It's estimated that about half of Catholic marriages involve a non-Catholic, though statistics are hard to find. No independent agency has made a serious study of this phenomenon, and civil marriage licenses do not ask people to give their religion. For a few years in the 1950s, Iowa and Indiana requested religion on their marriage-license applications, and studies based on that limited data show that there were a large number of interfaith marriages. A study in New England of Armenian Apostolic ceremonies showed that today some 90 percent of their members' marriages involve a nonchurch member. And a spokesman for the Greek Orthodox church recognized that many church members marry outside the ancient faith.

"Our church recognizes a Catholic ceremony, though we sometimes suggest that couples be married in both churches. Today there is so much more mixing, more traveling, more freedom for young people than when I grew up. They can see things happening on television immediately that it must have taken months to tell people about in the old days. We try to encourage young people to come to our church camps, to join the social groups, and to meet others from the same background. But there are so many opportunities for them to meet others here in America. They meet, they fall in love, they want to marry, they do not understand the old ways. Perhaps in the end, this may be the best way of all for us in America, to recognize how we can understand each other's religion. But we certainly cannot go backward and close them up again the way it used to be."

Yet the statistics of some churches show that along with the growing trends to more liberal attitudes, there's been a steady membership increase in those religions that turn their back on the modern world, and insist on rigid adherence to strict Biblical tenets. Conservative Baptists, Jehovah's Witnesses, and the Mormons can point to hundreds of new congregants who choose the security of set rules over the modern emphasis on personal responsibility and situational ethics in the more liberal churches.

The new social changes can be difficult ones for many traditionalists, and particularly for many clergy, to accept. A 1978 study by the Council of Jewish Federations estimated that nearly 10 percent of all married Jews are in interfaith relationships, and that between 1966 and 1972 31.7 percent of all Jewish marriages involved a non-Jewish spouse. Another study by the rabbi of a New Haven, Connecticut, congregation showed that almost all second marriages involved a non-Jewish partner. However, there is virtually unanimous agreement among rabbis that interfaith marriages are to be deplored, and almost all rabbis refuse to officiate at such ceremonies. "It's a fraud and a sham," said one outspoken but typical Orthodox rabbi, "to officiate when both people are not Jewish because they cannot in any way be considered truly married, according to Jewish law." Those few rabbis who do perform such ceremonies feel that by welcoming the non-Jewish partner into the community there is far more chance that the children will be brought up as Jews.

However, a young Jewish woman married to a Swedish-Lutheran man described the problem of trying to do this. "We've joined a Reform temple, because my husband is very happy for the children to have a Jewish upbringing," she said, "and on High Holy Days we all attend. One New Year, the rabbi gave a sermon on interfaith marriages, how they were destroying Judaism and breaking up Jewish families. He could see us sitting there with my parents, who were visiting, and they were really shocked, and I was very embarrassed. Afterward, I called him up and asked him how he could have done such a thing. He was quite taken by surprise, and said he had always considered us a Jewish family and didn't think what he had said had anything to do with us. I said he was insensitive to the realities of what was happening in the world and that I respected my husband's background and his heritage as much as my own, and when we go to Sweden, we go to church with his family. At Christmas, this year, which happened to fall at the same time as Hanukkah, I called him up again and invited him over. I wanted him to see our Christmas tree with the Star of David on top, and the way we light the Hanukkah candles every night. He came, but I don't think he really understood what I was saying at all."

Nothing has prepared the leaders of traditional religions for the complexities of dual-faith allegiances that they may find in their communities. Their congregants are usually forced to find their own solutions to these complex issues, ignoring their religious leaders who often seem to be immersed in their own brand of worldliness, insensitive to individual spiritual needs.

In a 1978 study by Dr. Steven Huberman, research director of the Union of American Hebrew Congregations, of some four-hundred same-faith and interfaith Jewish families, he found that in 25 percent of the mixed-faith families the non-Jewish partner converted to Judaism, and in 75 percent of the cases the partner retained his or her original faith. However even among the converts, Christmas still posed sensitive problems, and 26 percent of them continued to observe the holiday, though as a secular celebration. One woman remarked, "Christmas was always so much fun—it's a great family celebration. When I convert, I want to be a good Jew, but sneak in Christmas."

"We seem to be losing sight of the need to listen to every member of our congregation," said a Presbyterian minister, "as if success in religion depends on numbers, on who has the most members. We need to become more flexible and to see our congregants as individual human beings and not simply preach to a crowd."

My own childhood was steeped in the strict rules of an Orthodox Jewish household, which in my earlier years I relished and enjoyed. But as I grew into adolescence, I was disturbed that women were considered unworthy to take part in services and were not encouraged to become active leaders. Instead men were in charge of everything while women subtly maneuvered from the home. The traditional Jewish prayers recited by every adult male in the morning still contain the blessing: "Thank you, Lord, for not making me a woman." To me, the options for a woman did not appear to include any possibility for study or travel or work that did not conform to the strict dictates of Orthodox Jewish law, and that looked depressingly limited. The rules began to seem foolish, the observances slowly fell away, and the beliefs seemed impossible to accept as I struggled to find a path that provided some of the challenges and satisfactions that I wanted out of life. It was a painful time of change, and there are still scars that may never heal because it is difficult for both parents and children to face the rejection of a traditional way of life.

When I met my husband, he had traveled a similar path leading away from a strict Methodist upbringing. The two of us found that we had arrived at the same point in our thinking.

We shared similar ethical values; we did not pretend to have solutions to the complex questions of life or death, but we felt better able to deal with our uncertainty than with the absolute answers that our religions had provided; and our characters and temperaments were inclined toward individuality and independence rather than commitment to a particular group or community. Because our proposed marriage caused a certain amount of criticism from our parents, we talked with a marriage guidance counselor about our concerns. He listened carefully, and then suggested we take the advice of the Book of Genesis, chapter 2, verse 24:

"Therefore shall a man leave his father and his mother, and shall cleave unto his wife: and they shall be one flesh."

Together we agreed to share both our heritages with our children, and so we have told them the truth as we see it. We celebrate those holidays that we feel comfortable with; we light the eight candles at Hanukkah; and share the story of the Maccabees fighting for religious freedom and the traditional *"Maoz Tsur"* song. We also have a Christmas tree, with its symbols of family sharing and reunion, and explain the reasons behind the celebrations. We have enjoyed a family Passover seder, where we read the story of the Jews' escape from the slavery of Egypt, with its wider implications for freedom and for the meaning of Israel to Jews today. And my husband explains the significance of Easter as a time of rebirth. We have never joined any religious organization though we have attended a variety of services. We feel it's important for our children to understand what happens in churches and synagogues, and to recognize the diversity of religious experiences in the world today.

This book grew from a short piece I wrote on interfaith families and the growing realization that parents are the main sources of their children's religious training, even if they "don't do anything." The research took me across the country to spend hundreds of hours with men and women who shared their deepest beliefs and personal experiences with me. In particular, there were seventy-five families, reflecting a wide diversity of faiths, whom I interviewed in depth. Scores of individuals spoke with me on the phone, talked informally or wrote to me, and I also had the benefit of communication with many religious leaders who provided information and suggestions.

I had hoped to find out what children believed and how they felt about religion. But after a few informal discussions it became clear that the complex ideas of religious faith wash past most children, and they simply repeat what they have been told by parents and teachers. It is not until they reach the teens, and later, that they begin to assess their philosophy and beliefs and examine their own personal values and ethics. Many children do not ever reach that stage of questioning, but simply continue to repeat what they were taught and pass it on to their own children.

It seemed difficult to accept as faith and understanding the religious ideas that children absorb from their parents in their early years. I realized it was far more important to talk with the parents about their beliefs and practices and what they were sharing with their children, than to ask children questions that their understanding was not ready to comprehend. A child of seven when asked about God will repeat what he has been taught about God; a child of seventeen is more likely to think about what he has been taught about God and how he feels and thinks and believes in relation to that education. But often it is not until the late teens and twenties that such thinking is clarified.

My research showed that character and personality were far more influential in religious decisions than denomination. Tolerant and understanding men and women can be found adhering to the most orthodox of traditions, just as bigoted and intolerant people

can exist within the most open-minded of liberal communities. I
learned to look at the person every time, not the label. The Catholic
priest who left after eighteen years in the priesthood was as individual in his attitudes as the young couple who joined the Unification
church and believed that the Reverend Moon was the Messiah. It
was essential for me to listen, to hear what people were really saying, and to understand their answers and comments within the context of their lives, not their religious labels. Sometimes it was difficult to listen objectively to ideas that sounded absurd or even
dangerous, but at other times a comment or explanation would
come as a dazzling ray of clarity to dispel my own confusion and
change my own thinking and attitude.

The most exhausting conversations were often with people who
were deeply involved in their faith and had a tremendous zeal to
share it, whom I found emotionally sympathetic as individuals. All
the persuasion, understanding, and charm they possessed would
spill out as they told me of their beliefs and concepts and their total
happiness with the path they had chosen, while I sat taking notes
and struggling for objectivity. Despite the enthusiasm of more than
one of my interviewees, I did not choose a new religious path. But I
did learn a new respect for the integrity and intelligence of people
from a wide range of backgrounds who had made a purposeful commitment to a variety of religions and who showed me their dedication and sincerity in following their faiths.

For me, this book has been a fascinating exploration of what is
really happening to religion within American families, from the perspective of the true educators, the parents. It's not a summary of
theological approaches from learned scholars in ivory towers, nor is
it a collection of philosophical statements from religious leaders. It
is a sampling of true experiences of family life with children of all
ages. I spoke to small children who had not yet begun to question
and to their grandparents who wonder if the religious practices of
the past will live on in this new generation.

Conversations with parents, the people who will have the most
immediate influence on the future of religion in America, often
turned into a discussion of our own childhood experiences. Again
and again, I watched parents look back in surprise at the extent to

which the religious ideas they had been taught as children were still with them emotionally, playing an active if undiscerned role in their lives, even though they no longer believed in them.

Your religious beliefs are like your first language. No matter how fluent you become in another tongue, the language you learned first will always be with you, invading your thoughts and your dreams, slipping out in moments of stress and intensity, shaping your response to the world. The ideas we absorb and the emotional ties we form in the earliest years affect our development for the rest of our life, and religious influences are a part of the picture. We can never completely erase them, even if we eventually reject them. We must acknowledge them as a permanent part of our experiences and identity.

One of the things that struck me more as I listened and learned was the similarities of idea and practice that crossed the boundaries of different religious labels. Rituals in many faiths are marked by the lighting of candles. The concept of a day of rest is echoed in many religious communities. And the subservient "handmaiden" role of women is the accepted pattern in most religions.

A woman who had been brought up in the Episcopal church and then married a Jew felt that it was only when she began to learn about her husband's Jewish faith that she really understood her own. "It's impossible to understand that Jesus was a rabbi and a teacher in the community until you understand something of what that means," she said. "I don't think Christians really grasp the importance of much that's in the New Testament until they know something of Judaism."

I have attempted a panoramic examination of the practice of religion in America today and have tried to make my observations from an open, ecumenical viewpoint that rejoices in the diversity and variety on the scene. There is no summary of faiths, no comparison of one with the other, but a sharing of personal family experiences by men and women with a range of different backgrounds. This view may disconcert or anger those who believe their way alone is the correct one and that all others should be brought round to this recognition. But religion, interpreted as a complex pattern of faith, belief, values, and morals as well as rituals and observances, is a matter of individual decision and responsibility. If we choose to reject the religion in which we were raised, we must find our own answers for the difficult questions that life presents. In this book you will find how a number of different families have accomplished that task, ranging from the devotion of a Lutheran-Jewish partnership to the commitment of a Japanese-American Buddhist family. Some families feel that their lives are healthier without religion while others happily follow in the paths of their parents and grandparents. And some find themselves caught in the midst of unexpected changes and must find their own solutions to those dilemmas.

But in all cases, it is clear that parents have the responsibility for what their children learn about life, values, ethics, and religion. If parents make a firm commitment to a particular church, or if parents casually decide to "do nothing," the child will learn from that, because children learn from watching and listening and thinking, and a parent's basic attitude toward life and faith is as important as anything he may say, in words, about his beliefs.

The families you will meet are not perfect, nor do they have all the answers to the difficult questions about teaching children religious ideas today. But they have thought seriously about religion, tradition, ethical values, formal observances, and they provide valuable insights into the ways in which parents are bringing up American children in families with religion and without.

2

What if I marry someone of another faith?

onna and Edward's home is on the third floor of an old four-story stucco apartment building, constructed round a central courtyard that boasts a worn patch of grass amid the paving stones. The structure is set back from the road, behind a scraggly hedge, beyond which buses and trucks rumble by on a busy street. From Donna and Edward's window you can see the Greek restaurant opposite, the pizza house on the corner, the Indian import store, and the dry cleaners with its noticeboard covered with posters and announcements of local entertainment and a large "No Parking" sign.

Inside the heavy glass-paned door of the apartment house it's dark and cool, and walking up the wide stairs I am aware of the solid permanence of the older architectural style. Edward opens the door of the apartment, and as I follow him down the corridor to the sitting room, we come into a pleasantly restful room with windows that show the tops of trees and the clouds hovering in the blue sky. Shelves of books line one wall of the room, and the furniture is worn and secondhand-not-quite-antique in style. There's a rush mat on the floor, and the old wood still gleams around it. There are some framed prints on the wall and a big table by the window covered with books and papers, as if someone was working and writing.

Two-year-old Joseph is delighted to see a visitor and runs around the room, not quite ready for bed. He climbs on to Donna's lap demanding to be fed, and she opens her simple cotton shirt and nurses him for a few minutes. He settles down, begins to rub his eyes and yawn, and Edward gets up to carry him off to bed. But Joseph watches him walking over and wriggles away just before Edward bends down to pick him up and runs off down the corridor. Then he notices his blue toy rabbit under the table, and picks it up, tucking the soft fuzzy shape under his arm close to him and putting his thumb in his mouth.

"Are you ready for bed?" Edward asks, in a reasonable voice, as Joseph stands there with a vacant look on his face.

"No," says the little boy firmly and turns away.

It was a perfect example of the contrariness of two-year-olds. My technique with my own children had been a recognized limit for both of us, like, "Well, you have five more minutes, and then it's bedtime." That meant if they didn't want to go then, there would be a confrontation but they also knew they could cooperate gracefully and not lose face.

But like many other parents who truly respect the rights of children, Donna and Edward believed that Joseph would go to bed when he was ready, that he knew what was best for him, and that as long as they offered him the options, he'd choose the right one, in his own good time.

In finding solutions to their unusual religious situation, they have applied the same open-ended approach. They have avoided saying, "My religion is this way, and this is what I believe," or "We have different religions." Instead, they have said: "We both care deeply about our individual religions, and we have brought them together so that they are completely equal in our lives as a family."

Listening to how they came to that conclusion, and hearing about the effort and commitment they have invested to find it and carry it out, made me feel intellectually and emotionally exhausted. There's no question, though, that for them the decision is right, and their sincerity, involvement, and study have been thoroughgoing and dedicated. They have spent years in theological discussion, religious research, and personal examination, to find exactly the right path for both of them and for their children.

Edward is thirty-eight and a university teacher of English literature. His background is typical of many American Jews today. He grew up in a suburban Jewish community where he was bar mitzvahed and confirmed at the age of sixteen in the local Reform Jewish temple, to which his parents belonged.

In America today, there are three religious divisions of Judaism, all agreeing on fundamental beliefs and patterns of behavior and on the authority of the Bible, but differing in their interpretations of the details of observance of the laws that bind Jews and in their willingness to graft modern ideas and practices onto the ancient traditions. The Orthodox community adheres to the most traditional rulings and follows the more extreme dictates, such as having men and women sit separately at services and keeping strict dietary laws like not mixing milk and meat. The Conservatives have kept some of the old traditions but adapted to some of the newer trends, like having part of the service in English, not Hebrew, and in allowing participation by women. The Reform movement began as a strong liberal group that rejected most traditional practices to emphasize faith and ethical behavior above all, but in recent years they have brought back such ceremonies as the bar mitzvah, as well as other traditional observances, in response to the desire of many members who wanted to restore some of the more visible aspects of their heritage. There are more Jews who belong to Conservative and Reform temples than to Orthodox ones, and there is a certain amount of criticism and friction among the groups. However because Judaism has always affirmed the right of every individual to approach God directly, there is also a great deal of allowance made for individual interpretation of Judaism's laws and observances. Much of Judaic study is based on reading and discussing the variety of rabbinic analyses of Biblical passages, which have been preserved over the centuries.

Judaism affirms that there is only one God, and its laws demand a belief in His existence. But the issue of faith in God is not a crucial one for a Jew; it's possible to observe the many laws of Judaism, be a respected member of the community, and yet not be concerned with the spiritual implications of faith. One Reform Jewish seminary gave its students a questionnaire on the first day, asking if they believed in God. Five students said they were "not sure," and one stated he "did not believe there was a God." As one of the rabbis noted: "It's pretty unusual even to ask that question at any seminary and to expect an honest answer, but we did because we know these young people can be good Jews and responsible leaders of the community even without a belief in God, because of the way in which they lead their lives."

Other Jews may strongly disagree with this viewpoint—and, in fact, there is a great deal of disagreement, debating, and discussion about religion at all levels of Judaism, and very few topics on which you can find complete agreement throughout the community, some 5 million strong in America today. The classic story is that if three Jews sit down to argue a point of Jewish law, there will be at least four opinions.

When Edward was growing up, he didn't question his religion very much. "I went to Hebrew school, and to the public high school," he said. "There was some anti-Semitism in high school, but since about 40 percent of the students were Jewish, we controlled the student activities, and it never affected me very much. Some parents did pull their children out of the school and send them to a Jewish day school, but I felt secure enough in my Jewishness, and had the support of my closest friends, so I was not particularly bothered by the anti-Semitism." Furthermore, he learned something from it.

He became aware that anti-Semitism often had nothing to do with religious reactions. "I knew that most of the gentiles in school were not particularly observant of their religion, and were not committed to their Christianity," he said, "and it didn't seem to mean much to them. Their anti-Semitic remarks didn't stem from any religious concerns—it was just a habit of prejudice they'd picked up from their parents." After school, he went to college, where he spent most of his time running the newspaper, and then came to teach at a local college. He met Donna when a friend invited him to double-date.

Donna looked up and smiled at him. "I remember that very well, that first time, because although we liked each other immediately, we talked even at that early stage about religion, and we decided very quickly that we should not see each other again. We felt we just should not go on with this because of the religious differences."

Our teachings in childhood and the ideas we absorb from family and friends about religion instill in most of us a subtle, and sometimes not so subtle, mistrust of those who are not part of the same religious group. We know our own religion and its group, and we are In, while the others are considered Outsiders and Different. We may learn something about the religion of our parents, but very little about any other religion as we grow up. As we mature, we carry these inbred suspicions with us, uncomfortable with those who hold different religious beliefs, even though our views and attitudes may be liberal, open, tolerant in many other areas. Until our discriminatory attitudes are challenged by personal confrontation, we are never forced to rethink our childhood attitudes or suppositions. We simply believe our stereotypes.

At their first meeting, Edward and Donna recognized their mutual attraction, and perhaps for reasons they could not define then, immediately came to a mutual decision that they had no future together. It was not based on any argument, any comment, any disagreement. They had enjoyed each other's company very much. But in an unthinking response to taboos of which they were only half conscious, both felt an instinctive "Don't touch" reaction, though their conscious minds and emotions cried, "Take hold."

Judaism is especially strong in instilling a "Don't touch" mentality, because Judaism is more than a faith. It is a historical tradition of race and people, passed on through the family, from generation to generation. The legal definition of a Jew, according to rabbinic authorities, is a child born of a Jewish mother. Converts are frowned upon, and the Orthodox regulations for conversion are designed to deter all but the most persistent. Reform and Conservative Judaism have less stringent regulations, but no branch of Judaism ever accepts the idea of proselytizing or sending missionaries out into the world to convert others. In fact the process of conversion to Judaism today demands serious study and commitment to a Jewish way of life and its laws, far beyond the simple statement of faith and belief that most Christian churches require for conversion. Because so few newcomers are welcomed to the faith, it is essential for the preservation and future of Judaism that its young people marry only other Jews, which is why the pressures on young people to marry within the faith ("within the Tribe," as it is sometimes expressed) can sometimes be so extreme.

While Edward's reactions to the prospect of intermarriage were based on that upbringing, Donna's concerns were based on her own deeply personal commitment to her Christianity. The daughter of a successful business executive, she grew up in the 1950s, moving from city to city as her parents relocated wherever her father's company sent him. Because of all the moving, she formed no strong commitment to a single church. "We were always changing churches. Mostly we went to small Methodist churches," she remembers, "because my father's parents were very involved in Methodism, and my mother's father was a Baptist minister. But I went to Sunday school regularly."

It was while she was at college in the Midwest, studying art and European literature, that she began to attend a Lutheran church. "I liked the fact there was a certain decorum in the services, and the emphasis on a sermon and the hymns and the music," she said. So at a time when many of her friends were dropping away from their childhood faiths, Donna realized she had found a church that gave her a great deal of spiritual and emotional satisfaction, and she began to attend regularly and to be interested in religious ideas. "Before I met Edward, I was involved with two men, both of whom later became ministers," she said.

"I even considered going to divinity school myself, but there were no scholarships for women. For me, being a Christian was an important part of my identity. Many of my close friends were Christians or in theology." Her religious interest led her to decide to go to graduate school in education, and so she came to the academic community in which they now live. She soon joined the Lutheran church and became an active church member, attending services regularly.

The Lutheran church has a membership of some 9 million in

America, and about 70 million worldwide, mainly in Scandinavia. There are three divisions of the church in America—the Lutheran Church in America (LCA), the Lutheran Church-Missouri Synod (LC-MS), which is the most conservative group, and the American Lutheran Church (ALC). All three groups have been formed by mergers with other smaller churches, and today have created a Lutheran Council which acts as a central agency. There are also some nine other smaller groups of independent Lutheran churches.

Lutheranism takes its name from Martin Luther, who in 1517 in Germany protested many of the corrupt practices of the Roman Catholic church; as followers joined his rebellion, Protestantism took shape. The Lutheran church is marked by a concern for faith as an essential part of religion as well as a deep belief that the way you live must reflect the faith you profess. There's an emphasis on high ethical standards without strict rules and regulations, and the church has always been a leader in interchurch assemblies because of a strong belief in cooperation among Christians everywhere.

Two of the divisions, the LCA and ALC, have allowed women to be ordained as priests since 1970, and women have also been given suffrage rights and a voice in church organization. Divorce is frowned on, but a recent ruling agreed that "some marriages become so badly eroded by infidelity and selfishness that to end them is less evil than to try to keep them going." Birth control is now recognized as the responsibility of the couple or individual woman, but only the LCA has said publicly that abortion is as well.

Lutherans believe that "sin is not specific wrongdoing (this is the result of sin) but the basic condition of our personality." They do not have special reverence for saints, believing that every true Christian is a saint and that the only hope for mankind is to be rescued by the gift of salvation from God. It is through faith in Christ that a new life begins, and it is nourished by the word of the Bible and the sacraments. The goal of the Christian life is the perfect existence that will finally be ours when we can be completely obedient to our Creator, and those who live and die in faith in Christ will live with him eternally, freed from the limitations of time and space.

Because there are so few requirements common to all Lutheran churches, congregational worship and philosophies can vary a great deal. A cathedral in a Swedish city, for example, may take an approach very different from that of a church in a small Midwest American farm community. And churches in cosmopolitan city areas will reflect the views of those congregants and not those of more conservative members in other Lutheran churches. The church Donna attended was one of the more liberal open churches and not part of the Missouri Synod.

With little knowledge of each other's backgrounds, Edward and Donna continued to meet on occasion and talk to each other, despite their reservations. This was not a case of the disillusioned Lutheran meeting the disbelieving Jew and finding that they had a great deal in common, which is the basis for many successful interfaith marriages. It was an aware Jew talking with a committed Christian, trying to discover their true points of commonality; it was a serious intellectual relationship.

When Edward mentioned Donna to his parents, he met with criticism and opposition to any idea of their involvement. "My father is a lawyer," said Edward, "and he deals mainly with domestic problems. So he knew by rote all the statistics on divorce—and especially divorce in interfaith situations—and the problems that come up and how important religion is in marriage." Edward added: "He deeply believed that you could never really trust anyone who was not Jewish, no matter how friendly you became. He felt you could never really rely on them, that they would turn on you at some point and show their anti-Semitism, and that you could only trust Jews."

The attitude of Edward's parents reflected their own upbringing and their memories of the Second World War when Hitler's rise to power in Germany led to the destruction of a thriving and apparently well-assimilated German Jewish community. And it reflected the long history of Jewish persecution, highlighted by events ranging from the twelfth-century pogrom in York, England, which led to the banishment of Jews from that country until Oliver Cromwell readmitted them in the seventeenth century, to the Spanish Inquisition of the fifteenth century, to the pogroms of Russia in the early years of this century. To Jews steeped in these stories, non-Jews can rarely be seen as individuals or people; they are always the Outsiders, the potential persecutors, not to be trusted in personal relationships though it's acceptable to do business with them. Such feelings are part of the emotional core of Judaism, and have contributed much to the reputation of Jews for "clannishness."

But in America today, the ghetto walls have broken down and given way to an openness which makes it impossible to re-create the tightly cohesive Jewish communities of Europe's past. As he grew up, Edward watched many of his school friends marry, often to people of different religions, and later he heard of their divorces.

"My father asserted that it was the religious difference that caused the divorce," said Edward, "but looking back I can see that many of them married for the wrong reasons. They were too young, they hadn't decided what they wanted to do with their lives, and in some cases it was pressure from the parents that forced the kids to get married in the first place. Some of them didn't know what else to do; they could see all their friends getting married, and they just followed the crowd."

He thought for a moment.

"It seemed to me that it was too simple to say that marriages break down because of religious differences. I knew that many of the people I'd grown up with weren't too interested in religion anyway."

As I listened to them now, it was easy to see why Edward was attracted to Donna, and she to him. They are both interested in literature, fascinated by the philosophical concepts of religion, eager to discuss their involvement with ideas and feelings, and openly liberal in their outlook. They are also both quiet and serious, more likely to choose an evening at home reading a book than a night on the town.

"Over a period of three years, we kept going together, and then breaking up," said Donna, smiling. "We were so aware from the beginning that we should not get married that we talked about it incessantly."

One of the pleasures of an interfaith relationship is that, if you are interested in religion, it provides a unique and constant topic for discussion and analysis. If you're not enthralled with the idea of talking about religion, you should think seriously about ending the relationship because the subject doesn't go away. For Donna and

Edward, their different religious backgrounds provided a stimulating area of conversation, which they both enjoyed exploring to the full.

"The question of children really bothered us," said Edward. "We discussed that a great deal. How could we bring up a child in one religion when neither of us wanted to reject the other? We met people from different religions and asked them for their solutions. But most of them said that one partner gave up his or her faith and took up the other one, or else it was a matter of indifference to them, and they didn't bother with any religion for their children."

Edward and Donna felt that neither of these solutions was right for them. Edward began to go to church with Donna, and she went to a Reform temple with him. He found: "The Lutheran church was based a great deal on Christology, and that was a different world to me, so that it took a long time to get used to what they were saying and to feel something other than an outsider." She went to a series of Hebrew classes at a local temple and graduated with a certificate of proficiency. With Edward, she attended a Yom Kippur (Day of Atonement) service which she found "overwhelming and solemn and inspiring."

Both of them became very much aware that Jesus himself was Jewish and had been educated by rabbis to be a teacher. Donna could see more and more clearly that the roots of Christianity were in Judaism, and Edward began to analyze the development of Christian thinking from its Jewish sources.

He explained how his experiences began to change his thinking: "Over the years I realized that I had come to feel the distinctions between Judaism and Christianity were not like this"—and he held his two hands apart in front of him, the fingers extended—"but like this"—and he brought his two hands together and linked the fingers. "It was the substance of what our two faiths did for us that was important, and we saw that we had far more in common than in separateness."

For three years the two of them agonized over their involvement. Finally, they decided to marry and to bring up any children within both their religious traditions. The wedding took place in a Lutheran church with a specially designed ceremony to take into account

Edward's Jewish background. Both sets of parents came to the wedding ("they had seen us both going through so much pain and suffering that it was almost a relief when we said we would get married") and many friends. It was a joyous occasion that they both enjoy talking about.

The rising rate of such dual-faith ceremonies is confounding religious leaders. Only a handful of ministers of most established faiths will officiate at such weddings, and only a minority welcome two-faith families into their communities if the nonfaith partner will not convert. But it's clear that one in three Jewish marriages today involves a non-Jew and about half of the Catholic marriages involve a non-Catholic. A New York lawyer, who is Jewish and married to a non-Jew, looked surprised when asked about his marriage. "I don't think anything of it now—everyone I know seems to be intermarried."

It's hard to bring out any studies or statistics that show that such marriages are better or worse than any other kinds of marriages. It's hard even to arrive at an accurate assessment of the number of intermarriages. Religious affiliation is not requested on marriage forms, and there are few places where they can be analyzed outside of religious organizations.

In 1953, Iowa requested religious information on marriage application forms, and in 1959 Indiana did the same for a couple of years, and the few studies available are based on that data. Two Purdue University professors, Harold T. Christensen and Kenneth E. Barber, analyzed some 24,000 marriage-license application forms of Indiana residents in 1960, and found that one-ninth of all the marriages crossed faith lines—defined as Catholic, Protestant, and Jewish. Most cross-faith weddings were civil ceremonies not religious. Analyzing the background of the couples, the study showed that they tended to

belong to minority religious groups
have been married previously
be older than the average person marrying
be in high status occupations
reside in urban areas
be pregnant at the time of marriage.

In following up divorce statistics for the same sample, the researchers found that while "interfaith marriages showed *slightly* higher divorce percentages, the difference was so slight, and the record search which produced the percentage so short, as to make one wary of the results."

Christensen and Barber also noted that often there was more conflict in same-faith marriages where one partner was far more religiously devout than the other partner, or held more rigidly to certain observances, than there was in dual-faith marriages. In 1955, Dr. Jerold S. Heiss interviewed over 1,100 New Yorkers in a cross section of Manhattan for his thesis "Interfaith Marriage in an Urban Age." He concluded that such marriages were only occasionally apt to be less happy than same-faith marriages, and that the major threats to the success of interfaith marriages came from pressures from family, church, and society.

The reasons for the increase in interfaith families have in the past been attributed to lack of education, lack of religious upbringing, and parental failure to give religious direction. But studies show otherwise. Today, young people have far greater opportunities for travel, for study, for meeting people from different backgrounds at school, college, or work. There's an atmosphere of openness in America that enables barriers to be crossed and cross-cultural meetings to take place in an unprecedented way. Interfaith, interethnic, and interracial marriages increase and flourish in this atmosphere of tolerance, despite exhortations from the pulpit urging parents to keep their youngsters within the fold, marrying only their fellow religionists. But the dominant messages in society today are about equality and about respect for the individual regardless of race, creed, or religion.

Young people who absorb these heady idealistic ideas of the present, however, are often brought up short to find little support from leaders of traditional religious groups when they decide to marry across faith lines. Like Donna and Edward, they are forced to evaluate what they want to do and to create their own uncharted routes, usually condemned by religious leaders.

A couple of years after Donna and Edward's marriage, their son,

Joseph, was born. His arrival had been lovingly timed, and they had carefully planned the details of his religious training.

"The old neat distinctions were not relevant anymore," said Donna, "and we knew we wanted to bring him up in both our faiths, to share both our backgrounds."

In his parents' eyes, Joseph is a Jewish child. They followed the Biblical tradition of a circumcision a week after his birth, with a rabbi and mohel (religious circumciser) present to perform the ceremony of cutting the foreskin of the baby's penis. The ceremony was held at the home of a Lutheran pastor friend, and other friends from both faiths were there to read from the Book of Genesis, and to recite poetry and other carefully selected passages.

In his parents' eyes, Joseph also has a place in the Lutheran church. When he was a few months old, a special welcoming ceremony was held at the church, led by the pastor. Babies are usually baptized in the church. "But we were sure we did not want a baptism, because we didn't feel it was authentic," explained Edward. A baptism means that the baby has become a member of the Lutheran church. Edward and Donna preferred to adapt the ceremony for adult baptism, with variations they wrote themselves, to welcome Joseph into the church.

Donna was aware of the differences between the two ceremonies. "It's clear to me that a child is *born* Jewish," she said, "whereas there's no way you can be born a Christian because it's a different experience. That's made me realize that no matter what he decides later, it is important that Joseph have a Jewish education so that he knows who his people are."

This difference between Judaism and Christianity is a crucial one in many mixed marriages and can affect how the children are brought up in many ways. For even if a Jew observes no laws, keeps no Holy Days, never attends temple, he or she is still counted a Jew if born of a Jewish mother. In Israel today, this fact is causing a great deal of controversy, where non-Jews have settled in the country, married, and are raising as Jews children who may not be counted as Jewish under the law. To strict adherents of this definition, the fact that Joseph will be educated in a Hebrew school and will learn Jewish law and observances will not be enough to make him a Jew, unless he converts to Judaism or Donna converts. Others believe that if Joseph lives a Jewish life in a Jewish community, his actions and practices will show that he is a Jew. Donna and Edward know that under the strict interpretation of Jewish law Joseph cannot be a "born" Jew because of his mother's Christianity, but Donna does not feel she wants to give up her faith.

"But I do think of him as being raised more Jewish than Christian," she said thoughtfully, "and though he goes to church with me now and likes the music, and I want him to understand some of his mother's faith, the family emphasis will probably be Jewish."

Since the early months of Joseph's life, the dual family commitment has continued. At Christmas time, the family visits Donna's parents in the Midwest, "and we have a big family celebration with lots of presents and a tree, and we all go to church," said Donna. "It's a very traditional way of celebrating—though we've been talking about Christmas and reassessing what it is supposed to mean for us as a family. I think next year we may celebrate it here quietly at home for once, because the emphasis on materialism and presents and food sometimes doesn't feel right to me."

Edward nodded. "Yes," he said, leaning forward, "we began to feel that it should be a more simple personal event in a family setting that we would choose. Donna was working with a group once that encouraged people to spend time making their own gifts and trying to do something positive to help others and make the world a better place at Christmas, not just buy presents. That's the kind of feeling we'd like our family Christmas to have."

They also celebrate Hanukkah, the Jewish festival that commemorates the bravery of the Maccabeus family in fighting the oppression of those who tried to destroy their religion. Every night for eight nights they light the candles in the menorah and retell the story. Passover, too, is a significant part of their lives, and Edward has introduced its observance to Donna's church group. "One of the Sunday school teachers invited me to come and talk to her class about Passover, so I brought in some matzo and grape juice and explained what the seder was like and what happened," he said. "She suggested we might have a seder at the church the next year, and I agreed. But I insisted that it be authentic, with kosher food, and follow the traditional pattern of observance."

That year at Passover about eighty parents, children, and church members attended a seder, led by Edward and based on a temple seder written by a rabbi in Philadelphia, Pennsylvania.

"I try to use examples of slavery and imprisonment and liberation, so that we can see the relevance of the story of the Jews' escape from Egypt in modern terms," said Edward. "We also have a time of intercession, which is always part of the Lutheran church service, when anyone can stand up and say what they feel, which I think is important. One year we had a refugee from Chile with us, and he spoke, and another year we had a Russian Jewish immigrant. We try to encourage everybody to join in, so that it becomes a communal experience. Last year we had nearly a hundred people, and this year we had a hundred and seventy."

So ahead of young Joseph lie seders at a church, and quiet noncommercialized Christmas celebrations that will emphasize caring for others. He'll go to Hebrew school and perhaps to Lutheran Sunday school. His parents are united in their approach and wholly committed to their dual solution. Indeed, the time, energy, and enthusiasm they spend on the religious aspect of their lives amazes their friends and family.

"No one we know does as much as we do," said Donna, smiling, "and some people think we're crazy. But we've found it very satisfying so far, and it doesn't seem too much for us."

For many couples faced with the decision of bringing up a child in an interfaith situation, support from an organized religious group is crucial. But from other interviews, it's clear to me that the sympathy and support that Donna and Edward found in the intellectual academic community in which they live are the exception, not the rule. One mother described how she called her local Jewish temple, where she and her husband had attended a few services, to enroll her child in the Hebrew school. The secretary said she had to join in her husband's name, and since he was not Jewish, the child could not be enrolled in the school. "I was so mad and hurt that I blew up at her over the phone," said the woman, "but when I told my husband, he shrugged and said I might as well convert." In another case, a conservative church refused to permit a child to attend the Sunday school unless she had been baptized; when the parents demurred, it was suggested that the family move to another neighborhood. In both these cases—and there are many more—unsympathetic responses from established religious centers have completely turned off—and away—couples who might perhaps have become as sincere and devoted congregants as Donna and Edward.

But as I talked with religious leaders, it became clear that duality of faith is a difficult concept for them to accept. I mentioned Donna and Edward to one liberal rabbi and asked him how he felt.

"That's a terrible solution," he said emphatically. "It may be beautiful for the parents, but it's no good at all for the child. He doesn't know who he is or where he belongs."

I pointed out that his parents felt that he knew very well who he was because of the tremendous emphasis on religion in the home and that he belonged in two places since he has friends in the church and in the Jewish community and two sets of loving grandparents.

"That child is not a Jew," said the rabbi. "And he has no place in the Jewish community unless the mother converts. The rabbis involved in helping that couple are doing no good for anyone, and it should not be permitted. The wife should convert to Judaism and be done with it."

A member of the Lutheran church education department saw the issue in a different light. "If the child attends classes at the church and then when he is older decides he wants to be confirmed within the church, that is his decision," he said. "His upbringing depends on his parents, and if they are members of the church, they can bring him to classes and have him confirmed here."

One of the few places that even recognizes the plight of interfaith families is a temple run by Reform Rabbi Roy Rosenberg, in New York, where services are carefully designed to meet the needs of dual-faith families. Rabbi Irwin Fishbein has established a Rabbinic Center for Research and Counseling in Westfield, New Jersey. He pointed out "very little has been done and there is very little information about what happens to a couple and their children and the psychological adjustment and religious orientation after interfaith marriages." His center provides counseling and a list of rabbis who will perform interfaith ceremonies. And in Culver City, Los Angeles, Rabbi Allen Maller, who has written many articles on interfaith marriage, holds discussion groups at his temple for interfaith couples.

Donna and Edward represent an extreme commitment for couples involved in the complicated task of raising a child in a dual-faith marriage. But there are several human and social factors that would seem to point to success and happiness for this family and its unique solutions that might not be true in many other cases.

First, they were both from warm and loving families who, while not initially supportive of the marriage, eventually came round and found themselves able to rejoice in their children's happiness. Secondly, they met at a time of maturity; they had both been involved with other people before they met, had finished college, and were working and living their own lives. They had reached the stage of decision making in their adult lives, where they could recognize the real problems in their relationship and deal with them rationally. Neither of them spoke of falling madly in love or of eloping in a rash moment of passion. They were educated, intelligent, and articulate, well aware of what they were entering into and ready to cope with their problems in a thoughtful, realistic way.

Third, they happened to live in a community remarkably sensitive and open to ecumenical and interfaith ideas. While they were going out, they became involved in an interreligious community organization which met regularly for discussions and social-action programs. This gave them an opportunity to share the experience of interfaith situations among friends and to see the benefits as well as the problems. The ease with which they found religious leaders to advise, support, and encourage their efforts is not always the case, as others who have found only criticism and opposition have told me.

But those who are truly determined to follow their own path, no matter how unusual, seem to be able to find a way. One young man, now studying to be a Baptist minister, met his wife-to-be, a Roman Catholic, when they were both working for VISTA, a social work

agency, in the South. They spent a great deal of time discussing
their religious backgrounds, and after a certain amount of parental
opposition ("my parents never trusted Catholics," he said) they
were married, agreeing to keep their religions and bring up their
children within both their faiths.

When their daughter was about to be born, they had long discussions on the issue of baptism. In the Baptist church, the baptism
ceremony is a sign of an adult decision to join the church and is one
of the fundamental principles of the church. Babies are never baptized. In the Catholic church, all babies ar baptized.

"I talked to the dean of the divinity school where I'm studying
and did a lot of research and reading," said the father, "and I became quite an authority on baptism. My wife and I also talked
about it a great deal and about what the ceremony should mean to
us and our baby. We finally decided that the ideal solution was to
have a Roman Catholic priest administer baptism in the Baptist
church. Our Baptist minister agreed to the concept, and a friend of
ours, a young Jesuit priest, said he would be glad to perform the
baptism.

We told the congregation what we planned to do beforehand. We
created the service ourselves to be part of a regular Sunday morning
service, and though it's against canon law, we felt it was the right
thing for both of us to do."

Once again, the serious commitment of both parents found a solution to an issue that theologians might have considered an impossible confrontation. Both parents were sure that their child's baptism should be authentic and reflect both their backgrounds.

So during a Sunday service, the Catholic priest came to the Baptist church in his robes, and joined the minister. The two parents
brought their baby daughter up to him.

"Usually Catholics sprinkle water over the baby but Baptists im-
merse," explained the father. "We wanted to have an authentic baptism with one change. He followed the Catholic baptismal service
until the sprinkling, when he put the baby in the baby bath, which
we had brought in with some water, and dunked her in it. My father
and my wife's mother were the godparents. It was a very special
ceremony for all of us because it brought all of us together." With

great pride, he showed me some slightly fuzzy color photographs of the ceremony. Was there any community reaction, I wondered, or criticism of such an unorthodox ceremony?

He grinned. "Well, frankly it totally violates the Baptist tenets, which say you must not baptize a baby, and some people did comment on that. But only one member quit the church because he disapproved of the whole thing. We had announced it two Sundays before it happened, so that people would know, and there was quite a bit of discussion. But most people understood why we wanted to do it and what we were trying to do. We both felt that we had contributed something to this first religious ceremony for our child, and we hope that's what we're going to continue doing for her as she grows up."

These radical alterations of traditional ceremonies and celebrations often seem shocking to conventional followers of religious beliefs. But when I spoke to a family counselor who specializes in situations that have a religious basis because his work is affiliated with several churches, he recognized the validity of such actions.

"If these couples are open and honest and consistent in what they are doing, any problems that may arise in their marriages will probably have nothing at all to do with religion," he said. Of the many couples and individuals he has seen, he has arrived at this conclusion: "People who come to this office for assistance don't come because they have a religious problem but because they have difficulties or stress in their personal lives. I've found that someone reared in an orthodox background of any kind who wants to marry someone reared in a liberal or reform background, where both were very active in their communities, is, at first glance, very unusual. You have to ask then, What was it that made them interested enough to pursue courtship and marriage? How did they meet? What made them continue the relationship? And it often comes out that they really wanted to overthrow their own background and find another way of life. They can be very comfortable with the other person's background and in fact are eager to accept it, even though at first glance that might have seemed impossible."

His experiences have shown though that sometimes a crisis is precipitated when children come along.

"If problems start to arise after the child is born, you can see that there was a religious conflict that had not been resolved," he said. "Sometimes decisions about children had not been made, and the difficulties begin when these decisions have to be faced. But it's difficult to say that religion is the major cause of conflict, because there are so many other factors."

For any marriage to succeed there have to be several areas of compatibility—social, economic, educational, emotional, cultural, political, ethnic, and religious. The more areas of agreement and mutual sharing there are, the more likely the marriage is to succeed in terms of the happiness and satisfaction of both partners. Every marriage has a different pattern, and for some the religious similarities are insignificant beside the chasmic differences in education or the gulf in their political outlook. For others, the differences in religion may be the deep and critical ones, far outweighing compatibility in other areas. One woman commented: "The main problem with our marriage was that he was a man and I was a woman."

A minister of the liberal Unitarian Universalist Association knows that other churches often send couples to them when they cannot perform a wedding or other ceremony because of interfaith difficulties. "I'm very proud to have a reputation for openness, for faith without prescription," he said. "To me, that is the most religious thing any church can do. It shows a church that says, We honor you and your needs, and we want to serve you in ways that you want. My experience has been that people who enter a dual-faith marriage have demonstrated that they are looking at human values ahead of sectarian values. They have moved away from rivalries and dissent among faiths, and have come to the discovery of commonly shared humanity."

In a pamphlet on intermarriage, the Unitarian view shows a strong positive attitude toward the complexities of such marriages that's often lacking in other religions:

If it is true that adjustments are more difficult, it is also true that when an adequate effort is made, there will be a deeper sympathy and a larger understanding because struggle was necessary. There will be a closer togetherness. There can be a far richer family fellowship because two great traditions and cultures have been blended together, each one making its own unique contribution to the whole.

For many parents struggling with the day-to-day decisions of bringing up their children, the truly deep understanding they have been forced to reach because of their interfaith relationship may give them a security and strength in their marriage that helps them to deal with other problems, and which those involved in same-faith marriages may never discover.

It's hard to see what will happen to any child as he or she grows up. But the love, care, and devotion that Donna and Edward have shared with their son, as well as the openness of their beliefs and feelings, seem to be a good foundation for a family life based on honesty and sincerity. If Donna had reluctantly allowed herself to be converted to Judaism, how much of her subtle, or even obvious, discomfort at this pressure would she have passed on to her child? And if Edward had tried to shuck off his Jewish background and pretend he was Lutheran, how uncomfortable would he have felt denying his true beliefs and feelings? It is hard to believe that any marriage can last with such basic deceptions, or that any child could benefit from them.

A family that begins its life in conflict and disagreement is unlikely to find easy solutions later on. A couple who follows a path that other people say is right but that does not feel right for them is courting disaster. Several people commented that if you give up religious beliefs "because it's the easiest thing to do" and convert, they may resurface later in life.

Donna and Edward spent painful times examining their own beliefs and deepest feelings about their values and attitudes before they decided to marry and have children. As Donna said, "It wasn't easy, and other people may not want to do it, but it was right for us."

3

How can you create
your own religious
solutions?

oyce has that sun-tanned charm and relaxed casualness that so many women seem to acquire from living in California. She's married to Arthur, a successful movie producer, responsible for several popular feature films. They own a spacious sprawling house, and their lives are an enviable mixture of parties with friends from the world of entertainment, the high pressures associated with Arthur's work, and the easygoing pleasures of the Los Angeles life-style which they can share happily with their three young children.

"When we first arrived here from San Francisco, I didn't like it," said Joyce, as we ordered avocado salad and fresh orange juice in a coffee shop. "I grew up in New York, in a Jewish family with little interest in religion, and came out West after college. Arthur's parents are Irish Catholic, with some German thrown in, and he was an altar boy, went to college, and was still going to church when we met. Our relationship broke off and then was on again, and my parents told me they didn't want me going out with Catholics, but there was nothing they could do. When Arthur asked me to marry him, we spent a long time talking about religion, because it meant so much to him. He felt strongly that we had to get married in a church, for example."

In response to Arthur's needs, the two of them attended ten pre-marital classes with a Catholic priest. "Basically it seemed to me that both religions were saying the same thing," said Joyce, "though I had one argument with the priest about baptism, because I thought that was ridiculous. And Arthur and I had an enormous fight about symbols in the home. I didn't want the Virgin Mary hanging up everywhere, and Arthur was very pulled toward that kind of thing."

The Catholic priest who agreed to marry them in a small chapel created a special service with no reference to Jesus, the Father, the Son, or the Holy Ghost, in order to avoid offending Joyce's parents. After the marriage, Arthur still liked to attend church, but Joyce found it stifling and uninspiring.

"I didn't enjoy the pageantry and the ritual of the service because I like a time to reflect," she said. "I could see the value of religion for the family, but I didn't go along with most of the church stuff." After they had adopted two children, Joyce found herself taking them to church with her. "I hated it," she said frankly, "because other parents would be sitting there pinching their children to make them sit still, and behave, or else I had to sit in the crying room with other mothers and not participate in the service. I was in a very confused state of mind and hated the hypocrisy of having to hurt my children if we went to church. Then one weekend I went to San Francisco to visit a college roommate who was married."

Joyce poured out her difficulties with Arthur and his religious concerns, the long hours and unpredictable working life that the movie business demands, and the sense of uselessness that came from not teaching anymore, as she had before she married.

"Among other things, my friend talked about Creative Initiative, and said they were an educational institution which gave seminars," she said, "and that I should go. When I got back to Los Angeles, someone called me and said the first seminar was starting in the city and did I want to come with my husband? Arthur agreed to come with me, and I was so starved to get into relationships with other people that I could hardly wait for the day." She still remembers that first meeting clearly, in the living room of a house, with about sixteen people there.

"The course was called 'Challenge for Change' she remembers, "and it dealt with reality and how we perceived it in our lives. We went away for a weekend retreat with the group, and then attended the seminar for several weeks. Arthur was willing to come because he could see it was helping our relationship. No one ever said it was religiously based, but it felt as if it was. For us, the beginning was in 1970, when we started to go to the seminars because it made us talk to each other, find out who we are, where we're going, and helped us resolve a lot of our feelings about our beliefs and our feelings for each other."

She thought for a moment, trying to describe what had happened: "It was an experience of being with other individuals on the same journey and not being alienated from them." She sighed. "In Hollywood, the way we were living, we'd been going to a lot of parties and getting drunk, with hangovers the next day. There's a lot of womanizing and talking about it. I knew very clearly what was a right family and what was a wrong family. This showed me how to hold on to what I thought was important and take responsibility for it."

Creative Initiative began in California in 1968. Its roots go back to the early 1900s when Henry Burton Sharman, a chemistry professor at the University of Toronto, became concerned that students and others believed that there was a conflict between science and religion. Sharman believed that an attitude of free open-minded investigation, which is the essence of science, should also be the basis of a modern approach to religion. He left teaching and entered the University of Chicago where he received a Ph.D. in Semitics and Greek. His book, which he edited in 1917, is called *Records in the Life of Jesus* (Harpers), and displays writings of Matthew, Mark, and Luke in parallel examples for critical examination. He began teaching six-week seminars based on this material at a wilderness camp in Canada. One of the couples who attended were Dr. Harry Rathbun, a law professor at Stanford University, and his wife Emilia. They returned to Stanford convinced that Sharman's ideas were right, and in 1946 began teaching similar seminars to their students. Today, Harry is in his eighties, and Emilia in her seventies, and they live in Palo Alto, near the university, still active in their work.

Harry, a tall straight-backed man with bushy white hair and a neatly trimmed white beard, has startlingly blue eyes behind his glasses and an air of quiet concern as you talk to him. Emilia is a well-built woman, with a vivacity that is very compelling. White hair frames her animated face, and when we met, she was wearing a canary-yellow sweater, yellow pants, and a red and purple over-shirt. She spoke with the convincing fluency of one who has explained her life's work many times before:

"I was born in Mexico, and my father was American and my mother Mexican. Though she was Catholic, neither of them were very interested in religion or took it seriously, because they were very intellectual. Everything Sharman said made sense to me when we met, and after Harry and I went on this seminar, we came back deciding to carry on Sharman's work. He believed that university professors were the ideal people to mediate religion to students, and from that day to this, it has been the central focus of our lives.

"We run seminars, and over the years more than forty thousand people have gone through the discussion groups, weekends, and the seminars. When Sharman began, the idea of a discussion group where the participants investigated the material themselves and provided the answers was not a popular idea. The group leader was there only to keep the people's minds on the material, and it was an incredibly interesting experience for all of us."

The Rathbuns' two children are now grown; Richard served in the Peace Corps in Nepal, and traveled around the world with his wife, Carolyn. Juana, the Rathbuns' daughter, her husband, and their three children are deeply involved in the work of Creative Initiative.

"The idea is to undertake to live a life of perfection," said Emilia, "but it becomes extraordinarily difficult when you see the discrepancy between the life you are living and the set standards of religion. We try to investigate the needs of individuals and to help them overcome anger, egocentricity, injustice, and the other negative human emotions that divide them from their full human potential." Over the years, Emilia herself has undergone changes in her thinking. At one period, she went out to the churches to run seminars for women in church groups, but eventually returned to the university.

"In the 1960s, I had a clear inspiration," she said, "of an approaching Third Age. It is an age of universal spirit and truth. There will be no leader. It will be an Age of Community, when the world will be living in total communion. The Second Age is the one which Jesus started, and the First Age was the one before he came. In this Third Age, it is not blasphemous to assume that every individual should call upon himself to attain a relationship with God. The issue of authority has to be placed in the individual lives of every person. In the past, authority was emphasized in the church or in the Book or in Jesus. But today the authority has to be rooted within every individual." She stressed however that there were no particular individuals. "We"—she gestured to Harry and herself— "as two individuals in the community become totally erased. We are not leaders in any sense. We do not believe in cults based on personality or on personal experiences. The individual must be his own authority as a result of seeing the truth for himself and verifying it for himself."

To clarify the seminar ideas, Harry, who was a professor of law for thirty years before retiring in 1960, and others wrote *Creative Initiative—Guide to Fulfillment,* which was published in 1976. The book's cover has a twelve-pointed star surrounded by a circular rainbow, a symbol of the spiritual journey to fulfillment. The seven chapters contain ideas from Buddhism, Judaism, Christianity, psychology, psychiatry, philosophy, poetry, literature, and Alcoholics Anonymous.

The tone is of do-good ethics rooted in today's middle-class concerns. For example, a list of twenty-four "threats to our survival" includes among others "explosive racial tensions, the energy crisis, the high social cost of highway accidents" and "the aberrational indoctrination of our children through television."

These were the ideas that Joyce heard at that first seminar, ideas she values for having transformed her family life.

"Parents are the true teachers of religion for their children," she said. "Sure, you can send your children to learn religion in a Sunday school, but the intelligent child will see that the whole thing is about human relationships and nonviolence and being loving. It comes back to how the father and mother relate to each other. If children see that their parents are committed to the same goal, they will accept religion. Otherwise it is just lip service."

Those who accept the ideas follow the celebrations that are part of Community. "We start the year off with New Beginnings, which is in September, around the time of Yom Kippur, the Jewish Day of Atonement, and we ask ourselves, How can I start anew and afresh in a relationship? Then we celebrate Human Rights Day on December 10, and last year we put together a Bless Man pageant, with some three hundred people, including children, participating, to stress the message that we are one spirit and one community and one world."

There are special programs for children, where they go backpacking and camping in the mountains "to talk with their peer group about feelings and relationships and God," and there are other programs for fathers and sons and mothers and daughters.

"There is a special ceremony for men called Adam and for women called Eve," said Joyce. "We look on the Bible story as a positive myth. It's the desire to know more. We say, Yes, I desire to know more—I am searching for the truth, and we act out the story." There is also another ceremony for women called the Dawn Ceremony, "where a few women prepare a set of questions and ideas for meditation and a group of women get together for a day or a few hours, and act out some events, and it's like group therapy—but the goal is higher. We all want to act with totality and to say at all times that we are making the world a better place. They used to give out bracelets"—and she showed me the simple gold-link bracelet she wore—"as a symbol of woman linked to woman, but people began to feel it didn't mean anything and the symbol became separate from the event. And some people wear this twelve-pointed star"—she pointed to the gold star she wore—"to symbolize man's journey to be with God."

When a woman is pregnant, there's a ceremony where the girls in Community come to bring a blessing for the expected baby. "And we light candles and show that the baby is loved before it's born and sometimes we bring material things, small gifts to express our caring."

Young boys have an Eagles ceremony, marking the passage from childhood into adulthood, and usually held when a boy is about thirteen. Each young man is asked to consider the issues of Totality, Identity, and Love, to study these issues in relationship to David, Moses, and Jesus, and to discuss them with his father and one other adult male in Creative Initiative. Then he must give a talk on each subject to his peers. The program usually culminates in a weekend retreat for the young men and their fathers, usually with a solo overnight during which each young man spends the night alone in the wilderness, contemplating his life and his goals for the future. At the end of the weekend, the boys are recognized as men, and considered full members of Community. A similar rite-of-passage marks the transition to womanhood for the girls. "It's not done by rote because we try to do nothing by rote," said Joyce.

Those within Community should not smoke, drink, or engage in premarital sex. "We know how hard it is if one parent wants to join and not the other because it puts an unnecessary strain on the relationship, so we don't allow it," Joyce said calmly. "We don't try to reach minorities or poor people. We know that it's ridiculous to say, What do you want with God, when you cannot even feed your children. We want to reach the large mass of middle-class people who are not satisfied and who want more from life. Most people start on this journey when they have food and shelter, and their basic needs are met."

There are now some 1,800 followers, mostly on the West Coast, with a large group in Palo Alto. Beverly, who has been an active member for some years, is a beautifully dressed woman with great poise and charm. She chose her words carefully and precisely as she described how the religious upbringing of her two sons was different from her own.

"My parents chose anything that was fashionable so I went to the local Protestant church because there was a feeling that we should go to church because we were very American and did the right thing."

One summer she went to a teenage Bible camp and was given a Bible for memorizing the most verses. "I was very involved in wanting boyfriends and often in the doldrums," she remembers. "It was an awful time. Someone sent me off into the woods to pray about it,

and I went off and had a sense of being surrounded by light, feeling
that someone or something was telling me that things were going to
be all right. That's all that happened, but I have never forgotten it."

She worked as a buyer in a high-fashion store after college, and
when she met Don, she was completely uninvolved in religion. "He
was Jewish and wanted a rabbi to marry us, but they all said no, so
we were married in a nonreligious ceremony in his home," she said.
"We didn't discuss how we would bring up our children because it
didn't seem important, and afterward we didn't do anything religious at all. A friend suggested that we go to one of the Creative
Initiative seminars, and I was very surprised that Don agreed to go.
Don was really an atheist at that time. He had not had a concept of
something outside of him before, and he saw all authority as negative, but he came out believing in something greater than himself.
The seminar concentrated on the historical facts about Jesus, and
Don argued back and forth with the leader who read from Sharman's book. Then we'd discuss what he said. As we discussed the
ideas about Jesus, and about what had happened at that time, Don
came up with his own realization that there had to be some kind of
plan, some kind of author. It made a tremendous difference and led
us into a much deeper relationship and commitment to each other.

"I was having my own experiences in trying to come to terms
with the complexities of universal concepts. When we began, I was
eight months pregnant with our second son, and I didn't see any necessity for passing anything on in terms of religion. I thought it
would happen by osmosis. But after I had my second child, I had
this deep sense of wanting to share and pass on to my boys a sense
of a religious heritage, to help them to see where mankind had come
from in this universe. I wanted them to feel a sense of awe and won-
derment about the universe and to have some sense of their own
place in it. That to me is what religion is all about."

Beverly's sons are now six and ten years old, and since that
seminar, they have participated in the celebrations and events of
Creative Initiative. "At holiday times we get together with another
family, and we act out, for example, the story of Adam and Eve.
Last time my husband played God, I played the snake, and the other couple played Adam and Eve. Then the children played it back

to us, and it was amazing how they pick up the points every single time. And if we go on a trip to the beach, for example, we'll talk about the sand and say, Let's try to count the grains, and see if we can. We also talk about authority and what leaders should offer, and we stress respect for adults. But we also know that if you hit your brother, he will hit you back, and if you share with someone, he is more likely to share with you."

Beverly has found that other parents will often ask her what religion she is involved with "because the children have interesting points of view about things. And people see how we work with our children and spend a great deal of time with them, doing things." She paused and said: "It's hard to explain that it's religion because many middle-class people don't understand that it's teaching values that is really important. When you value life itself, then that is what makes you act in a certain way. We keep telling our children things and training them, and we hope it is sinking in. I think it is absolutely critical to have some kind of religious education and training. It is the most important thing—the gold thread that ties the world family together. It gives the children a solid base, and I'd recommend it for anybody."

For Joyce, it has become a vital part of her marriage and family life. "Arthur and I lead seminars together, and it gives us a goal outside of his work," she said. "The children are now nine, eight, and five, and we can see how much they have gained from our involvement in Community."

California seems to be particularly receptive to the creation of small independent religious groups. The yellow pages of the phone books have columns of listings under "Churches" unlike those in any other area. Usually groups begin under the influence of a strong leader, thrive while the leader is actively involved, and slowly decline after the leader leaves or dies, rarely able to continue under their own momentum. In some cases they may fall apart when discord among members causes a split or when a particular philosophy is unacceptable to the majority of the members. In other groups, key members may move out of the area, and the core of enthusiasts is too small to continue on its own.

Though the Rathbuns deny their leadership, their strong commitment and enthusiasm for the ideas of Creative Initiative are a key factor in the organization. They talk of their son continuing their work in the movement and of others carrying on the seminars and the teaching. But their sincere involvement and belief in the work is a vital part of the group's healthy growth, and their willingness to devote time and energy to its development has been essential in keeping its followers in step with the original concepts. Should they step down and withdraw entirely from their involvement, there might well be a slow decline in the organization, as happens in so many other similar California groups, until only a skeleton corps of followers remains.

Michael and Sarah, like many of the couples in Creative Initiative, have worked hard at creating a personally meaningful religious experience, but they have done so within the context of a faith which is thousands of years old, much to their own surprise and that of their friends and relatives. When they met, they found they were in agreement about religion; neither of them had any interest at all in giving their children a religious upbringing or in any kind of involvement with religious practices.

"We were married on my uncle's farm, outside in a field," said Michael, "by a chaplain from college, who was black. We had designed the ceremony ourselves, with readings from James Agee and Camus, and all our family and friends were there. At the end, the chaplain said, Shalom, and that was about as much religion as we could handle then."

"Michael's cousin was married a couple of days later on the roof of the Hotel Pierre in New York, in a ceremony that had everything you're supposed to have," said Sarah, "and it was quite a contrast for us."

"Politics was our religion then," said Michael, a dark-haired, handsome man now working as a journalist and writer in New York. "It had always been that way when I was growing up. My mother was a political activist and sent groups of women to Mississippi to help voter registration and worked to try to get Jews out of concentration camps in the 1940s. We grew up knowing we were supposed to fight for social justice, and that was what was important. I knew we were Jewish, but Judaism was always associated in my mind with the struggle for social justice, and later, when I met other Jews, it was a great shock to find that many of them were apathetic about social issues."

For Sarah, her childhood experience of religion had been marked by conflict and harshness.

"When I was born, there was a big fight over whether or not I should be baptized," she said. "I was told that my grandmother, who was Episcopal and very high church and a strong influence on my mother, was adamant that I should be baptized in the Episcopal church. My father was an atheist and against all religions, and he would not allow it. He was in the navy, so we moved around a lot with him. When I was about seven or eight, we lived near my grandmother and spent a great deal of time with her. She was a hard, stern person, who believed in a very punishing God, and in the sinfulness of humanity. Looking back now I can see that such an attitude can be a very destructive influence for children, when it gets passed on. I have strong memories from those years of absolutely hating the Crucifixion and the idea of Jesus as Christ, because of the emphasis my grandmother put on the suffering and cruelty. Later on when we moved to another town, I can remember reading *The Diary of Anne Frank,* and I identified with that book very strongly, because Anne was about my age, and so young and alive and full of enthusiasm, and yet she didn't understand the cruelty and harshness that had forced them to be hidden."

She laughed and looked over at Michael. "We often talk about my experiences and say that I was programmed to marry a Jew and Mike was programmed to marry a gentile, and that's how we got together."

They both grew up in affluent middle-class families and went on to Ivy League colleges, but they did not meet until they were working in Maryland and Mississippi in the civil rights movement of the 1960s, registering black voters. For Mike his only contact with Judaism had been when he'd spent his junior year in Israel on a kibbutz (communal farm).

"I went to Israel promising myself that I would not meet any Americans for that year, so I didn't," he said, "and it was really an experience. I didn't know any Jewish history and knew nothing about Zionism, so I took the country as I found it. I know a lot of Jews are disappointed when they come to Israel, looking for some kind of Utopia, a perfect solution to their Jewish problems. But I came with no expectations. I saw that life there is tougher, and I liked the people and respected them a lot. For a time I thought I might study Orthodox Judaism there."

But he didn't and instead became involved in civil rights. After meeting Sarah, the two decided to go to graduate school in Chicago where she took a degree in social work. Then they married and spent their first two years in Ecuador with the Peace Corps.

"That's where we first began to be aware of Judaism," said Michael. "We made friends with some Jews there, and they invited us to our first seder. And while we were there, I began to think about being Jewish and what it meant to me. This came up particularly since some of the Americans were very ignorant about what was going on in Ecuador, and were also very anti-Semitic. It wasn't like when I was in my New England prep school, where anti-Semitism was an accepted social attitude. When they said things like Fuck you, Jew boy, it was simply because that was the way they had been brought up to think about Jews. In Ecuador it was a more pervasive belief that Jews were bad, unworthy people. The anti-Jewish feelings were there in school, but they didn't seem serious the way they did in Ecuador."

Their daughter Kara was born soon after they came back from South America. They didn't have any religious ceremonies, but instead held a party for friends and relatives, where everyone was appointed as godparents for the baby, following the South American custom. "So now she has forty godparents," said Sarah delightedly. Michael found a job on a weekly newspaper, and Sarah began taking photographs, both working out of their apartment.

It's a small apartment in an old building, where the bathroom is strung with washing lines filled with Sarah's photographs clipped up to drip and dry. The living room has Michael's desk against one wall, with a typewriter, books, and assorted papers and notes on top. The phone is on the floor by his chair, and when it rang, he bent down and picked up the receiver, swung his chair round, and tipped it back to talk with one foot on the edge of the desk.

"When we first came back from South America, we really were not interested in religion because it was the height of the anti-Vietnam movement, and we were involved in that. We just forgot about our experience with Jews in Ecuador," said Michael. "Then at one period I was sent to Harrisburg, Pennsylvania, to cover the Harrisburg trials of the Catholics who had burned draft cards and made other protest efforts."

Michael had gone as a reporter, but during the trial he became aware of his own complex attitudes toward the Catholic leaders, like the Berrigan brothers, whose political viewpoint he shared. "I liked the Catholic left a lot," he said slowly, "but I felt worried when they said they were burning draft cards because Jesus Christ was leading them. I could accept that for *them,* but I felt that it excluded all the other people working to end the war. And I remember sitting in a house in Harrisburg watching TV when the Palestinians attacked the Israeli athletes at the Munich Olympic Games. And there were other people sitting there, cheering on the Palestinians for what they'd done. It bothered me a great deal, and when I got back from the trial, I was exhausted, and I started to think about being Jewish and why I had been worried by what I'd heard."

He met some friends who told him about the poor Jews living in New York; they felt neglected by the rich Jews of the city whose only concerns were blacks and Vietnam. He went to investigate and wrote a long and moving piece about their experiences, which evoked a tremendous response from readers.

"Sarah and I started to talk about being Jewish and what it meant to us and why it bothered me to see poor Jews and to hear anti-Semitic comments, and we both wondered what our children were learning," said Michael.

Their daughter Kara, who was three, and their son Enrico, who was two, were both in a day-care center.

"One day one of the teachers said, Let's have a Hanukkah party," Sarah said, "because it was in December, and there were a lot of Christmas and holiday celebrations going on. It seemed like a great idea, and I was very enthusiastic. I like the idea of formal rituals and ceremonies. So we had the party, and we invited parents and children, and lighted the candles on a menorah, and one of the teachers told the story of Hanukkah, and it was lovely."

"Later, when we began talking to our friends about my feelings about being Jewish and what it meant, it turned out that our Hanukkah party had meant a lot to people," said Michael. "So we started to figure out how to do a Passover seder. We didn't want to do a Freedom seder, which we'd participated in a couple of times during the anti-Vietnam protests. We wanted to have a Jewish seder. It was a kind of Jewish pride that we wanted to share with each other, and which we wanted to separate from our political involvement."

So with an informal group of like-minded friends, they carefully set up a religious Passover seder, reading the story of the freeing of the Hebrew slaves in Egypt and the cruelties of Pharaoh and the sufferings of the ten plagues and the courage of Moses and his brother Aaron, in a Haggada which Sarah bought Michael as a present.

"Nothing had prepared me for this involvement with Judaism," said Mike slowly. "My maternal grandparents were Jews, but later in their life they called themselves Christian Scientists, because my grandmother converted when she was sick. My father's father was an Orthodox Jew, but I never knew my grandmother because he divorced her soon after the marriage. And my parents were secularized Jews, though in the last years of his life my father began to share my growing interest in religion." Michael's parents died a few years ago.

The group began to look forward to Hanukkah and to Passover, and to talk about how their own Jewish experiences had made them reject their childhood faith. One woman remembered the High Holy Days as a time when the women came to the temple to show off their mink coats, and another spoke angrily of the "chrome temple" that she attended as a child, with tickets for High Holy Days services priced so that those who paid the most sat near to the rabbi and those who paid the least were relegated to the gym in the basement. For Mike, "I wanted to fill a void I felt in my own life. I wanted my life to reflect the sense of community, the stability of ceremony, that I had seen as a journalist covering blacks in the south, Italians in the north Bronx, Jews on the Lower East Side. I wanted to belong to something that would let me feel a direct, personal connection to my heritage." They began to talk of what they would pass on to their own children.

No one in the group had a strong Jewish education or knew much about the traditions they wanted to share. So they approached members of a New York *havura* ("group"), an assemblage of mostly religious Jews in their twenties and thirties who observed the traditions of Judaism independent of rabbi or temple. With their assistance, a school or heder was set up, meeting every Friday afternoon in a New York apartment, for children of all the group members.

"Each class begins with one of the teachers telling a story from the Torah [first five books of the Old Testament] and then they move into learning centers where they draw pictures or improvise a play based on the story," Sarah explained. "It depends on the age level of the group. And there's also some learning of the Hebrew letters. Then there's a second story, usually a fable or an allegory based on some moral idea, and finally a song to welcome the Sabbath day, which begins on Friday evening, and one of the children collects *tzedakah,* or charity money. Over the years they've done so many exciting things because the teachers are absolutely superb— like putting together a newspaper with editorials about Jacob's land transactions with Esau and making up a newscast for station WJEW. We're not really *Shabbat* [Sabbath] observers, though I wish we were sometimes. It's a nice idea to have a really peaceful day, no work, no interruptions. We do light candles on Friday night, and after the children's school there's a special kiddush ceremony for the Sabbath over a glass of wine."

All of the events and lessons at the Friday afternoon sessions are carefully planned. The teachers meet each week for several hours to plan each session, and every two weeks they spend an evening with the parents to discuss how major episodes should be presented. "That means we all have to evaluate our own feelings about Abraham's willingness to sacrifice Isaac or the cunning Jacob displays toward Esau," noted Michael, "and so the parents end up studying the Torah too, and for some of us this is the first time we've ever done that."

There's quite a lot of healthy argument, discussion, exchange of opinions on every issue. When the teachers first wanted to apply for a foundation grant to set the school up on a more permanent basis, there were mixed emotions. Some parents worried that the fund raising and financial base would change the participatory informal nature of the school, and others thought success might swamp the intimate atmosphere. But a small grant has changed little, and the school is thriving.

"We also have a *hevra* (group) of people in their twenties and thirties who come together for services," said Michael. "There's no rabbi, and men and women lead the services and both wear *tallithim* [prayer shawls]. We try to keep the old traditions, and we come together on Yom Kippur and Rosh Hashanah and Purim. Sometimes we go on a retreat, where we stay up all night and study the Torah until five o'clock in the morning and then repeat the Ten Commandments at dawn." He looked down for a moment, a little self-conscious, and then said: "And once a week I've been going to an Orthodox rabbi and studying Torah with him."

But this involvement with and commitment to Judaism has brought his interfaith marriage into new focus. As Sarah said, "When Mike was doing the story about the poor Jews, he'd say he was Jewish, but he would never tell anybody about his marriage to me."

"The people on the Lower East Side are not ready for it," said Mike defensively. "They don't want to hear about mixed marriage."

"And Mike was not ready to defend it then," said Sarah. "We always used to say to the children, You're half gentile and half Jewish. One day when Kara was about eight she said, I'm half Jewish, and I'm half Christian. I said, No, you're not, you're half Jewish and half Anglo-Saxon, but you are not a Christian because you have not been baptized. And she said, You mean I can say I am Jewish all the time, and I said yes. And she said, Well, I didn't want to hurt your feelings."

She and Mike exchanged smiles at the story, and Mike said, "I remember about three years ago when they had that Purim party and the puppet play, and Enrico was watching the story of Haman saying he was going to kill all the Jews, and he said, Well, he won't get me because I am not Jewish. Today, they know they are Jewish, and they have a really strong Jewish education. They've started to learn Hebrew and sing Hebrew songs, and they really love the school. There's nothing taught by rote, like in many Hebrew schools, and the teachers are fantastic. All the families are involved, because the teachers wanted that from the beginning. We do know of a few other groups like ours, and a few of us really want this idea to spread, because we believe anybody can do it. You need good teachers and involved parents and that's all."

Mike and Sarah are aware that "we live a fully Jewish life and more so than most people. But our backgrounds are strange because Sarah is open to Judaism, and Mike is open to Christianity."

Sarah feels "in some sense I am a Ruthian Jew, like Ruth in the Bible. But I don't want to convert. My experiences in services have taught me that I don't like that style of prayer, that it is not meaningful to me. I feel, though, that for the kids it is difficult to be both Jewish and Christian, and I feel very supportive of their Jewish education, because I know that Jews are both an ethnic and religious group. I am also the reason why we started in on a lot of this stuff, because I feel it is a part of a real tradition. I love the feeling of tradition, that sense that you are participating in ceremonies that have been going on for thousands of years. It's not a mission, you are not helping people find religion. It's just a tradition. I suppose if Mike's parents had wanted me to convert very much, I would have done it. But it would have been hypocritical."

Mike nodded and said, "I think there are real problems in an interfaith marriage, but I don't see how you can give any general advice, because each couple is different in how they feel about it. I also think there are fights to be waged, and one of them is the whole tradition of religion being passed on by the religion of the mother, as Judaism rules. When we were in Israel visiting, we had a lot of fights with Israelis about our mixed marriage. I don't like to think that some day some rabbi will say that because Sarah is not Jewish, the children are not Jewish. The whole Talmudic idea of conversion and the methods of conversion that exist are so hollow in many cases that it's not worth taking them seriously."

At present, Mike and Sarah's children are a long way from learning about the traditional rulings. Their education is a unique blend of modern educational theories and ancient stories and customs. Last year in preparation for Passover, the children made their own Haggada to read at seder. When Kara asked, "What's the Egyptian side of the story?" the teacher picked up her question, and there was a long discussion about how the Egyptians must have viewed the events of Moses' begging for the slaves' freedom and the sufferings of the ten plagues. It was decided to hold a trial on the issue that "If God kept hardening Pharaoh's heart about releasing the Israelites, was he really guilty?" There was much preparation, and the trial went off very successfully. Kara was the judge, and after Pharaoh had been found guilty, she gave her summing up:

"Pharaohism is not a good thing. People should not be like Pharaoh, and should not keep slaves because it is wrong. But Pharaoh could not do anything else because he was king, so he is sentenced to a year's probation to reform his ways and stop keeping slaves. And it's very important for every one of us to fight Pharaohism and stop it happening again."

Both Joyce and Arthur and Sarah and Mike felt a need for a structure of belief which would unify them as a family, provide an identity for their children, and give meaning and hope to their everyday lives. Joyce and Arthur came to choose a path for themselves that brought together their disparate religious backgrounds in a new modern philosophic interpretation. Creative Initiative provides for its hundreds of followers a core of community and commitment, and encourages individuals to take responsibility for their actions and for the education of their children. These ideas are firmly based in ancient Judeo-Christian teachings, but set within a framework that is relevant to current concerns and disciplines such as ecology and psychology.

For Mike and Sarah, their involvement in working to solve some of the social problems of the world today led them to a different solution; they turned back to traditional heritage and adapted it to their twentieth-century needs. The practices and observances they have chosen reach back thousands of years into the history of the modern world, spoken in a language that predates Latin and Greek. Yet at the same time their interpretation of their traditional religion is rooted in a framework of modern concepts, within which women can take part in services and discussion replaces rote—practices that have no precedent in Judaism's ancient rituals. They have reconciled an ancient faith with the present, while Joyce and Arthur have chosen a newly formulated faith to sustain the traditional values of their past, while also taking into account the findings of modern psychology and science.

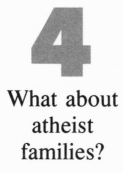

What about
atheist
families?

"When people say to us, Oh, you're atheists, so you don't believe in anything, I get very cross. Because I believe in a great many things. I just don't happen to believe in what they believe in, but that doesn't mean that I don't believe in anything at all."

Francesca has no hesitation in expressing her views about her independence from traditional religious ideas. She and her husband, James, live with their ten-year-old daughter, Nicoletta, in a rambling white frame Victorian house high on a river bank facing the city skyline. Inside, their apartment has gleaming wood floors, a few rugs, and comfortable antique furnishings. Their favorite sitting area is a long narrow room running the width of the east side of the house, its wide windows filled with spiky spider plants, large rubber trees, and a flourishing mass of greenery facing the vista of rippling river, open sky, and bright sunlight.

A few paintings and prints hang on the white-painted walls. In the window one of Francesca's woven textile creations swings, and through the glass doors leading to the rest of the house, the triangular shape of her gleaming gold harp, just acquired for her music lessons, stands silhouetted against the big old sofa. The overall effect is one of a friendly, comfortable eclecticism of style.

Francesca was born in southern Sicily and came to America with her parents when she was ten. She is now a well-built woman in her thirties, with a prominent Roman nose in a strong open face and brown-gold hair to her shoulders. She was wearing a beige shirt-dress, and spoke English fluently, only faintly accented with the lilt of her native Italian.

"I spent my first year here in a Catholic elementary school with a strong program in reading and writing," she said, "and that year convinced me that I would be a nonpracticing Catholic. It was in the early 1950s, in the midst of the anti-Communist McCarthy era. In Italy, I had met people of all political convictions, and I was not ready to put people into boxes or to deny their differences. But in the school everything had to be black or white. Their unethical system meant that because of a political name, someone was in or out. If you were involved in any kind of divergent thinking, in any area, at any level, or at any time, you were a Communist. It was a very difficult place for me. But when I told the school at the end of the year that I was going to a public high school, they offered me a scholarship and tried to stop me leaving. After that year though, it was the end of Catholicism for me."

Looking back, she tried to explain her rejection of her family's faith. "My parents were Catholics, but in Italy it is very different being Catholic than in America," she said. "It's more like Jews in Israel—we are Catholic more by culture and environment than by conviction. The traditional aspects were more important than the religious ones. We didn't go to church much when we came here, though I liked the ritual and the color of the services. In the school I found that I could not accept the dogmas, I could not accept the tenets of the faith. The kinds of things we were told in school were not questioned at all, because it was a very homogenous community. For example, we were told that you could not eat meat on Fridays. That was very difficult for me to accept because my grandmother's brother was married to a Jewish woman, and they used to eat meat on Fridays. It occurred to me that if there was a God who was concerned about people eating meat on Fridays, he must be a very narrow, very petty God indeed if he could not accept that.

How could he have such human characteristics that were so unreasonable, unloving, unconcerned, and unintelligent?"

Her own family did not reject the tenets of their faith but she was always encouraged to question and discuss things.

"The nuns, in school, made it very clear that questions were not encouraged," she remembers. "I remember wondering about the Greeks who lived before Jesus was born. Would they go to heaven if they did not know about heaven and hell then and if they believed different things? It seemed to me very unjust that someone's belief in heaven or hell depended on whether they were born after Christ or not. I wanted to know if the people born earlier were all in hell, and why they were there if it was not their fault when they were born. But no one wanted to answer questions like that. Religion was presented to me in very narrow terms, and I could not accept it at all. You simply believed and accepted what they told you."

She went on to attend a public high school for four years, which she found much more congenial, and then to study for and attain her master's degree in fine arts. She works with textiles and fibers, making batik, weaving, and creating individual hangings and art pieces. Last year she began teaching art in her old high school, "so it feels as if I have come full circle."

She said, "When I was in college, I considered myself an atheist. My mother minded that, but more from social reasons than religious concerns, I think. She felt a certain pressure to conform. She thought, How could her child not be like everyone else's child? It was many years before she could accept me for what I am."

It was while attending a course on Italian art that she met James. He's a soft-spoken man, with a neatly trimmed beard, glasses, and soft sandy hair, and an air of calm that balances Francesca's assertive exuberance. He works as a free-lance art director and also teaches.

"My parents were medium-strict Roman Catholics, I'd say, and sent me to parochial school for the first eight years," he explained. "I was baptized, confirmed—yes, I did all the proper things, and at the time I enjoyed it. But by the time I was about fifteen I began to have more questions than answers. I stopped going to church, and there was a lot of resistance from my parents when I said I did not want to go. They tried to convince me that I was doing the wrong thing. But after I graduated from high school, I didn't go to church again." He took his master's degree in art at Syracuse University, and during his college years began to think and formalize his philosophy about religion.

"The first year when they gave us some forms to fill out that asked for religion, I put down that I was Roman Catholic. The second year, I put down that I was an agnostic, and the third year I didn't put down anything. In the past few years, I have come to call myself an atheist, because I realized it was a chicken attitude to call myself an agnostic."

He thought for a moment and said:

"I have very negative feelings about most traditional religions, particularly in the United States where people have many choices. Religion seems to ignore those choices. I really associate most traditional religions with ignorance, because I cannot understand how anyone can think they have an absolute answer. You only have to look around the world today to see that there are many choices, many options, many answers. How can there be only one?"

He and Francesca met, fell in love, and agreed to marry within three months.

"I was twenty-three and James was twenty-eight, and we talked a great deal about how we felt and what we believed," said Francesca. "I knew that I wanted to be married by the Catholic church because it was the only thing I had any connection with—and ideally by my uncle who was a priest in Italy. But we realized our parents could not be involved if we went to Italy, so in the end we were married here in the church attached to the school I had attended. We had to attend the pre-Cana conferences for couples, because we were not practicing Catholics. They were not very helpful. Most of the couples were very young, and the priest said things like, Marriage is not for going out, it's not for going to nightclubs, but it's for being home, washing diapers. I'd never been to a nightclub in my life, and I don't think any of the others had either. The image of marriage that was presented was one of dutiful commitment—the fun was out of it. Even when they separated the sexes to give sex information, there was no doctor or nurse—only the priest—and I remember thinking, How would *he* know? Then, when we met with a priest to set the wedding date, my ideas about the hypocrisy and insincerity of the church were confirmed. We'd wanted to marry on a Sunday in July, and then go to Europe for our honeymoon the next day. The priest looked at us and said, Well, on Sunday afternoons we don't do any weddings because after the last mass we usually scoot out of here and go and play golf. We ended up with the shortest, simplest form of ceremony, with no mass. They just took our names and addresses, wanted to see our birth certificates and baptismal certificates, and asked if we had both been confirmed. Fortunately I was not asked how I felt about raising a child as Catholic. The only reason we went through with the ceremony was because we felt we had to be married in a way that was acceptable to our parents."

When they came back from their honeymoon, they did not join any church. Occasionally they listened to the radio broadcasts of the Ethical Culture Society in New York and found themselves in agreement with those philosophies. Created in 1876, by Felix Adler, a young professor of religious history and literature, the society emphasizes belief in the inherent worth and dignity of every human being, in democratic organizations and the practice of democratic ideals, as well as faith in the possibilities of human growth, change, and improvement and an active respect for the interdependence of all people and all life on this planet. Twenty-five local Societies make up the American Ethical Union, which develops national programs. In the past, members have been active in civil-rights and personal-liberty efforts, social-action causes such as the founding of the Legal Aid Society and the Visiting Nurse Association, and the establishment of three schools.

James explained: "The real impetus for us to get involved with any group was our child, who we felt needed some kind of religious identity within a group. One day when Nicoletta was about five, she came home from school and wanted to know if she was Christian or Jewish. That's when we decided it was time for some form of Sunday school, because we explained that we were atheists and not really either one. We joined the local Ethical Culture Society, and we enjoy it very much and feel that we gain from being involved. But unfortunately we know that the ideas of the group appeal particularly to nonjoiners, as we were, and that the number of people who agree with the philosophy of Ethical Culture is far greater than the few thousand who have joined. I'm not sure what we can do about that, since there's a great emphasis on individual decision making and people coming to Ethical Culture, not us going out to find them."

Francesca explained: "We wanted Nicoletta to learn about many religions, to meet other people who believe as we do, and to have an opportunity to share experiences with other children who come from families with similar outlooks. I always remember for example asking my grandmother, who died recently at the age of ninety-three and whom I was very close to as a child, what is a Jew. She'd grown up in a narrow, rigid environment, but she simply said, They are like we are, but they pray to God in a different way. I thought that was a wonderful reply, because it did not make me think of Jews as different human beings. And that is the kind of attitude I want Nicoletta to have."

In the younger age classes, she learns about ethical awareness, a sense of membership in the group, and concern for the feelings of others. Later she will move into classes that discuss ethical problems and moral values and the importance of decision making. Some of the curriculum will be based on the pioneering research of Lawrence Kohlberg, professor of education and social psychology at Harvard University. Kohlberg wondered, as Piaget had, how children learn moral and ethical ideas. He put together a series of moral dilemmas and as his thesis presented them to a group of boys, and then analyzed their replies. Since 1957 he has repeated the experiment every three years, and today his first subjects are in their thirties. His results show a pattern of development involving six possible stages of increasing complexity and maturity, through which an individual can pass as he develops his own standards of morality and ethics, much as Piaget presented the stages of cognitive development which young children experience. Kohlberg defines the six stages of moral development as follows:

STAGE 1: The child defers to the superiority of the parent or other adult, and the emphasis is on punishment and obedience.

STAGE 2: The child will obey or agree to behave if he can see some immediate benefit in return.

STAGE 3: The child behaves to gain the approval of others, and conforms in order to please. This is sometimes called the "good boy-nice girl" orientation.

STAGE 4: The child obeys rules for the sake of maintaining the social order, or from concern for the wider community, rather than for the immediate narrow group.

STAGE 5: The child obeys in response to a contract between those who are in charge and those who follow the rules laid down, based on a democratic system of equality. This is called the "social contract, legalistic" orientation.

STAGE 6: This stage requires a highly sophisticated and abstract sense of morality rarely, if ever, achieved in real life by children or even adults. Here individuals achieve resolutions to the dilemmas based on ethical principles applied universally, consistently, and logically. People make ethical decisions that take into consideration every point of view in a totally objective way. Kohlberg explains: "Personally chosen moral principles are also principles of justice, the principles any member of society would choose for that society if he did not know what his position was to be in the society, and in which he might be the least advantaged."

Kohlberg also groups his six stages into three pairs of developmental areas:

PRECONVENTIONAL (STAGES 1 and 2): Usually found in children from four to ten years old. Children here are often well behaved, but they interpret labels of good and bad in terms of their physical consequences or because of the physical power of those who set the rules.

CONVENTIONAL (STAGES 3 and 4): Usually described as confor-
mist. A child is concerned with conforming to the social order
and with maintaining, supporting, and justifying that order.

POSTCONVENTIONAL (STAGES 5 and 6): Characterized by a recognition of moral principles that are accepted because they have a
validity of their own, apart from any outside authority.

Kohlberg, who uses Piaget's open-ended approach to interview-
ing children, asserts that "adults seldom listen to children's moralizing. If a child throws back a few adult clichés and behaves himself, most parents—and many anthropologists and psychologists as
well—think that the child has adopted or internalized the appropriate parental standards. Actually, as soon as we talk to children
about morality, we find that they have many ways of making judgments which are not internalized from the outside and which do not
come in any direct or obvious way from parents, teachers, or even
peers."

In the courses that Nicoletta takes at Sunday school, she will be
presented with well-known Kohlberg dilemmas like the following:

In Europe, a woman was near death from a special kind of cancer.
There was one drug that the doctors thought might save her. It was a
form of radium that a druggist in the same town had recently discovered. The drug was expensive to make, but the druggist was charging
ten times what the drug cost him to make. He paid $200 for the radium
and charged $2,000 for a small dose of the drug. The sick woman's hus-
band, Heinz, went to everyone he knew to borrow the money, but he
could only get together about $1,000, which is half of what it cost. He
told the druggist that his wife was dying, and asked him to sell it
cheaper or let him pay later. But the druggist said: "No, I discovered
the drug, and I'm going to make money from it." So Heinz gets desper-
ate and considers breaking into the man's store to steal the drug for his
wife. What should he do?

Kohlberg points out that this, and the other dilemmas, have been
chosen "because they generate cognitive conflict, uncertainty about
what is right, about the adequacy of the current moral beliefs the
student holds," and because they cause disagreement among students, forcing them to argue among themselves.

This dilemma is frequently debated as a prime example of a moral issue, because it pits the issue of right to life against the rights of property. In analyzing the replies, Kohlberg chooses to look at the ways people think about moral values, rather than whether they pick life or property. Ambivalence of decision is a constant in Kohlberg's analyses, and there are no hard-and-fast answers on right and wrong, no flat statement that, yes, he should steal the drug or, no, he should not steal the drug. But in reading through the study material, one can see that there is general agreement among those at Stage 5, which is presumably a more morally developed stance than Stage 1, that the right to life takes precedence over the right to property.

The individual answers of young people involved in Kohlberg's study are interpreted according to criteria which are not clearly spelled out in the research. However, this reply, by Tommy, age ten, is considered to be Stage 1:

"Heinz shouldn't steal; he should buy the drug. If he steals the drug, he might get put in jail and have to put the drug back anyway. But maybe Heinz should steal the drug because his wife might be an important lady like Betsy Ross; she made the flag."

Three years later, at age thirteen, Tommy is at Stage 2 and says: "Heinz should steal the drug to save his wife's life. He might get sent to jail, but he'd still have his wife." When asked if he should steal the drug if it was for a friend, not his wife, he said: "That's going too far. He could be in jail while his friend is alive and free. I don't think a friend would do that for him."

At age sixteen, Tommy, at Stage 3, feels: "If I was Heinz, I would have stolen the drug for my wife. You can't put a price on love, no amount of gifts make love. You can't put a price on life either."

And at age twenty-one, he has reached Stage 4 when he says: "When you get married, you take a vow to love and cherish your wife. Marriage is not only love, it's an obligation. Like a legal contract."

There has been some professional criticism of this research by others in the field, who believe that the criteria are unclear and ill-defined. In one study of 957 individuals, for example, 45 percent could not be placed in one stage or another. Others complain that the stages lack standardization and point to the scoring manual which has comments like "ambiguous" and "guess." Further, it has been pointed out that even once a person's stage has been established, you cannot predict how he will behave in a moral situation. Indeed, when Kohlberg and an associate did a study of his original group later, many who had been at Stage 4 were found to have regressed inexplicably to Stage 2.

However, in a long analysis of how moral thinking is taught (in the February 1979 issue of *Psychology Today* magazine), Howard Muson notes: "Kohlberg's cognitive theory remains the most exciting one around. Many experts agree with Piaget that moral judgment does seem to unfold in a developmental pattern, and Kohlberg's theory has provided the most comprehensive effort to describe it to date."

In recent years Kohlberg has been involved in studies showing that these methods can be used to upgrade the level of moral judgment by at least one stage, and sometimes more if the teacher is capable of helping the child "experience the type of conflict that leads to an awareness of the greater adequacy of the next stage." His methods have been tried in a prison program, and in the setting up of self-governing justice communities in a few high schools, where students create a communally drawn constitution and engage in small-group discussions about moral and personal dilemmas, in order to raise the participants' level of moral development and awareness.

He believes that moral reasoning and ethical behavior can be taught independently of religious doctrines. In recent years, several courses have been instituted in schools to bring these ideas to students. Usually called something like "Moral Reasoning" or "Ethics," they cover such topics as honesty, fairness, responsibility, and respect for human beings, and they use dilemmas like those of Kohlberg plus other systems of values clarification and philosophical concepts.

The government is involved in funding some of these experimental projects through the U.S. Office of Education's National Diffusion Network. One of the projects is Curriculum for Meeting Modern Problems, which deals with moral and ethical issues and which is used in elementary schools in Lakewood City, Ohio, and distributed by the state.

Ralph Mosher, a Boston University professor of education, feels that the major emphasis of these new courses is to teach children "to think more systematically, more deeply, in a more principled way about moral and ethical issues in their own lives, in their personal interactions, and in the classroom."

This trend is the result of a long history of change as parents begin to reclaim responsibility for the moral and ethical education of their children. Until recently, such education was assumed by the church, attached to religious practice and observance or included in religious schools' curricula. Today, when many parents find themselves estranged from the ideas of any traditional religious group and yet eager for their children to learn and examine the ideas of ethics and morality, ethical education independent of religion seems an ideal solution.

Contrary to traditional notions about the importance of a religious upbringing, Kohlberg's studies show that forces both inside and outside the family play an important part in developing a child's moral sense, and that "religion and religious education do not appear to play any unique role." He has found that children who are exposed to a wide variety of social experiences, who have a chance to express their ideas, to take on different roles and lifestyles within the family, at school, and in their peer group seem to develop the most advanced sense of moral judgment.

Parents who encourage a child to share views openly, who invite advice, ideas, suggestions, who involve the child honestly in family decisions and responsibilities and who welcome questions, conversation, and discussion on issues of right and wrong and the reasons behind decisions that the child is involved with are helping the child develop a set of moral and ethical principles. But children who are not encouraged to question or express their thoughts and ideas, who are not given an opportunity to experience different roles in the family or the community and who have limited social interchanges are often those who do not grow beyond an early stage of moral development. So far there has been no research to evaluate whether these exchanges have to be experienced personally or whether children can gain such ideas through literature, movies, or even television, in order to absorb their impact.

Starr Williams, the education program director for the Unitarian Universalist Association, has been teaching in religious Sunday schools for twenty-five years, and though she did not quote Kohlberg's research, she had experienced at first hand those children who had little chance for personal expression.

"Over the years, the most difficult and deprived children in my classes were those who came from families where nothing was discussed," she said from her Boston office.

"It doesn't matter what is talked about usually, or how it's said, as long as families talked together. Those families who never had real conversations with their children deprived them of any understanding of what was going on. It doesn't matter what the background is—religious, irreligious, married, divorced, whatever—but at one time every child's curiosity is aroused, and he or she wants to ask questions. If that curiosity is stifled, repressed, silenced from the first moment, there's a kind of freezing in the child's understanding of the world and how it works. It's hard to define why you can spot those children so easily. You feel sorry for them and what they have missed, but it's often very difficult to encourage them to develop an awareness about the world when it's been crushed for so long."

For Nicoletta, there has always been an openness of communication between herself and her parents and a warm willingness to talk about anything and everything.

"We talk about what's right and what's wrong," said Francesca, "and I explain that it is wrong to steal because it hurts somebody else. I think it is very dangerous to tell children not to steal because they will go to hell, because when they grow older, if they do steal anything and don't go to hell, they'll think there's nothing wrong in doing it. Stealing is ethically not right, that's all."

But many parents wonder about those ultimate life crises for which religion seems to provide such reassuring answers and solutions. What does an atheist family do in the event of death? James did not hesitate in replying: "Unfortunately a few people Nicoletta was very close to have died recently, including her grandmother.

We don't talk about heaven because we don't believe in it. We explain that death is part of life and that everyone will die at some time."

Francesca said: "We know that the idea of death upsets her, because she wants to be sure that we will be around. When we went to pick up my harp recently"—and she gestured toward the harp standing in the other room—"we put it in its big case and just managed to fit it in the car, where it stuck out the back. The case is very wide and big, and it looks a bit like a coffin, and as we drove back, Julia was sitting in the back of the car and could see that many people looked at it with a strange expression. I realized what she was thinking, and I said to her, When I die, why don't you just put me in the harp case, and I'll be very comfortable. She said something about being afraid she might die first, and I remembered so well as she said it how I had felt about dying and not wanting to suffer the loss of other people. We talked about it, and I told her how I felt, and I said it would not be normal for a child to die before the parents, because usually the natural order is for the parents to die first. I said it's unlikely that she would die first, and we certainly hope to be around for a good long time, anyway."

James said: "My personal feeling is that I would like to be cremated, and I would like to have my ashes buried and have a tree planted on the spot. When people in our family have died, it's our custom to make a gift to the library in their memory. We usually give books that would have been of interest to that person, because it is something that goes on. Books will serve the living, and in death, you reassert life."

Francesca said: "My own personal feeling is that immortality is achieved by the things you do and the things you leave."

"If Nicoletta asks about things like that," added James, "we talk about them and explain to her what we believe, and answer her questions as honestly and openly as we can."

Both Francesca's and James's families have criticisms of their non-Catholic lives. "At first there was a certain amount of pressure to baptize Nicoletta," recalls Francesca, "especially from my mother. In the end, when we were in Italy, we decided to ask my uncle the priest to baptize her and invite another aunt and uncle to be godparents, not so much because of the religious ceremony but as an affirmation of our involvement with my Italian family."

Francesca would have much preferred to have had a naming ceremony, which is suggested by Ethical Culture. "Recently one of the Sunday school teachers had a baby and invited all the children to the ceremony, and it was really lovely," she said.

James said: "I don't believe that a child is born in sin; I think that a child is born completely innocent. This is a basic disagreement I have with Catholicism and with the concept of baptism. Since I don't believe man is born evil or incomplete, I don't think you need baptism. I also can't believe in the Virgin Birth or the notion that God has a son. I cannot accept a human being as a god figure. To me, Jesus was a human being, obviously ahead of his time in many ways and a very influential being, but as far as I am concerned he was a man. In Catholicism, these are important philosophic differences." He also expressed his concern at the pressures to bring back prayer to public schools ("I'm not against prayer, if people want to pray, but it has no place in schools") and added with a twinkle: "I'm always vaguely disturbed by the phrase 'In God We Trust' on all the money we have—it really doesn't seem to belong there."

Francesca nodded her agreement as he spoke. But since Catholicism was part of her culture as well as her religion, she still likes to mark the ritual of Christian festivals with celebrations.

"I am concerned that our child should not grow up with negative feelings about one religion, and since she is learning about other religions in Sunday school, she has a good understanding, which pleases me. We celebrate Christian holidays in a nonreligious way, because I grew up with the cultural emphasis of Catholicism, and our celebrations now have nothing to do with the church. I don't feel I have to discard the celebrations which I enjoy just because I am not a practicing Catholic. This Easter, for example, we are planning a true Sicilian feast with a whole range of traditional foods. And on Saint Cecilia's day [November 22]—she's the patron saint of music—I sent my harp teacher a special card. He told me, "I'm Jewish, you know," so I explained that Saint Cecilia doesn't care if you are Jewish, she will still look after you."

They have a Christmas tree and an exchange of gifts, and each year decorate the tree with hand-painted eggs, colorful and enameled, which they make themselves. "We send out Christmas cards which we design and make ourselves—James does the calligraphy, and I do the design, and some of our friends say they are keeping them from year to year for their collection." She brought out this year's card, a simple rectangle with the numbers of the year in cut-out numerals, with colorful batik material showing through the space, and a quotation beautifully written in calligraphy along the side: *La terra provvede abbastanza per nutrire ognuno, ma non abbastanza per soddisfare l'ingordigia degli avari.* "Earth provides enough to satisfy everyone's need, but not enough to satisfy everyone's greed."

"We know that ritual is a very important part of human existence, and one of the problems of a purely ethical way of life is a lack of established rituals, of ceremonies, and of the hocus-pocus that most children love," said James.

"So we have created some special traditions for Nicoletta's birthday," said Francesca. "We put up a big orange tent in the yard, and we serve only natural foods. We are always concerned about what we eat, and forbid candies and sugared foods usually. For the party, the children who come make favors or little gifts and then we serve a special supper buffet style. This year I put out baskets of yarn and sticks, and they made woven "eyes of God" symbols [*occhi di Dio*], and every child took one home. They usually have a wonderful time, and it's a change from the bowling parties and the skating parties." They have attended a Passover seder, given by Jewish friends of theirs who are also atheists, "which was much more an explanation of the ceremony than a complete service," said Francesca.

Their positive and constructive attitude toward their rejection of their childhood religion has come from an ongoing, serious analysis of what they believe and how they want to live their lives, not an unthinking petulant denial. Far from "doing nothing," they actively seek ways in which to embody the high ethical standards and strong humanist philosophy which they espouse. They welcome discussions with their daughter about religion and are actively involved in the Ethical Culture group in their community.

"It's no good just sending a child to Sunday school, because unless she sees that her parents support the same ideas, she won't follow them," said Francesca firmly.

While James was happy to abandon all practices and observances from his Catholic upbringing, Francesca saw that they were an important part of her cultural and ethnic inheritance and incorporated them into her humanist life-style. For her, celebrating Easter is a cultural event, like celebrating the Fourth of July in America, and quite separate from the heavily religious emphasis it has for Christians and Catholics in this country. She has realized that she needs to share those ethnic experiences within her own family as she did when she was a child, because they are an integral part of her emotional life. These Nicoletta will share with her as she grows up.

It is hard to foretell whether Nicoletta will continue to follow the path of free-thinking independence that her parents have chosen, and in which she is being educated. Perhaps she will find her inclinations turn more toward a traditional faith and old-fashioned rituals, like those her father has rejected, or decide to worship a God whose existence her parents deny.

Francesca admits that she has changed over the years since her childhood rejection of her faith. "I am more tolerant now than when I was at the university," she said, "and I realize that there are values that are important in Christianity that I share, and that are now part of Western civilization. You cannot take Christianity out of Western civilization, because it is a part of the literature and the art and the music.

"Some people who reject Catholicism refuse to recognize that and won't go into the Sistine Chapel in Vatican City, for example, to see Michelangelo's work, because they oppose the Pope. But I think that's cutting off your nose to spite your face. I appreciate the art and the architecture of Christianity, and I love religious music. Handel's *Messiah* is a wonderful celebration of Christmas that we always enjoy."

James agreed. "I have rejected the philosophy, but I still like the artistic aspects—the architecture, the music. The trouble with the Catholic church is that it is a package; there are no shaded areas. You either take it all, or you leave it.

"In Protestantism there are many more shades, from liberal to conservative, and so there are far more choices. At one time, I became interested in looking at the Unitarian church, because I feel it has much in common with Ethical Culture, and I can't think why the two of them don't get together."

Francesca interrupted firmly: "I would have no interest in joining the Unitarian church because it is a branch of Christianity, and even though it is the most liberal branch, I have rejected Christianity. That's the association I have, and it would be very difficult to go beyond that association."

James smiled, unperturbed by her firm denial. "I'll have to look into it some more," he said calmly.

As I left, Francesca talked about the old lady who, after many years of living here, had sold them their lovely house.

"She told us how she invited the monsignor from the cathedral and some other people for dinner on Friday. She served meat, because she was not at all religious, and the monsignor took a ham sandwich with everyone else. One man said to him, How can you do that? He replied, If something is offered with a good heart, you should accept it gracefully and not offend the giver. I often think of that story since we moved in, because it's a philosophy I believe in."

5

Can children remain religious in a secular society?

When Susanna's alarm buzzed at 5:30, she opened her eyes, confused for a moment as she wondered why she was awake so early. Of course—it was the regular early-morning Bible study group in an hour. The sun was already shining through the window shade, reflecting on the dull-green rug by her bed. She rolled over and lifted a corner of the shade to look out at the first early-morning signs of life. A car drove by and turned the corner toward the city. She could hear the steady hum of traffic from the buses, trucks, and cars on the main road.

She pushed off the sheets and padded across the room to the bathroom next door. It was strange being the only one at home now that the five older children had left. The frantic early-morning scenes when she and her sister had to fight to get in before the four boys seemed like another lifetime. Now the bathroom towels were neatly folded on the rails where her mother had put them yesterday, three toothbrushes hung on the hooks with spaces between them, and the tube of toothpaste had the top on.

She pulled the plastic shower curtain back and turned on the hot water.

Half an hour later, Bible, notebook, and pencils in hand, she came downstairs to meet her mother in the kitchen.

"Ready?" Rita asked her, and Susanna nodded as she gulped a glass of orange juice Rita had poured out for her.

Then she followed her mother through the back door, down the steps, and out to the car parked in the driveway.

The noise of the two car doors slamming reverberated in the street where most blinds were still down, and the revving of the engine sounded like a truck in the early-morning silence. Rita backed out of the driveway and drove along several other side streets for about five miles before pulling up outside a small two-story frame house, much like the one they had left. Susanna got out and slammed the door. "See you at seven-thirty," called Rita as she drove off, and Susanna nodded and went up to the front door to ring the bell.

Inside were five other girls, all between fourteen and eighteen, ready to study the Bible. As in many other Mormon families, Susanna's life and her family's too revolve around the church and related activities. During the week, most mornings begin with her study group, where a mother leads discussion on the Old and New Testaments, and on the history of the Church of Jesus Christ of Latter-Day Saints. The church was founded by Joseph Smith in Fayette, Seneca County, New York, on April 6, 1830, some ten years after Smith had a vision telling him to "restore" the gospel of Jesus Christ. The church believes that the Bible is the word of God, and complementary works accepted as scriptures are contained in the Book of Mormon. That also gives details of visits Jesus made to earth after his ascension. The name Mormon comes from one of the later prophets.

Susanna has learned church history and theology through the years, and now, in tenth grade at the local public high school, she is looking ahead to see where it all leads. We talked in the comfortable family living room.

"It's hard going to high school sometimes—well, it's hard growing up with mostly Catholics around. In school I like Spanish, anatomy, and physiology, and I think I would like to go to Utah, to Brigham Young University. That's the Mormon university, and my sister went there. I'd like to go to school and see what it's like to be around Mormon kids for a while.

"At one time we had only two Mormon kids in school, but now there are about eight. Next year there won't be so many because some are leaving. There are no fights or anything because I'm a Mormon, but kids think I'm really strange."

Mormon rules ban drinking and smoking, and discourage drinking tea and coffee too. Susanna has found that "if there's a party and I'm invited and there's smoking or drinking, I usually just say I don't smoke or drink—it's no big deal. Some kids might think that's strange and look down on you for a while, but it doesn't make any difference with my friends." She's a member of her high school junior-varsity basketball team, and last year wanted to go to a basketball camp but went to a church camp instead.

Outside school her life revolves around the social life of the church. From the age of three, she attended the Primary on Thursdays, where she learned Bible stories and the stories of Jesus. When she turned twelve, she moved into the Aronic Priesthood for Young Women (AYPW) which, she explained, "is named after Aaron, Moses' brother, because we believe that the truth was passed down through him." Usually on Wednesdays she attends activity nights, which include a class or lesson for the AYPW, and once a month there's a "Super Saturday," when youngsters from the seven nearby wards in the Stake Area come together for church activities and a dance.

A husband and wife from the church usually run the youth groups, and there's a separate Aronic Priesthood for Young Men. Because this area does not have many Mormon members, they drive from many miles away to attend the Stake Area meetings.

Susanna's views on her role as a young woman seem to be firmly based on her religious upbringing and uninfluenced by the present turmoil of women's rights.

"The church says we would like you to get married, but you are not forced to get married, and you have to marry the right person," she said. "Women are also told to be prepared with an education, so that if anything happens to your husband, you should be able to work. We have been told by our prophet that our place is in the home to bring up children and that we should not get involved with the Equal Rights Amendment."

The Mormon church is headed by a prophet, two counselors, and fourteen apostles, and only men can hold these positions. Susanna has watched the prophet speak on television frequently, when there are special broadcasts of the regular general conference of the church aired across the country.

Despite the flood of news about women's independence and the options for independent lives, careers, and jobs, Susanna's mind has been carefully focused on Biblical standards of womanhood. The Mormon church, for example, is against birth control, and its public statements emphasize that it is "unalterably opposed to all forms of abortion." It permits sex only within marriage, deplores divorce, and considers homosexuality as sinful as adultery, "which is second only to murder in seriousness." Susanna has learned to ignore information reaching her which is opposed to the teachings of her religion and to accept the way of life she sees in her family and church. The lessons and teachings of the Mormon church are based on the Bible, and they place women very firmly in the home, caring for the children which they have without benefit of family planning or other options. These ideas Susanna has absorbed. Public turmoil and anguish about racial equality also wash by her in a church that only recently recognized the rights of its black male members to be priests.

She was a little shy and unsure of herself as we talked and concerned that she say the right thing ("My mother said I wasn't to sit there and say I don't know," she admitted). She answered questions directly, simply, and thoughtfully, but perhaps felt hesitant to air her doubts and indecisions with an outsider. When her parents came in, she let them talk and answer my questions even when directed to her, uneasy about replying without first glancing at her mother to say, "Is that right, Ma?"

Joe, Susanna's father, has served as a policeman for some thirty years, and his kind, lined face must have seen many other sides of life. But it's Rita's influence that has determined the family's strong commitment to the church. She's a tall attractive woman with a firm voice that's come from years of setting standards and rules for six children. Today, she is president of the church women's organization and has undiminished enthusiasm for talking about her Mormon faith and its benefits. She grew up outside Salt Lake City, Utah, and comes from several generations of Mormons. She met Joe in the 1940s, when he was stationed at an army camp near her home, and friends introduced them.

"We were always taught to mingle with all kinds of people, even though we were told to marry within the church," she said.

Joe, who was a practicing Catholic when they met, grinned and said: "I didn't even know what a Mormon was then."

Rita said: "When I told my parents that I wanted to marry Joe, they kind of disagreed, because they felt it would be a difficult road. We came from a long line of Mormons, and they were concerned that I not give up my faith. But my husband promised my parents and me that, according to his way of thinking, it is the mother who makes the decisions about how to raise the children and who provides the religious education for the family, and he gave me complete freedom to teach the children whatever I felt was right."

Joe added: "I thought she'd drop it when we moved East."

But Rita said: "I really felt I had the true church, and so our children were raised in my church. I think it's very important to come to some agreement about children before marriage, because we've been married thirty-one years now, and I've learned that we have to be very flexible, and we have to work together, and it's a constant working out."

Rita was aware that her situation was different from that of her parents. "We live in a predominantly Catholic neighborhood, and we have raised our children in the Mormon religion, but we raised them to be tolerant," she said. "We always understood that my husband would take the children to his church sometimes, and he also came to church with us. We discussed it fully. We were always very much aware of what we were doing. The Mormon religion is a twenty-four-hour-a-day religion, so you are constantly on the go."

This complete commitment and family involvement typifies Mormon life, and it's supported by a tithe of 10 percent on all members. Over the years, Joe has seen many sides of the faith, and particularly remembers a time when his son was seriously ill.

"I came home one day, and my boy, our second son, was very sick, and we rushed him to Children's Hospital," he said. "My wife called a Mormon priest and asked him if he could do a special blessing. The elders came to the hospital, and they administered upon him and laid hands on his head. He had a marvelous recovery within twenty-four hours."

Rita explained: "It was spinal meningitis, and one of the worst cases the doctors had ever seen. The people at the hospital claimed it was a miracle. But it wasn't that. It was a spiritual experience."

The boy, their second oldest son, was told what happened, and was determined to become a doctor so that he could help people in the same way as he had been helped. "But I always felt he wasn't cut out for doctoring," said Joe philosophically. "He didn't seem to be right for it. For two years, he was sent to South America to do his mission for the church, and after that he married a Mormon girl, and worked as an assistant in a hospital for a while. That's when he realized that he didn't want to be a doctor, but I knew it all along. So he's studying now for a Ph.D. in immunology—that's it, isn't it, Rita?"

"Yes." She nodded, proud of her son's achievements. "He's at the university, and he's doing research, which he really enjoys. Things work out in the end."

Joe's experience with his son's miraculous cure did not instantly convert him to Mormonism. Indeed, he readily admits that he enjoyed leading his own style of life, with his own values and beliefs.

"The children used to ask me, How come you don't join the church?" he explained with a grin. "And I would say, I'll join the church when I feel I can be a good Mormon. I didn't want to join just for the sake of calling myself a Mormon if I didn't believe it and didn't behave like one. I used to smoke, and I liked to take an occasional highball, and the kids would see me smoking my cigarettes and drinking, and they'd say, How come you can smoke and drink and we can't? And I used to tell them, Listen to your mother—I never had the benefit of a Mormon upbringing, that's why I do these things."

But last year, after thirty years of marriage, Joe came to a decision. "I became a Mormon because now I really want to do it. I have always supported my wife in her religious commitment, but my own decision to join is something that grew over the years. You have to understand the Mormon religion—it's something you live within yourself. When I think of all my bad faults, it's amazing to me now that, at my late age, I have a religion that is a twenty-four-hour-a-day thing for me. I feel that I have found what I was looking for all my life. And you know, the Mormon church really thinks of everything. These rules like not drinking coffee or tea, they've had for years, and now they're finding out all the things you can get from drinking it. And keeping food stored in case of emergency; we have six months' supplies ready, including water. When we had the snowstorm last year, I know it wasn't any trouble for Mormon families because we were well prepared."

Their four sons, now twenty-nine, twenty-seven, twenty-five, and twenty-three, are living away from home and their daughter of twenty-one is in Utah. Their eldest son married a Catholic, and Rita clearly feels some pain at that. "I have given the children the best we can give them," she said, "and I think it is better to go to some church than no church at all. I could never disown him for marrying a Catholic, because after all, that's what I did. But I felt it was my duty as a mother to talk with him about it. There was a little— you know—resentment, but we knew it was a matter of his choice. Even as teenagers, it was always up to them to do what they chose."

Joe added: "The ideal marriage is both to be of the same religion. Religious beliefs are the spiritual core of the family, and if you really get involved in your religion, it makes for a happier home life for everybody."

Now that he has joined the church, he and Rita are considering having a wedding in a Mormon temple. Mormon weddings that take place in a temple between two approved church members are consecrated to go beyond the concept of "till death do us part" and continue through "time and all eternity." Rita said: "We believe in the hereafter, and the ideal marriage for the Mormon is to be sealed in the temple, for all eternity."

Susanna has absorbed these concepts from her parents and in her church education. She has watched her mother bringing up six children, chauffeuring them to and from meetings, church services, and activities. She has seen the immense amount of time and energy expended on religion and its many demands, and she has followed the rules she has been taught throughout her life even when they come in conflict with outside society.

The family's church involvement has filled Susanna's time so that she has not developed other interests or social contacts. Among the 2.5 million members of today's Mormon church, there is the same kind of activity in the families of the 7,000 congregations around the country. The solid religious family orientation has resolutely turned its back on the changes of the twentieth century and ignored the freedom of opportunity available to young women today in favor of continued adherence to strictly interpreted Biblical standards and beliefs.

Two of Susanna's brothers, aged twenty-three and twenty-five, are doing their two-year periods of service in a poor South American community, one of the paths the church encourages young people to follow. Her sister is now living in Utah, designing clothes, and Susanna thinks of joining her but is still unsure of her own path.

Trina was a friend of Susanna's sister before she and her family of five, also devout Mormons, moved to Washington, D.C. Now in her twenties, she is studying theater, and her childhood ideas about her faith have changed in the past few years. She looks back at her involvement in the church with new eyes.

"I was brought up real strict," she said, when we met at a party. Sipping a glass of wine, she explained: "In our family my mother was really into the whole thing, though my father was never too dedicated. She had four daughters and then a son. She did everything—the services, the meetings, it was her whole life. We went to church all the time that I can remember."

She ran a hand through her fluffy brown hair and laughed as she said: "I can remember getting up at five-thirty in the morning for those classes before school—are they still going on? I can't believe it now but that's what I did because I was so into it. When we were living in Washington, it was a very open liberal community, and there aren't too many Mormons there, so we were kind of isolated. After high school I went out to Brigham Young University in Utah, and I planned to study there. But when I got there, it was such a shock! I couldn't believe the prejudice, the narrowness, the rigidity of the kind of people I met there. It was just incredible to me. It was so different from Washington and what I had grown up with, and it was very difficult for me to accept. I began to wonder if that was the kind of life I wanted. I finally quit after a year, because I just couldn't take it anymore."

She transferred to a college back in the East with a good theater program to finish her studies. Now she's sharing an apartment with another woman, has a boyfriend in the theater, and earns money as a part-time typist at the college. She has also found changes in her own family.

"My mother has begun to change in the last few years. She found a job for a few months, and it was the first time in her life that she had earned money. Now she's decided she wants to teach, and she has enrolled at the university to get her degree, and she's really serious and involved with it. She was always so busy with the church and doing things with the church. She's suddenly realized that she must have some time to do things for herself for once. It's been great to talk with her now, because she understands what I am going through."

Her childhood and teenage years seem like another world to Trina today, almost as if they had happened to another person.

"Every now and then I wonder what would have happened to me if I'd gotten married at eighteen or nineteen," she said, "which you are encouraged to do. What would have happened if I'd not gone on to college? I suppose I would never have questioned any of it, and never been exposed to other ideas and other people. It's really a little scary when you think about it, with the kids growing up in it today. I can't believe that Susanna is still going through the whole thing, the early-morning classes and everything. I wonder if she'll change. It's such a demanding way of living when you're in it, and it takes up so much time. Sometimes I wonder how I could have spent all those hours studying and in church."

Trina isn't totally cut off from her Mormon background, however, since she still sees old friends when she returns home, and keeps in touch with some of them. "Sometimes when I hear about Mor-

mon girlfriends I used to have, I am surprised to realize that they
are still in it, still doing everything, still believing everything. It's
strange to realize that they would disapprove of what I'm doing and
my way of life now. I just couldn't take it anymore, and I realize
that I'm completely out of it now, thank goodness. But when I was
growing up and at home, I never questioned it or thought about it
at all. It was just something I did."

It's hard to imagine Susanna rejecting the beliefs and ideas she
now holds so strongly. But the early teenage years are rarely times
of decision about religious or ethical values. Change and rethinking
are much more likely to come in the late teens or early twenties,
when people are forced to choose their own paths of behavior. It is
impossible to predict why one child, like Trina, will reject her background in the Mormon faith while her good friend, Susanna's sister,
loves the life she has found in Utah and hopes to stay there permanently.

It seems usual for children like Susanna, who are brought up to
accept traditional values and who enjoy following the observances
and rituals of religion, to continue them without question through
their adolescence. They are generally unconcerned about the conflict between their views and the prevailing views of the society outside. They acquire such confidence in their own beliefs and faith
that they can brush off the contradictions and criticisms.

But at some point in their lives, generally in the late teens or
more often in the early twenties, a decision is made, whether from
the cumulative effects of personal experience or in response to a
particular situation. At this crucial time in their lives they either
choose to follow the same path into adulthood, or reject it and find
another. For Susanna, at the age of sixteen, the church and her family provide a full and active social and educational life, and she finds
it difficult to imagine any alternatives.

But for Trina, who comes from the same background, the moment of crisis came when she found herself in a totally Mormon setting in which she did not feel comfortable. She was forced to reexamine her childhood beliefs realistically, and she came to reject

them because they conflicted with more strongly held ideals of liberal philosophy and egalitarian politics which she had unconsciously absorbed and assimilated in Washington.

Even Trina however is not yet at a point where one can be sure what her decision means, because it is only when she is faced with bringing up her own children that she will feel the full import of making a decision about which religious path to follow.

Boston, Massachusetts, is the spiritual home of Christian Scientists, as Salt Lake City, Utah, is of the Mormons. It was here that Mary Baker Eddy (1821–1910) left her Congregationalist background to create a church "designed to commemorate the word and works of our Master, which should reinstate primitive Christianity and its lost element of healing." Her book, *Science and Health with Key to the Scriptures,* is the basic textbook of interpretation for Christian Science beliefs together with the Bible. The new Christian Science Church Center is in the heart of Boston, an imposing area with its huge domed church, wide stone plazas, and spacious reflecting pool edged by tall buildings. It is an architectural landmark, which has been built around The Mother Church, The First Church of Christ, Scientist, to serve as headquarters for the international organization.

Anne, a member of the church, is a charming New England lady, with her simply cut gray hair combed back. When we met in town, she wore a tailored skirt and jacket over a simple blouse, and white gloves which she carefully removed. She has written children's books and is now writing for Christian Science publications. She and her husband, who is in publishing, have three grown children.

Anne first went to a Christian Science church with her mother when she was about six years old. She remembers it well. "Because it was then that my mother found the answers to her questions about life," she explained. "She was healed of a variety of physical ailments by it. So I used to go to church with her. When I was sixteen, I made my own commitment to Christian Science by joining the Mother Church in Boston and the branch church in my home town."

Anne met her husband through friends, and though his mother and grandmother had been Christian Scientists, he had been confirmed in the Episcopal church in college.

"But he knew I was a Christian Scientist, and because of his family background he knew what he was getting into," she said. "He was quite willing to let me care for the children's physical needs through the application of Christian Science, as long as they were well taken care of. You show your adherence to your teachings by your actions, and you can trust in God to take care of you. When you have sickness, you don't have to go to doctors."

Since the Christian Science church has no clergy, they were married by a Presbyterian minister. "He was most concerned about the fact that we came from different religions, and urged us to give up both our religions and take up one we could share," she remembers. "But neither of us wanted to do that, so we married agreeing to disagree." She added: "Of course my experiences have shown me that religion is a uniting force, not a divisive one. After all, we believe in one God, don't we, and the differences in religion are not too important, are they?' She has the calm certainty of a woman who has not had her convictions challenged by experience, and never had occasion to doubt that the world agrees with her.

In the first five years of their marriage, their three children were born, and Anne was forced to deal with the realities of her religious commitment. "My husband, of course, worried about the physical care of the children, because Christian Science heals, as Christ Jesus did, through an understanding of the nature of God and a reliance on His power and willingness to maintain His creation in good health without the use of drugs.

"Of course, we obey laws about immunization, quarantine, and health examinations, but where there is a choice, we do not go to doctors or take drugs. We believe that prayer prevents sickness, accidents, and other physical and mental problems, besides healing them when they do occur."

She was not deterred by her husband's skepticism, but found that "I was forced to dig into the study of the Bible and the writings of Mary Baker Eddy to prove that I understood my religion and could practice its teachings, as well as just talk about them. It meant a deep and sometimes arduous and agonizing mental commitment."

After their first child was born, she remembers that she took him to a pediatrician, to see if perhaps she would be able to combine her beliefs with medical methods without conflict. "But I realized that I could never do that, and I was much happier with my wholehearted commitment to my faith than I would ever have been trying to mix medical and spiritual methods of healing."

Her faith was rewarded in that her children had very little trouble. "One child had her tonsils out, and two needed glasses," she noted, "but they missed very few days of school, and they have never been involved in an accident or had any serious diseases."

However, she was well aware of how the outside world regards those who choose to reject the marvels of modern medicine in favor of faith. "Generally, one's stand is not understood in the neighborhood," she said. "Other people see Christian Science attitudes toward health quite negatively. When your child is out with a snivelly cold and another child complains, they say, Oh, they're Christian Science, and they don't do anything. Of course, that's not true, but that's the way people interpret it. My children had contagious diseases very mildly, and we certainly obeyed all the rules about quarantine."

The children all went regularly to church services with their mother, and also attended special services at the local Episcopal church, where their father went. At one point, his church held a series on family life education for teenagers, which Anne described as "excellent." There was a constant devotion to religion and its ideas within the family every day, and both parents set an example by their individual but sincere commitment.

"Looking back, I'd say churchgoing united our family," Anne commented, "and appreciation of the Bible was a common bond. My husband and I were firmly agreed that the Ten Commandments were good rules to live by and govern our children with. From my own experience I would say that what appear to be differences in religion don't have to make any more problems in a marriage than do differences in the color of two people's eyes, because often religious differences are only labels."

Her three children today have found their own ways and fol-

lowed that philosophy. Her son married a Protestant, and neither of
them has become involved with any church. Her second daughter
married a Catholic, and Anne admitted to feelings of concern when
that wedding took place.

"I was always concerned about the possibility that they would
marry Catholics, and in this case, the mother-in-law goes regularly
to a Catholic church," she said. "When my younger daughter and
her husband had their children, his mother was determined to have
them baptized. But my daughter said no, and her husband backed
her up. So my daughter comes with me to the Christian Science
church and brings the children along, and they are going to the
Sunday school now."

Her first daughter, Grace, married a young man she met in high
school who had been raised as a Unitarian. He grew up in the town
where they now live. It is a peaceful farming community that is
slowly turning into a commuter suburb. They own five acres of rolling grasslands and uncut woods, which they hope to develop so that
they can grow their own food. The small house nestles in a slope
among tall day lilies and azalea bushes. The day I went to visit her,
we sat and talked on the grass by the house, where the sun felt
warm through the denim of my jeans. A soft wind rustled the tops
of the trees that hid the houses below, and a bee buzzed among the
clover on the ground. A low stone wall hid the curving country
road, and only the occasional growl of a plane in the sky reminded
us of civilization.

"I feel sorry for people who don't believe in anything and don't
have any religion," said Grace, in a soft quiet voice but with an
echo of the certainty that Anne expressed. "They just won't know
what to do when the cataclysm comes, because they won't have
anything to hold on to, and they will just fall apart." She picked a
blade of grass and twisted it in her hands, her eyes wide and honest,
her heart-shaped face almost childlike in the sunshine.

"The main point of Christian Science is a better understanding of
God," she said. "It's a theology and a way of life, not a list of rules.
But there are rules for becoming a church member, requiring you to
study weekly Bible lessons and do correlative readings from Mary

Baker Eddy. You declare that you are truly a Christian Scientist in your way of life, and you don't drink or smoke. It's also suggested that you don't drink stimulants like coffee or tea. It's a very intelligent religion, and there's an answer to every question you may have about life."

She thought about that for a moment and then added: "You may not accept it at first, but if you think about those things long enough, you can understand them. Christian Science has a different belief about healing and the miracles that Jesus Christ performed, which were actually based on scientific principles of healing."

With her own belief and her faith in Christian Science, how was she able to marry someone of a different faith?

"The Unitarian church is not that far from the beliefs of Christian Science," she replied, "since they are both New England religions and both come from Congregationalist backgrounds. And there are points about Unitarianism which I really like—for example, the idea that man can improve himself and make progress through work and faith. Christian Science starts from the point of view that man is already perfect. But usually in families, the real problem is whether the non-Christian Science parent will allow the Christian Science parent to look after the physical well-being of the children."

She glanced at me and then at the house where her young son lay sleeping. "We have talked about it, my husband and I, and we decided that I don't want that particular responsibility. When our son gets sick, we take him to the doctor. But Christian Science is preventive as well as curative, so he is rarely sick, and he's had all the shots he's supposed to have."

Her husband likes to sing in the choir at the Unitarian church. "So we find ourselves going to both churches," she explained. "I usually take our son with me to the Christian Science church with Mother, because my husband goes off very early on Sundays, though sometimes I go with him then. We plan to send Michael to Sunday school when he's old enough, and alternate one week at the Christian Science school and one week at the Unitarian."

At holidays they find themselves more often at the Unitarian church, "because the services are more interesting since the minister is really an outstanding person and gives really sharp sermons," said Grace.

Her life has revolved around her son and her community since she stopped working as a secretary four years ago. "I think now that I have the best job in the world, because I can do so much," she said, "but I know you have to motivate yourself to do the things you really want to do, and working in an office was not very interesting."

She glanced at her watch. "I ought to check up on Michael because he usually wakes up around now," she said. We got up from the grass and walked over to my car, parked on the gravel. She said: "Religion is not something I ever felt I had to think through, so that I don't have answers with great significance or portentous implications. My husband and I are two people who are married, and part of us is our religious faith. What counts is that we both feel strong because we know where we stand. We have something to rely on that is not the other person. I think that's the value of religion in a family, that God is beyond the human rule and the vagaries of life and chance."

As I drove off down the quiet winding road edged with bushes and trees, I glimpsed Grace walking back toward her house in the bright sunshine, its roof nestling in the gentle slope of the rolling farmland, surrounded by the orange-gold flowers of tall day lilies.

It was hard to imagine that her family would ever feel problems or pressures from the outside world, in this peaceful rural town, or meet events that would turn them away from the religious path they had chosen so easily and simply. For Grace, maturing into an adult had not shaken her commitment to her Christian Science upbringing or made her question or reexamine her childhood faith. Instead, she had grafted onto it her husband's Unitarian ideas, and brought both philosophies together in her daily life and churchgoing. Her faith was open and ready to absorb ideas that complemented her own, and she did not imagine there was any need to question or criticize them. It was easy to see why she felt sorry for those who did not hold the same sturdy convictions or who were not prepared for some future crisis by a deeply sincere faith in God.

What happens
if parents
change?

arola was never very interested in religion. She grew up with an open-minded and secular approach to life based on liberal humanistic ideas. But her two marriages have given her a unique insight into the effect of religious pressures on family life and her own two children, now teenagers.

She teaches full time at a private university in the communications department, drawing on her impressive background in news reporting and feature writing. Her office has a worn brown wooden desk and regulation swivel chair. On the wall is the classic poster of Golda Meir with the words "But can she type?" underneath, and next to it is a blown-up photograph of surf breaking over rocks. There are a few front-page tearsheets from newspapers with headlines of "Nixon Resigns" and "First Man Walks on Moon," and some mimeoed notices about university schedules and changes. The plain windows are set high in the wall, to discourage students from peering or breaking in, and below are a couple of shelves of books and some folders and notebooks.

The first time I went to see her, in her office, Carola was wearing a denim skirt, striped shirt, and sandals. The old black telephone on her desk rang a few times, and she answered it immediately, giving straightforward replies, checking a grade in a looseleaf folder on her desk, urging a student not to skip a class, recommending a name to another teacher, looking up a phone number in her card index box. It was easy to picture her in a busy city newspaper office, hot on the tail of a breaking story, but more difficult to realize that she was a rabbi's wife, which was part of the reason I had come to interview her.

"My parents were not religious Jews, but I grew up in New York City, and so much of the cultural atmosphere of the city was Jewish that it was the environment I absorbed," she said. "We didn't celebrate the Jewish holidays, but my grandmother always invited the whole family every year for a Passover seder, and I remember it as a big party. Until recently I never realized you did anything besides have a big feast, because we never read from the Haggada. My grandmother liked to keep kosher, and when she came to visit us, she always brought her own pots and pans, because she knew my mother didn't keep a kosher home, and she wouldn't eat out of our pans."

Strong ethnic and religious influences in New York color the experiences of everyone who lives there. Its large Jewish population (more than the total population of Israel) are visibly absent on Jewish holy days, when the streets in some areas are practically deserted. If you live in New York, it is hard to ignore the symbols of Hanukkah with its candles, or Passover matzo in the supermarkets, even if you have no interest in their significance.

Carola's knowledge and understanding of what it meant to be a Jew was influenced both by the environment of the city in which she grew up and the family life she experienced. Within her own family, she saw that her mother did not follow many of the customs that her grandmother and other Jewish people held dear, and yet that those differences in outlook were superseded by family feelings of love and respect. She saw no breach between mother and daughter because of religious differences in observance and practice. In the city around her she saw a wide variety of interpretations of Judaism and Jewish identity. She absorbed the outwardly visible symbols of the faith into which she had been born, but knew nothing of the Biblical and philosophical background of the Jews. Although she would not have hesitated to call herself a Jew, she would have found it difficult if asked to define exactly what that meant.

At college she joined a Catholic sorority, "because it was known for throwing the best parties, and having a great social life, and my last two years of high school had been miserable," she said frankly. "I wanted to make up for earlier bad times, and I threw myself into everything."

She edited the student newspaper, dated Catholic boys with enthusiasm, and decided to make journalism her career. Her one serious involvement—"I suppose we were engaged"—ended after she and her fiancé agreed to work for a while after college and then drifted apart. She spent a year working on a magazine in New York, and then found a job in the Midwest as a reporter on a daily newspaper. She moved there, started work immediately, and soon afterward met her first husband.

"He was seven years older than I, and was one of the editors on the paper," she said, fiddling with a paper clip. "I knew then there were problems, because his first marriage was just ending after three years."

Carola had fallen in love and in her euphoria had decided that her beloved was perfect. Although they avoided discussing many other crucial personal issues before marrying, they did discuss their religious backgrounds.

"Until he was about sixteen, he'd been a strict Southern Baptist, and his father was a deacon at the church. We talked about it a lot, because it had been very important to him. I didn't know anything about Southern Baptists."

They talked about his experiences growing up as a Southern Baptist, and he explained that he had totally rejected those religious ideas. When it came time to talk of marriage, they both agreed to a civil ceremony and were married by a justice of the peace. When their daughter was born a year later, and their son two years after that, they discussed religion again.

"We attended several services at the Unitarian Universalist church, and we met the minister and talked to him," said Carola. "We felt it was something we both wanted to join, and I liked it from the beginning. You didn't have to give a letter of intent or state that your beliefs agreed with theirs or anything like that. You could believe what you wanted to believe, and it was just the right place for us. It was very free flowing, and I always felt very comfortable there."

Unitarian Universalists are one of the smaller denominations in America today, with some 200,000 members in about a thousand congregations. In general they rely on their own reason and personal understanding, seeking guidance from many religious thinkers in a diversity of cultures and traditions, and emphasizing the worth of all human beings. Some churches refuse to acknowledge the Unitarians as Christians because they do not believe in the Trinity, nor do they recognize Jesus as "Lord and Saviour." Most Unitarians do not believe that morality and decency are the exclusive possession of Christians, and, unlike many Christian sects, they stress the importance of life on earth independent of life after death.

Besides deciding to make a religious commitment to a faith new to both of them, Carola and Jim also made one other major decision after they married: to start their married life in a new atmosphere. So the two of them arranged to be transferred to a newspaper in a different state, on the East Coast. They soon adjusted to the new area and settled into the community, both busy in their newspaper life and the daily pressures of meeting deadlines.

It was here that they joined the Unitarian Universalist church, and enrolled their two children in the Sunday school. Their energy and enthusiasm singled them out as active members, and they attended services regularly, became leaders of the youth group, and made many new friends within the church.

Many other couples in demanding dual careers would never have bothered to expend the energy and time involved in dealing actively with questions of a religious nature, or to follow through so positively with a commitment once a decision was made. But for Carola and Jim it was a very worthwhile investment of their time, which may well have prolonged their marriage. It's interesting to speculate that the religious involvement itself may have been a reflection of uncertainty and conflict in other areas, and an escape from such problems.

The church provided their family with one arena in which there was unanimity and complete agreement—in vivid contrast to the troubled, strife-ridden realities of a marriage which was slowly crumbling in other areas.

Carola also felt that their religious commitment provided a healthy alternative to the frenzied pace of their daily work.

"We were both so tied up with the newspaper and meeting newspaper people that it was good to have another life that had nothing to do with the world of journalism," she said. "We always had a Christmas tree and parties and friends over to celebrate." The children understood Christmas as an experience in the Unitarian tradition—recognizing it as a time of religious significance, and also as a season of celebration, part of the winter solstice festivities that are pre-Christian in origin, marked today as a time of family rejoicing and togetherness. "They learned something about Hanukkah too at the Sunday school, but they always thought of themselves as Unitarians," added Carola. "There was never any question in their minds that they might be Baptist or Jewish. It was a very positive experience for all of us in every way."

The conflicts that came had nothing to do with religion, but were a result of the differences in their cultural experiences and expectations of the family, and quite specifically, Jim's inability to face his reservations about a wife who worked in the same professional field.

Carola had not really understood the depth of their cultural differences in terms of a family until she and Jim visited his parents.

"They had been unable to come to the wedding because they were quite a bit older than my parents, and it was a long way for them to travel from Oklahoma," she said, "and Jim didn't seem to mind. So we went out to see them soon after our first child was born. Somehow they seemed to be operating with a lot less warmth than my own parents and seemed very much older. There was less friendliness, less emotion—it was very hard for me to accept. We went to the Baptist church with them, and it was like being in a foreign country." She mentioned the Woody Allen movie *Annie Hall* to describe her feelings about the contrast between her own Jewish-oriented childhood and the cooler Protestant style of her in-laws.

The visit to Jim's family had no immediate results, but it did give Carola a sobering insight into the vast cultural differences that separated her husband and herself. Although religion continued to serve as a unifying and stabilizing force in their daily lives, as the weeks and months stretched on, it became impossible to bridge the growing conflicts in other areas.

Carola saw their marriage collapse under the weight of disagreements about almost every important aspect of their lives.

"Jim had always expected that I would stop working after we got married and be a home person," she said, "but I had told him I never wanted to stop, and so I went on working as a reporter. When our second child was born, I stayed home for about a year and a half, because I felt the baby needed that attention, and then went back to work again. But Jim never seemed to respect my contribution in his field. There was never any feeling that we were in the marriage together, working together, the two of us against the world. He never liked my criticizing the newspaper at breakfast or talking about work with him at home. He couldn't accept it from me as his wife, although he had enjoyed those kinds of discussions when we were dating."

For Carola, it seemed a natural extension of her life at work to talk about the placement of particular news stories, the coverage of issues, and the news decisions behind the headlines when at home with her husband. But while Jim might have accepted these comments when they were friends and co-workers, he found it difficult to accept them from his wife in an informal family situation. He wanted work and family life kept strictly separate.

Carola's ideas of marriage were based largely on what she had seen in her parents' home. She had grown up in a family where her father and mother were both teachers. She remembers "how my parents were always sitting around, talking about their day at school, complaining about terrible principals and interference by school boards, sharing information on how they coped with parents." From those memories she had formed an idealistic concept of two working parents who cooperate, share with each other, and exchange their daily experiences. She imagined that unanimity and mutual support flowed naturally from a joint career commitment within a family.

But newspaper life is very different from the educational world.

There are no long summer vacations, no days off for legal holidays, no free weekends, none of the stability of a settled curriculum. It's a pattern of life that is frenzied, unpredictable, competitive, and unstructured in its exhausting demands, based on the hard realities of the commercial world and the instant decision and the deadline. And of course Jim was very different from Carola's father. For Carola, the first crisis came when Jim was made assistant managing editor of the paper they worked on. One of his first steps was to tell her that, because of conflict of interest and pressure from the management, she could no longer be a member of the staff.

"Looking back now, I think it was because he wanted it that way, he wanted to stop me working," she said. "But at the time I managed not to see the reality. I went to the other paper in town, explained the situation, and a few months later, the editor called me and gave me a job there."

To an outsider, hearing this situation described, it seems that there must be hidden icebergs of unexpressed feelings between a husband who fires his wife the moment he receives a promotion and a wife who then goes to work for a rival concern. There was no consideration of other options, for either or them, no discussion of other positions in journalism. The fact that they were both working in a fiercely competitive world, where too many bright journalists are always chasing too few good jobs, only exacerbated a tense marital situation.

The next crisis came when Jim was promoted to managing editor, and told Carola she could not work on any other journal in town. Carola was deeply hurt. It was a bitter blow to her image of their marriage.

"I was at a very low ebb," she said slowly. "I had been married five years, had two children, and I didn't know what to do. Then I got a call from a junior college in the city, asking me if I'd like to teach a journalism course. I had always vowed I wouldn't teach, but I finally decided to give it a try. At the back of my mind was the thought that if I was ever to get away from Jim and his interfering influence on my newspaper career, I had better try something else. I started teaching that fall, and to my amazement I found out that I did it very well, it was fun, and I loved it."

She also began to see a therapist and unburden some of her experiences as a wife and mother.

"To my surprise, after hearing what I had been through, my therapist asked if I had ever thought of having an affair. The idea had never occurred to me. I was at such a low point in my life that I couldn't imagine anyone ever finding me attractive again."

Her growing confidence in her teaching ability, and her slow realization that her marriage had become intolerable and destructive, gave her the courage to tell Jim that she thought they should separate.

"It wasn't a discussion, because he always acted very calm and cool," she remembered, "and I just said he should move out, and he agreed. He always behaved as if nothing I did could ever hurt him or reach him.

"We talked about money as one aspect of the separation agreement and later in terms of a divorce. I had to ask Jim to help pay for the house and children's expenses. That had always been another major source of disagreement between us. We were both very tight about money, which is a very bad situation for marriage partners. One of them should be relaxed about it. With us, we would save and skimp for a goal, and then when we reached it, we never knew how to enjoy it."

During the next year, she followed the painful steps of obtaining a divorce, which was finally completed eighteen months later. Living on her own again, she reacted strongly against the rigidity of her life with Jim, and threw herself into sensitivity encounter groups and human-potential-movement activity, "meeting all kinds of crazy people." She was running encounter groups for a local church, when the church set up a meeting to open a Free School in the neighborhood. She went to the meeting and met Eli.

"The first time I saw him, he was this guy with long hair, wearing a guru shirt," she said, with a grin. "He asked me about my experiences working with groups, and we went to have coffee to talk about it. That's when he told me he was a Reform rabbi. I was very surprised. I had never met a rabbi before, and I certainly never imagined that they would be anything like him. I also thought he was self-centered and arrogant—and weird."

Eli began to call Carola to talk, invite her out, discuss ideas. She decided to meet him for lunch and tell him exactly what she thought of him.

"We met and started talking, and I told him that I felt he was too egotistic and self-centered. It somehow never occurred to me to hold back or try to be tactful," she recalls, thinking back to Jim and how unmoved he always was when she tried to talk about what was wrong in their marriage. "To my amazement, I saw that I had really hurt Eli by what I had said and that he cared what I thought of him and what my opinion was." She recognized that confrontation as a turning point in her life and in their relationship. "I began to wonder about my own behavior and reactions and feelings, and why I felt I had to be cruel to him. We began to see each other, and when he was transferred to another city as an assistant rabbi, I really missed him. He invited me to visit him with the children, and when we saw each other again, we realized that we had a very good understanding of each other, that we loved each other. And soon after that, he asked me to marry him."

The fact that Carola was divorced was not an impediment to her marrying Eli, because Jewish law recognizes divorce by mutual consent. But Eli's parents were most concerned that their son was marrying a divorcee who had been married to a Baptist and who had two young children. Carola's parents had been saddened by the breakup of her marriage to Jim, whom they had liked very much, but supported her in her decision to marry Eli. Both sets of parents came to the wedding, held in the temple where Eli was working and performed by the rabbi who had appointed him as an assistant.

Carola and her two children moved a thousand miles northwest to join Eli in their new lives as Jews. For all of them it was a traumatic change. According to Jewish law, a Jew is someone born of a Jewish mother, so that Carola and her children were immediately accepted within the community without any need for conversion. But the two children had always had a strong identity as Unitarians, as a result of their parents' active religious involvement, and knew little of Jewish teachings. Eli was head of the religious school at the temple, and it was agreed that they should both be enrolled immediately.

"I didn't know anything at all about Judaism, so I couldn't have taught them anything," said Carola, "and I was looking frantically for a newspaper job in the area. It was very difficult to find one, but I had no intention of getting involved in the temple as the rabbi's wife. I finally found a job editing a group of suburban newspapers which was very convenient in every way except for the fact that I had to work on Friday nights. I almost lost my husband's job for him, because I didn't understand that I had a role to play as a rabbi's wife, whether I wanted to accept it or not, because it was expected in the congregation."

In most Jewish communities, the rabbi's wife is expected to be a public figure, serve on committees, run the women's organizations, and set the tone for the other women in the temple.

Carola never felt she could fit that image, so she quietly avoided becoming actively involved in these activities.

Because Friday was an exceptionally busy day at the newspaper, where she edited the Sunday section, she generally found she was not able to go to Friday evening services. Eli did not like going without her, and frequently they both stayed away. However, it was an unwritten expectation that the rabbi's assistant should attend all services. When Eli's contract came up for renewal by the temple board, his many absences from Friday night services were sharply criticized.

"It was very painful for him," sighed Carola, "and for me. Quite frankly, I never felt as comfortable in a temple as I had in the Unitarian services. One time before I met Eli, I took the children to the bar mitzvah of a cousin of mine at an Orthodox synagogue. It went on and on for hours in Hebrew and was so boring that we never went back again to another service. Of course the services at Eli's temple, which is Reform, were mostly in English, and we could understand them. But I never get as much out of them as I used to find in the Unitarian services. However, Eli and I talked about Friday services, and I realized that if I was interested in having my husband further his career, I would have to go on Friday night. He didn't want me to stop working, I knew. But it was important for his job that I attend the services. Now I usually do go. The few occasions that I don't, we always stay at home, and I light the candles, and we don't go out or do anything."

This conflict over Carola's work was entirely different from the conflicts she had experienced with Jim. She and Eli had managed to reach a compromise which was satisfactory to both and responsive to each person's needs. But for her two children it was a much more complicated situation.

"Melissa was eleven when we moved, and we agreed that she would attend the Hebrew school and be confirmed in a ceremony with her class," said Carola. "Adam was only nine, and we decided he should join the Hebrew school and be encouraged to study for his bar mitzvah at thirteen, which demanded much more knowledge and preparation than a confirmation ceremony. At that time it seemed like a great way to help both of them get involved in the Jewish way of life, meet other children, and learn about Judaism.

"But when we first sent them to the school, they were both very much surprised by the material because it was so different from the Unitarian curriculum. Instead of a general exposure to a variety of religious and philosophical ideas, there was a complete change of emphasis to learn about only one path and one concept. There was an insistence on learning a new language and a whole new pattern of thinking. Both of them went through a culture shock adjusting to the idea that they were now Jewish. Jim and I had always stressed that they were Unitarians and agreed with the liberal ideas of the Unitarian church and its inclusivity. Here it was clearly impossible for them to be both Jewish and Unitarian. They had to change their allegiance, absorb new beliefs, and think of themselves as Jews for the first time in their lives. And they had to do it just because we said so, not because they had come to that realization themselves. I didn't stop to analyze how unfair we were being to force them into that situation, how dishonest in some ways, because there didn't seem to be any other acceptable alternative."

For Melissa and Adam, it must have seemed as if their entire world was disintegrating. After a while, Melissa apparently accepted the change, and began to make friends and fit in. Adam, however, hated the Hebrew school from the start and was totally opposed to the idea of having a bar mitzvah. Both children found themselves totally unprepared for a change in their values and beliefs that demanded new adherences and beliefs. Up until then, their only religious experience had been attendance at a friendly liberal church once a week on Sundays. Now they found themselves in a different city, a different environment, with a new father whose life revolved around a religious institution about which they knew nothing, and where he and their mother hoped they would soon be as sincerely and completely involved as he was.

Adam found himself forced into an impossible situation. His stepfather demanded that he go to the classes, which he disliked, and his mother supported the idea. The religious dilemma was only one of a number of problems (though probably the hardest) which Adam was facing as he struggled to adjust to his new father, the new family, the new town, and the new school. Both Adam and Melissa had had a religious education which did little to prepare them for what Eli expected. After their parents separated, they spent weekends with their father, who did not attend church. Only Carola continued to go to Unitarian services "because it was important to my own life at that time."

The structure of the religious community in which Eli worked demanded a certain amount of conformity to recognized rules and social conventions. Carola forced herself to join the temple women's organizations, though because she was working, she was unable to attend the daytime meetings. But it would have been unthinkable for her two children not to attend the religious school which their rabbi-father headed. Eli and Carola sincerely believed that Hebrew school would help the children adjust by providing a Jewish education and knowledge of their new faith. Slowly, Melissa began to fit into the group, find friends, accept the situation. But for Adam, the conflict became even more bitter, especially as the time neared for his bar mitzva at thirteen years of age.

"One day there was a terrible confrontation," said Carola. "Adam had been making long-distance calls to Jim and telling him what was happening. Jim called me one day and said that he hoped we weren't pushing Adam into doing something that he didn't believe in because he didn't think that was a good idea. Adam was sure that he didn't want to have a bar mitzvah, and after one fight with Eli, he yelled, "If my mother hadn't married you, you wouldn't have to do this to me!" It was the final point in a long battle between the two of them, one which I knew represented much more than the bar mitzvah. It was very hard for Adam to realize that I wanted to be with Eli and not his own father, and even though he liked Eli, he resented having to do things for him." Carola knew that the religious issue was deeply rooted in the personal conflicts within the family, which all of them were forced to face. She supported Eli's wish to educate her children as Jews, yet she knew why Adam balked at it.

The stage was set for a classic parent-child conflict. There was no question that, according to Jewish law, Adam should have had the religious ceremony that would admit him into the Jewish community as an adult. Yet at the same time his ambivalence at accepting the ideas of his new father and his natural conflict about the changed family situation made the bar mitzvah issue more complex and emotional than a simple religious confrontation.

The end could have been a bitter and never-forgiven duel between adamant stepfather and rebellious stepson. But Eli and Carola had founded their marriage on a humanity and understanding of each other as individuals that was stronger than the rules and regulations. Eli was able to bring the same kind of attitude to his stepson; he recognized that, despite his own beliefs and faith, the child's feelings had to be given priority over his own standing in the community. He couldn't force Adam to participate in a religious ceremony he didn't believe in.

Carola remembers the discussion with emotion: "Eli came to me and said that if Adam was really upset with the whole thing to this extent, he did not have to go through with it. He could see no good at all in pressuring the child to do it if he didn't want to, and it was putting a tremendous strain on all of us as a family. It was a tremendous concession for him to make, and yet he felt it was absolutely the right thing to do, because he cared about Adam."

Since then, Adam has stopped going to Hebrew school and is not having a bar mitzvah. The bitter conflict has ended, and there's a new harmony within the family. Once again, the humanity of con-

cern for each other as individuals took precedence over strict adherence to religious rules, and caring for a child's feelings and beliefs
was more important to Eli then stern demands to observe a traditional ceremony. For Carola and Eli, religion had become an added
and positive element in their own mutually compatible relationship,
together with their cultural similarities, a readiness to adapt to the
needs and demands of each others' lives and a willingness to listen
to the individual needs of their children.

But parents can change and find themselves faced with situations
that they never imagined they would encounter. Relationships that
begin firmly founded in love and trust crumble unexpectedly, and
children are thrown into experiences that no parent could dream of
preparing them for.

For Marilyn, the idea that one of her three children would ever
have a bar mitzvah never crossed her mind. Her own childhood and
her marriage seemed to be leading her in a totally different direction.

"My family was Jewish but antireligious," she said when we met
on the patio in back of her suburban home, while her two sons,
Franklin, sixteen, and Caleb, thirteen, tried to wash their large dog.
Her seventeen-year-old daughter was away on vacation. "My father
was a physician in a small town, and we were the only Jewish family
besides some cousins of ours. When we first arrived, the local priest
preached a sermon in the Catholic church urging parishioners not
to go to a Jewish doctor, and I experienced a lot of anti-Semitism as
a child. But I found out that Jesus was a Jew, so I used to bring that
up a lot to argue with them."

In her teens she began to think about religion and decided she
would join the Unitarian church, "because I felt I could agree with
their ideas," she said. "I went to talk with the minister, and he listened to what I had to say and then urged me to talk with a rabbi
first, because I told him that I believed that my true religion was Judaism. I went to the city near us and met with a rabbi there a couple
of times. I was surprised to find that I had a Jewish philosophy
about life and humanity. I believed in the importance of living here

and now, listening to your conscience, having a debt to society, and living responsibly for yourself."

At an age when many young people begin to think about creating an identity independent of their families, Marilyn was concerned about reclaiming her family's Jewish heritage for herself, and finding her identity within it. The stolidly antireligious views of her family had not disguised the Jewish cultural values they had subconsciously accepted in their ideas of ethical behavior, respect for learning, and concepts of social responsibility, which Marilyn had absorbed to make her a part of Jewish philosophical concepts far more than Christian or Muslim cultures.

But Marilyn's own strongly independent character brought her into conflict with her parents. Because her father refused to pay for her tuition at the college where she wanted to study, she left home at nineteen and moved into an apartment, supporting herself by a variety of jobs in offices and laboratories. When she met Bernard at a college party, she went home afterward and told her roommate, "I am going to marry that man." She recalls: "I knew when I saw him that we would get married, right from the start."

The streak of rigid independence and self-sufficiency that is part of Marilyn's character persuaded her that the immediate attraction she felt would overcome the many differences she and Bernard knew existed between them. He was a brilliant medical student, with many years of study ahead of him. His parents were European and Chinese and had brought him up as a strict Catholic, and he still considered himself an actively practicing Catholic. He deeply believed in the tenets of the Catholic faith and attended church regularly.

The two of them weathered four tempestuous years of courtship, with frictions not only between themselves but with criticism from both sets of parents. Marilyn's father, for example, could not understand how an intelligent young man could ever accept the teachings of the Catholic church. "My father once asked me how I could go out with someone who still believed in the virgin birth," remembers Marilyn. "And then Bernard liked to read the funnies in the Sunday papers, and my father felt that was really terrible. My father was a highly intellectual socialist thinker. In our house we only saw *The New Republic* and other serious left-wing papers, and my father could not understand Bernard at all."

Perhaps partly in response to this extreme opposition, the relationship continued. Eventually, they began to talk of marriage and what kind of ceremony they could have. Bernard knew he could never give up his Catholic faith, but Marilyn still felt she was Jewish and didn't want to give up her religious identity, either. "We talked to a rabbi and asked him to marry us," she said, "but when he found out Bernard wasn't Jewish, he refused to see us, so that was that. So we went to the Catholic church, and they agreed to marry us as long as I took instruction, and they insisted that Bernard come along to the classes with me. I felt I had no particular beliefs myself and that I had no right not to support what was important to him. So that's what we did."

They were married in a Paulist Mission Center, "which his parents objected to because it wasn't a church, and my parents didn't like because it was a religious ceremony," said Marilyn with a grin.

But the religious conflicts which had seemed so insuperable before the wedding came into quite a different focus after the ceremony.

"The first Sunday after we had been married, I woke Bernard up early in the morning to go to church, as he'd always done," said Marilyn. "He said, I've never slept late in my life on Sunday, and I'll go to the next mass. So I woke him up later, but he said that he didn't want to go to church then either. Finally, the third time I went in, he said, I don't intend to get up and go to church on Sunday again. And you know, he never did. He never ever could explain why it happened; and I never ever understood why he made me go through the instruction and the Catholic ceremony if he could just stop like that. I had thought his faith was really important to him. Now suddenly it didn't seem to mean anything at all, and I couldn't understand that. I never went to church again either because I had not converted to Catholicism, and I certainly wasn't going to observe it if he didn't care."

Bernard's sudden about-face was a devastating shock for Marilyn. The only explanation she ever heard that in any way sounded plausible was from a conversation with her husband's sister, who repeated a discussion she had once had with her brother. He said he had always seen religion as a crutch, which he needed as a young single man, but now that he was married, he no longer felt in need of a crutch.

Marilyn, however, wanted her children to share in some kind of family religious celebrations, and she made sure that every possible event was exuberantly marked—"Chinese New Year, Jewish New Year, American New Year, Hanukkah, Easter," she said, waving her hands. "You name it, and we celebrated it."

She added: "I was quite willing to bring up the children as Catholics, and before we married, Bernard and I used to have long talks about religion because I was very interested in his beliefs. Since I didn't have any religion, I could perfectly well accept whatever was important to him. At first when we started going together, he said he didn't believe in birth control, he believed in self-control. But he found that quite impossible. After we married, I didn't use birth control, because I had physical problems with all the available methods, and when I started taking the pill I landed in the hospital with clots on my lung and cardiac arrest." Her three children were born within five years, and after several serious illnesses, she had her tubes tied. She is now writing a book about her experiences.

Although Marilyn had resolved her feelings about religion in bringing up her children, there were many other aspects of the marriage that were very difficult for her to accept, mainly stemming from the differences between the strict Catholic family life Bernard had experienced and the liberal secularism of Marilyn's background. The Oriental attitude toward women was another critical part of Bernard's heritage, which became more and more offensive to Marilyn.

"He had firm ideas on what a woman was, how she should behave, what a wife should do," said Marilyn. "He encouraged me to go back to school, but he rarely helped in looking after the children when they were little. He was always busy at the hospital, working there."

She sighed. "For example, when we'd finished dinner he would go into the other room, clap his hands or snap his fingers, for me to bring in the coffee. It was what he expected and how he had been brought up. It was a very Oriental outlook. One day when he did that, I came into the other room and sat down too. He looked at me and said, "I want my coffee," and snapped his fingers. And I said, "I want my coffee," and snapped my fingers. He didn't know what to do, because he had never experienced that."

Of such mundane incidents is marital strife composed. The deep underlying conflicts between Marilyn and Bernard were rooted in disagreements about religion, the role of women, and the division of responsibilities in a marriage.

"When I first got married, I did things that were important to my husband," said Marilyn, reassessing eighteen years of marriage. "I remember how I entertained his medical friends, visited his family, and stayed at home looking after the children. But as I got older, I realized I had to start thinking about who I was as an individual, and I began to develop my own identity. I think that's the most important thing for a woman to know before she gets married. My advice to any young woman today is to find herself a satisfying job, a career, something for herself so that she can understand where she is before she goes into a marriage. My identity problems and dissatisfaction with my role in the marriage may have been intensifed by the growing strength of the women's movement and my involvement in local politics. But whatever caused it, I realized that I had to become my own person, take responsibility for myself, find out what I wanted to do."

For many women who grew up in the 1950s the changes in the past twenty years in attitudes toward marriage and motherhood have come as a shock. Having immersed themselves in their husbands' careers, their children's development, and the care of their home, they suddenly find themselves alienated from their own needs and feelings of worth. Each woman struggles for a solution in her own way, by completing her education, finding a job, traveling, changing her life-style. But it is hard unlearning the lessons of twenty years ago when selfless marriage and parenting were considered their own reward.

Marilyn remembers the change in her own attitudes as beginning when her Jewish awareness reemerged after being swamped and stifled by her husband's influence. Redefining herself as a Jew was her own way of reestablishing her identity and becoming independent. Her decision to do this came after a period of crisis in her life.

"When the children were young, I was very ill for a time, and afterward I began to think about my own Jewish identity. But it was not until a few years ago that I said, that's it, I don't want to celebrate Christmas anymore. I don't want to celebrate any of the Christian festivals."

During the years of her marriage ("I don't regret it—it was a damn difficult marriage but certainly not dull") she slowly began to feel drawn back to Judaism, and increasingly alienated from her husband's background. She remembers: "I got to the point where I felt, damn, why are you making me celebrate Christmas? That's how I began to feel, although in fact no one was making me do it. I'd ask myself, why don't you want your children to be bar mitzvahed, or at least to have some kind of religious education? I always felt as a kid that my parents denied me any opportunity to reject Judaism by not teaching me anything, and this preyed on my mind about my own family. It was a feeling that grew during the last years of my marriage—that I wanted to mark my Jewishness by celebrating Jewish holidays and asserting the fact that I was Jewish, to my children and my husband."

Although her rededication to her Jewish faith was an extreme act under her circumstances, her observance of it follows a moderate, not extreme, path.

"I can't stand the community idea of joining a temple, so I didn't join one," she said. "I don't believe in keeping the Day of Atonement [Yom Kippur] because I don't believe there is any way you can atone for sins. We don't keep a really kosher home, because I don't want to, but I do try to observe the Jewish Holy Days. I wouldn't work on them, and I don't send the children to school then, because I don't want to insult other Jews."

Recently she visited Israel and came back to America convinced that only by living in Israel could she find her personal fulfillment as a Jew. The experience of visiting a country where Jews are in the majority can be an intoxicating experience after a lifetime in a non-Jewish environment. There's a sense of emotional freedom that

comes to Jews in Israel like that of black Americans in Africa or
Italian Catholics in Rome, where identity problems melt away—
temporarily—though the majority of travelers still come "home" to
America. For Marilyn, with her uneven history of involvement in
her Jewish roots, the idea of moving to Israel must seem the perfect
answer to her problems of identity, a unique opportunity to im-
merse herself completely in her Jewishness.

At present she talks seriously of selling her house, learning Hebrew, finding a job in Israel, settling there. Her children listen to
her plans and evaluate them from their own perspectives. Franklin
has prevailed upon her to wait until he is through high school next
year. Her daughter, now working, is sure she doesn't want to go
with her. Caleb will live with his father while finishing school. Both
the older children see their mother's religious awareness as something that reflects her own personal thinking. They join her in family observances and rituals, like the seder at Passover, but their own
beliefs are unclear, though the daughter has recently expressed interest in learning something about Judaism. All of the children visit
their father often, and spend vacation time with him. To the two
older children, their parents' divorce appears to be a rational resolution of many years of family conflicts; their mother's new religious
attitudes are simply one more aspect of the many recent changes in
their family life. But Caleb, the youngest child, has been hardest hit
by the disruption of the family, including his mother's religious re-
awakening, and he has taken the most decisive steps to join her.

He was much younger when the visible disagreements between
his parents became more obvious, and he was about nine when the
marriage began to enter a crisis. He probably suffered the feelings of
insecurity most severely as the separation became more evident, and
like many young children who grow up with the daily pain of
watching parents fight, he felt that he should ally himself with one
of them. Caleb saw that his mother had found an identity in a new
religious commitment, and he decided he wanted to join her in that.
When he was about eleven, he suddenly told her that he would like
to have a bar mitzvah at the age of thirteen. For him, the question
of his identity was still so closely linked to his mother that he may

have felt that only by showing his religious preference could he be sure of proving his allegiance.

Marilyn knew that the decision had many complex meanings for Caleb. Though her husband was no longer living at home, she considered the effects of the ceremony on both of them.

"I wasn't too enthusiastic about the idea at first," she admitted, "because I didn't know what it involved for Caleb or for the rest of the family. There's a temple just down the road, so I went down to talk with the rabbi, and he was great. He said that Caleb could enroll in the Hebrew school and study for the bar mitzvah and that there was no need for me to join the temple if I didn't want to. So we went ahead."

At first, when her husband heard of the plan, he was very skeptical and said to Caleb, "I suppose your mother expects me to pay for the whole thing."

Marilyn explained: "He thought that Caleb was just responding to what he saw happening to his Jewish friends and that he wanted the status and the presents and the party. But when Caleb visited him he saw that Caleb was sincerely concerned about missing his classes and that he was eager to show how he could read his portion. Bernard realized that Caleb was doing it because of his religious feelings, and after that he became totally supportive of his efforts, agreeing to pay for half the expenses of the celebration."

Caleb himself is always delighted to talk about his decision to become actively Jewish. He's a serious-faced, bespectacled child with a grasp of language that makes him sound like a miniature adult at times, and the assertiveness that the youngest child often has to learn in order to survive.

"I thought that everyone else in the family is not Jewish," he said, "and nobody had ever had a bar mitzvah. So I thought I would like to have one, because I had thought of it, and probably no one else had wanted to have a bar mitzvah in our family. When my father was here, he would not have let us do anything like that. When I first told him about it, he said, How can your mother do this? So I had to explain that I wanted to have it, and I said, Why not? I will try it, and it will give me a little education, and I'll learn a little about Judaism, and it will do me good. So I started going to the temple Hebrew school."

A bar mitzvah is the official ceremony of recognition by the Jewish community that a young man of thirteen is now a full male member of the community and can take his place as an adult in the services. On the Sabbath morning nearest to his thirteenth birthday, the boy is called to read that day's portion of the Bible from the scroll, accompanied by the traditional blessings. A large part of the religious tradition has often been swamped by lavish celebrations, parties, and an abundance of presents to accompany the religious event.

However, Caleb and his mother decided that only family and close friends would attend his celebration. He went regularly to his classes and lessons with the cantor, looking forward to the fall day when the ceremony would take place.

It was a fine sunny autumn morning. His relatives from other towns and different faiths had driven and flown in for the occasion. He wore a new suit and, accompanied by his mother, brother, and sister, went to the temple down the road. His father met them there.

The service began, and the family sat and waited until the scrolls were brought out from the ark and carried to the large reading table and unrolled. The rabbi called out Caleb's name, and, feeling a little shaky, he got up from his place between his parents and went up the steps to the dais.

"The two older children were very proud of Caleb's efforts in following through on his bar mitzvah," said Marilyn later. "They very much wanted to participate in the ceremony and were allowed to close the doors of the ark. I think they were both a little jealous of the amount of attention Caleb received, but their own religious instincts were nil. They seemed to have no inclination to do anything like that themselves."

The rabbi beckoned Caleb to the lectern table and lifted off the velvet cloth that covered the open-end scroll. He said the initial blessing and then turned to Caleb who stood beside him. Caleb opened his mouth to chant the blessing he had so carefully learned, and to his surprise his voice came out sounding much smaller in the crowded temple than it had in his own room.

At the end of the first blessing the rabbi said, "Amen," and a few men in the congregation echoed the word. Then the rabbi gave him the silver pointer to mark the beginning of the familiar Hebrew verses which he had recited so many times in the singsong chanting that has been handed down over the centuries.

He took a deep breath and began with the first word, remembering not to stumble at the one point he always stumbled, and stuttering only once. At the end of the verse, he turned back to the prayer book and read the concluding blessings, his voice growing steadier and louder.

He felt an enormous sense of relief and was delighted that he had not muffed that one line. He glanced around at the faces of the congregation and saw his mother looking at him and gave her a big grin.

Marilyn, seeing the smile, felt overwhelmed. A few rows away her ex-husband's family were sitting. Marilyn's sister and her family and her own mother sat beside her. Other relatives and friends from her many years in the community filled the temple. She had never expected to find herself sitting in a temple, attending the traditional bar mitzvah of her younger son, in the midst of a Jewish community she had never wanted to join.

But she was here because she had chosen to affirm her birthright of Judaism. Her son had followed her lead and her ex-husband had supported him in that choice, once convinced of its sincerity. They had all been brought together as a family again, on this occasion of Caleb's bar mitzvah, a time of rejoicing in which they could all share.

For Carola and Eli, the same ceremony had been rejected because it had threatened the very core of the family life for very different reasons. But the pressures and tensions within both families had not made them forget the essential concern for the individual child; their love and respect for each other and their children had triumphed over all other considerations.

7

What happens if long-held religious traditions change?

D uncan and Victor come from a long line of devout Irish Catholics. As third-generation Americans, their lives reflect the effects of the profound changes in the Catholic church resulting from the historic decisions of the Vatican Councils of the 1960s. The two brothers entered the priesthood in the fifties, each sincerely committed to the celibate religious life. But each found that the ripples of change that began to affect the church's teachings had personal reverberations as well, and both left the priesthood.

Today Duncan, a psychotherapist, is married to a Methodist woman and has two young children; while Victor, a communications counselor, is married to a divorced woman with two children, and has had two more children with her.

When their grandparents arrived in America in the early years of this century, the idea that two generations later the family would see priests marrying and divorce accepted was unthinkable. Coming from Ireland to make a new life, they raised their children in total acceptance of the church's teachings. Mike, their eldest son and Duncan and Victor's father, was trained as a dental technician, specializing in working with gold for fillings and false teeth. For years, he never earned more than a hundred dollars a week.

When he married Maureen, they brought five children into the world—first Duncan, then three daughters, and then Victor. Mike was forced to moonlight as a banjo player to make enough to feed the family. Every evening at five o'clock he would come home, kiss his wife, and go to bed. At half past six, he would come out to eat supper, in tuxedo and bow tie, with his family. Then he would be out of the door by seven, his banjo under his arm, to play in Irish clubs and halls, coming home when the children were fast asleep.

Victor remembers growing up in those years with nostalgia. "Our parents were always good role models for us," he said. "They were very devout Catholics, and my father still gets down on his knees every night and says his prayers and in the morning too. The church was part of our life as kids. The atmosphere in our family was deeply religious, and none of us ever rebelled or rejected it as we grew up. As children, it would never have occurred to us not to go to church. Of course, we were the ones who made the noise and caused a lot of trouble, but we would never have considered *not* going at all. It was part of our reality. In some ways, the priests themselves were like the old Barry Fitzgerald model in the movies."

He laughed. "You know, I can still remember on summer days, that we would all be out on the streets because no one could afford to go away. The priest would come down the road in his car, beep his horn, and pick up a group of kids and take us to the beach. We'd be having a grand time, and then all of a sudden he'd beep his horn loudly, and we'd all come running and throw ourselves into the car, with wet swimsuits, soaking wet, and he'd drive like crazy to the city, because he had to hear confessions at four o'clock. He'd stop the car outside the church, and we'd watch him running up the steps, pulling on his cassock." He grinned delightedly at the memory. "Where we lived, of course, almost everyone on the street was Irish Catholic too, and I had a very warm, very secure childhood."

Today that community has changed, and most of the children he knew are grown and departed for other parts of the country, or for the greener suburbs.

Duncan looks back at his childhood as a time when his path was clearly set. "I always knew I wanted to go into the priesthood," he said, "even earlier than high school. I suppose I was influenced by the parish priest, and I went to a Catholic school and my family was very religious. I was baptized, confirmed, the whole bit. After school I chose to enter the Jesuit order that ran the school, because I liked the community life of the society. If I'd chosen to be a parish priest, there would have been no opportunity to teach, which was something I had always wanted to do. The idea of living in the Jesuit community as an active teaching member appealed to me."

In the 1950s, when he began his seminary life, America was in a period of social stability. It was still some years before the issues raised by the birth-control pill, legal abortion, women's liberation, Vietnam, Watergate, or the Vatican Councils. Duncan enjoyed studying, and later thrived in the atmosphere of education and learning, after his ordination when he became a teacher. He holds a master's degree in philosophy, a doctorate in theology, and other academic honors. But as the ripples of change from the Vatican Councils began to make their impact on thinking and teaching within the church, he slowly came to the realization that he had chosen the wrong vocation.

"What happened to me was that the life of a priest became insupportable, particularly after I had met Patricia and realized that I wanted to marry her," he explained. "But I never felt any rejection of the Catholic church or its teachings, or of the idea of the priesthood. I continue to feel a very powerful loyalty to the church. But it was my own personal experience that led me to feel I must leave the priesthood and find my own path."

During those years there was a great deal of unrest and upheaval for many young men in Catholic seminaries. A Gallup Opinion Index Poll in April 1971 showed that 37 percent of those seminarians who were under forty had considered leaving the religious life. Their reasons included these:

frustrated-discouraged when cannot communicate (24 percent)
wanted to get married (17 percent)
religion is irrelevant (13 percent)
too many rules, regulations (13 percent).

Other complaints included serious communication gaps between the hierarchy (Pope and bishops) and the people. And 76 percent felt there was a communications gap between the priests and the people. In another study, over half the seminarians questioned believed priests should be permitted to marry, and 60 percent disapproved of the rule which excommunicated priests who do marry. However, in April 1979, the Pope made a major statement emphasizing the importance of celibacy in the priesthood as "a matter of keeping one's word to Christ."

According to the 1970 *Catholic Almanac,* between 1963 and 1968 over 7,000 priests asked for permission to leave the priesthood, and a Gallup Poll estimated that "perhaps 2,500 Roman Catholic clergymen, or 4 percent of all priests in the United States, are dropping out annually."

Much of this reaction was in response to the atmosphere of change brought in by the Vatican Council innovations, which ruled, for example, that the mass could be celebrated in a language other than Latin, that eating meat on Friday was no longer a sin, and that nuns might wear a shortened uniform much simpler than the traditional habit. Because the Catholic church is considered the divinely appointed custodian of the Bible and has the final word on what is meant in any specific passage, these new rulings affected every Catholic. For some, the changes came as a welcome response to the realities of practice in everyday life; for others, they were a slap in the face to orthodoxy and conservatism. One church in Dickinson, Texas, now has a priest who follows the extreme conservative French Archbishop Marcel Lefebvre, and has rejected all changes and the mass in English. They and other communities believe that the changes show the church has fallen into the hands of the devil, and a Texas bumper sticker reads: "The true Catholic church never changes."

Duncan knew that his own parents were surprised by many of the innovations and yet, being sincere Catholics, accepted them. However, he was sensitive to the tremendous shock and anguish they would feel about his leaving the priesthood. But he could not deny that, as he and Patricia grew to know each other, he had fallen in love with her and was determined to marry her.

Patricia is a quiet, serious woman from Indiana. Her family was

Catholic, but when the priest left the local parish, a Methodist minister came in and took it over.

"The community was a strongly united Hungarian one," she recalls, "so we all stayed in the church because we wanted to remain together as a congregation. I enjoyed going to the Sunday school and was always active and involved in what was going on."

After training at a teacher's college, she taught first grade for a year, and then decided to take her master's degree in religious education. So she came to the same community where Duncan was teaching.

"Because I was new in town, a friend invited others in the religious-education field to meet me when I first arrived, and that's how I met Duncan," Patricia said. "He was teaching in the Catholic high school, and I was going to be helping with the young group on Sunday evenings at the church, so we saw quite a bit of each other. And on Sundays we used to meet afterward, a group of us, and talk about our work."

Duncan added: "Once we stayed up until two in the morning to have a big discussion about celibacy." They both laughed at the memory, but neither would say how the discussion concluded.

"The differences in our religious backgrounds were the least of my concerns at that time," said Duncan. "I didn't know what to do about my dissatisfaction with the life I was leading as a priest and my involvement with Patricia, which I knew was getting serious. I can remember going to see the movie *Guess Who's Coming to Dinner* with my brother, Victor, and afterward I said to him, I think I'm going to be leaving the order. He was very surprised and said that it would be hard on our parents. I didn't even mention Patricia to him then, because I knew that was an additional problem." He sighed and said regretfully, "In an Irish Catholic family the most terrible thing to happen is for a son to leave the priesthood. The ultimate goal of every good Catholic parent is to have a son in the priesthood, because it's a visible sign of his good upbringing and education. But the idea that he might one day leave is unthinkable. What is he then? Can someone ever stop being a priest? How should they treat him? It's a feeling of shame, I suppose, for them and their hopes, and it is very hard to accept."

He had arranged for Patricia and her friend to be invited to his home for Thanksgiving ("we said they were homeless waifs from the Midwest"), and his parents had liked her.

Later when she graduated, her mother had come to the ceremony and met and liked Duncan. But he knew that the obstacles to his leaving the priesthood and marrying were still enormous.

"I realized that I had to take one thing at a time and that the first thing I had to do was to tell my parents that I was leaving," said Duncan. "At the time I was seeing a psychiatrist, and he kept urging me to leave because it was bad for my own health. I used that as one reason to explain to my parents why it was essential for me to leave. But they found it very hard at first."

Nothing had prepared Duncan's parents for this incredible event. Brought up in a strict conservative tradition and deeply loyal to their faith, they experienced his departure from the priesthood as a cataclysmic reversal of their life's dreams and prayers for their eldest son. How could he quit? What would he do? How could they explain his behavior to their friends? But Duncan was right in realizing that their love for him would eventually triumph. Gradually they began to talk with him, ask questions, listen to what he had to say. They realized that he could not reach the high ideals he had set for himself, and that his pain and feelings of failure were as disturbing to him as the fact of his leaving was to them.

Slowly they came to see that he had no other alternative but to leave, and they began to accept the inevitable. Since Duncan had no desire to make a break with the church, he went through the process of being laicized. Then, very gently, he began to talk to his parents about marrying Patricia. He also found himself a position as a social worker and counselor, and applied to the church for permission to marry. It was granted.

Before the marriage, Patricia visited a priest in her parish for the premarital investigation necessary for a mixed marriage.

"He asked me, Will you bring up the children in the Catholic church, which Duncan didn't think he should have asked, but I had no problems with that," said Patricia. "I do feel that our children will be Catholics, but they will have the benefits of both religions."

"Neither of us wanted to join the other's religion," said Duncan, "but what we wanted for our wedding ceremony, and have striven for in our marriage, was to do justice to both faiths."

The ecumenical ceremony took place in Patricia's Methodist church in Indiana, and was presided over by Victor, Duncan's brother (who was still a priest then), and a Methodist minister.

"Normally a priest would lead us through the ceremony," said Duncan, "but we both knew the formula from memory, and so we recited the marriage vows to each other. The priest and the minister were more like witnesses. Having been a priest, I knew all the ins and outs of canon law, and while the presence of a priest is essential for a Catholic wedding, he does not have to say all the vows. We conducted the marriage ceremony so that neither of us felt we were doing anything compromising to our beliefs." They had chosen to follow their own uniquely independent path, and each of them stressed that they felt what they were doing was acceptable within the tenets of their faith.

Today, Duncan and Patricia live some twenty miles from the family-counseling center where he works, in a simple shingled house on a hill where three roads meet. The steps leading to the enclosed front porch are steep, and the front door opens into a narrow hallway. The staircase on the left leads up to the second floor. On the right, is the living room where we sat and talked. Duncan, a solidly built man with glasses, thinning hair, and a round face and easy smile, chose a worn leather armchair facing the sofa where I sat, and Patricia preferred the other armchair, covered in a tweedy fabric. The room was plain, but cozy and friendly.

"When we first started going to church and when I first came back to the church, I wondered how people would feel about a laicized priest," said Duncan. "But it was very extraordinary, like a complete confirmation and acceptance, out in the open. I have no doubt in my mind that there are a lot of really conservative people around, who would be very upset at a priest leaving and marrying a Protestant. But we were lucky, because the monsignor in our church is an outstanding human being, and he set the tone for the parish, so it has never been an issue here."

From upstairs, his comments were interrupted by a plaintive

voice as we chatted: "Who's talking to you?" Patricia looked at Duncan and smiled, and went to the bottom of the stairs. "It's a lady who's come to talk with us—now go to sleep!" she called in a stern voice. "You don't know her." There was silence for a few moments, and then the voice called again in panic: "Mom, I can't find my paper animal for school." Patricia shook her head and called, "It's in the kitchen waiting for you, and there's to be no more talking." There was the sound of voices upstairs, then some thumping, and then a cry. Duncan looked at Patricia and said, "My turn." He clumped up the stairs, and there was the sound of talking. When he came down, it was quiet upstairs, and he smiled at Patricia. "Nothing to it—just beat them senseless," he said cheerfully. Patricia gave him a reproving look as she poured out the coffee: "Now look, what's she going to write about us if you say things like that?" They both laughed, and Duncan said with a twinkle: "I only knocked them half-senseless."

Now that they are parents, bringing up their own children, what decisions have they made about religious education? Have they found any problems or conflicts about what to do?

Their son is now seven and their daughter five.

"Both the Catholic and the Methodist churches believe there is only one baptism," explained Duncan, "so my obligation as a Catholic is to have them baptized in a Catholic church. We had a priest present for both baptisms as well as a Methodist minister, and they performed the ceremonies in our Catholic church. We didn't change any of the words in the ceremony about bringing up the children in the Catholic church. The Methodist minister gave the blessing, and the pouring of the water was done by the priest. Both our parents were there, and so far we have found a tremendous amount of support for what we wanted to do. There's not a single sour note."

In terms of his own experiences in the church, Duncan still feels himself to be a sincere and devout Catholic. "I find it difficult to accept those teachings dealing with conjugal morality and birth control, and I think in time these should be and probably will be reformed. But I don't go around publicly criticizing Catholicism, although I am aware of the controversial areas and the kinds of moral theology that are being discussed at present, and I hope that some of the aspects of the past will soon yield to change. My thinking was more rigid when I was a priest. My allegiance to papal teaching was a fierce loyalty rather than a reasoned commitment, and that's one of the things that has changed at this point in my life."

Both Patricia and he have agreed that the children will receive a thorough Catholic education.

"Our son studies religion in the parish Sunday school, and will learn the whole graduated educational curriculum as he moves up. He will receive First Communion in second grade. The parish leans toward the liberal, but there are some conservative elements, so the educational program is one that has gradually absorbed the changes and improvements of the recent past. We are very happy with what our son is learning there."

Patricia nodded. "We have also taken him to the Methodist church with me, because we want him to feel comfortable in both places. We feel that the children will be Catholics, but they will have the benefit of both religions. For a time I was the co-organizer of the Catholic education program in our parish, and Duncan has given a seminar at the Methodist church on marriage, so we both actively recognize the importance of each other's backgrounds."

With their parents the children attend the Sunday folk mass, "where there are a lot of instrumentalists and music, and the children are free to move around the church and walk in the aisles instead of being forced to sit still." Duncan admitted: "Sometimes they don't want to go, and at other times they seem to enjoy it. For my wife and me, it's an occasion when we see many of our friends, and we look forward to being there for mass."

For their daughter, "it is our answers to her questions that will provide her religious education until she goes to Sunday school. Both the kids know that I was a priest, because I have told them, and it would not be a surprise to them now. I'm not sure how they will cope later when they are taught that priests don't marry, but we will tell them the truth and answer the questions as best we can."

It is Patricia's influence in the home that has provided a variety of religious experiences for the children. "We pray together for grace at meals in the evening, and we pray for other persons who might be ill or in some adverse situation, and we pray for them by name. It's become a regular part of our family life," said Patricia. There are also books of Bible stories around, which the children like to read or have read to them. And at Advent, the period before Christmas, Patricia makes an Advent chain of paper. There is a link for each day, and each day a link is taken off the chain and broken open by the children to reveal a particular message like "Do something nice for your sister" or "Think of a child in some other part of the world" as a way of stressing the giving and sharing aspects of Christmas.

Duncan says: "I don't have any active worries about the children's religious education at present. I hope that they will get a less anxious treatment of sexual morality than was the case when I was a boy. If I thought they would receive the kind of education I had, I'd be more concerned. The atmosphere however has generally changed—there's no longer the emphasis on weekly reminders of the negatives, which I had, like that masturbation is a grave evil. Today, such things would simply not get the kind of attention that they did in the past. Theologians are now thinking and talking in ways that were unimagined twenty-five years ago. Eventually the essence of what they are proposing will be absorbed and made part of the church's thinking."

Since their son began attending the Catholic Sunday school, Patricia has stopped going to Methodist services, realizing that it would be impossible to do full justice to both churches; she feels extremely comfortable in their parish church.

How would Duncan feel if his own children turned their backs on Catholicism and rejected it as they grew up? He paused and said:

"I would feel rejection, and I would feel emotionally hurt. Yes, I would. But hopefully I would be tolerant, and assuming that it was a mature decision, something that they had thought about, I would feel sad, but hopefully—though you can never tell until it really happens—I would be accepting of it."

Duncan has not lost his original deep faith in the church, despite his personal reactions to life as a priest. He and Patricia are part of a growing trend in these days of upheaval and rearrangement within the church; they have both held fast to the religious beliefs of their youth, while rejoicing in the changes that have made their way of life acceptable within the framework of traditional religious observance.

"I continue to feel a powerful loyalty to the church," added Duncan. "I am very reluctant to be openly critical of the church in any way that might seem disdaining. Roman Catholicism is in my blood, something I drank in with my mother's milk, it is a part of me. I would feel greatly disloyal if I became critical of the priesthood or the church. It was my own personal experiences that led me to where I am today.

"Had I just quit the church and walked out without permission, there would have been a great deal more pain for my parents," said Duncan, looking back. "But I left with permission, and the marriage also had the ecclesiastical permission of the church and the bishop. So in that way it was acceptable to my parents. I know I could not have done it any other way."

It is important to realize that fifty years ago he would not have been able to leave at all. Permission was given so rarely, or was known to be so difficult to attain, that it was never applied for. Priests who left the priesthood were ostracized and isolated. To leave because of a woman was regarded as a terrible and demeaning failure, beyond redemption or acceptance. None were able to share their ecumenical life-styles as openly as he and Patricia do, and many withdrew into anonymity, to nurse the scars of their experiences.

But despite the many changes in the Catholic church, Duncan and Patricia understand better than most lay people the importance and extent of their deviation from accepted religious practice. They know from their studies how their behavior differs from orthodoxy, and yet they decided that because of their love they would think the impossible and dare to marry across religious barriers, to bring up children within their two faiths. The reforms brought about by Vatican II made their decision part of the spirit of change that is abroad in Catholicism today, and helped to encourage the radical steps they took, but even so their decision has required a level of commitment, energy, and maturity which are rare.

At present their son is in a public school "and because of his involvement in the parish, I have no reservations about his religious education and would not move him now to a parochial school," said Duncan, "though we might send him to a Catholic high school. I am very comfortable in the church, in my faith, and in the way of life we have chosen for ourselves and our children."

Many parents who remember their childhood Catholic education in the 1940s and 1950s are amazed to visit Catholic schools today. "The whole way of teaching and the emphasis of the curriculum is quite different from the way I remember when I went—it's incredible!" said one mother, the first few weeks after her children had been attending a church Sunday school in New York. And Caryl Rivers, who attended Catholic high school and college and wrote a book about her experiences, said, "After I married a non-Catholic and dropped away from my religion, I never imagined that I would ever be able to go back to my college or to meet the nuns again on a friendly basis. But the changes in attitude in the past few years have been remarkable. I was invited back to meet with them, and I went, and it was an incredibly friendly experience. I would never have believed that things could be so different in those institutions."

These changes reflect not only the new thinking of the church but also the influence of American culture and ideals. The emphasis on the importance and worth of the individual and the equality of all people, no matter what the label, brings pressure on those rules and practices which seem to discriminate or give particular power to some and not others. In America, more than in any other country with a large Catholic population, you can find priests who have left their calling and married, and nuns who still work within the church but have a husband and children. Because of the new atmosphere of freedom in the church, they see no conflict between their personal decisions and their formal religious beliefs.

In Duncan's family, two of his sisters married Catholics, and another sister entered a convent. His youngest brother, Victor, spent two years in the navy after high school and then, as Victor remembers it now, "I came back and told my father I was going into the seminary to become a priest. My father said, You don't have to do this, you know, and I said, It's something I have always wanted to do, and anyway, I can't think of anything else to do. Partly I realize now it was wanting to be like my big brother, because you always find in families that the youngest wants to do what the older kids are doing."

He was in the seminary for eight years, "and it was a lot of fun. I had some fairly strong opinions, and it was a very exciting time to be there, because it was when the Second Vatican Council took place. I actually read all those documents because I was fascinated by what was happening. There were all kinds of people in the seminary, from the very liberal to extreme archconservatives."

At one point there was talk of retrenchment and going back to teaching everything in Latin, but a group of Victor's teachers threatened to resign if that happened, and eventually the idea was dropped. Ordained in 1965, Victor spent three and a half years in one parish and then a year and a half in another.

"I liked being a priest, and I was very excited by it," he said. "But people kept saying to me, 'You just don't know what it's like in the world.' I began to think I ought to find out. As a result of the Vatican Council, the priests were embroiled at two levels—the insular protection that the church gave the priesthood had gone, and yet the priests were still not close enough to the people. For example I seldom wore a collar, and I felt we should model ourselves on the worker priests in France who live with the community and are an integral part of it. The image of the priesthood today is wrong, with the Roman collars and that kind of thing. I wanted to change that mood, and try an experimental ministry and work in industry."

When he presented this idea to his bishop, it was disallowed. Victor had already had trouble with the bishop on a couple of other occasions, like the time he married an Episcopal doctor and a Catholic nurse and administered communion to everyone present, which was not permitted. He began to wonder if he would be able to remain within the priesthood.

"Even though he rejected my idea for the experimental ministry, the bishop gave me a leave of absence to try it outside his jurisdiction," Victor said. "So I began to work as a lay-priest. I had gone through a certain crisis of faith because I had counseled a number of marriages and families that were breaking up, and I could see clearly what was wrong. I disagreed with the church on a lot of things—birth control, divorce—but the church would not accept the insights of psychology that are part of today's knowledge. I found it incredibly frustrating to have to counsel couples and individuals without violating the laws of the church. I'd see a young boy marrying because he had found a woman to go to bed with and the young girl marrying because she had a boy, and it was a pathetic sort of latching-on process, not an act of free consent." He sighed. "One young couple were living together and came to me for advice, and I tried to talk to them about the responsibilities of a church marriage and what it meant. In the end the girl decided I was right and threw the boy out, and then came back to me for help so that they could get back together again." He grinned mischievously. "I don't know how I got into that one!"

His knowledge of the church and its teachings has given him an unusual perspective on recent changes. "I see the church as growing and changing, shedding one skin and taking on another," he said.

"I know that it may be a relatively painful process of shedding. You don't just throw the old away because now it is no good; you try to make something better of it." He thought and said: "My crisis in faith was that I envisioned the Ten Commandments as a freeing set of laws, in the sense that if all men lived, or tried to live, by those laws, there could be freedom from suspicion and misbehavior. But I could see that my sense of religion and my sense of Jesus and the church, and the intent of Judaism and Christianity to be a freeing process, had been subverted."

On a more immediate, personal level, he recognized that he was lonely. "I was ready for a more intimate life," he admitted. "I wanted the kind of personal security that comes from intimacy with one other person and that desire became a stronger and stronger force in my life. Although I had close friends, I certainly didn't have a woman." As all these pressures began to grow, he left the parish priesthood to work independently as a lay priest. His first step was to go to college for a degree in interpersonal relationships. For two years he worked in a shipyard, and then moved to a large industrial company where he trains professionals in better communications methods.

In the year after he left the priesthood, he was involved in running community workshops and that was where he first met Kate.

She's a slim beautiful woman with soft auburn hair pulled casually back, a calm smile, and effervescent energy. When we met, she was wearing a loose cotton shirt over a T-shirt and jeans and still spoke with a trace of her native Welsh accent.

"All my aunts and uncles were Catholics, but I was brought up as an Anglican," she said. The youngest in her family, she went to university and has a law degree. "I came to America when I was twenty-one, to travel, and met my first husband here. He was ten years older than I was, but he wasn't too interested in religion though he went to the Unitarian church." The marriage was a difficult one, especially after the two children were born. Kate needed a community and a church to fulfill her spiritual needs; her husband was uninterested.

"I attended an Episcopal church regularly, and I would take the children with me," she explained. "They went regularly to the Episcopal Sunday school, which provided much the same education as the Anglican church did, and they were baptized there as infants. They learned Bible stories and basic Christian principles. Then after we moved to the suburbs, and Victor and I had become friends, I attended a mass at Victor's church, and for me it felt like coming home. I had been looking for a community which integrated church life with community life and didn't just exist on Sunday mornings."

During this period her marriage was gradually collapsing. The critical event was her husband's losing his job—and not telling her. "For six months he 'went to work' every morning, pretending to have somewhere to go," she said, still surprised that it had happened, "and I realize now that it was a tremendous blow to his ego to be without a job, and that he felt he could not face admitting it to me. But I was very angry at him for not sharing it with me, and it was the beginning of a long, drawn-out painful situation, which ended in a divorce."

Kate went to work, and her mother came from Wales to help her care for the children. She found a job running workshops on skill training for an order of Catholic priests, which until then had been extremely reclusive but now wanted to open up the order to the community. "They began a community chapel, admitted women as day students, and ran neighborhood programs," she explained. "But the rector was fired for being too avant-garde, and his successor kept going off on retreats, because he was too overwhelmed with what had been set up." She laughed and added: "So I was left to cope with the whole program, which was very interesting."

She continued to attend the Catholic church, and finally decided to convert to Catholicism, "which was a wondrous thing for me," she said.

She explained to her children that she was going to join the Catholic church. "Emily was seven or eight then, and Mark was only about five. Emily wanted to identify with me, and so she received her First Communion in the Catholic church soon after I joined. But neither of them was confirmed in the church. I explained that I wanted to belong to a community, and in fact the details of the differences were not very complicated—it was only like a different name. The Christian identification had been there all along anyway. At first Emily decided she wanted to go for instruction, which she did for a while, but she only came to church because I took her and Mark. Mark was never very interested at all. During this period Victor came around as a friend, so that the children grew to know him very well. They never knew him as a priest, and in the Anglican church the vicar had had a wife, so they were not worried on that score when we told them we were getting married.

"I don't think the fact that he had been a priest bothered either of them—he had been out of the priesthood for four years by the time we married, and we had been on beach trips and other trips together. So it was a gradual building of our own family community."

When Victor and Kate began talking of marriage, he knew he would be excommunicated automatically if he married because he was still officially a priest and had taken a vow of celibacy, and also because he was marrying a divorcée. Since 1974 when they married, he has been officially laicized by the church, and the penalties of excommunication for marrying divorcées have been withdrawn. This is partly in recognition of the realities of Catholic divorce statistics, which are almost equal to the national average. In 1971 there were some 3,000 church annulments, but about 120,000 Catholics obtained civil divorces. In 1977 the U.S. National Conference of Catholic Bishops announced that the Pope had lifted the excommunication penalty for Catholics who remarry after divorce so that they can now hear mass though they may not receive the sacraments.

"Now it's left to the conscience of the individual to recognize what he's doing and make sure it is consistent with the teachings of the Catholic church," explained Victor.

"Before we married, we discussed a great many ideas and beliefs we had about our religion," said Kate. "Victor is more hung up on the legality of what it means to be a member of the church than I am. I felt that in some ways our marriage was a religious act, showing a spirit of ecumenicism that went far beyond the usual demands of marriage."

Victor added: "We both share a Celtic tradition, and it's that spirit that unites us, a strong humanist spirit. We both enjoy working with people, having a good time with people, and we both feel that the religion is there."

In the marriage ceremony, they celebrated that philosophy. Held in the garden of Kate's suburban house, it was presided over by a Catholic priest and a friend who was a Unitarian minister. Both sets of parents and Kate's children were there, and home-baked bread and jugs of wine were shared afterward with the friends who came to join the celebration.

A year later their son Neville was born, and now, three years later, Kate is expecting their second child. Kate's two children, both teenagers now, live with them and their son, together with two large red setter dogs and a fluffy cat.

"My children don't want to come to church with us," said Kate. "We invite them when we go. I'll say, We are going to church and would you like to come? But we don't press them to come when they say no. We have seen so many teenagers who are in church physically because their parents have demanded they come and yet who are not there at all spiritually. I have always hoped they would go to church, but I don't want it to be a hollow experience, just a ritual which has no meaning for them."

Their own father is not attending any church at present, "and so from their perspective you may or you may not go to church," Kate realized. "They can see both options, and that's okay with me. I hope at some point they will think about it. We do have discussions about religion. Emily has a good knowledge of the Bible, and they both have a fair grounding in the Scriptures, and they certainly have had experience in attending church; but at this point in their lives they don't have any identification with any particular group. When we talk about religion, we get into issues like abortion that the church has taken a stand on, and their views tend more toward nonchurch thinking. They don't ridicule other points of view though—they recognize the validity of other ways of doing things because of their own experiences. In school, they have a lot of Catholic friends and Jewish friends, and they seem to be quite tolerant and understanding of others. Other kids that I meet in church seem to be very much like my kids, which is to say nowhere in terms of religion. They don't seem to see that religion is particularly important. They see it as one of the things that adults say you have to do or they won't leave you alone."

Victor is finding it hard to learn the complex role of stepfather to teenagers. "I know that there are stages in growing up, and these are formative years, where their own ideas are taking shape. In the teenage years, they begin to choose their own way, and that's what Emily and Mark are doing now. I would frankly like them to go to church with us. But I think that at forty-one I am becoming a reflection of my parents. I am very categorical and concrete in expecting things of the kids, and yet sometimes I don't do them myself. I'm becoming like a typical Irish Catholic father and just like so many other fathers I've known. I'm also learning that every teenager in the history of the world needs to rebel, and I am trying not to yell so much. But we do set rules and strive for some discipline, because we stress that we now live in a community of four adults who have to be considerate of each other. They will say, It's not fair, but the whole point is that they are establishing themselves, and doing that causes conflict. I know they have to become independent, but it's a hard time. Kate copes with it masterfully."

With their own son, the religious path has been much clearer. "He comes with us to adult services when there's a folk mass," Kate explained, "and he knows that it is Jesus' house, and he'll say, Hello, Jesus and Good-bye, Jesus, when we go. We feel it is important that he just come with us and see that this is something we do. He is not in the Sunday school yet, but he will go later on. There are Christmas candles at home, and when we have large family gatherings, we say grace. The older children just accept the fact that we take Neville along with us and that he enjoys it. They are often involved with their own lives, and though I would like them to come with us, I am more concerned that they have a place to go where they can share in the community, a place that they can turn to for help. They do have a community which they belong to, but it is not religiously based, and they don't have a strong identification with something that would support and fortify them if they were to need it. It's not even the religiosity or the ritual which I wish they could have; it's not anything as heavy as that. It is much more a strong community involvement that I wish for them. You drift so much during the teenage years, and some kind of organized community involvement would give them an anchor." She sighed.

"I guess it is not a survival need for them, so they don't want to look. But it is so different from my own upbringing, and Victor's too. I never had any options. I didn't question whether we were part of a church or not, or whether we should or should not be. It was just always there. I guess I have been tentative about religious involvement with the children of my first marriage, because my husband's lack of identification made me less emphatic about my faith. I should have been stronger about integrating our home life with church life, but it's difficult if your husband isn't interested."

Victor plans to bring up Neville and the new baby in the Catholic church, "because I want them to appreciate the history of the church, the background, the philosophy. They will learn about it from an ecumenical standpoint and about the differences between Protestantism and Catholicism. Today our church like many others shares its education program with a local Protestant church, and the whole orientation toward a unified Christian education has made the concept of heresy obsolete. I see that gradually the churches are coming together, slowly. And as we study more of Christian history, we realize that, if you don't study Judaism, you cannot understand Christianity. The whole history of the Bible is about the favored role of the Jews, so how can they be despised or punished in any way? That's the kind of open mentality I want my children to have. I have no antipathy, no grudge against the church because I believe that the process of change is always a traumatic one. After ten years of working in industry, the role of the church seems to me even more important. That doesn't mean that I go to church every Sunday—I don't, I admit it—but the priesthood has been the most outstanding part of my professional life, and I have no regrets. I can remember looking at my father, and thinking he was way behind the times in his religious thinking"—Victor chuckled—"and when my kids look at me, they may see exactly the same thing, and they'll say to me, How could you drag your feet and cling to those ideas? I plan to bring up my children as Catholics, but with the same alternatives as other children have."

Victor's hopes for his children and Duncan's interfaith decisions present a startling contrast to the unquestioning devotion of their parents to the traditional Catholic rituals and observances. Yet neither of them has found it hard to keep his faith, and continue his allegiance to the church of his childhood.

At the age of seven, Duncan's eldest child has already absorbed many ideas of the Catholic church that will be with him for life, and Victor's young son is already learning about the experience of churchgoing. For both Patricia and Kate, marrying priests has meant a deepening and expanding of their own religious feelings and a strong commitment to the faith of their husbands. For Patricia it is tempered with the Methodism of her own upbringing; for Kate, it is like a return to the traditions and rituals of her childhood.

Duncan and Victor are not bitter about their years in the priesthood, and both see that time as one of challenge and enrichment which ended when their personal needs demanded precedence in their lives. They still deeply believe in the tenets of their faith, and in the philosophy of the Roman Catholic church, while at the same time accepting the changes that have recently been implemented. Both of them are determined to ensure that the children they are responsible for bringing up will be given a thorough education in the church and its teachings, and yet will also absorb their fathers' own more unusual and ecumenical ideas.

8

Are there families without religious problems?

Valerie's welcome was sincerely warm and unaffected on the telephone and in person. Her pleasant face has an open smile that makes you want to tell her your difficulties because she offers an immediate sympathy of friendship and understanding.

The hot summer day I visited her, she was wearing a loose blue shift, sandals, and no makeup, her dark short hair simply combed back. She led me into the family living room to sit in comfortable armchairs facing the long window that overlooked the street.

"Excuse the mess," she said, waving a hand to the other side of the room, where an unpainted wall led to the kitchen area. "My husband has been redoing the kitchen as a summer project, and it takes forever." Two stepladders, planks of wood, and cans of paint, half-covered by a paint-spattered canvas drop cloth, stood by the wall. "It will be great when it's finished because we planned exactly how we wanted it, but"—she sighed—"it's getting tough living on the picnic table without a kitchen."

But her unfinished kitchen and the 90 degree temperature did not stop her from inviting me to talk about how she was bringing up

Rosemarie and Brett, aged nine and seven, within the traditions of the Methodist religion.

She had made a point of setting aside the time to talk, for when Brett came rushing into the house, she looked round to see if anything was wrong and then said: "I told you and Rosemarie to play outside while I am talking to this lady, so please go out." Brett eyed both of us, decided his mother meant what she said, and ran out, banging the front door noisily behind him.

"It's so interesting now," she said, after I explained what the interview would cover, "because Brett's best friend is Jewish. The two of them have deep philosophical conversations about God and religion and ask each other questions. I don't like to intrude, but I try to listen because it is so fascinating. The other day, while I was getting dinner, Brett came in and asked, Is God in your heart or up in heaven? So I explained that God is all around us, and he is in every place, in your heart and in heaven and in everywhere. Brett went to the phone and dialed his friend's number, and I heard him say, 'She says God is in your heart.' I was quite worried because I didn't want to cause problems. I know the family are Orthodox Jews, and I hoped they believed the same things about God because I didn't want the boys to have an argument. But they are just great, the two of them. They just talk to each other, and ask questions and discuss things."

This kind of experience was not part of Valerie's upbringing. Her Methodist parents were very involved with the church, and she grew up in a small community with many other United Methodist families, unlike the large church she now attends in an area with families of many different religious backgrounds.

"I was baptized and then later went to Sunday school, and when I was twelve, I was confirmed," she explained. "That is the step you take when you join the church, and at the time, it was something I just automatically did. I don't remember thinking about it particularly. There was a terrific group of kids whom I was very close to, and we went to camp together and to church camp and to high school. We had a marvelous leader in the church, and it was such a good friendship for all of us. I remember when I was fifteen, sixteen, seventeen, I would break my neck to get to church, because it was a big social thing, and all my close friends were there. The Methodist Youth Fellowship had a young people's group that met on Sunday evenings, and I always went along and met my friends there. It was probably the happiest time of my teenage life."

She went on to a Methodist university, which her older sister had attended. "In 1959, we followed the rules like sheep in some ways, I think," she said. "It was nice and peaceful. No one seemed to have a cause, there was no rebellion, and we just accepted things that now seem wrong because they were part of the system. We didn't try to change them, we just went along with what was done. I remember the one thing we did make a fight about was changing the dorm hours so that we could have people visiting till later, and we won that. But it wasn't anything like the kind of rebellion in the 1960s—we never thought of things like that. We were really very obedient."

She remembers going through a period of thinking about the church and her faith.

"I suppose it was the questioning stage of youth, but we didn't question very much then. I call it my Christian agnostic time. I wondered, Was Jesus really Christ? Did it really happen? I didn't reject the ideas, but I did think about it seriously and consider them. Then I looked around at people I admired, people who had much better brains than mine, and I saw that they believed it. We used to talk among my friends, and some of them were turned off and dropped away. But the ones I admired the most, who had very good minds, had a deep faith. So I accepted it, and I stayed within the church."

She studied nursing in college, worked in a Methodist hospital, and, as a head nurse, taught communicable-disease techniques. One vacation, she visited a cousin in California, "and he took me to a party," she said. "That's where I met my husband-to-be. We started dating, and I decided it was time for a change from Chicago and moved out here." She found a nursing job, and they continued to date.

Geoffrey, a research engineer, was from Canada. He had been brought up within the Anglican church, which is not far from Methodism in its beliefs.

"When we met, Geoffrey wasn't going to church, so we never really talked about religion," said Valerie. "I liked to go to church on occasion, so I'd say, Let's go to church, and he would say, Fine, let's go, and we'd go to the Methodist church together. It was understood between us, and we never really discussed it because it was never any problem."

They were married sixteen years ago in Valerie's hometown church, and then came back to live in California. Their mutually compatible religious arrangements flowed easily from Valerie's sincere commitment to a faith in which Geoffrey felt perfectly comfortable because it did not conflict with his own religious background or beliefs. The two of them found it natural and straightforward to become members of a Methodist community and to bring up their children within the church.

The Methodist church was founded in England in 1738 when John Wesley broke away from the Anglican church to spread his belief that rules and individual efforts at self-perfection would not help people, only faith in God's mercy. The Church of England refused to recognize his views, so he appointed his own leaders, and his followers traveled throughout the country to spread his message. In America, the Methodist Episcopal church was organized in 1784 in Maryland, and today there are some 40,000 churches with about 10 million members in what is now called the United Methodist church. Total Methodist church membership is around 13 million today. The church has always been active in social work and missionary efforts, accepts the ideas of birth control, divorce, women ordained as ministers, and ecumenical endeavors.

"Our oldest daughter Lynn was baptized in the church here, and so was Rosemarie," said Valerie, "and Brett was baptized in the Lutheran church when we visited my sister who's Lutheran. That's not a problem, since the baptism is recognized by the Methodist church. Now the children go to our church Sunday school and to regular public school during the week."

She looked down for a moment, considering her words, and then looked up and explained.

"We had a daughter, Lynn, and she died of leukemia seven years ago in September," she said in a calm voice. "We didn't know she had it until she was three and a half, and she lived until she was seven." She paused, and then went on, feeling it was important to describe how she felt and why she wanted to talk about it, her voice a little tense:

"We tried to let her lead a normal life within the limits of the disease. When she had a remission, she went to school and to church and did everything she could do. She would go into the hospital when she lost the remission. For the last six months she was in the hospital, and I am thankful that she was in a coma at the end and not in pain, so that she never knew what hit her. When she was outside with us, she led a normal life as far as she could."

Valerie looked back and said, "Our family is very close. My mother moved out here and then my brother did, and they all came round to help. The church was very helpful to us, because of our friends there, though we didn't have time to go to services too often. When my daughter was in isolation and no one could visit her, I stayed with her all day and then my husband would come in and stay with her all evening. My mother looked after the children. People would come by and take the children out or invite them over to give my mother a break. One lady, who knew Lynn from church, brought her a fresh rose from her garden every day. When Lynn died, there was a memorial service, and friends from church came and fixed the whole meal for us. They recognized that we wanted to be left alone while she was alive, because it was such a long, drawn-out thing, but they were always there when we needed them."

Did she find herself turning to the church's teachings during that time?

"Well, I believe pain and suffering can come in several ways. It can be self-inflicted, or it sometimes just seems to happen. It's another mystery of the universe. Why does one person have more suffering than another person? Why do some things happen to some people and not to others? There's a trite saying—a cliché really, and I don't like clichés except that it's true—that the Lord only gives you what you can bear. It's amazing what an awful lot you can take when you think you cannot stand it one more minute. And then when you look back, you think, Yes, I did do that, and I can take it. But I didn't want it." She paused a moment.

"Coping with pain and suffering wasn't anything that the church taught me. Most people who have their heads halfway right can cope with it. It's something I learned from thinking about it myself and talking about it with other people. The teachings of the Methodist church don't say suffering is God's wrath or punishment. That's definitely not our way. In the Methodist view the Lord is a loving God and a forgiving God, and that is an essential belief. Why these things happen to us is just one of the mysteries of this life."

For those uninvolved with religion, it seems as though those who belong to a church must find great support in their faith during times of crisis. But Valerie found that family, friends, her own knowledge, and experience provided as much support as her church. In this she is like many others.

A study in New Haven in 1967 and 1968 asked a random sample of almost one thousand adults about changes in their religious behavior in response to crises or life events, including the death of a loved one. The results showed that people who suffered the most crises or traumas were least likely to attend church frequently or to be affiliated with a church because of these events. Indeed, as situations became more painful, they participated less and less in organized religious activities, though many did turn to private prayer.

Did the formal teachings of her religion help Valerie explain death to her two young children?

"Well, when Lynn died, Brett was only a baby of five months and Rosemarie was two and a half, and they didn't really understand what was going on," she said. "But now they are old enough to realize what happened. A couple of years ago I saw a Phil Donahue talk show on television on the subject of death and how parents deal with terminal illness. It was interesting to hear how different people had coped and how they had explained death to their children. It made me realize that because my children were so young, I was let off the hook a little bit, while it was all happening."

Children learn about death whether their parents have a religious viewpoint or not. A child learns everything he knows from the daily interaction between parent and child, brother and sister, friend and neighbor, teacher and student etc. Religion is only one part of the fabric of that interchange.

When a child asks "What is death?" he does not consider the question to be of greater or lesser importance than "Why is the ball round?" But the child will absorb the words of the parent's reply, no matter what it is, and more important, will remember the manner in which the explanation was given. A parent who takes the child into a separate room and gives a long solemn speech about heaven, hell, death, and eternity and then ends the discussion without allowing for any questions, can easily terrify a child beyond reason. A parent who explains personal beliefs about death in a normal straightforward voice, and tries to understand *why* the child asked the question in the first place, presents a very different image of death. It is much more important to recognize the child's level of understanding about death than to go into the intricacies of religious and philosophical beliefs on the subject, more important to be open to questions and discussion than to present a cut-and-dried analysis.

Both Valerie and Geoffrey are very open and informal in talking about Lynn's death.

"We recently had our tape recorder fixed, and we got out all the old tapes we made when the children were little and played them," said Valerie. "Lynn was on several of them, and she was singing and talking and pretending to be the host of a radio show. She was a kind of ham, she loved to perform. And she was saying things like, 'I'd like you to meet my sister, so here's Rosemarie and she's two years old!' and you can hear Rosemarie making noises and giggling because she didn't know what was going on. The children love to listen to them, and we talk about Lynn and what she did and what she was like, and what we all did as a family when they were little."

When Brett and Rosemarie ask where Lynn is now, Valerie's reply is based on her religious beliefs.

"I tell them Lynn has died and gone to heaven," she said quietly. "Last year my father died, so we talked about his death, and how they were both in heaven, and it was very natural. They want to know where heaven is, and what it's like there, and what Lynn is doing. So I ask them, Do you remember what it was like before you were born? They say no. So then I say, I don't remember what it was like before I was born, either, and I haven't died yet, so I don't know what it is like to die or what heaven is like or what happens afterward. But I believe that there is something prepared for us after death, just like something was prepared for us before we were born. We don't know what it's like because we have not been there, but we know it's there. I am much more comfortable explaining it like this to them, because it is the truth. I think they recognize that I truly don't know and yet I can go on accepting it even though I haven't seen it."

When Brett and Rosemarie first began going to the church Sunday school a few years ago, Valerie was disappointed with the program and what they were doing.

"I talked with my friends," she remembers, "and we looked around our neighborhood to see what other kinds of church schools there were. We noticed that the Jewish temple school seemed to have a lot of children, and they seemed to be learning quite a bit. So we said, Why don't we Methodists get with it? We called the temple and had a meeting with them to find out how they ran such a successful religious school. They explained that they pay their teachers and have a curriculum geared to the age level of the children, and the teachers are trained to teach at the specific age levels."

She laughed. "So we decided to do the same. We managed to apply for a grant for some extra money for the pilot project, and we hired teachers and paid them, and we also used some church volunteers. When Brett began Sunday school, his teacher happened to be just great for children his age; the room had all kinds of stimulating books and materials, and he really enjoyed going. When we go to church on Sunday and they see us going, they are happy to go to Sunday school, and they like what they learn."

The pilot project ran for three years, using a variety of teachers, including several Catholics and an Episcopal seminarian, as well as qualified church members.

"Older people used to be in the majority as members of the church," said Valerie, "but the success of the school encouraged young parents to join. There are over a hundred children in it now, and much more communication between parents and teachers and students. When the new minister came in a couple of years ago, he felt he could persuade people to donate teaching time instead of paying, and he's managed to do it. The curriculum is based on a Methodist one from head office. But independent teachers have freedom to use their own ideas, and it's not a hard-and-fast outline. We give Bibles to children who complete the fourth grade and certificates to children who complete other grades. It's providing a fabulous education for our children.

"We still pay kindergarten teachers, though everyone else is a volunteer. Rosemarie has an excellent teacher, who is really encouraging the children to study the Bible seriously. She's finding it quite hard work for the first time."

Both Brett and Rosemarie sing in the Angels Choir and "on Palm Sunday the choir comes in carrying palms," said Valerie. "Both children understand that Jesus is the son of God and what the significance of the ritual is, because Jesus came into Jerusalem on Palm Sunday."

Before Easter the family talks about the coming celebration. "We talk about Lent and what it means," said Valerie, "and because of Brett's friend, we talk about Passover and what that means to Jews and to us. The children understand that Lent is the time we prepare for Easter, and they know about the Crucifixion and how Jesus was crucified. In the Sunday school today, they seem to learn much more about the reasons why it happened than I ever knew, because they study the political atmosphere of the times and the reasons why things happened. They know about Barabbas, and about the political pressures of that era which led to crucifixions. I didn't get any of that education when I was a child, and I didn't even know there were any politics involved. Now the teachers take them back to that time to give them a historical background and a broader understanding of what went on during those events."

The lessons of the church and Sunday school are reinforced by the observances and atmosphere at home.

"I try to make religion an ongoing part of our lives," explained Valerie. "We have grace before meals, and we hold hands. It's not mandatory, but it is something we like to do. Then for the four Sundays of Advent, we read every week from a special Advent book. It has Scripture quotations in it, and Bible stories including the story of Jesus. We light Advent candles and make Advent wreaths, and after dinner we'll have a discussion with the children about what it means and why we do this, so that they understand what it's all about as a preparation for Christmas. We also have a special Advent calendar, made of felt and shaped like a Christmas tree. There are twenty-four miniatures also in felt, with little hooks, and every day one child takes out one of the miniatures and hangs it on the tree. There's a manger and Joseph and Mary and a donkey and a sheep, and slowly you can see the whole story being told."

In Sunday school the children study the story of Jesus and prepare for his birthday. "We usually have a big family celebration, and go to church and sing carols together," said Valerie, "and they really understand the significance of the celebration."

The first decision for Brett and Rosemarie will come in a few years, when they are around fourteen years old.

"My husband and I have decided that we will let them make up their own minds then as to whether or not they want to be confirmed in the church," said Valerie. "We want this to be the first religious choice they make on their own. They will attend confirmation classes at the Sunday school, and after that they can decide whether they want to be confirmed as members of the church. Of course, it is nothing that you have to do, because you can be confirmed at any time. They were accepted into the church when they were baptized as babies. Confirmation is the conscious decision to join the church. We will certainly encourage them to join, but who knows? Rosemarie will be approaching adolescence, and I've been talking with other parents, who find that children often rebel at that age and don't want to be confirmed if they're not with a group of friends who are going along with it too. They lose interest in the church if their friends are not involved."

Looking back at her own experiences, she admitted: "It was so different when I was growing up, because I had such a strong group of friends in the church. Now Rosemarie has a couple of girlfriends from church who are in her school class, but other than that, her friends come from all kinds of different backgrounds, because we live in a very mixed area. She doesn't have the same support and church friends that I had. But then a lot of other things are different today as well."

How will she feel if her children reject Methodism? "I don't care if they don't go to church later, as long as they learn to cope with life and be happy and make the most of it. But I hope that they keep their religion because it will give them something to sustain them throughout their lives, no matter what happens. It's very important to have something. When the fear sets in, when you have the loss of any loved one, if you think there's nothing to hang on to, you are in trouble. It is very important to have something. That is what we are trying to do for the children, to give them something that will give them a faith, whatever form it comes in. It's all we can do, really—offer it to them. It's like education—you can only bring them to something that is outside their experience and offer it to them, but you can't force them to accept it. Yet if you don't bring it to them, they don't know about it."

Valerie has kept working as a nurse part-time while her children have been growing up and is now taking some nursing courses and hopes to move into a more responsible position in the fall. "I know that looking after the house, the children, my husband isn't enough for me—I need to know that I am doing something for myself as well," she said firmly. Her faith has provided an anchor for her life in everything she has done, and despite the trauma of her daughter's illness and death, she has not rejected her religion or its beliefs. Looking back, she finds her faith has always been a strong, visible part of her life, and despite her suffering, she believes that God and religion have helped her to cope and have little to do with the pain she has experienced.

Yet she is aware that her two children may not choose to follow her path. She sees the changes in the social and communal life that they lead, and knows that those influences may in the end prove stronger than the teachings of church and home. She stills holds firmly to her Methodist beliefs and ideas, and shares them in a loving and positive way with her children and is supported by her husband. Yet there is no guarantee that Brett or Rosemarie will automatically accept those teachings, or pass them on to their families when they are adults.

Valerie's devotion to her faith reflects the sincere commitment of many other families throughout America today who are members of churches, active in the community, and concerned about the religious upbringing of their children within traditional guidelines. Valerie has an open view of religion and shares that philosophy with her children. But like those who take a more isolationist stand in the religious upbringing of their children, she must face the knowledge that the pressures of the world outside may be more effective than parental urgings.

Parents who are confident of their religious beliefs and happy to follow them still realize that the most they can do is share their faith and observances with their children, and hope that it will prove a benefit. But there is no more security in that upbringing than in the millions of "unchurched" American parents who watch their youngsters searching out allegiances to religious groups they have never understood.

9

When is religion
a source of
parent-teenager
conflict?

When Simon was growing up in Ohio, he absorbed the strict teachings of the Pentecostal church where his father was a minister. In his late teens he began to question some of the regulations of the church, and at the same time chafed against the authority of his father. He decided in his twenties that he still accepted the teachings of his faith, but that he needed to temper his father's interpretation of it with a more liberal, flexible approach involving fewer rules. Today, married with two young sons, he works as a family counselor in a Pentecostal church in the Midwest.

"The church is very conservative theologically, and I am also conservative," he said. His plain cream-painted office had a big desk with a worn swivel chair, a bookcase against the wall by the door, two low armchairs, and a coffee table to one side where we sat, and a view of drab gray buildings opposite through the dust-smeared window.

"But there are different kinds of conservatives," he went on. "You can have a very oppressive, conforming kind of faith, but often it is not the theology itself that is oppressive, but the interpretation of that theology. There are two faces of Christianity: one face is positive, it stresses enjoyment and teaches us to rejoice in being a Christian, and that tends to be the liberal view; while the other is a depressing, depriving attitude, stressing how unworthy I am to be a Christian, and that tends to be the conservative view."

Going to church and Sunday school regularly were a large part of Simon's childhood, and the strict teachings were reiterated at home.

"My father would not buy a newspaper on Sunday, because that was the Lord's Day," he remembers. "So he used to buy the paper on Saturday night in Toledo, Ohio, and I would find the comics stuffed down the back of the couch, because we were not allowed to see the comics on Sunday at all. And we were never allowed to watch football games on TV on Sunday. The idea is that if you are not worthy, you have to make lots of laws and rules to help yourself be more worthy."

His mother died when he was eleven, and he and his brother were brought up by his father and traveled with him to different churches where he preached. It was when he spent four years in Bible college after school that he began to examine his own religious beliefs.

"I didn't reject religion, but I had to go through a reevaluation of how I saw God and what sort of image he had for me," he explained. "It was all very Freudian, I know, because of my father's attitude. My conflict with my father was because he was a very strict taskmaster, and he saw God in the same way. I could not accept God as a heavy authority figure. I wanted to find a more loving image for the kind of God I could accept. I had to reject the authoritarian thinking in order to find out what I wanted to believe. It was hard for me to ask questions, because I knew that that was bound to cause conflict between my father and me. But in fact I never really questioned the basic tenets of my faith. My problem was with the legalistic interpretations of that faith, rather than the emotional or spiritual center of it."

After Bible college, he wanted to apply for a military chaplaincy, but to qualify he had to have seminary training. Since there was no Pentecostal seminary, he went to a Protestant seminary in Boston, Massachusetts, and graduated as a chaplain.

"That really broadened my horizons," he said fervently, "and had I been foolish enough to go to a Pentecostal church seminary, had there been one, I would never have acquired any other perspective on religious matters. All through my childhood I had been told that other people, who did not belong to the Pentecostal church, did not have a devoted faith and were not committed to Christ. But in the seminary I met many people who certainly had faith and were committed to Christ. That seminary was a very good experience for me."

It was his experiences there that helped him to reshape his religious beliefs and arrive at a more humane, less strict interpretation of his faith. He took a doctorate in pastoral counseling, and has served in three church communities as a counselor since then.

"Most of the problems I see as a family counselor focus around teenagers, and the religious conflicts that develop between them and their parents," he said. "But religion alone cannot be faulted. The ways in which parents communicate with their children are often negative and punitive, and it's very often the taskmaster approach. In conservative religious families, the God thing begins very early, and the parents communicate with their children only through rules. While I recognize the importance of rules, it's also very important to show love in the process of imposing stern discipline, and flexibility is essential with growing children."

In many strict religious families, a "coalition with God" technique is used to make children behave. An excerpt from a study in 1947 by R. R. Sears, E. E. Maccoby, and H. Levin illustrates this method:

QUESTION: What do you do if your child denies something you are sure she has done?
MOTHER: She may deny it at first, but she'll usually tell me. She's deathly afraid of being punished, not by me, but we've told her that any little girl who tells a lie, God always does something terrible to them, and she's deathly afraid of that. Like, for instance, up the street a little boy was hit by an automobile, and Cathy was quite sure it was because he did something wrong at some time, and God punished him. Maybe it's not the right thing, but we let her believe it.

Another study, in 1957, by Professor Clyde Z. Nunn, examined interviews with 367 families in Nashville, Tennessee, who used the "coalition with God" methods. He found that "certain ineffectual, limited, and somewhat powerless parents" are most likely to use the coalition techniques, "to gain some degree of indirect control over their children." They are using an external agent, God, to back up their authority. However, children brought up in this way often turn the aggression they would normally feel toward a parent who punishes them for doing wrong, against themselves, feeling that it is their fault. Nunn found that this conserved the cohesion of the family, since the aggression and anger were not expressed to other family members. "A third person introduced into the parent-child relationship has the effect of avoiding the polarization of conflict," he states, "and avoids the loss of cohesion within the family unit."

Adolescents who question the truth of their parents' "coalition with God" often begin to find difficulty in respecting their parents' religious beliefs and may go through a phase of rejecting these beliefs completely.

"If the adolescent is emotionally healthy, it's fine to work through the 'I don't want this and I won't be that' stage," Simon observed. "But often other pressures cause complications, and then I see the traumas that result. The adolescent is struggling for independence, a separate way of life, and his rejection of religion is only one aspect of that struggle. I know that whenever there's a family day in church, it's very hard to get teenagers to sit with their parents, because it reminds them that they are still children, and they don't want to be treated like that. But for strict parents this is very hard to accept because they expect their children to obey them and to obey the rules of their religion. They cannot recognize the natural underlying pressures for independence."

Looking back at his own experiences, he feels: "When I was growing up, though the rules were strict, I knew what they were. As I grew older, I had to form my own judgments about those rules. But I did have boundaries, and I was constantly fighting to see which rules I wanted to accept and which rules I didn't. People who can fight against boundaries have something against which to grow because they are forced to make a choice. I know that I never had a problem with my identity when I was growing up, and a lot of the children I see today seem to come from homes where there are so

few rules to follow they have nothing to fight against. They sometimes have a problem working out who they are and what they believe, because of the laissez-faire, anything-goes attitude in the
home. Often they are the ones who join Jesus cults or religious sects
because they are looking for structure and boundaries to stop themselves from going too far."

Today Simon is married and has two young sons, one aged three
and one a few months. He continues to be "very much committed
to my Christian faith. While I don't totally agree with strict adherence to rules and regulations, I am not opposed to it in terms of providing structure for a child. As for bringing up my sons, there has to
be consistency so that if we say something, that's what goes. But I
know that it may be hard for my sons to accept our views on sexual
relationships later on. I have very firm views about what is and is
not appropriate in these matters, and my views are very much tied
up with the Scriptures. Theater, movies, books, television—I am
not sure exactly what I will do about them, but there will be restrictions, and that may also be a big problem for our children, since
they may resent our limits."

He has seen several families whose crisis has been precipitated by
adolescent sexual curiosity coming into conflict with strict antisex-
ual church teachings. Recently, he counseled a couple who were
quite unable to deal with their teenage son's sexuality.

"They explained that they wanted to send their fifteen-year-old
son away to an institution because he had 'assaulted' a nine-year-old
girl, and they wanted some advice on what to do. They were convinced that their son was mentally sick and must be removed from
society."

He sighed. "We talked about it, and I asked them to tell me exactly what happened. The whole story came to light when the
mother of the girl went to the police, and the affair had become a
community scandal. It turned out that the boy had known the girl
for some time, they were neighbors and went to the same church.
Both children told the police exactly the same story. Apparently the
boy asked the girl to come into the woods near the house, which she
did, and then asked her to take off her clothes. She did so, and he
looked at her and touched her, and then told her to get dressed, and

they went back. There was no assault, the girl was not raped, and it certainly wasn't an attack, since the girl went quite willingly and was not upset afterward. In fact she said she had done this before. It was when she told her mother and the mother became hysterical and called the police that the situation got out of hand. After the police had heard the story, they suggested she drop the charges because there was no case. But the boy's parents were horrified and embarrassed by the whole experience, and were determined to show their disapproval of what they considered to be extremely perverted behavior."

Understanding the beliefs and background of the family, Simon knew what the boy was experiencing. "The parents' comments showed that this was a home with a great deal of repression, where sex was a taboo subject and where sexual topics were never mentioned. None of the three boys in the family were allowed to date before the age of sixteen. In some ways I agree with that and in other ways I know that it depends very much on the maturity of the child. The mother, who had only sisters, admitted she didn't understand boys and so had left decisions entirely to her husband, who was a strict authoritarian. He lived absolutely by the rules of the church, and interpreted family relationships from the viewpoint of religious beliefs. There was no recognition of the possibility of any sexual overtures outside of marriage. The girl and her mother, who was divorced, were both church members and the parents felt they had a great responsibility to show the boy he must go straight because of their position in the church community. Their moral expectations had always been clear, and they could not imagine why their son had flaunted them so obviously. There was no way they could understand what had made him behave like that, though when considered objectively, it was not that surprising."

He leaned back in his chair, gesturing with his hands. "The kid is on his own, he's fifteen years old, his body is experiencing all sorts of new feelings, he's really curious about girls, and he wants to know what they're like. And he has no sisters. But he can't ask his father or his mother about girls, and as the eldest, he can't ask his brothers. There are no magazines lying around the house, no sex information books that some parents leave available, no outlet for his adolescent curiosity, no one to answer his questions. So he dreams up this way to find out. In less rigid families where such curiosity is recognized as an accepted part of growing up, there would be a variety of legitimate, acceptable ways of satisfying his need to know."

The boy himself refused to discuss the incident and, according to the parents, felt no remorse for it. "That bothered the parents," said Simon, "but the boy probably found it impossible to try to explain what happened and was trying to deny the whole thing. The parents wanted me to tell them if they were doing everything in accordance with the Scriptures, but I wasn't going to get into a Biblical argument. The parents are very strict followers of the church rules and the Bible, and accept its teachings without question. Their son's behavior was so unacceptable to them that they were on the verge of rejecting him as their son because of what he'd done." He leaned forward and said: "What I tried to do was to concentrate on the normalcy of what had occurred, and to help them to realize that the boy was only expressing a human curiosity that many young people feel, and that he wasn't a sex maniac or a rapist who should be put into an institution. Because of my own background, they were at least willing to listen to me, and in the end they agreed to let me speak with the boy, and then they would reconsider their original decision to send him away."

For Simon, it is not the church and its teachings which are guilty in a case like this, but the people who convert those beliefs into rigid rules. "I had found myself in a similarly repressive situation when I was growing up and had to fight against some of the restrictions," he said, "but the atmosphere of my family, and the attitude of my parents, particularly my father, was not quite as extreme in its approach to sex as this family's. My brother and I managed to find out what we wanted to know, though we certainly didn't learn it at home, and never discussed it with my parents. This couple however, were new members of the church and felt they had to adhere to the rules as faithfully as possible. They had no idea why their son wouldn't do exactly as they told him, because he always had up until then."

For many adolescents, even from families whose attitude toward sex is far less repressive and hysterical, the first confrontation over religion may come with the awakening sexuality of the teenage years, and the difficulty of balancing these new feelings with the teachings of the church. In response to this dilemma, much discussion and research has taken place among middle-of-the-road church leaders, hoping to reevaluate traditional attitudes toward sexuality and bring them more in line with modern knowledge.

In 1975, the Office of Sexuality, Marriage, and Family Ministries of the National Council of Churches published *A Synoptic of Recent Denominational Statements on Sexuality,* together with a study paper, *Abortion.* Compiled by William H. Genné, the *Synoptic* contains separate statements on different issues from the American Baptist churches, American Lutheran Church, Christian Church (Disciples of Christ), Lutheran Church in America, Moravian Church in America, Presbyterian Church in the United States and Canada, Reformed Church, United Church of Christ, United Methodist Church, and United Presbyterian Church of the United States.

The American Lutheran Church in a 1970 statement said: "In the expression of a man's sexuality, it is the integrity of his relationships which determines the meaning of his actions. Man does not merely have sexual relations; he demonstrates his true humanity in personal relationships, the most intimate of which are sexual." And the United Methodist Church states:

"Sexuality is a good gift from God and is a fundamental means of realizing life-in-community. This gift includes all that it means to be male and female and is not limited to coital behavior. All expressions of human sexuality affect the emergence of genuine personhood, and should reflect a concern for personal integrity, relational fidelity, and the equality of men and women."

The Reformed Church in America feels "the sin of adultery must not be magnified so as to obscure our common need for grace," and the Lutheran Church in America believes that "people have a right not to have children, without being accused of selfishness or a betrayal of the divine plan, and every child has the right to be a wanted child." Topics like sexual intercourse outside marriage are considered—"we question whether society has the right to impose celibacy or celibate standards on those who do not choose them," says the United Presbyterian Church in the U.S.A.—as well as artificial insemination, sterilization, and abortion.

The United Presbyterian Church in the U.S.A. spent three hours at its one hundred eighty-second General Assembly in 1970 debating the conclusions of a report prepared for its membership by a task-force committee of church leaders and lay people. The report, "Sexuality and the Human Community" was accepted for "study and appropriate action" by a vote of 485 in favor and 250 against. It has now been sent out to every church for consideration by the community. The report states:

The church, when reflecting on God's work of ordering creation, has often been tempted to see its task in reflecting on sexuality as one of ordering too. The emphasis then becomes one of restraint, prohibition, legalism and the definition of limits. . . . The attempts by some theologians to encourage Christians to appreciate the fact that our sexuality can be fun as well as functional has thrown some of our fellow faithful into paroxysms of fear and guilt. . . . We consider it a matter of the highest importance in the Christian formation of children that they be equipped with a realistic understanding and appreciation of their own and others' sexuality. . . . Our hope is that Christians will participate in the formulation of sex education programs in the schools and, by their participation, will help establish in these programs a healthy, informed and affirmative view of human sexuality.

A resolution called "for increased opportunities for specialized education for clergymen in all areas of human sexuality." The Assembly also passed by a small margin an additional statement reaffirming among other things "our adherence to the moral law of God as revealed in the Old and New Testaments that adultery, prostitution, fornication, and/or the practice of homosexuality is sin." While some of the views in the *Synoptic* are only the opinions of various church committees and have not been adopted as policy, they do reflect the thinking of a wide range of concerned Christians on sensitive issues of sexuality from the standpoint of modern knowledge and awareness.

Human Sexuality: New Directions in American Catholic Thought,
a study published by the Catholic Theological Society of America in

1977, shows that significant changes are sweeping through the Roman Catholic church too. The society is an organization of lay and ordained scholars and has no legislative authority within the church, but its influence is far-reaching.

The study suggests that "an intimate expression of love between two honest other-centered friends of long standing may be less immoral than the same intimate expression between a married couple who are selfish and self-serving, dishonest and irresponsible." Premarital intercourse, the study notes, can be an appropriate expression of commitment and intimacy when meeting certain criteria of moral decision making. Such an act should be evaluated by asking oneself whether it is "self-liberating (does it have a wholesome self-interest?); other-enriching (is it sensitive, considerate, thoughtful, compassionate, understanding, supportive, and does it contribute positively to the growth process of the other?); honest (does it avoid evasion/deception and not betray mutual trust?); faithful (does it encourage stable relationships?); socially responsible (does it hold positive societal implications?); life-serving (does it respect the relationships between creative and integrative aspects?), joyous (does it reflect the passionate celebration of life?)."

In discussing the issue of masturbation, the study comments: "There is no clear explicit moral prohibition of masturbation in either the Old Testament or the New Testament . . . persons who occasionally masturbate must *not* therefore be automatically judged in the state of mortal sin." The conclusion states: "Guidelines will serve to enlighten the judgment of conscience; they cannot replace it. The well-formed individual conscience responsive to principles, values, and guidelines remains the ultimate subjective source for evaluating the morality of particular sexual expression." This revolutionary approach to traditional teachings is still highly controversial, but does reflect the thinking of many influential teachers and scholars in the Catholic community.

Judaism has rarely taken as ascetic a view of sex as Christianity, though some Orthodox regulations are as stringent in their details as Christian rulings. Rabbi Roland B. Gittelsohn explains in *Judaism and Marriage: My Beloved Is Mine:* "Judaism looks with emphatic favor on marriage and on sex within marriage. It believes that intercourse between husbands and wives is desirable and wholesome; that God intended it not only as a means to propagate the human species but also to fortify and reinforce their love."

But fear of sexuality—both their own and their children's—is common to people of all faiths, and many people, no matter what their religious leaders may say, continue to emphasize the sinfulness of all sexual activity. When extreme teachings of this sort are absorbed by children, the resulting problems often surface only in adulthood.

Eli Chesen, M.D., was a psychiatry resident at a Phoenix, Arizona, medical center when he wrote his book *Religion May Be Hazardous to Your Health*, resulting from his experiences with patients reacting to childhood religious experiences. He believes that children under seven should never have any formal religious education, because they learn naive and confusing concepts that will only conflict with later ideas. After seven, there can be Sunday school and Bible instruction, with abstract ideas about God and heaven being brought in around the age of twelve or thirteen. From the age of thirteen, it is the parents who must be solely responsible for the education, by avoiding dogmatic and authoritarian statements, being honest, and setting a good example. "When in doubt," he cautions, "do nothing."

Chesen writes:

If one were to accept at face value most of the teachings and preachings emanating from the pulpit and the Bible, one would have to become a paragon of virtue. This is especially true for the more dogmatic and fundamentalist churches, because in these settings the moralizing can be repetitive, intense and supported with great—even mortal—fear. If the child who is exposed to all this is hearing the same messages at home, and/or if he tends to be quite naïve and suggestible, the unconscious storage locker may be put to the ultimate test. He soon finds that he is unable to live up to his religious authority to the letter and finds it necessary to repress whatever he cannot handle. The more he must live up to satisfying the expectations set up by his church, the more he must repress and the more strained his unconscious will become.

Chesen has seen the results of such repression because "it shows up clinically in vast numbers of cases of impotence and frigidity, which usually involve people who learned as children that sex is dirty and not to be enjoyed. It is often easy for the clinician to understand through the patient's history why he or she is impotent or frigid, but it is quite a different matter to treat these people successfully. The sex-is-tainted attitude becomes deeply entrenched and though the patient may see the light on an intellectual level, he finds it difficult to undo the problem emotionally and psychologically." He describes how one woman, brought up with constant preaching against the evils of dancing, swearing, drinking, and lovemaking had a psychotic reaction due to intense feelings of guilt, when she became involved in a sexual affair at the age of eighteen.

"Her mind was unable to reconcile the highly competitive paradox in a healthy manner," writes Chesen, "between her intense religious teachings on one side and biological sexual drives on the other, and so the result was devastating."

Because the more repressive aspects of the Christian attitude toward sex have permeated the society in which we live today, the negative implications have been embedded in our laws, our customs, and our everyday patterns of living. They are perpetuated by our behavior and unconscious attitudes. But while religion can be a destructive influence, it is the family's interpretation of a religion's teachings that the child absorbs and by which he is most profoundly affected, for good or ill.

One man, married and the father of two school-age children, looks back at his childhood in Virginia, growing up in a strict Southern Baptist community, and can clearly recognize the careful distinction his parents drew between religious rules and ethical behavior.

"Both my parents were brought up in Texas, where their families set the usual strict bans on dancing, card playing, smoking, and drinking," he said, "which go with that kind of upbringing. In my home, there was no hard liquor or wine, and nobody smoked. But my parents had decided that they would reject the hard line of their own childhood and would not be repressive about normal children's behavior or teenage attitudes. They taught me to have a strong sense of ethics, but there was never any punishment attached to other activities. They never smoked or drank, but there was always a six-pack of beer in the fridge for anyone who wanted it. In high school my friends and I played cards and danced like crazy at parties, and I know my parents would not have minded if they had caught me. It was made clear that there was never any serious religious significance attached to these rules. But I knew if they caught me lying or doing something to hurt someone or breaking one of the basic rules of ethical behavior, it would be quite different. There was very little discussion about sex, and no sexual information directly from either of them, because they made it clear they did not want to talk about it. But I could read what I wanted, and there were no prohibitions on studying or going to the library to look things up."

The family was very involved in the local Baptist church, and he remembers sitting through many sermons and discussions about the evils of smoking or drinking. "But my parents always drew a line between those rules and the important rules," he said. "When I went to college, I experienced a certain amount of rejection of religion, and the props began to fall away from some of the more silly stuff I had been taught in Sunday school. But I was fortunate in meeting a man who taught me to recognize what was important about my faith. I spent a great deal of time talking about it with him, thinking it through, and I went back to it."

He is now an active member of the American Baptist Church, "which is more liberal, more intellectual, less evangelical, less spiritual" than the Southern Baptist church, and he and his wife and children live in a Baptist community building, and are deeply involved in social work, community activities, and the church Sunday school.

Often the religious conflicts that adolescents experience within their families are rooted in their need for independence in the face of strong pressures to conform to traditional observances and community rules. The rebellion against religious practices may serve as a smoke screen to cover up the true roots of the problems. A child who first stands up to an authoritarian father on religious grounds may actually be challenging the father's power, not his religious beliefs. And similarly, a parent who bitterly opposes a child's romantic relationship on the grounds that it is religiously inappropriate,

may be reacting to feelings of rejection and fear as the child begins
to lead an independent life and move away.

Polly's three children are now grown up. Her eldest, a son age
thirty, is a rabbi working a thousand miles away in Massachusetts.
Her second child, a twenty-six-year-old daughter, now divorced,
lives nearby with her baby; and her youngest, a daughter, age twenty-five, lives a few miles away in her own apartment and works in a
law office as a paralegal. Polly and her husband live quietly in the
community where they settled soon after they married, visiting their
son on Jewish holidays and enjoying their time together. But she admits that this is the first time in ten years that they have felt so relaxed, and she still feels sad looking back at the pain they have experienced.

"My husband was not particularly crazy about religion when we
married, though his parents were very religious and were members
of the temple," she said. "We were married at home by a rabbi, and
we didn't join a temple until our son was ten, because we couldn't
really afford the fees. The training for the bar mitzvah usually begins then, so he and the two girls went to classes. My son really
seemed to take to it, and he got high marks. He was bar mitzvahed
at thirteen, and then elected to go on for confirmation at sixteen,
and did very well. I think the girls tended to be more social than
educational in their orientation. They didn't care for the schooling
and never completed any studies. I was lucky to get them through
high school!"

The family lived in a Reform Jewish community, and felt comfortably involved in its social life although not tremendously religious themselves. Then at the age of thirteen, Dana, their older
daughter, made friends with a boy who lived in the neighborhood
and who came from a Baptist family.

"When it began, my husband and son were upset because the boy
was not Jewish, and because Dana was seeing so much of him," said
Polly. "He was her first boyfriend, and he was over at our house all
the time. Every day he'd come over, and he was around constantly."

It might have been treated casually as a high-school romance or a first love that might flourish and then fade as the two young people grew up. But the additional tensions of the religious concerns lent the relationship, and the parents' reaction to it, a seriousness that was perhaps unnecessary.

"By then our son had become quite religious, and he never liked the idea of the boy coming over and going out with Dana," said Polly. "My husband was absolutely furious about it all, and he kept telling me I had to get the boy out of the house and that we had to do something to stop it. But there wasn't anything to do. If we had banned the relationship, they'd have gone on meeting secretly. At one point I said, Let's move from the area, but where were we going to move? And why should we have to move? He was her first boyfriend, and she never really looked at anyone else or went out with anyone else. He kept coming over after school, and they were together all the time. I heard from her friends later that she skipped most of her last term in high school to be with him. They were deeply involved with each other."

The crisis came when Dana told her family that they were going to get married. "That was terrible," Polly recalled, "because she was much too young to get married. My husband and my son both talked to her. They kept trying to tell her about religion and how she was Jewish and how she should not marry someone who was not Jewish, because of all the problems there would be."

Polly sighed. "But she was not listening to what anyone said. She would sit and ask about things, and my son would be very nice and explain things, and she would not really be listening to him. I knew that it wasn't religion that was going to change her mind, because a girl like that, who had never been out with anyone else and is in love, can't imagine not going on with it. It was really not the Jewish thing that bothered me. Dana was just too young to get married to this guy and too inexperienced to realize what it meant, and he wasn't the right person for her. But my husband went on and on about how he wasn't Jewish and she shouldn't marry him and we would have to throw her out if she was going to go with him."

They had met when Dana was thirteen, and the romance had continued until Dana was eighteen, when the two were finally married. "The relationship was a continuing upset for everyone throughout all those years," said Polly, "and she never dated any-one else. We finally agreed to the marriage, and since we could not have her married in the temple, by a rabbi, they agreed to be mar-ried through the Unitarian church in our home. I felt it was impor-tant to keep her with us and to show her that we still loved her, though my husband wanted to give her up. I tried to be soft and show that we were still there if she wanted to turn to us. I said, If this is the way it is, this is the way it is."

Looking back, Polly said: "I don't think we could have done any-thing that we didn't do that would have made any difference. She wasn't listening to us. Perhaps if we had reacted differently to the fact that he wasn't Jewish, perhaps if she had met him when she was older, perhaps if we had moved somewhere else, it might have helped. But I don't know."

She thought for a moment, and then went on: "Well, after they were married, they moved to the next county, because he had a job as a police officer and had to live near his work. Then he decided he wanted to finish his high-school education, which he had never done, and he went back while she took a job as a secretary to sup-port him. In the end, he never did finish, and for a while he worked in our business, but he was never comfortable with my husband. And so he went back to being a police officer. My daughter kept in touch with us, because I thought that was important.

One time she went to Las Vegas on vacation, and she had lost a lot of weight and was very thin and attractive. Men started paying attention to her, and this had never happened to her before. She was amazed at how marvelous it felt, and she told me that she had start-ed to get feelings of being attracted to other men. I tried to dissuade her from thinking like that, since after all she was married. But it was the first time in her life that she realized she was an attractive woman and that other men, besides that first boyfriend, might like her. Anyway, nothing came of it then, and they decided to have a baby, because they thought it might help their marriage."

Dana became pregnant and two years ago gave birth to a baby boy. "They had talked about having children, and he said it would be okay to bring up the child Jewish," said Polly, "because Dana decided that's what she wanted to do. But after the baby was brought into the world, he changed his mind. He wanted the child to be a Baptist."

It's hard to judge how much of the parental support that Polly and her husband continued to offer her daughter caused some of the conflict between Dana and her husband. Often interference from outside can cause problems in an interfaith marriage that did not exist before. But in this case Dana and her husband allowed the disagreement over how their baby should be brought up to become a major issue, and the marriage began to disintegrate. Last winter Dana called her mother and said she was going to leave her husband because "I have been walking on eggs for so many years that I have to get away." She moved out, found a place to live near her parents, and has now filed for divorce.

"She does not blame anyone but herself for it all," said Polly sadly, "but it is a difficult time for her now. She realizes that we did not do anything to stop her marrying the man she said she wanted, but she has become much more aware of her Judaism and now goes to the temple on Friday evening and to singles services. What happened was that she finally grew up, and he didn't. Actually we all had a lot of growing to do, but he wasn't able to keep pace with her, and she came to see that she had a life of her own to live."

Adolescents from religious families often find, in struggling for their own identity, that their clashes with their parents are complicated by the confusion between personal and emotional issues on the one hand, and religious issues on the other.

Polly today feels that things are "working out" for her daughter at last, since she has now realized the importance of a life of her own and since she has also returned to the Jewish fold and begun to observe Judaic customs.

There's often the feeling among Jewish communities when one member "marries out" that a subsequent divorce is almost beneficial, since it proves conclusively that the relationship was doomed from the start and has simply run its course to failure. Relatives and friends who directly or indirectly express this attitude provide constant irritation to an interfaith relationship and, in cases like Dana's, where the marriage faced many other problems as well, may only further confuse the major issues of the conflicts.

Polly still wonders sometimes what she might have done to make things turn out differently, but she says: "I don't think anything would have done much good. We fought very hard, but I tried to be loving. I believe it is very important for your children to be able to talk with you, not to make them feel it is a closed book. I think that's what kept our daughter loving us and that's why she wants to be near us. Her husband is trying to hurt her now and is threatening to take the baby out of state and make trouble for her. But we hope he will find someone else and fall in love and settle down." Polly looked back on the difficult years of her daughter's courtship and said: "At the time, the religious problem seemed very important, especially to my husband. Of course, we would both have much preferred that she marry a Jewish boy, but the real problem was that she was much too young to get married and had no experience of the world or of other men. I still don't know how you can reach a teenager who's in love for the first time, and somehow show her that life goes on afterward, and marrying so young isn't the best thing in the world for her."

The years of adolescence are confusing and difficult for both parents and children, and religion may in many cases be used as a scapegoat for real or imagined injustices and repression. Sometimes the disagreement is substantive and real, and a growing child may come to feel, on the basis of serious reflection and personal experience, that the old ways are not right for him, and that he must reject the religion in which he grew up.

But adolescent confrontations on religious grounds are often more complex than they appear, and can cover up the realities of disagreements that are deeper and more painful than a change of viewpoint on religion. It's vital for parents to recognize the true roots of their conflicts with their children and not be misled by the hysteria occasioned by religious arguments. Such arguments are often only a smoke screen for the normal problems of adolescence.

10

What happens to children in those new sects?

la lives with her husband Bana and their two-year-old son, Krala, in a four-story brick house with elegantly curving banisters, gleaming parquet floors, and high ceilings. A pink rosebush blooms in the small garden just by the front steps, and a low wall divides the garden from the street. Tall shady trees line the roadway, turning to vivid color in autumn.

The other houses in this part of town have gracious facades, fancy brickwork, and the curving bay windows that marked nineteenth-century Georgian building, symbols of success for the city's leaders in politics, arts, and society when they were constructed. But over the years, high taxes and rising prices have driven most of the families out to the suburbs, and the spacious ballrooms and fireplaced bedrooms now serve as modernized offices for fashionable architects or expensive apartments.

Ala lives here because the house belongs to a nonprofit, tax-exempt religious organization, the International Society for Krishna Consciousness, sometimes called ISKCON, and popularly known as the Hare Krishnas because of the devotees' constant chanting of that phrase.

The long pale-orange robes, tinkling bells, and shaved heads of

167

the men accompanied by women in soft saris and shawls are commonplace in many cities now, and the "Hare Krishna" chanting is a familiar sound.

On warm days Ala joins the group from her house when they set out to attract new converts at one of the major intersections nearby. Their route through a public park leads past beds of tulips in the spring and bright marigolds and roses in the summer. The simple orange robes contrast sharply with the soft green of trees and grass, and as the group streams through the park in an uneven line, dogs in the vicinity bark sharply at the monotonous beat of the drum, birds picking at spilled popcorn scatter from the ground into nearby trees, and a little girl climbs off her tricycle and runs to her mother. But the group is impervious to the reactions of the outside world. Walking steadily in sandals or bare feet, they cross the park, follow the path round the corner to the busy street, all the while chanting, "Hare Krishna, Hare Krishna," to the beat of the drum held by their leader.

As they reach the busy intersection, their chanting is almost drowned in the noise of the traffic and the rock music from a transistor radio. They spread out into a circle by the subway entrance, where people are constantly coming up the dark stairs into the sunlight, and there they stand, chanting, stamping their feet, clapping their hands, throwing themselves into the activity. Passersby glance, stop, listen, and Ala and the other women begin conversations, hand out leaflets, answer questions, talk eagerly with a fervent warmth. The bells jingle, the drum beats, and the gleaming bald heads shake as the circle increases the intensity of the chanting: "Hare Krishna, Hare Krishna." The ice-cream vendor eyes them with hostility, and wheels his van to the far side of the subway station, away from their performance. But this is their work, and they are oblivious, happily involved in chanting, singing, and dancing.

The Society for Krishna Consciousness was founded in America by his Divine Grace A. C. Bhaktivedanta Swami Prabhupada, who arrived in the United States in 1965. He wanted to combine the philosophies of Indian spiritual wisdom with American resourcefulness to arrive at a new form of Hinduism. When he died in 1977 at the age of eighty one, the society claimed some 10,000 followers and a $16 million income.

The money is said to come from the sale of books and publications, but large contributions from enthusiastic young Americans who join to find awareness of God through a strict spiritual discipline of chanting, meditation, and diet provide a major source of financial support, as does street begging by followers. Alfred Ford, a great grandson of the Ford Motor Company founder, and George Harrison, the former Beatle, have been substantial donors, among others.

Ala herself had little money when she joined. We met one morning in a sunny room on the second floor of the society's house, where the sound of men drilling in the street outside punctuated the conversation. The floor of the room was bare, its wooden boards gleaming and clean. There were no rugs, no chairs, no curtains, no pictures. The fireplace grate was swept clean, and Ala's two-year-old son, Krala, wearing only a diaper on his sturdy sun-tanned body, was sitting in it, looking up at the chimney and chewing on a breadstick.

There was a heavy smell of incense everywhere in the house, clinging to everything. Later I found that my hair, my clothes, even my notebook had absorbed the odor, and even now, months later, the Krishna magazines still carry that faint smell.

Ala was sitting on the floor in front of a tray with several bowls on it. There were cooked peppers, a mixture of vegetables, fresh peaches, and a white plastic bucket with breadsticks. She wore a long orange sari-like robe, with a thin organza shawl wrapped loosely over her shoulders and head. Her dark hair was wavy and to her shoulders, and her face had a lovely piquancy with wide dark eyes and an animated smile.

She was now twenty-nine and had been a Hare Krishna member for nearly six years. Assured that I was not a critic but only interested in how she had come to the decision to bring up her son in the society, she talked with fluency and enthusiasm, delighted to share her experiences.

"I was born in Ohio, and both my parents are Jewish," she began,

arranging the flimsy shawl around her face. "My father was Orthodox when he was younger and my mother was not so strict. The
more wealthy they became, the less religious they were, though my
father still has some religious feeling. I have a brother and sister,
and none of us went to Hebrew school every day, but we did go to
Sabbath school. I was never interested in it, because it was merely a
social gathering. All my friends went to the same temple, and we
met there and it was very social. You knew that when you got to
ninth grade, you could leave, and I left." Ala at least had been given
some education in the faith of her parents but her own lack of interest, or the way in which it was presented, made it unimportant to
her.

About 70 percent of the parents of Krishna devotees were members of established religious groups, and two-thirds of devotees had
attended their parents' church or temple regularly. A mid-1970s
analysis of Krishna devotees showed that family affiliations included 18 percent Roman Catholic, 14.5 percent Jewish, 13 percent
Methodist, 7 percent Presbyterian, 5.5 percent Episcopal, 4 percent
Congregational, 3.5 percent Jehovah's Witnesses, 2 percent Mormon, and 25 percent who said their parents had no religion.

After high school, Ala went to a college in the Midwest. "I went
just because everyone else was going, and I didn't know what else I
wanted to do," she said. "But I quit college after a short time. The
main goal of most of the women I knew there was to find a husband." Later as we talked, the real reason for her leaving became
clear. But she first expounded her interpretation of it through
Krishna doctrine.

"Basically women in this day and age are encouraged to go out
and search for a mate, and that demeans them," she said. "They are
not getting proper protection. Krishna says women are like children
and need protection. They have to be protected from society. In Vedic society, girls are married at a very young age so there is no need
to seek for a sex partner. In America, we think that the motivation
of life is to have a sex partner, and we find the sex partner who is
the nicest. Then we marry him, and if it doesn't work out, we get divorced. But in India, they know that women need protection all the

time. Traditionally in devout Hindu families, the husband leaves home after many years, and the wife goes to live with the son. This means that throughout her whole life she is protected. Krishna says that when the woman is not protected, there is unwanted progeny. Basically the husband is head of the family and is considered the spiritual master, and he teaches his wife how to develop her spiritual life. The woman should be very chaste and faithful, and then she will be satisfied."

Ala was scornful of ideas that women might have of leading independent lives and developing their own talents.

"Women's libbers will not be submissive, and so they are frustrated," she said firmly. "Women's lib is a male plot to get free prostitution."

The Bhagavad Gita, the holy book for Hare Krishna followers, is quite specific on the subject of women:

When irreligion is prominent in the family, O Krishna, the women of the family become corrupt, and from the degradation of womanhood, O descendant of Vrsni, comes unwanted progeny ... women are generally not very intelligent and therefore not trustworthy. So the different family traditions of religious activities should always engage them.

Ala said suddenly: "I am the perfect example of the woman who needs protection, because I had an illegitimate child and that is one of the reasons I quit college. Having to give up my child was bad, but I am very glad I didn't keep him because he was just born out of lust, and he would have been terrible."

Her attitude toward the incident was strangely detached. She seemed to feel no responsibility for the child or for what had happened to him, since that was part of another life—a life before she found Krishna. According to her understanding of her new religion, the illegitimate child was not her fault, but the fault of society for not protecting her adequately. Her newfound devotion to Krishna now separated her from that sinful society and her past experiences.

"Outside society is based on sex life," she went on, "and although you think we have no sex life in Krishna Consciousness, we have something better. We have Krishna. Sex is not taboo. But it is said that man is butter, and woman is fire, and if they meet, the butter melts. They should not meet except in marriage, or they will always be thinking of the opposite sex and not of God."

Ala had clearly warmed to her topic and continued: "It is all in the scriptures, and there are lots of examples. There is the story of one Brahmin who had lusty desires which he could not control. He fell into a very debauched life, and married a prostitute and began stealing. Even when he was eighty, he was still having a sex life"—Ala's face expressed her disgust—"and that was when he had his last child. The sex life degrades us actually. This man was beginning to forget about God, but he called his last child by the name of God, Narya. Just at the time of his death, as he was dying, he called out for his youngest son. Because he called out God's name, he was saved from a terrible death."

She had recited the story with a vivacity and conviction which were impressive. It was a story she knew well, and she seemed to embrace its message wholeheartedly. She explained: "We cannot have sex unless we try for children, and then, when we are pregnant, no sex. "When you are married and try for a child, there are special prayers and chanting. You chant fifty rounds and there are at least six special rounds of chanting, and on certain days you prepare yourself to have a boy or a girl. The preparation is to concentrate and to fix yourself upon God. At the time of conception, the consciousness of the parents determines the kind of child that will be born."

She glanced at Krala, who had been running round the room during her dissertation and had now begun to climb on to the high radiator by the open window to see what was happening in the street below. She ran over to him, lifted him down, and closed the window, after which she returned to her seat on the floor to continue the discussion.

"These children are not ordinary," she went on. "They are great souls, they are devotees. My child knows more Sanskrit now than I will ever know. He knows all the prayers and all the personalities, and he is a God-conscious child. It is a real joy to a family to bring up a God-conscious child."

She called to Krala, as he struggled to climb on to the radiator

again, "Come and have some breakfast now, or you'll be hungry."
He turned and came over a little reluctantly, looking at the food.
Then he took another breadstick and ran off to sit in the fireplace
again. "He'll only eat the breadsticks," she said, taking some vegetables and sounding like many other mothers.

Ala had first encountered the Hare Krishnas through a friend of
her brother's, who took her to a Sunday feast at a temple, where she
read some of the literature.

"After college I worked as a secretary for a while, and then I was
a hippie—you know, drugs, sex, anything—and then I gave it all up
and tried yoga, but it was all cheating," she said. "I liked the Hare
Krishna ideas but I avoided committing myself. Then I went out to
Germany to look up an old boyfriend, and when it didn't work out,
I went into a Hare Krishna temple there and just stayed." The temple was run by two Americans, but everyone else spoke German.

"When I was in high school, they offered German and French,
and I thought what a terrible language German was and who could
ever use it," she remembered. "Now here I was in Germany. It was
one of the preordained paths of the Hare Krishna that I should
come to them and that I should need to learn German in the temple
so that I could study with them. That is their way—everything is
planned. The longer I studied in the temple, the more I knew it was
the right thing to do. I was twenty-four, and I stayed for two
years."

Marriages are arranged by temple presidents, sometimes on request, sometimes by decree. Celibacy is highly prized and marriage
considered unimportant. Bana was active in the German Hare
Krishna movement, and had been single since the departure of his
wife, soon after he joined the Hare Krishnas. When he met Ala, he
wrote the temple president saying that he knew that it would probably not be possible for him to marry again, but he would like to.
Since he and Ala had met in the German temple, he was given permission to marry her, and they took part in a religious wedding
ceremony in the temple in 1974. Both Bana and Ala had completed
the initiation ceremonies and spent more than two years in the temple in order to qualify for marriage.

But afterward their lives barely changed. They returned to the

United States in 1975, and Bana was given a room in the main building while Ala lives in the house next door. "Living separately is the best situation, or it is an agitation for the unmarried students in the temple," she explained.

The essence of the Hare Krishna philosophy is based on strict adherence to four rules based on Hindu philsophy:

1. No illicit sexual connections. Sex is permitted only within marriage and then only to produce children. The emphasis in life is on celibacy and involvement with the spiritual.

2. No eating of meat, fish, or eggs. Only vegetables, fruit, cheese, and dairy products are permitted.

3. No gambling or speculation of any kind. This in some cases is taken to mean no questioning or thinking outside of the teachings of Krishna.

4. No intoxicants of any kind, such as alcohol, tea, coffee; devotees drink hot milk, rice drinks, fruit juices.

The society is ruled by a spiritual master who is descended from a long line of spiritual masters, and he instructs disciples and appoints certain qualified ones to take positions as temple presidents or leaders.

The most important part of the spiritual process is the chanting of God's name in the incessant Hare Krishna chant. Children come to the temple ceremonies and join in the chanting, and are involved in temple activities. The children are also taught Sanskrit, and as one temple leader expressed it: "That is the best language. English is designed for business and sex; Sanskrit is designed for spiritual values."

In every temple the same daily regimen is followed. Devotees rise about 3 A.M. for a cold shower, then apply dabs of *tilaka* (white clay) before the first ceremony in the temple. Each devotee has a set of beads, usually carried in a small cotton bag, with which they chant mantras. After meditation there is another service of chanting for half an hour, followed by a 7:30 class on interpretations of the Vedic scriptures, usually led by the leader. Breakfast, the main meal of the day, is served at 8:30, after which people leave for their individual duties, sometimes spreading the word in the streets or working at a regular job to bring money to the temple, or doing manual labor on one of the temple farms, which is where Bana spends his days.

Around the middle of the day, devotees may return for another ceremony in the temple, then go out again. Those working in the temple may hold a ceremony at 4:00; at 5:00, all adherents return. They take showers and prepare themselves for the evening classes and devotions, perhaps taking a light snack beforehand. At 7:00 there are more ceremonies, then a period for study, and final prayers at 9:00.

There may be a milk or fruit drink before bed at around 9:30, and then the devotees unroll the rush mats they sleep on, and the day is over.

Every hour is carefully structured, organized, and planned to allow no spare time, no free moments, and little opportunity for concentration on anything that might detract from worship and work for Krishna. This strong commitment cements a bond of community among those who choose to follow the path.

For Ala, most of her days are spent in the temple, cleaning, caring for her child, praying, and talking with the other women there. Her outings are few, but she spoke to me of an impending trip to a local doctor. "I think my son has impetigo, a skin infection," she said, glancing at him as he sat in the corner, "and my husband will come with us to the outpatient clinic at the hospital, because it is not good for a woman to go alone."

I asked her how her parents felt about her decision to join the Hare Krishnas and now bring up her child within it. She gave a mischievous grin: "They freaked out," she said. "I wrote them regularly when I was in Germany, and I still have contact with them. When we came back, my husband and I visited them, and my husband was preaching to my father, and he seemed to understand deep down, but my mother really doesn't understand the movement at all and doesn't like it. There's a woman in Connecticut who tries to help parents understand what is happening to their children and I asked her to write to my parents, which she did. My mother wrote her a very rude letter in return. So I've just written my father a ten-page letter explaining what I believe and why I'm doing what I am doing. I remember that my grandmother used to talk about God all the time, and it used to drive me crazy, but now I know why she did it."

From the point of view of parents, it is almost impossible to understand why intelligent young people will willingly give up the opportunities of the world to seclude themselves in a narrow, authoritarian, and demanding Indian religion. The dean of a major divinity school explained why he felt Jewish youngsters were perhaps more susceptible to such influences than others:

"For many Jews the essence of their upbringing has been a deep suspicion and mistrust of Christianity and the Christian community," he said. "That is of course understandable within the context of history, since Christians have been the source of persecution and discrimination against the Jews from the Crusades through the Middle Ages, the Spanish Inquisition, and most recently the Holocaust in Germany. So this means that when young Jews find themselves in rebellion against their religion, they find it difficult to turn to a Christian church because of their deeply ingrained suspicion of all things Christian. But many of them find they can accept the new cults and alien Eastern religions much more comfortably, because they do not have to overcome quite the same childhood prejudices in accepting these new beliefs. There is always hesitation at a very profound level about any kind of conversion to Christianity. But if they join some strange new faith, they can feel that they are striking out in a new direction, that they are pioneers who have seen the light."

One family, which has been very active in trying to rescue their daughter from the Hare Krishnas, was told in a final court ruling that now that she is over twenty-one, they cannot impose their wishes on her, no matter how humane or disinterested their concern. Because of the threats and harassment the parents say they have received from members of the Krishna organization, the mother would only discuss her experiences for this book over the phone after an assurance of total anonymity.

"My daughter was in a private high school, and one day the teacher invited a group of Hare Krishna people in to speak at the assembly. Apparently at the end, my daughter went up to the group and announced that she wanted to join. She was fifteen. They told her to leave school and move out of the family and join them, because it was a waste of time to learn science and technology. That evening she came home and told us what she planned to do. I was extremely upset, and I asked her how she could think of doing such a thing. She said that she had been told that people who joined were fulfilling themselves as *better* Jews and Christians because Hare Krishna is compatible with any religion. I tried to point out why that was impossible to accept, but she was adamant. Finally, we said that at least she should finish high school first, because she was still a minor. I went to the temple to speak to the leader, who had a degree from a university. I said, Look, you have had some education, and you know how much that means and how important that is. At least let the girl finish and get a high-school diploma. And so we agreed that she could finish school. So she went back, and got more involved in school life and made some new friends. Things were looking pretty good, and she said she wanted to go on to college."

While their daughter was at college, the parents learned from a couple of her friends that the Hare Krishna people were visiting her.

"They went to see her at college, and they'd talk to her, and they kept going back," said her mother. "I feel they never let her settle down and make friends there. They kept talking to her until one day she just disappeared from the university. I was always very worried about her, both for her psychological and her physical well-being, because she has a hereditary medical problem and is supposed to have a special diet. Their diet is vegetarian and high in all the things she is not supposed to eat. Because they are not allowed to indulge themselves, if she feels hungry, she can't eat anything."

The family went to the local Hare Krishna temple to see if their daughter was there. "They told us they didn't know where she was. They said things like, You so-called Jewish parents who send your daughter to so-called Jewish schools are no good, and we just tried to keep calm and ignore them. We only wanted to know where she was. We called the police and sat and waited on the temple steps. It's an old house in one of the suburbs. But no one would tell us where she was. Finally, a detective went in, spoke to the leader, and came out and told us she had been sent away to another part of the country."

Later they learned that the Krishna group had come to the college again, persuaded their daughter to go to the bank, where she had taken out all her money and given it to them, and then had sent her off to another city where she signed up for welfare so that she could get the necessary medication for her condition.

"They never even thought of the morality of what they were doing," said the mother angrily. "They'll steal or lie or do anything that they think is helping Krishna—because everything is permissible if it is for Krishna."

Once the parents had found out where their daughter was, the father flew out to make sure she was all right.

"She was standing on a street corner, peddling things and making between one hundred and three hundred a day," the mother said. "She had developed a skin infection which my husband said should be treated. But our daughter said, Only if the master will let me. She wouldn't make any decision herself. So my husband went to the temple and asked the president if he could take our daughter to the hospital to treat the infection. The president said, She is having a spiritual problem. There is no need for her to go. But she got much sicker, and finally a couple of days later the president realized that and said she could go. She was in the hospital for ten days with a serious infection. During that period my husband talked with her, and they came to an agreement: We would not make any trouble for the temple on the grounds that they had kidnapped a minor, and she would come home and live with us, but could continue to be involved with them."

She sighed. "But they interfered with the bargain, and instead of letting her stay with the temple near us, they kept sending her to other places on traveling missions, and as soon as she got too sick, so that they did not know what to do, they would send her home to us. When she stayed with us, she would steal things from the house and take them to the temple. I know because she admitted it when we asked her about it. We asked her if she thought that was right, and she said, Everything is right and good if it is for Krishna."

She paused for a moment. "My feeling is that hyperreligiosity is a kind of illness, and it should be dealt with as an illness. I believe that my child was at a particularly vulnerable age when she first saw the Krishna people, and that's how she got caught. She was the only child in the school who was affected like that. My daughter now thinks she sees and talks to God every day, and she tells us about it. If any of my other children started saying things like that, I would know they were sick, and I would arrange for treatment before it was too late."

Her experiences have led her and her husband to come into contact with many other parents whose children have been persuaded to join sects. She has found that the pattern of making contact with a child, talking him into joining, then demanding he give his money to the group and detach himself from family and friends, is a common one.

The Krishna book, the Bhaktivedanta, is clear on the lack of importance attached to family:

As for detachment from children, wife and house, it is not meant that one should have no feeling for them. . . . But when they are not favorable to spiritual progress, then we should not be attached to them. The best process for making the home nice is to live in Krishna Consciousness. . . . But if it is not congenial, not favorable for spiritual advancement, then family life should be abandoned. In all cases, one should be detached from the happiness and distress of family life, because the world can never be fully happy or fully miserable.

I asked the mother why she persisted in trying to make her daughter leave the Krishna movement if she seemed to find satisfaction and happiness there. Surely it was foolish to interfere?

"I believe that my daughter does not know the difference between her soul and her body, and that she is truly sick. If you have someone who is sick because he's a drug addict or an alcoholic, you can leave him alone and let him destroy himself. Or you can try to get him off the drug and help him back into real life. Or maybe you know someone who is physically ill—say, a cripple, who can't walk. You can either leave him in a wheelchair, with other cripples, abandoned, forgotten, or you can use therapy and other methods of rehabilitation to encourage him to be more useful and involved with society." She paused again, and then sighed:

"For the most part, it is a big problem for society. The only people dedicated enough to risk the harassment and litigation which so often occur are those who are directly involved, like the parents, and that makes it twice as hard. As soon as the kid finds out that his parents are rallying against Krishna, he cuts off all contact with them. There are some parents who have not heard from their children for five years because they are unfavorable to the movement. And it is very easy to be unfavorable to the movement. If you don't give enough money, that's unfavorable. And if you say something critical, that's unfavorable. There is no neutral stand—you are either for Krishna, or you are against Krishna. They say to us that we don't understand Krishna, or we have not seen the light, or we don't have the true meaning to life."

She went on: "What disturbs me the most is the blind obedience they demand from their followers and the way in which they totally deny any individual thinking. They also say in their magazines that they plan to take over this country, and I find that very disturbing. Their rule about no speculation is extended far beyond the concept of gambling, you know, to include any kind of creative thinking, argument, or education outside of Krishna. They demand total conformity from their devotees. The concept of freedom of thought is completely alien to them."

Her daughter was married off to a man in the temple several years older than she, "but I don't think that makes much difference," said her mother frankly, "because they don't care about family life at all. I think they just arranged the marriage to put another obstacle in the path of us reaching her. We have completely lost touch with her since then and don't hear from her at all."

In the Krishna movement literature, a devotee describes the perfect person:

Krishna consciousness is a very important movement to bring all living entities back to their original consciousness. Just as there are many mental hospitals, like Bellevue, established for the purpose of bringing a crazy man back to his original consciousness, similarly the purpose of

Krishna consciousness is to bring all crazy men back to their original consciousness. Anyone who is not Krishna conscious may be understood to be more or less crazy.

A philosophy which eliminates the possibilities of any other options, ideas, or concepts is the essence of the education which Ala's young son is absorbing daily. He sees no television, hears no radio programs, reads no picture books. Only the ideas and practices of the other temple members reach him. He is absorbing potentially destructive ideas about the sinfulness of his body and the importance of his spirit soul.

Ala, who spends most of her time with him, explained: "When he is of school age, we will take him to another temple where there is a school for Krishna consciousness. Later, the boys will go to school in India. It is not encouraged that parents go too, because you have to break the parent-child attachment so that the child can become attached to Krishna. You see, now we are on the bodily platform and thinking with the body. There are different levels of consciousness, and we move up to them. By our desires we are creating our own Karma, and I desire what I think about. Association is also very important, so we try to associate only with other devotees, because people outside are not of nice character."

Ala commented that in college she had always been interested in philosophy, "but it was such a drag there. Here I can practice philosophy and talk about it. I always like to talk with people and listen to them. Before there was really no meaning to my life. Everything I did ended up in failure because I was not satisfied. Krishna consciousness is very scientific."

I asked if Krala received regular health care. She shook her head emphatically.

"My son has had no shots for diphtheria, polio, or anything else," she said. "Most devotees don't give their children shots because we don't believe in puncturing the skin." I pointed out that there were now several vaccines which could be taken orally. She shook her head again.

"We just don't believe in these medicines because we have found out that scientists are cheaters too. We have some information about these different shots, and we know that they are used to cause diseases in children and to keep down the population."

What about the virtual disappearance of child polio cases since the Salk vaccine had been introduced?

Ala gave me a conspiratorial look. "We have information that we read in our magazines, and we don't give shots at all." That seemed to close the discussion for her.

However there are exceptions to this stance on doctors. If illness forces devotees to miss attendance at services, they are allowed to seek medical help.

"We like to go to Indian doctors when we can, and there are some nice Indian doctors around here," said Ala. "Last winter I was sick for a week and could not attend worship, so I went to a Western doctor, and he helped me. So it is permitted."

Ala's sources of information on medicine and any other topic are limited to the religious books and the *Back to Godhead* magazines, published by the Los Angeles Bhaktivedanta Book Trust. The copy which I read had a long article asserting that the American space journey to the moon never took place because it was not written about in the Vedic scriptures. Most of the issues have colorful Indian-style pictures on the cover and elaborate drawings of scenes from the Hindu literature inside together with descriptions of successful festivals, accounts of growing membership, and a couple of religious commentaries on the scriptures.

But in looking through a pile of recent newspaper clippings about Hare Krishna activities, I found another face of the movement, which seems to be in sharp contrast to the image of joyous devotion and spirituality presented in the Krishna publications.

In Moundsville, West Virginia, about an hour's drive from Pittsburgh, Pennsylvania, a Krishna community has been set up called New Vrindaban. Set on 1,500 acres of farmland which the community owns, there are about 375 devotees under their leader Kirtanananda Swami, once known as Keith Ham. In 1973 there was an incident involving a man from Kentucky who came to find his fifteen-year-old daughter at the farm, and later burst into the farmhouse firing a gun and wounding four Krishnas. Since then, the Krishnas have been stockpiling weapons, including military surplus, and one member has a federal firearms dealer's license. They assert it is for self-defense against the local community, who are critical of some of the group's practices, but Marshall County Sheriff Robert L. Lightner told a *Washington Post* reporter:

"It doesn't make any sense to me why a peace-loving, nature-loving, religion-loving people should have an arsenal." The swami stated: "There are demons and there are devotees, and they are always at loggerheads." "Demons" is how Krishna devotees refer to anyone who is not a Krishna supporter or "devotee." "You'll never convince the demons to become devotees or the devotees to become demons. So they are always destined to fight."

In 1977, newspapers in Calcutta reported an incident in India involving Krishna members who were building a huge temple complex called Chandrodaya Mandir in Mayapur. They opened fire on local villagers, injuring eighteen, including three children. The incident was confirmed by a U.S. State Department official in Washington, D.C. Apparently a local farmer had come to protest about Krishna group cattle grazing in his paddy fields and was beaten up, after which local villagers came to rescue him, whereupon the Krishna group began shooting. Police estimated that some twenty or thirty rounds were expended, and three villagers were admitted to the district hospital in serious condition. Four American citizens, one Canadian, and a Frenchman from the community were arrested for the shooting.

In another case, Alexander Kulik was found guilty in an Orange County, California, court in January 1979 of transporting $1 million worth of heroin, found in his car. He told the jury that for the past several years he had been the personal fund raiser for A. C. Bhaktivedanta Swami Prabhupada, the late founder of the Krishna movement, and had channeled more than $2 million to the leader. He is one of seven defendants in a murder case involving the death of another Krishna leader, Stephen John Bovan.

There are many other alarming incidents involving Hare Krishna members who were collecting money under false pretenses by pretending to be representatives of legitimate charitable organizations, buying large amounts of real estate in Los Angeles, and raising the rents in apartment buildings they own, and following poor hygiene and health routines that led to outbreaks of hepatitis on their farms. They were forced to close the harshly primitive school they ran for several years in Dallas, Texas, and from there they moved the children to India.

But news of these incidents will never reach Ala, Bana, or their young son, who live an insulated, protected life within the temple, learning only what the Krishna publications choose to tell them.

While I was talking with Ala, her husband wandered in and out of the room, occasionally looking at his little boy, who was sitting on the floor. Bana spends most of his days on the farmland the community rents about a hundred miles outside the city, but he had agreed to let me interview him on one of his days at the temple. As we began our conversation, he slid to the floor and leaned his shaved head back against the wall. Wearing glasses, dressed in baggy white tunic and pants, and holding a cotton bag with his mantra beads in one hand, he looked quite serious and ascetic.

He spoke slowly, hesitating as he thought about my questions, thinking while he answered. It was very unlike the fluently emotional outpourings that I had been listening to from his wife. He sat staring into space most of the time, never turning his head and avoiding my direct gaze almost entirely, so that I wondered whether looking at a strange woman was prohibited. His voice was flat, monotonous, and almost devoid of expression.

Brought up in an Episcopal family, he had been baptized and confirmed in the church. After high school, he chose to study forestry and botany at the University of Oregon. But when he was drafted for the war in Vietnam, he dropped out and skipped across the border to Canada, like many other young men of his age.

"I was living on my own and I didn't know too many people," he said slowly, "and I met this priest of a Hare Krishna temple. He invited me to the Sunday feast, to visit the temple. So I went, and I liked it. In the summer of 1966 I moved into the temple. I did all the initiation there, and after about a year, I was sent to Europe to open up centers. I'd been through music, art, work, traveling—I always felt I had to do something spiritual in order to be satisfied." He paused and looked down at his bag of mantra beads. "Nothing was any good, and I knew that for me it was Hare Krishna."

After he and Ala came back to America, he explained, he settled in at this temple to work on the farm, freed from the pressure of the draft by President Ford's amnesty.

"I enjoy working on the farm, and we grow our own vegetables there. We have just started so we're not able to provide for the whole community yet. But there are about sixty-five of us, and we hope to become totally self-sufficient."

Ala, who had been sitting glancing at him while he spoke, suddenly interrupted.

"In all the other religions there was never any mention of God," she said, "though by the sound vibration of the word there was something awesome and supreme about it. But there was no mention of developing love for God. The purpose of this religion is to serve God. Even though the Bible says so, there is no mention of God in most of the churches—they talk of bingo and pollution in the sermons, but there is no religion. When I came into Krishna consciousness, I could see that everything I had done was a form of looking for Krishna. All those rituals you go through in other religions are meaningless social functions, with the emphasis on bodily relationships, on family rather than on God. For example, I hated my father's sister, but she always had to be invited to our family ceremonies. I know I am not this body, I am all spirit, and the purpose of life is to serve God. All the other entanglements are relationships which can satisfy only if Krishna is the center. I am a spirit, and my son, my child, is a spirit soul, and I am trying to serve God."

Bana, who had glanced briefly at Ala when she interrupted, got up and walked over to the window while she spoke, to watch over Krala, who had once again climbed on to the radiator to look down into the street. Bana lifted him down, but Krala immediately scrambled back up with a mischievous grin, so Bana helped him to stand steady on the radiator.

Ala continued to talk with animation: "Once, I thought there was no meaning to life. But Hare Krishna gave a meaning to my life, and God sent his messenger showing that I was not what I should be. The purpose of true religion is to teach us how to serve God in our daily life. Only Krishna consciousness can teach us that."

She explained that more and more people were joining and working for Krishna, and she went on at length about how impressed she
was that they would devote so much effort—growing food, printing
magazines, writing books—"just for Krishna." It was hard to stop
her outpouring or to make any comment on her passionate devotion. Bana stood by the window, just behind Krala with his shaved
head and the traditional lock of hair in the middle "so Krishna can
grab you and pull you to heaven,' as the child looked through the
window at the daily life of twentieth-century America. Ala and
Bana had become isolated from that life, and intended that their son
should also be isolated from it. He would never be part of the world
he glimpsed through the window, never understand how it worked.
He would absorb the mystical ideas of a strange religion rooted in
Indian concepts, which deny the realities of the body in favor of the
intangibles of mind and spirit. He would never learn the history of
America or of other societies in the world, never understand the
composition of the atmosphere or why water gets hot. He would
never play a game of baseball in a friend's backyard, never read the
story of Tom Sawyer, never be taught the beliefs of American democracy or a free society.

Instead he will learn that all who do not believe in Krishna are
"demons" and crazy, and that he must not associate with them. He
will learn that he can steal, lie, and do anything that will help
Krishna. He will learn to obey the temple leaders without question
and let them make his decisions about work and marriage for him.

I said good-bye to the three of them, then went down the wide
main stairs, put my shoes on in the hallway, and banged the solid
front door shut behind me. Walking down the tree-lined street away
from the house, I looked at the children on the sidewalk with a new
interest. Here a little girl was wheeling a bicycle, there two boys
chased an excited puppy on a leash, and nearby a mother stood
holding her child, who licked a dripping ice-cream cone, beside another woman with a baby carriage. Across the street, a line of
schoolchildren, unevenly paired, walked toward the park on an out-
ing.

They were only yards away from little Krala at his window, but it
felt like a million miles.

11

Does the ethnic family have a future?

Gray-white clouds filled the sky, diffusing the rays of the summer sun into a shadowless light that reflected onto the still lake edged with spiky rushes. Around the lake a gravel path ran, widened into a parking lot, and then disappeared between the shrubs to cover the miles to an unseen highway. Rolling hills of thick green trees stretched on all sides, protecting the oasis of peacefulness.

On a rowboat in the middle of the lake sat two boys quietly fishing, their poles dark stripes against the bright water, the ripples from their lines undulating to the bank. A man sitting on a frayed canvas chair on the old wooden pier occasionally glanced at the boys. It was like a scene from a Japanese print of clear water, light sky, dark trees, and two tiny figures in a boat. But the sound of a car revving slowly as it came into the parking area transformed the Japanese miniature back into the everyday reality of a California state park on a humid August afternoon.

One of the boys turned as he glimpsed the car and watched as it stopped and a woman got out. She waved a hand, and he waved back, and the two boys began to reel in their lines. The woman leaned on the front of the car, watching the peaceful scene. Her smooth dark hair was tied back with a silk scarf, and her cotton skirt and pastel-pink shirt were crisply clean. She watched the boys row the boat to the shore.

The man got up from his chair as the boat bumped the pier, and took a length of worn rope from the boy to tie the boat to a wooden rail. As the boys carried their fishing lines and gear to the car, the woman asked:

"Catch anything?"

"Naw," said the boy who waved, in the bored tone that teenagers seem to develop instinctively for talking to their mothers. The two boys got into the car, and Irene revved up and drove away through the trees to the highway. She listened as the two of them agreed to meet at the baseball field later and wondered idly if she should suggest taking them swimming. Her older daughter had gone to the beach with a friend, and the younger one was happy in a local summer day camp. She liked the children to enjoy the freedom of the summer, but she herself had never experienced the opportunities they seemed to take for granted. After she dropped off the other boy, she and her son drove silently to their house a few blocks away, on a quiet suburban street shaded by trees and shrubs. Their house was like the other low California ranch houses in the neighborhood, painted white or brown or cream, with lawns of drying grass dotted with vivid yellow dandelions. But inside were the first signs of the unusual ethnic upbringing which distinguished this family from all the others.

Tall screens divided the living room from the hallway, framed Japanese brush paintings adorned the wall. A large grand piano stood by the living-room window, and a fluffy Pekingese yapped excitedly as Irene came into the house.

Irene offered me a mug of tea, which she set on the low glass coffee table by the sofa. Her face and features were distinctively Japanese, and her demeanor promised modesty, shyness, and a sense of withdrawal. But when she sat down to talk, she expressed her views on her upbringing and her Buddhist beliefs with the articulate firmness of a woman who lives in a culture where women are encouraged to be independent and express their opinions. She is an American woman of the present, far removed from the heritage of submissive obedience of her Japanese ancestry.

She and her husband are Shin-Buddhists, followers of the Jodu Shinshu sect of Buddhism. The temple they attend has a religious school where she teaches every Sunday. Her three children, now seventeen, fifteen, and twelve, have learned the principles and ideals of Buddhism and live by them. Yet at the same time because there are no Buddhist schools, they attend secular public schools. Irene and her husband believe that education is essential in order to succeed today.

"My children live in two different worlds," she explained. "On the one hand they are part of the Anglo community in school. Then they have their Buddhist friends, whom they meet in temple, and that is a completely different experience for them. Some 270 families from all around come to the temple, so that there's a very large Japanese-American-Buddhist group. We are active in the temple because we want the children to get to know other people from the same background. We want them to experience the Japanese-American community while they are still young so that they can make their own choice later. We want them to know that this is one religion. But we know we can only guide them so far. They will have to make their own choice later."

Buddhism is the name given by Westerners to the vast synthesis of teachings, now over 2,500 years old, attributed to Gautama, the Buddha, the Sage of the Sakyan clan. Later, these ideas were developed as they spread from India to other lands. In his own days, his teachings were known as Dhamma, meaning that which is right and is as it ought to be. They were also called Buddha-vacan, the word or speech of the Buddha, or even Buddha-sasana, the message, teaching, instruction, or dispensation of the Buddha.

Buddhism recognizes no God or Godhead. Life is not considered a preparation for eternity, but a discipline for governing man's attitude to the here and now. If the discipline is adhered to with true diligence, it will lead on gradually to what is the best and highest good, a state of mind (called Nirvana) which is reached when material things are completely transcended so that they do not attract, repel, or even impinge on the senses. "Immaterial things are more peaceful than material, cessation is more peaceful than immaterial things." (Itivuttaka p. 62)

Irene believes that the state of Nirvana "is not a place but a state of being. The highest spiritual good is nonego. Clinging to our ego is the immediate source of unhappiness and suffering. If we can come to understand that we can eliminate the ego, then we are not going to be affected by things that happen to us that we don't want to have happen nor by things that we want, that do not come to us." Irene feels that such dissatisfaction brings unhappiness. She understands that "human beings can never attain a state of egolessness, but we strive for those ideals. We strive to understand the totality of what is real, to see things as they are. We often talk of the 'suchness' of things, a way of recognizing things as they truly are. If we find an understanding of the 'suchness' of life we reach the highest spiritual attainment, and there would be no suffering if we could do that. But until then, we experience an enormous range of suffering, from the loss of a loved one to other less painful losses. We can attain our highest state when we can accept things as they are." Buddhism in the Jodu Shinshu sect emphasizes man's inability to become completely free of ego. True religious merit, it affirms, is the result of a selfless act.

Buddhism began in India. Then it traveled to China, and came to Japan between 550 and 600, by way of Korea, when several Korean princes sent gifts of images, Sutras, and missionaries to the Japanese imperial court. They arrived with promises that these Buddhist symbols would ensure national welfare. Buddhism was finally accepted when the pro-Buddhist supporters won control of the imperial house. Scriptures, art, and craftsmen were brought from Korea and China, and Japanese monks were sent abroad to study. In the seventh-century, temples were founded, clergymen ordained, and the four classical schools were introduced. Between 1150 and 1300 Buddhism became the dominant religion of the people of Japan. Today Shinto-Buddhism in Japan claims some 55 million adherents, almost half the population.

At the end of the nineteenth century, immigrants from Japan brought the modern ideas of Buddhism to the United States. The

first two priests of the Buddhist Churches of America arrived on
the West Coast in 1899, and in 1974 Buddhism celebrated its seven-
ty-fifth anniversary in this country. From California the early temple communities spread slowly. Today there are many different
sects with a total membership of about 500,000, mostly on the West
Coast.

Irene's grandparents came to America and brought up their children here, but neither Irene's parents nor any of her immediate
family have ever lived in Japan. "We are Americans of Japanese de-
scent," she said firmly, "so how could I go *back* to Japan when I
have never been there?"

The cultural influences acting on Irene's family are related more
to their religious beliefs than their ethnic background. "We are
Shin-Buddhists," explained Irene, "and that is the way of life we
follow. We are not strict vegetarians, because that is not an emphasis in my religion. I sometimes cook Japanese foods, but that takes a
great deal of preparation so I have to do it when I am not working,
but I cook a great many other ethnic foods."

For her children, it is the family's involvement in the Buddhist
temple which has shown them the differences in the Japanese-
American way of life. "That is where they have learned our orientation," she said, "and at home we talk about our experiences in the
life-style of America, from living here for three generations. The
temple and its religious teachings have influenced my children's values."

There are as many varieties of sects in Buddhism as there are
church interpretations of Christianity. While there is general acceptance of the basic teachings of Buddha, other ideas can be interpreted in vastly different ways. Jodu Shinshu is a division of Mahayana
Buddhism, and is based on four central beliefs: *samsara* (transmi-
gration), *merit, puja* (worship), and *worshipful personages. Samsara*
is a Hindu belief which, if interpreted literally, maps out the six
planes of temporal life. Shin-Buddhists interpret it metaphorically,
seeing the six realms (such as the realm of ghosts, of titans, of animals) as the six stages of the human condition, in which we experience deep pain or sorrow, or again happiness and satisfaction. The
realm that goes beyond them is the highest realm of Enlightenment

and a human being can only reach that through merit. *Merit* comes only from Amida-Buddha in Shin-Buddhism. Only one Buddha is worshiped, Amida-Buddha, which means Immeasureable Life and Light. Other Buddhist sects believe that spiritual credit can come from doing good deeds, thinking good thoughts, giving charity, writing out the scriptures, or painting religious pictures, among others. *Puja* (worship) has a wide variety of interpretations, as in many other faiths. But in Buddhism there is a basic wish expressed for Enlightenment, in which all self-centered desires must be given up and the wish for the welfare of all beings made central for each individual. Some sects worship the sacred symbols, such as the Three Jewels, Buddha, Dharma, and Samgha, to whom gifts and services are offered, but that is considered a lower form of *puja*. *Worshipful personages* are the many Indian, Chinese, and other saints and divinities who have become part of the legends of Buddhism. But the greatest worship is given to the Bodhisattvas and Buddhas who have unlimited merit, insight, and power. These personages are symbolic of Enlightened Beings, and they are worshiped because they are manifestations of the Enlightened State. Many people will either choose a particular Buddha who seems to be the best for their needs in striving for Enlightenment or else will worship all of them in turn.

Irene believes: "The only way to understand what living Buddhism is truly like is to live in an Eastern country. I would welcome an opportunity to live in a Buddhist country for a few years, to have the feeling of belonging to it. Maybe after that experience I would not want to come back to America, but maybe I would. I also would like my children to have that experience, because it would be important for them."

She added: "It is hard for them to gain a sense of identity when they are in a minority, and excluded from the mainstream of American society. It would be good to live in a culture where people feel strongly about the same kinds of things that you feel strongly about, a culture that is in harmony with you. It is very important for all human beings. Here I feel I always have to explain my Buddhism. There, I would not have to do that all the time."

Looking back at her own childhood, she felt that the pressures from the outside world were not as intense as those her children face today.

"When I was growing up, we never questioned the ideas of Buddhism," she said. "From my earliest childhood, and from the time I can consciously remember things, we just followed Buddhism automatically. Sundays would come along, and we would start the day by going to Sunday services. It was never anything to be questioned. All our close friends went to the Buddhist temple. We lived in an area with a great many other Japanese-American families, and so I grew up in an ethnic environment. It's fashionable nowadays to look down on closed ethnic environments, and to object to their exclusivity and their parochialism. But it is very different when you see these communities from the inside. When people talk of enclaves of ethnics, they must remember that often such separatism has developed because of outside discrimination and hostility, so that we have found it safer and more comfortable to be with people who think the same way as we do and who live the same kinds of lives. When the majority community does not follow the same beliefs, observe the same practices, hold the same values, it is often essential to have a tight ethnic group to provide security for those who hold on to those ideas. The Buddhist temple provided that security for us, and it served a social and cultural purpose as well as a religious one for those who were interested in the religious aspects. For Japanese-Americans here, the Buddhist temple has become a multipurpose institution because it provides a focus for all of us."

Her husband grew up in the same Buddhist community and at university chose to live in a Buddhist dormitory.

"We both had the same education, the same cultural exposure, and the same knowledge of our religion and heritage," said Irene, looking back at nineteen years of marriage. She paused and said: "Before you can understand the significance of our religious situation, you must understand the history of Asian-Americans in this country, so that you will know why it is important to us to preserve our heritage. For many years, laws were passed against Chinese and Japanese immigrants, and those in America were not permitted citizenship until 1952. There was much discrimination and ostracism. I know they must have endured a great deal of pain and humiliation."

Irene herself remembers the years of the 1940s when as a child she saw her family and thousands of others herded into internment camps in America. The wave of anti-Japanese feeling that swept the country after the bombing of Pearl Harbor and during the Second World War crystallized public opinion against the many Japanese-Americans who had never lived in Japan and had made their home in this country for years.

"I used to wonder how my Issei, that is my grandmother and her generation, managed to survive," said Irene somberly. "They had such awful experiences in terms of racism and discrimination. Yet somehow they have maintained this peace and serenity in themselves. It is not something you can teach, and it is not something you can talk about. It is their perspective on life.

"When I look at our religion today, it seems to be developing to the point where it's becoming similar to the Christian format and not so much like the practices in Japan. This is partly in response to fears of ostracism, I believe, and because we have many cultural and visual differences from the Anglo community, we have allowed our Buddhist practices to be influenced in such a way as to mitigate the other differences.

"Over the years, there have been changes in the language of the ceremonies, so that more and more English words are used." She shook her head. "I don't believe that this is a good trend. I believe it is better to be more traditional, and I would like to see appropriate Japanese or Indian or Sanskrit words used to explain Buddhist concepts or parts of a service. Often these words convey nuances of meaning which are impossible to translate accurately into English."

Describing the services, she explained: "People who come to them say that the Sutra chanting is like a Christian prayer chant and that the gathas are like the hymns—but they are not really exactly the same. When people, including Westerners, converted to Buddhism, many of them wrote songs that were Christian in style although Buddhist in philosophy. The end result seems to be that the Buddhist expression is set to Christian music. Personally I would like to see more music developed with a significantly Eastern feeling, that was more traditional, more Buddhist." She thought and said: "In Japan you live your Buddhism every day, not only on one day a week for Sunday school classes. It is a very different experience."

Irene's parents, the Nisei, might have felt sensitive to feelings of ostracism and therefore welcomed efforts to bring their religious practices into the cultural mainstream. But Irene, a Sansei (third generation) Japanese-American, feels the need to return to more authentic roots and to emphasize those Buddhist beliefs and practices that differentiate her upbringing from that of many other Americans.

In their childhood years, she and her husband experienced the close-knit isolation of an ethnic and religious community forced to rely on itself because of hostility and oppression from the outside world. Today her children are responding to a new freedom and openness in interracial and interethnic communications, which Irene fears may be only a temporary change. She and her husband grew up united in an unquestioning commitment to Buddhism and their Japanese heritage, amid the security of family and friends who supported their beliefs. But now they can see that the pervasive cultural influences of today's American society are reaching their children with a far stronger impact than they had imagined possible. They moved from their closed community seeking a better educational standard for their children. They found it, but they also found new problems of cultural and religious conflict as minorities isolated in the American mainstream.

"When we married, I don't ever remember talking about how we would bring up our children," said Irene. "Without ever thinking much about it, I guess we simply assumed that things would turn out right. My life has been fairly harmonious in many things. Life seemed simpler then, and we didn't ask so many questions. We were less aware of other options than our children are today. In a great many ways I expected my life to continue as it had done when I was a child, and I did not worry about it."

Soon after their marriage, Irene and her husband moved to another city in California, far from the close community life they had always known. They chose the city because of its excellent public-school system, as they felt their children would benefit from a high standard of education. But today, they wonder if it was the best decision.

"This is primarily an Anglo neighborhood," said Irene, "though there are a few Asian-Americans, a few black Americans, and some American Indians. But it is predominantly white. Its schools have an excellent reputation, but now that I know a little better, I am not sure that I would make the same decision about moving here. For example, at the elementary-school level, where only children from the same neighborhood attend, it has been very difficult for my children. Often they have been the only Japanese-Americans in the school. They have few other friends from the temple or the Buddhist community in this immediate area. It is very different from my own school experience, where I was part of a large Japanese community.

"In the middle school it's a bit better because they draw children from a pool of six schools from neighboring areas, and that means a bigger mixture of backgrounds and ethnicity. Though it still is not very many. In the high school there are a few more, but my children have always felt isolation."

One of Irene's greatest concerns has been the unconscious and often accidental slights to their beliefs and heritage which her children have suffered in their education.

"Even in the public schools, where there is supposed to be no religion, it is assumed that everyone has a Biblical background and that the ideas of the Bible are generally accepted," she said. "I can't remember specific examples because that kind of parochialism is something very pervasive and constant. But it is hard for our children, and it is hard for atheistic children and any others from different upbringings to feel that they belong to a school system when ideas that are not part of their background are generally accepted. I feel that a sincere effort should be made to introduce children to other philosophies, other ideas about religion, and to make them aware of other ways of life that exist in America."

The story of Adam and Eve, for example, is generally accepted as part of the education that every child should absorb, and the symbolism of offering an apple is often quoted in literature or in daily life as an image of temptation. For those children who have never heard the story, or who have never been exposed to the idea of an apple as an evil fruit to be avoided, such allusions must seem meaningless and foolish. Why would apples be wicked? What is wrong with accepting them? In time, it is probable that they will learn the story and understand the illusion. But will the other children learn the legends that fill the Buddhist literature or understand some of the symbolism of other stories?

"I am not saying that they should not teach the Christian concepts that are so prevalent in our schools," said Irene, "because I think it is important for children to know about these things. But we should also teach in schools, and in homes and in churches, something about accepting different concepts and different beliefs. This should be 'as well as' and not simply 'instead of.' So many times one thing simply replaces another, instead of adding to it and enriching education. In music for example, it might be interesting for children to learn something of Eastern music and other kinds of music, instead of just Western music." What do her own children listen to?

"Well, the two girls and my son hear Buddhist music in the temple, and my daughters play the organ for services so that they do know it," she said, and then sighed. "But at home, of course, they listen to that rock music and popular music all the time because that is what they like to hear. So I don't stop them."

As Irene's children reach adulthood, she is beginning to look ahead to assess those choices she knows they must face someday.

"There are no rules within Buddhism about marrying a non-Buddhist," she said. "It is an individual family expectation. But the pressures today are more social than religious. I don't know how I would feel emotionally if one of my children married someone not Japanese and not Buddhist. Intellectually I can understand that it is not wrong, but at the same time, it would be very difficult. Though I could accept it because my child's happiness would be of prime importance. Both parts of our heritage are important, and we care about our children continuing these traditions because I believe it is important for all children to have some kind of religious training, and to understand their heritage."

Buddhism encourages independence of thought and emphasizes personal interpretation and individual action, rather than community effort. Irene remembers that during the Vietnam War "those of us in the temple wanted to see more collective involvement in such social issues, but the Buddhist temples never took a stand on the war. It is not the Buddhist way. Within Buddhism you will always find a wide range of opinions and views on social issues."

Irene and her husband believe that their involvement in their Buddhist faith has preserved the family's identity as Japanese-Americans and stopped its absorption into the mainstream of Christian-oriented American life. But they can see that their children are affected by the non-Buddhist beliefs and practices they see around them, and find little to reinforce the Buddhist teachings they learn in the temple and from their parents.

The new opportunities that are now open for her children may also take them further from their ethnic and religious background, and tempt them to move into the American way of life, rejecting their heritage. Irene hopes that her children have seen and heard enough of their own background to encourage them to keep their ancestral faith and not reject their ethnicity and obliterate the past.

For children brought up in minority religious communities today, the delicate balance they must try to maintain between the education of the modern world and the ancient practices and beliefs of their parents can lead to great tension. For some, the long-held ideas and observances become an albatross hanging around their necks, marking them for life, ostracizing them from the world, dooming them to failure, and leading them to reject their past. For others, the old ways provide a secure umbilical cord to the years before their birth, linking them to the history and traditions of the past, and giving them strong emotional ties to it. For some children, the old religious ways are easy to follow and comforting to keep; for others, they are impossible to accept and a burden to continue. It's hard to explain why some children respond happily and follow religious traditions wholeheartedly while others reject them in anger.

Irwin chose to accept the teachings of the Armenian Orthodox church when he married, despite his more liberal upbringing of mixed Catholic and Protestant religious ideas.

"We lived in an Armenian neighborhood when I was a child," he said, "and then we moved. When I first brought my future wife home, I didn't realize she was Armenian until my father asked me if she was Syrian or Armenian. My mother had always said to me when I was growing up, It doesn't matter how you pray as long as you pray. She always said that to me. So when my wife started me going to the Armenian church, I found that I enjoyed it. I like the structure, the order. It is a definite ritual."

His wife, with her short dark hair, dark eyes, and creamy complexion, was not from any immediately identifiable ethnic group. Her own family had been in Turkey in 1915 when the Turks overran the Armenian nation and killed thousands and thousands of men, women, and children, destroying the country and its people. Today only a small part of Armenia is still a separate nation, within the Russian borders, but many Armenian refugees and their children now make trips from the United States to visit the Old Country, for the ethnic feeling continues to be very strong.

Irwin is a tall, well-built man with light-brown hair, thinning a little on the sides, and a strong face with a pointed nose. He works as a management consultant, and we talked in the open backyard of his suburban house, under a shady apple tree on the grass.

"In the Armenian church, the male is still dominant," he said calmly. "At the wedding the priest explained in English the role of the male and the female in the Armenian family, and it is still very traditional. Women cannot be acolytes in the church, and right now at the Sunday school there's a girl who wants to be an acolyte, and there's just no way she can be one. People who find unstructured religion unsatisfactory can really respond to the Armenian church, because it gives you something to appreciate. There are no kneelers, because you stand most of the time, which goes back to the very beginning of what the church was like. In the days of abstinence, you eat no meat and no fish, and that lasts forty days. You are not supposed to cross your legs in church, and women should be covered, and there are lots of other customs like that which are maintained in their original form, which I approve of. Today morality seems to be unimportant. I don't know where the next generation is going. In my office, there are women in their twenties and thirties, and the way they carry on, the things they are saying and doing shock me. The whole society seems to be coming to an end for me."

When the first Armenians arrived in America, they set up their Armenian Apostolic churches following the rites of the Eastern Orthodox church, but with the unique stamp of Armenia in the language, the music, and also the food. Today there are twenty-nine Armenian Apostolic Churches of America and fifty-eight Diocesan Armenian Churches of America, with a total membership of about half a million.

The differences between Orthodox churches and Catholic churches date back to the schism of 1054, when the church broke into an Eastern and a Western church. Among the beliefs which separate them are the Orthodox church's refusal to accept the infallibility of the Pope (believing that only the church as a whole can be considered infallible), its denial of the existence of purgatory, and various disagreements over the concept of the virgin birth. In the Orthodox church priests may marry, though bishops and higher officials may not.

Following the seven ecumenical councils of the early years of the Christian church, Orthodox followers accept the creed of orthodoxy (the Nicene Creed), dating back to A.D. 381.

For Irwin, it was satisfying to accept the creed and the more stringent demands of the church. He brought his daughter, now fifteen, and his son, eighteen, to Sunday school from the beginning of their education and became involved in teaching there himself.

"That's how I learned so much about the church," he said. "It broadened me quite a bit. I would never have known what happened in Turkey if I had not become involved here. It is like a new vista for me. It is a whole new culture and a whole new history, which is fascinating because the Armenians were the first people to embrace Christianity, as a nation."

He is proud of his children's awareness of their ethnic origins. "My son was in the Boy Scout troop at church, and he was awarded the Ararat medal, which is one of the highest honors in the church, and he was so delighted. You know, I think it meant more to him than the Eagle Scout award he won later on. He's going to college next year, and he found out that there is an Armenian community in the town he's going to. So he said to me, I'm going to look into the Armenian club down there and see what's happening. When he talks about people who aren't Armenians, he calls them 'Odar,' which means outsider, and then he says, But not you, Dad, to me. I know that I have been accepted by the community—and I was chairman of the religious-education department last year. Sometimes it is a bit clannish, because I don't really understand the language yet, but that's only taught on Saturdays at a special school. I understand enough to guess what's going on when they start talking Armenian. And I just love the food. My wife cooks up great banquets of Armenian foods for our friends."

At the Armenian church, the minister has seen many changes taking place within the community as his Armenian congregants become more Americanized.

"Over 90 percent of the marriages in our churches involve non-Armenians," he said, "so we have a lot of 'Odar' people coming into the community. Anyone who has been baptized in a Christian church is welcome, but sometimes there's a bit of discrimination from the family at first. Usually it disappears if the outsider joins the church, and often the convert becomes even more enthusiastic about religion than the church member. It seems to me that the further people are from their ethnic roots, the more they need to identify with their religious roots, because that is a stronger link for them with their past and with their heritage. Today, the Armenian community has more in common with other Americans than with the Armenians living in Lebanon or in Russia. We have become acculturated to this life-style and its values. Our children learn here, absorb education here, accept the culture and the foods here. The new generations cannot speak the old language and don't understand the services unless they are in English. The influences of American culture are stronger than the influences of the Armenian church in life-style and education. But the church, our faith, our observances will continue to be a strong part of our cultural traditions and beliefs, as long as people bring up their children to observe and understand them."

Though Irwin and his wife have brought up their children within an ancient religious tradition, they find no conflict between the values and standards of the church, and the underlying values and standards of American society. Irwin hopes that his religious heritage will give his children high moral standards and strong beliefs so that they will want to remain within the faith. But there is a basic compatibility between what he wants for his children and what society offers them.

Irene and her husband have also tried to share their strong feelings about the values and standards of their faith with their children, but unlike Irwin, they feel threatened and undermined daily by the messages their children hear from the society outside and its dominant themes based on Judeo-Christian principles.

They have tried to make their children aware of other Japanese-Americans and their unique way of life. But they know that when their children reach adulthood, they may choose to reject the paths of their parents, because the conflict is too painful.

"Buddhists who marry Christians in America usually find it very hard to balance the two," said Irene, "and even though they may keep their Buddhist philosophies, they frequently stop going to church. There is no religious pressure, because anyone can go to a Buddhist temple and all are welcome under any circumstances. But the community can exert much pressure even to the point of ostracism."

There is no baptism in Buddhism because it is believed that we are all born with a Buddha nature.

In some cases, marriages between Buddhists of Japanese-American background and Western Christians have resulted in a certain isolation for the Buddhist partner, because of the pulls toward the Western way of life. This can be a painful experience for both partners, and conflicts within the ethnic group can cause new problems.

Irene is already confronting conflict and criticism about their upbringing from her children.

"My son and my older daughter sometimes say, Why do we have

to go to temple? and explain that they don't want to go with us," she said. "I think it is to test our own religious commitment as much as it is a desire to stay home on Sunday. Up till now I have said that it's important for them to come, and so they do. But though it is not a sensitive issue in our family, we do talk about it, and who can tell what will happen in the future?"

She added: "One of the problems is that we live in an affluent and materialistic culture, so that many people don't take religion seriously. It is only when you face suffering in some form that you feel that there must be something more important to turn to, and then you revert back to your childhood training and your religion on many occasions. But it is hard to explain that to a child."

Her son ran down the stairs holding a baseball mitt and ball in his hand.

"Back later, Mom," he said, putting on a red baseball cap that lay on the chair, and straightening his Los Angeles T-shirt.

"Supper's at six," she called, as he went to the door, "have a good game."

" 'Bye," he said and banged the door behind him.

12

So what have you found out?

While I was working on this book, people often asked me, "What discoveries have you made? What's the best religion? Which is the ideal way to teach children about religion? What do children respond to?"

Sadly, those questions have no single answer. There is no simple philosophy waiting to answer all the problems of belief and faith for every one of us. I would have been delighted to discover one and to recommend it as the perfect religious panacea for you, for me, for our children, for the world. Many of the religious tracts I read and many of the people I spoke to fervently asserted that they indeed had found the right way, the only path, the true faith, and urged others to "Join me" or "Be saved by us." But somehow my doubts always overwhelmed the rhetoric of those who were sure that there is only one answer and that they had it.

Reading, talking, listening, and thinking about children and religion today have only increased my suspicions of instant religious solutions. The range of philosophies, the depth of interpretations, the varieties of individuals and families provide so many choices that it would be foolish to demand that we all follow one path.

I have come to realize, as I listened to the many people I interviewed, that my own beliefs were often in conflict with the ideas they expressed and the philosophies they believed. Faith asserts you should "believe, accept, and all will be well." For me, that leap has always been difficult. I want to have things explained, think about them, and then decide whether or not to accept them. But religious faith demands a step into the unknown, a willingness to take things on trust, and a capacity for belief without confirmation.

My sympathies seem to lie with the second-century Roman emperor Marcus Aurelius, whose *Meditations* expound the philosophy of the Stoics. He believed that life is simply a short span of existence ("this boundless abyss of the past and of the future into which all things disappear") and that man's own reasoning and thinking are the best judges of honorable living. The true purpose of life, according to the Stoics, is an awareness of an honest goal, founded on self-examination and consciousness. There should also be a commitment to what one knows to be right, no matter what others say or do:

It is a man's duty to comfort himself, and wait for his natural dissolution and not be vexed at the delay, but rest in these two ideas: first, that nothing will happen to me which is not in harmony with the nature of the universe; and second, that it is in my power never to act contrary to my god and divinity, for there is no man who can compel me to this.

This pragmatic assertion that we must take total responsibility for ourselves in a calm, dispassionate way is not in vogue today. There are emotional adherents of every faith and thoughtfully intellectual adherents too. But at the heart of religious faith is a quantum leap into accepting a belief in something intangible. Once you have chosen your path and jumped, you are free to vary the intensity of your devotion to the belief and the seriousness of your commitment to the observances. But the leap itself is crucial, and common to all religious believers.

No matter what our religious faith or our philosophy of life, all of us must make certain decisions about how to bring up our children. Yet in the past months, I have found it impossible to define exactly how a child absorbs his or her religious beliefs. Each child is unique, a reflection of his family and community, which he interprets by means of his character and personality. It's difficult to evaluate how a child benefits from religious education, because so much depends on the manner in which it is presented, the honesty and awareness of the parents who teach, and the individual experience of the child. And it is equally difficult to judge what a child misses for lack of a definitive religious doctrine in the home, because so many other experiences may provide a sound education in ethical values, moral behavior, and religious philosophy unrelated to a specific doctrine.

Every child interprets messages about religion from an independent perspective. Sometimes children brought up in strict religious families reject the restrictions and break away from the faith. Others may feel that the parents were not strict enough and become even more ardent followers of the faith they grew up in. Children growing up in liberal families may feel that they lack concrete beliefs and choose to follow a demanding, regimented philosophy. Others rejoice in the freedom and openness of their family's tolerance, and continue to follow those ideas.

Often brothers and sisters in the same family choose diametrically opposite paths to follow, in religion as in other ways, for reasons that seem almost impossible to comprehend, as for example the devout Catholic family where two brothers left the priesthood to marry while their sister continues in her life as a nun.

For Geoffrey, his life has come full circle. Now a social worker in his late twenties, he was given a strong Quaker upbringing by his mother and the Quaker school he attended.

"My mother was always taking me to meetings and to the peace demonstrations she was always going to," he said. "I can still remember protesting the execution of the Rosenbergs and how people burst into tears when the news came that they were dead. In my late teens I found that I could not accept many of the ideas I had grown up with. I dropped out of college, broke away from the Quakers, and became very active in groups protesting the war in Vietnam. One day, I went to a march round the war memorial in Cincinnati and found myself behind a father and his little girl. The child was crying, and I felt so angry at the man because it reminded me of the way my mother used to drag me to protests. I walked around behind them. The father was talking to the child, and I found myself listening to what he was saying. He told her why we were doing this and what was important about it and how Quakers feel about war and why it was wrong. He was talking to her very quietly and calmly, and I began to cry. It was like hearing things I had known for a long time and forgotten. I asked him if we could have coffee after the demonstration, and we did. On his suggestion I decided to go to a Quaker meeting again. Since then, I have become much more involved in the community, and I feel I have found a place for myself and a real faith that I thought I had completely lost."

But for others, that childhood rejection is complete and remains a constant source of exacerbation between parent and child. Sharon was brought up in a strongly Protestant church, and went regularly to Sunday school and services.

"I met Bill in college," she said, "and we are both musicians, and that commitment was the most important one for us. When we decided to get married, my parents objected strongly because Bill was Jewish. His parents liked me, and we were married with their blessing. After our children were born, we spent several months in Israel, and when I came back, I knew I wanted to convert to Judaism." The family is now actively involved in a Reform temple, and, after several years in Hebrew school, her son was bar mitzvahed. But her parents refuse to accept her change.

"Even after fifteen years of marriage, my parents cannot accept the fact that I have rejected my Protestant upbringing," said Sharon. "My mother kept nagging me to baptize the children when they were young, which of course I did not do. They never want to hear about my involvement with the temple. When they were here for a while, the first day of Hanukkah came, and I told the children we would celebrate it a day later because I could not face lighting the candles with them there. I knew they would never understand it. They are still both devout members of the church, and though this is painful to realize, they will never accept my change of faith."

From the many experiences I have heard from parents, grandparents, children, and others, there is an unending variety and diversity of religious experience, in acceptance and rejection. But echoing through the stories, the anecdotes, the facts, two patterns of family attitudes and style emerged. Again and again they surfaced, cutting across all boundaries of faith, ethnicity, culture, economics, or education, and reflecting personal characteristics that were far stronger than other attributes. These two distinct patterns seemed to permeate every denomination and separate the attitudes of those involved in the religious education of their children.

I call the adherents of these two ways of life the Oaks and the Willows.

The Oaks believe that religious instruction is essential for their children and are deeply hurt when their children express views contrary to their teachings and often reject the child because of unacceptable religious views.

The Willows believe that children should learn about religion, and observe it, but recognize that in adulthood children often choose a different path. They may be deeply hurt when children express views contrary to their teachings, but they try to recognize the needs of the individual child and to keep channels of communication open.

A father talked of the confrontation he experienced when his son, who had been brought up within the Protestant church the family has always attended regularly, told him he wanted to marry his Roman Catholic girlfriend.

"We had known her since they met two years before," said the father, "and we liked her very much. But I knew that the girl's family were strict Roman Catholics, and I suggested that they first talk to a priest in her church. Unfortunately he was most unhelpful. They came back to me and said they both wanted to marry in our church because they refused to be married in the Catholic church. We finally agreed to have a meeting with the parents. The girl's mother was very emotional and kept making accusations about our son taking her daughter away from the church. Finally she stood up and said, My religion is everything to me, and I cannot permit this marriage to take place. My wife, who is usually very quiet and doesn't like arguments, spoke up and said, These last two years have been the most difficult years of my life because my religion has always meant a great deal to me and is a very important part of my life. I know exactly how you feel. The woman looked at her and burst into tears. I think it was the first time she realized that the situation was the same for both of us because we too cared about our faith. In the end we agreed that they should marry in our church, and since then we have become good friends."

The Oaks usually choose authoritarian instruction for their children, stressing rote teaching and solid regulation as the best method of instruction. Generally the education will concentrate solely on their faith and not deal with others at all.

The Willows feel that religious education should be carefully planned to meet the educational abilities of the child, and should provide the child with information on which to base an adult choice later.

The Oaks usually have answers to every question about faith, life, death, religion, values, and behavior. They are not concerned with the changing patterns of social attitudes toward issues like homosexuality, abortion, premarital sex, the role of women, or divorce; they know where they stand.

The Willows have answers to many questions but are inclined to hesitate on complex issues, and often admit to a certain ambivalence on topics that seem different today from the way they seemed in Biblical times. They find themselves ready to consider changes in traditional patterns of behavior in the light of modern thinking.

The issue of women in the pulpit, for example, has caused a great deal of soul searching among many religious groups. In some cases, women are simply denied such leadership options. In others, acceptance has seemed natural and uncomplicated. The Episcopal church in recent years has faced much dissent in its decision to ordain women priests. Several members and church communities have withdrawn from the church to found their own organization in protest against the decision. Yet the mainstream of the Episcopal membership has accepted the change, and women now serve as priests within the church.

The Oaks are always certain that their way is right and everyone else is therefore wrong. This is especially evident in some of the more extreme sects, where any method is acceptable to persuade new converts to join, including illegal activities such as lying, stealing, or misrepresentation. The followers of the Reverend Moon call this "heavenly deception."

The Willows are sure that their way is right for them, but recognize that other people might prefer a different path.

The Oaks believe that they are superior in morality, honesty, and righteousness to other groups, and are suspicious and wary of outsiders, believing that the outside world is sinful and dangerous.

A devout family of Jehovah's Witnesses living in a Kingdom Hall expressed their concerns about their four-year-old son attending the local public-school kindergarten.

"We are living in a wicked and degenerate world," said the father, who works as a bookkeeper to support his family. "We know that there are dangers, and we are cautious and protective. For example, we will not let our child go to Christmas parties, because the birth of Jesus is not ordained as a celebration in the Bible, and we would not let him attend a Passover service. We cannot allow him to do something we do not believe in, but we are not bigoted or closed-minded. It's just that as far as worship is concerned, it has to be kept pure."

The Willows believe that their group has high standards of morality and ethical behavior, but recognize that people in other groups also behave honorably and that the evil in the world is balanced by the good. The Muslim faith allows marriages between those who are considered "the people of the book," including all those whose faiths follow the teachings of the Bible.

The Oaks wait hopefully for the day when everyone in the world, by force, persuasion, legislation, or miracle, will come round to their way of thinking and leave their erroneous beliefs.

The Willows believe that the world is a better place if there is a real variety of religious ideas and practices, freely followed and openly accepted, to encourage the essential concept of democracy and understanding. They are vehemently opposed to the idea of one group imposing its beliefs on the rest of the world.

The Oaks are generally very concerned with the minutiae of observance and trational practice, and feel those who adhere to their faith should be as attentive to such details as is humanly possible.

The Willows tend to be more concerned with ethical behavior and honest practice, and less with the details of observance or ritual, understanding that for some people such practices may not seem very important.

Several religious groups have rules about not eating specific foods—like alcohol, tea, coffee, pork, shellfish—and many people find such demands helpful and supportive in their daily faith, a constant reminder of their religious beliefs. But within every faith there are those for whom such rules are elevated to the status of commandments, to be observed with a stringency bordering on the neurotic, while there are others for whom they are simply a part of life, accepted as a pattern of behavior which they are happy to follow as one way of expressing their beliefs.

Parenthood is always uncertain, perplexing, and inconclusive. There are no Pulitzer prizes for teaching your children that it is wrong to lie, steal, or cheat. There are no televised awards ceremonies for helping children recognize that discussion and awareness can solve problems more successfully than violence and fighting.

The love, respect, and concern for each child as an individual, which are essentials of parenting, depend little on the intricacies of religious belief and much more on the personal character of the parents and those intangible attributes of kindness, warmth, common sense, discipline, awareness, and a ready sense of humor.

Children are born with individual characteristics and talent, and parents learn to help develop these into the personality that is uniquely theirs. Religion can be a part of this development, but it is only one part. The strength of any religious group is its reinforcement of the efforts of conscientious parents to instill ideas of morality and ethics. Yet at the same time, religion often inculcates ideas which many parents find impossible to accept, so that some parents today have decided to teach their children without the influence of any particular religious group. From the families I've met, it seems clear that it is possible to bring up honest, ethical, aware, and loving children without involvement in a religious organization. And it is also possible to bring up open-minded, thinking, and intelligently aware children within the framework of an established religious community.

For children, religion in a family is one of the givens, like going to baseball games or reading books at bedtime. Young children rarely question why their parents follow or reject a religious way of life. They simply accept it as a part of their family experience. As they grow up, and reach adolescence and adulthood, they may think about what they have learned. Perhaps they will simply accept it without question. They may consider the manner in which traditions were observed, the honesty with which religious teachings were followed, the sincerity of parental devotion. They may examine the acceptability of the beliefs and tenets they have been taught in the light of their own needs and personality.

For them, the time of decision will come when they have children of their own, and they must choose whether to pass on the faith of their childhood, or to choose new and different paths along which to lead the next generation.

APPENDIX

In this book you have met many people who have chosen to follow their own interpretation of a religious faith, often blending the traditions and beliefs of two faiths to give added meaning to their family lives. To celebrate important family events, some of these men and women have devised religious ceremonies that reflect their mixed heritage.

Although I have sought written examples, few such ceremonies are put down on paper. Often they are carefully created for a specific event or occasion, and then spoken but not recorded. However, I have found a few examples of ecumenicism that reflect the diversity of today's religious experiences and include them here in the hope of encouraging other families to create ceremonies of their own. (If you know of other ceremonies reflecting individual family beliefs and celebrations that you would like to share, please send them to me c/o Clarkson N. Potter Inc., One Park Avenue, New York, N.Y. 10016, and I will include them in future editions.)

Also included in this Appendix is a list of organizations that can offer assistance in answering any questions you may have on a particular aspect of this subject.

Ecumenical Services, Ceremonies, and Curriculum

Ecumenical or marriage interfaith service

(Prepared by Reverend Melvin Hawthorne, Church Center for the United Nations, New York, N.Y.)

In behalf of _____ and _____ I welcome you to this significant service in the Church Center for the United Nations. As Minister of the Chapel, I invite you to come often to this chapel whose purpose is world peace.

Because of the location, this chapel reflects the internationalism and the universalism of the United Nations. To this chapel of all faiths have come persons from many nations, races, and religions to declare their love for each other and to establish new homes by their marriage. The Universal Declaration on Human Rights affirms that "men and women of full age, without any limitation due to race, nationality, or religion, have the right to marry and found a family." So in keeping with this principle of universal brotherhood, _____ and _____ have come to unite themselves in marriage.

I wish to say to you who are present as friends or relatives that this is your service as well as theirs. The future of their home depends upon you as well as upon them. By your thoughts, your feelings, and your acts toward them on this day and in days to come, you can strengthen or weaken the vows they are taking. Your presence implies that you are giving positive support to this marriage.

I hope you will pledge your love not only to each other but to all people of the world and you will make peace-making a concern of your life together. A noble purpose of your life is to share love. Unless you share love, you will lose love. Love is not to be kept; it is to be shared.

Love has a broader meaning than just your personal feelings for each other. Love is like justice and beauty. Love is difficult to explain and describe, but is the ingredient of life which motivates and leads us to goals beyond our own ambitions. Every action which heals, cultivates, and protects—that is a part of love, too.

Love is present in a look, a touch, a smile, a tear. Love expresses itself through actions, feelings, and thoughts. The writer of Corinthians sought to capture the importance of love when he wrote:

> Love is patient and kind; love is not jealous or boastful; it is not arrogant or rude. Love does not insist on its own way; it rejoices in the right. Love bears all things, believes all things, hopes all things, endures all things . . . there are three things that last forever: faith, hope, and love, and the greatest of them all is love.

The vows which you are about to take are a public confirmation of your trust and love for each other. In a spiritual sense, you began your married life when you decided clearly to marry each other. At this moment you express that decision publicly that your friends may know your will, celebrate with you, and understand your assumption of responsibility for each other and for children who may be born to you.

_____, do you wish to have _____, as your wife? Do you?
GROOM: I do.

_____, do you wish to have _____, as your husband? Do you?
BRIDE: I do.

> (The following part of the service, known as "giving away" the bride may be omitted, or may involve the father of the bride, or the father and mother of the bride, or all four parents.)

Mr. _____, do you give your approval and blessing to this marriage?
FATHER (or someone acting for him, or father and mother): Yes.

GROOM (repeating after the minister, phrase by phrase):

_____, I want you to be my wife. I promise to be true to you in good times and in bad, in sickness and in health. I will love you and honor you all the days of my life.

BRIDE:

_____, I want you to be my husband. I promise to be true to you in good times and in bad, in sickness and in health. I will love you and honor you all the days of my life.

In this moment that you have expressed your vows to each other, we have tried to experience with you the depth of this relationship that has drawn you together.

A paraphrased verse of Elizabeth Browning gives a challenge to those who choose to love with the commitment you have just expressed.

> If you must love one another, let it be
> for love's sake only.
> Do not say I love her for her smile—her look—
> Her way of speaking gently—or for trick of
> thought that agrees with me.
> For these things in themselves may be changed.
> Or changed for you—and love, may be undone.
> Neither love her for pity's sake wiping her
> cheeks dry—
> A creature might forget to weep
> And lose your love thereby!
> But love each other for love's sake, that evermore
> You may love on, through an eternity.

> Elizabeth Barrett Browning

Do you have symbols of your sincerity and love?

(The minister receives the rings from whoever has them and places them on the altar.)

Rings are circular in shape, which suggests that there is no ending to them. It is our hope that they will symbolize the love that is between you which will have no ending to it.

Rings are also made of precious metals—suggesting a quality about them which is priceless. It is our hope that your love will be of such quality that it will inspire us to a life of love among all races and nations. Such a love is priceless.

_____, will you receive this ring from _____, as a sign of his love and sincerity, and will you wear it as a symbol of your own love and sincerity to him? Will you?

BRIDE: I will.

(Groom places ring on third finger of left hand of bride.)

_____, will you receive this ring from _____, as a sign of her love and sincerity, and will you wear it as a symbol of your own love and sincerity to her? Will you?

GROOM: I will.

(Bride places ring on third finger of left hand of groom.)

_____ and _____ have come to this place today to share their lives of love in marriage. They have said in our presence that they wish to be husband and wife. They have given pledges to each other. They have given and received rings. Therefore, I now affirm that you are husband and wife, Mr. and Mrs. _____, and express the hope that in all of your togetherness, you will feel as tenderly toward each other as you do during this day. And as citizens of the world you will help to establish the reign of love among the races, nations, and religions of this earth.

May God bless you and keep you.

May God make his face to shine upon you and be gracious unto you.

May God lift up his countenance upon you and give you peace and happiness, now and evermore.

Amen.

Jewish-Catholic
interfaith marriage
service

PRIEST:

Good friends of _____ and _____, we welcome you to the Church Center for the United Nations. We believe that it is God's will that men should beat their swords into plowshares, that they should sit unafraid under their vines and fig trees, and that they should be blest in peacemaking. The Hebrew prophet Isaiah expressed the hope of bringing people closer together when he declared, "My House shall be called the House of worship for all the peoples of the earth." The Psalmist exclaimed, "Behold how good and how pleasant it is for brethren to dwell together in unity." (Psalm 133.1)

The sixteenth article of the Universal Declaration of Human Rights affirms that "men and women of full age, without any limitation due to race, nationality, or religion, have the right to marry and found a family."

Today we have standing together at the altar a bride and groom who are of different faiths. They symbolize a lesson in love and brotherhood and harmony, admonishing us to seek and find the elements that bring us closer to one another. They believe that there is nothing in their faiths which prevents their marriage. They see each other as objects of love and worthy of the sacrament of marriage. This is a concrete expression of that spirit of human unity which we are seeing manifested so much in this part of the twentieth century between whites and blacks, Protestants and Catholics, Jews and Christians, Marxists and believers.

To quote the scriptures, "This is the day the Lord has made, let us rejoice and be glad in it."

Invocation by the Rabbi
(given in English and in Hebrew)

Rejoice in the Lord all the earth. Serve the Lord with gladness, come before His Presence with cheerfulness. Enter His gates with thanksgiving, and His courts with gratitude. Give thanks unto Him and bless His Name. For the Lord is good and His mercy endureth forever. (Psalm 100, verses 1, 2, 4 and 5)

Blessed be he who comes in the Name of the Lord. We bless you out of the House of the Lord. (Psalm 118.26)

O God, supremely blessed, supreme in might and glory, guide and bless this groom and this bride.

Our God, and God of our Fathers grant Thy choicest blessing to this groom _____ and to this bride _____ who are about to enter the Holy Covenant of Marriage. They seek Thee O God, out of the joy of their troth that their devotion to each other may gain Thy favor. Hopefully they look forward to the morrow that under Thy protection they may establish a home of their own, filled with the spirit of love, loyalty, faithfulness, commitment, and dedication to each other's happiness and well-being.

Teach them O God that unless Thou dost build the house, they who build it labor in vain. Hallow their love, bind their lives together, and help them to face the future with faith in one another and with unshakable confidence in Thy Divine Providence. Guide them through every trial and temptation. In Thy grace, join them unto each other with a love that shall not falter, neither will it fade, and cause them to approach the time-tested, age-old institution of marriage with understanding hearts, courage, confidence, and faith. Amen.

Scripture Readings by the Priest

As we prepare for the solemn and joyful moment when _____

and _____ exchange their marriage vows, it is good for us to reflect thoughtfully on the Scriptures, concerning love and marriage.

Then God said: "Let us make man in our image, after our likeness; and let him have dominion over the fish of the sea, and over the birds of the air, and over the cattle, and over all the earth, and over every creeping thing that creeps upon the earth." So, God created man, in His own image, in the image of God, He created him; male and female He created them. And God blessed them. And God saw everything that He made, and behold it was very good.

"And I will show you a still more excellent way. If I speak in the tongues of men and of angels, but have not love, I am a noisy gong or a clanging cymbal. And if I have prophetic powers, and understand all mysteries and all knowledge, and if I have all faith, so as to remove mountains, but have not love, I am nothing. If I give away all I have, and if I deliver my body to be burned, but have not love, I gain nothing."

"Love is patient and kind: love is not jealous or boastful; it is not arrogant or rude. Love does not insist on its own way; it is not irritable or resentful; it does not rejoice at wrong, but rejoices in the right. Love bears all things, believes all things, hopes all things, endures all things. . . . So faith, hope, love abide, these three; but the greatest of these is love."

Exhortation

This union then is most serious, because it will bind you together for life in a relationship so close and so intimate that it will profoundly influence your whole future. That future, with its hopes and disappointments, its success and its failures, its pleasures and its pains, its joys and sorrows, is hidden from your eyes. You know that these elements are mingled in every life and are to be expected in your own. And so, not knowing what is before you, you take each other for better or for worse, for richer or for poorer, in sickness and in health, until death.

RABBI:

Questions for Parents (optional)

Mr. and Mrs. _____, _____ wishes to marry _____. In this does she have your approval and blessing?

(Same question to other parents.)

PRIEST: _____, do you wish to have _____ as your wife?
GROOM: I do.

_____, do you wish to have _____ as your husband?
BRIDE: I do.
PRIEST: GROOM (repeating phrase by phrase):

_____, I take you to be my wife. I promise to be true to you in good times and in bad, in sickness and in health. I will love you and honor you all the days of my life.

BRIDE: _____, I take you to be my husband. I promise to be true to you in good times and in bad, in sickness and in health. I will love you and honor you all the days of my life.

Blessing and Exchange of Rings

RABBI: *Avinu She-ba-Shamayim barech at ha-Tabo-oth ha-zoth/ha-Eleh/.* . . . Heavenly Father may it be good in Thy sight to bless (these) ring(s). May (they) bring cheer, joy, gladness, success and prosperity, lasting happiness and harmony to the recipients, both to the bride and to the groom in the holy wedlock of matrimony.

Dear _____, with this ring I thee wed, and by it be Thou consecrated unto me, as my wedded _____ according to the Laws of God and Man.

The Seven Benedictions and the Wine Ceremony
(given in English and in Hebrew)

RABBI: Praised be Thou O Lord, our God, Ruler of the Universe who fashioned man in Thine image and created woman to be his helpmate throughout life. Blessed be Thou O Lord who implanted in this world of ours love and joy, gladness and happiness, friendship and brotherhood, harmony and peace. May it be Thy will O God that these Thy children receive a fair share in Thy gifts to mankind, and may Thy richest blessing accompany them in all their undertakings. Praised be Thou O Lord who fillest the hearts of the bride and the groom with cheer, joy, gladness and happiness.

Amen.

As together you now drink from this cup, so may you, under God's guidance in perfect union and devotion to each other, draw contentment, comfort and felicity from the cup of life that is in store for you, now that you are united in the holy wedlock of matrimony.

Amen.

Bride and Groom Drink from the Goblet

Thou, Source of all life and all joy, sanctify the covenant which this Groom and this Bride are consummating in Thy Name. Bestow upon them Thy gifts of friendship, of love and of peace. Make them rejoice in the sweetness of that family union which is founded on purity and fidelity, on duty and religious consecration. Be with them at this hour of their gladness, bless their covenant and seal their bond of wedlock with love everlasting.

Amen.

Confirmation of the Wedding Bond

PRIEST: Forasmuch as you, _____ and _____, have consented together in holy wedlock, and therefore have pledged your faith to each other, by the authority of the Catholic Church I ratify and bless the bond of marriage which you have contracted.

Amen.

I call upon all of you here present to be witnesses of this holy union which I have blessed. "Man must not separate what God has joined together."

RABBI: This Interfaith Marriage Ceremony is drawing to its conclusion. I join the Catholic Priest in ratifying the confirmation of your marriage vows. And I am doing so by the virtue of the ecclesiastical authority vested in me at the time of my ordination. Therefore, I do hereby declare your marriage to be valid and binding, and I do hereby pronounce you Miss _____ and you Mr. _____ to be husband and wife in the sight of God and man.

Benediction

RABBI: Both of us invoke upon you an ancient blessing taken from the Book of Numbers, a Scripture we mutually hold sacred. May God be with you and help you develop together. May you enjoy peace of home, of mind and of heart together.

Y'bharekh'khah Adonoy w'yishm'rekhah:

PRIEST: May the Lord bless you and keep watch over you.

RABBI: *Ya-er Adonoy panaw elekhah wiy'chunekkah:*

PRIEST: May the Lord cause His face to shine upon you and be gracious unto you.

RABBI: *Yissah Adonoy panaw elekhah, w'yasem l'khah shalom:*

PRIEST: May the Lord lift His countenance upon you and grant you the blessings of peace and of health and happiness and harmony—with each other, with your loved ones, with your fellowmen, and with your God—now and forevermore.

Amen.

RABBI: Congratulations to you—break the glass and kiss the bride.

Service at Lutheran church to welcome interfaith baby

At our 11 A.M. service, Joseph is being welcomed as part of our community of Faith. The parents, Donna and Edward, decided to base a marriage upon the full affirmation of the Jewish and Christian faith together with the liturgical life that makes them rich with meaning. This is a real witness of a new relation between Jews and Christians which gives hope for Paul's hopeful vision that there be one Israel. We wish to do everything we can to help them in this reversal of effort . . . most meaningful in our time.

Entrance into the Community of Faith of Joseph

Introduction

> The Lord be with you.
> AND ALSO WITH YOU,
>
> "We rejoiced, because they said to us:
> 'We shall go into the house of the Lord.'
>
> "OUR FEET ARE ALREADY STANDING WITHIN THY
> GATES, O JERUSALEM."   (Psalm 121)

Donna and Edward bring before this congregation their child, Joseph, desiring to make public their intention to raise him in the company of faith in prayer, in the study of scripture and in witness to the gospel.

Dear friends, we rejoice to receive Joseph into the household of faith, and we extend to him our community in the gospel which binds us in worship, learning, witness and responsibility for others. We rejoice in your desire that Joseph be nourished in God's word and learn God's loving purpose for him and for all creation.

Let us Pray. Lord God Almighty, our gracious Mother and Father, we pray for the sponsors and the parents who affirm their faith this day. Fill them with the Holy Spirit that they may guide this child's growth in faith, hope and love.

Donna and Edward: *Boruch atah Adonoi Elohenu Melech Haolam shehehiyahnu v'kimanu v'hiahnu lazman hazeh.*

> BLESSED ART THOU, O LORD OUR GOD, RULER OF THE UNIVERSE, WHO HAS SUSTAINED US IN LIFE AND BEING AND BROUGHT US TO THIS VERY MOMENT.

Holy God, mighty Creator: We give you thanks, for in the beginning your Spirit moved over the waters and you created heaven and earth. By your grace you nourish and sustain us and all that lives.

We give you thanks O Lord for the gift of this child, and for the new life which brings to us hope and promise. Pour out your Holy Spirit upon him and daily increase in him your gifts of grace, the spirit of wisdom and understanding, the spirit of counsel and power, the spirit of knowledge and reverence, and always and ever the spirit of wonder and awe in your presence.

Amen.

Psalm 95
"Let the heavens be glad, and let the earth rejoice;
   let the sea roar and the fulness thereof;
   let the field exult and all that is herein.

THEN ALL THE TREES OF THE FOREST SHALL BE JOYFUL
BEFORE THE LORD, WHO COMES
WHO COMES TO RULE THE EARTH.

The Holy One will rule the world with justice,
   and the peoples with truth."

The Ministers, laying their hand on the child, say:
Joseph, may God strengthen in you the gift of the Holy Spirit, to deepen your faith, to direct your life, to empower you for service, to give you patience in suffering, and to bring you to life everlasting.

Amen.

God has given us this new brother. We receive him with love and assure him of our joy over his entrance into our fellowship.

WE WELCOME YOU INTO THE LORD'S FAMILY AND INTO THE HOPE OF THE HOLY ONE WHOSE RULE IS AND IS TO COME.

Curriculum:
How can I know
what to believe?

The following is an excerpt from a new curriculum for sixth grade
through Junior High in the American Ethical Union classes, by
Charlene Brotman. Entitled "How can I know what to believe," the
curriculum is designed for about twenty class sessions, and can be
obtained from the AEU, 2 West 64 Street, New York, N.Y. 10023,
for $30.

Contents:
What do I believe about people?
  Focus:
  Part I   What do I believe about the nature of people? *(1 session)*
  Part II   What a monk named Erasmus believed about people. *(2 sessions)*
  Part III What do humanists believe about people? *(2 sessions)*
  Part IV   Affirming the strengths within people. *(1 session)*
What do I believe about God?
  Focus:
  Part I   Two men who never wanted to be God. *(1 session)*
  Part II   Was Jesus human or God? *(1 session)*
  Part III Ideas of God and good as a reflection of human values and needs. *(1 session)*
  Part IV   Theist, deist, agnostic and atheist . . . *(2 sessions)*
  Part V   Ideas about God. *(1 session)*
What do I believe about Death?
  Focus:
  Part I   Issue of life after death. *(1 session)*
  Part II   Accepting death as a natural part of life. *(2 to 3 sessions)*
What do I believe about religion?
  Focus:
  Part I   Defining what is "being religious." *(2 sessions)*

Part II   Freedom of religious thought. *(3 sessions)*
Part III   We have the responsibility to think honestly ... *(1 session)*
What do I believe about believing?
Focus: Our believing involves both knowing and valuing. *(1 to 2 sessions)*

What Do I Believe about God, Part III
(Ideas of God and good as a reflection of human values and needs.)

A comic book format provides students with the following dialogue between a questioning boy and a wise girl.

BOY: Do you believe in God?
GIRL: Which God?
BOY: Whaddya mean, *which* God?
GIRL: Do you mean the God described in this ancient story from India (the Upanishads)?

FATHER: My son, put this lump of salt into this pan of water. . . . Now, give me back the salt!
SON: But I don't see it anymore.
FATHER: Then taste the water from *this* end of the pan.
SON: It tastes salty.
FATHER: And taste the water from this *farther* end of the pan, and from the *middle* too.
SON: It *all* tastes salty.
FATHER: My son, as the salt is hidden in the water, so is God hidden in all the world. God is spirit, as you yourself are spirit. God is hidden in you. God *is* you and you are part of God.

BOY (indignant): Hold it—hold it—I mean God in the Bible! Do you believe in the God in the Bible?
GIRL: *Which* God in the Bible?
BOY (very upset): Whaddya mean *which* God in the Bible!
GIRL: Do you mean the God who commanded Moses to say to the people:

At the first day of you month you shall offer a burnt offering to the Lord: two young bulls, one ram, seven male lambs ... without blemish. ... (Numbers 28:11) Also one male goat for a sin offering. (Numbers 28:15)

Or do you mean the God of Isaiah:

I have no desire for the blood of bulls and sheep and he-goats. ...
Cease to do evil and learn to do right! (Isaiah 1:11–17)

And the God of Amos:

Even though you offer me your burnt offerings ... I will not accept them. But let Justice roll down like waters and Righteousness like an everflowing stream. (Amos 5:21–24)

Do you mean the God who instructed Joshua on conquering the land of Palestine for the Hebrews:

Hamstring their horses, and burn their chariots. ... (Joshua 11:6)
Leave no survivors. ... (Joshua 10:40) Set an ambush for the city. (Joshua 8:2)

Or do you mean the God of Micah:

And what does the Lord require of you but to do justice, and to love kindness, and to walk humbly with your God? (Micah 6:8)

Do you mean household gods—like the idols Rachel stole from her father and hid in her camel saddle? (See Genesis 29–32 to find out what happened.) Do you mean the manlike God of Adam and Eve who "walked in the garden in the cool of the evening" and who "made garments of skins for Adam and his wife"? (Genesis 3:8, 3:21) Do you mean the God who descended to Mount Sinai in thunder and lightning, with the blast of trumpets and the mountain smoking? Or do you mean the *Father* God of Jesus:

If you then, bad as you are, know how to give your children what is good for them, how much more will your heavenly Father give good things to those who ask him! (Matthew 7:11)

Do you mean Paul's God who damns non-Christians regardless of how good a life they lead? Paul: "No one comes to the Father but through Christ."

If you confess with your lips that Jesus is Lord and believe in your heart that God raised him from the dead, you will be saved. (Romans 10:9) He who does not believe is condemned already because he has not believed in the name of the only Son of God. (John 3:18) He who believes and is baptized will be saved; but he who does not believe will be damned. (Mark 16:16)

Or do you mean Jonah's God who forgives people who are sincerely sorry—*regardless* of whether they are Jews or *non*-Jews? (You can find out more about Jonah, the whale, and the wicked men of Nineveh in the Book of Jonah in the Bible.)

BOY: I don't get it! Why are there so many different ideas of God in the Bible?

GIRL: 'Cause it was written by many different people over a period of more than a thousand years—and it was edited and re-edited and added to. . . . So—which God *do* you mean? What do *you* believe?

BOY: Ummmmmmmmm

GIRL: You know, a famous minister once said:

Better believe in no God than to believe in a *cruel* God. If the God you believe in is small and mean . . . the smaller and meaner *you* will be!

Men have believed in a cruel God who will send a large part of the human race to an endless Hell, and by this belief all their cruelty was confirmed. They got the idea that the torture chambers of the Earth were but replicas of the great torture chamber of *God*.

Take care what kind of God you believe in! Some of the people who do not believe in God at all are more merciful, truth loving, and just than are some who do. (Harry Emerson Fosdick)

Then there's Sir Julian Huxley's point of view . . .

BOY: So what's his view?

GIRL: He says "God is a hypothesis constructed by man to help him understand what existence is all about."

BOY: But then—what does he put his *faith* in?

SIR JULIAN HUXLEY: My faith is in the possibilities of *Man*.

BOY: Hummmmmmmm

Resource List

The following list of religious organizations and centers is designed to help those who would like more specific information on a particular topic.

Headquarters of U.S. Religious Bodies
(Year organized in parentheses)

Advent Christian Church (1854)—Pres., Rev. Joe Tom Tate. Exec. V.P., Rev. Adrian B. Shepard, Box 23152, Charlotte, NC 28212

Adventists, Seventh-Day, General Conference of (1863)—Pres., Robert H. Pierson. Sec., C.O. Franz, 6840 Eastern Ave. NW, Takoma Park, Wash., DC 20012.

African Methodist Episcopal Zion Church (1796)—Senior Bishop, Herbert Shaw. Sec., Board of Bishops, Bishop Charles H. Foggie, 1200 Windermere Dr., Pittsburgh, PA 15218.

American Ethical Union; Exec. Dir. Jean S. Kotkin, 2 West 64 Street, N.Y., NY 10023.

Antiochian Orthodox Archdiocese of Toledo, Ohio (1936)—Archbishop Metropolitan, Michael G. Shaheen, 2656 Pemberton Dr., Toledo, OH 43606.

Antiochian Orthodox Christian Archdiocese (formerly **Syrian Antiochian Orthodox Church**) (1894)—Head of Archdiocese Metropolitan, Archbishop Philip (Saliba), 358 Mountain Rd., Englewood, NJ 07631.

Armenian Church of America, Diocese of the (1889)—Primate, Most Rev. Archbishop Torkom Manoogian. Sec., Very Rev. Zaven Arzoumanian, 630 Second Ave., N.Y., NY 10016.

Assemblies of God (1914)—Gen. Supt., Thomas F. Zimmerman. Gen Sec., Joseph R. Flower, 1445 Boonville Ave., Springfield, MO 65802.

Augustana Evangelical Luthern Church. See *The Lutheran Church in America.*

Baha'i Faith—About 5,500 communities, groups and isolated centers in the U.S. Sec., Natl. Spiritual Assembly, Glenford E. Mitchell, 536 Sheridan Rd., Wilmette, IL 60091.

Baptist Association, American (1905)—Pres., Dr. Roy M. Reed. Sec., Dr. L. Chester Guinn, 4605 N. State Line, Texarkana, TX 75501.

Baptist Association of America, Conservative (1947)—Pres., Rev. Robert P. Dugan, Jr. Sec., Rev. Carl E. Abrahamsen, Jr., P.O. Box 66, Wheaton, IL 60187.

Baptist Churches in the U.S.A., American. (1907)—Pres., Dr. Charles Z. Smith. Gen. Sec., Rev. Dr. Robert Campbell, Valley Forge, PA 19481.

Baptist Churches, Unified Free Will (1964)—Pres., Bishop Caldwell Thomas. Exec. Sec., Ernest Leonard, P.O. Box 4255, Newark, N.J. 07112.

Baptist Convention, Southern (1845)—Pres., Jaroy Weber. Exec. Sec., Dr. Porter Routh, 460 James Robertson Parkway, Nashville, TN 37219.

Baptists, General (1611)—Moderator, Rev. Harlen Webber. Clerk, Vern Whitten, 1629 Stinson Ave., Evansville, IN 47712.

Baptist General Conference (1879)—Gen. Sec., Warren Magnuson, 1233 Central St., Evanston, IL 60201.

Baptist General Conference, North American (1865)—Moderator, Delmar Wesseler. Exec. Sec., Dr. G. K. Zimmerman, 1 So. 210 Summit Ave., Oakbrook Terrace, Villa Park, IL 60181.

Baptist, Natl. Assn. of Free Will (1727)—Moderator, Dr. J. D. O'Donnell. Exec. Sec., Rufus Coffey, P.O. Box 1088, Nashville, TN 37202.

Baptist, National, Convention of America (1880)—Pres., Dr. James C. Sams, 1724 Jefferson St., Jacksonville, FL.

Baptist Missionary Assn. of America (formerly **North American Baptist Assn.**) (1950)—Pres., Rev. Kenneth Bobo. Gen. Sec., Craig Branham, 720 Main St., Little Rock, AR 72201.

Buddhist Churches of America (1914)—Bishop Kenryu Takashi Tsuji, 1710 Octavia St., San Francisco, CA 94109.

Bulgarian Eastern Orthodox Church (1909)—Most Rev. Joseph. Metropolitan. 312 W. 101st St., N.Y., NY 10025.

Calvary Grace Christian Churches of Faith (1898)—Internatl. Gen. Supt., Rev. Dr. Herman Keck, Jr., P.O. Box 14576, Ft. Lauderdale, FL 33302.

Calvary Grace Church of Faith (1874)—Rev. A. C. Spern, Internatl. Gen. Supt., P.O. Box 333, Rillton, PA 15678.

Christian Church (Disciples of Christ) (1809)—Gen. Minister and Pres., Dr. Kenneth L. Teegarden, Box 1986, Indianapolis, IN 46206.

Christian Endeavor, International Society of (1881)—Pres., Dr. LaVerne H. Boss. Gen. Sec., Rev. Charles W. Barner, 1221 East Broad St., P.O. Box 1110, Columbus, OH 43216.

Christian and Missionary Alliance (1887)—Pres., Dr. Nathan Bailey. Sec., Dr. R. W. Battles, 350 N. Highland Ave., Nyack, NY 10960.

Christian Reformed Church (1857)—Stated Clerk, Rev. William P. Brink, 2850 Kalamazoo Ave., SE, Grand Rapids, MI 49508.

Church of the Brethren (1719)—Gen. Sec., General Board, S. Loren Bowman, 1451 Dundee Ave., Elgin, IL 60120.

Church of Christ, Scientist (1879)—The Mother Church, The First Church of Christ, Scientist, in Boston, Mass. Pres., Mrs. Naomi Price. First Reader, Clem W. Collins. Second Reader, Jane O. Robbins. Clerk, George W. Ledbetter. Christian Science Center, Boston, MA 02115.

Church of God (Anderson, Ind.) (1880)—Exec. Sec., W. E. Reed, Box 2420, Anderson, IN 46011.

Church of God, The (1903)—General Overseer, Bishop Voy M. Bullen, 2504 Arrow Wood Dr., SE, Huntsville, AL 35803.

Church of Jesus Christ of Latter-Day Saints (Mormon) (1830)—Pres., Spencer W. Kimball. Pres. of the Council of Twelve Apostles, Ezra Taft Benson, 47 E. South Temple St., Salt Lake City, UT 84111.

Church of Jesus Christ of Latter-Day Saints, Reorganized (1830)—Pres., W. Wallace Smith. Commissioner of Communications, Elroy Hanton, Saints Auditorium, Independence, MO 64051.

Church of the Nazarene (1908)—Gen. Sec., B. Edgar Johnson, 6401 The Paseo, Kansas City, MO 64131.

Churches of Christ—No central organization. B. C. Goodpasture, editor, the Gospel Advocate, 1006 Elm Hill Rd., Nashville, TN 37210.

Churches of God, Gen. Conference (1825)—Pres., Dr. K. E. Boldosser. Sec., Rev. Harry G. Cadamore, 1934 Candlewick Dr., Findlay, OH 45840.

Congregational Christian Churches, General Council. See *United Church of Christ.*

Congregational Christian Churches, Natl. Assn. of (1955)—Moderator, Alexander S. Irvine. Exec. Sec., Rev. Dr. Erwin A. Britton, P.O. Box 1620, Oak Creek, WI 53154.

Evangelical Christian Churches (1966)—Pres., Dr. Kenneth T. Giles, P.O. Box 174, Jacksonville, FL 32219.

Evangelical Christian Churches, California Synod (1966)—Pres.-Treas., Dr. Richard W. Hart Sr., P.O. Box 399, Huntington Park, CA 90255.

Evangelical Lutheran Synod (Norwegian Synod) (1918)—Pres., Rev. G. M. Orvick. Sec., Rev. Alf Merseth, 106 13th St., S., Northwood, IA 50459.

Evangelical Methodist Church (1946)—Gen. Sec., Rev. R. D. Driggers, 3036 N. Meridan, Wichita, KS 67204.

Evangelical and Reformed Church. See *United Church of Christ.*

Finnish Evangelical Lutheran Church (Suomi Synod.) See *Lutheran Church.*

Foursquare Gospel, International Church of the (1927)—Pres., Dr. Rolf M. McPherson. Sec., Dr. Leland B. Edwards, 1100 Glendale Blvd., Los Angeles, CA 90026.

Free Methodist Church of North America (1860)—Sec., Board of Bishops, 901 College, Winona Lake, IN 46590.

Friends, General Conference of the Religious Society of (1900)—Chmn., C. Lloyd Bailey, Gen. Sec., Howard W. Bartram, 1520 Race St., Philadelphia, PA 19102.

Friends United Meeting (formerly Five Years Meeting of Friends) (1902)—Presiding Clerk, J. Binford Farlow. Gen. Sec., Lorton G. Heusel, 101 Quaker Hill Dr., Richmond, IN 47374.

Greek Orthodox Church of North and South America (1864)—Primate, the Most Rev. Archbishop Iakovos Chan., Very Rev. George J. Bacopulos, 10 E. 79th St., N.Y., NY 10021.

Hebrew Congregations, Union of American—Pres., Rabbi Alexander M. Schindler, 838 Fifth Ave., N.Y., NY 10021.

Holy Church on the Rock—Pres., Elder F.R. Willis, Pactolus, N.C. 27834.

Independent Fundamental Churches of America (1930)—Pres., Rev. Donald Hurlburt. Exec. Dir., Rev. Bryan J. Jones, Box 242, Westchester, IL 60153.

Jehovah's Witnesses (1884)—Chairmanship (rotating) of Governing Body, Watch Tower Bible and Tract Society. Pres., Nathan H. Knorr, 124 Columbia Heights, Brooklyn, NY 11201.

Jewish Congregations of America, Union of Orthodox—Pres., Harold M. Jacobs. Natl. Dir., Rabbi David Cohen, 116 East 27th St., N.Y., NY 10016.

Jewish Interfaith, Rabbinic Center for Research and Counseling—Dir., Rabbi Irwin H. Fishbein, 128 East Dudley Ave., Westfield, NJ 07090.

Latter-Day Saints. See *Church of Jesus Christ.*

Lutheran Brethren of America, Church of the (1900)—Pres., Rev. Everald H. Strom, Box 655, Fergus Falls, MN 56537.

Lutheran Church, The American (1961)—Pres., Dr. David W. Preus. Sec., Dr. A. R. Mickelson, 422 S. 5th St., Minneapolis, MN 55415.

Lutheran Church in America, The (estab. 1962 by consolidation of **Amer. Evangelical Lutheran Ch.** (1874), **Augustans Evangelical Luthern Ch.** (1860), **Finnish Evangelical Lutheran Ch.** (1890) and **The United Lutheran Ch. in Amer.** (1918)—Pres., Rev. Robert J. Marshall. Sec., Rev. James R. Crumley Jr., 231 Madison Ave., N.Y., NY 10016.

Lutheran Church-Missouri Synod (1847)—Pres., Dr. J. A. O. Preus. Sec., Rev. Herbert A. Mueller, 500 N. Broadway, St. Louis, MO 63102.

Lutheran Confession, Church of the (1961)—Pres., Rev. Egbert Albrecht, 213 Spring St., Mankata, MN 56001.

Lutheran World Federation, U.S.A. National Committee of the (formed Jan. 1, 1967, former **National Lutheran Council**)—Gen. Sec., Rev. Paul A. Wee, 315 Park Ave. South, N.Y., NY 10010.

Mennonite Church (1690)—Moderator, Edward B. Stoltzfus. Sec., Paul N. Kraybill, 528 East Madison St., Lombard, IL 60148.

Methodist Church, The United formed 1968 from union of **The Methodist Church** (1784) and the **Evangelical United Brethren Church** (1767)—Council of Bishops Pres., Bishop W. Ralph Ward. Sec., Bishop Ralph T. Alton, 1100 W. 42nd St., Indianapolis, IN 46208.

Moravian Church (Unitas Fratrum) (1740)—**Northern Province:** Hq., 69 West Church St., P.O. Box 1245, Bethlehem, PA 18018; Pres., Provincial Elders' Conf., Dr. J. S. Groenfeldt. **Southern Province:** Hq., 459 S. Church St., Winston-Salem, NC 27101; Pres., Provincial Elders' Conf., Dr. Richard F. Amos.

National Council of Churches (1950)—475 Riverside Drive, N.Y., NY 10027.

New Jerusalem in the U.S.A., General Convention of the (1782)—Pres., Rev. Eric J. Zacharias. Rec. Sec., Mrs. Wilfred G. Rice, 983 Fellsway, Apt. 8, Medford, MA 02155.

Open Bible Standard Churches (1919)—Gen. Supt., Raymond E. Smith. Sec.-Treas., O. Ralph Isbill, 2020 Bell Ave., Des Moines, IA 50315.

Orthodox Church in America (formerly **Russian Orthodox Catholic Ch. of Amer.**) (1794)—Primate, Metropolitan Archbishop Ireney. Chancellor, Very Rev. Daniel Hubiak, Rte. 25A, P.O. Box 675, Syosset, NY 11791.

Pentecostal Church of God of America (1919)—Gen. Supt., Dr. R. D. Heard, 211 Main St., Joplin, MO 64801.

Pentecostal Church, United (1945)—Gen. Supt., Stanley W. Chambers. Gen. Sec., Robert L. McFarland, 8855 Dunn Rd., Hazelwood, MO 63042.

Presbyterian Church, Cumberland (1810)—Moderator, Roy E. Blakeburn, Stated Clerk, T.V. Warnick, Memphis, TN 38104.

Presbyterian Church in the U.S. (1861)—Moderator, Rev. Paul M. Edris. Stated Clerk, Rev. James E. Andrews, 341 Ponce de Leon Ave., NE, Atlanta, GA 30308.

Presbyterian Church in the U.S.A., The United (formed 1958 through merger of the **Presbyterian Ch. in the U.S.A.** (1706) and the **United Presbyt. Ch. of N. America** (1858)—Moderator, Robert C. Lamar. Stated Clerk, Ruling Elder William P. Thompson, 475 Riverside Dr., N.Y., NY 10027.

Protestant Episcopal Church, The (1789)—Presiding Bishop, Pres. of Exec. Council, Rt. Rev. John M. Allin, 815 Second Ave., N.Y., NY 10017.

Rabbinical Alliance of America—Pres., Rabbi David B. Hollander, 156 Fifth Ave., N.Y., NY 10010.

Rabbinical Assembly, The—Pres., Rabbi Stanley Rabinowitz. Exec. V.P., Rabbi W. Kelman, 3080 Broadway, N.Y., NY 10027.

Rabbinical Council of America—Pres., Rabbi Fabian Schonfeld. Exec. V.P., Rabbi Israel Klavan, 220 Park Ave. South, N.Y., NY 10003.

Rabbis, Central Conference of American—Pres., Rabbi Arthur J. Lelyveld. Exec. V.P., Rabbi Joseph B. Glaser, 790 Madison Ave., N.Y., NY 10021.

Reformed Church in America (1628)—Pres., Rev. Bert Van Soest. Gen. Sec., Rev. Marion de Velder, D.D., 475 Riverside Dr., N.Y., NY 10027.

Reformed Episcopal Church (1873)—Pres. and Presiding Bishop, Rev. Theophilus J. Herter. Sec., Rev. D. Ellsworth Raudenbush, 560 Fountain St., Havre de Grace, MD 21078.

Reformed Presbyterian Church, Evangelical Synod (Apr. 6, 1965, union of the **Reformed Presbyterian Ch., General Synod** and the **Evangelical Presbyterian Ch.**)—Moderator, Rev. Paul H. Alexander. Stated Clerk, Dr. Paul R. Gilchrist, 107 Hardy Rd., Lookout Mountain, TN 37350.

Regular Baptist Churches, General Assn. of (1932)—Natl. Rep., Dr. Joseph M. Stowell, 180 Oakton Boulevard, Des Plaines, IL 60018.

Roman Catholic Church—National Conference of Catholic Bishops. Pres., Archbishop Joseph J. Bernardin. Sec., Bishop James S. Rausch, 1312 Massachusetts Ave. NW, Washington, D. C. 20005.

Romanian Orthodox Episcopate of America (1929)—Archbishop Valerian D.

Trifa. Sec., Rev. Lawrence C. Lazar, 2522 Grey Tower Rd., Jackson, MI 49201.

Russian Orthodox Church Outside Russia (1920)—Pres., Council of Bishops, Most Rev. Metropolitan Philaret, 75 East 93rd St., N.Y., NY 10028.

Salvation Army, The (1865 in Eng., 1880 in America)—Natl. Cmdr., William E. Chamberlain. Natl. Chief Sec., Col. George Nelting. Natl. Hq., 120-130 W. 14th St., N.Y., NY 10011.

Seamen's Church Institute of N.Y. (1834)—Dir., Rev. John M. Mulligan. Sec., Alfred Lee Loomis III, 15 State St., N.Y., NY 10004.

Serbian Eastern Orthodox Church—Diocese for U.S., Canada and Europe. Bishops: Most Rev. Dionisije and Iriney. Sec., Very Rev. Aleksandar Ivanovich, St. Sava Monastery, Libertyville, IL 60048.

Serbian Eastern Orthodox Church in U.S. and Canada—Bishops: Rt. Rev. Bishop Firmilian, Midwest Diocese, 5701 N. Redwood Dr., Chicago, IL 60631. Rt. Rev. Gregory Western Diocese, 2511 W. Garvey Ave., Alhambra, CA 91803. Rev. Sava, Eastern U.S. and Canadian Diocese, Way Hollow Rd., Edgeworth, PA 15143.

Synagogue Council of America—Pres., Joseph H. Lookstein. Exec. V.P., Rabbi Henry Siegman, 432 Park Ave. South, N.Y., NY 10016.

Ukrainian Orthodox Church of the U.S.A. (1919)—Metropolitan Most Rev. Mstyslav S. Skrypnyk, Box 495, South Bound Brook, NJ 08880.

Unitarian Universalist Assn. (formed 1961 by merger of the **American Unitarian Assn.** (1825) and the **Universalist Church of America** (1793)—Pres., Rev. Robert Nelson West. Moderator, Dr. Joseph L. Fisher. Sec., Russell F. Benson, 25 Beacon St., Boston, MA 02108.

United Church of Christ (formed 1957 through union of the **General Council of the Congregational Christian Churches** with the **Evangelical and Reformed Ch.**)— Pres., Rev. Dr. Robert V. Moss, Jr. Sec., Rev. Dr. Joseph H. Evans, 297 Park Ave. South, N.Y., NY 10010.

United Sons & Daughters of True Holiness Assn. (1912)—Gen. Sec., Elder B. W. Shoffner, 109 Daniel St., Greensboro, NC 27401.

United Synagogue of America—Pres., Arthur Levine. Exec. Vice Pres., Dr. Benjamin Z. Kreitman, 3080 Broadway, N.Y., NY 10027.

Volunteers of America (1896)—Commander-in-Chief, Gen. John F. McMahon. Natl. Field Sec., Lt. Colonel Belle Leach. Hq., 340 West 85th St., N.Y., NY 10024.

Wesleyan Church, The (1968) (organized through the merger of the **Pilgrim Holiness Ch.** (1897) and the **Wesleyan Methodist Ch. of America** (1943)—Gen. Superintendents, Dr. Robert W. McIntyre, Dr. M. H. Snyder, Dr. J. D. Abbott, Dr. V. A. Mitchell. Sec., D. Wayne Brown, Box 2000, Marion, IN 46952.

Wisconsin Evangelical Lutheran Synod (1850)—Pres., Rev. Oscar Naumann, 3512 W. North Ave., Milwaukee, WI 53208. Sec., Prof. Heinrich J. Vogel, 11757 N. Seminary Drive 65W, Mequon, WI 53092.

World Council of Churches, U.S. Conference for the—Chmn., Dr. Robert J. Marshall. Exec. Sec., Rev. Charles H. Long Jr. 475 Riverside Dr., N.Y., NY 10027.

BIBLIOGRAPHY
(prepared with assistance from June Beittel)

Texts

The Bible. Containing the Old and New Testament. Authorized King James Version. London: Collins' Clear-Type Press.

The Book of Common Prayer and Administration of the Sacraments and Other Rites and Ceremonies of the Church. (Episcopal) Certified by Charles Mortimer Guilbert. Kingsport, TN: Kingsport Press, 1977.

The Book of Mormon. Translated by Joseph Smith. Salt Lake City, UT: The Church of Jesus Christ of Latter-Day Saints, 1961.

Prabhupāda, A. C. Bhaktivedanta Swami. *Bhagavad-gītā As It Is.* New York: Macmillan, First Collier Books Edition, 1972. Complete edition with original Sanskrit text; Roman transliteration; English equivalents, translation and elaborate purports.

Riev, E. V., ed. *The Koran.* Middlesex, England: Penguin Books, 1956. A new translation by N. J. Dawood.

General reference

Archdeacon Methodios, ed. *Greek Orthodox Archdiocese of North and South America. 1977 Yearbook.* Available from Greek Orthodox Archdiocese of North and South America, 8–10 East 79th Street, New York, NY 10021.

Beit-Hallahmi, Benjamin, ed. *Research in Religious Behavior: Selected Readings.* Monterey, CA: Brooks/Cole Publishing Company, 1973.

Berry, Gerald L. *Religions of the World.* New York: Harper & Row, 1956.

Black, Algernon D. *The First Book of Ethics.* New York: Franklin Watts, 1965.

Black, Algernon D. *Without Burnt Offerings:* Ceremonies of Humanism. New York: Viking Press, 1974.

Boas, Guy, and Gilkes, Antony, eds. *Selections from the Old Testament.* London: Macmillan, 1944.

Brickner, Balfour. *Know How to Answer.* . . . New York: The Department of Inter-religious Activities, Union of American Hebrew Congregations, 1977.

Dewey, John. *A Common Faith.* Clinton, MA: The Colonial Press, 1972.

Doppelt, Frederic A., and Polish, David. *A Guide for Reform Jews.* Rev. ed. by David Polish. New York: KTAV Publishing House, 1973.

Finestein, Israel. *A Short History of Anglo-Jewry.* London: Lincolns-Prager, 1957.

Fishman, Isidore. *Introduction to Judaism.* 3rd ed. London: Valentine, Mitchell and Company, 1962.

Fowler, Floyd J. *1975 Community Survey: A Study of the Jewish Population of Greater Boston.* Boston: Combined Jewish Philanthropies of Greater Boston, 1977.

Greeley, Andrew. *The American Catholic: A Social Portrait.* New York: Basic Books, 1977.

Greeley, Andrew. *Why Can't They Be More Like Us: America's White Ethnic Groups.* New York: E. P. Dutton, 1971.

Greenfield, Robert. *The Spiritual Supermarket: An Account of Gurus Gone Public in America.* New York: Saturday Review Press/E. P. Dutton, 1975.

Hoffer, Eric. *The True Believer: Thoughts on the Nature of Mass Movements.* New York: Time Inc., 1963.

Holm, Jean. *The Study of Religions.* New York: A Crossroad Book/Seabury Press, 1977.

Judah, J. Stillson. *Hare Krishna and the Counterculture.* New York: John Wiley & Sons, 1974.

Kellet, Ernest E. *A Short History of Religions.* Middlesex, England: Penguin Books, 1962.

Kertzer, Morris N. *What Is a Jew?* Rev. ed. New York: Collier Books, 1961.

Landis, Benson Y. *Religion in the United States.* New York: Barnes & Noble Inc., 1965.

McLoughlin, William G., and Bellah, Robert N., eds. *Religion in America.* Boston: Beacon Press, 1966. Published in paperback by Beacon Press in 1968.

Mouat, Kat. *What Humanism Is About.* London: Barrie and Rockliff, 1963.

Multimedia Religious Education and Adult Discussion Program Kits for Unitarian Universalist Churches and Fellowships. Available from Curriculum Development Office, 25 Beacon Street, Boston, MA 02108.

Muzzey, David S. Introduction to *Ethics as a Religion,* by James F. Hornback. New York: Frederick Ungar, 1951. Published by the American Ethical Union in 1967.

Posner, Raphael, ed. *Popular History of Jewish Civilization: Hasidism.* Compiled by Aryeh Rubinstein. Jerusalem: Keter Publishing House Jerusalem, 1975. Published in the Western Hemisphere by Leon Amiel Publisher.

Pyle, E. H., and Williamson, S. G. *Introducing Christianity.* David and Helen Kimble, eds. Middlesex, England: Penguin Books, 1961.

Rathbun, Harry J. *Creative Initiative: Guide to Fulfillment.* Palo Alto, CA: Creative Initiative Foundation, 1976.

Rosten, Leo, ed. *Religions of America.* Updated and revised. New York: Simon and Schuster, 1975.

Seltzer, Sanford. *Jews and Non-Jews.* New York: Union of American Hebrew Congregations, 1976.

Sklare, Marshall. *America's Jews.* A volume in the Random House series Ethnic Groups in Comparative Perspective, New York: Random House, 1971.

Sklare, Marshall. *Conservative Judaism: An American Religious Movement.* New, augmented ed. New York: Schocken Books, 1972.

Sklare, Marshall, ed. *The Jew in American Society.* New York: Behrman House, 1974.

Spalding, Arthur W. *Who Is the Greatest?* (Seventh-Day Adventist) Mountain View, CA: Pacific Press Publishing Association, 1941.

Stendahl, Krister. *Paul Among the Jews and the Gentiles.* New York: Fortress Press, 1976.

Stoltzfus, Eli L. *The Serenity and Value of Amish Country Living.* Lancaster, PA, 1969. Copies available from Eli L. Stoltzfus, 69 Strasburg Pike, R.F.D. #4, Lancaster, PA 17602.

Strassfeld, Michael, and Strassfeld, Sharon. eds. *The Second Jewish Catalog Sources and Resources.* Philadelphia: The Jewish Publication Society of America, 1976.

Strober, Gerald S. *American Jews: Community in Crisis.* New York: Doubleday, 1974.

White, Ellen G. *Education.* Mountain View, CA: Pacific Press Publishing Association, 1952.

Zaehner, R. C., ed. *The Concise Encyclopedia of Living Faiths.* Boston: Beacon Press, 1959.

Interpretive works

Allport, Gordon W. *The Individual and His Religion, a Psychological Interpretation.* New York: Macmillan, 1950.

Argyle, Michael, and Beit-Hallahmi, Benjamin. *Social Psychology of Religion.* Boston: Routledge and Kegan, 1975.

Chesen, Eli S. *Religion May Be Hazardous to Your Health.* New York: Collier Books, 1972.

Cogley, John, ed. Introduction to *Religion in a Secular Age: The Search for Final Meaning* by Arthur Toynbee. London: Praeger, 1968.

Fromm, Erich. *The Crisis of Psychoanalysis.* Greenwich, CT: Fawcett Premier Books, 1970.

Fromm, Erich. *The Dogma of Christ and Other Essays on Religion, Psychology and Culture.* New York: Doubleday, 1963.

The Geography of Faith: Conversations Between Daniel Berrigan When Underground and Robert Coles. Boston: Beacon Press, 1972.

Grant, Michael. *Jesus: A Historian's View of the Gospels.* New York: Charles Scribner's Sons, 1977.

Journal for the Scientific Study of Religion. Storrs, CT: Society for the Scientific Study of Religion, University of Connecticut, 1961.

Weber, Max. Introduction to *The Sociology of Religion* by Talcott Parsons. Translated by Ephraim Fischoff. 4th ed. Boston: Beacon Press, 1963.

Wills, Garry. *Bare Ruined Choirs: Doubt, Prophecy, and Radical Religion.* Garden City, NY: Doubleday, 1972.

Zilboorg, Gregory. *Psychoanalysis and Religion.* New York: Farrar, Straus and Cudahy, 1962.

Marriage and family

Anderson, Clifford R. *How to Have a Happy Home.* (Seventh-Day Adventist) Nashville, TN: Southern Publishing Association, 1973.

Bainton, Roland. *What Christianity Says about Sex, Love and Marriage.* New York: Association Press, 1957.

Bernard, Jessie. *The Future of Marriage.* New York: Bantam Books, 1972.

Christensen, Harold T., ed. *Handbook of Marriage and the Family.* Chicago: Rand McNally, 1964.

Clinebell, Howard J., Jr., ed. *Growth Counseling for Marriage Enrichment: Pre-Marriage and the Early Years.* Philadelphia: Fortress Press, 1975.

Gittelsohn, Roland B. *My Beloved Is Mine—Judaism and Marriage.* New York: Union of American Hebrew Congregations, 1969.

Kuhn, Jerold R. *Marriage Counseling: Fact or Fallacy?* Hollywood, CA: Newcastle Publishing Company, 1973.

Novak, Michael, ed. *The Experience of Marriage: The Testimony of Catholic Laymen.* New York: Macmillan, 1965.

Olthuis, James. *I Pledge You My Troth: A Christian View of Marriage, Family and Friendship.* New York: Harper & Row, 1975.

100 Years of Marriage and Divorce Statistics. Vital and Health Statistics, Series 21, no. 24 (1973). Rockville, MD: National Center for Health Statistics. A DHEW publication containing data from the National Vital Statistics System.

Rogers, Carl R. *Becoming Partners: Marriage and Its Alternatives.* New York: Delacorte Press, 1972.

Russell, Bertrand. *Marriage and Morals.* New York: Bantam Books, 1929.

Seligson, Marcia. *The Eternal Bliss Machine: America's Ways of Wedding.* New York: William Morrow, 1973.

Sherry, Paul H., ed. Topic of entire issue: "Is the Family Dead?" *Journal of Current Social Issues* 14 (1977).

Sussman, Marvin B., ed. *Sourcebook in Marriage and the Family.* Boston: Houghton Mifflin, 1974.

Thomas, Darwin L.; Gecas, Victor; Weigen, Andrew; and Rooney, Elizabeth. *Family, Socialization and the Adolescent.* Lexington, MA: D. C. Heath, 1974.

White, Ellen G. *The Adventist Home: Counsels to Seventh-Day Adventist Families as Set Forth in the Writings of Ellen G. White.* Nashville, TN: Southern Publishing Association, 1952.

Yorburg, Betty. *The Changing Family.* New York: Columbia University Press, 1973.

Intermarriage

A Guide for Planning and Conducting Interreligious Institutes for Jewish and Christian Religious School Teachers and Educators. 1977 rev. ed. Prepared by Balfour Brickner. New York: The Department of Interreligious Affairs of the Union of American Hebrew Congregations, 1977.

Barron, Milton L., ed. *The Blending American: Patterns of Intermarriage.* Chicago: Quandrangle Books, 1972.

Christensen, Harold T., and Barber, Kenneth E. "Interfaith versus Intrafaith Marriage in Indiana." *Journal of Marriage and the Family* 29 (1967).

Colman, Hila. *Mixed Marriage Daughter.* New York: William Morrow, 1968.

Eichhorn, David Max. *Jewish Intermarriages Fact and Fiction.* Satellite Beach, FL: Satellite Books, 1974.

Final Report: Commission on the Theology of Marriage and Its Application to Mixed Marriages. June 27, 1975. Commended by John Cardinal Willebrands and Donald Cantuar. Washington, D.C.: Publications Office United States Catholic Conference, 1976.

Gordon, Albert I. *Intermarriage: Interfaith, Interracial, Interethnic.* Boston: Beacon Press, 1964.

Heiss, Jerrold S. "Premarital Characteristics of Religiously Intermarried." *American Sociological Review* 25 (1960): 341–47.

Huberman, Steven. "Jews and Non-Jews: Falling in Love." *Union of American Hebrew Congregations/Journal of Jewish Communal Service* 55 (1979).

Packouz, Kalman. *How to Stop an Intermarriage: A Practical Guide for Parents.* Jerusalem: Graph-Press, 1976.

Rosenthal, Erich. "Jewish Intermarriage in Indiana." *American Jewish Year Book* 68 (1967): 243–64.

Rosenthal, Erich. "Studies of Jewish Intermarriage in the United States." *American Jewish Year Book* 64 (1963): 3–53.

Rosten, Philip M. " 'The Mischling'; Child of the Jewish-Gentile Marriage." Honors paper, Harvard University, 1960.

Silver, Samuel M. *Mixed Marriage: Between Jew and Christian.* New York: Arco Publishing Company, 1977.

Related reading

Appel, John J. "Christian Science and the Jews." *Jewish Social Studies* 31 (1969): 100–121.

Berman, Louis. *Jews and Intermarriage: A Study in Personality and Culture.* New York: Thomas Yoseloff, 1968.

Cahnman, Werner J., ed. *Intermarriage and Jewish Life.* New York: Hertzl Press, 1963.

Caplovitz, David, and Levy, Harry. *Interreligious Dating Among College Students.* Processed, New York: Bureau of Applied Social Research of Columbia University, 1965.

Davis, Moshe. "Mixed Marriage in Western Jewry: Historical Background to the Jewish Response." *The Jewish Journal of Sociology* 10 (1968): 177–220.

Drachsler, Julius. *Democracy and Assimilation.* New York: Macmillan, 1920.

Feldman, Ephraim. "Intermarriage, Historically Considered." *Yearbook of the Central Conference of American Rabbis* 19 (1909): 271–307.

Heiss, Jerold S. "Interfaith Marriage and Marital Outcome." *Marriage and Family Living* 23 (1961): 228–33.

Intermarriage and the Future of the American Jew. By the Federation of Jewish Philanthropies of New York, Commission on Synagogue Relations. New York: Federation of Jewish Philanthropies, 1965.

Lazerwitz, Bernard. "Intermarriage and Conversion: A Guide for Future Research." *The Jewish Journal of Sociology* 13 (1971): 41–63.

Levinson, Maria H., and Levinson, Daniel J. "Jews Who Intermarry: Socio-Psychological Bases of Ethnic Identity and Change." *YIVO Annual of Jewish Social Science* 12 (1958–59): 106–28.

Mayer, John E. *Jewish-Gentile Courtships.* New York: The Free Press, 1961.

The Psychological Implications of Intermarriage: Proceedings of a Conference. By the Federation of Jewish Philanthropies of New York, Commission on Synagogue Relations. New York: Federation of Jewish Philanthropies, 1966.

Rubenstein, Richard L. "Intermarriage and Conversion." *The Reconstructionist* 28 (1962): 11–21.

Schoenfield, Eugene. "Intermarriage and the Small Town: The Jewish Case." *Journal of Marriage and the Family* 31 (1969): 61–64.

Sklare, Marshall. "Intermarriage and the Jewish Future." *Commentary* 37 (1964): 46–52.

Sklare, Marshall. "Intermarriage and Jewish Survival." *Commentary* 49 (1970): 51–58.

Stern, Malcolm H. "Jewish Marriage and Intermarriage in the Federal Period (1776–1840)." *American Jewish Archives* 19 (1967): 142–43.

Development and adolescence

Elkind, David. *Perceptual Development in Children.* New York: International University Press, 1966. See especially the chapter on "The Developmental Psychology of Religion."

Inhelder, Barbel, and Piaget, Jean. *The Growth of Logical Thinking from Childhood to Adolescence.* Translated by Anne Parsons and Stanley Milgram. New York: Basic Books, 1958.

Your Youth: Getting the Best Out of It. New York: (Jehovah's Witnesses) Watch Tower Bible and Tract Society of New York, 1976.

Feminism and religion

Barron McBride, Angela. *The Growth and Development of Mothers.* New York: Harper & Row, 1973.

Barron McBride, Angela. *A Married Feminist.* New York: Harper & Row, 1976.

De Beauvoir, Simone. *The Second Sex.* Translated and edited by H. M. Parshley. New York: Vintage Books, 1952.

Cunneen, Sally. *Sex: Female; Religion: Catholic.* New York: Holt, Rinehart & Winston, 1968.

Millett, Kate. *Sexual Politics.* New York: Avon Books, 1970.

Parvey, Constance F. "The Theology and Leadership of Women in the New Testament." *Religion and Sexism,* Rosemary Radford Ruether, ed. New York: Simon and Schuster, 1974.

Priesand, Sally. Introduction to *Judaism and the New Woman* by Bess Myerson. New York: Behrman House, 1975.

A Resource Guide for Women in the Seminary. By the Commission on Women in Ministry. New York: Division of Education and Ministry, National Council of the Churches of Christ in the U.S.A., 1976.

Education of children

Adler, Alfred. Introduction to *The Education of Children* by Rudolph Dreikurs. Translated by Eleanore and Friedrich Jensen. New York: Greenberg, 1930.

Fahs, Sophia L. *Today's Children and Yesterday's Heritage: A Philosophy of Creative Religious Development.* Boston: Beacon Press, 1952.

Goff, Nancy. *Not by Myself.* Valley Forge, PA: American Baptist Board of Education and Publication, 1971. (Learner's book and teacher's guide—second semester.)

Holmes, Urban T. *Young Children and the Eucharist.* New York: Seabury Press, 1972.

Jones, Jessie O. *The Spiritual Education of Our Children.* New York: Viking Press, 1960.

Junior: Bible and Life Graded Series 2 (December 1976, January, February 1977). Valley Forge, PA: American Baptist Churches, (Workbook and teacher's manual).

Mayle, Peter. *Will I Go to Heaven?* New York: Corwin Books, 1976.

Rothchild, John, and Wolf, Susan. *Children of the Counterculture.* New York: Doubleday, 1976.

Thorn, Emily. *A Teacher's Guide for Algernon Black's "First Book of Ethics."* New York: American Ethical Union, 1977.

Westerhoff, John H., III. *Values for Tomorrow's Children: An Alternative Future for Education in the Church.* Philadelphia: Pilgrim Press, 1973.

Westerhoff, John H., III. *Will Our Children Have Faith?* New York: Seabury Press, 1976.

Index